The
Anti-Apartheid
Reader

THE ANTI-APARTHEID READER

THE STRUGGLE AGAINST WHITE RACIST RULE IN SOUTH AFRICA

Edited by

DAVID MERMELSTEIN

Grove Press
New York

Published by Grove Press, Inc.
920 Broadway
New York, N.Y. 10010

Library of Congress Cataloging-in-Publication Data
The Anti-Apartheid Reader
   Bibliography: p.
   Includes index.
   1. South Africa—Politics and government—1978—
2. South Africa—Race relations. 3. South Africa—
Foreign relations—Africa, Southern. 4. Africa,
Southern—Foreign relations—South Africa. 5. South
Africa—Foreign relations—United States. 6. United
States—Foreign relations—South Africa.
I. Mermelstein, David, 1933-
DT779.952.S66 1986   305.8′00968   86-45242
ISBN 0-394-55488-4
ISBN 0-394-62223-5 (pbk.)

Manufactured in the United States of America
Designed by Irving Perkins Associates
First Edition 1987

10 9 8 7 6 5 4 3 2 1

CONTENTS

SOUTHERN AFRICA

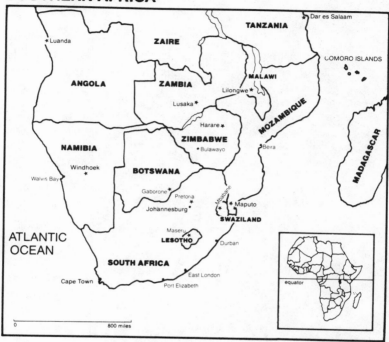

South Africa in Relation to the United States

Kevin Danaher and the Institute for Policy Studies

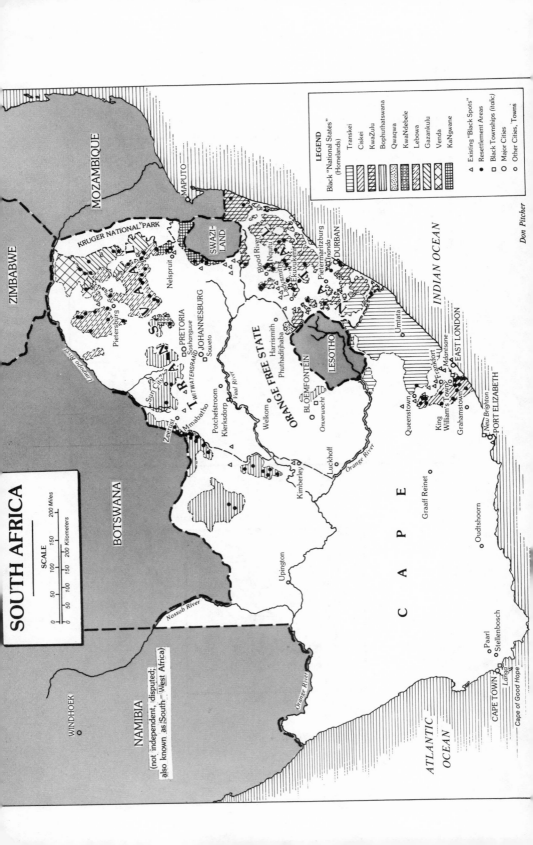

SOUTH AFRICA

SCALE

0   50   100   150   200 Miles

0   50   100   150   200 Kilometers

ATLANTIC OCEAN

INDIAN OCEAN

ZIMBABWE

MOZAMBIQUE

MAPUTO

KRUGER NATIONAL PARK

SWAZILAND

BOTSWANA

NAMIBIA
(not independent, disputed;
also known as (South-) West Africa)

WINDHOEK

Nossob River

Orange River

Limpopo River

TRANSVAAL

Pietersburg

PRETORIA
Soshanguve
Nelspruit

JOHANNESBURG
Soweto
WITWATERSRAND

Vaal River

Sun City
Mmabatho

Zeerust

Potchefstroom
Klerksdorp

Kimberley

Luckhoff

Upington

ORANGE FREE STATE

Welkom

Harrismith
Phuthaditjhaba

BLOEMFONTEIN
Onverwacht

LESOTHO

Blood River
Ladysmith
Nqutu

Pietermaritzburg
DURBAN
Inanda

NATAL

Umtata

Queenstown
Frankfort
King William's Town
Mdantsane
Grahamstown
EAST LONDON

New Brighton
PORT ELIZABETH

Graaff Reinet

Oudtshoorn

C A P E

Paarl
Stellenbosch
CAPE TOWN
Langa
Cape of Good Hope

Orange River

Don Pitcher

LEGEND

Black "National States"
(Homelands)

	Transkei
	Ciskei
	KwaZulu
	Bophuthatswana
	Qwaqwa
	KwaNdebele
	Lebowa
	Gazankulu
	Venda
	KaNgwane

△ Existing "Black Spots"
● Resettlement Areas
□ Black Townships (italic)
◉ Major Cities
○ Other Cities, Towns

SOUTH AFRICA IN BRIEF

PEOPLE

POPULATION (1984 est.): 32.6 million

African	24.1 million	74.0%
White	4.8 "	14.7%
Coloured	2.8 "	8.6%
Asian	.9 "	2.7%

ANNUAL GROWTH RATE: Africans: 2.8%;
Whites: 0.8%;   Coloureds: 1.8%;
Asians: 1.8%;   Overall: 2.5%

POP. DENSITY: 62.08 per sq. mi.

URBAN (1972): 47.9%

LANGUAGES: Official—English and Afrikaans; Zulu, Xhosa, North and South Sotho, Tswana, others

RELIGIONS: English-oriented—Anglican, Methodist, Catholic; Afrikaans-speaking —Dutch Reformed; also traditional African, Hindu, Muslim and Jewish

GEOGRAPHY

AREA: 435,868 sq. mi. (equivalent to N.M., Tex., La. combined) [listed as 472,359 by U.S. State Dep't (Oct. 1985) and others but this includes the enclave at Walvis Bay, in Namibia]

LOCATION: At the southern tip of Africa, bordered on the north, from west to east, Namibia, Botswana, Zimbabwe, and on the northeast by Mozambique and Swaziland, and surrounds Lesotho

CAPITAL: Administrative—Pretoria (pop. 1.0 million). *Legislative*—Cape Town (1.7 million). *Judicial*—Bloemfontein (0.2 million). *Other cities*—Johannesburg (1.9 million), Durban (0.9 million).

TERRAIN: The country has a narrow coastal zone and an extensive interior plateau with altitudes ranging from 1,000 to 2,000 meters (3,000–6,000 ft.) above sea level. South Africa lacks important arterial rivers or lakes, so extensive water conservation and control are necessary. The coastline is about 4,300 kilometers (2,700 mi.) long.

CLIMATE: South Africa's climate is generally moderate, with sunny days and cool nights. The seasons are reversed because the country is in the Southern Hemisphere. The average mean temperature is remarkably uniform, the most southerly point having a mean yearly temperature of 16.5°C (61.8°F), while Johannesburg, about 1,600 kilometers (1,000 mi.) to the northeast and 1,700 meters (5,700 ft.) higher, has an annual mean temperature of 16°C (60.8°F). Mean annual precipitation ranges from less than 12.7 centimeters (5 in.) along the west coast to 102 centimeters (40 in.) or more in the east.

MAJOR RIVERS: Orange, Vaal, Limpopo, Fish

GOVERNMENT AND POLITICAL

TYPE: Executive—president, tricameral Parliament with one chamber each for whites, coloureds, and Indians, under a new constitution effective September 3, 1984.

INDEPENDENCE: May 31, 1910, Union of South Africa was created; became sovereign state within British Empire in 1934; May 31, 1961, became republic; October 1961, left the British Commonwealth.

CONSTITUTION: (effective September 3, 1984).

ADMINISTRATIVE SUBDIVISIONS: Provincial governments of the Transvaal, Orange Free State, Cape of Good Hope, and Natal; ten separate "homelands" administered in areas set aside for black Africans.

"HOMELANDS"

Bantustan ("Tribe")	No. of Pieces	Date of "independence"	De Facto African Population 1976 (1000s)	Chief "Minister" or "President"
Bophuthatswana Tswana	7	1977	1,154	Chief Lucas Mangope
Ciskei Xhosa	18	1981	475	Chief Lennox Sebe
Gazankulu Shangaan	4		333	Professor Hudson Ntsanwisi
KaNgwane Swazi	3		209	Enos Mabuza

Bantustan ("Tribe")	No. of Pieces	Date of "independence"	De Facto African Population 1976 (1000s)	Chief "Minister" or "President"
KwaNdebele S. Ndebele	1		150	Simon Skosana
Kwazulu Zulu	44		2,891	Chief Gatsha Buthelezi
Lebowa N. Sotho N. Ndebele Pedi	14		1,388	Dr. Cedric Phatudi
QwaQwa S. Sotho			91	Chief T. K. Mopeli
Transkei Xhosa	3	1976	2,391	Chief Kaizer Matanzima
Venda Venda	3	1979	339	Chief Patrick Mphaphu

POLITICAL PARTIES: White—National Party, Progressive Federal Party, New Republic Party, Conservative Party, Reconstituted National Party. *Coloured*—Labor Party, Freedom Party, People's Congress Party, Reformed Freedom Party, New Convention People's Party. *Indian*—National People's Party, Solidarity.

NATIONAL PARTY HEADS OF GOVERNMENT:

D. F. Malan	1948–1954
J. G. Strijdom	1954–1958
H. F. Verwoerd	1958–1966
B. J. Vorster	1966–1978
P. W. Botha	1978–

ECONOMY

GNP (1983): $75.5 billion

GDP (1983): $73.2 billion.

ANNUAL GROWTH RATE (GDP): +12.6% nominal, −3.1% real.

PER CAPITA GNP: $5,239.

NATURAL RESOURCES: Nearly all essential minerals except oil.

AGRICULTURE (1983): 4.7% of GNP. *Products*—corn, wool, dairy products, wheat, sugarcane, tobacco, citrus fruits. *Cultivated land*—12%.

MINING: 15.1% of GNP.

MANUFACTURING: 23% of GNP.

INDUSTRY: Types—minerals, automobiles, fabricated material, machinery, textiles, chemicals, fertilizer.

TRADE: Exports—$18.2 billion: gold, diamonds, corn, wool, sugar, fruit, fish products, metals, metallic ores, metal products, coal. *Major markets*—US, Switzerland, Japan, UK. *Imports*—$14.4 billion: machinery, electrical equipment, transportation equipment, office machinery and data processing equipment, metal products. *Major suppliers*—US, FRG, Japan, UK.

DEFENSE EXPENDITURES: $2.84 billion budgeted (1983/84)

EMPLOYMENT AND MONTHLY WAGES: May 1983

Mining	employed	wage
African	613,452	$260
White	78,020	$1395
Coloured	9,581	$450
Indian	659	$690
Manufacturing		
African	748,700	$320
White	316,600	$1290
Coloured	240,800	$365
Indian	86,400	$460

AGRICULTURE: 1.3 million Africans work on white farms, average wage $28 to $40 per month plus in kind payments—minimal housing, corn or "mealie" meal

DOMESTIC WORK: 700,000 Africans, primarily women, salaries commonly range from $40 to $80 a month

AFRICAN UNEMPLOYMENT (1985 est): Cape Town 19%, Pretoria 24%, Johannesburg 28%, youth 50% +

OFFICIAL EXCHANGE RATE (Jan 10, 1986): US $1 = R2.439 or 1 Rand= $0.41 [(1980) 1 Rand=$1.30]

US-SOUTH AFRICA ECONOMIC TIES

U.S. COMPANIES IN SOUTH AFRICA, 1982: More than 350 U.S. Companies have subsidiaries in South Africa

U.S. PERCENTAGE OF TOTAL FOREIGN DIRECT INVESTMENT IN SOUTH AFRICA: Approximately 20%, second only to Britain

AVERAGE RATE OF RETURN ON U.S. INVESTMENT: 1979–1982, 18.7%

MAJOR US CORPORATE OPERATIONS IN SOUTH AFRICA: Direct investments—Mobil Oil ($426 million/3,577 workers); Caltex [Standard Oil of California and Texaco] ($334 million/2,238 workers); General Motors ($243 million/5,038 workers); Goodyear ($97 million/2,797 workers); Union Carbide ($54.5 million/2,465 workers); SOHIO [Kennecott] ($345 million/2,259 workers); Ford ($213 million/6,509 workers); Newmont ($127 million/13,535 workers); General Electric ($93 million/5,130 workers). Other Involvement—Fluor ($4.7 billion contract for oil from coal facility/17,300 workers); Burroughs Corp. ($6 million annual sales/558 workers); Control Data Corporation ($17.8 million annual sales/330 workers); IBM ($262 million annual sales/1,800 workers).

U.S. BANK LOANS TO SOUTH AFRICA (JUNE, 1983): $3.88 billion. Significant lenders: Bankers Trust (NY), BankAmerica (CA), Chase Manhattan (NY), Chemical Bank (NY), Citibank (NY), Continental Illinois (IL), First Boston (MA), First Chicago (IL), Manufacturers Hanover (NY), Morgan Guaranty (NY).

HEALTH

MORTALITY (1980): Infant mortality rates per 1000 live births—Whites: 13; Indians: 24; Coloureds: 62; Africans: 90. Life expectancy—White men: 67; African men: 55; White women: 74; African women: 60

MALNUTRITION (Conservative estimates): 2.9 million black children under the age of 15

DOCTOR/PATIENT RATIOS: Whites—1:330; Africans—1:19,000; Coloureds—1:12,000; Indians—1:730

EDUCATION

PER CAPITA SPENDING ON EDUCATION, 1980/81: Whites—$1,115; Africans—$170; Coloureds—$310; Indians—$625.

TEACHER/PUPIL RATIOS, 1982: Whites—1:18; Africans—1:39; Coloureds—1:27; Indians—1:24.

CHRONOLOGY

Millennia	Ancestors of San and Khoikhoi in South Africa
Circa 300	Ancesters of Bantu-speaking Africans settle in South Africa
1488	Bartholomeu Dias discovers Cape of Good Hope
1652 (Apr 6)	Dutch East India Co. establishes a trading station on the site of present-day Cape Town, in vicinity of Khoi and San pastoralists
1658	Slaves imported from West Africa
1659	First battles by the Khoi against dispossession
1688	Arrival of French Huguenot settlers
1702	Major clash between settlers and Xhosa near the Fish River
1806	Second and permanent occupation of the Cape by the British
1834	End of Cape slavery
1836	Beginning of the Great Trek
1843	British annex Natal
1845–75	Segregation introduced throughout Natal under British rule
1852	Independence of Afrikaners in the Orange Free State recognized by the British
1854	Independence of Afrikaners in Transvaal recognized by the British
1860	Indian indentured labor introduced in Natal
1867	Discovery of diamonds
1877	British annex the Transvaal
1878	Xhosa final battlefield defeat
1886	Gold discovered on the Witwatersrand
1890	Cecil Rhodes is Prime Minister of Cape Colony; German South West Africa created
1894	Natal Indian Congress formed, Mohandas Gandhi, president
1899–1902	Anglo-Boer War, ended by Treaty of Vereeniging, May 31, 1902

xvii

1910 (May 31)	Union of South Africa established, Louis Botha first Prime Minister
1912 (Jan 8)	Founding at Bloemfontein of the South African Native National Congress, which changed its name in 1925 to the African National Congress (ANC)
1913	Natives Land Act, prevents Africans from acquiring land outside of "reserves," then 7% of land area
1918	Broederbond formed
1919	Jan Smuts becomes Prime Minister at death of Botha
1920	South Africa given mandate by League of Nations to administer former German colony (Namibia)
1921	South African Communist Party founded
1922	Rand revolt—strike of white miners over decision to increase proportion of blacks
1924	Victory of Nationalist Party-Labour Party Pact, Hertzog Prime Minister
1933	Hertzog invites Smuts to form coalition government
1934	"Purified" Nationalist Party formed under Malan. United Party "fused" from Nationalist Party and South African Party; Hertzog remains Prime Minister
1936	Native Trust and Land Act, increasing "reserves" to 13%. Elimination of African parliamentary voting rights
1938	Centenary of Great Trek celebrated
1939	Smuts again becomes Prime Minister, leads South Africa into war on the side of Britain, against opposition of Hertzog and the Nationalist Party (which was sympathetic to Nazi Germany)
1946	African mine workers strike
1948 (May 26)	Victory of Malan's Nationalist Party
1949	Prohibition of Mixed Marriages Act
1950	Immorality Amendment Act; Suppression of Communism Act; Group Areas Act
1951	Bantu Authorities Act; Coloureds in Cape Province removed from Parliamentary Voter Roll
1952	Defiance campaign launched by ANC and South African Indian Congress
1953	Bantu Education Act; Public Safety Act
1954	Strijdom becomes Prime Minister
1955 (June 26)	Freedom Charter adopted at Kliptown
1956 (Aug 9)	20,000 women protest in Pretoria the extension of passes to women
1956–61	Treason Trial: 156 leaders of congress movement charged, ultimately acquitted of High Treason
1958	Verwoerd becomes Prime Minister
1959	Formation of Pan-Africanist Congress
1960 (Mar 30)	Sharpeville Massacre; State of Emergency declared, March 30; ANC and PAC banned. Ovamboland Peoples Organization reor-

ganized as the South West African People's Organization (SWAPO)

1961 South Africa becomes a republic, leaves the Commonwealth. Chief Albert Luthuli, President of ANC, wins Nobel Peace Prize. Umkonto We Suzwe formed. U.N. General Assembly votes for sanctions against South Africa

1964 Mandela, Sisulu, others, sentenced to life imprisonment

1966 Vorster becomes Prime Minister

1967 Terrorism Act provides for indefinite detention without trial

1969 South African Student Organization (SASO) formed

1973 Wave of strikes by black workers in Durban

1974 Rightist Portuguese dictatorship overthrown, leading to independence for Mozambique and Angola, in 1975

1975 South African troops cross into Angola for the first time; Cuban troops defend Marxist Angolan government

1976 Soweto revolt begins (June 16). Transkei, first "homeland" designated independent

1976–77 Continuous unrest—over 700 deaths, detentions, stay-aways, school boycotts

1977 Steve Biko, Black Consciousness movement leader, killed while in detention. U.N. Security Council imposes mandatory arms embargo on South Africa

1978 Muldergate scandal; Botha becomes Prime Minister. 867 killed in South African raid of SWAPO refugee camp, mostly women and children. Security Council adopts Resolution 435 calling for free elections in Namibia, accepted by SWAPO

1979 U.S. Vela Satellite detects intense double flash of light (characteristic of an atomic blast) near South Africa

1980 Zimbabwe independence. ANC attack on SASOL coal-to-gas plant

1981 Abortive Geneva Conference on Namibia

1982 South Africa Defense Force raid on Maseru, Lesotho, kills 42. Conservative Party formed by defectors from National Party led by A. P. Treurnicht and F. Hartzenburg. Neil Aggett, first white to die in detention

1983 Whites give 66% approval to a new constitution with limited power-sharing for coloureds and Asians. Formation of United Democratic Front (UDF), a coalition of over 600 groups

1984 Nkomati Accords, restricting ANC activities inside Mozambique borders. Sept 3—new constitution promulgated; September—current phase of revolutionary unrest begins; Bishop Desmond M. Tutu awarded Nobel Peace Prize

1985 Desmond M. Tutu elected Anglican Bishop of Johannesburg. Mixed Marriages Act repealed; Immorality Act amended to allow inter-racial sexual relations. July 20—State of Emergency imposed; mass detentions. Aug 27–Sept 2—foreign and stock exchanges closed; four-month moratorium on foreign debt repayment declared. Sept 9—Reagan Administration imposes mild economic sanctions on South Africa by executive order (heading off stronger Congressional actions). Sept 13—South African business leaders meet with ANC leaders in Zambia

1986 (Jan)   After a year and a half of unrest, approximately 1000 blacks are dead, a majority unarmed and killed by the police and military authorities

January 2   More than 10,000 blacks attend a funeral rally in Port Elizabeth for Molly Blackburn, South Africa's most prominent anti-apartheid white activist, who died in a car crash in late December

January 19   Blockaded by South Africa, Lesotho's Prime Minister, Leabua Jonathan, is overthrown in a military coup. Within a week, ANC members are deported to undisclosed destinations in return for which the blockade is lifted

March 7   South Africa rescinds 1985 state-of-emergency decree, releasing what it says are the last 327 of almost 8000 persons detained

April 14   Desmond Tutu is elected first black Anglican Archbishop of Cape Town

May 1   1.5 million blacks stay away from work, in the biggest strike ever to occur in South Africa, calling for May Day to be designated an official public holiday

May 19   In the most spectacular military operation in the South African government's 25-year war against the ANC, ground and air forces struck its alleged guerrilla strongholds in the capitals of Zimbabwe, Botswana and Zambia

June 6   The Commonwealth 7-member eminent persons group abandons its 6-month effort to mediate a solution, attributing their failure to South Africa's unwillingness to legalize the ANC or free Nelson Mandela. Its 68-page report, issued June 12, calls for wide-ranging sanctions to avert "what could be the worst bloodbath since the Second World War"

June 12   The South African government declares a nationwide state of emergency. Virtually unlimited power is given to security forces. Severe restrictions are placed on media coverage. 1000 are said to be detained the first day. Government said decree was designed to forestall riots on June 16, the 10th anniversary of Soweto Uprising

June 25   South African Parliament passes a package of reforms, including an end of the pass law system which is to be replaced with uniform documents for all S.A. citizens. Citizenship is restored to about 20% of those blacks who lost it when tribal homelands they resided in were declared "independent"

July 22   Major address by President Reagan urging the S.A.G. to negotiate, but opposing sanctions as "historic act of folly," draws bi-partisan criticism for its lack of significant U.S. initiative, though it is praised in Pretoria

July 29   U.K. Foreign Secretary Sir Geoffrey Howe's week-long peace mission on behalf of the European Community ends in failure

August 8   Following the August 2–5 summit of 7 Commonwealth Heads of State, Margaret Thatcher agrees to limited economic sanctions but rejects the other 6 leaders' calls for more forceful sanctions

August 15   The U.S. Senate votes 84-14 to impose new sanctions on South Africa, a less stringent bill than previously passed by the House in June, but still a challenge to the Reagan administration, which has opposed any new sanctions at all

Mid-August   Estimates are that about 10,000 have been detained since the June 12 state of emergency was announced and that 2000 had died since the current phase of unrest began in September 1984

INTRODUCTION

In fall 1970, demonstrators massed outside the Cambridge, Massachusetts, headquarters of the Polaroid corporation. Polaroid produced a complex piece of photographic equipment known as ID-2, which in two minutes took and developed a person's picture (and duplicate), sealed it in unbreakable plastic and registered the subject's name and other information in a computer. ID-2 was being used by the South African government to help implement what are known as its "pass laws." Then, as now, these laws, which regulate the day-to-day movement of Africans, were key elements in the odious system of racial separation known as apartheid.[1]

Like other anti-apartheid protests held during the Vietnam era, this one soon faded from public view, though it did catch for a moment attention of the media.[2] While the U.S.'s role in South Africa, then, was considerable, few Americans, outside of a handful of liberals and radicals and members of several

[1] Shortly before this book went to press, President P. W. Botha announced that South Africa had rescinded the "pass" laws (which restricted the movement of those designated as black and required them to carry a passbook at all times). With hundreds of thousands of violators having been arrested yearly the reform appeared to be a significant concession. Unfortunately, under the new rules, racially designated identification documents will be required of everyone. Blacks will still be forbidden to live in white areas, and such institutions as schools and hospitals will remain strictly segregated. The attitude of South Africa's anti-apartheid activists to the new reform is best summed up in Bishop Tutu's warning to "beware of the small print."

[2] Years later, in 1977, Polaroid pulled out of South Africa when it learned that its distributor had been selling its equipment to the South African Government in violation of a 1971 agreement adopted by Polaroid in response to the rallies and boycotts. It is believed Polaroid was the first U.S. company to withdraw from South Africa for anti-apartheid reasons. (See *Facts on File,* 1977, p. 934. For an earlier account, see Daniel Schechter, *Ramparts Magazine,* March 1971.)

1

black organizations, seemed concerned with the plight of South African blacks. Fewer still thought the U.S. government should intervene on their behalf.

How times have changed! Within South Africa, black[3] resistance to apartheid is intensifying and becoming increasingly violent. Media coverage of events there has been extensive. Most public officials have condemned apartheid and called for its abolition. Resistance in South Africa and domestic pressure in America have forced the Reagan administration to impose mild economic sanctions in 1985—a move widely interpreted as a reluctant one intended to head off even stronger measures being proposed in the Congress.

So much has South Africa appeared in recent headlines that many of its leading figures are now well known. Those in the forefront are Nelson Mandela, the imprisoned leader of the African National Congress (ANC), a man many believe would be South Africa's head of state under a democratic system of one person-one vote; Winnie Mandela, Nelson's wife, a heroic resister to apartheid in her own right; Bishop Desmond M. Tutu, the black South African recipient of the 1984 Nobel Peace Prize, who has captured the hearts of many in this country with his eloquence, dignity and sense of humor; and, on the other side, Pieter W. Botha, the Afrikaner[4] President, who, like a twentieth-century King Canute, seems intent on holding back the inevitable tide of black power in South Africa.

The media, then, have not done their job badly. Enough grains of fact have been separated from the sensationalist chaff to provide the average American with a rudimentary knowledge of events in South Africa. Nonetheless, popular news coverage—especially television—has its limits. It is all but impossible to encapsulate such a complex reality for an audience which lacks background. Moreover, the U.S. media are sometimes the witting, or unwitting, tools of the South African government, which budgets considerable sums to disinform and muddy the waters.

It is not surprising, then, that there are misconceptions about America's role. This is illustrated by the questions asked of Bishop Tutu in a U.S.

---

[3] In this Introduction, as in most of the readings in this book, black is being used as it is increasingly used in South Africa, especially among those resisting apartheid, to include Africans, "coloureds" (South Africans of Afro-European descent) and Asians. Black consciousness leaders and others have argued that the old collective term for Asians (or Indians) and the "coloureds"—non-white—was subtly racist, implying some kind of ideal white standard against which people were to be judged. Coloured, often capitalized, is frequently put in quotes (or preceded by the modifier "so-called") to avoid insult and to express distaste at politically motivated racial delineations. In this volume, one in which articles were written by a variety of people, it was generally expedient to omit the qualifiers and simply refer to persons of mixed race as coloured.

[4] The National Party, the party of Afrikaner nationalism, came to power in 1948. Afrikaners are descendants of Dutch, German and Huguenot settlers. They speak Afrikaans, an offshoot of seventeenth-century Dutch.

audience-participation show: "Why should the American people heed your call for sanctions against South Africa? Don't we have enough problems of our own?" The questioner ignores what is central to the issue. When Polaroid was being picketed in 1970, the U.S. corporate presence in South Africa was sizable; nearly two decades later it is immense. Our total financial commitment, including bank loans, shareholding and direct investment, is estimated at $14 billion, a tidy sum in anyone's ledger (see Reading 67). Over 250 U.S. companies have subsidiaries in South Africa[5] and the U.S. share of direct foreign investment was about 20%, second only to that of Britain.[6] Apartheid's oppression is programmed with *American* computers, especially those from IBM, but also from Burroughs, NCR, Sperry Univac and Control Data, among others (see Reading 66). Such realities underscore the fact that we are not innocent bystanders but deeply involved participants.

Another misconception about South Africa is that apartheid is simply that country's version of Jim Crow, the system of legal segregation that existed in the American South for nearly a century. From this perspective, the fact that South African laws against interracial marriage have recently been rescinded and that hotels and restaurants catering to an international clientele have been desegregated—aspects of what in South Africa are known as "petty apartheid" —is wrongly taken to mean that apartheid is at last being dismantled.

Unfortunately, such is not the case. Whereas black Americans were "unconstitutionally" denied their basic citizenship rights until the civil rights movement forced government to honor them, Africans in South Africa have no such rights. They are not even *second-class* citizens. None of the reforms of the past few years, introduced by the Afrikaners under domestic and foreign pressure, have altered the central fact of South African life, that the vast majority of blacks—Africans—are disenfranchised in the land of their birth.

Nor are the bantustans or so-called homelands being dismantled. These homelands are the barren wastelands—the spatial expression of apartheid— to which literally millions of the "unneeded"—the old, disabled, unskilled, mothers and children—have been forcibly removed, there to eke out a bare subsistence, often not even that. (On forcible removals, see Readings 19 through 21. For a discussion of premature death and malnutrition in South Africa, much of it taking place in the "homelands," see Reading 25.)

Ideologically, there was nothing in the system of segregation that prevailed in the United States to equal the racist vision of Verwoerd and the other architects of apartheid.[7] The South African policymakers sought, through the

[5] *The Wall Street Journal,* February 27, 1986. The number is decreasing because of divestment pressure. In 1985, 28 U.S. firms left South Africa and no new ones entered.

[6] *Southern African Perspectives*, January 1984.

[7] For three recent studies comparing the segregation system in the U.S. South with apartheid and its forerunners, see George M. Fredrickson, *White Supremacy: A Comparative Study in Ameri-*

homeland system, to create a totally white South Africa—in a land over 80% black. It was to be serviced by black "guest" workers from Ciskei, Bophuthat-swana, KwaNdebele or one of the other seven pseudo-states engineered into existence. For the Afrikaner traditionalist, who believed race-mixing was evil, that it would inevitably lead to a tragic dilution of blood, the bantustan system was "a dream come true." For 20 million Africans, however, this dream has turned into an endless and bitter nightmare.[8]

This volume is conceived as an accessible source book for anyone wanting to go beyond the headlines and television images for a deeper understanding of how apartheid came into being; of what reality lies behind the alien vocabu-lary—Boers and bantustans, black spots and sjamboks; and of what life is like for those subject to apartheid's countless indignities, people brutalized from the cradle to the grave. The struggles of blacks, who have resisted white tyranny as best they could, are recorded throughout the book. Although domestic and international opposition have forced the Afrikaner government to introduce "reforms," material presented in this volume suggests that both in intent and impact such reforms may serve to strengthen apartheid, not eradicate it. Several readings also focus on the fact that the South African problem is not just a question of color, but also one of class: clear economic factors lie behind racial subjugation.

There is considerable material on Namibia, the occupied colony fast becom-ing South Africa's Vietnam, and material on South Africa's policies in the rest of Southern Africa including Mozambique, Angola and Zimbabwe. Most im-portant for many Americans are sections on the role of the United States in South Africa—past, present and projected—in particular, the readings which evaluate "constructive engagement," the Reagan administration's euphemism for its warm relationship with the government of South Africa.

As the title implies, this book has not reprinted a full range of arguments used to justify the system of apartheid, though enough material is presented to enable the reader to understand the Boer point of view.[9] Nor does this anthology pretend to political neutrality in U.S. policy matters. While there are differences among the various authors, the general point of view is that the

---

can and South African History (New York: Oxford University Press, 1981); John Cell, *The Highest Stage of White Supremacy: The Origins of Segregation in South Africa and the American South* (Cambridge: Cambridge University Press, 1982); and Stanley Greenberg, *Race and State in Capitalist Development: Comparative Perspectives* (New Haven: Yale University Press, 1980).

8 Even for the Afrikaner purist, there was the vexing anomaly of the "coloured," the embarrassing offspring of a considerable African-Afrikaner miscegenation. If the Asians, in theory, could be sent back to India, where were the coloureds to live? No conceivable area could be designated *their* tribal homeland.

9 Boer, a synonym for Afrikaner, is used here generically as any white, be he or she Afrikaner or English-speaking, who supports apartheid. Without capitals, *boer* is the Afrikaans word for farmer.

policies of the Reagan administration have been misguided at best, if not cynical reflections of the fact that geo-political considerations, and corporate profits, come before human rights. American policy in South Africa during the Reagan years has made communism, not racism, the central issue. This East-West formulation is not shared by most contributors to this volume.

In discussions of the future of South Africa, there are many allusions to its being five or ten minutes to midnight (or even "five minutes after midnight"!). In a final section in the book, entitled "South Africa's Future," one which is necessarily conjectural, the prevailing view is that we have at long last reached a point when time is really running out on the Afrikaner state. Its powerful military and even the sympathetic ear of the current occupant of the White House will not help.[10] Whites cannot monopolize power much longer.

Just over a decade ago South Africa's most important neighbors—Angola, Mozambique and Rhodesia (Zimbabwe)—had governments that were friendly and white; today they are black and Marxist. Moreover, with the birth rates of blacks inside South Africa much higher than those of whites, the internal demographics are increasingly adverse to white rule. Perhaps, what is most significant is what is intangible. By all accounts, blacks now appear to believe in their heart of hearts that they are going to win. Winnie Mandela's statement read at a funeral for 17 riot victims, attended by 25,000, captures the mood: "No bullets or armies can stop an idea whose time has come."[11]

Afrikaners, in turn, must be disheartened by the fact that South Africa's most distinguished business leaders have made pilgrimages to Lusaka, Zambia, to pay homage to Oliver Tambo, exiled leader of the outlawed African National Congress. In Pretoria's eyes, this is a terrorist organization controlled by Communists. Other signs also point to an ebbing of whites' confidence. Emigration of whites, for instance, long a topic of conversation, is a small but growing reality.[12]Conscientious objection to enforcing brutal colonial rule in Namibia, also marginal, is growing, and no longer confined to religious sects such as Jehovah's Witnesses.[13]

Most important, the low-level civil war which began in September 1984 and has resulted in the deaths of over 2,000—mostly black victims of police fire

[10] Early in his term, President Reagan praised South Africa as "a country that has stood beside us in every war we've ever fought. . . ." The Union of South Africa did indeed decide to fight on the Commonwealth side in World War II. But the National Party—those in power since 1948—did not support that decision. Many of its members were pro-Nazi and some, including John Vorster, later to become Prime Minister, were in fact interned as threats to the war effort.

[11] *The New York Times,* March 6, 1986.

[12] See "White South Africans Flee Country, Fearing a Grim Future There," *The Wall Street Journal,* December 13, 1985. While most of the whites emigrating are English-speaking, and liberal, small numbers of Afrikaners are also leaving, and as many as 3% said they would be gone within five years.

[13] See David L. Goodman, "South Africa: Whites Who Won't Fight," *The Progressive,* September 1985.

—shows no sign of abating. Young blacks in the urban townships, openly contemptuous of the police, often pay for their bravery with their lives. Even the ANC, which reluctantly sloughed off a long tradition of non-violent opposition to white minority rule in the early 1960s and which then carefully limited its violence to "hard" targets like SASOL installations (coal-to-gasification plants) or police stations, "softened" its targets in 1985 to include personnel in areas deemed to be war zones.

Given the turmoil, it is hardly surprising that the South African government has not thought it politic to defend by name the apartheid system it created. It has tried, thus far without success, to popularize such substitutes as "cooperative coexistence" or "joint responsibility."[14] It is commonplace now for National Party leaders to proclaim that the apartheid system is dead, or dying. If so, they apparently remain firmly committed to its putrefying essence— segregated residency in townships, the continued existence of the "homelands" and the denial of citizenship rights to blacks.

Euphemisms aside, what are Afrikaners to do? Botha has argued that they must "adapt or die," but his cosmetic tinkering has not appeased the blacks and only alarmed the diehards (see Reading 40). In short, the Afrikaner, confused and troubled, is split between two alternatives, both of which seem prescriptions for failure. On the one hand, the Afrikaner fears that genuine concessions would be taken as a sign of weakness and end up strengthening the resolve of those demanding nothing less than a black-ruled South Africa. On the other hand, he fears that stronger doses of repression would be equally counterproductive. Not only would that raise domestic violence to new levels, it might induce a future government of the United States to impose meaningful —even devastating—sanctions.

Unwilling to move forward, with genuine reform, or move backward, to the total repression extremist Afrikaners are advocating, the Botha government has adopted, ironically, the old-fashioned British way of the stiff upper lip— it is attempting to muddle through. But this avoidance of choice, in the context of escalating strife, has consequences that also point to disaster, namely the gradual withdrawal of international capital and the continuous increase in the civil and military cost of maintaining the system. In short, more-of-the-same threatens to undermine the Western living standards of the white minority, the creation of which was in part the purpose of the apartheid system in the first place. Even worse, the violence in the black townships—shadowing what has happened in Beirut—threatens to invade the white suburbs.

---

[14] Like the Red Queen in *Alice in Wonderland,* Afrikaners have the habit of making words mean what they want them to mean, an example being the new name for the 1952 law requiring all Africans previously exempted from the pass laws, including women, to carry a "reference book," which functioned in the same way as the existing pass. It was called the Natives (Abolition of Passes and Coordination of Documents) Act (see Reading 9).

If it is an overstatement, then, to suggest the Afrikaners are huddled in their *laagers* [an encampment protected by a circle of covered wagons], they are in fact increasingly besieged. From a die-hard Afrikaner perspective, what is at issue is not just the survival of their own unique culture but the survival of Western Civilization itself in its Southern African outpost.[15] What gives them encouragement, if not hope, is the fact that their black opposition lacks unity.

There is, for example, "inter-black" antagonism, such as the historic animosity between Africans and Indians which exploded in the riots of 1949. The creation in September 1984 of a tricameral parliament in which coloureds and Indians were each given representation, but which totally excluded Africans, was a transparent attempt to isolate Africans from other racial groups. Although this particular effort at divide-and-rule backfired, and helped touch off the current crisis, the fact remains that there exists a degree of disunity based on culture differences and disproportionate racial privilege.

Intra-African disunity, on the other hand, may be even more significant. Afrikaners have a habit of overstating tribal hostilities among Africans, in order to argue that a black-ruled South Africa would degenerate into Idi Amin's Uganda. Tribal animosities are not wholly figments of the Afrikaner imagination. The recent outbreak of violence in December 1985 between Zulu and Pondo is a case in point, although the argument can be made that it was the "homeland" policy of the white government which touched it off. Moreover, there are the traditional sources of disunity that show up in any movement seeking power—those of ideology, opportunism and sectarianism.[16]

Many anticipate a greater degree of black unity will develop as the by-product of the struggle. But what if it doesn't? Other scenarios then become possible, including confederation or even partition. The black townships, for instance, are coming under the control of young militants who answer to no one (see Reading 74). Conceivably, Natal could in time be dominated by a coalition of liberal whites and conservative Zulus under the leadership of Gatsha Buthelezi,[17] while the more radical African National Congress would

---

[15] Since Western Civilization is permeated with racism, there may be an ironical truth to this. When Mahatma Ghandi was once asked his view of Western Civilization, he replied that "it would be a very good idea."

[16] In the South African context, the question of political disunity may transcend ordinary formulations. The Afrikaner poet, Breyton Breytenbach, who spent seven years in an Afrikaner prison for his involvement in anti-apartheid activity, has warned, "Don't ever trust a *boer.* His two faces are the result of a tragically flawed culture. Don't put your faith in any other category of South African either—the system of the *boer,* the elemental presence of discrimination and oppression, have tainted and corrupted one and all." *The True Confessions of an Albino Terrorist* (New York, 1983), p. 161.

[17] It is interesting to note that the chairman of South Africa's largest supermarket chain, Raymond Ackerman, has attempted to organize a coalition of business groups, whites from the liberal Progressive Federal Party and blacks from Buthelezi's conservative Inkatha movement. (See

carve out a zone of control in its strongholds. Other centers of black power may develop in areas and industries employing unionized workers, whose numbers have increased spectacularly (see Readings 16 and 45). It is at least possible that a series of Afrikaner compromises, or unspectacular retreats, could in time lead to the creation of a loose, *de facto* confederation. History occasionally creates unexpected, unwanted and even ironical outcomes to intractable problems—ironical, because the Balkanization the Afrikaners currently seek as a means of maintaining power could turn out to be a Balkanization others impose on them, substantially stripping them of power.

But if "partition" is one solution to South Africa's crisis, black majority rule in a unitary state undoubtedly is the outcome most authorities expect will eventually take place. It is even possible, implausible though it appears at present, that a compromise can be worked out in which majority rule is phased in (see the range of scenarios discussed in Reading 78).

What appears to agitate the Reagan administration most about this potential turn of events is that majority rule might not simply replace whites with blacks, but in the end might replace them with Marxist-Leninists closely allied to the Soviet Union. Granted the revulsion Reagan's Washington feels for any variety of Marxism, what in the last analysis does it really fear? It is doubtful that it comes down to the strategic value of South Africa's sea lanes or even its precious minerals, factors often cited for why South Africa must remain in the Western camp (see Reading 62). Loss of investments aside—and as previously noted, in South Africa, the sums are huge—Washington seems to be afraid of the further erosion of U.S. ideological hegemony (for a brief analysis of the Reaganite world view, see Reading 58). If the U.S. is unable to stop a revolution it believes, or claims to believe, is ultimately "made in Moscow," the State Department fears that the Soviet Union will perceive America as an international "wimp." Permitting South Africa, or any nation to which we have made a commitment, to fall into the Communist orbit would be considered a national humiliation.

For this reason, the official view in Washington since 1981, until recently, has been that authoritarian regimes like Pinochet's in Chile, or Botha's in South Africa, had to be supported. Any U.S. attempt to rid these countries of their dictators could pave the way for the seizure of power by totalitarian Communists who would turn their countries into Soviet satellites. Once in power, Soviet-backed totalitarianism, unlike authoritarianism, is thought to be permanent.

This argument was originally formulated by Jeane Kirkpatrick and won her the position as ambassador to the United Nations, a post she has since relin-

---

"Big Business Prepares for Change," *Euromoney,* December 1985.) For a skeptical view of the Natal option, see Reading 75.

quished.[18] Recent cases of the overthrown dictators in Haiti and the Philippines make it appear the authoritarian-totalitarian argument has either been modified or abandoned. With their regimes crumbling, the United States did withdraw its support for Duvalier and Marcos and welcomed their replacements, but in neither situation was there an imminent possibility of a Communist takeover. Washington presumably feared that if Marcos remained, there was a greater likelihood that Communists would gain control than if he were ousted. Since then, the White House has announced it will oppose dictatorships of the anti-Communist right as well as of the pro-Communist left. Apparently, the Reagan administration has concluded that each situation has to be decided on its merits, Kirkpatrick's formulation to the contrary.

South Africa is different. If the white regime falls, Communist rule becomes an immediate possibility. Unlike the United States, the Soviet Union has long opposed apartheid without equivocation. Blacks in South Africa—or many of them—are not unappreciative. Not only does the African National Congress, the symbol of black resistance, have Communists in its inner circle (see Reading 28), it is indebted to the Soviet Union for its military aid. (Non-military aid has been given the ANC by such countries as Sweden, Norway, Austria and Italy, among others.) To American conservatives, like Richard Viguerie and the Rev. Jerry Falwell, not to speak of Ronald Reagan, the ANC is simply a Soviet surrogate. Should it triumph, Moscow would then call the tune (see Reading 63).

Nonetheless, most observers do not quite believe the African National Congress is a puppet of the South African Communist Party (quite apart from the question of whether the latter has its strings pulled from Moscow). In fact, in the eyes of the canny and highly respected financial weekly, *The Economist,* handing over power to the ANC may be the most effective way to *forestall* a Communist take-over (see Reading 75).

Whatever its ideological preconceptions, a black-ruled South Africa will most likely be influenced by the fact that the capitalist West has far more to offer it materially than the Communist East. If the other nations of southern Africa can serve as examples, it is clear that nationalism has been more of a force than Marxist ideology and that such Marxist states as Angola, Mozambique and Zimbabwe have been highly pragmatic in their relations with the West.

Unfortunately, the sympathy black South Africans once had for America has eroded sharply during the Reagan years. America is viewed, alas, as a bed partner of their oppressors, even if the affair shows signs of strain. If U.S.

---

[18] The original article, "Dictatorships and Double Standards" appeared in *Commentary,* November 1979. It was reprinted in Gettleman, et al., *El Salvador: Central America in the New Cold War* (New York: Grove Press, 1987), where it was trenchantly criticized by Michael Walzer and Tom J. Farer.

policy changes are not made soon, it may be that Reagan, Helms and Falwell will push South Africa toward the revolution they most detest.

Should black rule come, what of the fate of the South African whites? For its part, the African National Congress has long been committed to a racially unified society. Its Freedom Charter is known for its clause that South Africa belongs to all its people—black and white (see Reading 30). If the ANC takes power, will its leadership have the will and clout to enforce this historic commitment in a milieu in which millions of blacks are deeply embittered? Significantly, in January 1986 thousands of blacks attended the funeral of Molly Blackburn, a white anti-apartheid activist who died in an automobile crash. In neighboring Zimbabwe, white farmers who remained after the long, bloody, racial civil war, have experienced a high degree of prosperity.[19] Another positive sign is the fact that black leaders have denounced racism without equivocation. They have insisted their people hate white supremacy without hating whites.

Finally, some have suggested that conditions for blacks, rather than improving, might even deteriorate with majority rule. It is easy to dismiss what is implicit here as a variety of racism. Boers are forever posing worst-case scenarios—Idi Amin and Uganda are favorite examples—to justify continued white rule. Given the horrors blacks must bear under apartheid, it is not very likely they would fare worse under black rule.

But after centuries of *white* rule, blacks might have to undergo a lengthy period of little or no economic improvement, especially if they take over an economy which has suffered in the transition. Nor, in the short run, will it be easy for blacks to make economic progress if they do not have available the skills possessed by the white managerial elite.

The degree of success or failure of black majority rule should not be judged by its short-term economic results. The long-term possibilities are encouraging. South Africa's black population is educated and literate (in spite of the failures of apartheid education), and more so than most black African states at the time of their independence. Forming most of the industrial working class, blacks are also largely urban. They will have at their disposal the infrastructure their labor and the apartheid system created. The minerals, for example, that formed the basis for South African wealth will benefit blacks as they did whites. In short, unique opportunities exist in South Africa that were not always available to the rest of black Africa.

In the last analysis, the precondition for human progress in South Africa is the dismantling of apartheid. As the most powerful capitalist nation, the United States could hasten the process and thereby reduce the transitional

---

[19] See "They Lost Civil War, But White Farmers Prosper in Zimbabwe," *The Wall Street Journal,* February 13, 1986.

costs. Increasingly, Americans are learning of the cruelty of South Africa's system of racial oppression. Even in the pragmatic, career-oriented mood of campus life in America today, more than 100,000 students have demonstrated against apartheid.[20]

Sooner or later, majority rule will prevail. Unfortunately, a firm American commitment to bringing it about apparently awaits another presidency. Delay has the disadvantage of alienating people of color the world over, but especially those destined to take power in South Africa. This being the case, does American foreign policy make sense, even in its own terms?

Time is fast running out on Afrikaner rule. Has it not run out also on America's South African policy?

In the readings which follow, considerations of space have necessitated the omission of most footnotes in the original articles and occasioned considerable condensing. Because much of the subject matter is interrelated, topics overlap in some sections. Readers interested in learning more about South Africa are referred to the bibliographical guide in the appendix. Those seeking to take an active role in the anti-apartheid struggle are provided with a list of action-oriented organizations in the appendix. In the preparation of this book, I would like to thank Lily Middleton, of the Polytechnic University library, my colleagues Marvin E. Gettleman, Leonard Leeb and especially Louis Menashe, Barbara B. Brown of Boston University, David Curzon of the United Nations, David Gelber of *60 Minutes,* Milton Mankoff of Queens College, Holcomb B. Noble of *The New York Times,* Lloyd Davis Raines of Herzfeld & Stern, Judith Stein of City College of New York, present and past staff of Grove Press, including Lisa Rosset and Walter Bode, and especially my wife, Cindy Hounsell, and most of all, Andy Taylor, formerly of *60 Minutes*, whose help was indispensable.

David Mermelstein
October 1986

[20] See Bill Hall, "The Kids Aren't All Right," *In These Times,* Dec. 25–Jan. 15, 1985–86.

PART ONE

OVERVIEWS

Chapter I:

PERSPECTIVES ON CONTEMPORARY SOUTH AFRICA

1. APARTHEID: THIS TERRIBLE DREAM

by CHIEF ALBERT J. LUTHULI*

In 1961, Chief Albert J. Luthuli, the deeply religious President General of the African National Congress, was awarded the Nobel Peace Prize. At the time, Luthuli was banned and restricted to his home in rural Natal. Permitted to attend the ceremonies in Oslo, he delivered the traditional address on December 11, 1961 (excerpts from which appear below). Chief Luthuli died in 1967.

In years gone by, some of the greatest men of our century have stood here to receive this Award, men whose names and deeds have enriched the pages of human history, men whom future generations will regard as having shaped the world of our time. No one could be left unmoved to be plucked from the village of Groutville, a name many of you have never heard before and which does not even feature on many maps—to be plucked from banishment in a rural backwater, to be lifted out of the narrow confines of South Africa's internal politics and be placed here in the shadow of these great figures. It is a great honor to me to stand on this rostrum where many of the great men of our times have stood before.

The Nobel Peace Award that has brought me here has for me a threefold significance. On the one hand it is a tribute to my humble contribution to

*Luthuli is often spelled without an *h*. Although the editors spell his name as above, some readings in this volume do not.

efforts by democrats on both sides of the color line to find a peaceful solution to the race problem. . . .

On the other hand the Award is a democratic declaration of solidarity with those who fight to widen the area of liberty in my part of the world. As such, it is the sort of gesture which gives me, and millions who think as I do, tremendous encouragement. . . .

From yet another angle, it is a welcome recognition of the role played by the African people during the last fifty years to establish, peacefully, a society in which merit and not race, would fix the position of the individual in the life of the nation. . . .

Though I speak of Africa as a single entity, it is divided in many ways— by race, language, history and custom; by political, economic and ethnic frontiers. But in truth, despite these multiple divisions, Africa has a single common purpose and a single goal—the achievement of its own independence. All Africa, both lands which have won their political victories, but have still to overcome the legacy of economic backwardness, and lands like my own whose political battles have still to be waged to their conclusion—all Africa has this single aim; our goal is a united Africa in which the standards of life and liberty are constantly expanding; in which the ancient legacy of illiteracy and disease is swept aside, in which the dignity of man is rescued from beneath the heels of colonialism which have trampled it. This goal, pursued by millions of our people with revolutionary zeal, by means of books, representations, demonstrations, and in some places armed force provoked by the adamancy of white rule, carries the only real promise of peace in Africa. Whatever means have been used, the efforts have gone to end alien rule and race oppression.

There is a paradox in the fact that Africa qualifies for such an Award in its age of turmoil and revolution. How great is the paradox and how much greater the honor that an Award in support of peace and the brotherhood of man should come to one who is a citizen of a country where the brotherhood of man is an illegal doctrine, outlawed, banned, censured, proscribed and prohibited; where to work, talk or campaign for the realization in fact and deed of the brotherhood of man is hazardous, punished with banishment, or confinement without trial, or imprisonment; where effective democratic channels to peaceful settlement of the race problem have never existed these 300 years; and where white minority power rests on the most heavily armed and equipped military machine in Africa. This is South Africa.

Even here, where white rule seems determined not to change its mind for the better, the spirit of Africa's militant struggle for liberty, equality and independence asserts itself. I, together with thousands of my countrymen, have in the course of the struggle for these ideals, been harassed, and imprisoned, but we are not deterred in our quest for a new age in which we shall live in peace and in brotherhood.

It is not necessary for me to speak at length about South Africa; its social system, its politics, its economics and its laws have forced themselves on the attention of the world. It is a museum piece in our time, a hangover from the dark past of mankind, a relic of an age which everywhere else is dead or dying. Here the cult of race superiority and of white supremacy is worshipped like a god. Few white people escape corruption and many of their children learn to believe that white men are unquestionably superior, efficient, clever, industrious and capable; that black men are, equally unquestionably, inferior, slothful, stupid, evil and clumsy. On the basis of the mythology that "the lowest amongst them is higher than the highest amongst us," it is claimed that white men build everything that is worthwhile in the country; its cities, its industries, its mines and its agriculture, and that they alone are thus fitted and entitled as of right to own and control these things, whilst black men are only temporary sojourners in these cities, fitted only for menial labor, and unfit to share political power. The Prime Minister of South Africa, Dr. Verwoerd, then Minister of Bantu Affairs, when explaining his government's policy on African education had this to say: "There is no place for him (the African) in the European community above the level of certain forms of labor."

There is little new in this mythology. Every part of Africa which has been subject to white conquest has, at one time or another, and in one guise or another, suffered from it, even in its virulent form of the slavery that obtained in Africa up to the nineteenth century.

The mitigating feature in the gloom of those far-off days was the shaft of light sunk by Christian missions, a shaft of light to which we owe our initial enlightenment. With successive governments of the time doing little or nothing to ameliorate the harrowing suffering of the black man at the hands of slave-drivers, men like Dr. David Livingstone and Dr. John Philip and other illustrious men of God stood for social justice in the face of overwhelming odds. It is worth noting that the names I have referred to are still anathema to some South Africans. . . .

There is nothing new in South Africa's *apartheid* ideas, but South Africa is unique in this: The ideas not only survive in our modern age, but are stubbornly defended, extended and bolstered up by legislation at the time when in the major part of the world they are now largely historical and are either being shamefacedly hidden behind concealing formulations, or are being steadily scrapped. These ideas survive in South Africa because those who sponsor them profit from them. They provide moral whitewash for the conditions which exist in the country: for the fact that the country is ruled exclusively by a white government elected by an exclusively white electorate which is a privileged minority; for the fact that 87 percent of the land and all the best agricultural land within reach of town, market and railways is reserved for white ownership and occupation and now through the recent Group Areas legislation non-whites are losing more land to white greed; for the fact that all skilled and highly paid jobs are for whites only; for the fact that all universities of any academic merit are an exclusive preserve of whites; for the fact that the education of every white child costs about £64 p.a. whilst that of an African child costs about £9 p.a. and that of an Indian child or Coloured child costs about £20 p.a.; for the fact that white education is universal and compulsory up to the age of 16, whilst education for the non-white children is scarce and inadequate, and for the fact that almost one million Africans a year are arrested and gaoled or fined for breaches of innumerable pass and permit laws which do not apply to whites. . . .

I, as a Christian, have always felt that there is one thing above all about *"apartheid"* or "separate development" that is unforgivable. It seems utterly indifferent to the suffering of individual persons, who lose their land, their homes, their jobs, in the pursuit of what is surely the most terrible dream in the world. This terrible dream is not held on to by a crackpot group on the fringe of society, or by Ku Klux Klansmen, of whom we have a sprinkling. It is the deliberate policy of a government, supported actively by a large part of the white population, and tolerated passively by an overwhelming white majority, but now fortunately rejected by an encouraging white minority who have thrown their lot with non-whites who are overwhelmingly opposed to so-called separate development.

Thus it is that the golden age of Africa's independence is also the dark age of South Africa's decline and retrogression, brought about by men who, when revolutionary changes that entrenched fundamental human rights were taking place in Europe, were closed in on the tip of South Africa—and so missed the wind of progressive change. . . .

But beneath the surface there is a spirit of defiance. The people of South Africa have never been a docile lot, least of all the African people. We have a long tradition of struggle for our national rights, reaching back to the very beginnings of white settlement and conquest 300 years ago.

Our history is one of opposition to domination, of protest and refusal to submit to tyranny. Consider some of our great names; the great warrior and nation-builder Shaka, who welded tribes together into the Zulu nation from which I spring; Moshoeshoe, the statesman and nation-builder who fathered the Basuto nation and placed Basutoland [now named Lesotho] beyond the reach of the claws of the South African whites; Hintsa of the Xhosas who chose death rather than surrender his territory to white invaders. All these and other royal names, as well as other great chieftains, resisted manfully white intrusion.

Consider also the sturdiness of the stock that nurtured the foregoing great names. I refer to our forebears, who in the trekking from the north to the southernmost tip of Africa centuries ago braved rivers that are perennially swollen; hacked their way through treacherous jungle and forest; survived the plagues of the then untamed lethal diseases of a multifarious nature that abounded in Equatorial Africa and wrested themselves from the gaping mouths of the beasts of prey. They endured it all. They settled in these parts of Africa to build a future worthwhile for us their offspring.

Whilst the social and political conditions have changed and the problems we face are different, we too, their progeny, find ourselves facing a situation where we have to struggle for our very survival as human beings. Although methods of struggle may differ from time to time, the universal human strivings for liberty remain unchanged. We, in our situation, have chosen the path of non-violence of our own volition. Along this path we have organized many heroic campaigns. All the strength of progressive leadership in South Africa, all my life and strength, has been given to the pursuance of this method, in an attempt to avert disaster in the interests of South Africa, and [they] have bravely paid the penalties for it.

It may well be that South Africa's social system is a monument to racialism and race oppression, but its people are the living testimony to the unconquerable spirit of mankind. Down the years, against seemingly overwhelming odds, they have sought the goal of fuller life and liberty, striving with incredible determination and fortitude for the right to live as men—free men. . . .

If today this peace Award is given to South Africa through a black man, it is not because we in South Africa have won our fight for peace and human brotherhood. Far from it. Perhaps we stand farther from victory than any other people in Africa. But nothing which we have suffered at the hands of the government has turned us from our chosen path of disciplined resistance. It is for this, I believe, that this Award is given.

How easy it would have been in South Africa for the natural feelings of resentment at white domination to have been turned into feelings of hatred and a desire for revenge against the white community. Here, where every day in every aspect of life, every non-white comes up against the ubiquitous sign "Europeans Only," and the equally ubiquitous policeman to enforce it—here it could well be expected that a racialism equal to that of their oppressors would flourish to counter the white arrogance towards blacks. That it has not done so is no accident. It is because, deliberately and advisedly, African leadership for the past 50 years, with the inspiration of the African National Congress which I had the honor to lead for the last decade or so until it was banned, had set itself steadfastly against racial vaingloriousness.

We knew that in so doing we passed up opportunities for easy demogogic appeal to the natural passions of a people denied freedom and liberty; we discarded the chance of an easy and expedient emotional appeal. Our vision has always been that of a non-racial democratic South Africa which upholds the rights of all who live in our country to remain there as full citizens with equal rights and responsibilities with all others. For the consummation of this ideal we have labored unflinchingly. We shall continue to labor unflinchingly.

2. *GUARDING "THE GATES OF PARADISE"**

by NADINE GORDIMER

Nadine Gordimer, the distinguished South African novelist and short story writer, is the author of Burger's Daughter *and, most recently,* Something Out There.

We whites in south Africa present an updated version of the tale of the emperor's clothes; we are not aware of our nakedness—ethical, moral, and fatal—clothed as we are in our own skin. This morning on the radio the news of the withdrawal of more foreign diplomats from South Africa, and the continuing threat of the withdrawal by foreign banks, was followed by a burst of pop-music defiance by the state-owned South African Broadcasting Corporation, on behalf of Afrikaners and English-speaking whites. *"Allies,"* yelled a disco idol, "We're allies, with our backs against the w-a-ll. . . ."
✻ There is an old misconception still current abroad: the Afrikaners are the baddies and the English-speakers, the angels among whites in our country. The categories do not fall so neatly into place. Not all Afrikaners support the state of emergency and the sadistic police and army actions that led up to it, and not all English-speakers would implode apartheid tomorrow if it were possible to prevail against the Afrikaner army that mans the Afrikaner fortress.

The misconception surprises me. Anyone who follows the reports of foreign press correspondents in South Africa must be aware that in November 1983, the Prime Minister, Mr. P. W. Botha, received an overwhelming "yes" vote for his new Constitution, with its tricameral parliament for whites, Indians and coloreds (people of mixed race)—and the total exclusion of the black majority. The referendum held was open to whites only, both Afrikaners and English-speakers; Mr. Botha could not have received a mandate if the English-speaking whites had voted "no." "Yes," they said, voting along with supporters of Mr. Botha's National Party. "Yes," they said, 23.5 million black people shall have no say in the central government of South Africa.

And "yes," said the Reagan Government too, entering into constructive engagement with a policy destructive of justice and human dignity, while mumbling obeisance to abhorrence of apartheid like those lapsed believers who cross themselves when entering a church.

* * *

From The New York Times Magazine, September 8, 1985.

There is no special position of non-Afrikaner whites in South Africa, nor has there been for a very long time.

The actual division among whites in our country falls between the majority —Afrikaner and English-speaking—who support the new Constitution, whether directly or circuitously, as a valid move toward "accommodating black aspirations" (let us not invoke justice), and the minority—English-speaking and Afrikaner—who oppose the Constitution as irremediably unjust and unjustifiable. Fewer Afrikaners than English-speakers oppose apartheid, but the English-speakers who uphold the central government of South Africa represent a majority in their language group.

When blacks speak about the "Boer" these days, they're not just referring to Afrikaners; the term has become a generic rather than an ethnic one. It is likely to refer to a mode of behavior, an attitude of mind, a *position*. The nomenclature encompasses all whites who voluntarily and knowingly collaborate in oppression of blacks. Not all Afrikaners are "Boer," and many English-speakers with pedigrees dating back to the 1820 settlers are. . . . States of mind and ways of life under crisis would be expected more or less to follow the lines of division, and I believe that states of mind do. Everywhere I go, I sense a relaxation of the facial muscles among whites who had appeared to be tasting the ashes of the good life when Soweto was on fire in the week before the state of emergency was declared in July. Approval of the state's action is not often explicit in my company, because it is known that I belong to the minority within the white minority that opposes the Constitution as a new order of oppression in contempt of justice, and sees the state of emergency as an act of desperation: a demonstration of the failure of the Government's atrocious "new deal" only a few months after it was instituted. The general feeling among whites is that fear has been staved off—at least for a while.

The police dogs are guarding the gates of paradise. Keep away from roads that pass where the blacks and the police-army are contained in their vortex of violence, and life can go on as usual. One can turn one's attention to matters that affect one directly and can be dealt with without bloodying one's hands: lobbying all over the world against disinvestment and sports boycotts. These are areas where sophisticated people understand one another in economic and leisure self-interests: for many, the only brotherhood that transcends nation and race.

There is a physical and mental cordoning-off of "areas of unrest." The police and army take care of the first matter, and that extraordinary sense of whiteness, of having always been different, always favored, always shielded from the vulnerabilities of poverty and powerlessness, takes care of the second.

As for the less worldly among the white majority, they express openly their approval of Government violence in the last few months, and there is a group that believes there has not been enough of it. "The Government should shoot the lot." This remark was offered to my friend, the photographer David Goldblatt, in all crazy seriousness; there are whites in whose subconscious the power of the gun in a white man's hand is magical (like his skin?) and could wipe out an entire population more than five times as large as that of the whites.

In bizarre historical twinship, this is the obverse of the teachings of the mid-19th-century prophetess Nongqause, of the Xhosa tribe. Nongqause told her people that by following her instructions they could cause all those who wore trousers—the white men—to be swept away by a whirlwind. . . .

It is not true that the South African Government is bent on genocide, as some black demagogues have averred (the black man is too useful for that); but it is true that the unconscious will to genocide is there in some whites.

So is belief in the old biblical justification for apartheid, that blacks are the descendents of Ham, although even the Dutch Reformed Church has embarrassedly repudiated this. Over lunch on his father's Transvaal farm recently, I met a handsome young Afrikaner on leave from military service. Grace was said. When the young man lifted his bowed head, he gave an exposition of biblical justification that was all his own, I think: blacks are the descendents of Cain and a curse on humankind. I did not rise to the bait; but my eyes must have betrayed that I could scarcely believe my ears. Later, among the women of the family, I was shown their new acquisition, a pristine white dishwasher that had replaced the black maid. The young Afrikaner took the opportunity to fire at me, "Yes, it's a good white Kaffir girl."

During the weeks that led up to the state of emergency, the Eastern Cape black townships had become ungovernable. Violence was horrific in the vicinity of Grahamstown. The white town of Grahamstown is the English 1820 Settlers' Association showpiece answer to the Afrikaner Voortrekker Monument at Pretoria. Soldiers and armored vehicles had taken the place of cultural festival visitors.

It was only when, closer to home, Soweto became a hell to which Johannesburg's black workers returned each night as best they could (buses would not venture farther than Soweto boundaries) that white faces in Johannesburg became strained. Until then, most whites in South Africa were in a state of anguish over the outcome of the New Zealand Government's determination to stop a rugby team's tour of South Africa.

The minority within the white minority did not have to wait for any declaration to be aware of an emergency beyond the nation's rugby fields. Some leaders had been warning for months that an uprising was inevitable: built into the new Constitution as its own consequence. Outstanding among them were Bishop Desmond M. Tutu; the Rev. Beyers Naudé, general secretary of the

South African Council of Churches, and the Rev. Allan Boesak, president of the World Alliance of Reformed Churches and a founder of the United Democratic Front—who was detained in August on the eve of an illegal protest march and the widespread violence that followed.

Also there was Sheena Duncan of the Black Sash—a women's organization that has done more than any other source to expose the appalling forced removals of black rural people. Government policy has meant that in the past 25 years, one in ten blacks has been moved to make way for whites.

The Government was arresting trade union leaders and leaders of the United Democratic Front, an organization which recognizes no racial or color distinctions and stands for a unitary state in South Africa. And just as, abroad, one may mutter abhorrence of apartheid and go on funding it morally and materially, so the Government was busy reiterating a litany of dedication to consultation and change, while arresting almost every black leader with any claim to be consulted about change.

On the minority side of the dividing line between white and white, a new organization had grown in urgent response to the deployment of 7,000 troops against the people of the black township of Sebokeng, 40 miles south of Johannesburg, last October. This force included young army recruits. Resistance to conscription—while still rare—was suddenly no longer some fringe defection on religious grounds by a handful of Seventh-day Adventists, but a wave of revulsion against "defending one's country" by maiming, killing and breaking into the humble homes of black people.

In this horrifying domestic context, a group called the End Conscription Campaign held a three-day gathering in Johannesburg. A large crowd of young men and their families debated the moral issues of conscientious objection and defined their position not as pacifist but as a refusal to defend apartheid.

I gave a reading there of poetry by South African writers, black and white, in whose work, like that of playwrights, lately, resistance to military service has been the theme. The subject has to be handled gingerly, whether in poetry or platform prose; it is a treasonable offense in South Africa to incite anyone to refuse military service. The E.C.C. is not yet a mass movement, and maybe will not become one, but the Government is sufficiently alarmed by it to have detained several members.

Again, there is a strange historical twinship. Even after 1960, when the South African revolution may be said to have begun, the sons of liberal and left-wing families docilely accepted, *force majeure,* the obligation to do military service, if with a sense of resentment and shame. At the same time whites who support black liberation have long wondered why blacks have not turned significantly against the informers and collaborators among their own people.

Now, young whites have at last found the courage to fulfill the chief provision blacks demand of them if they are to prove their commitment to the black cause: to refuse to fight to protect racism. Meanwhile, young blacks themselves have reached the stage of desperation that leads them to hunt down and destroy those who are their own people in terms of skin, but not loyalty.

Both developments—the first positive, the second tragic—are the direct result of the new Constitution. The blacks were not consulted about it, rejected it, and are now in a continuous state of rebellion, out of bottomless frustration at finding themselves finally cast out, in civic and even physical terms, from their own country. The Government deals with this rebellion by sending in white soldiers to terrorize blacks into temporary submission; young whites are confronted with the loathsome "duty" it was surely always clear racism eventually would demand.

For years, when one asked blacks why they allowed black police to raid and arrest them, they would answer: "Our brothers have to do what whites tell them. We are all victims together." Now, black youths are confronted with what surely always was clear would be the ultimate distortion of their lives by apartheid: brothers, co-opted as police informers and city dignitaries by white power, becoming enemies.

Many of us who belong to the minority within the minority already were accustomed, before the state of emergency, to using the telephone for the kind of call not made outside thriller movies in your country.

When the South African Defence Force raided the capital of one of our neighboring countries, Botswana, earlier this year, we feared for the lives of black and white friends living in exile there.

For some days, we could piece together their fate only by exchanging guarded word-of-mouth news. For my fellow writer, Sipho Sepamla, the news was bad. He traveled across the border to Botswana to the funeral of a relative murdered in the raid. We were nervous about his doing so, since the brutal raid—which resulted in indiscriminate killing, so that even children died—was purportedly against African National Congress revolutionaries, and the demonstration of any connection with even random victims could rub off as guilt by association.

With the beginning of the state of emergency came mass arrests, and severe penalties for revealing without authority the identity of any detainee. The names we know are confined to those permitted by the police to be published. Who can say how many others there are? So our ominous kind of morning gossip has increased—and there remains the fear that the individual one calls may not answer because he or she has been taken.

Some of us have friends among those who are the accused in the treason trials in session or about to commence, mainly trade unionists and leaders of the United Democratic Front. I telephone my old friend, Cassim Saloojee, a social worker and an officer in the United Democratic Front. He is at home on bail after many weeks of detention before being formally charged with treason. One discovers, these days, that genuine cheerfulness exists, and it is a byproduct of courage. He has only one complaint, which is expressed in a way that catches me out—"I've been spending my time watching pornographic films," he says.

With my tactfully unshockable laugh, I suddenly remember that active resistance to apartheid is "political pornography." The films he has been viewing are video cassettes of public meetings made by the United Democratic Front as records of their activities. They have been seized by the state. For the purposes of their own defense, the accused must study what may now be used as evidence against them. "Ninety hours of viewing. . . ."

The case is sub judice, so I suppose I cannot give here my version of whether the particular meetings I attended (the U.D.F. is a nonracial, nonviolent and legally constituted movement) could possibly be construed as violent and treasonous, but I hope that among all that footage there is at least recorded the time when the crowd in a Johannesburg hall heard that there was police harassment of some supporters in the foyer, and, from the platform, Cassim Saloojee succeeded in preventing the crowd from streaming out to seek a confrontation that doubtless would have resulted in police violence.

While writing this letter, I have received a call from Colin Coleman, a young white student at the University of the Witwatersrand, down the road, himself a veteran of detention. His brother is now in detention for the second time.

At last, after more than two weeks, Colin Coleman's parents have managed to get permission to visit Neil Coleman in prison. Like well over a thousand others, he has not been charged. The parents are founder members of the well-established Detainees' Parents Support Committee. This title and status indicate the enduring state of mind that prevails among white people like these, stoic but unintimidatedly active on the part of all prisoners of conscience, black and white, whether or not in the family.

Colin called to ask me to take part in a panel discussion on South African culture to be held by the students' Academic Freedom Committee. Irrelevant while we are in a state of emergency? Concurrently with engagement in the political struggle for the end of apartheid, there exists an awareness of the need for a new conception of culture, particulary among whites. Young people like Colin Coleman are aware that a *change of consciousness,* of the white sense of self, has to be achieved along with a change of regime, if, when blacks do sit down to consult with whites, there is to be anything to talk about.

The arts in South Africa sometimes do bear relation to the real entities of South African life in the way that the euphemisms and evasions of white politics do not. This is increasingly evident in the bold themes explored by blacks and whites in South Africa's theater and literature.

* * *

These are the *states of mind* of the majority of white South Africans, and of the minority within the white population. Within the first group, the majority, the preoccupations of the second are no more than newspaper stories you, too, read thousands of miles away: so long as the Caspir armored monsters patrol the black townships and even mass funerals are banned, the majority feel safe, since there is no possibility that they may be imprisoned for a too-active sense of justice, or find any member of their families or their friends in detention, on trial, or in danger of losing a life in right-wing terrorist attacks. There isn't any possibility that one of their lawyers might be gunned down, as was Victoria Mxenge, a member of a treason trial defense team, outside her home near Durban in July.

The *conditions of life,* for whites, are a different matter. Even those few whites who have members of their families in prison themselves continue to wake up every morning as I do, to the song of weaver birds and the mechanical-sounding whir of crested barbets in a white suburb. Soweto is only eight miles from my house; if I did not have friends living there, I should not be aware of the battles of stones against guns and tear gas that are going on in its streets, for images on a TV screen come by satellite as easily from the other side of the world as from eight miles away, and may be comprehended as equally distanced from the viewer. How is it possible that the winter sun is shining, the randy doves are announcing spring, the domestic workers from the back-yards are placing bets on Fah Fee, the numbers game, with the Chinese runner, as usual every afternoon?

In terms of *ways of life,* conditions of daily living are sinisterly much the same for all whites, those who manage to ignore the crisis in our country, and those for whom it is the determining state of mind. Some go to protest meetings; others play golf. All of us go home to quiet streets, outings to the theater and cinema, good meals and secure shelter for the night. Meanwhile, in the black townships, thousands of children no longer go to school, fathers and sons disappear into police vans or lie shot in the dark streets, social gatherings are around coffins and social intercourse is confined to mourning.

The night the state of emergency was declared, I was at a party held at an alternative education center, the Open School, in the downtown area where banks and the glass palaces of mining companies run down into Indian stores and black bus queues. The school is directed by Colin and Dolphine Smuts (black, despite their Afrikaans surname), for black youths and children who study drama, painting, dance and music there—subjects not offered by Government's "Bantu" education. The occasion was a celebration: the school, which had been in danger of closure for lack of funds, was to receive a Ford Foundation grant. Colin had not known until the evening began whether the new ban of gatherings might not be served on the celebration. Dolphine had gone ahead and prepared food.

There were polite speeches, music, drumming and the declamatory performance of poetry that has been part of resistance rhetoric since young people began to compose in prison during the Soweto uprisings in 1976 and which sets such gatherings apart from their counterparts in other countries. Soweto was sealed off by military roadblocks. Yet the black guests had come through somehow, thoroughly frisked in the "elegantly casual" clothes we all, black and white, wear to honor this kind of occasion. I asked a couple I had not met before what it was like to be in Soweto now, looking at them in the inhibited, slightly awed way one tries not to reveal to people who have emerged alive from some unimaginable ordeal. The man took a bite from a leg of chicken and washed it down with his drink. "In your street, one day it's all right. The next day, you can cross the street when a Caspir comes round the corner, and you'll die. It's like Beirut."

Yes, if you want to know what it's like here, it's more like Beirut than he knew. I remember a film I once saw, where the camera moved from destruction and its hateful cacophony in the streets to a villa where people were lunching on a terrace, and there were birds and flowers. That's what it's like. I also remember something said by a character in a novel I wrote ten years ago. "How long can we go on getting away scot free?"

3. THE SOUTH AFRICAN WASTELAND*

by BREYTEN BREYTENBACH

Breyten Breytenbach, the Afrikaner poet, is the author of The True Confessions of an Albino Terrorist *(New York: Farrar, Straus and Giroux, 1983). He was arrested in South Africa in 1975 and charged with terrorism. Sentenced to nine years in prison, he served seven and was released in 1982, thanks to an intervention by President Mitterrand. He now lives in Paris.*

What is the true nature of the South African state? I propose two series of answers. Talking of South Africa as a reality, one could say that it is a fairly developed industrial state, the economic giant of the region—using, for instance, 60 percent of all the electricity generated on the continent. That it is self-sufficient, and endowed with excessive natural riches, with space enough for all, and room for expansion. That it is the granary of the subcontinent. That

*From *The New Republic,* November 4, 1985.

it is a land laid waste by recurrent droughts and erosion and mismanagement, its arable surfaces diminishing yearly. That it is a Third World country, showing all the archaic features of a feudal society, with the vast majority of its citizens living or dying under the breadline. That it is a country made up of a rich patchwork of cultures, but due to acculturation, centuries of mixing, and a long exposure to American clichés, exhibiting a distinctly recognizable South African culture, making it different from Zimbabwe and Mozambique. That it is a country where differences are enforced and exploited and rewarded by the privileges of discrimination. That it is a country cut off from the world, where thinking and political activity are smothered. That it is a depoliticized wasteland, where the mind is stultified by imported dogmas ill-equipped to provide solutions to local discrepancies—neo-Nazism and Stalinism, to name but two. That it is a country rich in theoretical innovation, with minds stretching to provide sensemaking interpretations of its peculiar social realities, finding novel forms of political expression, inventive structures. That it is a country of the devil, of alcoholism, of despair, of heart ailments, of hereditary high blood pressure, of obesity, of hard-heartedness, of wasted bones, of apathy, of crusted-over insensitivity, of daily violence and nightly murder. That it is a country, also, of tenderness and hope and generosity and hospitality, where the believers are truly involved in the burning issues scorching the communities. That it is a place where you find Africa's foremost military force consisting of white professionals and conscripts and black volunteers, capable of both orthodox and irregular forms of warfare, ready to strike fast and far beyond its borders; a land where the army, made up of jittery young whites, brainwashed, taking to drugs, and brutal black flunkies, is employed in the squashing of internal uprisings—an occupation force. That it is a land of rain and wind and dust; of storms and isolation; a land crisscrossed by borders; a land of death and regeneration; of death mentality, suicide mentality; of border paranoia, revolutionary elan.

My second group of answers would touch upon the world of difference between pretensions and reality, upon the world of madness, of calculated madness, of sublimated madness. Those in power in Pretoria claim that, as the arbiters of peace and progress, they are carrying the illuminating force of Western civilization into the heathen darkness, that they are God's lonely soldiers battling against communism and barbarism. Many of them even believe it. Some powerful individuals abroad do too, or pretend to. Those in power in Pretoria fully insist that they are the only ones who can assure Western capitalist investment in the subcontinent. In the process of so pretending, they are, inter alia, corrupting the power brokers of the West—often, alas, so easily corruptible. They are also raping Africa; but that would seem to be by the way, as the West closes a complacent eye and leers tolerantly at those goings-on as just healthy sexual romping. They say that they are uplifting the natives, near and far. They can even be heard to boast that they know and understand Africa and the Africans.

The truth? Communism has found, objectively, a recruiting agent in the South African regime, embodying boldly the basest manifestations of capitalist colonialism. The rulers are destabilizing and ruining the region, and mortally humiliating the entire continent. They are destroying the credibility and the viability of Western values. They are endangering, in the long run, whatever strategic and financial interests the West may have in the area. They cannot know the Africans, or even themselves. How can the master ever understand the slave? Control and repression are not tools of perception.

The veritable nature of the South African state is that it is totalitarian. A totalitarian system is found, I think, where a single party expressed in a structure of power, usually operating on behalf of some homogeneous ideology, rules the state to the exclusion, or more likely the repression, of any valid alternative. The dominant establishment may well range from a centralized democracy to a seemingly democratic multiparty setup; in certain instances dissent may be allowed, and opposition tolerated, but only to maintain the appearance of tolerance, or to the extent that resistance may be incorporated into the oppressive system, to make it stronger by rendering it more flexible.

And since a totalitarian system is always run by a minority, military and police methods must be used to impose the system on the majority. Repression, with its concomitants of violence and corruption, will inevitably be justified in the name of the state's supposed security, which is the highest good and ideal; the state is God's carcass inhabited by the good and the just. Arbitrary administrative measures take precedence over representational politics. The army and the police, particularly the security police and the intelligence advisers, become the mainstay of the regime. Totalitarianism promotes a police state —not necessarily because the streets will be crawling with policemen, but because treachery and informing will be the name of the game, indeed a survival technique, and because people living in such a state will camouflage their true beliefs and pretend to opinions of convenience. Finally, the power elite, more likely than not, will be organized as an occult brotherhood, or a lodge, or a league.

South African totalitarianism's claim to fame, however, lies in its constitutional, institutionalized, structural, and codified racism—covering all forms of human intercourse and enterprise: politics, economics, religion, social life, culture, sports, sex. It is unique in its alternative solutions to all the problems of cultural and economic coexistence, solutions such as camps, homelands, border industries, mass removals, classification, repression, and crisis control. It is unique in its shaping of new forms of colonialism, just when we thought that history was at last pointing the other way. It is unique in its introduction of massive state violence against its own citizens, in a controlled enlarging of the limits of acceptable violence. It is unique in its conscious banalization of inhumanity. It is the cutting edge of a new realpolitik, expressed in the callousness to hunger and poverty and death.

What does this state aim for? To perpetuate itself; to increase the good fortune of those loyal to it, whose interest it promotes. Since it is totalitarian and expansionist, but also encircled from within and without by growing numbers of agitators, antagonists, barbarians, and others like myself, it must extend its hegemony, particularly if it wishes to preserve its privileges. And so, despite breakdowns, fuck-ups, and temporary setbacks, it moves along the suppurating lines of big apartheid, farming out the indigenous majority to manageable homelands, depriving them of their nationality as South Africans, ultimately aiming to regroup them together, with the neighboring client states or colonies, in a constellation of Southern African states with white South Africa secured by the constructive approval it gets from the United States.

Does the South African state evolve? Is it amenable to pressure? No, it has shown no evolution, except for an adjustment to changing circumstances, a refinement of the theoretical matrix underpinning the praxis, an introduction of some flexibility to make it more resilient, all still in terms of overall goals and basic assumptions that have not undergone even an iota of change. Nobody can tell, in fact, how it would react if it were put under real pressure; no effective pressure, apart from low-level internal resistance flaring up sporadically, has ever been brought to bear upon it.

Ideally, as things are moving now, there could come a point when the rulers of South Africa become enmeshed in the pretense of affecting structural and conceptual changes, when they unleash more momentum than they can handle. I have always maintained that it is not important to expect the racist to undergo a change of heart; he should be forced by circumstances, rather, to *pretend* that he is not a racist. Eventually the posture will come to have content. But I'm not optimistic. First, because the rulers have enough blanket control to guide events and direct them. Second, because Afrikaner consciousness is grounded in a profound willingness to self-destruct. This armors their fanaticism. The Afrikaner, with the rigid sense of insecurity of the half-breed, is culturally incapable of absorbing or translating or accommodating transformation, let alone of provoking it.

What are the real problems, then, the true obstacles, facing the South African state as construed and run by the white elite?

(1) Demographic pressure. They cannot breed fast enough, and a tribal survival instinct may well be blemished. Nor can they incorporate sufficient numbers of foreign whites fast enough without submerging their identity. And

even if they were to succeed in making real allies of the two co-opted minorities, the Indian and the Coloured, the dike would not withstand the flood; and they have run out of minorities by now.

(2) Economic pressure. They can only safeguard their own privileges by allowing the economic growth, and ultimately the integration, of the blacks, which doctrine of course forbids; and there is not enough money to go around. A certain Dr. Frank Shostak, an economic researcher, foresees that during 1985 we shall see the price of gold slithering to somewhere between $270 and $300 an ounce; that the prime interest rate will be 35 percent, and the South African rand will not be worth much more than 25 cents, and that it may well plunge to ten cents; that there will be zero economic growth probably until 1988. (To compare, when I was in prison the gold price was reaching for $500 an ounce, and the rand used to be pegged to the dollar on a one-on-one basis. Perhaps I should have stayed in prison.)

The fat of the land is turning rancid. Economic and financial hardship will accentuate the rifts in their own ranks. The far right will become more militant, more influential. And then—resistance. For there is just no way that they can, once and for all, eradicate black political consciousness, or prevent it from evolving specifically South African forms of struggle against South African totalitarianism. Time, you may say, is black.

Who is the opposition? Ultimately, the ruling elite is confronting the South African people. I'm not for a moment attempting to deny the South Africanness, the *Africanité,* of those now ruling. I am saying, however, that the opposition, too, is patriotic, that it comes from within, in the name of the healing of the South African nation. More precisely, effective opposition more and more clearly situates itself in relation to the aims and the practices of the political avant-garde and mass organizations of South African history, foremost among them the African National Congress. In a land of crude extremes, the liberal alternative is a nonstarter, a nonadaptable transplant from more clement climes, ill-equipped to do battle with nationalism and extremism. In the final analysis, liberalism of the old-fashioned kind can but fit a more humane mask over the embittered features of the clowns running the show.

The battle lines are thus drawn. On the one hand, the white minority, with some Coloured and Indian and minimal black support, using a fearsome repressive machinery, having a monopoly on power, strong in a favored position as caretakers for Western interests; on the other, the black majority, with some Coloured and Indian and white support, led by the ANC or by organizations hewing to the same line. What does the opposition propose? The opposition programs are vague, but there are the zero demands that cannot be negotiated: a unitary state, unconditional citizenship for all majority government. These are the essentials. They can perhaps even be reduced to: one people, one nation. (Those words were written on the flag that covered the coffin of Steve Biko when he was carried to his grave.) Beyond that there are obviously many concerns—freedom of movement, land ownership, equality of opportunity, decent and free education, and so on. But what matters now is the quality and the lucidity of the opposition struggle—the extent to which, by their principles and their choices, the resistance organizations show the way to moral acuity and nation-building. Oppression sharpens the mind; resistance cleans it.

The opposition, of course, is not homogeneous. There are real differences of approach, though far less than the Bothas of this world would have us believe. Influential factions may be against violence, but all thinking is defined by the simple fact of the Boer having the gun, and using it. He is quite literally calling the shots. People may not look upon violent resistance as the decisive component of liberation, but no one expects the process to be violence-free. How do you talk to the man who has been killing hundreds of your youngsters over the last year?

There are essentially still two major resistance groupings—the "charterists" (referring to the 1955 Freedom Charter) such as the ANC and the UDF, and the Black Consciousness movements such as the Black Forum and AZAPO (Azanian People's Organization). Differences in analysis, appraisal, and approach have led to internecine community violence. In a ham-fisted way the government tried to exacerbate this. The ideological positions of the two currents are not static; they have been evolving, are partially overlapping. Black Consciousness is now perhaps more Marxist-influenced than used to be the case. . . . All of this demands a clearer exegesis than I'm capable of.

Opposition? I prefer to speak of resistance. We cannot, as yet, talk of a general uprising. The situation cannot be described as either an insurrection or a revolution, although aspects of a revolution are present—such as an indigenous mind-freeing, a willingness to be self-reliant, the purging of informers, collaborators, lackeys, police spies. What we do have is the flaring up of a low-level civil war. Black resistance now is significantly different from previous eruptions (Sharpeville and after during the 1960s, Soweto in 1976), in that the locus of mobilization is inside the country; all strata of the population are involved; the backdrop is one of dire economic hardship; the people are more resolute and more desperate, and political awareness is at a much higher general level; there has been an accumulation of militant experiences; liberation is not seen to be a wave breaking over the borders; and trade unions have hardened their political role (despite the relative failure of the recent mine workers' strike).

The South African majority is painfully forging—as oppressed peoples always have had to—its own physical and ideological tools in the liberation struggle against a peculiarly South African blend of exploitation, repression, and corruption. This struggle is not necessarily well coordinated. It is unclear to what extent the ANC is present, despite its international recognition and the people's mythical identification with ANC colors and songs. One of the heartening elements, even if it can be disruptive, is the ongoing ideological debate on anything from the role of trade unions to the pros and cons of violent or nonviolent strategies to the duplicity of official United States reactions.

What are the possible scenarios? Again, I don't think there is any cause for optimism. There will be blood and suffering, treachery and bestiality. Those in power will stretch their claws to the Congo. Where among the nations of the world can the political will be found to thwart them? And who in Africa, or what combination of forces, can mobilize the necessary economic and military power to prevent the implementation of their schemes? This is the first, the most gruesome, alternative. But they will be building on sand. For how long could they maintain the state of drawn-out war, beset by eternal unrest, needed to impose such a Pax Africana?

The second possibility hinges on rapid deterioration—a cave-in of the national economy and a wide-scale, well-coordinated black uprising. I don't think that is likely, either. But the ferocious commitment to the struggle of those presently fighting with bare hands, and their willingness not only to endure suffering, general unemployment, no electricity or water in the townships, but actually to sacrifice themselves, could become a decisive factor. The government is showing a willingness to use troops for internal security purposes. Now they cannot undo the escalation. They have been maneuvered into the classical trap of being an occupation force.

A third possibility I have already alluded to: that the powers would lose control over the attempts at reform and adaptation. If the politicians fail, will the army then take over? Why not? Or need it be pointed out that the military forces already, surreptitiously and then sometimes quite openly, are in command? What of the fact that we have now, in the best banana tradition, a professional soldier as minister of defense? Look at Namibia. Isn't it really only a military province? Surely the negotiations can be described as essentially a military process. Look at the way foreign policy toward Angola, Zimbabwe, Mozambique is conceived, and put into application, as acts of war.

When P. W. Botha came to power in 1978 (by what I described elsewhere as a "camouflaged coup d'état"), as the culmination of the carefully engineered "Information Scandal," which brought down B. J. Vorster and scratched from the race Botha's rival, Connie Mulder, then minister of the interior, it meant that military thinking would thenceforth largely define the future. Botha was minister of defense; he now had grouped around him a generation of Green Beret-type "interventionist" anti-guerrilla strategists. Through this ascendancy the new "pragmatic" constitutional thinking can be traced, the shift in power from Parliament or party caucus to a National Security Council can be explained, South Africa's military meddling near (and far) in Africa can be understood.

It's perhaps useless to speculate about a Jericho solution—that all-encompassing and purifying revolution inexplicably bringing down the walls. What can be more plausibly foreseen is that the official white opposition, the progressives, will focus on three areas of dispute: urbanization, influx-control, the nationality question. The browns in parliament will want to do away with the laws of apartheid. They are puppets who must show that they can dance without strings. The blacks will harden and diversify their total rejection and opposition. Economic or trade union action will become more important. The psychological freeing from dependency through a re-valorized consciousness will again become relevant. But they will suffer from the split between Black Consciousness and "charterists," meaning essentially the ANC-UDF.

The African National Congress will go into crisis. Deprived effectively of bases, the external headquarters now finds its primacy as the architect of a developing armed struggle threatened. Paradoxically, the ANC inside the country is growing in strength and popularity. Does this mean that the outside leadership may lose its grip on events inside? Is that perhaps one of the reasons why the ANC may now be interested in talking to the South African government?

I think that on one side the struggle will be more diversified, become more complex, and on the other side there will be repeated offensive actions launched by the whites, to shore up their recently confirmed position of regional dominance. Botha will swing through Africa. There will be regional alliances and development aid from abroad funneled through the white government. There will be the occasional military incursion alternating with economic throttle to weaken Zimbabwe and Zambia. They will play footsie with Zaire. They will ignore Tanzania, and have no reason to be reminded of the existence of Malawi, except as a feeding trough for RNM, the Mozambique rebels. They will pray that the Cubans do not leave Angola too soon, so that they may continue extrapolating their internal contradictions into an East-West conflict.

It is true, at the same time, that many average South African whites are at the moment deeply shaken and despondent because of recent events, and the confusing signals flashed at them by the leaders; true that some conscripts seem to be reluctant, even in the name of "emergency," to be marching on the townships against the "adversary" or the "enemy" (as blacks are referred to) —but there the opposition Progressive Federal Party may suggest succor by propagating an end to conscription and a strengthening of the professional army! True, also, that many observers now consider Botha a lame-duck president. But then, incapacity, rigidity, blustering, stupidity, and any number of self-inflicted foot wounds never disqualified an Afrikaner politico. Just look, for instance, at the fine career of Louis le Grange, minister of law and order.

If you think in terms of survival and attrition, if you take into account that the government is ready, if need be, to do away with the residual vestiges of white democracy, if you believe (as government leaders do) that they are facing a flabby and, at best, hypocritical West, and a dissolute and bribe-weakened Africa ever hovering on the brink of tribal genocide—then you can see why and how they do not consider themselves seriously challenged yet. (Although they don't underestimate the Total Onslaught!) They cannot seriously be challenged from within their own ranks, since they man the only lifeboat provided for the whites.

Concerned outsiders will be well advised to remember that they are facing a South African political-military cast unrestrained by moral boundaries, profoundly (finally self-destructively) motivated by a fanaticism that cannot conceive of anything less than a monopoly of power. Their guidelines are *adapt or change,* better still, *dye or die* (and not *adapt or die,* as P. W. Botha so disingenuously averred). They will dye if they have to, but the ultimate barrier remains: for the whites, barring some exceptions, the blacks, barring some exceptions, are not human the same way they are.

So what else is new? Given the rulers' declared and illustrated resolve to use force against all comers, and given their considerable police and military power, it doesn't seem as if they have been weakened by events. Criticism leveled at them by business community spokesmen may reflect differences in priorities and degrees of anguish that are more apparent than real. To the extent that these concerns of the free marketeers tend to confuse and defuse international solidarity expressed through sanctions or divestment, it suits the regime no end. In any event, the government (I sense) expects to have turned the corner. The world is doing its worst and it isn't good enough. International queasiness is dying down, and traditional interests are being reasserted. The possibility of international orchestration leading to the political, economic, and military isolation of South Africa now seems remote. South Africa's backers (Ronald Reagan's America, Margaret Thatcher's Britain, Helmut Kohl's Germany . . .) are still stronger than the dispersed opponents.

At the time of this writing, in late September, it is clear that internal turmoil has not yet seriously impaired the white regime's regional aggressiveness or its capacity for exporting unrest: it is again intervening abroad in Angola, in support of UNITA. Similarly, the world abroad is probably belatedly discovering the harsh but dialectically agile adversaries so well known to South African freedom fighters. The government's response to mounting pressure from inside and outside the country has been standard: promises, doublespeak, obfuscating the real problems, one step forward and two in the kisser, shooting the messengers of ill tidings. Even blackmail and threats: it is enlightening to see a Botha wag a warning pie-stained finger at the whole world, promising dire consequences and burnt hands, in exactly the same mad way as when talking to those subjects "who don't know their place" or, God forbid, "who agitate!" And, ah, to see the South African government use on you, America, the well-tried repressive technique of alternating the "bad" Botha with the "good" Botha!

Changes? It is true that some of the most hoary apartheid fixtures have been modified or abolished—the law prohibiting "mixed" marriages and that declaring "mixed" sex "immoral." Many more will probably disappear from the books. They must, if the minimal support of Coloureds and Indians is to be retained. It will all be done with a great to-do—taking the padlocks off the stable doors after the horses have been shot. And not a damn essential will be altered. Unrest may die down temporarily, yes, but I don't doubt that the war will continue.

While we were all looking the other way, at apartheid, the nature of power control and the depth of Western involvement in Southern Africa were modified, consolidated, and are in the process of being revealed now as much more naked and ferocious than we ever thought.

The situation being extraordinarily complex, the writer, if he really wants to write, if he wants to hone his craft, must face the splitting of the mind, the supping with the devil, the writing in dribbles from the corner of the mouth, but also the exhilarating challenge of rising to the need. But how? We don't even speak the same meanings. If you say "man," quite innocently, in Afrikaans, you are of necessity referring to a white; the language has other derogatory terms for indicating the Other. Similarly, "peace" in the white mouth demands maintaining a strict order by law, protecting the status quo, everybody "knowing his place." For the black, this peace spells poverty, oppression, alienation, indignity, humiliation, and being driven to the despair of violence in the bitter quest for the recognition of his essential being. Justice is white. Imagine a black who has raped a white not being sentenced to the rope. Imagine a white condemned to death for raping a black. Imagine what it is like to be, naturally, by birth, an alien in your country, needing a pass to move through it and a permit allowing you to settle there temporarily, on sufferance. Think of how many black males attain adulthood without a sojourn in prison.

Do you believe that beauty is the same, then, for black and white—or politics, or commitment, or literary and intellectual quality? And yet we all speak the same words seen through different prisms of ache. The best black writing comes from the profound shared popular aspiration toward freedom, but this identification does not help with the conundrum of not having an audience, not really; and neither does it of necessity confer quality on the work. As for the whites, despite the fact that some of them, some of us, are passionate observers, and sometime diligent escapees into the exquisitely vibrating space of a literary no-man's-land, we are alienated, marginalized, depoliticized, irrelevant. The heart is shrinking.

And yet the task remains the same—to keep the word alive, or uncontaminated, or at least to allow it to have a meaning, to be a conduit of awareness. To remember that writing imposes an obligation of dignity, even if idiotically so, in the Dostoevskian sense. To try not to confuse writing with politics, given the fact that writing *is* politics. To keep up the noise level, to create confusion at least, to be an undermining campaigner for alternatives, that is for thinking. To fight against the laming of the palate. To keep an uncivil tongue in the head. To write against that fate worse than death, the wooden tongue clacking away in the wooden orifice in order to produce the wooden singsong praises to the big bang-bang and the fluttering flag. Not to knuckle down to oversimplification. To write like a bat out of hell, always screeching for the line of truth. To accept the compromise to survive, publishing by hook or by crook or by samizdat, beating the breast and gnashing the teeth, if you are that way inclined.

Propagating violence? Condoning mayhem? Penning prose poems to some homegrown Stalin? No. The craft excludes that. To accept, though with humility and compassion, that we have, that we all have, areas of rottenness within us, that which was stolen and killed by the censor, or weakened by fear. The white writer, moreover, must avoid the twin paternalist pitfalls of either trying to speak in the place of the oppressed blacks, or indulging in special pleading when it comes to their work. He must, at all costs, avoid having himself or his work be tainted by the epithets of martyrdom or courageous actions. Someone once said to me that there are two forms of corruption, the corruption of power and the corruption of suffering. The one needs to be avoided as badly as the other.

I have set these bleak thoughts about totalitarianism, and the role of the writer in a totalitarian situation, in South Africa, partly because it is the totalitarian situation that I know best, to the extent that a white living away from that country, with its hidden majority, can pretend to know it at all; but mainly because South Africa is at one and the same time a unique case, and a microcosm of the many problems bedeviling colonial societies, or imperialist outposts, or multicultural nations, or simply developing countries; and also, if I may be for a moment a little imperialist myself, because the solution to the South African problem will be exemplary to the world, and will set Africa on the road to freedom.

4. APARTHEID: AN EVIL SYSTEM

by BISHOP DESMOND M. TUTU

The following is Bishop Desmond M. Tutu's Nobel Peace Prize address, delivered in Oslo, December 10, 1984.

Your Majesty, members of the Royal Family, Mr. Chairman, Ladies and Gentlemen:

Before I left South Africa, a land I love passionately, we had an emergency meeting of the Executive Committee of the South African Council of Churches with the leaders of our member churches. We called the meeting because of the deepening crisis in our land, which has claimed nearly 200 lives this year alone. We visited some of the troublespots on the Witwatersrand. I went with others to the East Rand. We visited the home of an old lady. She told us that she looked after her grandson and the children of neighbors while their parents were at work. One day the police chased some pupils who had been boycotting classes, but they disappeared between the township houses. The police drove down the old lady's street. She was sitting at the back of the house in her kitchen, whilst her charges were playing in the front of the house in the yard. Her daughter rushed into the house, calling out to her to come quickly. The old lady dashed out of the kitchen into the living room. Her grandson had fallen just inside the door, dead. He had been shot in the back by the police. He was six years old. A few weeks later, a white mother, trying to register her black servant for work, drove through a black township. Black rioters stoned her car and killed her baby of a few months old, the first white casualty of the current unrest in South Africa. Such deaths are two too many. These are part of the high cost of apartheid.

Every day in a squatter camp near Cape Town, called K.T.O., the authorities have been demolishing flimsy plastic shelters which black mothers have erected because they were taking their marriage vows seriously. They have been reduced to sitting on soaking mattresses, with their household effects strewn round their feet, and whimpering babies on their laps, in the cold Cape winter rain. Every day the authorities have carried out these callous demolitions. What heinous crime have these women committed, to be hounded like criminals in this manner? All they wanted is to be with their husbands, the fathers of their children. Everywhere else in the world they would be highly commended, but in South Africa, a land which claims to be Christian, and which boasts a public holiday called Family Day, these gallant women are treated so inhumanely, and yet all they want is to have a decent and stable family life. Unfortunately, in the land of their birth, it is a criminal offence for them to live happily with their husbands and the fathers of their children. Black family life is thus being undermined, not accidentally, but by deliberate Government policy. It is part of the price human beings, God's children, are called to pay for apartheid. An unacceptable price.

I come from a beautiful land, richly endowed by God with wonderful natural resources, wide expanses, rolling mountains, singing birds, bright shining stars out of blue skies, with radiant sunshine, golden sunshine. There is enough of the good things that come from God's bounty, there is enough for everyone, but apartheid has confirmed some in their selfishness, causing them to grasp greedily a disproportionate share, the lion's share, because of their power. They have taken 87 percent of the land, though being only about 20 percent of our population. The rest have had to make do with the remaining 13 percent. Apartheid has decreed the politics of exclusion. Seventy-three percent of the population is excluded from any meaningful participation in the political decision-making processes of the land of their birth. The new constitution, making provision for three chambers, for whites, coloureds, and Indians, mentions blacks only once, and thereafter ignores them completely. Thus this new constitution, lauded in parts of the West as a step in the right direction, entrenches racism and ethnicity. The constitutional committees are composed in the ratio of four whites to two coloureds and one Indian. Zero black. Two plus one can never equal, let alone be more than, four. Hence this constitution perpetuates by law and entrenches white minority rule. Blacks are expected to exercise their political ambitions in unviable, poverty-striken, arid, bantustan homelands, ghettoes of misery, inexhaustible reservoirs of cheap black labor, bantustans into which South Africa is being balkanized. Blacks are systematically being stripped of their South African citizenship and being turned into aliens in the land of their birth. This is apartheid's final solution, just as Nazism had its final solution for the Jews in Hitler's Aryan madness. The South African Government is smart. Aliens can claim but very few rights, least of all political rights.

In pursuance of apartheid's ideological racist dream, over 3,000,000 of God's children have been uprooted from their homes, which have been demolished, whilst they have then been dumped in the bantustan homeland resettlement camps. I say dumped advisedly; only things or rubbish is dumped, not human beings. Apartheid has, however, ensured that God's children, just because they are black, should be treated as if they were things, and not as of infinite value as being created in the image of God. These dumping grounds are far from where work and food can be procured easily. Children starve, suffer from the often irreversible consequences of malnutrition—this happens to them not accidentally, but by deliberate Government policy. They starve in a land that could be the bread basket of Africa, a land that normally is a net exporter of food.

The father leaves his family in the bantustan homeland, there eking out a miserable existence, whilst he, if he is lucky, goes to the so-called white man's town as a migrant, to live an unnatural life in a single sex hostel for 11 months of the year, being prey there to prostitution, drunkenness, and worse. This migratory labor policy is declared Government policy, and has been condemned, even by the white D.R.C. [Dutch Reformed Church], not noted for being quick to criticise the Government, as a cancer in our society. This cancer, eating away at the vitals of black family life, is deliberate Government policy. It is part of the cost of apartheid, exorbitant in terms of human suffering.

Apartheid has spawned discriminatory education, such as Bantu Education, education for serfdom, ensuring that the Government spends only about one tenth on one black child per annum for education what it spends on a white child. It is education that is decidedly separate and unequal. It is to be wantonly wasteful of human resources, because so many of God's children are prevented, by deliberate Government policy, from attaining to their fullest potential. South Africa is paying a heavy price already for this iniquitous policy because there is a desperate shortage of skilled manpower, a direct result of the short-sighted schemes of the racist regime. It is a moral universe that we inhabit, and good and right and equity matter in the universe of the God we worship. And so, in this matter, the South African Government and its supporters are being properly hoisted with their own petard.

Apartheid is upheld by a phalanx of iniquitous laws, such as the Population Registration Act, which decrees that all South Africans must be classified ethnically, and duly registered according to these race categories. Many times, in the same family one child has been classified white whilst another, with a slightly darker hue, has been classified coloured, with all the horrible consequences for the latter of being shut out from membership of a greatly privileged caste. There have, as a result, been several child suicides. This is too high a price to pay for racial purity, for it is doubtful whether any end, however desirable, can justify such a means. There are laws, such as the Prohibition of Mixed Marriages Act, which regard marriages between a white and a person of another race as illegal. Race becomes an impediment to a valid marriage. Two persons who have fallen in love are prevented by race from consummating their love in the marriage bond. Something beautiful is made to be sordid and ugly. The Immorality Act decrees that fornication and adultery are illegal if they happen between a white and one of another race. The police are reduced to the level of peeping Toms to catch couples red-handed. Many whites have committed suicide rather than face the disastrous consequences that follow in the train of even just being charged under this law. The cost is too great and intolerable.

Such an evil system, totally indefensible by normally acceptable methods, relies on a whole phalanx of draconian laws such as the security legislation which is almost peculiar to South Africa. There are the laws which permit the indefinite detention of persons whom the Minister of Law and Order has decided are a threat to the security of the State. They are detained at his pleasure, in solitary confinement, without access to their family, their own doctor, or a lawyer. That is severe punishment when the evidence apparently available to the Minister has not been tested in an open court—perhaps it could stand up to such rigorous scrutiny, perhaps not; we are never to know. It is a far too convenient device for a repressive regime, and the minister would have to be extra special not to succumb to the temptation to curcumvent the awkward process of testing his evidence in an open court, and thus he lets his power under the law to be open to the abuse where he is both judge and prosecutor. Many, too many, have died mysteriously in detention. All this is too costly in terms of human lives. The minister is able, too, to place people under banning orders without being subjected to the annoyance of the checks and balances of due process. A banned person for three or five years becomes a nonperson, who cannot be quoted during the period of her banning order. She cannot attend a gathering, which means more than one other person. Two persons together talking to a banned person are a gathering! She cannot attend the wedding or funeral of even her own child without special permission. She must be at home from 6:00 P.M. of one day to 6:00 A.M. of the next and on all public holidays, and from 6:00 P.M. on Fridays until 6:00 A.M. on Mondays for three years. She cannot go on holiday outside the magisterial area to which she has been confined. She cannot go to the cinema, nor to a picnic. That is severe punishment, inflicted without the evidence allegedly justifying it being made available to the banned person, nor having it scrutinized in a court of law. It is a serious erosion and violation of basic human rights, of which blacks have precious few in the land of their birth. They do not enjoy the rights of freedom of movement and association. They do not enjoy freedom of security of tenure, the right to participate in the making of decisions that affect their lives. In short, this land, richly endowed in so many ways, is sadly lacking in justice.

Once a Zambian and a South African, it is said, were talking. The Zambian then boasted about their Minister of Naval Affairs. The South African asked,

"But you have no navy, no access to the sea. How then can you have a Minister of Naval Affairs?" The Zambian retorted, "Well, in South Africa you have a Minister of Justice, don't you?"

It is against this system that our people have sought to protest peacefully since 1912 at least, with the founding of the African National Congress. They have used the conventional methods of peaceful protest—petitions, demonstrations, deputations, and even a passive resistance campaign. A tribute to our people's commitment to peaceful change is the fact that the only South Africans to win the Nobel Peace Prize are both black. Our people are peace-loving to a fault. The response of the authorities has been an escalating intransigence and violence, the violence of police dogs, tear gas, detention without trial, exile, and even death. Our people protested peacefully against the Pass Laws in 1960, and 69 of them were killed on March 21, 1960, at Sharpeville, many shot in the back running away. Our children protested against inferior education, singing songs and displaying placards and marching peacefully. Many in 1976, on June 16th and subsequent times, were killed or imprisoned. Over 500 people died in that uprising. Many children went into exile. The whereabouts of many are unknown to their parents. At present, to protest that self-same discriminatory education, and the exclusion of blacks from the new constitutional dispensation, the sham local black government, rising unemployment, increased rents and General Sales Tax, our people have boycotted and demonstrated. They have staged a successful two-day stay away. Over 150 people have been killed. It is far too high a price to pay. There has been little revulsion or outrage at this wanton destruction of human life in the West. In parenthesis, can somebody please explain to me something that has puzzled me. When a priest goes missing and is subsequently found dead, the media in the West carry his story in very extensive coverage. I am glad that the death of one person can cause so much concern. But in the self-same week when this priest is found dead, the South African Police kill 24 blacks who had been participating in the protest, and 6,000 blacks are sacked for being similarly involved, and you are lucky to get that much coverage. Are we being told something I do not want to believe, that we blacks are expendable and that blood is thicker than water, that when it comes to the crunch, you cannot trust whites, that they will club together against us? I don't want to believe that is the message being conveyed to us.

Be that as it may, we see before us a land bereft of much justice, and therefore without peace and security. Unrest is endemic, and will remain an unchanging feature of the South African scene until apartheid, the root cause of it all, is finally dismantled. At this time, the Army is being quartered on the civilian population. There is a civil war being waged. South Africans are on either side. When the ANC [African National Congress] and the PAC [Pan-Africanist Congress] were banned in 1960, they declared that they had no option but to carry out the armed struggle. We in the SACC [South African Council of Churches] have said we are opposed to all forms of violence—that of a repressive and unjust system, and that of those who seek to overthrow that system. However, we have added that we understand those who say they have had to adopt what is a last resort for them. Violence is not being introduced into the South African situation de novo from outside by those who are called terrorists or freedom fighters, depending on whether you are an oppressed or an oppressor. The South African situation is violent already, and the primary violence is that of apartheid, the violence of forced population removals, of inferior education, of detention without trial, of the migratory labor systems, etc.

There is war on the border of our country. South African faces follow South African. South African soldiers are fighting against Namibians who oppose the illegal occupation of their country by South Africa, which has sought to extend its repressive systems of apartheid, unjust and exploitative.

There is no peace in Southern Africa. There is no peace because there is no justice. There can be no real peace and security until there be first justice enjoyed by all the inhabitants of that beautiful land. The Bible knows nothing about peace without justice, for that would be crying "peace, peace, where there is no peace." God's Shalom, peace, involves inevitably righteousness, justice, wholeness, fullness of life, participation in decision making, goodness, laughter, joy, compassion, sharing and reconciliation. . . .

PART TWO

APARTHEID SOCIETY

Chapter II:

HISTORICAL BACKGROUND TO APARTHEID

5. *SOUTH AFRICA: FROM SETTLEMENT TO UNION**

by ERNEST HARSCH

Ernest Harsch is the co-author of Angola: The Hidden History of Washington's War *(1976). He writes frequently on South Africa for the biweekly* Intercontinental Press, *of which he is managing editor.*

Foundations of Colonial-Settler State

The roots of colonial rule and white supremacy in South Africa run deep. They stretch back more than three hundred years. From the very beginning, when the first Dutch settlers started to arrive in the seventeenth and eighteenth centuries, the history of white colonization was one of conquest, plunder, and dispossession of the indigenous Black peoples and societies. . . .

In 1652, the Dutch East India Company, then one of the largest colonial trading monopolies in the world, dispatched Jan van Riebeeck and a handful of other company employees to the Cape of Good Hope at the tip of South Africa. The company's initial aim was limited to setting up a refreshment station for its trading ships sailing to and from the Dutch colonies in Asia.

But once started, the company was impelled further down the road of colonization. Just a few years after van Riebeeck's arrival, the company agreed

*From South Africa: White Rule, Black Revolt (New York, 1980).

to allow some of its employees to settle there as "free burghers," obliged to sell their produce to the company. The settlers were allocated about twenty-eight acres of land each.

Since the Cape had already been settled many hundreds of years earlier by the San and Khoikhoi, the land the company so generously gave the white settlers had to be first acquired through conquest and guile. The encroachment of white settlers on traditional Khoikhoi grazing lands resulted in the first colonial wars. Together with the establishment of unequal trade relations that siphoned off Khoikhoi cattle into European hands, these wars greatly undermined traditional Khoikhoi society and broke its organized resistance to further white advances.

After the defeat of the Khoikhoi, the settlers turned their attention to the San. The San sought to defend their hunting grounds, but, like the Khoikhoi, were overwhelmed by superior European firepower and later virtually wiped out.

At least for the time being, these wars of dispossession provided the settlers with one of the main prerequisites for white prosperity: abundant land. What they still lacked in sufficient amounts was cheap labor power to work the land. These twin concerns—land and labor—were to recur time and again throughout South African history, serving as touchstones for much of the colonialist legislation directed toward the exploitation of the Black population.

In the early years of the Cape Colony, the settlers were unable to attract enough laborers from among the Khoikhoi or San. As long as the Khoikhoi were able to live off their cattle and the San off their hunting grounds, they would not willingly submit to employment by the conquerors. Van Riebeeck complained that "the natives here are not to be induced to work." It was to take decades before Khoikhoi society had disintegrated to such an extent that they were compelled by economic necessity to seek jobs with whites.

To supply the settlers' immediate labor demands, the Dutch East India Company agreed in 1657–58, after repeated requests by van Riebeeck, to allow the importation of slaves into the Cape. By the end of the following century, about twenty-five thousand slaves (most of them African, but also many from Asia) had been pressed into servitude in the Cape Colony.

As the number of slaves increased, the social restrictions and laws against them were stiffened. In 1760, one of the first versions of South Africa's infamous pass laws was adopted to restrict their freedom of movement. It was similar to the more extensive and elaborate pass laws of later years, which are now among the white regime's principal instruments of control over the Black population as a whole. According to the 1760 law, every slave traveling "from the town to the country or from the country to town" was required to carry a pass signed by the slave owner authorizing the journey.

As in all slave societies, the punishments meted out in South Africa were barbaric. Severe beatings by slave owners were administered routinely and the use of torture against slaves was legally sanctioned. Even minor offenses were punished with whippings, binding in chains, branding, or cutting off of ears. Upon recapture, slaves who had tried to escape were usually mutilated. More serious "crimes"—such as raising a hand against a slave owner—brought mandatory death sentences, carried out by strangulation, breaking on a wheel, decapitation, quartering and chopping off of limbs, and burning.

Throughout the eighteenth century, slavery was the predominant form of labor. Slaves from India, Ceylon, and other Asian countries performed almost all of the jobs in the mechanical trades in Cape Town. Outside of the city itself most of the slaves were put to work on white-owned farms. Thanks to slave labor, wheat and wine production increased substantially.

Although the number of "free" wage laborers did not rise appreciably until the following century, when slavery was formally abolished, some Khoikhoi did begin to seek work with white employers in the eighteenth century. By 1800, many of the fifteen thousand Khoikhoi living in the Cape Colony were employed as servants or laborers.

The large-scale importation of slaves was a momentous development in South African history. While the institution of slavery itself did not survive beyond the early part of the nineteenth century, it left a strong imprint on future social relations through the entrenchment of the master-servant relationship. The importation of slaves—and later the emergence of a class of landless Black laborers from within South Africa—tended to close the door to the settlement of large numbers of poor and unskilled whites. Those whites who did settle in South Africa in that period rapidly became part of a privileged layer. According to a report in 1743, ". . . the majority of the farmers in this Colony are not farmers in the real sense of the word, but owners of plantations, and . . . many of them consider it a shame to work with their hands."

The white settler population nevertheless continued to grow at a steady, though modest, rate. And so did the land area occupied by them. White-owned farms of six thousand acres or more became common. The sons of plantation owners soon came to expect large farms of their own as a virtual birthright. This system of white land tenancy led to a rapid expansion of the colony's frontiers.

The dispersion of the Boers (the Dutch word for farmers) inevitably brought them into contact with yet more African peoples and led to a new wave of colonial wars. In 1779 the first of a long series of wars against the Xhosa began. But Xhosa society was more developed and organized than that of the Khoikhoi and San, making them much more formidable opponents. The armed conflict along the eastern border of the Cape Colony was thus to drag on for another century.

* * *

The last two decades of the eighteenth century marked the twilight of Dutch colonial rule in South Africa. In the 1780s, the Dutch East India Company began to founder under an avalanche of debts. Despite efforts to generate more revenues and cut back on costs in the Cape and other colonies, the company went bankrupt in 1794. The following year the Cape was occupied for the first time by British troops.

By that time, industrial Britain was already a mighty imperialist power, with a vast colonial empire of its own. The biggest prize in it was India, and the Cape assumed a strategic and commercial importance in relation to the naval and trade routes to India. As long as Britain's Dutch allies were in firm control of the Cape, those routes were considered relatively secure. But after the French revolution and the subsequent French defeat of the Dutch royalist forces, the British colonialists feared that their French rivals would press onward to occupy the Cape and thus jeopardize British dominance in India itself. The British occupation of the Cape in 1795 was designed to forestall such a possibility.

The British takeover brought the colony into a period of economic growth. The white settlers were granted freedom of internal trade and the right to export their surplus produce. New towns sprang up and roads and bridges were built. Like the Dutch before them, British settlers began to arrive in South Africa. By 1820 the British recognized that the Cape was potentially the most important commercial port in the southern hemisphere and that it was a valuable market for British manufactured goods. From the position of economic isolation imposed by the former Dutch monopoly, the Cape Colony was now drawn into the main channels of world capitalist trade.

There was no fundamental difference between the policies of the British and the Dutch toward the indigenous African population. The British settlers enjoyed the same privileged status that the Boers had already carved out before them. Blacks were kept in a totally subservient position. In fact, the economic and military strength of the British colonialists enabled them to bolster and extend white supremacy in southern Africa far beyond what the Dutch had ever dreamed of achieving.

Only a few years after the British takeover, the new administration made its intentions clear by continuing the wars begun by the Dutch against the Xhosas. Farms of four thousand acres each—on land taken from the Xhosa —were parceled out to the settlers. "Though official reports told of deeds of soldiery daring," historian C. W. de Kiewiet wrote, "the real warfare was directed against the cattle and food supply of the Kaffirs [Xhosas]. Their fields were burned, their corn destroyed, and their cattle driven off. . . . Nothing was more calculated to bring them to their senses and, when the war was over, to leave them impoverished."

Over time, this policy not only had the desired effect of weakening Xhosa society, but also of inducing some Xhosas to seek employment with white farm owners. As early as the 1820s, there was a steady trickle of Xhosas into the colony, prompting the adoption of an ordinance giving passes to any Xhosa willing to work for whites.

As long as the Xhosas were able to defend themselves militarily, the policy was to push them back physically before the Cape's expanding borders. Once they had been defeated and impoverished, however, they were allowed into the colony, but only (at least in theory) on the basis of their labor as a conquered people. This was a pattern that was to unfold, slowly at first, throughout the subsequent wars on the eastern frontiers of the Cape.

By the early 1800s, those social forces in Britain favoring the abolition of slavery had gained the ascendancy. Among them were the new captains of industry, who viewed slavery as an inefficient and costly form of labor. Rather than buying slaves outright—and then having to provide at least a minimum of food and lodging whether the slaves were usefully employed at the moment or not—these entrepreneurs preferred to purchase only the actual labor time of so-called free workers.

The slave trade was formally abolished in the British Empire in 1807. The more than thirty-five thousand slaves in South Africa were officially "freed" in 1834, although they still had to be "apprenticed" to their old masters for four more years.

This signified the definitive transition of the Cape Colony from a slave-labor society into one in which the laws of the capitalist market were beginning to dominate. For Blacks, however, the change meant little real improvement in their material position; for many years wage levels rose only slightly above the former cost of slave subsistence.

Even before the abolition of slavery, "free" contract labor had become increasingly important in the Cape, much of it provided by the remnants of the Khoikhoi people, who had been almost completely landless since the end of the eighteenth century. The growing urbanization of the Khoikhoi threw them into close social contact with ex-slaves, other African peoples, and whites. Through years of intermarriage, the Khoikhoi gradually lost their specific ethnic identity and became absorbed into the racial category now known as Coloureds, which also includes descendants (usually mixed) of the San and other Africans, of Asian slaves, and of whites.

Since the abolition of slavery did not mean that the Cape had ceased to be a colonial society, Black workers—both Coloured and African—were still unable to experience much freedom, either on the labor market or in social life in general. They were fettered by various laws, pass regulations, and labor ordinances, such as the Masters and Servants Act of 1841, which made it a criminal offense for a worker to break a labor contract.

In the Eastern Cape, the wars against the Xhosa continued to disrupt African life, creating the prerequisite for an even larger supply of propertyless African laborers for the white farm owners by robbing the Xhosas of enormous herds of cattle and hundreds of square miles of land. Following a severe famine in 1857, about thirty thousand Xhosas were forced to seek work on the white-owned farms in the eastern districts of the Cape.

Various laws were enacted to control this African labor force. The Masters and Servants Act was repeatedly strengthened. The Kaffir Employment Act regulated the terms of employment of "Natives of Kafirland and other Native Foreigners," requiring them to sign labor contracts and carry passes.

The Xhosas, Coloureds, ex-slaves, and other Black peoples had no legal way of abolishing or altering the laws that governed them. Theoretically, some of them could gain the vote, but the property, income, and education qualifications were pegged so high that few of them actually did, leaving the government of the Cape a whites-only institution.

In the decade from 1836 to 1846, a number of social and economic factors affecting the Boer settlers in the Cape combined to prompt a mass migration beyond the colony's borders. Known as the Great Trek, the emigration of ten thousand settlers—one-sixth of the Cape's white population—rapidly extended the limits of white colonization and greatly affected the future history of southern Africa.

The trekkers cited a number of reasons for their original departure from the Cape. Some expressed dissatisfaction over the abolition of slavery and vowed to "preserve proper relations between master and servant" in the new regions that they conquered. Others complained about the "proud and defiant attitude" of the Xhosas. Perhaps one of the most important compulsions was the relative "shortage" of land and labor the growing Boer population faced within the confines of the colony. As they moved northward and eastward, the trekkers satisfied their economic wants by seizing yet more land and cattle and by forcing Africans to work for them.

Some of the first groups of trekkers skirted the remaining Xhosa regions and occupied land on the fringes of the Zulus' traditional territory in what is now southern Natal. After the Boers inflicted a major defeat on the Zulus, thousands of them streamed into the area, and in 1840 the trekkers proclaimed an independent white republic of Natalia. The Zulus within the republic were distributed among the settlers as laborers, with about five families working on each white-owned farm. Zulus captured in battle were "apprenticed." Passes were issued to Africans. Those Africans not needed to work for the Boers were subject to residential segregation.

British merchants in Cape Town feared that the Boers' Port Natal (Durban) would develop into a rival port to that of the Cape, so in 1843 the British annexed Natal as another direct colony and took over its administration.

The British continued many of the labor policies against the local African population developed by the Boers. Between 1845 and 1875 Theophilus Shepstone evolved a policy of territorial segregation in Natal that was to provide the model for the present apartheid regime's Bantustan program. As in the Cape, Africans in Natal theoretically had the franchise, but because of high property and other qualifications they were effectively denied the vote.

The British annexation prompted the Boers to trek once again, this time further into the interior. They set out to conquer the areas that are now the provinces of the Orange Free State and the Transvaal. The British colonialists tried to impose their direct political authority over these territories for a few years after 1848, but largely for financial reasons were compelled to pull back from any new expansionist undertakings. By 1854 they had agreed to withdraw south of the Orange River. This allowed the Boers to set up two independent white settler states, the Orange Free State and the South African Republic (Transvaal).

Before temporarily relinquishing their claims to the region north of the Orange River, however, the British helped the Boers establish themselves in the Orange Free State by waging two wars against the original inhabitants, the Sotho people. The Boers also conducted a few military campaigns of their own after the British departure. This combined British and Boer assault was eventually to leave most of the Sothos' land, especially the rich wheat fields west of the Caledon River, under white ownership, while the Sothos themselves retained only the territory that is now the formally independent country of Lesotho (then known as Basutoland), a mountainous, desolate region with only 13 percent of its land surface suitable for cultivation.

Farther to the north, beyond the Vaal River, the Boers carved out another white supremacist "republic," defeating the Ndebele, Sotho, Tswana, and other peoples in the region.

Both of the Boer republics were explicitly based on the principles of white supremacy. Neither had even a pretense of a franchise for Africans as the Cape and Natal did. The constitution of the Transvaal frankly stated, "The people want no equality of Blacks with white inhabitants, either in Church or State."

The African inhabitants were reduced to farm laborers or "squatters" on their former lands. They were required either to pay rent or to work for 90 to 180 days a year for their "right" to continue living on those lands. The land wars and the disruption of the African communal economy compelled many Africans to seek work with the white plantation owners.

Where these economic pressures did not yet bring forth enough laborers to satisfy the Boers, measures were adopted to force Africans onto the labor market. In the Orange Free State, Boer commando units burned Sotho crops in the hopes that they would be driven by hunger to seek work with white employers. In the Transvaal, military expeditions were sent out to capture African children, who were forced to work for the Boer landowners. Labor taxes were imposed, instituting a system of virtual forced labor. To control the African population, both white regimes introduced pass laws. The Transvaal regime developed an early form of "influx control," decreeing that Africans would not be allowed to live "too close to the vicinity of any town."

Over the years, the Boers in the two republics, as well as those who had stayed behind in the Cape, gradually acquired a new cultural and national identity. The Dutch that they spoke became modified, picking up a number of African and Malay words, expressions, and grammatical constructions from their Black servants, until it was transformed into a new language, which they called Afrikaans. They began to refer to themselves as Afrikaners. . . .

The Consolidation of White Supremacy

Diamonds and gold. Nothing else changed the settler colonies of southern Africa so radically and suddenly. By whetting the acquisitive appetites of hundreds of financiers, entrepreneurs, and adventurers in Europe and South Africa, they catapulted the previously little-known British and Boer states into the international limelight. They quickly spurred the growth of large-scale mining industries, drawing capital and labor toward the mine fields at a rate unprecedented on the African continent.

In a pattern that was to repeat itself time and again in later years, this rapid development and expansion of the capitalist mode of production was to bring with it an entrenchment, extension, and systemization of white racist rule. Where the one flourished, so did the other.

In 1870, extensive diamond fields were discovered at the site where the city of Kimberley now stands. One passing hindrance to the British colonialists in exploiting them was the fact that the diamond fields were on land that was occupied by the Griquas, a Coloured people. After first posing as protectors of the Griquas, the British annexed the area and threw the diamond fields open to white miners. When the Griquas finally rose in rebellion, they were brutally put down.

Barely a few years after the first diamonds were unearthed, about 15,000 whites, 10,000 Coloureds, and 20,000 Africans had poured onto the diamond diggings. The town of Kimberley mushroomed. The first sizable Black industrial work force was created; between 1871 and 1895, some 100,000 Africans worked at the mines, supporting another 400,000 with their wages.

With the aid of low Black wages, the dividends generated by the diamond mines were exceptionally high, reaching about £2 million to £3 million a year by 1910 on an issued capital of only about £10 million.

Out of the early jumble of hundreds of individual mining claims, one person, Cecil John Rhodes, managed to secure control over all of the Kimberley mines by 1889, under the name of De Beers Consolidated Mines. Rhodes's monopoly over the South African diamond mines enabled him to build De Beers into an international giant. "All but a tiny proportion of diamond production was controlled by De Beers," biographer Anthony Hocking wrote, "and all but a fraction of sales were handled by a single sales organization. De Beers and the [Diamond] Syndicate were so interlinked that they seemed inseparable. It was the most impregnable monopoly in the world."

As important as the diamond mines were in launching the industrial revolution in South Africa, they were soon dwarfed by the emergence of another mining industry—this time based on the extraction of gold.

White settlers first found gold in South Africa in the 1850s, but the major discoveries—the extensive gold veins along the Witwatersrand in the southern Transvaal—were made only in 1886. These veins were later revealed to be only part of a series of gold reefs that stretch in an arc for at least three hundred miles from Evander in the Transvaal to Welkom in the Orange Free State. For the white conquistadors, it was at last the discovery of a new El Dorado: South Africa's reefs hold by far the largest known gold deposits in the world.

The Boer government of the Transvaal proclaimed the Witwatersrand (or Rand for short) a public goldfield in 1886. Although the economy of the Boer republic was based on farming, the regime nevertheless opened the way for the further penetration of capitalist productive relations into the African interior.

Unlike the early diamond diggings, there was no room for individual claim holders or small mining companies on the Rand. The difficulties and costs of underground mining and of extracting gold from the ore-bearing rock required massive concentrations of capital and labor. The gold mining companies thus had to be heavily capitalized from the start. Much of the money for these operations came from the mining barons who had already made a killing in diamonds, as well as from foreign investors, predominantly British. Of the £200 million invested in the gold mines until 1932, roughly £120 million came from abroad.

By the turn of the century most of the gold industry was controlled by six mining finance houses, including Cecil Rhodes's Consolidated Goldfields of South Africa. These monopolies were in turn closely associated with each other through the Chamber of Mines, which sought to protect the interests of the gold industry as a whole.

In his study of the gold industry, Frederick A. Johnstone called it "the first really large-scale capitalist industry in South Africa." In fact, the Chamber of

Mines was the greatest single employer of labor in any one area of the world at the time.

The rapid development of the gold and diamond mines spurred capitalist economic growth throughout South Africa. By 1910 Johannesburg, which was bare pasture land before the opening of the gold fields, had surged ahead of both Cape Town and Kimberley to become the largest city in South Africa. Thousands of miles of railway were built. The gold mines directly influenced the growth of coal mining in the Transvaal and Natal, spurred the development of banking, and induced the beginnings of a manufacturing industry. The domestic market for agricultural produce was greatly widened, further enriching the white plantation owners. Trade expanded greatly.

Most importantly, this economic growth forged—and was dependent on the creation of—a numerous and powerful Black working class. Like magnets, the mines and other industries drew toward them hundreds of thousands of Black workers from throughout southern Africa.

Rather than breaking down the political and social restrictions on the Black population and creating a class of "free" Black workers, the white financiers and mining magnates who presided over this capitalist economic growth adapted the existing system of national oppression to their own ends, wedding white supremacy to class domination. To maintain high profit levels, the mineowners sought to keep labor costs at the barest minimum. They employed racial oppression to help create a large class of propertyless Blacks who had no option but to sell their labor power and to carry out unskilled work in the mines at ultralow wages.

One encumbrance the mineowners had to overcome, however, was the competition between the various mining companies in the recruitment of Black labor. Many Africans still had some access to land in the reserves (those areas that had not been directly seized for white land ownership) and thus were not compelled by economic necessity to seek full-time wage employment. This created a relative shortage of available mine labor. In order to attract workers, the companies were forced, to an extent, to outbid each other by offering slightly higher wages and better working conditions. According to a contemporary observer, "The dream of the mine manager is to cut down the cost of native labour by getting a larger and more regular supply. . . ."

Acting in the interests of the gold industry as a whole, the Chamber of Mines adopted two measures to prevent the labor shortage from raising wage costs and reducing profit levels. One was the hiring of African workers from beyond South Africa's borders and the other was the coordination of recruitment policies and the elimination of competition. Several bodies, including the Witwatersrand Native Labor Association and the Native Recruiting Corporation, were established to lessen competition, cut recruitment costs, and fix wages and working conditions more or less uniformly throughout the gold mining industry.

From its earliest days, a cornerstone of labor policy on the mines was the migratory labor system. To get a mining job, a Black worker had to sign a labor contract specifying a minimum amount of work required, ranging from about nine months for Africans recruited within South Africa up to fifteen months for those hired elsewhere. When the contract was over, the worker had to return home before being allowed to reapply for another stint in the mines. This prevented many Black workers from becoming permanently urbanized.

The entrenchment of this migratory labor system was absolutely central to the chamber's policy of driving down Black wages. The modest agricultural output in the African reserves (or in other African countries), to which the migrant workers remained tied, made it possible for the mineowners to pay them below what it would cost to maintain both the worker and his family in an urban setting. . . .

While working in the mines, Blacks were kept under tight rein. Breaking a labor contract was a criminal offense under the Masters and Servants Act, punishable by imprisonment. Strikes and other acts of "insubordination" were also illegal. One key mechanism of social control was the confinement of Black workers in prison-like compounds, called hostels. The compound housing system was first developed at the diamond mines, initially to prevent Africans from quitting their jobs or walking off with the fruits of their labor—the diamonds. When not actually working in the mines, they were obliged to stay in the compound areas during the whole period of the labor contract. This system was later extended to the rest of the mining industry.

Another important instrument of labor control was the pass. In 1895 the Transvaal government adopted a pass law drafted by the Chamber of Mines in order, according to a mine official, "to have a hold on the native." Within twenty-four hours of entering a labor district, an African seeking work had to obtain a special pass, which was good for only six days. If no employment was found in that time, he was subject to fines, imprisonment, and expulsion from the area. This short period weakened the bargaining position of the worker, forcing him to accept whatever job was offered. By controlling movement, the pass system also kept out "unwanted" Africans from the cities and restricted the workers' ability to quit or change jobs.

As a result of these combined measures, the Chamber of Mines was successful in reducing annual African mine wages from the equivalent of R78 [$90] in 1889 to R58 [$67] in 1897.

It was primarily the low wage costs achieved by the Chamber of Mines that made possible the profitable development of the gold mines. As the chamber itself acknowledged, "It was not so much the richness of these fields that attracted the necessary capital, as it was their apparent continuity and the fact that they could be worked efficiently by cheap native labour."

The tightening control over African workers was accompanied by increasing restrictions on the political rights of Africans in general. In 1865 the British-dominated settler state in Natal disenfranchised virtually all Africans. Cecil Rhodes, the diamond and gold baron who was also prime minister of the Cape Colony, adopted measures that struck some thirty thousand Africans off the voting rolls in the Cape as well.

The accelerating capitalist economic growth in South Africa, particularly the opening of the diamond and gold fields, created a tremendous appetite for cheap Black labor. But throughout this period the white capitalists were unable to fully satisfy their needs. The main obstacle they faced was the continued possession of or access to land by broad sections of the African population in the areas that were still nominally independent, and even in the conquered territories themselves.

To try to break those African ties to the land, the rise of mining was accompanied by the last stages of the white conquest and the wars of colonial dispossession. It ended by the turn of the century with the defeat and subjugation of the last independent African societies in South Africa.

Africans living beyond South Africa also fell victim to this colonial expansion. Lured on by rumors of more fabulous mineral wealth north of the Transvaal, Cecil Rhodes used the fortune he had made to establish the British South Africa Company in 1889 for the purpose of extending white domination even further into the interior of the continent. Through a combination of guile and military force, he subjugated the Ndebele and Shona peoples and carved out a personal empire, which was named after himself—Rhodesia.

The conquest of the African territories—and in many cases their actual incorporation into the British colonies and the Boer states—was insufficient by itself to create a class of propertyless wage earners. To be sure, a portion of the African population became proletarianized from a fairly early date, but many others continued to eke out an existence from the land, either as "squatters" or labor tenants on the white-owned farms or as more or less self-sufficient producers in the areas later demarcated as African reserves.

In fact, the growth of capitalist market relations provided an opening for the emergence of a small layer of African peasants, and even commercial farmers, who began to produce for the market in competition with white farm owners. The first sizable African peasantry, composed mostly of Mfengu, arose in the Ciskei area of the Eastern Cape around 1835, and later in the Transkei and northeastern Cape. This process accelerated after the rise of mining, which gave a further boost to agricultural production.

The growing economic weight of the African peasants worried the settlers and the colonial authorities. In Natal, the Native Affairs Commission of 1852–53 complained that African peasants were "rapidly becoming rich and independent" and that they "preferred the most independent state, and hence has arisen the uniformly insufficient supply of labour." In the white republics of the Orange Free State and the Transvaal the Boer settlers were too weak to push Africans off the land and Africans began to use their saved earnings to buy back the land that had originally been taken from them.

In response, the white plantation- and mineowners launched a political and economic war against the African peasants and subsistence farmers, attacking their position as sellers of agricultural produce and driving them off the land to serve as wage workers.

The first major campaign in this war began as early as the 1840s in Natal, where Theophilus Shepstone established the first Native Reserves, the forerunners of today's Bantustans, which serve as vast labor reservoirs. With the aim of impoverishing the Africans in the reserves and driving them onto the labor market to earn cash wages, an annual tax was imposed on every hut. The reserves themselves were fragmented and scattered with, according to Pierre van den Berghe, "the dual purpose of making farm labour more easily accessible to White farmers, and of averting the threat of large concentrations of Africans." Just before the British war against the Zulu state in 1879, Shepstone expressed the hope that the defeated Zulus would be "changed to labourers working for wages."

For the whites, this assault on African land ownership acquired a new urgency with the opening of the diamond and gold mines. As prime minister and minister of Native affairs of the Cape Colony, Cecil Rhodes once again led the charge. In 1894 he pushed through the Glen Grey Act, which he called his "Native Bill for South Africa." It imposed individual tenure on African land in the Glen Grey district that had previously been worked on a communal basis. The purpose was to limit the number of Africans with access to land and drive the rest out of the reserve to work. An annual hut tax was levied to push this process along. "Every black man cannot have three acres and a cow," Rhodes said. "We have to face the question and it must be brought home to them that in the future nine-tenths of them will have to spend their lives in daily labour, in physical work, in manual labour." The provisions of the Glen Grey Act were later extended to other parts of the country.

Combined with the further displacement of Africans from the land were other measures designed to drive them into the hands of white employers. Through law, social compulsion, and economic inducement, new wants were fostered among Africans, such as the use of European clothes and manufactured goods, which could only be obtained through purchase. To get money to buy, Africans first had to work. The imposition of hut taxes and other monetary levies, though a cruder form of compulsion, had the same effect.

Speaking in 1899 at an annual meeting of Consolidated Goldfields, one company official stated, "If we could only call upon one-half of the natives to give up three months of the year to work, that would be enough. We should try some cogent form of inducement, or practically compel the native through taxation or in some other way. . . ."

The efforts to draw Africans onto the labor market took effect only gradually —and could not be systematized for several more decades. The white employers were thus forced to look elsewhere, at least for the time being, for enough workers to fulfill their labor needs.

In Natal, the plantation owners along the coast brought in contract workers from India, the first of whom arrived in 1860. The Indian workers, mostly from the lower castes, were indentured to their white employers for a period of five years, after which they were allowed either to return home to India or to stay on in Natal. Most decided to stay. They were employed primarily in the burgeoning sugar plantations. Some got jobs as domestic servants. From 1876 to 1900, the number of Indians in Natal increased from ten thousand to sixty-five thousand, outnumbering the whites themselves. They soon constituted 90 percent of the labor force on the sugar plantations.

Not all of the Indians who came to South Africa were workers. Shortly after the first indentured laborers arrived, a significant number of Indian merchants immigrated to Natal to engage in trade. Fearing competition from this merchant class, as well as the potential political influence of the large Indian population, the authorities in Natal explicitly excluded Indians from voting in 1893 and four years later barred the entry of virtually all nonindentured Indians. Indian competition in trade was checked, and when Indian merchants began to move into the Transvaal in the 1880s they were shackled with further restraints.

The mineowners sent recruiters into other African countries as well. Between 1890 and 1899 the number of Africans employed in the gold mines alone increased from 14,000 to 97,000, about half of them coming from Portuguese East Africa (Mozambique). After the turn of the century the proportion reached about two-thirds. Migrant workers for the mines and other sectors were recruited from almost all the other countries of southern Africa, and even from as far away as Zanzibar.

The extension of white supremacy, the continued wars against the various African peoples, the rapid capitalist growth based on diamonds and gold, and the consequent demands for large numbers of African workers, all highlighted a key anomaly facing the white colonialists: This vast territory was still being ruled by four separate white settler states—the British colonies of the Cape and Natal and the Boer republics of the Orange Free State and Transvaal—whose policies were often uncoordinated and at times divergent. Many whites, mostly among the English-speaking population, saw this disunity as the chief obstacle to the effective entrenchment and protection of white supremacy, as well as to the unfettered growth of the newly emergent system of capitalist production.

Raising the well-worn alarm of a "Black peril," an English-language newspaper in the Orange Free State stridently declared in May 1851, "We see a war of races—the declared aim and intention of the black man being to drive the white man into the sea . . . and what we ask in the name of reason are we to present as a counterpose? We answer in one word UNION."

Such attitudes were prevalent in official circles as well. In 1858, Sir George Grey, the governor of the Cape Colony, stressed the advantages of white confederation or union, primarily in military terms. . . .

Broader British imperial interests were also involved, particularly at a time of sharpening competition among the European colonial powers over how to carve up the African continent. With the development of the gold mines, the Transvaal became the most important region of southern Africa, yet it was still outside direct British control. The British colonialists were concerned that the further strengthening of the Boer states, in alliance with a rival European power, could eventually challenge British dominance in southern Africa. In particular, there appeared to be the threat of a Boer alliance with imperial Germany, which had begun to conquer parts of South West Africa in the 1880s.

Rhodes, moreover, harbored extravagant ambitions of extending imperial control from the Cape all the way to Cairo—and further. In the first of his many wills he favored the "extension of British rule throughout the world . . . the entire Continent of Africa, the Holy Land, the Valley of the Euphrates, the islands of Cyprus and Candia [Crete], the whole of South America, islands of the Pacific not heretofore possessed by Great Britain, the whole of the Malay Archipelago, the sea-board of China and Japan, the ultimate recovery of the United States of America as an integral part of the British Empire. . . ." Closer to hand—and to the real world—he saw an independent Transvaal as a threat to the trade route between the Cape and his Rhodesian territories.

The mining companies generally concurred with the efforts to bring all of South Africa under a single administration. While the Boer regimes were not overly hostile to the companies, the mineowners viewed these regimes as inefficient and insufficiently attuned to the capitalists' own particular interests. They chafed at the Transvaal's expensive monopoly on dynamite sales, high taxes and railway rates, and obstacles to labor recruitment.

The British drive for consolidation helped fan the nationalist sentiments of the Afrikaners and met with increasing resistance. Following a steady build-up of political frictions and occasional armed confrontations over a period of more than two decades, the conflict between the British and the Afrikaners led inexorably toward war. In October 1899 the Anglo-Boer War finally broke out.

On the eve of the war, Sir Alfred Milner, the governor and high commissioner of the Cape, reminded all the antagonists involved, "The Anglo-Dutch friction is bad enough. But it is child's play compared with the antagonism of White and Black." That did not, however, prevent the British and Boer forces from conscripting as many as one hundred thousand Africans to provide them with labor and other services. The British even armed about ten thousand Africans to serve the imperial cause.

The war was an unequal one. On one side stood the mightiest imperialist power in the world, with an army seasoned in colonial warfare and with the backing of a highly industrialized economy. On the other were two weak settler states, based on an undeveloped agricultural economy that could not sustain a prolonged war effort, no matter how hard their irregular armies of farmer-soldiers fought.

The costs of the war were high. More than twenty thousand British and Afrikaner troops were killed and another twenty thousand Afrikaner civilians perished in the British internment centers (known as "concentration camps"). Although Black deaths were not included in the official casualty lists, at least twelve thousand Africans also died in internment camps during the war and several thousand of those who served with the British were executed upon capture by the Boer forces.

The war ended in 1902, with the British troops victorious, the Orange Free State and Transvaal annexed to the British Empire, and the capitalist mine-owners in Johannesburg ecstatic over the demise of the "backward" Boer states. The basic effect of the British victory, as Marxist sociologist Martin Legassick has pointed out, was "to ensure the establishment of a dominant capitalist mode of production throughout South Africa."

Having broken the independent military power of the Boer states, the English were more than willing to draw the Afrikaners into a common system of white rule. The Treaty of Vereeniging specifically allowed the Transvaal and Orange Free State to exclude Africans from voting. The British government distributed £7 million in free grants to white farmers in the Transvaal and Orange Free State and extended a £35 million loan to the two states. In 1907 both were granted "responsible government" and were once again governed by Afrikaner parties. In fact the two principal political figures in the Transvaal, Louis Botha and Jan Christian Smuts, had both been generals in the Boer military forces during the war. They were later to become the first two prime ministers of the Union of South Africa.

For Africans, the results of the British victory were soon obvious. When British troops marched into Johannesburg in mid-1900, African mine workers, apparently expecting improvements in their position, burned their passes and greeted the British. But the British "were swift to disillusion the demonstrators," historian Donald Denoon wrote, "handed out severe punishments for breaking the (Republican) law, and set the labourers to work on road and railway building at arbitrarily low wages." Encouraged by these measures, the mineowners slashed African wages by almost half, from more than fifty shillings a month to thirty shillings.

Negotiations for union among the four states were spurred after the end of the Anglo-Boer War partly by the emergence of new signs of Black unrest. A number of African, Coloured, and Indian political organizations were forged and a major Zulu rebellion shook Natal in 1906, reaffirming the dire need, from the viewpoint of the white supremacists, for an effective and uniform policy toward the Black majority.

The South Africa Act, passed by the British Parliament in 1909, provided for the formation of an independent Union of South Africa the following year. The four white settler states were incorporated as provinces. The provisions of the act entrenched the existing racist franchise laws, which barred all Blacks from voting in the Transvaal and Orange Free State, excluded almost all Africans and Indians from the voting rolls in Natal, and severely restricted the Black franchise in the Cape through high income, property, and literacy qualifications. The act specifically stated that all members of parliament had to be "of European descent."

The establishment of the Union capped the consolidation of white minority rule and signaled the forging of a long-standing political alliance among the various ruling strata: mining and agricultural, English and Afrikaans speaking.

Union also marked an important shift in the relations between the South African settler state and Britain. For the white South African ruling class, it brought political independence from the former imperial power (although strong political ties were still retained with Britain until 1961, when South Africa became a republic and withdrew from the British Commonwealth).

For the Black majority, however, the establishment of Union signified no qualitative change in their position as a subjugated people. They still remained enslaved by a colonial-settler state, with no voice in the government and with their few surviving political rights destined for elimination. They still remained alienated from their land. Their country continued to be plundered of its natural and human wealth by white capitalists, who employed force and coercion to extract colonial-type superprofits. They still faced national oppression in all spheres of life.

In effect, the new South African state simply took over from Britain the role of direct colonial power over the subject Black population. Though it was now independent, having its own economic and political interests to defend, it nevertheless continued to function as an imperialist outpost on the southern tip of the African continent, a position it holds to the present day.

6. THE POST-COLONIAL STATE*

by DONALD DENOON and BALAM NYEKO

Donald Denoon is a Senior Research Fellow at the Australian National University at Canberra. Balam Nyeko is a Senior Lecturer at the University of Zambia at Lusaka.

The centerpiece of southern African history in the twentieth century has been the South African state, the Union of four British colonies which assumed the status of a British Dominion from 1910 until 1961, and has been a republic since that time. That state has caused astonishment throughout its life. In Europe there was amazement from 1910 onward that Afrikaner generals behaved as loyal ministers of the British Crown. Among Africans at the time, and ever since then, there has been disbelief that a racially defined minority should be permitted (and should be able) to exercise power over a disfranchised majority for generation after generation. . . .

[Post-Union] politicians who sought to gain and to hold a parliamentary majority had to attend to the demands of the three political movements represented in parliament: white landowners, the white working class, and the mainly English-speaking members whose interests were linked to the mining industry. These three movements could be brought into harmony, but only with great effort and on a very fragile basis. And their interests could not be harmonized at all, if the further demands of educated Africans of Indians, or the African working class or the peasants were attended to. From the inception of the Union, therefore, ministers of the cabinet worked in two main directions: seeking ways to satisfy the demands of the major white political interests, and developing means of coercing the rest of the population.

The 1911 Mines and Works Act, for example, gave Union-wide effect to the job color bar which was already in force in the Transvaal mines. However, it did not satisfy the labor aristocracy in the mining industry, always nervous of being diluted in numbers and in wages by the wider employment of black miners. In the middle of 1913 Johannesburg miners went on strike, won concessions from the state, and organized themselves for a further strike. In the interval, the government mobilized the Union Defence Force, and in January 1914 when a strike broke out again, the UDF marched into Johannesburg, aimed cannon at the miners' headquarters, broke up the strike and deported the leaders of the movement. If the mineowners were satisfied by this demonstration of state support, the labor aristocracy was outraged—and in

*From *Southern Africa Since 1800* (London, 1984).

any case it was black miners whose interests were most seriously affected. Not only were a range of semi-skilled and skilled jobs permanently barred to them, but the mining industry was now better able to control black wage levels through agreement among employers. White miners and their working class allies could now organize themselves politically—and they did so very efficiently, winning the Transvaal provincial elections in 1914 for instance—but no such alternative was available to blacks.

The government moved from the mining industry's needs to those of white farmers, introducing and enacting the Native Land Act in 1913 which . . . consolidated the control of white landowners over their land, and made it almost impossible for African agricultural tenants to survive, unless they agreed to become wage laborers. Yet even this draconian measure was insufficient to satisfy landowners entirely. During 1912 Hertzog had been squeezed out of the cabinet, for expressing anti-imperial sentiments which upset English-speaking whites; and in January 1914 the Nationalist Party formed itself around him, in opposition to the governing South African Party. The Nationalists had their heartland in Hertzog's Orange Free State, whereas the SAP continued to be popular in the Transvaal, where the alliance between gold and maize had first emerged, and where landowners had gained the most advantage from that alliance. Once established, however, the Nationalist Party won support in the other provinces, wherever the sentiments of republicanism or the needs of Afrikaners were thought to be at risk. In any case, if politics was the art of balancing three major interest groups, inevitably those three groups would tend to crystallize out, the better to press their demands.

The outbreak of the Great War in 1914 provoked a further realignment of the party system. Constitutionally, South Africa was at war with Germany as soon as King George V declared war. The government was anxious to demonstrate its imperial loyalty, had attacked German forces in South West Africa. Not all Afrikaners felt so committed: a detachment of the UDF crossed the border to join the Germans; other Afrikaners rebelled and attempted to declare a republic; Hertzog and his supporters sought neutrality. The government's decision to send an army to occupy South West Africa alienated many of its earlier supporters. And in 1915 when elections were held, the Nationalists won 26 of the 130 seats, forcing the SAP (54) into a tacit alliance with the Unionists (40) in order to be sure of a majority. The powerful Labour Party was, for the moment, so badly divided on the war issue, that it won only four seats. Meanwhile the easy conquest of South West Africa was followed by Smuts' participation in the East African campaign, which persisted to the end of the war, and which was much more difficult to explain in terms of purely South African interests.

By the end of the war, then, the South African Government was an active (and publicly honored) participant in the British imperial alliance—but losing the sympathy of the Afrikaner constituencies. White landowners were inclined to believe that they could gain even more from Hertzog than from the SAP (especially after Botha died in 1919, leaving the leadership to the more aloof Smuts); white labor was alienated by the manifest influence of mine-owners over the SAP; the government depended increasingly upon the tolerance of the official opposition Unionists; and outside parliament African opinion was not only hostile, but (by the end of the war) increasingly self-confident, vocal and assertive.

During the 1920s, the state modified its shape and its purpose in response to opposition groups. Black opposition was suppressed by the police, by the UDF, and by white volunteers, both in rural areas and in the urban areas which were rapidly attracting a permanent black population. African opinion could not be conciliated without antagonizing the parliamentary parties, so an elaborate machinery of pass laws and a reinforced police force were called into existence. Black demands for land, for freedom of movement and association, or for a living wage, were met by force. The government was inclined to respond in much the same high-handed fashion when white workers threatened the peace. During the crisis of 1921–22, when mine managers determined to reduce the proportion and the wage levels of the white miners, the state supported management. The white workers took their revenge in 1924, when the Labour Party won 18 seats and—as junior partner to Hertzog's Nationalist Party—displaced the SAP (and the Unionists who had now joined it) from government.

Both the Nationalists and Labour had expressed a vague anti-capitalism in the election, and the Nationalists had linked that issue to anti-imperialism. In reality the new government was caught in the same triangular network which had paralysed the SAP. The white working class was becoming Afrikaner in its ethnic composition, and the coalition partners were anxious to relieve the misery of the unemployed poor whites. However, white unemployment was not to be relieved by attacking capital investment, nor by untying the imperial connection. Instead, the Pact government entrenched the position of those white miners who had kept their jobs despite the retrenchment of 1921; it attempted to create new job opportunities in manufacturing, and through the reservation of jobs in the public service; and the general loosening of commonwealth constitutional links satisfied the demand for greater autonomy. Now these measures irritated mining capitalists, but did not drive them out of business: the real victims were blacks whose lives were hedged around by an ever-increasing network of economic, political and social constraints. Two slogans were used to justify the policies—civilized labor to ensure a living wage for a large range of white workers, and "segregation" to exclude blacks from jobs, from permanent urban residence, and from many social and economic opportunities. In brief, the Pact government set about controlling the rapid urbanization and diversification of the economy, ensuring that blacks should take part in these processes only on terms which were acceptable to employers and to white workers.

Since the Pact government refrained from any direct assault on existing capital investment, and its own legislative program was soon enacted, the parliamentary divisions were increasingly irrelevant. Black—or any other—militancy could be controlled by the Riotous Assemblies Act (1927); the network of pass laws limited the mobility of African men; the government was committed to industrial development, symbolized by its establishment of ISCOR [Iron and Steel Corporation of South Africa]—what else was there to argue about? Feelers were put out from both sides of the parliamentary division, and eventually during 1933 and 1934 the existing parties merged into the United South African National Party, with Hertzog as Prime Minister and Smuts as his deputy, and only a few diehard imperial loyalists (the Dominion Party) and republicans (the Purified Nationalists) remaining outside the grand coalition or Fusion. For a while it seemed as if the absolute unity of the white population was within reach, since the new party included representatives of white labor, mining capital, and landowners. The stage was set for a final, and comprehensive, strategy to deal with the majority of the population.

The package of legislation which passed through parliament in 1936 dealt with two dimensions of African life which seemed as yet unclear. Industrial relations had been clarified by the solidification of the industrial color bar, and arbitration procedures which ignored African unions; the lives of urban Africans were determined by pass laws and residential segregation, a structure which assumed that Africans were inherently rural and came to town only for limited periods of employment in limited capacities. What remained unclear was how African rural area were to be controlled, and how Africans were to relate to the political system. The Native Trust and Land Act committed the government to acquire further land for African occupation—on a scale which would eventually bring about 13 percent of the South African land surface under African occupation. The Representation of Natives Act removed Cape Africans from the common voters' roll, and provided for their separate representation in both houses of parliament. The government was unmoved by the massive opposition of Africans to each of these measures. The value of African (and coloured) votes had already been cut in half by the enfranchisement of white (but not black) women in 1930; they possessed far too little electoral power to divert the Fusion government from its purposes. At the same time a Native Representative Council was set up, whose members could advise the government on matters concerning Africans—but whose advice could be ignored. Created in defiance of African opinion, the NRC was most unlikely to influence future government policy.

Demonstrating its disregard for African opinion, and abolishing white poverty, the Fusion government had little to fear from parliamentary opposition. The Purified Nationalists were slow to gather Afrikaners to their republican banner, the Dominion Party could hardly expect to win many seats except in Natal, and white trades unionists saw little point in breaking with a government which guaranteed not only jobs but also incomes.

Once again it was war which prompted a realignment of parliamentary parties. When world war broke out again in 1939, Hertzog (again) attempted to keep South Africa neutral, but a majority of the United Party (and a narrow majority of parliament) supported Smuts and the Allies. Hertzog's faction of the United Party was eventually merged into the Purified Nationalists under Dr. D. F. Malan's leadership. During the war, the drain of manpower into the armed forces placed a strain on mining and manufacturing, and led to a discreet employment of Africans in a wider range of jobs than had been available in the 1930s—but the government still outlawed any strike action by African unions. Although the government supported the Atlantic Charter with its resoundingly democratic aspirations—and the government was accused by Afrikaner nationalists of jeopardizing white security on that account—in reality the state remained firmly committed to preserving the existing pattern of race relations. That policy was good enough to win the general election of 1943, when the Nationalist opposition was itself divided: but in the long run it has never been sufficient for a political party merely to preserve the status quo.

When general elections were called again in 1948, the Nationalists had a program summed up in the vague term "apartheid," which served just as well as Hertzog's slogan of "segregation" in 1924; and by the narrowest of majorities, Malan's Nationalists came to power with the support of the survivors of Hertzog's faction. The Nationalist Party has won every subsequent election, and since 1948 the shifts in government policy have owed nothing to the interaction of political parties in parliament, and everything to strategic and tactical decisions made within the Nationalist Party to meet the increasingly committed opposition of extra-parliamentary forces.

In retrospect, three circumstances may be seen to have favored the entrenchment of a state explicitly committed to racial separation wherever possible. One of these is the 1910 constitution, which by enfranchising all adult white males, ensured that the interests of landowners, of white workers, and of the capital invested in mines (and then in manufacturing) would persistently demand attention. Conversely, the exclusion of all but a handful of the coloured and African population from participation in politics guaranteed that the burden of white demands would be carried by the disfranchised majority. Second, the overrepresentation of rural white voters ensured that landowners would hold a disproportionate share of political power. Conversely, the increasing Afrikaner proportion of the white population, and the steady drift of

Afrikaners into urban employment, ensured that mainly rural political parties would possess a bridgehead to urban constituencies, which were in any case liable to be divided between working class and lower middle class interests. Third, the constitutional and political link with imperial Britain proved to be a source of stability to the political system, rather than a means of changing it./African appeals to Westminster were always turned away empty-handed; and imperial officials made sure that South Africa's neighbors, under colonial administrations of various kinds, would not embarrass the Union government. As each new anti-imperial government came to office—in 1910, in 1924, and then in 1948—it turned from hostility to acquiescence in the imperial relationship. Though Afrikaners held office from 1910 onwards, it took half a century for the republic to come into being: The imperial links were allowed to fade away, rather than being snapped.

The cost of such a political process, however, was the persistent and ruthless alienation of the whole disfranchised population; not only Africans, but equally Indians (despite the representations of the Indian Government on their behalf) and coloureds (culminating in the removal of coloured voters from the common roll during the early 1950s). The impossibility of conciliating black interests meant a massive expansion of the forces of internal repression, until there was hardly a branch of government which was not directly involved in maintaining control over the black majority, whether in the rural reserves, or on white farms, or in the shanty towns and mining compounds.

In this sense, many of the Nationalist government's measures of the 1950s merely put the finishing touches to machinery which already existed. Racially mixed marriages were banned—but interracial sexuality had already been prohibited by the Immorality Act of 1927. The Population Registration machinery of the 1950s merely made it more difficult for individuals to sneak across the barriers of race which already existed. The provision of different syllabi for African school children (and then the provision of separate universities for different races in the late 1950s) took to a logical conclusion the actual segregation which already prevailed in almost every school in the country. The disenfranchisement of coloureds followed logically from the earlier removal of Africans to separate electoral rolls and representation. All of these measures were implicit in the 1910 constitution, and in the interaction of political forces represented by that document.

By the 1950s, then, all three enfranchised white groups had seized the opportunities presented to them by the constitution, and had entrenched their interests very deeply. The white working class—by now overwhelmingly Afrikaner—shared power in a government committed to protecting their jobs and their wage levels. White landowners had clear title to most of the land, and coercive powers over the rural labor force. International capital was reconciled (mainly by the state's manifest and ruthless control over unskilled labor) to taxes which subsidized and protected manufacturing industry. A fearsome battery of uniformed forces and bureaucrats and repressive laws controlled the lives of the population. Two circumstances, however, made it necessary for the government to seek a fresh approach to political institutions: the deterioration of South Africa's international position, and the massive development of internal opposition. A constitutional arrangement which was not very unusual in 1910 had become—by the middle of the century—offensive abroad, and intolerable at home.

7. *INTERNAL OPPOSITION**

by DONALD DENOON and BALAM NYEKO

Strictly speaking, we could trace internal opposition back to the foundation of the Cape Town garrison in the seventeenth century, when Khoi groups resisted the occupation of their land, and when free burghers opposed the privileges of the Company's officials. However, opposition has changed its form and purpose many times since then, and this is especially true in the hundred years following the mineral revolution. In this chapter, we will be concentrating on the internal opposition since the 1880s, seeing how new circumstances led to new conflicts and forms of organization.

In the 1880s, in the oldest colony, there were a number of well-educated Africans, including Mfengu and Xhosa in the east and coloureds in the west, who thought of themselves as representing the present and future aspirations of Africans generally. Their education admitted them to clerical and professional employment, and their jobs admitted them to the franchise. They usually linked themselves with Cape liberal politicians—professional and merchant men—and shared many of the optimistic views of that group. The Jabavus, Sogas, Walter Rubusana and others assumed that a general liberalization would eventually enfranchise more Africans—in the Cape and beyond—and it was not necessary to do more than encourage white people in that direction. They did not have a distinct voice in Cape politics, and they did not see themselves as an opposition. During the South African War for example, Jabavu's newspaper *Imvo* opposed the imperial cause (and was suppressed) while *Izwi* supported the empire. It was only in the years leading to Union that this group realized that South African affairs were running against them. Time was not on their side. They protested against the racial provisions of the Act

*From *Southern Africa Since 1800* (London, 1984).

of Union (and against many of the Union government's actions), but even then they shared a platform with the old white Cape liberals, and were slow to form a distinct movement.

Outside the Cape, African opposition was still voiced mainly by chiefs in the 1880s. The Tswana chiefs—Khama, Sechele and Gaseitsiwe—successfully negotiated with Britain, against incorporation into Rhodes's territories; and their successors (especially Tshekedi Khama) continued that diplomatic and defensive campaign through the twentieth century. In Lesotho it was the "sons of Moshoeshoe" who warned against moves to incorporate them, just as the royal family and leading chiefs of Swaziland were doing. The crucial role of chiefs in the 1880s is suggested by Zululand. By removing Cetshwayo, and subdividing his kingdom, the British authorities unleashed internal civil war which neutralized Zulu power in the 1880s. The removal of Sekhukhune from the Pedi chieftaincy in 1879 also neutralized the most powerful African society within the Transvaal.

The crucial role of chiefs is not very surprising, when we remind ourselves how late the independent chieftaincies survived. The Shona were conquered only in the 1890s (and had to be conquered twice), and Lobengula's Ndebele also went under in the 1890s. Portuguese conquest of the Gaza kingdom occurred in 1895, and was insecure for some years thereafter. Maharero led the Herero, and Hendrik Witbooi the Nama, against Germany as late as 1905. It was only the defeat of the chiefs, and their exile, which forced opponents of the colonial regimes to find alternative leaders.

Colonial and settler authorities continued to see kings and chiefs as the most likely leaders of revolt. In Rhodesia, the authorities resolutely refused to allow Lobengula's sons to be recognized by the Ndebele, preferring to send them away to school. Maharero's exile in Botswana and Witbooi's death removed the most likely leaders of renewed resistance to Germany. In Zululand, Natal officials insisted on putting Dinuzulu on trial, although there was no evidence to suggest that he had led the Zulu during the Bambatha campaign of 1907. In the Cape, resident magistrates kept a close watch on the southern Nguni (and East Griqua) chiefs. And undoubtedly the chiefly titles, and their holders, continued to enjoy the loyalty of many people, even after the chiefs lost their power to act independently.

By the end of the nineteenth century, however, new forces were forming. The western-educated clerks and journalists and teachers of the Cape were more visible than the chiefs, and spoke to a much wider audience. As individuals in the other territories returned from tertiary education, they also became prominent spokesmen: John Dube, for example, returned to Zululand from the USA in 1909, determined to apply some of the measures developed by black Americans. As conditions and prospects for western-educated people declined, so they were pushed toward outspoken opposition.

Social conditions and relationships were changing in other ways too. As numbers of men and some women were drawn into urban wage employment, they began to see themselves in a fresh light, confronting daily problems which the chiefs were quite unable to resolve. Miners, domestic servants and laundry workers lived for shorter or longer periods—quite outside the communities of their birth, in barracks or dormitories or shacks, among people from many different backgrounds. Even if the chiefs visited them in town, there was nothing the chiefs could do to improve urban living conditions. The migrants might cling to their family ties—but they also needed support among themselves.

There were also people who left their rural homes but did not find a niche in the labor market, and therefore turned to robbery, or illicit alcohol, or protection rackets. Johannesburg was the Mecca for these activities but they flourished around all the urban areas. Groups like "the regiment of the hills" which van Onselen has traced through Johannesburg police records, were certainly opposed by the state; but we should not consider their actions to be "opposition" to the state, since they were willing to rob or defraud everyone, irrespective of race, sex or creed.

In the early years of this century, there was opposition from chiefs, from the educated, from urban and rural workers, and from the unemployed. In isolation from each other, they could accomplish almost nothing. Was there some way they could combine? The South African War prompted the formation of congresses—the African Peoples Organization in the western Cape in 1902, led by Dr. Abdurahman and comprising mainly coloured people, and African congresses in the OFS, Transvaal and Natal. These associations were mainly led by the western-educated, and they responded angrily to the betrayal of African aspirations, notably Britain's acceptance of a racially exclusive franchise in the ex-republics. The particular grievances of members—exclusion from land and from trade—seemed to hinge upon exclusion from the franchise; and it was these measures (rather than industrial grievances) which drew most of their fire.

These articulate men were brought together, with a few of the diehard Cape liberals, in protest against the Act of Union. Their protests were overruled, and the new Union government proceeded to tidy up some inconsistencies in industrial and agrarian laws. It was clearly necessary to form a Union-wide and permanent association, to express African dismay and to seek amelioration. They met in January 1912 at Bloemfontein, agreed to create the South African Native National Congress, and proposed an ad hoc constitution. Paramount chiefs were to be lifetime members of an upper house, and it was expected that Lewanika of the Lozi, and Letsie II of Basutoland would belong, as well as the paramounts of Tswana and Sotho and Nguni communities. The scope of the SANNC [which came to be known as the African National

Congress (or ANC)] was conceived as Pan-African, rather than merely Union-wide. Indeed the aspiration of many leaders was to achieve common and non-racial equality with whites, rather than an exclusively African identity, even though it might require a mobilized African movement to reach that goal.

The inclusion of tribal leaders acknowledged their continuing prestige—and the impossibility of reaching rural Africans by other channels of communication. Inter-ethnic tensions persisted, and the executive committee had to balance them—four members from the Cape, including Rubusana (but not Jabavu, who refused to join), four from the Transvaal, including Makgatho, one from the OFS, and the Rev. John Dube from Natal as President. Though the African National Congress—as it came to be known—was widely spread, it did not have deep roots.

Strategies of Opposition

This shallow membership did not seem to matter at first, since most leaders believed that their rulers could be persuaded to amend their policies, by appeals to reason and humanity. When appeals failed to move the South African Government in 1914 and 1919, the ANC sent respectful delegations of well-spoken men to London to address the British Government, or the King. Only slowly did they realize that neither the King, nor the British Government, nor the South African political leaders would act on their behalf. The issues closest to ANC's heart—land, trading rights, job discrimination and the franchise—were subject to ruthless government action in the first years after Union.

Meanwhile other groups were taking actions and devising tactics which were worth thinking about. Indian indentured laborers in Natal from the 1860s sometimes stayed there when their indentures expired, and they were supplemented by others who came as merchants and clerks and professionals. Though they were usually British subjects, they experienced a wide range of discrimination in Natal and in the Transvaal (where a few had managed to settle). In the face of discrimination, and led by M. K. Gandhi, a young lawyer, they organized peaceful non-cooperation tactics, forcing the Transvaal and South African Governments to arrest them in large numbers. Later on in India, these techniques were perfected into *satyagraha* (passive resistance, or moral resistance) and undermined British imperial control. In South Africa, however, this technique was not effective.

ANC leaders established and maintained close relations with the APO under Abdurahman. However, although coloured people suffered much the same discrimination as other Africans, their situation in the western Cape was rather different and consultations did not lead to close cooperation. Essentially the ANC must either mobilize African mass support, or else find allies within the enfranchised white population. It was the second alternative—seeking white allies—which the ANC mainly preferred.

There were strong and committed enemies of the South African Government within the white population. The industrial working class as a whole was suspicious about the influence of capitalists over the state, and disappointed at Botha's and Smuts's collaboration. Strikes broke out on the Witwatersrand in 1907, 1913 and 1914, in protest against the dilution of the white labor force. However, the white miners preferred to struggle (and even to lose) on their own, rather than enlist African allies. If African workers were to be unionized, they would have to organize themselves.

It was, of course, difficult to mobilize African industrial workers even around Johannesburg. As contract workers from different parts of the region, spending only a few months together, and under the constant observation of employers, they could not easily agree to action. Their discontents were commonly expressed by short outbursts of anger, and ill-prepared action. After the South African War, for example, many simply stayed at home or worked in non-mining jobs. At the end of the First World War there was a more organized strike by black miners, whose living costs had increased during the war, but whose wages did not rise. The strike was suppressed violently in 1920.

Shortly afterwards, in 1921, the white miners struck once again, in protest against dismissals and dilution. On this occasion the strike escalated into a revolt—the famous Rand Revolt—before Smuts sent in the army to restore order. Within a few months, the white miners were seeking to regain by the ballot box what they lost in direct action. Eventually, in 1924, the Labour Party won enough seats to become junior partner in Hertzog's Pact government. However, there was absolutely no prospect of sympathy from the Labour Party, which indeed preferred to keep Africans out of jobs which white workers wanted. So what could be learned from these struggles?

No clear "lessons" could be deduced. Both white and black workers had used the strike strategy: but it did not yield results, perhaps because black and white did not strike together. White workers gained more through voting in elections—but African votes were so few that the same option was not really available. In any formal political alliance, representatives of African voters would form only a tiny minority.

In any event, it was not the ANC who took initiatives as a rule. Their commitment to the cause of individual westernized men, and their confidence in rational argument, as well as their pride in their own individual accomplishments, made them reluctant to initiate mass protests. The leaders did, however, adopt causes which emerged spontaneously from other oppressed groups. In 1913, women in the OFS marched peacefully against the extension of pass laws against them, and the ANC endorsed these protests. When miners struck work, ANC leaders would represent them. In brief, the leaders tolerated local mass protests, and even used these as evidence that humane change was necessary: but they would not incite such protests.

The leaders of the ANC were particularly weak in industrial matters which were usually outside their personal experience as pastors and teachers and clerks. They were overshadowed in this area by a quite new movement. In 1919, dock workers at Cape Town struck work, in favor of wage increases; and from this episode Clements Kadalie emerged onto the national stage. A young migrant from Nyasaland, with a secondary education and clerical experience in Rhodesia, he founded an organization known as ICU. Though not at first its secretary, he was always its dominant personality.

The ICU flourished in the Cape, where workers in Cape Town, Port Elizabeth and East London were eager to form large associations, and where the cooperation of a few whites could be expected. From the Cape it spread rapidly to the Witwatersrand and to Durban. At its peak it may have enrolled 100,000 members; but it was known to many more, who might well follow where it led. The question was where it would lead—the same question which ANC leaders had failed to resolve. If it were purely an industrial organization, then it should negotiate wage settlements for its members. If it were a political association, then it could bargain with Hertzog or prepare for extra-parliamentary agitation. In the event, all three tactics were used, none of them to great effect. Hertzog was surprised to enjoy ICU support in his 1924 election campaign; but he had no doubt that ICU was a threat to his coalition, and once in power he tried to harass and weaken it. When the small Communist Party protested against ICU indecision and financial muddle, Communists were expelled—but Kadalie was also uneasy with his few white liberal advisers. No clear strategy was laid down.

Kadalie hoped for international support, seeing (probably correctly) that ICU was too weak to force general economic or political changes on a stubborn South African Government. Once again he faced a choice, whether to seek support from Communist or non-Communist unions in Europe. And while he was away in Europe, his organization began to break up. By the time he gained a little support from the British Labor movement—and the aid of a full-time organizer from Scotland—it was too late. The provincial branches were pulling in separate directions. In the absence of a clear strategy, or of significant gains in wages, the rank and file grew impatient. In 1929 ICU broke up, leaving separate organizations in Rhodesia, Natal, the Transvaal, the Orange Free State and the Cape itself. . . .

Chapter III

AFRIKANERDOM

8. *THE APARTHEID LAWS IN BRIEF**

by FIONA McLACHLAN

Fiona McLachlan is associated with the Institute of Criminology, University of Cape Town, South Africa.

The Population Registration Act 30 of 1950

Upon the registration of a birth, each person is classified as white, Coloured or African. Coloureds and Africans are further divided into ethnic or other groups. Generally, a child will have the same classification as his/her parents, but for those who do not fall into any definite category, their status will be determined by criteria such as descent, appearance (hair, lips, nails, etc.), social acceptance, habits, speech and education. A person may apply for reclassification to another group or third parties may object to the official classification awarded.

Any classification other than white means fewer rights. This Act causes much human suffering as families are torn apart by different classifications.

Groups Areas Act 41 of 1950

In terms of this Act, separate geographical areas are set aside for use by different racial groups. White suburbs immediately surround the central and

*From United Nations Centre Against Apartheid: *Notes and Documents,* "Children in Prison: South Africa" (New York, 1985).

business districts of cities, while black residential suburbs (townships) are established on the outskirts. . . .

District Six in Cape Town is an example of the effects of this Act. In 1966, District Six was proclaimed a white area although 90 percent of its residents were Coloured. The consequences of this proclamation have been described as follows: the breakdown of supportive extended families, the end of many home industries, unemployment, increased living costs, women compelled to work and unsupervised children forced to run wild in the streets where many joined street gangs which "absorbed the ideology of the ruling class and replayed its tune on the streets in a particularly naked and brutal fashion." . . .

Pass Laws and Influx Control

Africans are subject to the greatest restrictions. The pass laws require all Africans over the age of 16 to apply to a Central Reference Bureau for identity documents. These are to be in their possession at all times and the police may arrest anyone failing to produce them on demand. The passbooks indicate whether an African has the "right" to be in a white area. The influx control laws forbid any African to be in a white area for more than 72 hours except in special circumstances. . . .

The Keystone of Apartheid: The Bantustan or "Homeland"

The intention behind the influx control laws is that all Africans must live in their respective "self-governing homelands." Therefore, unless an individual qualifies to live in a white area, he requires permission to work in "white" South Africa as a migrant contract laborer and may not bring his family to live with him. Furthermore, in terms of government homelands policy, once a homeland becomes "independent," its "citizens" automatically lose their South African citizenship, whether they live in the homeland or not.

The homelands comprise 13 percent of South Africa's land and need to support more than 70 percent of its population. The South African Government shifts the costs of housing, education and welfare to the homeland governments, yet all these areas are financially dependent upon South Africa.

As a result of the overcrowding in the homelands and consequent unemployment, poverty and overloaded services, thousands of Africans stream "illegally" to the major urban areas looking for work or to join their relatives in an attempt to maintain their family lives. During 1981, 1,329,000 migrant laborers and 745,500 commuters from the homelands alone were legally in South Africa. During the same year, 160,600 Africans were convicted of influx control and pass law offences. The Government has proposed further legislation to tighten up its enforcement of these laws despite warnings that it will never be able to tide the flow from the homelands. In addition, African communities are regularly forced to move from "black spots" within white South Africa as the Government attempts to consolidate the homelands.

"Petty" Apartheid

Apartheid controls many other aspects of life in South Africa as well. Public amenities, for example, beaches, restaurants, theatres, libraries and public transport are reserved for use by one race. . . . Africans are not allowed to own land (except in the "independent" homelands) and are only granted 99-year leaseholds over their property. Due to the shortage of houses, poverty and the influx of Africans from the homelands, African townships are overcrowded and "squatter" communities are a common sight on the outskirts of all major cities. Coloured and Indian areas are similarly overcrowded. . . .

9. THE ASCENDANCY OF AFRIKANERDOM*

by ROBERT I. ROTBERG

Robert I. Rotberg, a frequent visitor to southern Africa, is Professor of Political Science and History at Massachusetts Institute of Technology. His recent books include South Africa and Its Neighbors: Regional Security and Self-Interest, *co-author (1985);* Namibia: Political and Economic Prospects, *ed. (1983); and* Suffer the Future: Policy Choices in Southern Africa *(1980), from which the following is excerpted.*

The Triumph of Afrikanerdom

The triumph of the National party in the 1948 elections proved revolutionary in its impact on the politics of South Africa. Not only had Afrikaners, including many who had been interned in World War II for their pro-Nazi sympathies, successfully appealed to fears of black advancement and competition, but they had also promised to rewrite the statute book in order to guarantee permanent white dominance. Their 70 seats (of a total of 153) were sufficient, when allied with the Afrikaner party's 9 seats, to oust the United party of General Jan Christiaan Smuts and Jan Hofmeyr (which won 65 seats); they thus had a parliamentary majority large enough to undermine the system of representative democracy that had until then followed the British model. (The Labor party had won six of the remaining seats.) The hard-line Afrikaners who were the architects of the unexpected National party victory, and who con-

*From Suffer the Future: Policy Choices in Southern Africa (Cambridge, Mass., 1980).

trolled the party, lacked the inherited shared values of the Cape Dutch and the British. Instead, they took their triumph as a mandate to alter the social, economic, and particularly the political structure of the country. Most of all —as a cardinal dictum to which all else was secondary—the new governing class viewed its victory in ethnic-specific terms. Afrikaners had ousted the hated English and had thus reversed the military result of the Anglo-Boer War. Having done so, Afrikaners were determined never to risk being again ousted from power. Loss of power could threaten white hegemony and, more directly, the opportunity for Afrikaners to redress the humiliations of the past. . . .

The Mechanisms of Control

In 1949 the leaders of the National party began to behave in a manner that is not uncommon on the African continent. In order to entrench themselves in power forever, Nationalists early used legal and extralegal means to increase their own majority and to hinder the effectiveness of opposition groups inside and outside parliament, to eliminate dissent, and to emphasize conformity. Within their own party there has been an unusual emphasis upon rigid obedience and loyalty to decisions made by the hierarchy and confirmed by the caucus; the influence of a cohesive, shadowy secret society, the Broederbond (Band of Brothers), has been used to exert pressure on those who would break rank and seek rewards outside of the party or Afrikanerdom. Continued disproportionate representation of rural areas and some gerrymandering buttressed the dominance of the party. So has the ruthless elimination of dissent and the equation of most forms of dissent with communism, and of communism with treason.

The ability of the courts to interfere with the supremacy of parliament and to review and overturn legislation had to be curtailed. Constitutional provisions protecting the Coloured vote in the Cape and basic rights such as habeas corpus had to be rescinded. Once the unassailability of the ruling cadre of Afrikanerdom had been assured through deft and deliberate subversion of the rule of law and of representative democracy, the passage of legislation implementing and further safeguarding Afrikaner and National party dominance was easy and inexorable.

Color was the emotive factor. The National party leadership has always made its way politically by playing upon the electorate's fears of black power. Dread of the loss of privilege is real among the white community, but it has also been exacerbated and inflamed for political ends. In the wake of the mismanagement of independent African countries, and of disasters like the Congo and Idi Amin's Uganda, Afrikaners have had no lack of horrors on which to dilate. At the highest political levels, however, racial and color-based exclusiveness have been less ends in themselves than means capable of helping to ensure perpetual Afrikaner rule. It is power, and what power means, and not race as such, or at least not race primarily, that explains the Afrikaner political imperative.

Whatever the motive, the National party had campaigned on a platform of racial exclusion. Immediately after its electoral victory in 1948 the party extended the existing legislative prohibition against mixed marriages and private immorality to all kinds of transracial intercourse involving whites (and not just that between whites and Africans). It introduced the Population Registration Act to assign all persons to racial categories and the Group Areas Act to extend residential and commercial segregation to Coloureds and Asians (Africans were already affected by the Urban Areas Act of 1923). Under the Prevention of Illegal Squatting Act of 1951, the minister of native affairs could remove Africans from public and private land and send them to resettlement camps. The Native Laws Amendment Act of 1952 eliminated home ownership and other long-held rights of urban blacks; it restricted permanent residence in the urban areas to those who could prove that they had been born in the cities, who had lived there continuously for fifteen years, or who had worked continuously for the same employer for ten years. In 1952, parliament also passed the carefully named Natives (Abolition of Passes and Coordination of Documents) Act so as to require all Africans previously exempted from the pass laws, including women, to carry so-called reference books listing their places of origin, employment history, tax payments, and brushes with the police, and a photograph on their persons at all times. By enforcing this act, the government sought tightly to control the movement of Africans in and out of the urban areas; together with the Native Laws Amendment Act, the legislation was intended to stem the growth of the black population in the cities. . . .

In 1953 the Native Resettlement Act empowered the government to move African residents of Johannesburg to a new location twelve miles from the city. In 1956 and 1957 Sophiatown, the black freehold section outside Johannesburg, was rezoned for whites; Coloureds and Africans were forcibly removed. A similar implementation of the Group Areas Act enabled the government to begin to remove Coloureds from District Six in Cape Town in 1966 (a process that continued as late as 1979) and from Simonstown on False Bay. In another ten cities, and in numerous towns, the same procedure eliminated Africans, Coloureds, and Asians from commercial and residential competition with whites. A total of about 500,000 people have been removed from their homes under the Group Areas Act.

The Elimination of Dissent

Since Africans, Coloureds, Asians, and some brave whites protested the rewriting of South African laws and the denial of both civil rights and civil liberties that was intended by the new legislation, the government increased the number and power of its legal weapons to minimize and eliminate dissent. The Suppression of Communism Act of 1950 made the Communist party illegal. In addition, it permitted the minister of justice to declare kindred groups—that is, groups the aims of which were similar to those of communism—unlawful. Such construction might have had only a limited effect, but the law defined communism not only as Marxism-Leninism, but also as any related form of such a doctrine that attempted to bring about political, industrial, social, or economic change within South Africa by promoting disorder or by encouraging hostility between whites and nonwhites. Thus the minister of justice could, without effective immediate judicial review, decide that almost any organization opposing the government was communist, and thus unlawful. The act further gave the minister the right to "name" and then to restrict the movements of members and supporters of the bodies that he had declared unlawful. He could prohibit gatherings that he considered to be designed to further the ends of communism, broadly defined. However, the bill did not give the government the right to hamper the activities of persons who had renounced their membership in communist organizations. In 1951, therefore, the 1950 law was applied retroactively to anyone who had ever been a communist.

In 1953, to add to its arsenal, the government, assisted by the votes of six members added on questionable legal grounds from Southwest Africa (a lapsed mandate never legally incorporated into South Africa), passed two additional pieces of legislation. The Public Safety Act permitted the governor-general to proclaim emergencies of up to a year, during which summary arrests could be made and detentions without trials or judicial review could be authorized. The Criminal Law Amendment Act permitted imposition of heavy fines, long prison sentences, and corporal punishment of individuals convicted of inciting others to violence or threatening breaches of the peace.

Neither the rhetoric of Afrikanerdom in power nor the translation of that rhetoric into legislation seemed unduly to alarm the bulk of the white electorate. African hostility and fear was obvious, and some whites, and many Coloureds and Asians, protested what was seen as the perversion of South African practice and intent. Yet the United party opposed neither the Public Safety Act nor the Criminal Law Amendment Act. Nor did it speak out against the passage of the Reservation of Separate Amenities Act of 1953, which eliminated the requirement that separate facilities be equal and which thereby intensified the impact of all forms of segregation. The white electorate, aroused by the National party and encouraged to fear creeping communism and black power (and to equate the one with the other) apparently accepted that the party's ends justified any means, even the callous manipulation of the country's political processes. In 1953 the electorate increased the Nationalist majority to 94 of 159 seats. The United party won 57 seats and the Labour party, 5.

Succeeding elections swelled the parliamentary strength of the Nationalists. In 1958 they captured 103 seats; in 1961, 105; in 1966, 126 (of 166); in 1970, 118; in 1974, 123 (of 171); and in 1977, 132 (of 165). As it lost seats, so the United party lost its will. By the middle of the 1950s, it had ceased to present a viable political alternative to the National party in parliament. In the 1960s it generally followed the National party's lead—so much so that Helen Suzman, the lone survivor in the 1960s of 11 Progressives who had defected from the United party in 1959, single-handedly carried the banner of serious opposition to National party policy until she was joined by seven fellow Progressives in 1974 (two won by-elections) and four further refugees from the United party in 1975. By 1977 the renamed Progressive Federal party had won 17 seats (it won an eighteenth in 1979) and had become the official opposition.

Their electoral victories enabled the Nationalists to continue to rewrite the statute book in order to extend their parliamentary power, their control over all aspects of African, Coloured, and Asian life, and their insulation of the security apparatus from the normal (and hitherto expected) processes of judicial review. In 1955, for example, the government concluded a process begun in 1951. Defying the constitution, it enlarged the Senate from 48 to 89 members by giving some provinces more seats than others and by electing senators by a full majority vote of the party that controlled each province. The result was an unassailable two-thirds Nationalist majority of both houses of parliament. Earlier it had enlarged and packed the appellate division of the Supreme Court. Together, these actions, and the passage of the South African Amendment Act of 1956, brought about the removal of Coloureds from the voters rolls in the Cape, eliminating a right that had been entrenched in the Act of Union. The 1956 law also provided that no court could henceforth rule on the validity of a law passed by parliament.

Missionary societies had educated Africans from the beginnings of South Africa. In 1953 control over the content and administration of the education of Africans was transferred to the government. The State-Aided Institutions Act of 1957 gave the government the right (and the responsibility) to decide who could visit a library or any place of entertainment. Also in 1957, another Native Laws Amendment Act permitted the government to prohibit the holding of classes, any kind of entertainment, and church services if they were attended by Africans in an area that had been proclaimed "white" under the Group Areas Act. Thus Africans (domestic servants, for example) could not worship in white suburbs or attend night schools outside of urban locations. The curiously named Extension of University Education Bill, introduced in 1957 and finally approved in 1959, made it almost impossible for nonwhites to continue to attend universities, such as Cape Town and Witwatersrand, which had for decades opened their doors to all students. Instead, the state established ethnic universities, thereby compelling nearly all Coloureds to be educated only with Coloureds, Asians with Asians, and—for Africans—Zulu with Zulu (at the new University of Zululand), Xhosa with Xhosa (at the University of Fort Hare, opened originally as a multiethnic college in 1916), and Tswana, Venda, Pedi, Sotho, and others only with members of the same groups at the new University of the North. The act also made it a criminal offense for whites to attend the universities for nonwhites.

Throughout the 1950s and 1960s, there were many other legislative abridgements of freedom. Each was explained by the need to maintain security in the face of the perceived perils posed by black defiance or communist subversion. The result was the construction of a formidable security system, innumerable arrests, the employment of methods of detention and interrogation that were new to South Africa, major show trials, and—after the Sharpeville massacre of 1960—the overwhelming subordination of ordinary human rights to the declared political imperatives of the state (as interpreted by the oligarchy that had come to direct the fortunes of the National party). In 1962, for example, after B. Johannes Vorster had become minister of justice and Africans were for the first time resorting to urban sabotage and rural assaults, the police were empowered to detain subjects without charge, and in solitary confinement, for 12, then 90, then 180 days, and, eventually, for an unlimited period if authorized by a judge; after 1976, such suspects could be detained indefinitely, even without authorization. In 1962 sabotage was made a statutory offense. According to the General Law Amendment act, the so-called Sabotage Act, the definition of sabotage was construed to cover the illegal possession of weapons as well as willful destruction, tampering with property, and unlawful entry. In 1967 terrorism was defined by the legislature to include training for what could be defined loosely as activity harmful to the interests of the state, furthering the objects of communism, and sabotage as defined in the previous act. House arrest was legalized in 1962. The Prisons Act of 1959 had made the unauthorized reporting of conditions in prisons illegal; it also gave the state the power to hold suspects incommunicado. These provisions made it virtually impossible for allegations of mistreatment by prisoners to be proved.

The Structure of Domination

. . . The security police, the department [Department of National Security], and military intelligence have separate networks of informers, white and black. The state censors and controls publications and films (administering the Publications Act in fiscal 1977–78 cost R 235,000). It also opens mail, taps telephone conversations, has threatened and compelled the press to impose a degree of self-censorship, and uses the state-run television and radio services to disseminate propaganda. In the 1970s, too, state funds were used covertly to influence public opinion within South Africa and to attempt to manipulate the country's image overseas (the Muldergate scandal). Another mechanism of indoctrination is the state-run educational system, which is especially effective in the white sector.

Most of the time this control over information enables the political apparatus to hide and distort its real aims. The press is severely constrained by the Police Amendment Act and other legislation discussed earlier. In criminal cases the defense is often unable to learn the charge against its clients until trial, since discovery motions are usually thwarted on security grounds. . . .

Although less random and therefore less an instrument of terror than the state-licensed violence of Idi Amin's Uganda or François Duvalier's Haiti, the ability of the South African security apparatus to instill fear has become almost unlimited. In the five years before 1979, 45 Africans had died in police custody while undergoing interrogation. The death of Stephen Biko in 1977 was only the most notorious of these incidents. From 1950 through 1978, 1,385 whites, Coloureds, Indians, and Africans were the subjects of banning orders of varying severity under the Internal Security Act. Being banned, they were prevented from talking or being with more than one other person at a time (while saving the state the costs of their room and board in prison). They also had to report regularly to the police. By early 1979, a quarter of the total had fled the country. In the cases of others who had died, the banning orders continue and prevent them from being quoted; Robert Sobukwe was an example.

Including 21 Africans released from preventive detention toward the end of 1978 and immediately served with banning orders, 168 blacks and whites were banned and alive in South Africa in February 1979. Among their number were trade unionists; black-consciousness leaders; former members of the African National Congress, the Pan-Africanist Congress, and the Congress of Democrats; former officers of the Christian Institute; journalists; and students. Some could not find jobs as professionals, despite their training. Others were prohibited from working in their own professions; three recently banned black writers were forbidden in early 1979, for instance, to resume their former occupations as journalists. In March 1979 a former student leader was forbidden to attend her own wedding celebration. A black churchman likes to play tennis but is restricted by the terms of his banning order to singles: to play doubles would be to take part in an illegal gathering. Most banning orders apply for five years and are renewable.

In 1977, in the aftermath of the Soweto disturbances, as many as 800 persons were being detained without trial; in early 1979, however, the security police were holding only 64, all Africans, in prisons without benefit of counsel or access to relatives. (An additional 447 prisoners were serving long sentences on Robben Island, South Africa's Alcatraz, for offenses against the state; nine were under eighteen years of age.) Forty-five were being detained according to the provisions of section 6 of the Terrorism Act of 1967; it permits the police to detain suspected terrorists, or those who are presumed to have information about terrorism, broadly defined, for questioning indefinitely (if necessary, they may keep the detainees, uncharged, in solitary confinement). The police are not obligated to admit to holding a detainee, to inform his family of his detention, or ever to bring him before a court. The Internal Security Act of 1976 (the revamped Suppression of Communism Act) sanctions preventive detention of anyone whose activities are thought to endanger the security of the state or the maintenance of public order (sections 10 and 12b). . . .

Well before 1979, a pattern had been established. As soon as African or white dissenters became prominent or were thought to be influential, they were questioned and detained or banned. By 1978 serious, nonparliamentary internal opposition had therefore been driven underground, as it had been in the 1960s, and the bulk of the population—both white and black—had effectively been cowed.

. . . Despite the existence of a parliament and several parties, it is reasonable to describe the Republic as an authoritarian state with a police state potential that is already exercised over the vast majority of the inhabitants of the country. For purposes of handy description, at least, South Africa is run by an absolutist oligarchy capable of leading an electorate to which, throughout the 1970s, it gave only safe and unimaginative choices. . . .

South Africa's white leadership is consequently insulated by the successes of the last thirty years; by the rigidity and authoritarian quality of the party, the church, and Afrikaner life generally; by tradition buttressed by a revised legality and an extensive security and intelligence apparatus; by the powerlessness of countervailing corporate and other nonstate institutions; and—possibly most of all—by a clannish solidarity that still reacts to the danger of English as well as African aspirations.

The Ruling Oligarchy

. . . In cold, clinical terms . . . the electorate has become—for political purposes —subservient to the wishes of an oligarchy. The membership of the ruling cadre is largely drawn from the ranks of politicians. Historically the leadership of the Broederbond was often included, but the influence of this one-time informal network of power brokers waned under Prime Minister B. Johannes Vorster. Its leadership became comparatively enlightened, or liberal, but it was the strength of the country's purely political oligarchy that tended to diminish the importance of the Broederbond, as also the church, the Afrikaans-medium press, and Afrikaner-dominated commerce. . . .

Remaining an unacknowledged authoritarian state is not terribly difficult where the guardians of white control can point so easily at another alternative that is threatening to most whites. Black dominance—the black peril—fuels authoritarianism, justifies and legitimizes it for whites, and makes the concentration of power in a few hands that much more plausible and self-perpetuating. It was precisely the prevailing climate of fear and subservience that permitted South Africa's Department of Information to spend vast sums of money secretly, and on dubious projects—some of which distorted the direction of South African society—without the country, or even the entire cabinet, being informed. Among various schemes floated by Cornelius Mulder and Eschel Rhoodie, the secretary of information and the plan's "mastermind," were the covert purchase of leading American, British, and French news publications; using front men, the establishment of the *Citizen,* an English-language morning daily to compete with the liberal *Rand Daily Mail;* [1] the secret funding of research institutes, foreign-policy associations, economic seminars, and meetings of various kinds in South Africa and in the United States; the secret financing of programs of the Dutch Reformed Church in South Africa; the covert dispersal of funds to pro-South African front groups in Europe and the United States; gifts of money to European and American politicians; and, allegedly, covert giving to influence American senatorial races. The acknowledged total of all of this largesse was R 73 million, some of which was unaccounted for and some of which was devoted to junkets by Rhoodie and Mulder to funspots in Africa and elsewhere, as well as to the purchase of housing and other material benefits for private consumption. Roelof F. Botha, South Africa's foreign minister, subsequently called the projects of Mulder's Department of Information "naive and half-baked." They constituted an "amateurish attempt to serve South Africa's interests [and] in the process caused incalculable hardship to the country."

When the outlines of the department's usurpation of authority became known privately to journalists and to political gossips, it took a full year, charges by the Progressive Federal party in a parliamentary select committee, cautious comments in the English-language press, and jealousies within the cabinet to curtail its activities. Even then it was only because a courageous judge happened upon evidence of the misappropriation of foreign funds and —a rarity in South Africa—chose to speak out that what had long been known to the press and the opposition became public knowledge and politically consequential. Newspapers could not publish without the action of the judge, and only his action breached the cloak of secrecy with which the oligarchy had attempted to cover up extensive ministerial and governmental deceit.

The Vorster Era

In South Africa concentration of power came about gradually and naturally in the wake of the hegemony of the National party and the patterns of leadership associated with its heritage. As the Nationalists consolidated their power,

[1] The *Rand Daily Mail* closed its doors in the spring of 1985, the official reason given, its financial losses.—Ed.

so they concentrated the control of that power. Verwoerd brooked little disagreement within the party. Vorster, less well known and less ideological, acceded to his position in 1966 and spent the next four or five years buttressing his prominence with personal as well as positional control. He did so from within the party, as a manipulator as well as an architect, and then from about 1971 began to project himself onto the international stage. By doing so he gained credibility at home and increased stature within the party. Because he was thought indispensable, he was in a position to dominate the party as the party dominated South Africa, and as the leaders of black Africa dominate their own new positions. Like them, Vorster was a man for all seasons. A little less totally but nevertheless in the same ways, he came in the 1970s to personify the state. Behind a dour, delphic countenance and in consultation with political and military cronies, some of whom were interned with him during World War II, he carefully substituted his own for the public will. His was an authoritarianism on behalf of a ruling class and, in particular, on behalf of a majority of the ruling class. . . .

During the first half of the 1970s, Vorster established himself as a pragmatist capable of leading with imagination. Despite a reputation as a strong segregationist, he was capable of suspending ideology and of attempting to bring about an entente with a number of black African states, of welcoming black leaders and their wives to Pretoria, and of making the distinction—soon easily accepted—between the need to maintain apartheid at home and the irrelevance of color elsewhere. Vorster was capable of doing what was difficult for Verwoerd and his predecessors—concentrating the minds of his followers on power, not the principle nor the ideology of color for its own sake.

Vorster thus managed profoundly to alter the nature of the debate. He presided over a modification of the strict application of the color bar to all aspects of South African public life. In so doing he succeeded, admittedly at the eleventh hour, in making his own people aware of the necessity for movement. . . . Plagued by what was officially called deteriorating health, he resigned as prime minister in September 1978 without resolving any of his country's critical problems. (He became president but was also compelled to resign that position, in mid-1979, after his involvement in the Muldergate scandal became officially known.)

Separate development remained official dogma despite a widespread feeling that granting local independence to a handful of homelands, and the intention to make all Africans, no matter where they really resided and worked, putative citizens of the homelands, only obscured the demographic and political realities: blacks would continue to constitute a majority in all the urban centers of the country, and in the rural, white-farmed areas as well. No legislative fiction could eliminate their preponderance, their economic relevance to modern South Africa, their political salience, their capability, regardless of age, of being mobilized against prevailing norms, their antagonism to separate development, their distrust of homeland options, the increasing radicalization and nationalism of their politics, the increasing strength of the young in indigenous politics, their new refusal to prefer the option of embourgeoisement to shifts in political fortunes, and their determination to share power instead of merely demanding relaxations in social apartheid. Although many Afrikaner Nationalists, including Vorster and his cabinet ministers, understood how dramatically the politics of post-Portuguese coup and post-Soweto uprising South Africa had shifted from a focus on social rights to the quest for political power, the ruling oligarchy under Vorster rebuffed those within its own ranks who promoted innovative ways of responding to the aspirations of blacks. . . .

The Accession of Botha

P. W. Botha, who succeeded Vorster, inherited the kind of intransigent party posture that doubtless fitted his own temperament. With a reputation as a man who preferred fighting to negotiating, he seemed a natural successor to the Vorster of 1978. Yet he acceded to power over Mulder, who had developed a reputation for pragmatism, largely because of the burgeoning financial scandal that shortly after the election forced Mulder to resign his ministerial and party positions. Botha, too, was not solely the dogmatic, ostrichlike leader of the popular picture.

It is true that many South Africans, especially those of the more liberal wing of the National party and those allied to the Progressives, feared that Botha would not be equal to the challenges facing South Africa in the late 1970s and early 1980s. Those challenges were several. First, black unemployment in 1978 was rising to unprecedented levels; the black dwelling areas were restless; young blacks were still boycotting secondary schools; and violence was—more than ever before—a common accompaniment of daily race relations. One challenge was how best to accommodate black aspirations and black desires for effective political representation to white fears of the loss of power and privilege.

A second challenge was related to the first. Although in 1978 high gold prices had been cushioning the impact of recession on the country, South Africa's economy was weak. Reviving confidence in the future growth of the nation was linked to the first challenge, since Botha would be unable to attract the foreign investment that South Africa desperately needed to grow in real terms without restoring a belief in his country's essential stability.

A third challenge was that of isolation. Vorster refused to battle the West on every front. His willingness in 1977 and early 1978 to negotiate the future of Namibia resulted in the acceptance of a Western formula meant to convey legitimacy to a new government after elections to be supervised by the United Nations. But by coupling his resignation with an about-face on Namibia,

Vorster left for Botha the decision whether or not to do battle with the West, and thus potentially to invite broad economic sanctions against South Africa.

Botha, on his record, did not share Vorster's pragmatic belief that cooperation with the West was a useful way of securing the power of Afrikanerdom. He was reputed to see safety for Afrikaners in self-reliant antagonism and appeared, in 1978 and 1979, to oppose all foreign attempts to nudge South Africa into a political posture more acceptable to world opinion. He was suspected of thinking that world opinion was irrelevant.

Botha's critics said that as prime minister he would "hang tough"—that he was not the man for South Africa's season of discontent, or any season. They pointed to his volatility, his excitability in parliament as majority leader, and his reputation as a "cowboy."

Botha had been a member of parliament for thirty years and was sixty-two when he became prime minister. After studying law briefly at the University of the Orange Free State, he became an organizer for the National party, entered parliament (five years before Vorster), and became deputy minister of the interior, minister of Coloured affairs, minister of public works, and, beginning in 1966, minister of defense (a position that he retained after becoming prime minister) and leader of the House of Assembly. Botha was known as a tenacious politician. His contacts overseas were few, however, since he had ventured only rarely outside South Africa before 1978.

Botha is a prime minister sympathetic to some of the Afrikaner political stereotypes. He talks a hard line. Yet because he has long represented a constituency in the Cape Province, where most Coloureds reside, he has never favored extreme discriminatory measures against blacks. He has also spoken out against whites being too insistent on full supremacy over all blacks.

As Botha emerged from the first hundred days of his rule as prime minister, he began to respond to the West over Namibia and to the more liberal element within his own party by replacing Mulder with Koornhof and by refusing at first to give a senior position to Dr. Andries Treurnicht, the party's leading hard-liner. Later, in early 1979, he permitted Koornhof, the most articulate and adventurous liberal in the cabinet, to make Africans happy by promising not to destroy the 20,000-strong Crossroads squatter settlement near Cape Town (Koornhof's predecessors had bulldozed two such shantytowns). Koornhof, again with Botha's support, also agreed to maintain Alexandra township near Johannesburg as a residential area for black families rather than convert it into a high-rise hostel area for single migrant workers.

At about the same time as Koornhof, who had renamed the Ministry of Plural Relations the Ministry of Cooperation and Development, was showing more flexibility and courage than his colleagues over African housing arrangements, he unexpectedly began consulting with and taking advice from the African dwellers affected, from liberal and critical academics, and from opposition white politicians. Further, he appointed a large committee to recommend changes in the way the state regarded urban-dwelling blacks, thus hinting that the government was prepared to reevaluate previous policies based on the premise that Africans were to be regarded as temporary sojourners (out of the homelands) in the urban areas. In announcing the committee, Koornhof also did the unexpected: as members he nominated several Africans widely respected by militant blacks despite (or because of, which is the more remarkable) the fact that they had been imprisoned as enemies of the state less than two years ago.

Botha supported Koornhof in these actions against Treurnicht and other members of the National party. When Koornhof visited the United States in June and said that apartheid was "dying and dead," Botha defended him against attack from the right. Later Botha himself, in a hopeful speech to a provincial congress of his party, told his colleagues that South Africans must "adjust or die." "We are all South Africans and we must act in that spirit toward each other," he said. The chief goal for South Africa should be "to improve the quality of life of all the people in this country." He rejected both "one man, one vote" and total separation (old-fashioned apartheid) with white supremacy. He recognized what South African whites call multinationalism and foresaw the creation of—unspecified—constitutional structures that would give these so-called subordinate nations (to employ Botha's terminology) control over their "own destinies."

The tone of this rhetoric was new. Botha was attempting to redefine the ideology of the National party and of Afrikanerdom by giving to pragmatism the status of a refined theoretical set of formulae. He was insisting that Africans were not subjects to be controlled, but a part of the solution. Much of the old jargon was dismissed, which had symbolic value. So did a surprise visit by the prime minister to Soweto, South Africa's largest black city, in August 1979. He became the first major National party leader to set foot in the sprawling, 33-square-mile dormitory area 12 miles from Johannesburg. Although his visit was largely ignored by all but a few, and studiously disdained by radical Africans, it indicated a new official white sensitivity to the problems of minority rule. In Soweto Botha promised to transform the area into a city, under black control, but carefully said nothing about the political role of Soweto's 1.3 million inhabitants in the future South Africa. . . .

The history of Afrikaner politics is marked more by pragmatic responses to the realities of power than by ideological autarky. When it was essential to cooperate with the English, Afrikaners did so. When they were defeated in war, they made the most of the resulting bitterness, bided their time, returned victorious, and determined never again to be denied political primacy. But as the dream of unfettered control has met the dawn of modern politics, so Afrikaners have made accommodations, no matter how grudging and how token. Botha may be a leader capable of saying that Armageddon is preferable to tactical retreat, but if he is, he belies (and perhaps betrays) the lesson of Afrikanerdom. Whether he can respond in a visionary way to the needs of the changing political climate is questionable, but it may be that only a leader of his credentials can afford to think boldly enough to wrestle vigorously with the problems that most Afrikaners now know cannot be dismissed, and will not evaporate of their own accord.

10. ASPECTS OF REPRESSION*

by the INTERNATIONAL DEFENCE AND AID FUND FOR SOUTHERN AFRICA

The International Defence and Aid Fund for Southern Africa is a humanitarian organization which has worked consistently for peaceful and constructive solutions to the problems created by racial oppression in Southern Africa.

It sprang from Christian and humanist opposition to the evils and injustices of apartheid in Southern Africa. It is dedicated to the achievement of free, democratic, non-racial societies throughout Southern Africa.
The objects of the Fund are:—

(i) to aid, defend and rehabilitate the victims of unjust legislation and oppressive and arbitrary procedures,
(ii) to support their families and dependents,
(iii) to keep the conscience of the world alive to the issues at stake.

In accordance with these three objects, the Fund distributes its humanitarian aid to the victims of racial injustice without any discrimination on grounds of race, color, religious or political affiliation. The only criterion is that of genuine need.
The Fund runs a comprehensive information service on affairs in Southern Africa. This includes visual documentation. It produces a regular news bulletin 'FOCUS' on Political Repression in Southern Africa, and publishes pamphlets and books on all aspects of life in Southern Africa.
The Fund prides itself on the strict accuracy of all its information.

Banning and Banishment

Since 1948 about 200 people have been banished under the Black Administration Act and related laws, and 1,450 people banned under the Internal Security Act (formerly Suppression of Communism Act).

The restriction orders or bans vary in their scope, but most commonly people are prevented from attending any gatherings and are restricted to their homes from dusk to dawn and all weekend. Banned people are generally

*From *Apartheid: The Facts* (London, 1983).

JENNIFER FARLEY

prevented from carrying out their jobs. Sometimes this is done directly (as in the case of many journalists and teachers), or as a consequence of the restrictions on their movement, or just by being named as banned people.

The banning orders affect almost every aspect of people's lives. The vagueness of the provisions and the orders makes it virtually impossible for people not to break the law by contravening the restrictions, and prosecutions for contravention are common.

Africans, the only section of the population subject to banishment orders suffer even greater personal and material hardship in that they can be removed from their home, community and livelihood.

The banning order is renewable so that any person may be restricted for much longer than the original order.

Banning of Organizations and Meetings

Both mass organizations of the liberation movement and small organizations have been banned by the apartheid regime. This has had the effect both of forcing the organizations to work underground, and of making it an offense, punishable by imprisonment, to further their aims.

In 1950 the Communist Party of South Africa was banned under the Suppression of Communism Act. It later reconstituted itself as the South African Communist Party, operating underground.

In 1960 the *Unlawful Organizations Act* was passed and used to ban the African National Congress and the Pan-Africanist Congress. The Act was then used, along with the Suppression of Communism Act to ban several other organizations during the 1960s. In 1977 the Internal Security Act was used to ban 18 black consciousness organizations. . . .

There has been a general ban on all outdoor meetings since June 1976. The ban was imposed with the start of the uprising of that year, and kept in existence by successive annual renewals, most recently in April 1982. Only sports gatherings, indoor gatherings, funerals or meetings for which official permission has been granted, are exempt.

For two and a half months during 1980 as mass protests, education boycotts and strikes gathered force, all gatherings of a political nature of more than 10 people were banned. This covered indoor as well as outdoor meetings.

After the expiry of this ban, the ban on all outdoor meetings was again supplemented by bans on particular indoor meetings and funerals. The meetings prohibited by such bans have included several to commemorate events of resistance and repression, and memorial services for people who were active in the struggle for liberation. They have included meetings of workers on strike, and political protest meetings.

Funerals in particular have become a focus for political protest and the 1982

Internal Security Act introduced new measures to restrict this trend. Magistrates were empowered to prescribe the route and mode of transport for a funeral procession and enabled to ban all speeches, flags and posters from the ceremony.

In a move which recognized to what extent political trials had become a focus for resistance, the regime in 1982 banned all demonstrations even by an individual in the vicinity of a courthouse. In September 1982 police used tear gas to clear the public gallery at the end of a Treason Trial at the Pietermaritzburg Supreme Court.

Detention without Trial

Detention without trial is characterized by secrecy and lack of accountability by the security police. No detailed statistics of people in detention are provided. Families of detainees are rarely even told at which police station their relative is held. No court can order the release of a detainee. No visits or legal advice are allowed. . . .

The exact numbers of people detained at any time without trial is not known. The most reliable estimates indicate that in 1980 over 950 people were detained at various times under the various "security" laws and at least 967 in 1981. In addition an unknown number were detained under laws in force in bantustans. . . .

Children are subject to the same powers of detention and interrogation as adults. Of those detained during 1977–81, over 700 were juveniles, that is, under 18 years. Some have been held for very long periods. For example, 19 schoolchildren detained in early 1981 were held as potential witnesses in a trial in Kimberley for over 18 months. . . .

Torture and Death of Detainees

There is extensive evidence of torture of detainees, given by former detainees themselves. It is known that by 3 March 1983 at least 57 people had died while in the custody of security police since 1963, the year in which detention for 90 days without trial was introduced. (Of that number, three people died in detention while in the custody of the security police during the uprising of 1976, although they were reportedly not held under "security" laws.) The causes of death in detention are officially reported in such terms as "suicide," "falling out of a window," "falling down a stairwell," "brain injury" and so on.

Torture of detainees, sometimes so severe as to lead to death, is an integral part of the apartheid regime's practice of detaining people without trial for purposes of interrogation. Justifying detention without trial, a commission appointed by the government to review the security legislation said in its report published in 1982 that detention without trial was the most important and, to a large extent, the only means the police had of obtaining information about "subversive" activities. It also noted that information obtained in that way could be used as evidence in trials. Although the report did not say so it is also to a large extent the only source of "evidence" for trials.

There are powerful incentives to torture detainees in order to extract statements and "confessions," and to force people to give evidence. In addition, the conditions of secrecy under which people are detained allow the police to subject them to torture without fear of punishment or retribution. In the case of only one of the 57 deaths of political detainees have policemen been charged and in that case none were convicted. However, due to the nature of the detention laws and the secrecy involved, it has become virtually impossible for detainees to obtain redress through court action. An additional handicap is that charges must be laid within six months of an alleged assault—a period which often elapses while the detainee is still in custody.

Detainees are kept in solitary confinement which in itself has been condemned by legal experts and psychologists as severe torture by sensory deprivation. Detainees have been admitted to hospital for psychiatric care after suffering severe psychological damage. In other cases political trials have had to be stopped so that defendants could be examined by psychiatrists.

Detainees have described many forms of abuse—days of ceaseless interrogation during which they were deprived of sleep and forcibly kept standing; electric shock treatment and physical assault. Many reported that they had been hooded and partially suffocated and then revived.

The use of torture has been particularly intense and widespread during periods of major repressive operations, and the number of deaths in detention has been highest during such periods. . . .

11. APARTHEID: DIVINE CALLING*

by D. F. MALAN

On December 15, 1953, Rev. John E. Piersma, one of a group of Christian Reformed Church ministers in Grand Rapids, Michigan, wrote a letter to the Prime Minister of the Union of South Africa, Dr. D. F. Malan, asking for "a frank description of apartheid," one which could be used "to convince the American public." Reprinted below is Malan's reply of February 12, 1954.

*From *Apartheid: South Africa's Answer to a Major Problem* (Pretoria, State Information Office, 1954?).

... It must be appreciated from the outset that Apartheid, separation, segregation or differentiation—whatever the name given the traditional racial policy of South Africa—is part and parcel of the South African tradition as practiced since the first Dutch settlement at the Cape in 1652, and still supported by the large majority of white South Africans of the main political parties.

The deep-rooted color consciousness of the White South Africans—a phenomenon quite beyond the comprehension of the uninformed—arises from the fundamental difference between the two groups, White and Black. The difference in color is merely the physical manifestation of the contrast between two irreconcilable ways of life, between barbarism and civilization, between heathenism and Christianity, and finally between overwhelming numerical odds on the one hand and insignificant numbers on the other. . . . The racial differences are as pronounced today as they were 300 years ago. . . .

From the outset the European colonists were far out-numbered; there is no doubt that if they had succumbed to the temptation of assimilation, they would have been submerged in the Black heathendom of Africa as effectively as if they had been completely annihilated. Of necessity they had to arm and protect themselves against this ever-growing menace, and how could it better be done than by throwing an impenetrable armor around themselves—the armor of racial purity and self-preservation?

. . . [T]here is no parallel for the South African racial record of non-extermination, non-miscegenation, non-assimilation, but of preaching and practicing Christianity with the retention of racial identity and of mutual respect.

This then is the basis of Apartheid. . . . Apartheid is based on what the Afrikaner believes to be his divine calling and his privilege—to convert the heathen to Christianity without obliterating his national identity. And as you have addressed me in the first place as a Christian and a churchman, let me at the outset summarize for your consideration the point of view of the Dutch Reformed Church with which the other Afrikaans churches are fundamentally in agreement.

A considered statement [of principles] on behalf of the leaders of the Dutch Reformed Church . . . was issued a few months ago. . . . I may summarize these principles as follows:

1. Missionary work has been practiced in this country from the early beginnings as being the Christian duty of the settlers to the heathen. . . .

2. The Church believes that God in His Wisdom so disposed it that the first White men and women who settled at the foot of the Black continent were profoundly religious people, imbued with a very real zeal to bring the light of the Gospel to the heathen nations of Africa. These first South Africans lit a torch which was carried to the farthest corners of the sub-continent in the

course of the last three centuries and whose light now shines upon the greater part of all non-White peoples south of the Equator.

3. Whilst the Church regards the conversion of the heathen as a primary step in his march to civilization it is prepared to face and, in fact, to implement the implications of christianizing the heathen. . . .

4. In the early beginnings the Church used the blessings of civilization as a means to attract the heathen, but today the traditional concept of European guardianship has taken the form of fostering and financing to the full the social, educational and economic development of the non-White. . . . [T]he Church has at all times vouchsafed the various Black races the right and duty to retain their national identities. Christianity must not rob the non-White of his language and culture. Its function is to permeate and penetrate to the depths of his nationalism, whilst encouraging him to retain and refine those national customs and traditions which do not clash with the Christian tenets.

5. The traditional fear of the Afrikaner of racial equality (equalitarianism) between White and Black derives from his aversion to miscegenation. The Afrikaner has always believed very firmly that if he is to be true to his primary calling of bringing Christianity to the heathen, he must preserve his racial identity intact. The Church is, therefore, entirely opposed to intermarriage between Black and White and is committed to withstand everything that is calculated to facilitate it. . . . Whereas the Church . . . opposes the social equalitarianism which ignores racial and color differences between White and Black in everyday life, it is prepared to do all in its power to implement a social and cultural segregation which will rebound to the benefit of both sections.

6. But the duty of the Church has its bounds. It is wrong to expect the Church to enunciate a racial policy for the peoples of South Africa. . . .

7. The Bible is accepted as being the Word of God and the Dutch Reformed Church accepts the authority of Holy Writ as normative for all the political, social, cultural and religious activities in which man indulges. The Church acknowledges the basic rights of the State as a particular divine institution to regulate the lives and actions of its citizens.

Passing then from the historical and spiritual basis of apartheid to its everyday political application as practiced by the present South African Government, let me remind you that government is the art of the possible. It makes no sense, therefore, to criticize the policy of apartheid in the abstract and without due regard to facts and conditions as they exist and as they have been allowed to develop through the centuries. And may I emphasize that to consider only the rights of the Blacks would be precisely as immoral as to have regard only for the rights of the Whites.

I must ask you to give White South Africans credit for not being a nation of scheming reactionaries imbued with base and inhuman motives, not a nation of fools, blind to the gravity of their vital problem. They are normal human beings. They are a small nation, grappling with one of the most difficult problems in the world. To them millions of semi-barbarous Blacks look for guidance, justice and the Christian way of life.

Here a tremendous experiment is being tried; not that fraught with the bloodshed of annihilation, nor that colored by assimilation, but that inspired by a belief in the logical differentiation, with the acceptance of the basic human rights and responsibilities. Human rights and responsibilities can, however, only be exercised by human beings who are capable of appreciating their significance and it is here that my Government, dealing as it does with a still primitive non-White population, is faced with a major educational problem. . . . Today nearly 800,000 Bantu children are given their schooling free of charge, whereas many more attend technical and industrial schools and an ever-increasing number are being fitted at universities, hospitals and training establishments for the profession of doctors, nurses, policemen, clerks, demonstrators, artisans and builders.

. . . It is computed that every European taxpayer in our country "carries" more than four non-Whites in order to provide the latter with the essential services involving education, hospitalization, housing, etc.

For, apart from education, much is done for the physical rehabilitation of the Bantu in his own reserves—in many cases the best agricultural land available in our comparatively poor country. . . .

Allegations that the country's non-Whites are not accorded political rights are untrue. In the urban areas, Advisory Boards whose members are elected by the residents of Black urban residential areas, provide an adequate mouthpiece, whilst tribal authorities are now being established in terms of the Bantu Authorities Act in the rural areas. Through this means the Bantu are given the opportunity to play an active part in the administration of their own affairs and, as they develop, more responsibilities and duties, as well as privileges, are granted them until they are proved to be competent to govern themselves. . . .

Contrary to popular belief abroad, the Whites and Blacks are practically contemporary settlers in South Africa, the former migrating from Europe, the latter fleeing from the terror of Central African internecine wars of extermination.

It is only fifty years since South Africa, until then a poor country, has, through the discovery of its vast mineral resources, emerged from its pastoral era. Half a century of intense development has brought about the upliftment also of the Bantu far beyond that reached by him in any other country on the sub-continent. . . .

Theoretically the object of the policy of Apartheid could be fully achieved by dividing the country into two states, with all the Whites in one, all the Blacks in the other. For the foreseeable future, however, this is simply not practical politics. Whether in time to come we shall reach a stage where some such division, say on a federal basis, will be possible, is a matter we must leave to the future.

In any case, the full implementation of the policy of separate racial development will take very many years. Call it an experiment, if you like, and one could say it is an experiment which is as yet only in its initial stages. Many aspects of the problem are certainly still far from clear, and it would be unwise, even if it were possible, to draw up a blueprint for 50 years ahead. In more than one respect progress will have to be by trial and terror. And if in this process we should err, I ask you and your countrymen not to judge our efforts only by our incidental failures nor to reproach us for what you may at this great distance judge as being lack of the spirit of Christ.

Chapter IV

RACIAL CAPITALISM

12. THE DEVELOPMENT OF RACIAL CAPITALISM*

by ROBERT DAVIES, DAN O'MEARA and SIPHO DLAMINI

Robert H. Davies, Dan O'Meara and Sipho Dlamini are all on the staff of the Centre of African Studies, Eduardo Mondlane University, Maputo, Mozambique. Davies is the author of Capital, the State and White Labour in South Africa 1900–1960 *(1979).* O'Meara is the author of Volkskapitalisme: Class, Capital and Ideology in the Development of Afrikaner Nationalism, 1934–48 *(1983).* The Struggle for South Africa, *from which the following is excerpted, is a two volume reference guide to organizations, movements and institutions involved in the struggle for power in South Africa in the 1980s.*

Overview

Given the all-pervading nature of national oppression and racial discrimination in South Africa, apartheid and the forms of segregation which preceded it, have often been explained simply in terms of racial prejudice. Whites, or more especially the Afrikaans-speaking section of the white population, popularly known as the Boers, are presumed to suffer from intense racial prejudice, and this system of racial discrimination is the result. It is certainly true that

*From The Struggle for South Africa: A Reference Guide to Movements, Organizations and Institutions, Vol. I. (London, 1984).

most whites are highly racially prejudiced, but this explains little. In our view, explanations which stress only the racial component of the apartheid system and fail to explain the historical development and current functioning of the system, are positively misleading. Such types of explanation actually conceal the most important elements of the system.

The approach on which this book [*The Struggle for South Africa*] is based assumes from the outset that the various changing historical forms of national oppression and racism in South Africa are organically linked with, and have provided the fundamental basis for, the development of a capitalist economy in that country. In other words, the various complex and intersecting class struggles through which capitalist forms of production and relations of production were developed and consolidated under colonialism in South Africa, themselves generated racist ideologies and a racially structured hierarchy of economic and political power. The national oppression of black people in South Africa is a product of, and was indeed the necessary historical condition for, the development of capitalism in that country.

Apartheid, then, is much more than a system of intense racial discrimination. Fundamentally it, like the segregationist policies which preceded it, is a system of economic, social and political relations designed to produce cheap and controlled black labor, and so generate high rates of profit. As such, it serves both the dominant capitalist class—which benefits directly from the high levels of exploitation and rates of accumulation made possible by a cheap and controlled labor force—and certain other privileged classes in white society. While these latter are not themselves capitalists . . . they came to form a supporting alliance in the exercise of the white monopoly of power. Thus both the historical development and contemporary functioning of the apartheid system can only be properly understood through an analysis of, the contradictions around and the interlinked processes of capital accumulation, class struggle and national liberation.

Whilst in the late 1970s and the early 1980s the apartheid system has been and is being modified in various minor ways, it has always operated to secure cheap black labor through the following mechanisms:

1) a white monopoly of land ownership;
2) a comprehensive system of control over the movement of the black population in general and black workers in particular;
3) a political system which excludes all blacks and
4) a repressive state dominated by the military, police, and security services.

The Period of Mercantile Colonialism

Dutch Colonialism, 1652–1806

Dutch colonialism held sway over large parts of what is now the Cape Province from 1652–1806 (with an interruption 1795–1803). Between 1806 and 1910, all of present day South Africa came under British colonial rule. . . .

Dutch colonialism was notable for three things: firstly the rapid dispossession of the indigenous colonized population; secondly, the largely corrupt and inefficient rule of the Dutch East India Company officials; and thirdly, the establishment of a stratified settler population. . . .

The Cape colony was primarily intended to replenish the passing ships of the Dutch East India Company, thereby reducing the costs of its trade with the East Indies; Dutch colonial authorities constantly sought to reduce their administrative costs at the Cape. One of the most important measures in this regard was the early abandonment of the initial policy of using Company employees to produce supplies, in favor of encouraging the permanent settlement of white agriculturalists on land seized from the Khoisan inhabitants of the Western Cape. These white *vryboers* (free farmers) received no salary and produced on their own account, making extensive use of Khoisan slave labor. They were nevertheless subject to numerous restrictions and were obliged to sell their produce to the Company at fixed prices. Resistance to these conditions drove many of these colonists to seek to escape the jurisdiction of the rule of the Company. Over the 150 years of Dutch colonialism a significant differentiation developed amongst the settler population (which gradually came to speak a new, Dutch-derived language, later termed Afrikaans). Roughly speaking, in the areas around the Western Cape and present Boland districts, there developed a group of relatively large-scale landowners producing wheat, wine and other crops for sale to the Dutch East India Company's monopoly. They farmed almost exclusively with slave labor.

On the other hand, relatively large numbers of settlers trekked beyond the jurisdiction of the Company and established themselves as largely subsistence stock farmers in outlying areas on land expropriated from the Khoi pastoralists. By the mid 1700s, however, this form of settler colonial expansion became increasingly difficult as the settlers encountered the militarily powerful Xhosa people in the region of the Fish River. For 50 years a series of inconclusive wars for control of the grazing lands of the Zuurveld region were fought between Boer colonists and the Xhosa, with neither side able to impose itself finally on the other.

Thus the slow expansion of Dutch colonialism rested on the twin props of the expropriation of the land of the indigenous inhabitants, and their enslavement as farm and other types of laborers for their white colonial masters.

Accompanying these oppressive processes was the development of a strong racism justifying expropriation and enslavement in biblical terms. Extended discussions on the status in "the Divine Hierarchy of Being" of the enslaved Khoi, concluded that they were *skepsels*—i.e. creations of God, higher than animals but lower than "men" (whites). By the end of Dutch colonialism in 1806, colonial production at the Cape remained based on slave labor. . . .

British Colonialism after 1806

The British seized the Cape from the Dutch in 1806 to guarantee the security of British imperialism's vital sea-going trade with India. . . . Two interlinked processes set in motion a transformation of the political and social map of the region. Britain was in the process of the Industrial Revolution and emerging as the world's foremost capitalist power. Through its free trade policies, British imperialism sought to open the world market to its industrial goods. In the Cape colony this policy saw the gradual abolition of slavery (the slaves were only finally freed in 1838) and the relaxation of other measures of control over the labor market. The aim of this policy was not only to create a market for British industrial goods, but also to foster the development of commercial farming which would pay the costs of maintaining the colony. Commercial agriculture began to develop slowly under British rule. By the end of the 1860s, capitalist farming was established in parts of the Cape and Natal colonies; the black labor force, however, remained tightly controlled.

This British policy of relaxing controls over the labor and other markets increased the economic pressures on the Boer pastoralist colonists and led to increasing antagonism between them and the British authorities. The end result was the large-scale exodus from the Cape colony in the mid to late 1830s of the so-called *Voortrekkers*. These Boers now sought to colonize areas outside British control. . . .

The second crucial social process under way at the end of the 18th Century was the consolidation of numbers of small African chiefdoms into powerful kingdoms. The vast social disruptions this gave rise to—known as the *Mfecane* —completely reorganized the political map of southern Africa. By the mid-1830s, five powerful African kingdoms straddled much of the central and eastern areas of present day South Africa (the Zulu, Ndebele, Swazi, Basotho and Bapedi kingdoms). The expansion of Boer and British colonialism into the hinterland of South Africa after 1830 brought them into conflict with these various pre-capitalist societies. Again, whilst rifles and artillery generally proved superior to the assegai, the majority of these societies remained politically and economically independent throughout the period, and retained large and powerful armies. Yet they were increasingly incorporated in widespread trading networks with colonial capitalists and thus became increasingly dependent on British commodities.

. . . The Afrikaans-speaking Boer colonialists who had set up republics in the Transvaal and Orange Free State in the 1850s were engaged mainly in rentier forms of exploitation. They lived mainly off the rents in labor and in kind from the various squatters on their extensive landholdings. They justified this pre-capitalist form of colonial exploitation in terms of rigid racist ideologies which forbade any "equality in church or state" between white master and black servant.

In the British colony of the Cape, men of property (regardless of color) had been given a form of local self-government. Nevertheless, social relations in the Cape were also marked by a strong racism and racial patterns of power and privilege. However, under British rule, class position—the ownership or non-ownership of the means of production—rather than outright racial discrimination, determined the patterns of economic and political power. . . .

The Age of Imperialism and the "Segregation" Period of Capitalist Development

In the mid-1860s and mid-1880s, the world's largest deposits of first diamonds, and then gold, were discovered at Kimberley and Johannesburg respectively. Diamond mining began in 1867 and gold mining in 1886. The interest of the British metropolitan state in South Africa were transformed virtually overnight. South Africa was no longer an expensive unproductive burden on the British treasury, sustained to protect Britain's vital interests in India. Rather, South Africa was transformed from a colonial backwater into a central prop of British imperialism—itself now scrambling for colonies all over Africa.

The mineral discoveries shattered the existing social systems in what is today South Africa, hurling men and women into new types of social relations, forging new cultures and modes of living; it also transformed the political map of the region. The colonial conquest of the independent African societies was hastily completed between 1868 and 1881. All were now subject to some or other form of colonial rule. The British also sought to smash the independence of the Boer republics they had recognized in the 1850s. Following the Anglo-Boer war of 1899–1902, all of present day South Africa was incorporated into four British colonies. These were finally united as the existing four provinces of South Africa in 1910, and the white colonists were given internal self-rule (the vast majority of the black population remained without political rights). . . .

The development of the mining industry marked a fundamental turning point in South African history. Here first emerged capitalist production on a large scale; three aspects of this are significant. Firstly, it was in the mining industry that the *wage labor system of exploitation,* which distinguishes the capitalist mode of production from others, was first introduced into South

Africa on a significant scale. . . . Within three years of the opening of the Witwatersrand gold fields in 1886, over 17,000 African workers were employed in the mines, together with 11,000 whites. Twenty years later the figure had reached 200,000 black workers and 23,000 whites.

The mining industry was significant secondly because it created the conditions for the early development of capitalist production in agriculture and manufacturing. . . .

Thirdly and finally, it was in the mining industry that many of the institutions or forms of exploitation and consequent national oppression specific to South Africa were first developed in their modern form—the migrant labor system, pass laws, job color bars, the racial division of labor, compounds etc. These were later adapted and used in agriculture and industry. Thus it may be said that the forms of exploitation and relations which developed in the gold mining industry largely shaped the development of labor practices and social relations in other sectors for a long period.

The Mining Industry

The Witwatersrand gold fields were the largest hitherto discovered, but the ore was of a low grade, was very deep underground and widely scattered—and hence difficult and expensive to mine. To produce one ounce of gold, something like four tons of rock had to be brought to the surface. . . . With the commencement of deep-level mining in 1897, a rapid process of financial concentration and amalgamation began. This brought all mines under the control of six large groups of mining houses by about 1910. These great mining monopolies were the most powerful political force in South Africa; they fought for state policies which would speed up their own accumulation under these difficult constraints.

Secondly, the specific conditions in the mining industry led to the *establishment of highly exploitative and coercive social relations of production.* Measures were taken to compel African peasants to leave their land and enter mine labor. A pass law system was instituted to control the influx of African labor to the towns. The mineowners grouped themselves together in the Chamber of Mines and set about monopolizing the recruitment of mine labor and reducing competition between them for labor. . . . Through these monopolies, the Chamber was able to slash African mine wages in 1897 and hold them at these levels in real terms until the early 1970s. A highly restrictive contract system was also introduced together with the notorious compound system which barricaded tribally divided workers into enclosed and guarded compounds under very tightly policed conditions. All of this was based on a system of migrant labor.

Migrant labor was the key to the cheap labor policies of the mining industry. It presumed that African workers still had access to land in the rural areas and on completion of their contracts would return to these plots of land. Their families would be housed and fed in the rural areas through production on this land, and not out of the wages of the migrant worker. Thus wages could be kept very low. . . . These cheap labor policies were justified by a racist ideology directed exclusively against blacks. The measures facilitated a high rate of accumulation in the mining industry, and the migrant labor system enabled mining capitalists to overcome profitably the difficult technical conditions of the extraction of gold-bearing ore on the Witwatersrand.

The third product of the specific technical and price constraints of gold mining was the emergence of a rigid *racial division of labor.* When mining first commenced, the skilled work necessary for the extraction of ore was performed by labor imported from Europe or America for the purpose, generally assisted by gangs of unskilled black migrant workers. The wages of these white skilled workers were often dependent on the amount of gold-bearing rock mined, and they thus had a direct interest in intensifying and speeding up the labor process of the black work-gangs which they controlled. From the outset then, the formation of a proletariat in the mining industry was marked by a racial division. White workers were relatively highly paid and tended to be organized into trade unions; they also engaged in often militant struggles against capital to protect their interests.

With the introduction of deep-level mining in 1897, mining capitalists began a protracted attempt to "de-skill" the tasks performed by these relatively expensive white skilled workers. Through reorganizing labor processes, capital sought to replace more expensive whites with cheaper black workers, or at least push whites into the role of supervisors of ever larger gangs of black workers. These processes were fiercely resisted by white miners for 25 years, culminating in the great "Rand Revolt" of 1922. Under the slogan "Workers of the World Unite for a White South Africa," a general strike by white labor against such de-skilling measures by the Chamber of Mines led to a three month strike and armed revolt which was suppressed with great violence by the state.

These struggles of white labor against the bosses were not fought by organizing all mine workers, but by demanding job color bars which would compel the mineowners to reserve certain skilled and supervisory categories of work exclusively for whites. . . .

Thus the imperatives of capital accumulation produced a division of labor within the working class in which whites did skilled, highly-paid tasks, and black migrant workers performed unskilled or semi-skilled jobs for starvation wages. . . .

Thus from the beginnings of large-scale capitalist production in the mining industry, the national oppression of black workers and the African population generally, racism and racial discrimination, were actively fostered by both capital and white labor in pursuit of specific class and/or sectional interests. Through a complex process of struggle and concession, such racial discrimination also served as the ideological basis on which alliances were eventually forged between components of the capitalist ruling class and white labor after 1924. . . .

The Road to Capitalism in Agriculture

Capitalist agriculture in South Africa developed "from above." Pre-capitalist forms of production, in which white colonist landlords extracted various forms of rent from a surplus-producing peasantry, were transformed into capitalist production based on the large landholdings of such rentier landlords. This process of transformation was extremely uneven across the four provinces. But in every case, the intervention of the state was fundamental; in the process, the economic independence of the African peasantry was destroyed. They were chained to the land first as labor tenants (roughly 1913–1960) and then as contract wage laborers compelled by the apartheid system to continue working for white farmers. . . .

This process of transformation developed only through protracted class struggles. Immediately after the beginnings of diamond mining, it was in fact African peasants rather than the white landlords who first began supplying surplus produce for the large market created by the mines. For almost 50 years after 1865 there was a fierce struggle between these surplus-producing peasants who marketed their crops, and the white landlords. . . . Eventually, in 1913 was enacted the key piece of legislation which finally shattered the remaining economic independence of the African peasantry and intensified the process which was transforming them into landless wage laborers or labor tenants. The 1913 Land Act demarcated 8 percent of the total land area of South Africa as the only areas in which Africans could own land (extended to 13 percent in 1936). The rest was reserved for whites. Moreover, the Land Act also limited the number of African families which could live on one white farm, thereby breaking the back of the surplus-producing squatter peasants who had occupied so many "white" farms, particularly in the Transvaal and Orange Free State. These were now transformed into labor tenants, obliged to supply labor for newly emerging capitalist farmers. This Land Act not only secured labor for newly emerging capitalist agriculture, but by finally destroying the economic independence of the African peasantry, it also made their labor available to the mining industry. It is one of the fundamental pieces of legislation in the so-called segregation period of development of South African capitalism. . . .

One final point must, however, be noted: an important side-effect of this particular path of development of capitalism in agriculture was that very large numbers of smaller Boer landlords lost their land and were driven into penury in the cities. The emergence of the so-called "poor white problem" after 1890 was nothing less than the proletarianization of small white farmers (almost exclusively Afrikaans-speaking). By 1933 it was "conservatively" estimated that one-sixth of the white population of 1.8 million had been made "very poor" by the development of capitalist agriculture, whilst a further 30 percent were "poor" enough not to be able "adequately to feed or house their children."

The development of capitalism in agriculture thus proletarianized both black and white producers, but it did so unevenly. White, predominantly Afrikaans-speaking, proletarians could move freely to the cities whilst blacks were subject to forms of influx control and the hated pass system. However, among the urban poor, social segregation was not very strong and a number of sprawling slums sprang up in which both black and white lived. This tended to undermine the ideology of white supremacy so essential to capitalist exploitation in South Africa. It also raised the specter of joint struggle by the white and black urban poor. Moreover, the newly proletarianized whites had the vote and were thus a potential political force (one which, after 1933, the petty bourgeois militants of organized Afrikaner nationalism sought to mobilize for their own purposes). For these reasons, successive regimes fostered measures to "uplift" the poor whites.

The Development of Industrial Production

The development of the mining industry also stimulated the emergence of a manufacturing sector, producing various inputs for the mines such as dynamite, and on a larger scale, consumer wage goods. The tiny manufacturing sector received a further stimulus when the shortage of imported products during World War I resulted in increased demand for locally produced goods. The years between 1910 and 1920 saw the rapid expansion of local manufacturing.

However, this sector still remained fairly small; in the period before 1924 it was in the phase of manufacture as distinct from machinofacture. . . .

This situation began to change following the election of the Nationalist/Labour Pact government in 1924. The Pact came to power on a platform pledged, *inter alia,* to protect fledgling South African industries and a program of state provision of various infrastructural requirements for industry. Under the Pact, the state steel producer, ISCOR [Iron and Steel Corporation of South Africa] was established and protective tariffs were instituted for a wide range of local products. Equally importantly, through its Wage Act and state-controlled systems of national collective bargaining for industry, set up under the Industrial Conciliation Act, the wage policies of the regime favored the emergence of more efficient—that is more mechanized—producers. Thus, particularly in the 1930s, the old artisan/unskilled division of labor characteristic of manufacture began to break down; machinofacture began to emerge on a significant scale. This led to a rapid rise in the size of the African proletariat. By 1939, over 800,000 Africans were employed in manufacturing and mining.

White skilled workers began to resist the process of de-skilling these transformations implied. During this period, the white trade unions remained essentially craft based. They did not attempt to recruit new industrial workers (white or black) into their ranks, but strongly resisted attempts to introduce less skilled black or Afrikaner workers into what these unions considered skilled jobs. Their defense of the threatened position of white artisans and skilled workers produced strongly anti-black and anti-Afrikaner worker policies—and so provided fertile soil for the later mobilization of the latter into so-called "Christian national" trade unions by the petty bourgeois *Afrikaner Broederbond.*

Contradictions and Class Struggles

Thus by the outbreak of the Second World War in 1939, capitalist production had taken hold in mining, agriculture and industry. Capital accumulation in each of these sectors was based on the exploitation of a low wage, highly controlled African migrant labor force. This migrant labor system was itself dependent upon the state enforced system in which Africans were still deemed to have access to land in the reserve areas. The state also attempted to regulate the flow of African labor to the cities under the various influx control measures and through the many laws in operation. This was based on the "Stallard principle" that blacks were to be admitted to the cities only to "minister to the needs" of whites, and to leave the cities when they "ceased so to minister." In each of the three major sectors of capitalist production, the state had intervened decisively to foster the conditions of accumulation of capital, and control where necessary the struggles of African workers and peasants. This was the basic thrust of the gamut of "segregation" policies during this period.

There nevertheless remained important contradictions within the capitalist class which affected both its political organization and the thrust of state policies. Thus, whereas mining capital was monopoly capital virtually from the outset, and was based on high levels of investment (mainly from British and other external sources) and employed very large conglomerations of wage labor under fairly mechanized conditions of production, the situation in both industry and agriculture was very different. Unlike the "foreign capital" which still controlled the mining industry, agricultural and industrial capital were essentially local. Both sectors were characterized not by monopoly, but by a high level of production units owned largely by individual proprietors. . . . Moreover, both industry and agriculture were relatively "cost efficient" in international terms. This meant that the bulk of the small undertakings which made up these sectors were profitable only behind barriers of state protective tariffs and subsidies—which were paid for out of increased taxation of the monopoly and "imperialist oriented" mining industry. . . .

The development of capitalist production in all sectors of the economy was uneven in other senses as well. Leaving aside for the moment its differential impact on the white and black populations, within the white population it affected English and Afrikaans-speakers differentially. The only sector in which a significant group of Afrikaner capitalists emerged was within agriculture—where it has been estimated that in 1939 Afrikaner capitalist farmers controlled 85 percent of the turnover of all marketed produce. However, by 1939 agriculture was the least significant productive sector in terms of contribution to GDP. The share of Afrikaner-owned concerns in the turnover of other sectors ranged from 1 percent in mining, 3 percent in manufacturing, 5 percent in finance to 8 percent in commerce. The language of the urban economy was English, and Afrikaans-speakers were strongly discriminated against. Moreover, Afrikaans-speakers were clustered in the worst-off positions amongst whites in the capitalist economy. Leaving aside the massive poor white population (which consisted almost exclusively of Afrikaans-speakers), Afrikaner workers occupied the lowest categories of wage labor reserved for whites. In 1939, for example, almost 40 percent of adult white male Afrikaans-speakers occupied the categories of unskilled laborer, railway worker, mine worker and bricklayer—compared with 10 percent of other whites. This relatively disadvantaged position of Afrikaner capitalists, petty bourgeoisie and laborers provided a fertile base for their mobilization in terms of an anti-monopoly and racist Afrikaner nationalist ideology in the 1940s. Such an ideology was able to argue that "foreign" [i.e. British] capitalism had dispossessed and "exploited" all Afrikaners. Its answer was an "Afrikaner republic" which would be "free of the golden chains of British imperialism." The interests of all Afrikaners could then be advanced under a system of "state controlled private enterprise" through more intensive exploitation of the black population. . . .

The Crisis of Segregation 1940–1948 and the Coming to Power of the Nationalist Party

The Second World War produced a period of very rapid economic growth in South Africa: in particular it saw the massive expansion of industrial production. . . . Given the rapid expansion of industry, African workers began to enter into semi-skilled and even skilled positions in industry (and to a lesser extent, mining) on a large scale. This development was actively fostered by the United Party government which sought to create a low wage, skilled African workforce whilst simultaneously retraining white workers and shifting them upwards into supervisory positions.

The growth of the African proletariat during the war saw the rapid rise of a militant African trade union movement: by 1945 almost 40 percent of African industrial workers were unionized. The biggest union group, the Council of Non-European Trade Unions, claimed a membership of 158,000 workers in 119 affiliated unions. The collapse of the ability of reserve production to "subsidize" the pathetic wages of migrant labor led to fierce wage struggles in all sectors. The militant action of these unions and the rapid rise in strikes produced a steady rise in African industrial wages. The real earnings of African industrial workers rose by almost 50 percent in the period 1939–48, and the earnings gap between white and black workers closed slightly for the first time.

These continuing struggles by an increasingly organized working class were supplemented by an intensification of class struggle in all areas. In the rural areas of the Transvaal in particular, fierce conflicts erupted over attempts by capitalist farmers to intensify the exploitation of their labor tenants. There were reports of armed clashes, and the South African Air Force was used to quell disturbances in the northern Transvaal. So strong was the resistance of labor tenants that the government was forced to suspend the application of Chapter IV of the 1936 Natives' Land and Trust Act designed to restrict the access to land of labor tenants and so increase their exploitation. . . .

In this context of heightened class struggle, deep divisions emerged within the capitalist class; these fatally weakened the capacity of the ruling United Party to organize together all elements of capital, and so enabled the Nationalist Party to build against it a new alliance of class forces, and to take power with a narrow parliamentary majority—on a minority of votes cast—in May 1948.

Capitalists were divided primarily over the question of what to do about the disintegrating base of the migrant labor system, and hence the militant trade union struggles which erupted out of this. Industrial capital favored a policy of labor stabilization and controlled recognition of African trade unions—positions strongly rejected by mining and agricultural capital. Both these latter sections of the capitalist class experienced intense labor shortages during the war as workers flocked to the cities seeking the higher wages paid in industry. They both favored a policy of intensified influx control and the continuation of the migrant labor system. . . .

The unity of the capitalist class was further strained by a range of other issues such as housing, taxation policy, etc. Significantly strong differences also emerged over the appropriate response to the organized political demands of the oppressed class forces. Whilst no section of the capitalist class advocated an end to segregation and the introduction of non-racial democracy, or even a move in this direction, within influential intellectual circles of the bourgeoisie, pressure began to mount for the easing of some of the restrictions imposed on the black petty bourgeoisie by segregation. This carried the germ of a political strategy which sought to win political allies for the capitalist class amongst the black petty bourgeoisie, and which divided them from the workers. On the other hand, other sections of the capitalist class favored an intensification of repression and further segregation of the various race groups.

In this context of heightened class struggle, division within the capitalist class on all the vital issues of the day, and growing international pressure on South Africa through the United Nations (which first condemned segregation practices in 1947), the ruling United Party was unable to maintain its political cohesion. Originally formed in 1934 to organize together all sections of capital, it now tried to appease all conflicting demands and adopted vacillating and extremely contradictory politics. The Nationalist Party was able to seize on this and organize, for the first time, a new political alliance under the banner of a militant Afrikaner nationalist ideology.

In the 1948 elections, the Nationalist Party won support from four central groups, and welded these into a cohesive class alliance. In response to its severe labor shortage and acute pricing problems, and confronted with the vacillating policies of the UP, agricultural capital finally deserted the UP. The Nationalist Party promised farmers rigid influx control measures to stem the efflux of labor from white farms and general control over African workers. The NP also promised a pricing policy which would guarantee a higher rate of profit to agriculture. Whereas the NP had always been the party of agriculture in the Cape Province, following the formation of the United Party in 1934, it was the UP which was the primary agricultural party in the Transvaal and the Orange Free State. In 1948 these elements finally went over to the NP.

A second new element in the Afrikaner nationalist alliance in 1948, was specific strata of white workers, particularly in the mining, metal and building industries. The rapid influx of African workers into industry, their increasing incorporation in skilled and semi-skilled positions, the rapid rise in African industrial wages and the militancy of the African trade union movement in the period 1942–1946, all appeared to threaten the carefully carved out niche of privilege of white labor—particularly the Afrikaner workers who were clustered at the lower end of the job categories reserved for white labor. For much of this period the Labor Party was formally allied to the major party of capital, the ruling United Party. . . . The period 1936–1947 saw a major struggle for control of key unions between the craft-dominated established labor movement and petty bourgeois elements of the *Afrikaner Broederbond*. . . . By 1948 they [Afrikaner Nationalist Groups] had brought crucial strata of white labor into the Afrikaner nationalist alliance on the dual promise of rigid job color bars to protect their position against the entry of black semi-skilled and skilled labor, and increased welfare measures financed through an attack on monopoly profits. In 1948 the Nationalist Party committed itself to the nationalization of the gold-mining industry.

The Afrikaner petty bourgeoisie comprised the third element of this 1948

Afrikaner nationalist alliance. This class force had been the principal base of the Nationalist Party since its "purification" in 1934. Threatened by rising mass struggles, the economic advances of the African proletariat, the political demand for integration etc., this petty bourgeoisie gave its support to ever more exclusivist racist policies. It was the moving organizational force in the NP and in the formulation of its apartheid policies for the 1948 election.

Also out of this petty bourgeoisie, emerged the fourth class force organized in the nationalist alliance—small Afrikaner finance, commercial and manufacturing capital. . . .

This Afrikaner nationalist alliance thus consolidated under an Afrikaner nationalist ideology which had two major elements. The first was a strongly anti-monopoly rhetoric; and since these monopolies were conceived of in the ideology as "British," this also took the form of a strong rhetoric against "imperialism" and a pledge to transform South Africa into a republic. The second element was the policy of apartheid: this drew together the interests of each of these class forces and held out the promise of state policies to resolve their problems. It is, however, important to realize that while apartheid clearly promised to stem what it called "the flood of natives to the cities," and, more concretely, to push the unemployed back into the reserves and barricade them there behind the pass laws and tighter influx control measures, at no stage did it threaten the labor supply of any section of capital. It held out a scheme for the "efficient" channeling of labor to sectors where it was needed in the labor market through a system of state labor bureaus; and it promised to deal very firmly with any sign of resistance by the oppressed class forces. As such, it promised to resolve the crisis of segregation and raise the rate of exploitation and profit for all capitals.

13. *ECONOMIC GROWTH AND POLITICAL CHANGE: THE SOUTH AFRICAN CASE**

by STANLEY B. GREENBERG

Stanley B. Greenberg is Associate Director, Southern African Research Program, Yale University and author of Race and State in Capitalist Development: Comparative Perspectives (1980).

People of quite diverse social position and perspective have turned to economic growth as a source of political change in South Africa. Contained within

*From *The Journal of Modern African Studies,* 19, 4 (1981).

the concept of growth, they maintain, are processes—capital accumulation and class formation, business enterprise and markets, changing skill and capital requirements—that, at the very least, allow some blacks a more secure and higher living standard, that may bring greater equality between the races, or more profoundly, confound traditional racial lines and privileges. Indeed, some argue that growth undermines the foundations of the racial state. Many of those who posit a relationship between economics and politics, take the next logical step: supporting actions, including foreign investment, that foster economic growth and, presumably, political change in South Africa. . . .

Considerations on Theory

The presumed relationship between economic growth and political change is not simply a causal linkage but a theoretical statement about development and modernization. A change in a set of economic factors—in this instance, growth in the gross domestic product, the aggregate wealth, the composition of capital, and the labor force—produces changes in another set of social and political factors, including the social welfare, income shares, social relations, bargaining position, and political standing of various racial groups. . . .

The development model most frequently advanced to accommodate the economic-political linkage is the *dual economy.* In this view, South Africa is divided into two separate economies: one organized around subsistence production, with low productivity and considerable surplus labor; the other organized around capitalist production based on wage labor, higher productivity, and expanding markets. Labor is attracted to the "modern" sector by marginally higher wage rates and, because of widespread unemployment and labor surplus conditions in the "traditional" economy, tends to flood the developing urban labor markets. Growth under conditions of "unlimited" supplies of labor produces in the short term increases in wage employment but not higher living standards. With accelerating growth and an increasing capacity to absorb labor in the "modern" sector, the labor surplus is progressively exhausted, resulting in higher wage rates, lessening inequalities between the "modern" and "traditional" sectors, and an enhanced bargaining position for black labor. . . .

The critical steps in the dual economy model are the original state of labor surplus and the easy attractions of the "modern" sector, the eventual exhaustion of labor surpluses in the "traditional" economy, and the growing strategic position of black labor in the "modern" economy. The model presumes that racial exclusions and barriers originally associated with the two separate economies are increasingly called into question as blacks join the "modern" sector, and as the condition of labor surplus dissipates.

Noteworthy inconsistencies between these theoretical propositions and the historical record have placed the dual economy model in some doubt. In the first place, there is little evidence that Southern African economies prior to capitalist penetration were undeveloped—that is, plagued by labor surpluses and ready to respond to marginal wage inducements. They responded to the growing labor requirements of the white industrial and farming centers only after African landholdings and peasant production were radically constricted, and after a variety of political measures were employed to force Africans into the wage economy. . . .

The alternative development models posit very different relations between the "modern" and "traditional" economies and, as a consequence, a different kind of linkage between economics and politics. The two sectors are not viewed as separable and distinct. Indeed, the development of the capitalist sector depended upon the conscious *underdevelopment* of African peasant communities—the creation of labor control mechanisms, labor surpluses, and wage elasticities that did not previously exist. Entry into the "modern" sector did not represent some advance on peasant life but the culmination of processes that disintegrated and impoverished it.

Associated with the underdevelopment of African peasant society are a range of policies, practices, and institutions that are at the core of racial domination in South Africa. The native reserves and separate development policies, Harold Wolpe writes, were integral features of a development strategy that undermined African subsistence and commercial economies and created labor surplus areas throughout Southern Africa. These have provided "cheap" migrant labor, first to the farms and mines, and later to industry. . . .

This underdevelopment model presumes that the "unlimited" supplies of labor are not an original condition but the result of development, that growth maintains "cheap" labor through a process of migration and preservation of "traditional" economies—sometimes called "semi-proletarianization"—and that development under these conditions requires a form of structural unemployment in the African rural areas. The whole panoply of state racial policies, including separate development, are in no sense dysfunctional to growth or undermined by it: the policies are on the contrary an integral part of development. Controlled movement between the "traditional" and "modern" sectors has proved an essential feature in the emerging forms of racial domination and capitalist growth in Southern Africa. . . .

In the light of contemporary events, both the dual economy and underdevelopment models require revision: the former, because labor surpluses have proved enduring; the latter, since the disintegration of the 'traditional' economy has advanced so far that reserve areas no longer provide an effective income supplement. Wolpe himself posited:

apartheid . . . [is an] attempt to retain, in a modified form, the structure of the "traditional" societies, not, as in the past, for the purposes of ensuring an economic supplement to the wages of the migrant labour force, but for the purposes of reproducing and exercising control over a cheap African industrial labour force in or near the "homelands," not by means of preserving the precapitalist mode of production but by the political, social, economic and ideological enforcement of low levels of subsistence.

But Wolpe did not forsee other aspects of racial and labor policy, including the use of remittances and taxes from urban centers to finance, in effect, the preservation of African rural areas; nor did he foresee the growth of a landless, urban population in the Homelands. It is in this contemporary context, with widespread and enduring unemployment and impoverished reserve areas, that we must evaluate development models, and consider the effects of growth and investment.

A straightforward neo-classical approach might, despite the difficulties of the historical argument, simply restate the essentials of the dual economy model in a contemporary context: growth will draw labor out of the reserve areas and need only provide marginal wage inducements in the process; the cure for seemingly structural unemployment is a yet higher rate of growth and entry into the urban economy. Only then will a developing shortage of labor permit advances in material conditions and in the bargaining position by Africans in the market and in politics. Growth will fail to dissipate structural unemployment or create political leverage, however, if artificially high wage rates are imposed, or if other forms of state regulation limit opportunities for investment or attracting labor.

An extension or revision of the underdevelopment model must take into account what is variously called the segmented, split, or dual-labor market. This conception of development and contemporary events questions the neo-classical approach at its core argument—the relationship between investment and jobs. "An abstract link between an increase in the capital stock (investment) and an increase in employment," Alec Erwin writes, "is an exceedingly dangerous formalism." Growth takes place within a socio-economic and political context that provides unequal access to emerging opportunities, and an uncertain impact on African unemployment. At the simplest level, state controls on labor mobility, such as influx regulations, create market barriers and a formal dualism: to one side, workers (including some Africans) who receive a higher wage rate than they would have in the absence of such barriers; to the other side, workers (nearly all Africans) who face both a depressed wage rate and a condition of continuing labor surplus. Under these conditions, growth may exacerbate inequalities while failing to diminish unemployment; it may buttress those groups whose interests are served by that dualism and state role, and yet fail to enhance the bargaining position of African workers as a whole. . . .

Economic growth, if this view is correct, will create new forms of inequality, both between black and white, and among Africans; at the same time, it will foster a "marginal economic pole," increasingly redundant and superfluous. Rather than foster political reform, growth should generate African social and political marginality. Moreover, it may necessitate yet more refined measures for controlling the location, movements, and politics of the African majority. . . .

Growth and Politics

We considered two broad models at the outset of this article: dual economies emphasized the incorporation of labor into the "modern" sector, and the economic and political benefits that follow on that process; underdevelopment and split-labor markets emphasized the pauperization of the subsistence sector, controlled proletarianization, and class differentiation. While the dual economy perspective did not promise an immediate improvement in African living standards, it did suggest that rising welfare and declining economic inequality would follow on development and the exhaustion of labor surpluses in the "traditional" economy. It also implied that those developments would enhance black bargaining power, and undercut state efforts to limit African mobility and political rights. These propositions lay at the center of conventional business conceptions of economic growth and political change, and almost invariably assume beneficent consequences with the incorporation of Africans into industry and some automatic, if vague, linkage to political change: "they will be brought into the industrialization of the country and as such they will gradually move away from the apartheid system."

The underdevelopment and split-labor market perspectives emphasize, above all else, the creation and management of labor surpluses: first, in the undermining of subsistence agriculture; second, in the bottling up of African labor in the white rural areas and Homelands; and third, in the stratification of the African community, concentrating opportunities in the urban centers and redundancy in the rural areas. Growth so understood brings no necessary improvement in living standards or decline in income inequalities; indeed, with the intrusion of capital-intensive technologies, growth may contribute further to inequality and labor surplus conditions. State policies, constructed to manage labor surpluses and the labor market, will likely be elaborated so long as labor conditions threaten living standards in urban areas and the political ascendancy of whites in South Africa.

The evidence presented in this article provides very little support for the dual economy model, and its expectations about growth and political change.

The evidence is, for the most part, consistent with theoretical formulations on underdevelopment and split-labor markets.

(1) African living standards did not rise appreciably in the first century of capitalist development in South Africa, though African incomes in manufacturing may have begun to rise before World War II. The African labor force as a whole began making modest gains during the 1960s, followed by substantial progress in the early and mid-1970s. Still, it is difficult to use these income trends to sustain either perspective: significant African income gains did not come in the 1960s when the growth rate was high, but in the early 1970s when the growth rate was falling and unemployment rising.

(2) The stark inequalities between Africans and Europeans, one of the most skewed income distributions in the world, has not been appreciably diminished by economic growth, and may well have been enhanced by it. The post-war period up to 1970 brought widening inequalities in wages and incomes *per capita;* only since then has this historic pattern been offset. Still, there is very little reason to believe that the rate of population and economic growth, and the white community's likely tolerance for stagnant living standards, will permit a substantial erosion of this inequality over the long term.

(3) Though estimates of African unemployment vary considerably, virtually all the literature suggests that labor surpluses are substantial (between one-tenth and one-quarter of the labor force), that they have increased during the 1970s, and that they will continue to grow under the most likely economic circumstances. The evidence of "capital deepening," declining labor-absorptive capacity of manufacturing, and higher wage rates in the "modern" sector, suggest an emerging pattern of development in South Africa that may further exacerbate the labor surplus problem. Structural unemployment, contained within the growth process itself, belies pressures for "political reform" suggested by the dual economies model, and fosters, instead, increased state attempts to control the African labor market, and to fashion political arrangements consistent with the maintenance of African Homelands.

(4) Capitalist development has fundamentally altered the class landscape in South Africa. In the European community, and particularly among Afrikaners, development has brought businessmen in manufacture and commerce into increasing prominence, and has undercut the role of commercial farmers and white workers. It has, in effect, altered and fragmented the class alignments associated with racial domination, and has created groups whose interests and needs might well be served under alternative, less costly political and economic arrangements. Still, these emerging class actors have not automatically questioned the conventional racial structures. Only when political disorder has threatened the economic environment have businessmen in and outside of Afrikanerdom reconsidered their pervasive accommodation to racial customs.

(5) In the African community, development has brought a marked class

differentiation, with the population divided almost equally between white urban areas, migrant contract work, the white farms, and the Homelands. Though these groups differ in income, education, mobility, privileges, and status, they have not clearly chosen separate political paths. We do not know whether growth will bring further political fragmentation, or a convergence of groups opposed to race domination in South Africa. We do not know whether growing "privileges" for the urban African population will produce confrontation and pressures to dismantle the *apartheid* structure, or whether these "privileges" will prompt new forms of collaboration and a partial accommodation at the expense of other Africans.

This assessment of the impact of growth on patterns of race domination and African politics is in direct conflict with arguments that encourage foreign investment as a vehicle for "reforming" South Africa. Direct corporate investment and the provision of international credits may well permit higher wages for immediate employees, and may, under some circumstances, assist the organization of African trade unions. But such benefits, however worthwhile in themselves, should not be confused with change generally. Nor should these immediate benefits be evaluated without careful reference to the political-economic context of which they are a part.

Three cautionary points may be advanced for those urging "constructive engagement" in South Africa. First, one cannot recommend investment based on a belief, frequently expressed by businessmen, that such economic activity inexorably or even probably benefits Africans as a whole. The trends in living standards, inequality, and unemployment permit no compelling economic argument for growth and engagement.

Second, the pattern of United States investment, in particular, may reinforce processes that mitigate the presumed beneficial consequences of growth. Higher wage-rates for urban Africans seem unexceptionable, yet in the context of influx control, they may foster economic inequalities and exacerbate political divisions among Africans. Investment in the most advanced manufacturing sectors and technology transfers, under labor surplus and labor control conditions, may reinforce processes fostering African marginality, and may further the development of labor-repressive measures. Constructive engagement under these circumstances may unwittingly facilitate the initiatives of the South African Government to create a privileged urban African stratum, economically and politically divorced from the majority of the African population.

Third, arguments for constructive engagement which point to indirect political consequences, such as trade union organization, white class fragmentation, and the African population's growing strategic position in society, are shrouded in uncertainty. As our analysis of class formation and political scenarios suggests, such developments do not easily or automatically translate into changes in the overall racial framework and, under some circumstances, may buttress it.

There is no question that more than a century of capitalist development has shaped the political landscape in South Africa, and that the needs of developing capitalism place vital constraints on all political actors, black and white. But the importance of developmental factors, and the vagaries that surround future scenarios, should not be allowed to obscure the central importance of political processes in the contemporary period. Strikes, rather than growth rates, may account for the rapid wage advances and erosion of inequalities in the early 1970s; widespread township disorders in 1976 and 1977, rather than the pressures of growth—which, by that time, had nearly stalled—may account for the willingness of businessmen to support job opportunities, urban amenities, and trade union rights for Africans. The extent and nature of political disorder, the efficacy of the liberation movements, the forms of internal political organizations, the unity or disunity of the black community, and the response of the white community to such challenges, all contribute to the prospect for change in South Africa. Exclusive emphasis on economic growth and investment diverts attention from the political arena where the most immediate pressures for change operate.

14. *ECONOMIC EXPLOITATION**

by THE INTERNATIONAL DEFENCE AND AID FUND FOR SOUTHERN AFRICA

The International Defence and Aid Fund for Southern Africa is a London-based humanitarian organization opposing racial oppression in South Africa. (See headnote to Reading 10.)

Sectors of the Economy

The structure and development of the economy have been dominated by three sectors: agriculture, mining and, increasingly important, manufacturing industry. The needs and interests of the owners and employers in these sectors have been the principal factors in shaping the apartheid system.

Although domestic service is a shrinking sector, it still employs a substantial number of people, particularly African women. Two thirds of all women employed in 1970 worked in domestic service or agriculture, while a large proportion of women not formally employed were engaged in subsistence agriculture. . . .

*From *Apartheid: The Facts* (London, 1983).

Agriculture

Agricultural production ranges from subsistence farming to highly capital intensive commercial farming by big enterprises. Subsistence farming is carried out almost entirely by Africans, both in the bantustans and in "white" areas where many occupy land deserted by whites and some others continue to live as tenants of white farmers (in spite of such tenancy having been outlawed). There is some commercial farming by Africans, but on a relatively small scale: only 10 percent of agricultural production in the bantustans is marketed.

The African farming areas were mainly self-sufficient in the nineteenth century, producing a surplus which was successfully marketed at favorable prices. Since then, however, government policies have worked to the great advantage of white farmers and to the detriment of rural Africans. . . . Two thirds of those in the bantustans are landless.

. . . There were estimated to be 1,400,000 black workers on white-owned farms in "white" areas in 1982, mainly African. Conditions for black workers on these farms are generally bad and pay very low.

A report submitted in 1982 by the Farm Labor Project to a government commission of enquiry revealed that real wages of farm workers had declined in the past ten years. The report said that in many areas women were forced to steal food for their children and that diseases of malnutrition were found to be common among black children on white farms. . . .

In spite of the bad conditions workers are tied to farm work by the pass law system. Once categorized by a labor bureau as an agricultural laborer, a work seeker from the bantustans cannot take other work in a "white" area or go to a town or city. Likewise all Africans in "white" rural areas are registered as farm workers. Farm workers who retire or lose their jobs must go to a bantustan.

Mining

. . . From the start the demands of the mining sector for labor far exceeded the number of people in South Africa prepared to enter into wage labor. Steps were taken to induce more Africans to leave the land, by imposition of taxes and changes in the structure of land ownership. Workers were recruited from all over Southern Africa, both inside South Africa and from neighboring territories. To prevent the demand for labor causing a rise in wages, the mineowners centralized recruitment.

The mining industry is still largely dependent on the migrant labor system. Employers have also for a long time put obstacles in the way of trade union organization amongst black miners. When they have taken industrial action the workers have frequently been met with the armed force of the police. During 1982 when nearly 30,000 mine workers struck over low pay, thousands were simply dismissed and forcibly sent to the bantustans.

The mines are almost entirely owned by a few very large private corporations, with a substantial amount of foreign investment.

Manufacturing Industry

The process of industrialization has taken the South African economy from one with virtually no manufacturing industry at the turn of the century to one with a highly developed and sophisticated industrial sector, producing an increasingly wide range of goods. Profits from mining and from farming provided the finance for industrialization, together with a high level of foreign investment.

. . . In 1971 over 80 percent of South Africa's industrial output was produced in the four major metropolitan regions. It has for a long time been the aim of the regime to promote the development of industry in areas where use could be made of black labor without the workers living in or close to "white" areas. Known earlier as the "Border Industry" policy, it is currently described as a policy of "deconcentration." . . .

The rapid growth in trade union organization of black workers which characterized the 1970s and early 1980s was most heavily concentrated in the manufacturing sector, particularly in the metal products and motor industry.

The Bantustans in the Economy

Almost all economic activity is in the part of South Africa declared "white." In 1970 only one quarter of employed Africans lived in the bantustans, and a significant number of them were "commuters" who worked outside the bantustans. Of the rest of those who lived in the bantustans and were employed, over 60 percent were engaged in subsistence agriculture. As far as manufacturing, mining, transport and services are concerned, less than one tenth of the country's economic activity (measured in terms of numbers of people involved), took place in the bantustans in 1970. . . .

The fact that so little economic activity takes place in the bantustans is a reflection of their role in the economy, as suppliers of labor and depositories for the unemployed, the aged and the sick. The function of the bantustans is apparent from the composition of the population within their boundaries. There is a large number of "commuters" working in white areas, a large number of unemployed people, a high proportion of children and aged people, and a high proportion of women confined to the bantustans as a result of governmental policy of keeping the number of African women in the cities and towns as low as possible.

Migratory Labor

Under apartheid Africans are not treated as part of the permanent population of those parts of South Africa containing most of its wealth and resources. Their presence in those areas is, with relatively few exceptions, made legally dependent on their being employed. . . . "The basis on which the Bantu is present in the white areas is to sell their labor here and for nothing else" (M. C. Botha, later to become Minister of Labor/Manpower Utilization). . . .

The migrant labor system was originally created largely in order to meet the needs of the mineowners. It has been extended to manufacturing and other industries in order to reverse the tendency of industrialization to create a resident urban black working class. With the attempt to sever the last tenuous hold which Africans had on the land outside the bantustans, it has also been extended to agriculture.

Nearly a third of African workers in "white" South Africa are migrant workers. They work on contracts of up to a year in areas away from where their families live. About a quarter of a million came from neighboring states in 1980, almost all of them working in the mining industry. Over one million are South African workers. They are deemed to live in the bantustans and not in the areas in which they work. In fact, they reside in the areas in which they work for eleven months of every year, in a pattern which is often sustained throughout their working lives.

Migrant workers may not take their families with them to the area in which they work. Workers have no family life and are generally housed in mining or industrial compounds, in single sex hostels in the townships, or in "servants quarters" if they are domestic workers. Except in agriculture and domestic service, relatively few women are recruited as contract or migrant workers. . . .

Unable to prevent the growth of a permanently urbanized black work force, the regime has created a section of "commuters" alongside the migrants. Great regional townships have been established around major towns and cities, often just inside bantustan boundaries. Sometimes this has been by forced removals, sometimes by simply redrawing bantustan boundaries to include existing townships. In 1980 there were over 700,000 daily commuters, traveling each day up to 70 miles (113 km) in each direction, working in "white" areas and residing in bantustans. In addition there are weekly "commuters," traveling up to 400 miles (644 km) each way at weekends. . . .

Direction of Labor

The direction of African workers and the enforcement of the migratory system is brought about by a network of labor bureaus, in conjunction with the pass laws.

All men of working age (15–65) in the bantustans who are not self-employed (as commercial farmers, traders or professionals) must register as work seekers with the labor bureau in their area. Women have to register as work seekers if they want a job.

The entire future of a person is decided on first registering. At that point the labor bureau classifies the person into one of several categories of employment. Once classified workers cannot choose to change, unless it is to change to mine work or farm work. The worker seldom has much choice. Someone born in a rural community outside a bantustan area, for example, will generally remain classified as "Farm Labor" irrespective of educational qualifications: he or she will not be registered for work in an urban area unless the farmer agrees there is no shortage of farm labor elsewhere.

In such ways workers can be forced to remain for life in very bad working conditions for very little pay. . . .

The use of the labor bureaus, and pass laws, to direct African workers to the lowest paid jobs, and to prevent them changing their occupation, helps keep wages very low and weakens workers in relation to their employers.

15. POVERTY IN SOUTH AFRICA*

by AZIZA SEEDAT

Aziza Seedat, a South African doctor, is now living in exile in West Germany.

The Gross National Product (GNP) of South Africa is one of the highest in Africa and among the top 30 in the world, but the wealth is very unevenly distributed. Whites, comprising 15 percent of the population, received 64 percent of national income in 1977, while Africans (73.5 percent of the population) received 26 percent. On average, a white worker earns more than four times the monthly wage of an African.

Figures for average *per capita* incomes show even greater discrepancies: for the year 1974–75, *per capita* personal incomes for the main population groups

*From *Crippling a Nation: Health in Apartheid South Africa* (London, 1984).

were white R2,534, Indian R584, Coloured R496 and Africans R237—less than one tenth those of whites.

The comparison of *per capita* African incomes in South Africa with those elsewhere in Africa is also instructive, particularly as white South Africans are fond of claiming that "their" Africans are better off than Africans anywhere else. For 1980, the South African Institute of Race Relations calculated that the real *per capita* Gross National Product (GNP) in the bantustans (excluding KwaNdebele) ranged from R120 (Gazankulu) to R314 (Bophuthatswana). The *per capita* GNP in Nigeria (1978) was US$600 (c. R726 at late 1983 exchange rates); it was US$620 (R750) in Botswana (1978), US$440 (R532) in Angola (1979), US$240 (R290) in Mozambique and in Tanzania (1978), US$300 (R363) in Lesotho (1978) and US$380 (R460) in Kenya (1978), to cite a few examples.

The standard of living of Africans in South Africa is in general very low. The majority live in poverty because of inadequate wages and widespread unemployment. Agriculture and services employ the largest fractions of the African labor force—officially 18.6 and 22.6 percent respectively in 1980. There is no minimum wage for African farm workers in South Africa. In 1952 the average African farm laborer's income was assessed at just over £3 a month and there are figures to indicate that in real terms this average wage stayed almost constant between the discovery of minerals in South Africa (1870s and 1880s) and the end of the Second World War. The agricultural census of 1976 estimated average monthly cash wages for regular farm employees as R31.95 with rations valued at R9 provided. Official figures given in parliament in 1981 indicated that African farm workers could still be earning as little as R32 a month including the food provided by employers—cash wages alone were as low as R23 a month. A government commission was told in 1982 that some farm workers were earning R10 a month. Because of influx control laws farm workers cannot find work elsewhere.

The system that controls African workers functions to preserve cheap labour on the farms. The Labor Bureau classifies a person into one of several categories of employment; once classified, the worker cannot change (except to mine or farm work) and, in particular, he cannot escape from farm work. This system ensures that there is no competition in wages. Despite the fact that wage rates for Africans in manufacturing industry are considerably higher than those in farming and better than those in mining, the farms and mines are never short of labor. Africans in urban areas unemployed for more than four months (not necessarily consecutive) in any year may be arrested and sent to work in farming areas.

In the mining industry the ratio of white to black incomes actually widened from 9:1 in 1911 to nearly 20:1 in 1971. Although the ratio fell to just under 6:1 in 1981, the gap between average white and African monthly wages increased from R360 to R996. African wages have in general been increased over the last decade but they never approach white wages and in most years have been effectively eroded by inflation.

. . . [A]t any given time, a large proportion of African families in South Africa, even in the relatively affluent cities, is living below the breadline. Thus in 1976 a market research survey showed that two thirds of all African households had less than R80 a month on which to live, 25.4 percent had between R80 and R149 and only 11 percent had more than R150. Nearly a quarter had less than R20.

This was at a time when it was estimated that a family of five in Soweto needed R129 a month to survive. . . .

A number of surveys of average African household incomes have indicated that these incomes actually declined by 12.4 percent in real terms between 1976 and 1980. . . .

The percentage of each main population group living in poverty was calculated in 1978 as follows: white two percent, Colored 50 percent, Indian (on the East Rand) 20 percent and (in Durban) 50–60 percent, and African between 60 and 70 percent. The situation in the rural areas for Coloured and African families in particular tends to be worse. In Nqutu in the KwaZulu bantustan, for example, the average monthly income was reported to be R20 in 1980.

The claim that black wages in South Africa are rising, and with them the standard of living of Africans, must be measured against the high figures for unemployment. The exact extent is difficult to ascertain as comprehensive figures are not kept, but in 1978 it was estimated that over two million African workers were unemployed and that the total was increasing by 470 a day.

Private local surveys have found unemployment rates of 19 percent among Africans in Cape Town, 24 percent in Pretoria and 28 percent in Johannesburg and the Reef. Estimates for rural bantustan areas range up to 42 percent in Limehill, KwaZulu. Underemployment is common with Africans working seasonally in the farms and plantations, or obtaining jobs on short contracts for a few months before being laid off.

. . . A seminar at the University of the Witwatersrand in October 1982 was told that about 2.5 million people or 24 percent of the labor force were unemployed. Other estimates cited by the South African Institute of Race Relations place the unemployment figure at between 1.5 and 3 million.

THE POVERTY IS ARTIFICALLY CREATED. DISTORTION OF 1 GR. TOWARDS THE WORTH OF ANOTHER.

16. THE GROWTH OF UNIONS*

by DENIS MacSHANE, MARTIN PLAUT and DAVID WARD

Denis MacShane is a former BBC producer and president of the National Union of Journalists. His previous books include a study of Solidarity, the Polish union and a political biography of François Mitterand. He is currently an official of the International Metalworkers Federation. Martin Plaut was educated at the University of Cape Town and is currently a broadcaster with the BBC's Africa Service. David Ward works for the World Development Movement. He is co-author of the 1982 Spokesman pamphlet "Black Trade Unions in South Africa."

The 1973 Strikes in Durban

. . . The repression of the South African Congress of Trade Unions (SACTU) in the early 1960s and the indifference of the Trade Union Council of South Africa (TUCSA) to the needs of black workers meant that there was no leadership or trade union expression given to the rising tide of black industrial discontent. The following table shows the number of strikes by black workers 1962–1972.

STRIKES BY BLACK WORKERS: 1962–72

Year	No. of Disputes	Black workers on strike
1962	56	2,155
1963	61	3,101
1964	99	4,369
1965	84	3,540
1966	98	3,253
1967	76	2,874
1968	56	1,705
1969	78	4,232
1970	76	3,303
1971	69	4,196
1972	71	8,814

During this period of labor quiescence, the South African economy was expanding at a rate matched only by that of Japan. . . . But black workers, who by 1970 formed 78 percent of the workforce in the manufacturing and construction sector, and 90 percent in the mining sector, were not sharing in this

*From *Power! Black Workers, Their Unions and the Struggle for Freedom in South Africa* (Boston, 1984).

bonanza of rapidly increasing industrial development, nor in the sharp upturn in South Africa's national income following the increase in the price of gold after President Nixon suspended dollar convertibility in 1971. . . . Between 1961 and 1979 unemployment went up by 4,000 a month; between 1971 and 1975, the rate of increase in joblessness was 11,000 a month. In 1973, a survey showed that 80 percent of the African employees in British and South African controlled firms were paid below the Poverty Datum Line.

These problems were accutely felt in Durban, where 165,000 African workers constituted one of the largest groups of industrial workers in South Africa. The major industries are garment, textile, general engineering, food processing and tires (Dunlop). The factories are generally small, single-story affairs. In January 1973, a strike began in a brickworks. Two thousand workers went on strike for higher wages. They marched down the streets, chanting: "Man is dead, but his spirit still lives." They won a wage increase. The strikes spread to factories belonging to the Frame group, South Africa's largest textile employer and notorious for low wages and poor conditions. . . .

Help from "Outsiders"

By the end of 1973, about 100,000 workers in Durban had gone on strike. Strikes also hit other industrial centers elsewhere in South Africa, but Durban was the focal point for the 1973 strike wave. Employers and the government were aghast. The strike wave appeared to have come from nowhere. Its spontaneity was undeniable but effective. . . .

The wage levels against which the Durban strikers were protesting were extremely low, often less than R15 a week. Employers found that they could offer increases without much dent being made in their profits. The strikes were also embarrassing for foreign companies. American and European firms were suddenly and publicly exposed as paying wages which to public opinion in their own countries might seem little better than slave rates. The successful sporting boycott of South Africa had increased the country's sense of isolation and its need to cultivate its image as part of the Western community. Partly by skillful tactics involving staying inside workplaces for meetings, by not having any identifiable leaders, and avoiding major public demonstrations and partly by the short, sharp nature of the strikes the 1973 strikers avoided brutal police repression. Only 0.2 percent of the strikers were prosecuted. . . .

The bold steps taken by black workers in the "Durban" strikes of 1973 may, in retrospect, seem to have been destined to succeed. At the time that was certainly not the view. . . .

As Steve Friedman, the labor correspondent of the *Rand Daily Mail,* the country's most liberal newspaper, and one of the most respected labor analysts was to write later: "The initial wave of organisation was to prove as ephemeral as its predecessors. The banning of union leaders—all white intellectuals—began a decline which was to see paid-up union membership in the Durban area slump to something in the region of 2,000 by the mid-1970s. In retrospect, it seemed that the brief wave of unionism in the early Seventies was to be yet another chapter in the catalogue of the African union movement's failures."

But this pessimistic prognosis proved mistaken. The unions have succeeded, they have grown, and they have become a powerful force on the South African political scene. . . .

Economic Contradictions and the Role of Management

Like the economies of most other capitalist states, the South African economy has in the past two decades witnessed increasing monopolization. As South Africa followed other countries down the monetarist paths of the 1980s the rate of concentration increased. One company, the Anglo-American Corporation, holds 50 percent of all the shares listed on the Johannesburg stock exchange. According to the *Financial Mail,* the South African business and finance weekly, five general corporations and three insurance companies now control the bulk of South Africa's private-sector infrastructure. Apart from the mining industry—gold and coal—the big corporations now exercise effective control over, amongst others, the food sector, alcohol, tobacco, packaging, chemicals, insurance, motors and the press.

The public sector controls 58 percent of South Africa's fixed capital stock and contributes 26 percent to the country's GDP. One in three workers in South Africa is a state employee. The South African Iron and Steel Industrial Corporation (ISCOR), the Industrial Development Corporation (IDC), the Electricity Supply Commission (ESCOM), the Armaments Development and Production Corporation (ARMSCOR) and the South African Coal, Oil and Gas Corporation (SASOL) are among the major "parastatal" companies which are effectively government controlled. . . .

In May 1984, the *Financial Mail* noted: "Monopolies, ologopolies and cartels have become entrenched features of South Africa's economic life." Yet it is in just these sectors that the black unions have made the most substantial gains since 1973.

This is not accidental. During the 1973 strikes management had found itself at factory after factory facing a workforce that had simply walked off the job. Time and again managers found themselves faced with an angry crowd of workers who refused to elect leaders or engage in any kind of dialogue. As one worker insisted: "We don't need a committee. We need R30.00 a week." The reason for this reluctance to elect a leadership was clear—fear of victimization by management or the police. But as the manager of Coronation Brick Co., the company at which the strikes began, said, he was neither willing nor able "to negotiate with 1,500 workers on a football field." It was a dilemma that management was to come across time and again during the dispute. And for the more thoughtful managers it held a clear message—if you want to be able to conduct reasonable negotiations with workers in the future, you had better come to terms with the leaders that they throw up from the factory floor. Simple repression is not going to solve the problem. And one of the results of the increasing monopolization outlined above, was that these considerations spread rapidly through major sectors of the economy. Senior management realized that it could not achieve its goals of increased profits and a larger market share if it allowed local managers to simply remove any leader that stepped forward from amongst the workforce. This sophisticated analysis did not come easily, but it was assisted by two factors—the intense shortage of skilled labor and the international context within which many firms operated.

The shortage of skilled labor was probably the more important factor. According to a 1981 survey, the South African private sector had a skill shortage of 8 percent in terms of craftsmen and apprentices and 12.1 percent in terms of scientists, engineers and technicians. In 1982 there were 5,517 white apprentices under training in the metal engineering and 390 Africans. There were 807 coloured and 426 Asian apprentices in the same year. Although this was still not enough to provide the skills required by industry, it was a considerable advance from the situation in 1979, when no African apprentices were under training. With the white population static the employers had no alternative but to begin to train blacks for skilled positions.

. . . The Siemens chief executive, Wilfried Wentges said: "In 1966, we had only 10 blacks in skilled and semi-skilled wage-earning jobs. Now the number is 1,391, a most impressive result of untiring training. In 1966, only 2.4 percent of our African wage earners could be classified as skilled or semi-skilled, but now the proportion is 26 percent." Clearly no rational manager would be prepared to throw away the results of this "untiring training," and this gave black workers a bargaining strength that they had previously lacked.

The international investment in the South African economy is central to the country's development. According to the Business International survey cited above, there are between 2,000 and 2,500 foreign owned firms operating in South Africa. By far and away the largest number are British (1,200) followed by German (350) and US (340) concerns. Total foreign investment is in the region of $30 billion. About 20 percent of all industry in South Africa is accounted for by foreign investment.

Countries such as Japan are increasing their involvement but are doing so, for example, in the auto industry, by setting up wholly owned South African firms so that the fiction of non-Japanese involvement in the apartheid system is maintained. In fact South Africa exports more to Japan (15.6 percent) than to either the United States (12.3 percent) or Great Britain (13.7 percent). . . .

But the crucial point is that international companies are susceptible to international pressure in a way in which local companies are not. . . .

So although the campaign for sanctions against South Africa may have failed to achieve its ultimate objective, namely economic sanctions, it has helped to create a climate in which international companies are aware of the spotlight that is focused upon their activities. It was not accidental that the first company to recognize a black union in the 1970s was Smith and Nephew —a British subsidiary.

Unions and the State: Confusion, Concessions and Confrontations

. . . No one should be under any illusion about the dangers under which the unions operate in the country. Union leaders and activists have been banned, jailed and even killed. . . .

To this chilling list [omitted] could be added the death in detention of the trade union official, Neil Aggett in early 1982, and the detention and harassment of Thozamile Gqweta, the president of the South African Allied Workers Union. Not only were his mother and uncle burnt to death when the door of his house was wired shut, and the place then set ablaze, but his girlfriend was shot and he was taken into prison and so brutally treated that he became severely depressed and lost his memory.

But if this [repression] was the only response that the state had found to the unions they would, in all likelihood, have ceased to exist. In the wake of the 1973 strikes the state embarked upon an alternative approach. This change in emphasis was signaled by the introduction of the Bantu Labor Relations Regulations Amendment Act of 1973. The Act established two types of infactory committees which were meant to be available as means of communication between black workers and white management. The committees—"works" and "liaison" committees—were a deliberate attempt to forestall the development of trade unions, and were denounced as such.

They were generally passive instruments of management, and workers became dissatisfied with this poor substitute for genuine representation. Nonetheless, they did provide workers with the first taste of bargaining—a novel experience for many. By 1979 there were 312 works committees and 2,683 liaison committees in operation.

But a far more significant step was taken with the appointment in 1977 of a Commission of Inquiry into Labor Legislation led by Nicholaas Wiehahn. The Commission, which was set up in the wake of the 1976 Soweto uprising, reflected the government's concern that the union movement was consolidating its position, and that it was doing so entirely outside the parameters of government control. In particular the government was worried about the politicization of industrial relations as the "class of '76" (young blacks politicized by the Soweto uprising) began to enter the workforce.

In what was described by Steve Friedman as "a bizarre piece of symbolism" the Wiehahn Commission released its report on May Day 1979. The Commission recommended a number of measures, but perhaps the most important was the recognition that blacks could form their own unions. Although such unions had not been illegal, they now received official recognition. This change ended 60 years of government policy aimed at forcing black unions out of existence, and driving all Africans into the bantustans.

. . . The Commission hoped to bring the black unions under the official industrial relations system that had previously only been available to white unions. These were the Industrial Councils. These Councils govern the terms and conditions of particular industries, setting wages, hours and standards of employment. Previously only white or coloured and Asian union members were represented directly on the Industrial Councils. . . .

Now for the first time Africans would be allowed a place at the Industrial Council sessions. But only if they registered. This was something that the black unions rejected. For they saw the Industrial Councils as being remote from the real struggles that were taking place on the shop floor, and an attempt to remove the negotiations from the factories in which the unions had their real strength. The unions were as yet not strong enough to cope with negotiations on a national level. . . .

Strikes

If the response of the unions to the Wiehahn proposals was at best cool, the response from management was just the opposite. Many managers saw the Commission's recommendations as official endorsement of black unions, and the number of recognition agreements that were entered into by companies after Wiehahn snowballed. This process was accelerated by a rise in confidence on the part of workers, and a spate of bitter, but generally successful strikes that won nationwide coverage in the press. A strike at one of South Africa's best known food firms, Fattis and Monis, in their pasta factory in Cape Town in April 1979 was won after workers held out for seven months. After a community-wide boycott of the companies' products, and substantial sums of money had been donated by the public, the strikers won, and the union was recognized by the company. Hot on the heels of the settlement came a strike amongst stevedores on the Cape Town docks, and after a few days the employers there also gave in, and the docks were unionized. Not that the workers did not suffer reverses. A strike by meat workers collapsed, despite a four-month-long community boycott of all meat products. But the strike brought such a wave of bad publicity for the employers that many managers began to feel that it was not worth the poor image that was now associated with disregarding the unions.

As the following table indicates the confidence and combativity of black workers soared after the low that it had reached in 1977.

STRIKES BY BLACK WORKERS: 1973–83

Year	No. of Disputes	Black workers on strike
1973	370	98,029
1974	384	58,975
1975	276	23,295
1976	248	26,931
1977	90	15,091
1978	106	14,088
1979	101	17,323
1980	207	56,286
1981	342	84,705
1982	394	141,517
1983	336	64,469

. . . .

Yet the use of the strike weapon in South Africa has to be handled with care. For a start, most strikes are illegal; in fact there has been only one legal strike by a black union since 1981. To go on strike legally requires that a union first goes through a lengthy procedure designed to wear down union determination and to try and put as much time between the cause of the dispute and any industrial action undertaken to resolve it.

Once on strike, unions have to face further problems. Picketing is forbidden, though some unions have been gingerly organizing poster campaigns outside strike-hit workplaces. Strike pay is illegal. Under both the Internal Security Act and the Riotous Assembly Act the police can arrest strikers or unions' officials for organizing workers' meetings. Companies are legally entitled to dismiss workers during a strike. Inter-union rivalry has led to management successfully using others unions to help break strikes. During the Johannesburg municipal workers' strike, white citizens undertook what to them was the remarkable and unprecedented labor of rubbish disposal in order to undermine the strikers. . . .

17. THE SOURCES OF SOUTH AFRICAN OIL*

by OLUSOLA OJO

In the following article, the author refers to South Africa's SASOL plants, which produce oil from coal. A recent UN study [Paul Conlon, "South Africa's Attempt to Reduce Dependence on Imported Oil," Centre Against Apartheid, October 1985] downgrades SASOL's potential: (1) its cost is estimated at about $75 per barrel of oil equivalent, many times the official or spot price of oil; (2) its technology is antiquated. Conlon describes SASOL as a costly, white elephant. He also points out that attempts to discover oil through off-shore exploration have been futile, not to speak of costly. In the event of an effective oil embargo, South Africa's ability to survive would depend on three factors, all of which are state secrets: (a) SASOL's output (the estimated range is 55,000–75,000 barrels/day (bld); (b) South Africa's estimated consumption of oil, 250,000–320,000 bld; and (c) estimated stockpiles, the maximum estimate being 17.5 million tons or 15 months' consumption. (The general consensus is that the government's claim to have stored a three years' supply of crude in old mineshafts is exaggerated.) Making the most favorable assumptions as to South Africa's potential to survive, the longest period is 22 months (652 days). Presumably, financial confidence and backing would have dissipated much sooner. Conlon concludes that "the fuel-strategic situation of the minority government can only deteriorate." Dr. Ojo is a member of the Department of International Relations, University of Ife, Nigeria.

According to a 1973 OAU report, South Africa received about half of its oil from Iran at that time. The other principal sources were Iraq, Qatar and Saudi Arabia, all Arab states. However, in November 1973 the Arab oil-producing states agreed to embargo oil supplies to South Africa. But the Shah of Iran, because of his close ties with the South African authorities, refused to take a similar action despite appeals by the African states. Iran, in actual fact, stepped up its deliveries to the republic after the Arab boycott decision. According to one UN estimate, Iran supplied 90 percent of South Africa's oil needs in 1974 and 85 percent in 1975. These levels were maintained until the fall of the shah. Iranian crude oil was exported to South Africa in two ways. First, through direct export by the government-owned National Iranian Oil Company (NIOC) which had a long-standing contract to supply a refinery near Johannesburg. And secondly, Iranian oil was exported to the republic by the Iranian Consortium—BP, Shell, Mobil, Exxon, Texaco, Gulf, Standard Oil of California and Total.

After the Arabs had officially imposed their oil embargo, it became difficult to know the actual percentage of South Africa's oil originating from them. However, an analysis of the data obtained on tanker movements from Lloyds

*From *Southern Africa in the 1980s* (London, 1985).

of London in 1977 shows that oil did continue to flow from the Middle East, particularly from Bahrain, Iraq, Kuwait, Oman, Qatar, the United Arab Emirates (Abu Dhabi and Dubai) and Saudi Arabia. In June 1979 it was reported that South Africa had exchanged unknown amounts of gold bullion for Saudi-Arabian and Kuwaiti oil. Some quantities of oil also came from Indonesia and Brunei. With OPEC formally instituting an embargo against South Africa and the loss of Iranian supplies, Brunei became the only country openly selling oil to the republic. It now supplies about 8 percent of South Africa's oil needs.

South Africa receives some of its imported oil from the "spot market," although at a very high premium. It pays as much as a 60 percent premium over the already-high crude prices. The oil exporters have no control over this market which operates principally out of Rotterdam, Antwerp and Amsterdam but also from Hamburg, London, Paris, Milan, New York and Singapore. Usually the oil sold in the "spot market" is not subject to the restrictive terms of sale contracts entered into by oil exporters and oil companies. Purchases on the market are usually done by brokers. Thus, crude oil shipments may pass through a number of intermediaries and the oil itself may not be dispatched directly from the original oil-exporting country to South Africa.

South Africa also obtains some of its oil through "oil piracy," mainly through the manipulation of tankers. First, a tanker may be deliberately sunk after its cargo has been illegally discharged in South Africa. This was, in fact, what happened to the tanker SS *Salem* (ex-*South Sun*) sunk off the coast of Senegal in January 1980. The *Salem* had loaded 190,000 ton of Kuwaiti crude oil under sales contract between Kuwait and Pontoil, an Italian-based company. Investigation later revealed that the *Salem* headed for Europe with its cargo via the Cape of Good Hope. But while on the high seas Pontoil sold the *Salem*'s cargo to the Shell International Trading Co. for delivery to Europe. *Salem* later changed its name to *Lema* before it approached Durban, where it offloaded its cargo of crude oil and was filled with sea-water. It was deliberately sunk off the coast of Senegal in an attempt to conceal the oil theft. Two other Liberian-registered oil tankers—the *Albahaa B* and *Mycene*—sank off the African coast after the *Salem* incident under similar circumstances. The *Albahaa B*, a 240,000-ton tanker exploded and sank off the coast of Tanzania on its way back to the Middle East after it had offloaded its cargo in Durban. Like the *Albahaa B*, the *Mycene* also a 240,000-ton tanker mysteriously sank off the coast of Senegal with no traces of its oil cargo by the time it sank.

Secondly, there is "double-loading" of tankers. This is usually done in close collaboration between the oil companies, tanker owners and the South African government. Some tankers load crude oil destined for Europe from the Middle East, but later offload either part or all of the crude in South Africa. The tankers later proceed northward to load new supplies in one of the loading points on the west coast of Africa—in Cabinda, Port Harcourt, or Warri. In

May 1979 the Nigerian government seized a tanker, *VLCC Kudu,* which called at Port Harcourt to load crude after it was known to have discharged its previous cargo in South Africa. Thirdly, it is not uncommon for a tanker carrying crude oil to feign mechanical breakdown in the vicinity of South Africa. Its contents are offloaded to another vessel which then takes the oil to Durban or Cape Town; the original carrier subsequently proceeds back to the Middle East after "undergoing repairs."

Fourthly, international oil companies with the approval of some host governments also swap embargoed oil for non-embargoed oil which is then shipped to South Africa. This arrangement became widely known following the controversy between former British Foreign Minister, Dr. David Owen, and Lord Carrington, then Foreign Secretary, in June 1979. Under the arrangement the Conservative government of Margaret Thatcher agreed to pass North Sea oil to Conoco which then sent it to South Africa in exchange for embargoed oil.

Finally, South Africa gets some quantity of its oil from the synthetic production of oil. The first oil-from-coal plant—Sasol I—was opened in Sasolburg near Johannesburg in 1955. Its output of oil products in 1978 was about 5,000 barrels per day. Another oil-from-coal plant—Sasol II—was opened early in 1980. It was to produce about 45,000 b/d of oil products at full production in 1981.

18. ANGLO-AMERICAN CORPORATION*

by JOHN HOWLEY

Economic Notes *is published monthly by the Labor Research Association, which provides research and educational materials for labor unions. John Howley is an LRA Research Associate.*

The "American" in Anglo-American Corporation, South Africa's largest corporation, is no mistake. J. P. Morgan and other U.S. interests supplied half the capital when Anglo was founded in 1917. Anglo-American is now part of a complex web of financial, industrial and mining interests dominated by the Oppenheimer family, with assets estimated at $16 billion, $800 million in 1984 earnings, and 250,000 workers worldwide. Anglo-American is also the single largest foreign investor in the U.S.

Anglo has been South Africa's leading mining company since it was founded. In the post-World War II period, Anglo used the massive cash flow

*From *Economic Notes,* July–August, 1985.

generated by new gold fields to diversify its investments in South Africa and overseas. Currently, the Anglo group consists of several central holding companies, including the Anglo-American Corporation and DeBeers, which are tied together by interlocking directorships and mutual shareholdings. The group accounts for half of the value of all South Africa's exports and dominates national economies in southern Africa.

Black Miners

Although Anglo's holdings in manufacturing and finance are substantial, it has concentrated its interests in mining, with over 250 mining ventures in 22 countries. Anglo mined 240 tons of South African gold in 1984, with over 100,000 workers drawn from South Africa's gold mining workforce of 500,000 black miners. It is the largest single employer of black migrant labor in South Africa.

As such, Anglo increasingly comes into confrontation with the National Union of Mineworkers, which now represents over 130,000 black mine workers. Black miners earn less than $250 a month, or one-sixth of the wages paid to the country's 12,000 white miners. By law, no more than 3 percent of the black miners are allowed to live with their families near the mines; 97 percent must live in company barracks away from their families.

During a strike at the end of 1984, Anglo called in the police with dogs and batons to drive workers back into the mines. In April of this year, Anglo dismissed 14,000 miners from its Vaal Reefs mine—the largest gold mine in the world—after six weeks of slowdowns and work stoppages.

U.S. Holdings

In 1970, the Anglo group moved one of its major holding companies—the Minerals and Resources Corporation (MINORCO)—to Bermuda to funnel investments into the U.S. and Canada. Other Anglo holdings were transferred to MINORCO, including its 29 percent stake in the U.S.-based Engelhard Minerals and Chemicals, purchased from Charles Engelhard, the American metals tycoon who served as the model for Ian Fleming's Goldfinger. In 1981, Engelhard's commodity trading subsidiary—Phillip Brothers—was spun off and merged with the Salomon Brothers investments banking firm to form Phibro-Salomon Corporation.

Anglo is the largest single foreign investor in the U.S., with holdings that range from zinc and copper mines in the Yukon to natural gas deposits in Texas. The Anglo group's U.S. holdings now total over 100 companies, primarily in mining, construction, chemicals, manufactured steel products, and the energy industry.

MINORCO remains Anglo's key vehicle for expansion in the U.S. MINORCO holds 27 percent of Phibro, the world's largest trader of crude oil. Phibro, in turn, holds 100 percent of the New York-based Salomon Brothers, the largest investment banking firm in the U.S. In the first half of 1985, Salomon Brothers managed $14.7 billion of new corporate and public securities issues in the U.S. Salomon is the leading underwriter in the country, with nearly 20 percent of the total underwriting market. It specializes in the sale of large amounts of stock to a small number of institutional investors, and underwrites bonds for a number of municipal governments. In July, David Stockman, Reagan's Budget Director, announced that he would leave the Administration for a position at Salomon Brothers in the fall. Despite the obvious link to South African apartheid, Salomon Brothers assures U.S. institutional investors that it does not "engage in underwriting for the South African government or any of its agencies."

Another important U.S. Anglo holding is its 26 percent interest in Newmont Mining, held by Anglo's London-based Consolidated Gold Fields. Newmont, in turn, owns 27.5 percent of Peabody Coal, the largest U.S. coal producer.

Anglo-Citicorp

MINORCO's board is chaired by Harry Oppenheimer, who leads the Anglo group, and includes other Anglo representatives. It also includes Walter Wriston, the recently retired Chairman of the Board of Citicorp, and Felix Rohatyn, senior partner at Lazard Frères and chief architect of the New York City social service cutbacks of the 1970s. Rueben Richards, a Citicorp Executive Vice President, also sits on the boards of several other Anglo affiliates, including Engelhard, Phibro-Salomon, and Inspiration Resources, which is 60 percent owned by MINORCO and holds extensive interests in the U.S. oil, coal, and minerals industries.

Through these key connections, Citicorp has become Anglo's main U.S. partner. Citibank is the largest U.S. lender to South Africa and manager of the $100 million loan to African Explosives and Chemical, an Anglo company held through Consolidated Gold Fields.

Chapter V:

FORCED REMOVALS AND THE BANTUSTANS

19. FORCED RELOCATION*

by THE SURPLUS PEOPLE PROJECT REPORT

Over the past 20 years, the South African government has forcibly moved over 3.5 million people in implementation of apartheid. For three years, more than 50 members of the Surplus People Project analyzed this horrendous program. In 1983, it published a five volume report of its findings. Below are excerpts from its "General Overview."

Overview

Since the early 1960s the South African State has uprooted and relocated well over three and a half million people in the name of apartheid; approaching two million people at least are threatened with removal in the near future. The people who have been moved have, with the exception of a tiny number of whites affected by the Group Areas Act, been black. . . .

The removals described in this report have been forced. . . . Sometimes the violence with which people are removed is direct—police and guns, bulldozers demolished houses, arrests. Sometimes the violence is less overt—intimidation, rumor, cooption of community leaders, the pressure of shops and schools being closed and building restrictions imposed in areas due for removal. In these situations people may move themselves, without the State actively providing

*From *Forced Removals in South Africa,* Vol. 1, "General Overview" (Cape Town and Pietermaritzburg, 1983).

the transport, or they may agree to make use of State transport. Pretoria has been quick to describe these cases as "voluntary removals"—the age of forced removals, like apartheid, is dead according to the Department of Cooperation and Development. The mass of case study material . . . makes it very clear that such claims are false—a cynical misrepresentation of the submission of right-less people to the dictates of a repressive minority government as an act of positive choice. In a situation where blacks do not possess political rights or freedom of movement there can be no talk of them exercising a free choice about being removed. . . .

Historical Background

The Natives Land Act of 1913 delimited certain areas as African reserves (the "scheduled" areas) and laid down that henceforth no African could purchase or occupy independently land outside the reserves. It also prohibited whites from acquiring or occupying land in the reserves. The land scheduled in 1913 amounted to about 7 percent of the total area in South Africa. This land was concentrated in Natal and the Cape, where the largest reserves already existed, and excluded extensive areas already owned and occupied by Africans. How-ever, it was accepted by the SAP [South African Party] government of the time that further land would be added to the core reserved for African ownership in 1913; the precise boundaries of this would still have to be defined, after further investigation. . . .

The question of the released areas was finally taken up by the Native Trust and Land Act of 1936, passed once the fusion United Party of Hertzog and Smuts had come into office. This Act formed part of a "native policy" package deal. It released a total of 7.25 million morgen, to be added as "released areas" to the 10.5 million morgen that had been scheduled as reserves in 1913; combined, the scheduled and released areas would amount to some 13 percent of the total area of South Africa. The Act also established the South African Native Trust (SANT) as the registered owner and administrator of these areas.

Not all the released areas were specified in 1936. The outstanding amount of land that could not be specified in 1936 (largely because of the continued hostility of white farmers to making more land available for the reserves) was still to be acquired by the SANT; this amount was allocated across the four provinces on a quota basis. The land purchasing program of the SANT pro-ceeded very sluggishly in the ensuing decades and by 1974 20 percent of the area released in 1936 had still to be acquired. . . .

The National Party of D. F. Malan came to power [in 1948] at a time of great ferment in South Africa. The period after the Second World War was one of particularly rapid urbanization and industrialization. . . .

The first major step in the direction of incorporating tribalism into the system of political control of the African population came with the passage of the Bantu Authorities Act of 1951. This made provision for the establishment of tribal, regional and territorial authorities in the reserves, with limited powers of local government, and thereby incorporated the traditional tribal elite into the overall structures of domination.

At this stage, the manipulation of tribalism seems to have been more in the interests of administrative convenience and control and had less of the economic and political importance it was to assume in its full-grown, ethnic form at the end of the 1950s. Nevertheless, the social reorganization embodied in the Bantu Authorities Act of 1951 laid the foundation for a policy which was to seek the solution to unemployment, economic and political resistance, international qualms about white minority rule, and rapid urbanization (with the accompanying problems of a demand for housing and social services and the fear that it would eventually lead to a demand by those in the urban areas for the vote in a central parliament) in the development of the reserves as the true "homelands" of the African people. . . .

The great leap in policy implementation came at the end of the 1950s and was, at least partially, a response to the political activism of the dominated classes during the 1950s. During that time black antagonism to separate development increased enormously and became far more forceful: the Defiance Campaign, bus boycotts, the anti-pass campaigns, the Treason Trial demonstrations, etc. The pressure was further exacerbated by increased international hostility.

The strength of the internal opposition to separate development, expressed in a broad, united nationalism, suggested that the fragmentation strategy of bantu authorities was not working adequately, and it was now that the stress on ethnicity came fully into its own, with an ethnic franchise being "offered" as a substitute for a vote in the national political structure.

In the Promotion of Bantu Self-Government Act of 1959 the emphasis definitely shifts to nationhood. The Act was

> to provide for the gradual development of self-governing Bantu national units and for direct consultation between the Government of the Union and the said national units in regard to matters affecting the interests of such units.

The preamble states that "the Bantu peoples of the Union of South Africa do not constitute a homogeneous people, but from separate national units on the basis of language and culture." "National units" is a key term throughout the Act. Article 4 of the Act refers to "Representatives of Blacks in urban areas" and seems to be the first move to legislate for the binding of the Africans in urban areas to a "homeland." The remnants of parliamentary representation for Africans were abolished by means of the Act. Eight national units were recognized—North-Sotho, South-Sotho, Tswana, Zulu, Swazi, Xhosa, Tsonga and Venda. In a White Paper the Nationalist Government declared that the government was returning to the basic aims pursued before 1936, of identifying the various African communities with their "homelands" in the reserves and ensuring that Africans entered the "white" areas as migrants only.

The 1960s and 1970s saw a continuation along the path mapped out in 1959. . . .

[The following update is from a November 1985 newsletter put out by the National Committee Against Removals, which is composed of four regional organizations concerned with forced removals: The Association for Rural Advancement, Natal; the Grahamstown Rural Committee; the Surplus People Project, Western Cape; and the Transvaal Rural Action Committee. —ed.]

"No More Forced Removals"?

In February this year the Minister of Cooperation, Development and Education announced that removals had been suspended. NCAR members have, however, found evidence to the contrary in their day to day work. Three eastern Transvaal black spots and 52 rural townships have been reprieved, but most categories of removal have not been stopped. The current position remains confusing, not only for the affected people, but also for officials and politicians.

Superficially it appears that black spot removals are about to come to an end, but other indications contradict this. For instance, although the Western Transvaal black spot of Mathopestad has resisted removal for many years, the Deputy Minister of Land Affairs told representatives of the community on 19 September that their removal was still under consideration. And within a week the consolidation proposals for Lebowa, Gazankulu, KwaNdebele and KwaZulu involving the removal of hundreds of thousands of people were announced.

Consolidation

In spite of abundant proof that the Nationalist bantustan dream has failed, despite thousands of millions of wasted Rands and P. W. Botha's admitting that citizenship will have to be restored to those dispossessed of their land and rights as South Africans, the 1985 plans propose to strip at least half a million more people of their land in an attempt to reduce the number of separate, isolated pieces of bantustans.

Not even the figures for those threatened with removal quoted by Mr. Hendrik Tempel, current chairperson of the Commission for Cooperation and

Development, can be trusted. He claimed that only 42,000 people in Natal would be moved in terms of the plan, while AFRA calculated that 240,000 people from black spots and excised reserves would have to move. This figure does not even include the "landless chiefs" and their people on white-owned farms, the Commission threatened with removal. The 1975 plans have not been improved much—188 black spots in Natal remain under threat of relocation.

The Transvaal situation is similar. The Minister of Constitutional Development and Planning claimed that 125,000 would no longer have to be moved, but in the Central Transvaal black spots of Bloedfontein alone 15,000 people will have to move and the Minister's figure does not include those who will have to move "voluntarily." For example, against their will 100,000 non-Ndebeles in the Moutse area are still to be incorporated into KwaNdebele, scheduled to take independence in 1986. Should they leave their homes to escape "ethnic" conflict, their relocation will no doubt officially be termed "voluntary." For ten years the Moutse people have refused to move or be incorporated into KwaNdebele, yet this 1985 final plan gives them no option. Likewise the black-owned ethnically mixed farms of Bloedfontein and Geweerfontein are to be incorporated into Bophuthatswana and the residents moved to KwaNdebele.

Thus although land is granted to a bantustan, it does not mean that the people presently living on it will be allowed to remain there. This is also the situation at Madibogo in the Northern Cape where Sotho-speaking people are threatened with removal. Their land, which has been set aside for the Motlatla people who do not want to move from their Western Transvaal black spot, is to be consolidated into Bophuthatswana.

Many black communities are resisting their areas being incorporated into bantustans, particularly if there is a chance that that bantustan will take "independence," because P. W. Botha made it clear in his speech on 11 September that only those who permanently reside in S.A. may regain their S.A. citizenship. Even if some bantustans agree to dual citizenship, it is likely that the S.A. government would implement these plans as speedily as possible, knowing that Bophuthatswana, for example, will not agree to joint citizenship. The result would be a hollow reform. The old apartheid plan to rid S.A. of as many black people as possible, turning them into "foreigners," would then have succeeded.

Other Categories of Removal

Group Areas: While only 38,000 people or 4% of all those moved in terms of the Group Areas Act of 1950, are still to be moved, last month P. W. Botha categorically refused to repeal the Act.

Informal Settlements: During the first week of October Western Cape Development Board Officials accompanied by the SADF [South African Defense Force] demolished at least 60 shacks in Mbekweni outside Paarl.

More than 6,000 residents of Kabah informal settlement between KwaNobuhle and Langa, outside Uitenhage, have been served with eviction notices. The community is determined that none of its members will be forced to move.

Farm Evictions: More than one million farm workers and their families are to be moved off the white-owned farms. Their plight is extremely serious. They live in appalling poverty, and because of influx control, they have no choice but to move to the bantustans.

Betterment Planning and Internal Bantustan Relocation: People continue to be forced off their land for it to be used "more economically" or for the private use of the chosen few. In the Nqutu region of KwaZulu, for example, numerous people are evicted by local officials and sent to inhospitably dry areas.

Reforms: Influx Control

A close examination of the locally and internationally heralded recommendations of the report "An Urbanization Strategy for the Republic of South Africa," presented by the Committee on Constitutional Affairs of the President's Council on 12 September 1985, is necessary. The main recommendation was that "influx control in the RSA as applied at present in terms of Act 25 of 1945 be abolished." Subsequently the State President refused to scrap influx control and referred the report to the Minister of Constitutional Development and Planning to make recommendations to the cabinet for the reform of the system.

While welcoming the recommendation to scrap influx control, it is crucial to examine the context and reasons for the call in order to assess possible real consequences. Essentially, the existing "hidden" forms of urban influx control, such as clearance of slums and informal settlements, zoning and decentralization are to replace classic pass law control.

Some positive points were made in the report, for instance, on REMOVALS: "As far as possible, urbanized people should not be moved. However, where circumstances necessitate this, it should be done with the consent of those involved and in a community context." But the report only recommends the abolition of one act, the Urban Areas Act, which regulates the physical presence of Africans in the urban areas. It did not recommend the repeal of any legislation related to the right to work or occupy land in urban areas, neither did it consider rural influx control. In effect, it only dealt with one of the three aspects of influx control.

The report claims that South Africa no longer needs influx control, as such, because it can use direct and indirect means of control such as the Prevention of Illegal Squatting Act (52 of 1951), Slums Clearance (Act 76 of 1979), Groups Areas Act (41 of 1950), legislation relating to health controls and local authority measures such as zoning.

The committee recommended that classic influx control be replaced by "orderly urbanisation":

> Orderly urbanisation means that the process of urbanisation is ordered and directed mainly by indirect forms of control, but also by direct measures. Indirect measures consist mainly of incentives and restrictive measures based chiefly on market forces. Measures should not be applied that discriminate against certain population groups. Direct measures comprise legislation, ordinances and by-laws that direct and control. Orderly urbanisation implies freedom of movement for all citizens of the country. Orderly urbanisation also refers to the operation of economic and social forces and related requirements, and its object is not only the spatial ordering of urbanisation but also the accommodation of urban growth.

Planned site and service is to replace informal settlements. As P. W. Botha said at the Cape Nationalist Party Congress in September, the government would not tolerate "squatting." In South Africa the term "squatter" is liberally applied to anyone who is not living where the authorities require him or her to live, e.g., a person too young or too old to be working on a white-owned farm, a tenant on a black spot or mission station, a wife of a migrant worker living with him on a building site.

Economic Control

Economic rather than racial differentiation is the central theme throughout the report. The Committee argues for controls and incentives; e.g., "New arrivals in urban areas should obtain approved accommodations/site within a specified period" and indirect pressures such as subsidizing township developments in the "national states" more than in metropolitan areas so that people will be more "attracted" there. This is no different from the current policy.

The reference to "new towns" in S.A. and the "national states," e.g., Botsabelo (or Onverwacht, the huge relocation area 50km from Bloemfontein), is disturbing. Apparently the government is still talking about urbanization in the bantustans, i.e., closer settlements and townships like Ezakheni or Itsoseng. As has become the practice, another name change is proposed: "new towns," which sounds better than "closer settlements in border areas."

Black Local Authorities

The report urged that "[A]n extensive and comprehensive strategy to make these institutions more acceptable and effective appears to be essential" and they must have "adequate financial resources and effective planning," but that "[T]he costs of providing urban services and housing should be recovered from consumers and purchasers as far as possible." It seems, unrealistically, that the committee ignored the nationwide rejection of black local authorities and assumed that, with a change of image, they could be expected to administer "orderly urbanisation."

Conclusion

In conclusion, out of the confusion and contradictions, it seems that the state is taking communities' resistance seriously. The response is, however, uneven. In some cases those in authority appear to be relenting while they reorganize their means of control. Reform does not mean structural change: they have backed down on their promise to scrap influx control and have refused to repeal the Group Areas Act. It seems unlikely that a legal minimum wage or freedom of movement will be extended to farm workers, and consolidation plans continue in the same mould.

There is speculation that the PC proposal for "orderly urbanisation" is part of a bigger plan to extend the nine industrial development zones (which cross bantustan borders) into a new constitutional dispensation for a federal government. This may be the result of combined efforts of the government and big business since the Carlton Conference in 1979: a federal system in an attempt to stave off universal franchise in a unitary South Africa.

Between 1960 and 1980 the percentage of the total African population living in the bantusans rose from 39.5 percent to 54 percent. There will be no more black South Africans, Connie Mulder, then Minister of Plural Relations, said in 1978. Population relocation and an increasingly stringent application of influx control have been the major mechanisms by which this "reversal of the tide" has been achieved. The National States Constitution Act of 1970, which decrees that all Africans are citizens of one or other of the bantustans and the granting of independence to these territories—already achieved in the Transkei, Ciskei, Bophuthatswana and Venda—completes the process of dispossession.

However, not all relocation has been into the bantustans. A sizeable minority of the removals—between a quarter and a fifth—have affected Indian and coloured people. They have been removed mainly in terms of the Group Areas Act of 1950, which has enforced a system of rigid segregation in residential and trading areas between Indians, coloureds and whites (to the advantage of the latter) and forced Indian and coloured communities out of established areas, to the periphery of the towns and cities. . . .

REPRESSIVE REGEIME

20. RESETTLEMENT AT GLENMORE*

by THE SURPLUS PEOPLE PROJECT REPORT

The following resettlement at Glenmore is typical of many that have taken place in the implementation of apartheid. For a more general discussion, see the previous Reading.

The reactions of the Kenton residents threatened with relocation were as bitter as they were poignant. One man who had received a notice was a blind pensioner. He had lived at Kenton since 1956 working for one employer for 15 years. Most registered their opposition to the move. Some threatened to refuse to board the trucks. One old-age pensioner was dumbstruck:

I have not committed a crime. I have trusted the Christians all these years but now I have lost my trust.

A 66-year-old woman who had lived there for 25 years was more damnatory:

They make us work like donkeys and then they throw us out.

Following an outcry by various sectors the Kenton removals were temporarily halted after PFP [Progressive Federal Party] representations to Koornhof [Minister of Cooperation and Development]. ECAB [Eastern Cape Administration Board] also felt obliged to check whether any unregistered but employed residents had been issued with notices. The Klipfontein removals were, however, to go ahead. Klipfontein squatters had a history of fighting removals through the courts. After being told to move in 1976 they were allowed to remain after a successful court case. In March 1978 charges of illegal squatting were deferred on the grounds that there was no alternative housing available.

The Klipfontein squatters received no written notice at all. They were simply informed by a police sergeant that they were to be moved within a week. . . .

Despite the claims of Koch [of ECAB] and Koornhof that squatters would not be forced to move, newspaper reports and statements by squatters gave a radically different picture. One man, a father of three, said the removal squads had arrived at his two-roomed house and ordered him to break it down.

I told them I would not do it. The man in charge then told the others to take my furniture out and they broke the house down. . . .

*From *Forced Removals in South Africa,* Vol. 2, "The Eastern Cape" (Cape Town and Pietersmaritzburg, 1983).

Affidavits made at the time confirm that the community felt itself under pressure:

> ... That on the 5th April 1979 the officials of the Eastern Cape Administration Board came to my house and told me to move. I persist in my attitude not to move. That on the 9th April I was told by the ECAB official that "Kaffir you must break down your house, failing which we will do it or arrest you." On the 10th April 1979 a number of white officials came to my house, and instructed me to break my house down. There were about five officials including those from the ECAB. I demolished my house and shall not move.
>
> ... That the authorities came to our home on the 3rd April and that my mother informed them that we could not move because my father was in hospital. The authorities again came on Wednesday the 4th April. The officials from the Eastern Cape Administration Board then informed my mother that they were going to break the house down. When I returned to my house I found my mother on the truck and that all our personal possessions were on another lorry. My wife and children have been transferred involuntarily to Glenmore.

That I heard from friends about our pending removal on the 2.4.79. The ECAB officials came on the 3.4.79. They came again on 6.4.79. I saw Sergeant K*** in the township and I said that I shall not be leaving and he replied that we cannot remain in Klipfontein. K*** took a piece of paper and asked me to place my thumb print thereon. I refused and further said all the people must leave. Sergeant K*** took my hand and placed my thumb on his book. This was a blank piece of paper. My name was written on this paper in my presence. Sergeant K*** took my thumb on the ink stamp pad and thereafter he placed my thumbprint on this blank piece of paper on which he had written my name.

Initial Conditions at Glenmore

Conditions suffered in the initial weeks at Glenmore were nothing short of critical. Complaints of unemployment, hunger and cold were rife. The rations provided by the government were pitifully inadequate and many who had been gainfully employed in their places of origin were now "asking and borrowing" to stay alive.

A survey written up in June 1979 by a Rhodes University academic found that

> in 25 households there were 30 workseekers, but only one case of a family member employed at Glenmore. It also found that the average income of 25 households had

fallen from R60 a month to R27 a month, and that several households had no cash income at all.

The fall in income was attributed to the high number of men that had lost their jobs, forcing them to migrate to Port Elizabeth in search of employment. It was also claimed that many women who had previously worked part-time had lost their sources of income. It was also reported that of the 507 men who had sought employment at Glenmore only 10 percent had been successful.

There were complaints by the residents that the brackish water from the Fish River was making people ill. The water was tested and found to be passable by South African standards although some elements were very high —the saline trace was above the limit allowed by some other countries, for instance. Then there were numerous complaints of diarrhea, vomiting and bloody stools and children covered with pustules. As the first rations began to run out there were increasing reports of children with swollen feet and stomachs. When approached, a spokesman for the clinic said there had been no complaints of hunger and only one case of kwashiorkor. The spokesman was quick to add that the case "couldn't have started at Glenmore."

Agriculture in the initial weeks was understandably nonexistent. Many who had supplemented their incomes at Coega and Klipfontein with livestock and crops were now denied this source with little or no compensation. No one had, at that stage, been able to cultivate maize and other vegetables. Some of the Klipfontein people had brought their cattle but these quickly succumbed to the ticks and the tulp, a poisonous iris in the area. Newspaper reports indicated that stock deaths were averaging two a day, and by 18 June it was reported that a quarter of the cattle had already died. Officialdom ruled out compensation.

Begging, borrowing and sharing were the only avenues open to many to eke out a precarious existence. Rations dried up after the first few days and many pension payments had not been transferred to Glenmore at that stage, necessitating costly trips to collect the money. The Glenmore Action Group organized the World Vision to sponsor 2,000 kg of food each week for eight weeks, to be distributed to 200 families. This helped ameliorate the crisis in the short term.

The total of all these conditions materialized on 7 June when newspapers reported there had been 11 deaths at Glenmore—9 were children. Gastroenteritis, kidney inflammation, kwashiorkor and bronchial pneumonia were among the causes.

This critical state of affairs provides a sharp contrast to the words of ECAB Editor, Louis Koch, in his press statement:

> We believe that in moving the squatters here we have succeeded in bringing dignity to the lives of people who have been living in very unfavourable conditions. . . .

Conclusion

Following weeks of intimidation and legal battles, eventual removal and three subsequent years of poverty and privation, Glenmore's 4,200 residents face yet another move in the near future. It was reported in the *Eastern Province Herald* (Nov. 19, 1981) that they "are to be resettled once more at a camp currently being laid out near Peddie in the Ciskei.". . .

So they have to begin all over again against a background of the same utterings and promises that were made just three years ago. As one young mother of three said,

We will never get used to one place. We lead the life of a bird.

She speaks for 4,200 surplus people wanted neither by South Africa nor by the Ciskei, and doomed, it seems, to a future as grim as their immediate past.

21. THE FUTURE MEANS DEATH: TESTIMONY OF ONE FORCIBLY REMOVED*

by THE SURPLUS PEOPLE PROJECT REPORT

Sakhiwo Shode says he is twenty-eight but he looks at least forty-five. He is a man who has been completely demoralized by the forced removal to Eluk-hanyweni. He not only misses his land—"aches for it" he says, but feels that by not resisting on the day they were moved, he had given up any claim to being a man. . . . "That day, with the guns pointing at me, I thought better be alive and in a strange place than dead and under the ground. Now I know I was wrong. . . . I wasn't even a woman because some women spat on the guns but I did nothing." He is restless, sometimes he gets up and walks to the door, hits the door with his fist, turns back, circles the room. His mouth twitches and he looks at the ground during the whole of the conversation. . . . He seems obsessed by the fact that he did not resist, and during the course of the conversation he comes back to it again and again. . . .

For more than a year people talked about little else than the impending removal. But after all the years of insecurity and waiting, when the actual day on which they were to be removed arrived, they were totally unprepared for it. . . .

*From *Forced Removals in South Africa*, Vol. 2, "The Eastern Cape" (Capetown and Pietermaritzburg, 1983).

The lorries came early in the morning when they were still asleep. They were woken up by the loud voices and the knocking on the door. He and his father went to open the door. They heard women crying and they saw the lorries. There were two soldiers on the stoop and the one said: "You must go now, there are the lorries, get in now, get in." They had guns and Sakhiwo and his father turned and got dressed and then they dragged their furniture out. The furniture was thrown on the lorries and even before they got moving quite a few pieces were broken. Some people complained about it and they were told to take their complaints to court. Most of their furniture got broken on the way to Elukhanyweni, and all their crockery. The cattle were left behind. They were promised compensation but never received any. A few of the men resisted and they were put in jail. . . .

When asked whether he has any plans or hopes for the future, Sakhiwo says, . . . "I cannot talk about the future. To me the future means death. I don't have a future, you can see for yourself. When one says future you mean . . . you have a job and it means children, you see your children growing up and everything, and then again their children, your grandchildren. So you see, I don't have a future. It's just death.". . .

22. *BOPHUTHATSWANA: POVERTY AND GLITTER**

by RICHARD KNIGHT

Bophuthatswana is one of the ten "homelands" created by the South African government. It has become internationally known as the home of a casino resort, called Sun City, an island of glitter in a sea of poverty. Big name American performers and athletes earn rich rewards for appearances at this resort, which caters mainly to visiting white South Africans. Diversions forbidden elsewhere in South Africa flourish at Sun City. Many Americans are aware of its existence because of the protest album, "Sun City," which has sold about 300,000 copies in the United States. (There is also a video, a political pamphlet and a paperback book.) The songwriter and producer of the album is Little Steven Van Zandt, who previously played guitar with Bruce Springsteen. The poverty and the glitter are described by Richard Knight, Literature Director of The Africa Fund.

Bantustans, the fragmented areas designated for Africans, comprise only 13 percent of South Africa's territory. Yet these areas are to be the "homelands" for all Africans, or 72 percent of the population. Already the government has declared four of these bantustans, including Bophuthatswana, "independent,"

*From The Africa Fund (New York, 1984).

thus stripping 8 million people of their South African citizenship. The intention of the white minority government is to declare all ten bantustans independent, arriving at a time when, by the stroke of a white pen, every African will be a foreigner in South Africa. These pseudo-states are recognized by no government on earth except South Africa.

. . . Originally the land allotted for African occupation consisted of more than 100 separate scraps of territory. A proposed consolidation plan will reduce the number of pieces to 36. Out of this fragmented territory, the ten bantustans have been created.

History and Government

Bophuthatswana consists of seven pieces of land which are located in three different provinces of South Africa. The 1980 resident population is estimated at two million people with an annual growth rate of over 4 percent.

The South African government claims that each bantustan is the real homeland for a particular ethnic group, the Tswana in the case of Bophuthatswana. In fact, almost half of all Tswana live outside Bophuthatswana while one-third of Bophuthatswana residents are non-Tswana.

South Africa granted Bophuthatswana independence in December 1976. At that moment, every Tswana, whether living in the rest of South Africa or in Bophuthatswana, was stripped of South African citizenship and arbitrarily made a citizen of the new "country" even if they had never lived in, or visited the bantustan.

The white minority government justifies the complete absence of political rights for Africans in South Africa on the grounds that Africans will exercise these rights in the bantustans. The vast majority of Tswana reject this system. . . . In the first election for the national assembly in 1977, only 163,141 people or 12 percent of those eligible in Bophuthatswana cast a vote. Polling booths were set up in the urban areas outside the bantustans for Tswana residents to vote. Three hundred thousand Tswana live in Soweto, the black township outside Johannesburg. Only 600 voted in the 1977 election. In 1982, only 135 voted.

Since 1976 Chief Lucas Mangope has headed the government as President. If the vast majority of people in Bophuthatswana are poor, Mangope is not. In an area where the average income per capita is estimated between $339–$495, Chief Mangope receives a salary of $27,500 a year and runs an expense account.

Bophuthatswana is the showcase bantustan, and proudly boasts a bill of rights. On paper it guarantees equality before the law, the right to freedom from torture and inhuman and degrading punishment and the right to freedom and liberty. But in reality, opposition is curtailed. The government maintains the power of detention without trial and the right to declare any organization illegal. Local chiefs have considerable power, and can arrest and pass sentence for certain offenses. In 1982 three men died after being locked up by police on the orders of a local chief.

In spite of "independence," the movement of Africans is still rigidly controlled. Instead of the hated "passbook," Africans wishing to go to the white areas now carry a "passport," but to seek work outside the bantustan it is still necessary to go through the labor bureau. No one can just go to the city to look for a job.

Economy

So-called independence has not changed the basic economic function of Bophuthatswana as a labor reservoir for white-owned mines, farms and industry. . . . The bantustans are the poorest parts of South Africa, with only about 3 percent of South Africa's Gross Domestic Product produced in all the bantustans combined. . . .

Migrant Labor

There are few jobs in Bophuthatswana; unemployment was conservatively estimated at 19.4 percent in 1981. . . . Because Africans have no free access to the places where jobs are, they have little choice but to join the ranks of migrant workers.

The migrant workers from Bophuthatswana [236,000 in 1982] and elsewhere are usually hired on one year contracts, and are not allowed to take their families with them. They spend most of their lives far from home, living in squalid, single-sex, barracks-style hostels in the white areas. They rarely see their wives and children more than once a year, during brief visits home between contracts. Women, children and the elderly are left in the bantustans to survive as best they can on the meager remittances sent by family members, sometimes supplemented by subsistence agriculture. . . .

Commuters

In addition to providing migrant workers, Bophuthatswana provides some 163,000 "commuter" workers. These workers actually live in Bophuthatswana but "commute" by bus or train on a daily basis to jobs in the white areas. . . .

To be as near as possible to their place of employment, people have built squatter settlements in Bophuthatswana, especially near the Pretoria-Witwatersrand industrial areas. Over 40 percent of the Bophuthatswana population now lives in these squatter camps. They provide much of the labor for the industries of the southern Transvaal.

Agriculture, Mining and Manufacturing

Bophuthatswana is the only homeland with any significant mineral deposits. Bophuthatswana's mines, which are owned by South Africa's largest mining houses, provide the single largest amount—53 percent—of Bophuthaswana's GDP. About 30 percent of all platinum produced worldwide comes from Bophuthatswana. The U.S. firm Union Carbide owns a vanadium mine.

The mines, which employ some 40,000 people, impose many of the same restrictions on black advancement that exist in the rest of South Africa. . . .

Bophuthatswana has relatively little industrial development. . . .

Rejection and Resistance

Despite South African propaganda that the bantustans are an answer to African demands for political rights, the black majority has strongly resisted the imposition of phony "independence" for puppet states and continues to demand full citizenship in a united South Africa. . . .

Fearing the challenge to his rule, Mangope has openly sided with the white minority government. He told a group of parents that the police had been too lenient when dealing with strikes, that they should shoot indiscriminately. "In fact, I have told the police to even shoot my own child," Mangope said. . . .

The puppet leaders of the bantustans play their part, insisting that they are doing away with apartheid. The African majority knows better, understands that the bantustans are themselves apartheid. They will not be satisfied until they have equal access to the wealth of South Africa and full political rights in a unitary state.

Sun City

Sun City is a $90 million pleasure resort stuck into the vast rural poverty of Bophuthatswana. It plays a significant part in the South African effort to break out of its isolation and win back foreign favor. The large complex includes an artificial lake, a casino, soft porn movies, discoteques, and scantily clad chorus girls. Near by, the Pilanesberg game reserve was created for the tourists' delight by evicting 100 families from their homes. And there is the Superbowl, a large auditorium that regularly features big name international entertainers.

The Superbowl was opened by Frank Sinatra, who was paid $1.6 million for a nine day stand.

Artists going to Sun City justify themselves by claiming on the one hand that they are not political and on the other that they are not performing in South Africa but in an independent country. They choose to ignore the fact that Bophuthatswana's independence is entirely unrecognized outside South Africa and is rejected by the majority of South Africans.

The big bucks have drawn well-known American stars to Sun City. These include Millie Jackson, Cher, The Beach Boys, Glen Campbell and Linda Ronstadt.

Audiences are not officially segregated at Sun City. But the cost of the more expensive tickets often makes this the de facto reality. Liza Minnelli performed her opening night to a crowd of 4,500 people, of which about 200 were black. There was only one black face in the most expensive seats—the rest were high up in the auditorium in seats that sold for $13.00. And Southern Sun, which owns the hotel, admitted to giving tickets to blacks free. It does this not out of generosity but so that artists do not perform to all-white audiences. "I don't mind about anything except that I'm playing in front of mixed audiences," said Liza Minnelli, ignoring the fact that by performing there she was helping apartheid score propaganda points.

Sun City, sometimes called Sin City, exists as it does largely because of the apartheid fiction of independence. Laws in South Africa which make it illegal to gamble or for a black and white to have sex together do not apply in Bophuthatswana. It is not unusual for white men to come to Bophuthatswana to do what they cannot do in Johannesburg. This has led to a growth in prostitution. Apologists for Sun City suggest that this inter-race mixing will lead to changed attitudes of whites and thus to change in South Africa. But white men can go home to Johannesburg while black women must stay in the poverty of Bophuthatswana, and to suggest that casual integrated sex and black access to slot machines will break down the structures of apartheid is an insult to the long and costly struggle blacks have waged against the oppression of minority rule. . . .

The fact is that Sun City is controlled by political and economic interests that are part and parcel of apartheid. The Bophuthatswana government, which would not exist if it were not for apartheid, holds a minority interest in the resort, as do a number of South African companies. . . .

Not all performers have succumbed to the large sums offered to perform at Sun City. There is a growing list of those who have refused lucrative contracts, including Tony Bennett, Ben Vereen, Gladys Knight and the Pips, Elton John, Roberta Flack, The Kool (Newport) Jazz Festival and the Harlem Globetrotters. John McEnroe has twice refused million dollar offers to play in Sun City. As protests mount against those who do go to Sun City, the ranks of those who choose conscience over dollars will also surely grow.

23. THE BASIC HISTORICAL DECEPTION*

by JOHN C. LAURENCE

John C. Laurence is also the author of The Seeds of Disaster *(1968).*

To make the suggestion that much of the West's reporting of, and public comment on, the South African policy of apartheid takes place on an almost entirely superficial level is to invite strong reaction. After all, so many Westerners have been to South Africa, reported on apartheid at great length and even written books about it, that there does not appear to be much more to be said. But, in reality, there is. For the entire policy, and its central theme of dividing up South Africa into black "homelands" on one hand, and "white South Africa" on the other, is based on a deliberately fictionalized version of South African history. The fact that the West now largely accepts that counterfeit history, to such an extent that politicians and press alike now use South African propaganda terms such as "black homelands," "white South Africa," "black migrant labor" and so on, represents one of the most remarkable, worldwide propaganda successes in recent world history. . . .

The official version in brief is . . . that white and black reached South Africa at the same time, little more than three centuries ago, prior to which South Africa was largely or totally uninhabited; that black and white first met 500 miles east of Cape Town in 1770 as both groups were expanding; that they somehow settled quite different areas without conflict and without the whites taking any land that was originally black; that 87 percent of South Africa is therefore historically white because the whites were the first to settle it; and that the whites now generously allow the blacks to leave their homelands and work in the more prosperous areas—"white" South Africa. This is the moral justification of both the "black homelands" policy and of apartheid itself, which now claims that as the black majority never lived in any of the 87 percent of South Africa which is "white homeland," then the blacks have no right even to South African citizenship. . . .

The Historical Facts

Although the maps and statements of the all-white South African government quite clearly claim that the blacks, or Bantu as they will be specifically called now, did not enter South Africa until the seventeenth century A.D., they were

*From *Race, Propaganda and South Africa* (London, 1979).

in fact already settled in parts of South Africa by the tenth century A.D., and quite possibly even earlier.

Settlement by Africans of one kind or another over a good deal of what is now South Africa has been proved as far back as 20,000 years ago, but their exact description is uncertain. By very roughly 2,000 years ago, Africans of the Early Iron Age were settling extensively in South Africa, or were perhaps already there and were undergoing cultural changes as the first iron-smelting technologies filtered down from the north. There are clear cultural—and thus inevitably biological—links between these Early Iron Age peoples and those of the Later Iron Age, or Bantu, peoples whose increasingly widespread settlement of South Africa dates from at least 1,000 years ago. Thus the ancestors of most of the present-day Bantu inhabitants of South Africa—19½ million black South Africans in 1979—were already in South Africa 1,000 years ago, and some of these ancestors were there 2,000 or more years ago. . . .

Proof that there were Bantu in South Africa 1,000 years ago has, amongst other evidence, been clearly established by Scully and van der Merwe, writing in *World Archaeology* in October 1971. Their extensive research, backed by consistent radiocarbon datings, shows that the BaPhalaborwa tribe now living around the rich copper and phosphate deposits at Phalaborwa in the northern Transvaal had been living there continuously since at least 960, had been experienced miners with sophisticated smelting techniques, and had enjoyed a good and varied diet. (Today, the rich mineral deposits are classed by the government as part of the "traditional white South African homeland," despite the existence of many ancient Bantu mining tunnels up to 50 feet deep.)

Scattered across the Transvaal and Orange Free State "white homelands" of South Africa are hundreds of stone-walled, Bantu-built settlement sites, many of them dated to more than 900 years ago. One of them, a smelting furnace radiocarbon dated to 1060, is actually inside a "whites-only" Johannesburg inner suburb, Melville Koppies, and is almost on top of the Main Gold Reef, which white South Africa claims belongs to whites because of "prior white settlement." . . .

Many of the Bantu stone-built sites across the northern half of South Africa are of similar date—as well as large numbers mainly from the thirteenth to fifteenth centuries A.D.—and known to have been built by the Sotho and Venda peoples who have ever since then formed a substantial part of the South African population. . . . In June 1552—exactly 100 years before the first white settlement—the Portuguese vessel *San Joao* was wrecked on the Pondoland coast, 150 miles south of where Durban now stands. The survivors' diaries record that they met "very black" Africans who spoke in a clicking tongue: a description which fits only Bantu. Yet as recently as April 1977 the South African Education Department's magazine *Bantu* was still putting forward the long-discredited official version of history, as the basis of history teaching in black schools and colleges in South Africa. . . .

The reality, according to the professional historians, is that by then [the Great Trek of Boers in the 1830s] roughly half of South Africa had long been settled by Bantu. (And so it is fair to suggest that these areas, half the country, by the South African government's own definition are the true "black home-lands.") Yet when the whites arrived, the rest of South Africa, was by no means empty. Roughly south of center were the Bushmen, and the southern-most portion in the west had been settled by the Hottentots[1] for many centuries beforehand. Far from being "totally uninhabited," South Africa was fully inhabited, with perhaps a million brown and black people already there. In contrast, an official assessment as late as 1810 showed that even then, there were barely 30,000 whites in the whole of South Africa.

Three facts are thus fully established. The whites were by far the latecomers in South Africa. Whether one's point of reference is the time of the first white settlement in 1652 or the time of the major black/white contacts a century later, the blacks occupied a good one-half of South Africa before the whites arrived. And blacks have always greatly outnumbered whites in South Africa —so it is thus by definition a black man's country rather than a white man's despite white propaganda claiming exactly the opposite [and intended to "jus-tify" the Bantustan Policy], which actually gives each white, on average, 28 times more land—and its underlying mineral wealth—than each black.

Epilogue: Impact of South African Propaganda

The evidence that the papably untrue version of South Africa's history specifi-cally favored by the South African government has indeed been spread throughout the world, and is now in many influential quarters accepted as the truth, is not hard to find. The innocent believers of such propaganda are from all walks of life. As long ago as 1963, the October issue of the South African edition of the *Reader's Digest* carried part of the all-white government's ver-sion of history in an article pleading for "more time" for South Africa, written by a U.S. presidential adviser.

In more recent years, there is the interesting statement in the superbly produced 330-page coffee-table book *What About South Africa* (1971) that when the first white settlers landed at Table Bay in 1652, apart from "a few nomadic Hottentots . . . this fabulous country lay undisturbed by human inhabitants." The South African government bought 150,000 copies of this

---

[1] Modern scholars now use the indigenous words Khoikhoi for the Hottentot and San for Bush-man, the displaced terms having acquired derogatory overtones.

publication and mailed it free to influential politicians, industrialists, journalists and opinion-formers throughout the world. . . .

[In 1971] the British bank, Barclays DCO of London, was telling its British customers and shareholders in its glossy, full-colored booklet, "Emigrating to South Africa," that "The Bantu moved south into what is now South Africa, arriving there at about the same time as the first whites were establishing themselves at the Cape."

In its June 1973 issue *Armed Forces Journal International,* an influential American magazine circulated to armed-forces chiefs throughout the free world and extensively circulated within the Pentagon, carried a special fifteen-page supplement on South Africa. The introductory article, "A Policy of 'Separate Development,' " quoted white South Africans as saying, "Our ancestors arrived in this country (South Africa) to find vast, undeveloped areas that were virtually unpopulated. . . . The Bantu came later, attracted partly by the prosperity and security created by white vigor and industry."

Of this claim that the whites actually arrived in South Africa before the Bantu, the magazine commented in parenthesis: "The South Africans are historically correct here. Settlers in South Africa found only a few stone-age bushmen and Hottentots . . . the Bantus began arriving in what is now South Africa about the same time or a little later for the most part." The magazine gratefully acknowledged the source of this information as "the South African embassy in Washington.". . .

On 12 December 1974, as remarked on earlier, the British Broadcasting Corporation's BBC-2 TV program broadcast, in the interests of "balance," an official South African government film, *Black Man Alive.* This included the government's version of South Africa's racial history, with an animated map which showed black and whites arriving at about the same time, with the blacks avoiding the Transvaal areas where their pre-white ruins have for years been known to abound. As far as can be established, although the BBC has thus shown the untrue version of South Africa's history, it has never in any similar peak listening time shown the true version.

Visitors to South Africa are apparently unwittingly indoctrinated with the official version of history—sometimes in an extreme form—on the spot. In the book *The Other Side of the Coin—a Visit to South Africa* (1976) by Patience Strong is the interesting statement: "The Bantu . . . were not indigenous. They came after the Dutch and the British." A similar version is found in Alan Drury's *A Very Strange Society* (1968). And many books published in South Africa for worldwide consumption carry much the same story. "Bantu tribes from Central and East Africa invaded South Africa at the time when Europeans landed at the Cape," asserts the privately published *State of South Africa Year Book* (note that blacks "invade," but whites merely "land"), in issue after issue. Unsolicited free copies of this book have been received year after year by influential politicians and industrialists throughout the world. The source of such generosity is unknown. Professional historical works which refute the South African government's historical claims for the "homelands" policy and apartheid itself include: *Mapungubwe* by Prof. L. Fouche (1968), *The Pre-History of the Transvaal* by Prof. R. Mason (1962), *Southern Africa in the Iron Age* by Prof. B. Fagan (1965), *The Oxford History of South Africa,* Vol. I (1969), and *The Journal of African History,* the leading professional journal on the subject. See in particular Vol. XVIII, No. 2, 1977.

24. LIFE IN THE BANTUSTANS—FORCED BUSING AND QWAQWA: VEST-POCKET STATE*

by JOSEPH LELYVELD

Joseph Lelyveld has twice served as The New York Times *correspondent in South Africa and is currently foreign editor of that paper.*

Forced Busing

. . . [T]he population explosion in KwaNdebele, unlike the wider world, has little to do with breeding and practically everything to do with apartheid. In a period in which South Africa is alleged to be changing and phasing out apartheid, the expansion of [the bus company] Putco into the *bundu,* or bush, of the homeland provides as accurate a measure as can be found of the real thrust of change. The bus company had to draw its own maps, for its new routes were on roads that had just been cut; its buses came in right behind the bulldozers. In 1979 Putco started to run two buses a day from Pretoria to the resettlement camps of KwaNdebele. By 1980 there were 66 a day, which jumped to 105 in 1981; to 148 a day in 1981; then 220 a day in 1983 and 263 a day in 1984, when the government was expected to pay Putco a subsidy of $26.5 million to keep its buses rolling to the homeland. That worked out to about $25 a head a week, more than $1,000 for each "commuter" a year: a negative social investment that went up in gas fumes when it might just as easily have gone into new housing for the same black workers nearer the industrial centers if that had not violated the apartheid design. It was the price the white government was willing to pay—and go on paying, year after year —to halt the normal process of urbanization. The KwaNdebele bus subsidy

*From *Move Your Shadow: South Africa, Black and White* (New York, 1985).

—the government's largest single expense in the development of this homeland —was higher than the KwaNdebele gross domestic product. This is basic apartheid economics. It had to be so high because KwaNdebele, a state supposedly on the way to independence, was utterly devoid of a productive economy or resources. The racial doctrine sets the priorities: First you invent the country; then, if you can, an economy. In the meantime, there are the buses to carry the homeland's citizens to jobs in the nearest industrial center. In KwaNdebele's case that meant Pretoria, which is fifty-five miles distant at the homeland's nearest point. . . .

. . . I was not prepared for the visual shock of what Kwaggafontein had become in two and a half years. It was no longer just a spot in a rash of "closer settlements." Now it was a part of a nearly continuous resettlement belt. You drove through the Pretoria suburbs and then through more than forty miles of rich farm country before you hit it; then you could drive another forty miles, and it was seldom out of sight: a serpentine stream of metal shanties and mud houses the metal roofs of which were typically weighted down by small boulders to keep them from blowing off in the Transvaal's violent hailstorms. Such sights can be seen in other countries, usually as a result of famines or wars. I don't know where else they have been achieved as a result of planning. The hillside where the Ndulis had been dropped was now as densely settled as Soweto. It no longer looked like a hillside. What it had become was a slight swell in a sea of shanties. I turned off the highway there and followed a dirt road for five miles to see how far into the *bundu* the settlement now extended. This brought me to a place called Frisegewacht that seemed to be near the homeland's outer edge, for when I looked past the last shanty to the next rise, all I could see was open, unspoiled, empty grassland belonging to a white cattle farmer.

At Frisegewacht I met a man who had to get to work at a munitions factory in Brits by seven in the morning. The man was not an Ndebele by ethnic origins but a Swazi, and he had not been put here by GG [i.e., official government trucks]. He had come after being expelled from a white farming area because the Swazi homeland was too remote from any possibility of employment. Here at least he could live with his family. He was earning $85 a week, an unusually high wage for a black industrial worker, but he had a desperate problem. He was regularly late to work in Brits, which was on the other side of Pretoria, a distance of nearly 100 miles by road from where he lived, because the first Putco bus often didn't reach Frisegewacht until four-fifteen in the morning. His white supervisor—who lived, of course, in Brits—was not interested in excuses, so his job was in jeopardy. To be on the safe side, what he really needed, he said, was a bus that would come at three-thirty. As we chatted, a blue Putco bus came around the bend on a dirt track. Here we were, out in the veld, about 75 miles from Pretoria, more than 5 miles from the nearest highway. It would not have seemed much more incongruous to find a red London Transport double-decker there.

I asked the man who worked in Brits what time he got home. That depended, he said, on whether the Putco driver was willing to go to the last stop at Frisegewacht. Sometimes the driver turned around a couple of miles away, obliging his passengers to walk. On those nights, he said, he seldom got home before ten. On a good day this "commuter" left at four in the morning and returned, seventeen hours later, at nine at night. Then, if he ate quickly and went straight to bed, he got five hours' sleep. The vista across the veld from Frisegewacht, when you faced in the direction of the white farmer's grazing land, was fine. The climate was undoubtedly salubrious. The man could live with his family, and he was not badly paid. But Frisegewacht had to be mentioned, along with the mine compounds and single-sex hostels, as part of the South African gulag. It was frightening in a different way from the more remote "closer settlements" I had visited where migrancy was the only possible answer to unemployment. The harsh conditions and barrenness of such places, the absence of any visible economy, seemed to portend a breakdown in the system. Or so a visitor could imagine. But Kwaggafontein and Frisegewacht were actually taking root. Their black inhabitants, by their capacity for sheer endurance, were rescuing a seemingly harebrained scheme concocted by white ideologues and making it durable. There were little signs of commerce that I noticed as I drove back to the highway: shops selling groceries, meat, and even building materials, all trucked in from the white areas. Some of the shanties, hovels no longer, had been handsomely improved. For blacks in more remote areas, Kwaggafontein could represent a thin ray of economic possibility, a way out of the maze created by government regulations. GG no longer had to dump them here. Responding to heavy pressures and tiny incentives, they were coming on their own.

Wage earners, after all, lived here. They had cash in their pockets, and they were capable of turning a "closer settlement" whose reasons for being were strictly abstract into something like a community. In Pretoria, I was told, KwaNdebele was viewed with pride as a tremendous success for the racial planners: an answer to the problem of migrant labor, developed from nothing in little more than a decade. Blacks didn't want to live in towns, a high official told a friend of mine. They were much happier with their own kind out in the bush. The Afrikaans term he used was *doodgelukkig* ("dead happy"). That seemed singularly apt for emergent KwaNdebele, a nation of sleepwalkers.

To catch the first Putco bus from the Wolverkraal depot in KwaNdebele, the photographer David Goldblatt and I calculated, we would have to leave the Bundu Inn (a white hostelry that went "international" after finding itself in a homeland) no later than one-thirty in the morning. It is then that Kwa-

Ndebele's first "commuters" start to stir. Wolverkraal was even farther from Pretoria than Kwaggafontein or Frisegewacht. The black settlers of the new state who boarded the bus near there had to ride about 95 miles before transferring to local buses that would take them to factories where they worked, in areas where they were forbidden to live. That meant a minimum of 190 miles every working day in buses designed with hard seats for short hauls on city streets. They were fortunate in a sense—they did have work— but they were spending up to eight hours a day on buses. The distance they traveled annually, I calculated, came to more than a circumnavigation of the globe.

The Putco depot was just a fenced-off clearing in the bush with a tiny shack for the dispatcher and nothing else: no floodlights, no time clocks, no coffee machines, no grease pits. Rain during the night had cleansed the air and drained a layer of clouds that had glowered over the veld at sundown, leaving a light breeze and a full moon to limn the hulks of the ranked buses. I counted fifty-two of them. Two others, I was told, had left the yard at one in the morning to round up the drivers who stayed in nearby "closer settlements." One of these staff buses had then got stuck in the mud, so Putco was going to be a little behind schedule this morning in KwaNdebele. The engine of the other staff bus, which had rescued the stranded drivers, was the first night sound I heard.

It was about twenty past two when the lights inside the buses at the depot started to blink on one by one. Number 4174, which we boarded after being told that it would be the first out of the yard, had one bulb glowing dimly inside a red globe, another in a green globe, casting together an eerie light into a gloom made stygian, despite the clear night outside, by the coating of caked mud on the bus's windows. A sign near the cage in which the driver was encased declared that number 4174 was certified to carry 62 sitting passengers and 29 standing. I did another quick calculation. The fifty-two buses represented roughly one-fifth of the homeland's daily convoys to the white areas; the number of "commuters" who were thus being subsidized by South Africa to live beyond the pale—the pun was inadvertent but hard to erase—came to roughly 23,000 on the KwaNdebele run.

At two-forty in the morning, number 4174 left the depot and headed north and east, *away* from Pretoria, to pick up its first passengers at a place called Kameelrivier. In the Ndebele homeland, it seemed, all place-names were still in Afrikaans—the names, mostly, of the white farms the state had bought up in order to ghettoize the bush. The headlights showed six men and four women waiting patiently beside the dirt road, in what appeared to be the middle of nowhere, when the bus made its first stop, ten minutes late, at two-fifty. At that place and that hour, the sight of a couple of whites on the bus was as much to be expected as that of a couple of commuting walruses. Momentarily it startled the passengers out of their drowsiness. Once our presence was explained, it became possible to ask a few questions as the bus rattled to its next stop.

John Masango, the first man to board, said he worked six days a week at a construction site near Benoni, an industrial town forty miles on the far side of Pretoria, taking three buses each way. Even at the concessional rates arranged by the authorities for KwaNdebele, the total bus fares he paid out in a week gobbled up one-quarter of his wages. He was fifty-three years old, and on days when he was not required to work overtime, he could get back to Kameelrivier by eight-thirty at night. Only on Sundays did he ever see his home or his family in the light of day. Most nights, after washing, eating, and, as he put it, "taking care of family matters," he was able to get to sleep by ten or ten-fifteen. With four hours' sleep at home and a couple of hours' sleep on the bus, he managed to stay awake at work. It was important not to be caught napping; you could lose your job. While I was still thanking him for his patience, John Masango reached into a bag he was carrying and extracted a little rectangle of foam rubber about the size of a paperback book. He then pulled his blue knitted cap over his eyes and, leaning forward, pressed the foam rubber to the back of the seat in front of him; in the final step in this procedure, he rested his forehead against the foam rubber and dropped his hands to his lap. As far as I could tell, he was out like a light.

Emma Mokwena was on her way to a part-time job as a cleaning woman for an Afrikaner family called the Van der Walts who lived in one of the new suburban developments burgeoning on the veld between Pretoria and Johannesburg. She was expected at work by seven in the morning, in time to prepare breakfast for her employers, who rose to face the new day four and a half or five hours after she had to get up in KwaNdebele. She did not, however, have to serve the Van der Walts tea in bed, as live-in servants are often still expected to do in South Africa. She worked for them two days a week, for other families in the same suburb on other days. Usually she worked for seven hours, leaving at about two in the afternoon, in time to return to Kameelrivier to prepare dinner for her five children aged fourteen down to two and a half. In a month she earned about $120, of which a little more than $30 went in bus fares. It could have been worse, but fortunately her employers underwrote the $1.20 she spent each day getting from Pretoria to their homes and back. When she saw I was finished with my questions, Emma Mokwena pulled her blanket snug over her shoulders and unfolded the collar of her turtleneck sweater so it covered her face. She then leaned back in her seat, half-slumped against the woman with whom she had boarded, now similarly mummified.

By this time it was only three-twenty, and number 4174 had yet to reach the narrow ribbon of asphalt that connects KwaNdebele to Pretoria. But it had stopped by enough "closer settlements" to fill all its seats; anyone getting on beyond this point was bound to stand, not just this morning, but every morning in the week. There were still nearly two and a half hours to go to Pretoria. Thus some people *stood* on the bus nearly twelve hours a week. These calculations were beginning to make me more tired than the ride, which was grim enough, especially since I had lost my seat and was now standing, too, squeezed in next to a man who was managing to doze on his feet.

Another "commuter," a construction worker whose job was at a site in a section of Pretoria called Sunnyside, stood long enough to tell me that he had received several reprimands, each formally inscribed on his work record, for falling asleep on the job. This man represented a particularly telling example of the dramatic changes that have occurred in the lives of some South African blacks, for his family had been landowners in a "black spot" called Doornkop, from which they were expelled along with 12,000 others in 1969. The compensation his family got from a government that never ceases to profess its devotion to principles of private enterprise came to less than $300. The man smiled bitterly as he mentioned the figure. Then, excusing himself, he removed a folded piece of newspaper he had been carrying under his jacket and spread it neatly on the floor between his feet. Next, with the suppleness of a yogi, he collapsed himself into a seated position on the paper with his knees drawn up to his chin and dropped his head.

I looked around. Aside from the driver and one man who was smoking about four rows from the rear of the bus, David and I and a black Putco official who had graciously come along to run interference for us appeared to be the only persons out of more than ninety who had not now dozed off. The center aisle was packed with bodies wound around themselves like anchovies in a can. The motion of the bus threw some happenstance couples, men and women who got on at different stops, into intimate contract. A young woman's head slumped on the shoulder of the man seated next to her, who was too far gone to recognize his good fortune. Nearer the front a young man clutched restlessly in his sleep at the sleeping woman next to him. Some of the heads lolled backward, but most of the forms were bent forward like that of the man who carried the foam rubber. By three forty-five the bus had reached the highway, and the ride was now smoother. Their heads covered, blankets over their shoulders, the passengers swayed like Orthodox Jews in prayer. Or, in the eerie light of the two overhead bulbs, they could be seen as a congregation of specters, souls in purgatory.

Twice they were jostled into consciousness: once when number 4174 pulled off the highway onto the rough shoulder for a routine Putco checkoff; another time when the driver slammed on his brakes, barely missing a truck that had stopped by the side of the road as if to let him pass, then eased its way forward directly into our path. Shaken, our black driver got down to yell at the black driver of the truck. A small crowd gathered in the dark patch between the two sets of headlights. The truck driver expressed remorse. He had been giving a lift to three women, who were crowded into the cab of his truck with him, wrapped in blankets like the women on the bus, and asked the one who was nearest the window to tell him whether the coast was clear. Apparently without looking, she had mumbled something that he took to mean "go."

The first streaks of dawn showed on the outskirts of Pretoria. We saw plenty of blacks heading for work but no sign of white life as number 4174 proceeded through the first of several white neighborhoods until we came upon a jogger, a hyperventilating gray-haired man in his fifties wearing a T-shirt that had, stenciled on his chest in red as a greeting to all comers, including the passengers on a Putco bus, a blank "happy face" with a turned-up smile. Posters strung up on lampposts and trees by extremist white parties resisting the new constitutional proposals also seemed to mock the "commuters," who were excluded, in any case, from the supposed "new dispensation."

"Protect Our Future," the posters exhorted. "Remember Rhodesia."

It was October, and Pretoria's splendid jacarandas were in full blossom but seen from the vantage point of a black commuter bus, the sight left me indifferent. It was like looking at Bali or the Himalyas in tourist posters for holidays you would never take. It was only a few moments now until we turned into Marabastad, once a teeming black residential neighborhood at the very edge of Pretoria's downtown, at present a stretch of razed, overgrown real estate lying as a no-man's-land between the capital's commercial center and a tiny enclave of Indian-owned shops adjacent to the terminus where the buses from KwaNdebele disgorge their black passengers. Number 4174 ended its ride there at five-forty, exactly three hours after it had begun in the *bundu* at the Wolverkraal depot.

This left us leeward of a lavish new temple of apartheid: a combination rail and bus terminus called the Belle Ombre station, which will function one day, according to the dreams of the social engineers who do South Africa's long-range planning, as the hub for a series of bullet trains to the homelands. The first of these, a high-speed rail line into the nearest section of Bophuthatswana, had just begun operation, bringing back to Marabastad on a daily basis many of its old residents, or their descendants, in the status of aliens. At a quarter of six in the morning, there was piped music at the Belle Ombre station to cheer the homeland blacks on their way. A high-pitched pavilion with airy esplanades and structural piping painted in bright primary colors, the station seemed to exert a gravitational pull that sucked the groggy KwaNdebele "commuters" down its ramps to waiting Putco buses that would carry them on the next stage of their journeys to work.

Qwaqwa: Vest-Pocket State

The land set aside for human habitation in mountainous Qwaqwa, scarcely twenty-five square miles, filled up with nearly a quarter of a million people in a decade of resettlement. Supposedly the homeland for two million southern Sothos—the dominant black group in the Orange Free State, where blacks still outnumbered whites by more than three to one and where they haven't been permitted to own land for more than a century—Qwaqwa then had something like 88 percent of its nominal population living outside its borders. Even so, its overpopulation seemed so conspicuous and unnatural when I came upon this apparition of shanties and hovels for the first time—after driving for several hours through scenic national parks and open grazing land in and adjacent white area that looked like Idaho or Montana—that I found myself groping for Oriental comparisons. Did it remind me of Peshawar? Could Yemen look something like this? With level land fast running out near Phuthaditjhaba, the government center and capital of this vest-pocket state, newcomers were finding it necessary to hack their building sites out of steep slopes. For an hour or so, I experimented with taking pictures of these hillside settlements, hoping to get an image that conveyed the hivelike density of the place, but gave up in frustration. One picture of mud houses squeezed together in a barren landscape looked more or less like another. It wasn't the houses themselves that accounted for the overwhelming sense of abandonment and claustrophobia that you might expect to find in a refugee camp; it was the accumulation, the totality of them, with little in the way of a visible, supporting economy. It required a panoramic shot with a precise depth-of-field calculation, which was beyond my competence. And it required the immediate contrast of white South Africa, in all its plentitude and spaciousness, next door. How else could you make an image of exclusion?

I was still trying to put my finger on what it was that made this encampment masquerading as a nation seem so apparitional when I found in the waiting room of the chief minister in Phuthaditjhaba a bound volume of learned papers entitled *Ontwikkeling in Qwaqwa* ("Development in Qwaqwa"). The papers had been delivered at an "interdisciplinary," not to mention interracial, conference that had been held for black and white officials in the new homeland capital under the auspices of the University of the Orange Free State. Achieving a level of self-parody, it was a sublime example of the ability of white South Africans to blind themselves to the visible consequences of the policies they support, a kind of political double bookkeeping in which the tax evader seeks to make sure that the taxpayer's money is not wasted. Here was a group of Afrikaner academics worrying about the problems of "nation building" in a minuscule country that had no existence at all before 1974, except as a remote reserve for two obscure tribal clans. Now, as a result of the white government's resettlement efforts, it had blossomed before their eyes as a full-fledged "LDC" (less developed country). They had grown it themselves in their own social hothouse, and now whatever the World Bank had to say about Bangladesh or Gunnar Myrdal once said about India could be said by them about Qwaqwa. So I found a certain S. F. Coetzee pointing to the danger of "the high population growth rate in the LDCs" and "the high unemployment rate in the LDCs," as if these provided an explanatory context for "a developing country such as Qwaqwa." Unemployment, he tells us gravely, "is causal to a new phenomenon, to wit the so-called 'marginal men' or people who, due to their situation of unemployment, are not concerned with the community at large and therefore also not with development." P. H. du Preez painstakingly diagrams a community development program to bridge this gap. Qwaqwa, it appears, requires "initiators" to form "nuclear groups" that will then be responsible for the "activation" of "normative transformation in a non-directive manner." P. H. du Preez, identified as an employee of the Department of Cooperation and Development in Pretoria, which runs the resettlement programs, extracts a potentially subversive thought from the American sociology texts he is plagiarizing. "Responsible freedom," he says, "can only be realized in a democratic community."

There are a few paradoxes here, obviously, that he has to steer around. Most of Qwaqwa's nominal population lives outside its borders, where black "initiators" who encourage "activation" usually get into trouble. For reasons he does not mention, "responsible freedom" appears to be available only in an indigent community formed by uprooted people living on the earnings of absentee realties, and these absentees remain "marginal men" even when employed because they are legally barred from citizenship where they work. If P. H. du Preez dissociated like this in private life, he would be judged severely neurotic. But in South Africa it is possible for a white to earn a respectable living lecturing on community development and participatory democracy to black refugees from communities that have been destroyed by arbitrary laws enacted by whites, without blacks having had the slightest say.

The chief minister, a former school inspector named Kenneth Mopeli who had a photograph of South Africa's white president hanging over his desk, was also dissociating a bit. His distress became evident when, interrupting his account of the efforts his white advisers made to coax him to seek independence for Qwaqwa, a black aide entered the room and handed him a folded note with a look of great urgency. The chief minister read the note and scowled.

"I am very shocked," he said reprovingly. "I can see you are one of those foreign journalists who come to South Africa with preconceived ideas to write one-sided articles. It says here that you were taking pictures of poor houses and shanties."

I said there were certainly lots of shanties in Qwaqwa but I hadn't been focusing on the worst of them, only trying to take pictures that showed the density of population in his state. Some of the mud houses, I added, venturing to placate him, seemed to have been lovingly improved. Yes, there was poverty, the chief minister now acknowledged, but there were also some "points of light." He said the phrase first in Afrikaans, then translated. For instance, there were the eight houses the South African government had built for himself and members of his Cabinet at a coast of more than $1 million. When I said I would be happy to visit and photograph them, the chief minister became less tense. "Leaders should live in houses their people can be proud of," he said. There was now an uneasy, defensive note in his voice. Giving him the benefit of the doubt, I guessed that he was repeating a rationalization he could not entirely accept.

Phuthaditjhaba's ministerial mansions were on top of a hill, with a commanding view of resettlement blight and nearby mountains, including the flat-topped mesa, a near replica of Cape Town's Table Mountain, which gives Qwaqwa its name and stands as a symbolic barrier to white South Africa. There was a gate and a guardhouse at the only gap in the chain-metal fence surrounding the compound. Each residence came with a high alpine gable and a three-car garage. A swimming pool and a tennis court were under construction. Across a ravine that was filled with shanties there was another compound, visible through the fence, with a fence of its own and houses that were noticeably less opulent. This was the segregated enclave for the white officials who advised the Qwaqwa Cabinet. I was encouraged to wander through the chief minister's residence; then, preoccupied by two questions, I stood for a time on a rear patio where empty pint-size whiskey and brandy bottles were accumulating in a small pile. One question was what would happen to Qwaqwa and, specifically, these absurd mansions if the South African system ever collapsed. A decent successor regime, I speculated, could turn them into an old-age home, a mental institution, or a center for rural development; a nasty regime would take them over for local party and military leaders, in which case their purpose would not have greatly changed. The other question was more difficult. I couldn't decide whether I was right in my initial instinct to impute cynical motives to the white advisers who offered mansions and Mercedes cars to black homeland leaders they had cultivated and advanced. Perhaps it wasn't cynicism but zany, self-exposing idealism, really doing unto others what they would have others do unto them. Perhaps they needed to believe that this was what "nation building" was all about or that since people expect their leaders to live in big houses, the reverse can also hold true: that they'll accept as their leaders whoever is put in the only big houses they can see. Perhaps, I thought gloomily, they weren't entirely wrong. . . .

Chapter VI:

HEALTH AND EDUCATION

25. *HEALTH IN APARTHEID SOUTH AFRICA**

by AZIZA SEEDAT

A South African doctor, Aziza Seedat lives in exile in West Germany.

Overview

A country's basic health services are judged on two main criteria: the infant mortality rate and the life expectancy of its population.

A study of the health situation in South Africa reveals two distinct patterns of diseases for black and white people respectively. White South Africa has a pattern similar to that found in the developed countries: a low infant mortality rate (14.9 per 1,000 live births in 1978—similar to that in Britain) and a long life expectancy (64.5 years for white males and 72.3 for females for the period 1969–71). (The infant mortality rate measures the number of babies who die before their first birthday, not including those stillborn.)

Black South Africans, particularly Africans, have a health pattern similar to that of underdeveloped countries: high infant mortality rates and low life expectancies. It has been estimated that in some rural parts of South Africa, between 30 and 50 per cent of children die before their fifth birthday. In May

*From Crippling a Nation: Health in Apartheid South Africa (London, 1984).

169

1983, the infant mortality rate among Africans in Worcester, Cape Province, was reported to be 550 per 1,000.

Official figures of life expectancy for Africans have not been available since 1945–47 when the life expectancy for an African male was 36 years and that for a female, 37. At the time, this was 20 years less than the life expectancy of whites. Life expectancy figures have not been available since then because it has not been compulsory for Africans to register births or deaths, and authoritative demographic figures cannot be compiled.

The latest available official estimates give Africans life expectancies of 51.2 for males and 58.9 for females, for the period 1965–70, and an infant mortality rate of 100–110 per 1,000 live births for the year 1974.

It has been estimated that at least 50,000 deaths among black people annually are not registered. These occur mainly in the rural areas. Birth statistics for Africans are not published by the government. One consequence of the "independence" of the bantustans is that it becomes even more difficult to obtain statistics to cover them, while figures for "South Africa" (i.e., excluding the "independent" bantustans) conceal the true incidence of disease.

Official life expectancies for the years 1969–71 for Coloureds are 48.8 years for males and 56.1 for females, and for Indians, 59.3 for males and 63.9 for females. . . .

Because of the high standard of medical care for its white citizens, South Africa is often regarded as a country with a good health service. The now defunct South African Department of Information (in the late 1970s the center of a huge scandal involving dubious undercover activities and the secret use of vast amounts of state funds) published many books and glossy magazines presenting a favorable picture of South Africa, including its health services. . . .

However, if this propaganda is carefully scrutinized, it will be revealed to be a mixture of truths, half-truths and some outright lies. Photographs are carefully posed and selected. For example in 1977 the Department of Information published a pamphlet entitled *The Health of the People* including a full page color picture of an African patient on renal dialysis at Baragwanath Hospital—suggesting that such treatment was readily available for blacks.

Another distortion is the statement that "all the health services are available to all the inhabitants of the Republic irrespective of race, colour or religion" or the statement by a South African diplomat on BBC television that "we have only a few cases of malnutrition."

Furthermore, South African propaganda never compares facilities available for blacks in South Africa with those for whites in South Africa, but instead compares facilities available for blacks in South Africa with those for blacks elsewhere in Africa, and in so doing actually juggles with statistics to deceive the reader. For example, in *Health and Healing,* another pamphlet issued in 1969 by the Department of Information in Pretoria, figures are given for the ratio of the number of doctors per population in South Africa, but these are figures for *all* population groups combined. If the figures of the ratio of serving doctors to population are given for the different groups separately, it will be found that there are fewer serving black doctors per head of the black population than in any of the other African states mentioned, with the exception of Burundi, Chad, Rwanda, Upper Volta and Dahomey—countries much poorer than South Africa.

Figures for infant mortality quoted tend to be the very lowest figures. For example, *Health and Healing* has the figure of 68 per 1,000 for Soweto in 1968, but not mentioned is the figure of 269 per 1,000 for the previous year in Port Elizabeth. Other unreliable information is contained in the 1970 issue of *Report from South Africa,* another official publication. This cites a figure of 23,000 for the number of "Bantu nurses." Two years later, in April 1972, the figure was only 11,000 according to the same official magazine. . . .

. . . South Africa is a highly industrialized and wealthy country, but the ill-health of its black population, suffering from the diseases of poverty, malnutrition and deprivation, serves as a damning indictment of the apartheid regime.

Malnutrition and Infant Mortality

Malnutrition is the single biggest killer of black children in South Africa. One of the myths propagated by the South African government is that although poverty is a factor, "ignorance," "bad eating habits," "superstition" and "taboos" are largely to blame. The truth of the matter is that in the face of grinding poverty it is simply impossible to obtain enough of the right kind of food for adequate nutrition. . . .

The main diseases of malnutrition are kwashiorkor and marasmus. Kwashiorkor has been described as the most severe nutritional disease known. It characteristically follows weaning and results from a diet grossly deficient in milk and other high protein foods. There may be an associated deficiency of vitamins and calories. Marasmus is the childhood equivalent of starvation. It has its onset in the first year of life when supplementary feeding is not provided. It is due to a severe deficiency of calories together with some deficiencies in protein.

Incidence of Malnutrition

In *Health and Healing,* a South African government information pamphlet, it is stated that "kwashiorkor . . . was proclaimed notifiable in South Africa so that a clear picture of its incidence and distribution might be obtained." The figures that are given for the incidence of kwashiorkor amongst Africans from 1963 (15,477) to 1967 (9,765) suggest that it has declined.

Kwashiorkor in fact ceased to be a notifiable disease in 1967. The last official figures published for that year were: whites seven cases, Indians 12, Coloureds 1,046 and Africans 9,765 cases. When questioned as to whether kwashiorkor would again be declared a notifiable disease, the Minister replied that it would not. The reason given was that the notifications of kwashiorkor were "unreliable" due to the different interpretations of the diagnostic criteria in this field.

Medical and nursing staff throughout the black hospitals in South Africa, however, both urban and rural, report incidences of malnutrition of almost epidemic proportions. Their findings are confirmed by other sources. . . .

A survey conducted by the South African Institute of Race Relations in 1978 revealed that 50 percent of all two- to three-year-old children in the Ciskei were malnourished. . . .

Staff at a Bophuthatswana hospital serving a population of 100,000 people claimed in 1980 that as many as 40 percent of deaths were due to malnutrition. They estimated that 50,000 children would probably die directly or indirectly of malnutrition in the rural areas of South Africa and that a further 100,000 children's lives were at risk. . . .

Such news items are not uncommon in South Africa. The problem is long-standing and unchanging. During the 1980s, however, the situation has been aggravated by the worst drought that South Africa has experienced for two centuries—a drought that has not only affected South Africa but neighboring countries as well. In April 1983 the head of the Department of Paediatrics at the University of Natal, Professor Allie Moosa, claimed that South Africa's current death toll from malnutrition stood at 30,000 a year, or three to four an hour—the vast majority of the victims being children. His appeal to the South African government to take preventative action, however, met with little positive response. The Minister of Health, Dr. C. V. van der Merwe, said that responsibility for the high toll of dying children should be shared by those people who continued to "multiply uncontrollably." . . .

Infant Mortality

A survey in 1979 demonstrated the following:

- Mortality rates for both African and Coloured children aged one to four years were 13 times as high as for whites.
- The majority of deaths occurred in children under five years of age.
- Deaths below one year were six times higher among Africans and Coloureds than among whites.

. . . .

The South African government does not itself publish national figures for infant mortality rates among Africans. The only figures available, other than estimates, are those compiled by Medical Officers of Health in the main urban areas. These indicate infant mortality rates ranging up to over 300 deaths per 1,000 live births in certain areas. The latest available government estimate for the whole country (excluding the "independent" bantustans) is 100–110 per 1,000 live births, for the year 1974.

· ·

National infant mortality rates for the other population groups in 1978 were: white 14.9 per 1,000, Coloured 80.6 per 1,000 and Indian 25.3 per 1,000.

The high infant mortality rates among black South Africans occur in a country that, by comparison with the great majority of independent African countries, has a booming economy and prides itself on being a major exporter of food. In the early 1960s thousands of tons of surplus fruit and bananas were dumped to rot, 4,000 lbs of butter were exported to Britain at a loss, and 23 million bags of maize were in storage awaiting export. In 1976 the Dairy Board reported that farmers in Bloemfontein were pouring more than 10,000 liters of milk down the drain daily. In 1971, under the headline "Too much Food —South Africa's Dilemma," a newspaper report revealed that surplus milk powder was being fed to animals and that eggs were exported at a loss. . . .

Hospitals

In general white patients have better access to better facilities—less crowded hospitals, speedier referral, better equipped surgeries and so on. With few exceptions, all facilities are segregated, those for whites being amongst the best in the world and those for blacks being greatly inferior.

Some visiting doctors from abroad appear to be unaware of these discrepancies and praise conditions that their own patients and staff at home would find intolerable. Facilities at Baragwanath Hospital in Soweto, for example, have often been cited as an example of the superior medical care enjoyed by South African blacks compared to their counterparts elsewhere in Africa. . . .

Baragwanath Hospital is in fact acutely overcrowded. Situated on the edge of Soweto, it has an estimated 2,500 beds which, together with eight clinics, serve the whole of Soweto, estimated population more than one million. In its 1981–82 financial year, Baragwanath treated 112,000 in-patients and 1,620,-000 out-patients. In winter, bed occupancy in the medical and surgical wards can be up to 300 percent and 250 percent respectively. When a deputation from the Transvaal Provincial Council and the press visited the hospital in 1976 they found that "the situation at Baragwanath was one patient under the bed, two in the bed and two on the floor."

The photographs in official South African publications do not show the mattresses on the floor, the infants two to a cot, or the casualty department littered with patients sleeping on the floor or on hard wooden benches. Those on the floor include the acutely ill and injured, as well as the less seriously ill patients. Because of the critical shortage of beds, over 13,000 patients are discharged each year before their treatment is complete, according to Dr. van der Heever, the Superintendent of Baragwanath.

. . . Journalists who visited Ward 21 found that its 40 beds were occupied by 89 women and one child. Red stickers marked "Urgent" were stuck to the foreheads of critically ill patients and a doctor explained that "we have to do that. It's the only way we can indicate the urgency of a case. There are not enough doctors and too many patients to do things any other way here." Bedletters, giving the crucial medical and drugs history of each patient, often got lost in a confusion of movement as patients moved outside the wards during the day to give the doctors greater freedom to work inside. "Sometimes I haven't been able to find out what medication a patient was receiving," one doctor said. "People are not being treated properly here."

At night, when the patients all moved back into the wards, more than half slept on the floor. Doctors and nurses attending the sick had to step over bodies packing the spaces between and under the beds. "It is very hard for old grannies. If they have problems during the night we can't get to them easily. It is difficult to move," a nurse said. . . .

Appalling conditions were reported in the maternity unit at the Livingstone Hospital in Port Elizabeth in 1977, with women in labor lying two to a bed, on mattresses on the floor and on trolleys in the corridors. Meanwhile, there were empty beds in the white section of the hospital. Following the outcry, patients were accommodated in prefabricated buildings.

Five years and more later, pregnant women and those who had just given birth were still having to sleep two to a bed, or on the floor, at the Kalafong Hospital near Atteridgeville, Pretoria. Women in the maternity ward described it as a "squatter area," and said that the majority of inmates were sleeping on the floor with the same blankets they used before giving birth. Others claimed that they had to use blankets dirtied by other patients who had been discharged. . . .

Ambulance Apartheid

Ambulances, like other branches of the health services, are racially segregated. Such segregation persists despite the higher costs entailed by duplicating the service between population groups, and the risks to patients themselves when refused admission to ambulances, and hospitals themselves, on racial grounds.

Incidents of "ambulance apartheid" are described from time to time in the South African and overseas press. A particularly graphic account by a recent immigrant from Britain to South Africa was published in February 1983, for example:

> Walking home late at night through Hillbrow, Johannesburg, I came across a young white man dying from stab wounds.
> A black caretaker from a nearby block of flats was gently tending him.
> Alarmed by the ghastly wounds, I dashed to the nearest phone to call an ambulance.
> "Is he white?" inquired the woman with an Afrikaans accent on the end of the line.
> "The man is dying. What difference does his colour make?"
> "It depends which hospital we send an ambulance from," the woman replied.
> It shouldn't have shocked me—this is South Africa—but the cold face of apartheid *in extremis* chilled me into submission.
> I said the man was white and put the phone down.
> While waiting for the ambulance, I hailed a passing taxi and asked the driver to take the man to hospital.
> "What's the matter with him?" asked the Portuguese driver.
> "Two burglars stabbed him repeatedly in the face and neck with a screwdriver," I said.
> "Oh, he'll only get blood on my new seat covers."
> "But, for heaven's sake, the man is dying."
> "What colour is he?" the driver asked reluctantly.
> At that moment the ambulance arrived, ending this spirited debate on the Christian ethics of separate development.
> The ambulance had taken just four minutes, and the stabbed man's life was saved.
> Had he been black, an ambulance would have had to come from further away, lengthening the time of the journey and the odds on his survival.

Racial segregation in the health services means that patients often have to travel long distances to the nearest hospital catering for their population group. Some deaths inevitably result from the delays in initiating treatment. In theory, ambulance drivers are supposed to exercise their discretion in these matters, but in practice this seldom seems to happen. It is normal procedure for a driver to ascertain the population group of an injured person before setting out with an ambulance in response to an emergency call.

In July 1983, a nine-year-old African boy with serious head injuries resulting from a fall from the back of a farm lorry died after being refused admission to a hospital reserved for Indians. Zulinkosi Lindedu was taken to Northdale Hospital, north of Pietermaritzburg, after the accident on a nearby farm. He was refused admission and the farmer—himself an Indian—was told to take him to Edenvale Hospital, six miles away in the Kwazulu bantustan. The Northdale medical superintendent explained that the hospital was not allowed to admit Africans except in cases of "extreme emergency." Zulinkosi had seemed to be in a "stable condition."

Zulinkosi was taken to Edenvale in the farmer's pickup truck rather than an ambulance because, as a Northdale doctor explained, "it would have taken much longer to get an ambulance here than it takes to get from here to Edenvale by car." In the course of the journey, according to the farmer's son, the child went into a fit, and when he arrived at Edenvale was diagnosed as being in a critical condition. A white doctor ordered him to be transferred to Wentworth Hospital, Durban, 50 miles away, where there was a neurosurgical unit. Zulinkosi died the next day.

In August 1982, a month-long investigation in Balfour, southeast of Johannesburg, exonerated the town's ambulance service from any blame after an incident in which a black worker lay bleeding for five hours before being taken to hospital. The patient, Johan Botha, was given emergency treatment by a local doctor for serious open wounds caused by a drum of thinners exploding at the glass factory where he worked. The doctor then tried to arrange admission to hospital, but found that Balfour's black ambulance service was out of town. The company refused to allow Botha to be taken to hospital by car and eventually, after delay, an ambulance from a meat factory was used. . . .

In October 1982 the Johannesburg *Sunday Times* published a letter from a middle-aged woman, describing an incident outside a hotel in Maritzburg. The writer and her sister had gone to the aid of an African man trapped beneath a car. "I tried to get the white men around to lift the car off the man," she said. "They were disinclined to do so—many holding glasses in their hands. One told me: "Leave him, he smells. . . ."" The man was indeed grimy as well as being covered in blood.

"One man finally helped me and we lifted him onto the pavement while laughter rang out from the balcony of the hotel. I was told that the manager of the hotel had not phoned for an ambulance but had 'lodged a complaint with the police' about the incident." When the man was finally taken away in an ambulance the two women were told they would have to pay for this service.

26. RACISM AND EDUCATION IN SOUTH AFRICA*

by ERNEST F. DUBE

Professor Dube, a native of South Africa and member of the African National Congress, teaches at the State University of New York, Stony Brook.

The History of European-Influenced Education in South Africa

There is today a general agreement among South African educational historians that the European form of education was introduced into South Africa by missionaries and that the foundation of this form of education was laid by the Glasgow Mission Society in 1821. . . .

Prior to 1821, the ruling white settlers showed no interest in the education of any children, be they non-European or European, other than religious training. As a result of this lack of interest, the task of providing education for South African children fell into the hands of the missionaries, who used education as part of their method of African Christianization. As the missionary schools were the only schools available in South Africa (these schools were initially intended for African children and were built in mission stations located in African areas), white children who wanted education went to the mission schools, where they were taught the same lessons, by the same teachers, in the same classrooms with the African children.

The best-known school was set up by the Glasgow Mission Society in Lovedale, named after Dr. John Lovedale, the founder of the London Mission Society, who later became the chairman of the Glasgow Mission Society. . . .

In the early days of missionary-sponsored education, schools in South Africa were not segregated; that is, children of all "races" attended the same missionary schools. Only the dormitories and the eating facilities were segregated. . . .

By 1892 racism was clearly entrenched in the educational system. The reasons for this development are numerous. First, both the Afrikaans and English-speaking whites were displeased that missionaries had insisted on the legal rights for the Khoikhoi, Coloureds, and Africans. Since missionaries were playing an active part in the education of the Africans, white conservatives feared that integrated education would threaten white supremacy. Second, the settlers realized that educated Africans could bargain and choose from a range of employment opportunities and tended to have more resources than unedu-

*From *Harvard Educational Review* Vol. 55, No. 1 (February 1985).

cated Africans, or knew how to manage their resources better. Educated Africans were, therefore, not easy to satisfy with meager wages. Third, if Africans were given the best educational opportunities, they would compete with whites economically. Fourth, educating Africans in the same schools as whites would result in a multiracial society where whites would be minorities and, therefore, politically dominated by Africans. Whites believed that ignorance of Western political strategies among the Africans would dampen any quest for political liberation and prevent the traditional chiefs from publicizing to the international community the atrocities to which their people were being subjected.

School Segregation

School segregation as a stated policy began in Natal, a predominantly English-speaking colony which prided itself on its British heritage. A similar policy was adopted in the Cape region soon afterward. . . .

There seems to have been no other reason for introducing segregated schools in both the Cape and Natal other than racism. There was no argument presented to indicate friction between white and black children, nor was there any to indicate that black children were failing to learn as well as white children. Regarding the latter point, the existing evidence suggests equal competence. For instance, [one study of the origins of African education] cites Dr. James Stewart, a principal at Lovedale, who wrote that "excellent examination results were achieved by white and African students at Lovedale." Other evidence in support of equal competence of white and African children comes from Dr. R. H. W. Shepherd, also a principal at Lovedale, who wrote, "According to the records of the Cape Education Department between 1884 and 1886, Lovedale had 597 passes in Standards III, IV, and V, a higher number than was achieved by any of the 700 schools in the Colony. Its closest competitor was Wellington, a white girls' school with 411 passes." Although it might be argued that both Stewart and Shepherd were blowing their own horns, there can be no doubt that the majority of students at Lovedale were Africans, and therefore the larger number of successes were registered among African children. The effect of equal ability in school performance was seen by the colonialists as undermining the social perception of Africans as "inferior." Children who see firsthand the contradiction between social stereotypes and reality are not likely to embrace those stereotypes. The aim of segregation, then, was to prevent white children from learning of the true African ability directly through social intercourse at school. . . .

To reinforce racial stereotypes, in 1904 both the Cape and Natal enacted laws introducing compulsory education for all white children between the ages of seven and sixteen. The law was not extended to the nonwhites. Furthermore, in 1909, both the Afrikaaners and the English-speaking South Africans joined with the British in depriving nonwhite South Africans of a just say in the formation of the Union of South Africa. These laws barring nonwhite children were enacted before the formation of the Afrikaner Nationalist Party and long before the advent of the purified Nationalist Party of apartheid, the more radically conservative party which gained power in 1948 and which is the ruling party in South Africa today.

Native Education

The introduction of "Native Education," around 1920, for Africans in South Africa was a logical route to follow for a society that was already committed to racist practices. Its main purpose was to handicap African children with the introduction of an inferior syllabus, coupled with inadequate learning conditions and poorly educated teachers. These combined factors were intended to reinforce the existing belief of white superiority while simultaneously making African children believe that their lowly position in society was due to their inferior mental ability. Moreover, this system of education was intended to make both African and white children believe that they, by nature, have different destinies. Whereas segregated education was intended to impose mutual ignorance of each others' customs, values, and lifestyles upon white and African children, the curriculum for native education was designed to retard the intellectual development of Africans. . . .

In Natal, the argument for Native Education was less crude than that used in the Cape. In Natal, the government argued that English was a foreign language to African children and thus placed undue strain on their learning potentials. It was proposed that the mother tongue be used as a medium of instruction for African children in lower primary schools, with English taught as just another subject. At higher primary levels, English would be introduced as a medium of instruction and the mother tongue taught as just another subject. This argument was persuasive to many of the white people.

The most serious handicaps of Native Education, however, were the poorly trained teachers and the inadequate learning conditions for African children. The latter point was highlighted by Dr. O. D. Wollheim in his report on learning conditions under Native Education. By 1943 Wollheim was reported to have said:

> Native Education has been in appalling condition. . . . Buildings in most cases consist of tin shanties or wattle daub huts into which are crammed two or three times the number of pupils which the room should hold. The equipment is correspondingly pitiful. . . . The salaries paid to teachers are likewise appalling. . . . The teachers are

seriously overloaded, and one teacher will occasionally be found to be teaching from eighty to one hundred pupils in two or three different standards all in the same room.

. . . .

If the purpose of Native Education was to show concern for African children, why were these appalling conditions allowed? Why was there no improvement in school funding for African schools comparable to the funding for white schools?

Everything in Native Education supported the consolidation of racism in South Africa. Consider the following: African children had to be six years old to begin their schooling, while whites began at five years of age; African children had to spend two years in preschool before beginning their standardized primary education, compared to one year in preschool for white children; African children spent, on the average, thirteen years in school before qualifying for entrance to a university, while white children spent an average of only eleven years. The African children's syllabus was discontinuous, beginning with Native Education and then making a transition to general education, while the white children began with a syllabus that was continuous through to the university. Native Education failed to prepare Africans in mathematics and the physical sciences, while the white children had this foundation laid in lower primary classes which continued in higher primary grades. Finally, those African children who persevered and overcame the appalling conditions of the lower primary classes and who had also succeeded in making the transition into the upper grades found that their poor preparation deprived them of the possibility of continued studies in the physical sciences at university level.

Clearly, then, Native Education was intended to be "a road to nowhere" insofar as higher education was concerned. For most African children, all that was intended was that they should gain enough education to read labels and become better laborers.

Bantu Education

Native Education was introduced by whites with hidden aims. Bantu Education, by contrast, was introduced without any attempt at pretense. Its aims were clearly stated by its architect, Dr. Hendrik Verwoerd, then minister of Native Affairs under which the Department of Bantu Education was to be administered. When Verwoerd introduced the Bantu Education Bill before the all-white parliament in 1953, he opened the debate with an attack on missionary education, which he accused of teaching African children false expectations and directing them to "green pastures they would never be allowed to graze." African education, according to Verwoerd, must train and teach people in accordance with their opportunities mindful of the sphere in which they live. Furthermore, education must have its root entirely in the Native areas, Native environment, and in the Native community. The African, he thought, must be guided to serve his own community in all respects; there was no place for him in the European community above the level of certain forms of labor.

Clearly, Verwoerd had seen Native Education as not doing what it ought to do, which for him was to lower the Africans' expectations. There can be no clearer racist statement than Verwoerd's declaration of the aims of Bantu Education: Bantu Education was designed to meet labor demands of the growing secondary industries in South Africa. While Africans were needed for their labor, they were nonetheless made aware that they should aim no higher than certain forms of labor; they did not belong to the white community but to a separate group. Indeed, the Bantustans later were established as political entities.

Questions might now arise as to why the Afrikaners thought it necessary to introduce Bantu Education at all, and what Bantu Education was to achieve which Native Education had not. The problem with Native Education, insofar as the Afrikaner Nationalists were concerned, was that there were loopholes which could be exploited by Africans. One of those loopholes was that beginning in general education at Form II (corresponding to grades in the American system), Africans used the same syllabus as whites. The gap between the preparation Africans received in Form I under Native Education and the academic demands of general education in Form II could be overcome through trained and experienced teachers who adopted a sympathetic approach in teaching African children at this level. As it turned out, the missionary schools, in their competition for high results, began to recruit highly trained and experienced teachers, mainly from abroad. These teachers were joined by a growing number of newly qualified African teachers from Fort Hare University, who from their own personal experiences both understood the problems of the African child and approached their teaching tasks with a political commitment.

The combination of these two factors began to be noticed in the years 1945–1950 in matriculation results. African institutions in Natal—Mariannhill and Inkamana (both Catholic), Inanda Seminary, Adams College, and to a lesser extent, Pholela Institution—began to show excellent results. In Transvaal, St. Peters (an Anglican institution), Madibane High, and Orlando High also excelled. Similarly, in the Cape, Lovedale, Healdtown, Emfundisweni, and others produced excellent results. Since the examination for all students—whites, Africans, Coloureds, and Indians—was the same, taken at the same time, with the results published alphabetically by school in the same newspapers all over South Africa, it was possible to compare not only the schools but also the grades. Furthermore, since schools such as Mariannhill, Inkamana, Inanda, St. Peters, Lovedale, and Healdtown were not only competing very well with top white schools but were actually surpassing many of them, the African schools' success challenged the whites' image of superiority.

In order to prevent these embarrassing comparisons, the overtly racist system of Bantu Education was introduced. Teaching the Afrikaans language became compulsory and was raised to the level of English as a subject, even though Africans hated Afrikaans since they associated it with oppression. Unlike Native Education, which was introduced without any opposition from the Africans, Bantu Education was immediately met by strong opposition from parents and from the African National Congress, a liberation movement formed in 1912. In time, however, other issues became more important than Bantu Education. For instance, the restriction of movement among Africans had been extended to include women as well as men. Therefore opposition to Bantu Education was temporarily diverted. It was only to be taken up again by university students in 1959, when the apartheid principles involved in Bantu Education were extended to universities. . . .

The inferiority of education for African children under the Bantu Education system created in time a further and unexpected opposition—primary school and high school children rebelled. This was unexpected because, as previously mentioned, Bantu Education was intended to make African children accept their low position in society as divinely fated and not as a white social decision. In 1976 the Afrikaners introduced a policy whereby half of all subjects in secondary schools would be taught in Afrikaans. . . .

Since [the Soweto "student riots" in] 1976 the opposition to Bantu Education has continued to be led by children, thus creating a unique situation in which eleven-year-olds have been brought into government opposition. Between April and September 1984, more than 900,000 students have been involved in school boycotts over the issue of Bantu Education. Between August 20 and October 3, 1984, it was reported that 57 people died in South Africa, mainly children. In addition to this number, during early October, eight miners were shot dead by the police while they were exercising their legal right to strike when their demands were not being met by their employers.

The killing of children in 1976 led to a mass exodus of African children from South Africa to the bordering states of Tanzania, Mozambique, Zambia, and Angola. Most of these children, over a thousand of them, left home seeking to join *Umkhonto We Sizwe* (The Spear of the Nation), the military wing of the African National Congress (ANC). . . .

The exodus of so many children, from age eleven to young adulthood, caught the ANC unprepared. There were no arrangements for such a number, let alone for those so young. Most of these children left South Africa clearly intending to join the ANC freedom fighters. The ANC knew that the vast majority of them were either too young or politically unprepared for the tasks of the liberation army. The alternative was to get most of these children to school. The ANC was fortunate—so it believed initially—to find the Nigerian government prepared to take most of the children into its schools. The others were shared between Liberia, Lesotho, Botswana, and Swaziland. The ANC was, however, soon to discover that the South African children in Nigeria were experiencing a culture shock which they could not endure. To make matters worse, a government minister, who did not understand that these children were rebels and thus would find any imposition of authority unacceptable, tried to impose a student leader on them. When he left the hall where he had called them together to be addressed by this "leader," the students also left, en masse, to confront the ANC representative with a demand for tickets to go back to ANC headquarters in Lusaka, Zambia. The students had not come to the ANC office in Nigeria to plead but to serve an ultimatum: either give them tickets or they would walk to Lusaka—just as they had walked from South Africa to Botswana, Lesotho, and Swaziland.

As a result of the students' demands, the officials of ANC discovered for the first time that, although they had spoken of education in their Freedom Charter, they had never decided on the form that education would take. Since Zambia could not accommodate more than six hundred students all coming in at once, the alternative was to build a school for these South African children and others that might follow. The first thing the ANC officials did was to approach the governments in the Frontline States for land to build a school. Next, they established an education council to create a syllabus for the school. The first education council meeting took place in Tanzania on the site where the school was to be built. Since then, the council has met once a year to review the syllabus.

The Solomon Mahlangu Freedom College (SOMAFCO)

The school in Tanzania is named after Solomon Mahlangu, one of the African students who left South Africa after the June 16, 1976, student riots. Solomon Mahlangu was eighteen years old when he left home to join *Umkhonto We Sizwe* of the African National Congress. Together with two other comrades, he had returned to South Africa following their military training to establish bases inside the country. They were discovered by the security police and a gun battle ensued which left two civilians dead. Solomon and another comrade were captured.

Solomon's captured comrade was so beaten up and tortured that the South African court found him unfit to stand trial—he was judged insane. This meant that Solomon stood trial alone. Promises were made to him upon the condition that he denounce the ANC and accuse it of forcing him to enter their military camps and of indoctrinating him. He refused to do this and instead blamed the battle on apartheid. Even though Solomon was not accused of having killed the two civilians, he was accused of being an accomplice, and on April 6, 1979, at the age of twenty-one, he was the first freedom fighter to be sentenced to death and hanged. Throughout his ordeal Solomon displayed uncommon courage.[1] For this courage the ANC named its school in Tanzania after him. . . .

The major educational issues were resolved. First, English was to be the medium of instruction from kindergarten to matriculation. The reason for this was that there are five major languages in South Africa other than English, and a choice of one could lead to protest. Even if there were enough teachers to teach all African languages, there were not enough students to justify this. Second, it was decided that separation of mathematics and arithmetic was artificial and therefore unnecessary. Third, all students were required to take mathematics, English, the development of society, and the history of liberation struggle in South Africa. Optional subjects, such as biology, general science, geography, and agricultural science, were to be taught as well. Last, innovative teaching methods that were better suited to the learning styles of African children were developed. The SOMAFCO model was thought to meet the educational needs of African children more adequately than the racist systems that had existed before, and thus was adopted by the ANC as the most suitable prototype for further developments in education. . . .

27. BLACK EDUCATION IN SOUTH AFRICA*

by JOHN A. MARCUM

John A. Marcum, who served as Academic Vice Chancellor of the University of California at Santa Cruz from 1979 to 1984, headed a team of six senior U.S. university administrators who made an in-country study of South African higher education. The mission's findings are presented in Dr. Marcum's book, Education, Race, and Social Change in South Africa (1982).

. . . In *Apartheid and Education,* Peter Kallaway of the University of Cape Town discounts liberal initiatives for educational reform as a strategem to build an enlarged black middle class and integrate it into a basically unchanged and iniquitous political-economic system. Education is essentially a dependent variable, he argues, and schooling is a "mechanism of class domination."

---

[1] An example is his message to his mother on her last visit before his execution: My blood will nourish the tree which will bear the fruits of freedom. Tell my people that I love them and that they must continue the struggle. Do not worry about me but about those who are suffering. (Quoted in *Apartheid: The Facts*).—ed.

*From CSIS *Africa Notes,* April 15, 1985.

Constricted by a complicit "technicism" that responds to the demands of the prevailing system, educators focus on producing more vocationally trained manpower without challenging the underlying structures of racial separatism.

Even if one accepts that reform-minded whites in or out of government may seek to serve and preserve their own interests as they perceive them, the education-as-a-control-mechanism argument leaves at least one important question unposed and unanswered. What might be the *unintended consequences* of massively expanded and substantively improved black education?

. . . .

The End of Complacency

It was student anger, targeted on obligatory Afrikaans but grounded in pervasive resentment of the whole educational system, that sparked the violent explosion that spread out from the Soweto township near Johannesburg in 1976. . . . Having already moved some distance from the crude and narrow *(verkrampte)* stance of initial Verwoerdian apartheid doctrine toward a more pragmatic form of white hegemony, the government was by this time quietly relaxing the color bar in some professions and edging away from the disabling anachronism of Bantu education in response to manpower imperatives. The explosion of 1976, however, blasted Prime Minister B. J. Vorster's government out of its lingering complacency and embarrassed even previously indifferent whites into openly accepting a need for comprehensive educational reform—albeit still within a framework of communal segregation.

By this time, quantitative as contrasted to qualitative trends were already on an upswing. According to government statistics (which included the designated ethnic "homelands" for this period), between 1955 and 1975 African primary school enrollment rose from 970,000 to 3,380,000, secondary school enrollment from 35,000 to 318,000, and university enrollment from approximately 500 to 4,500. Comparable numbers were enrolled in University of South Africa [UNISA] correspondence courses. Over a 50-year period (1927–1977), the overall distribution of education had changed substantially, down from 53.6 percent white to 16.4 percent white.

In the late 1970s, the pace of change intensified. Government expenditure on African education (excluding capital expenditure and universities but including Homelands) rose from R68 million in 1972–73 to R298 million in 1980–81. This still left the government spending 10 times as much on each white as on each African student, however, and not all of the statistics were encouraging. In 1980 only 31,000 of the more than 600,000 African children who had entered school in 1969 reached the last year (standard 10) of secondary school—a 5 percent completion rate. In 1979, only 1,000 of the over 6,000 students then enrolled at the three universities then ascribed to Africans (Universities of the North, Fort Hare, and Zululand) successfully completed a course of study (generally three years), suggesting a dropout rate of at least 50 percent.

. . . .

Some Positive Developments

The magnitude of need and the inadequacies of government policy acknowledged, it would be unrealistic to gainsay the significance of the uneven change that is, in fact, beginning to take place in black education. That overall expenditure on African education has risen by a factor of five since 1978 and the ratio of expenditure on white and African pupils has begun to drop (from 10 to 1 down to under 8 to 1) represents a relative gain.

It is even possible to read the statistics concerning matric examination results as encouraging if one views them over the span of the last two decades and hypothesizes that the recent drop in the proportion of those succeeding is largely a transitional problem tied to rapid expansion. In 1960, only 716 Africans took the matric, 128 passed (17.9 percent), and 28 earned university entrance (3.9 percent); in 1983, 72,168 took the matric, 34,876 passed (48 percent), and 7,108 earned university entrance (9.8 percent). In 1990, 29,000 Africans are expected to earn university entrance and in 2000 the figure predicted is 65,000.

Beneath these statistical shifts, moreover, lies a developing factor of enormous potential, the cumulative impact of independent black initiatives. A growing legion of voluntary organizations unsullied by collaboration within the official administrative system and ranging from local parent and student groups to national organizations such as the Council for Black Education and Research is attempting to influence the trajectory of change in black education. By articulating interests, formulating priorities, and pressing demands from within the black community, these groups hope to realize informally some small measure of the influence on educational policy denied to them by virtue of African exclusion from the national political process.

Open Universities. In higher education, the initiative remains overwhelmingly in white hands, although increasing African demand (but not yet organized African leadership) is becoming an important catalyst at the university level. The tables on this page [omitted] demonstrate the pace at which white universities are now opening their doors. African universities are developing, and African enrollment is for the first time becoming more than a negligible proportion of the total enrollment of residential universities and University of South Africa (UNISA) correspondence programs. . . .

The Political Core of the Issue

In the final analysis, the effectiveness with which Africans are able to capitalize on the intended and unintended opportunities inherent in the expansion of black education will necessarily be a matter of political as well as educational significance.

. . . [I]t may be, as Professor J. P. de Lange believes, that the basic trend in South Africa is toward "the devolution of power" and an expansion of private enterprise; that resourceful use of technology—computers, video, educational television—will render a telescoped development of black education feasible even in a time of economic stringency; and that by the time of South Africa's next economic upswing an increased number of literate homes and a sharp rise in skill levels will enable South African blacks to attain an unprecedented level of social well-being. In either case, the expansion of black educational opportunity cannot but test and challenge fundamental structures of the South African system.

Professor de Lange has implied as much in commenting to the press: "We are creating a time bomb if we go on providing education and don't create a situation in which that education can be used." A situation in which that education can be fully used must presumably be a peaceable one of high social mobility possible only in a context of white-black political accommodation. The achievement of such accommodation, therefore, becomes an ever more urgent necessity as black education develops. It will require white (as well as black) leadership marked by moral courage and vision. . . .

PART THREE:

OPPOSITION AND RESISTANCE

Chapter VII:

BLACKS: ORGANIZATION AND IDEOLOGY IN THE FIGHT AGAINST APARTHEID

28. *REVOLUTION IN THE MAKING: BLACK POLITICS IN SOUTH AFRICA* (Parts III–IX, XI)*

by THOMAS G. KARIS

Thomas G. Karis is Executive Officer of the Doctoral Program in Political Science at the Graduate School of the City University of New York. He has traveled frequently to southern Africa, and was a foreign service officer in the American Embassy in Pretoria in the late 1950s. He is the editor, with Gwendolyn Carter, of the four-volume work, From Protest to Challenge: A Documentary History of African Politics in South Africa, 1882–1964.

III

As a legal organization, the ANC was ill-prepared to embark on a militant campaign. Its leaders, who had come of age in a relatively open political system, were even less prepared for clandestine activity. In prison and underground, ANC leaders inevitably found themselves dealing with popular demands for violent action, which they had to balance against their own concern

*From *Foreign Affairs,* Winter 1983/84.

that such action would leave deep bitterness and could be counterproductive.

In December 1961, Chief Albert Lutuli, president of the ANC, was allowed to travel to Oslo, Norway, to receive the Nobel Peace Prize in recognition of African patience during the 50 years of the ANC's legal existence. He read aloud President John F. Kennedy's congratulations on his record of "peaceful means" and repeated ANC calls for sanctions and external pressure.

A week later, on the day South African whites celebrate the defeat of the Zulus in 1828, the ANC's newly formed military wing, "Umkhonto We Sizwe" (Spear of the Nation), exploded home-made bombs at symbolic targets at times when no one would be injured. To protect rank-and-file members as well as Lutuli, efforts had been made to keep Umkhonto separate from the ANC. But in Oslo Lutuli ratified the ANC's historic turn when he spoke of the legitimacy of "armed force provoked by the adamancy of white rule." White and Indian communists participated in forming Umkhonto despite objections within their party to the feasibility of violence. The developing ANC-Communist Party alliance was given organizational expression in 1969 in the establishment of a Revolutionary Council with authority to direct Umkhonto and the armed struggle. The Council's vice-chairman under Tambo was Dr. Yusuf Dadoo, chairman of the Communist Party.

During the next decade, South Africa became a powerful police state, using detention and torture but also winning some black collaboration. The police smashed underground cells and demoralized the radical opposition. The unearthing of Umkhonto's headquarters in mid-1963 was followed by the sentencing to life imprisonment of Mandela and other major leaders. Tambo, who had been sent abroad, was cut off and had to add long-range military preparation to his diplomatic and propagandistic functions.

By the end of the 1960s, the ANC seemed to be little more than a shadowy presence in South Africa. At a conference in Tanzania in 1969, it emphasized the primacy of African "national consciousness" but also invited whites, Indians, and Coloureds to join. Meanwhile, in reaction to the political lull and passivity, South Africa saw the stirrings of what came to be called the Black Consciousness movement. Defining "black" to denote the status of racial oppression rather than color, a new generation of outspoken African, Coloured, and Indian students exerted a pervasive national influence for "psychological liberation" through their writings, meetings, and symbols of defiance. Steve Biko was to become the movement's internationally known spokesman before his brutal death at the hands of the security police in late 1977.

African workers also displayed a new sense of power in the 1970s. Nearly 100,000 workers in the Durban area went on strike in early 1973 with almost no visible leadership. The collapse of the Portuguese government and, in 1975, the coming to power of revolutionary governments in Mozambique and Angola heightened black expectations inside the Republic.

A new era in black protest was signaled on June 16, 1976, in Johannesburg's Soweto. A student demonstration against instruction in the Afrikaans language was met by guns and turned into an uprising. According to official statistics, 575 people died in the shooting and rioting that followed, 134 of them under the age of 18. Other estimates were much higher. Demonstrations, arson, and violence (mainly by the police) spread to many parts of the country. What made "Soweto" a watershed was the qualitatively new level of defiance and fearlessness among black youth. It also resulted in the first substantial exodus of blacks for guerrilla training. Most of them moved through Swaziland and gravitated to the ANC in Tanzania.

On October 19, 1977, the government cracked down, banning all the major Black Consciousness organizations. It also detained African leaders known for their moderation, together with a few of their white allies. In the face of the government's repressive capacities, it had become clear that the kind of spontaneous, loosely organized protest represented by Sharpeville and Soweto could not be effective.

IV

The six years since the 1977 crackdown have witnessed a revival in aboveground black politics and the burgeoning of black unions. These legal activities, at one end of the action spectrum, have been accompanied by a resurgence of the ANC at the other end, pursuing a long-term strategy of "armed struggle" coordinated with mass political pressures such as demonstrations, boycotts and strikes. In effect the opposition is pursuing two tracks, although there are already signs that the two could become linked at some point. . . .

The ANC's armed efforts for over 20 years have often been amateurish and abortive; they have also been marked by restraint. Its leaders acknowledge that its sabotage and small-scale guerrilla attacks have essentially been exercises in "armed propaganda." ANC guerrillas have attacked such targets as police stations, offices of government departments and officially sponsored black councils, and such symbolic targets of strategic significance as railway lines, oil depots, and electricity substations. The ANC has also taken responsibility for a small number of attacks on African policemen and the assassination of a few informers and state witnesses, actions obviously designed to deter such collaboration. But it has rejected the terrorism of indiscriminate killing and the assassination of white leaders, kidnapping, and other measures used by extremist groups elsewhere. . . .

Not until mid-1980 did ANC attacks appear seriously to worry the regime. At that time the ANC carried out its first major sabotage of strategically crucial facilities. Infiltrators cut through security fences and sabotaged three SASOL oil-from-coal plants 75 miles apart; no one was hurt.

On January 31, 1981, South African commandos made their first open crossing of the Mozambique border, destroying three ANC houses in Matola and killing 12 men (described as refugees by the ANC). They cut the ears off some.

After a lull of nearly two years in large-scale actions, in December 1982 helicopter-borne South African soldiers descended on Maseru, the capital of independent Lesotho, in a midnight raid. With cold-blooded deliberateness and with flares, bazookas, and machine guns, they sought out South Africans who they believed to be ANC activists in scattered houses and apartments. The invaders killed 42 people, including five women and two children. Some of the victims may have had military training; apparently most of them were refugees and visitors. Because of outdated intelligence, 12 Lesotho citizens were killed.

The ANC retaliated ten days later. In a salute to those killed in Maseru, four bombs in a staggered series over a period of 12 hours damaged the tightly guarded Koeberg nuclear power station under construction near Cape Town. Again no one was hurt.

Still stunned and infuriated by the Maseru raid, the ANC struck again on May 20, 1983, reaching a new level of violence and dramatic effect. A car bomb was exploded outside a military headquarters in downtown Pretoria at rush hour, killing 19 and injuring more than 200, including blacks. In targeting military personnel, the attack marked a shift in tactical emphasis. Three days later, South African planes attacked Matola in Mozambique, claiming 64 deaths, 41 of them ANC members. Although ANC members had occupied houses in Matola, the government of Mozambique asserted that they had left, and that the casualties were all civilian citizens of Mozambique—setting the total at six, including two children. . . .

Since the Pretoria attack, ANC leaders have engaged in an extended reexamination of their strategy, including problems of infiltration. The creation of a *cordon sanitaire* of black states can be expected to give greater impetus to ANC guerrilla training within the Republic's townships and depressed rural areas. Acknowledging "the reality" that countries bordering South Africa cannot provide bases, Oliver Tambo claimed in July 1983 that ANC guerrillas were being trained inside South Africa and that a political base had been created there. Yet the day appears many years away when the ANC underground, however linked to above-ground organizations, can seriously threaten the regime.

While the Pretoria bombing was a shock in some black quarters, the ANC's guerrilla actions also have a strong popular appeal, especially to angry and impatient young blacks, even as ANC activists and guerrillas are apprehended, jailed, sometimes tortured, killed in shootouts, and in a few cases hanged. Men whom whites regard as "terrorists" are acclaimed by blacks as "heroes and martyrs," says Bishop Desmond Tutu, general secretary of the South African

Council of Churches. For its part, the government remains implacable: one high Defense official has told the writer that the problem posed by the ANC can be dealt with by killing every one of its members. . . .

The best organized display of support for the ANC in almost a quarter-century occurred on August 20–21, 1983, near Cape Town. The defiant reading of a message of greetings and solidarity from Nelson Mandela and other ANC leaders in prison produced a standing ovation. It was the high point of a mass meeting of over 12,000 people, calling for the national launching of a United Democratic Front.

The UDF is now in being. Built up regionally since January, it is a locally based front—not an organization with individual members—of over 400 community, labor, religious, youth, and other organizations representing all races. Many of the organizations focus on local grievances. In its multiracialism, the UDF resembles the congress alliance of the 1950s but differs organizationally since the alliance was comprised only of national organizations. The UDF will be more difficult to decapitate. The membership of its affiliated groups is estimated to range from 1,000,000 to 1,500,000.

Seeking to encompass the widest possible opposition to the government's unfolding policy, the UDF has carefully avoided making adherence to the Freedom Charter a condition of membership. But its three presidents are veteran ANC activists: Oscar Mpetha, Archie Gumede, and Albertina Sisulu, the wife of Walter Sisulu, the ANC's imprisoned secretary-general. Its list of "patrons" includes Mandela, Sisulu, Govan Mbeki, and other prominent leaders or associates of the ANC.

Linked with them, however, are patrons and key officers who have not been identified with the ANC or were once prominent in the Black Consciousness movement. Among the former are Dr. Allan Boesak, president of the World Alliance of Reformed Churches; Reverend Beyers Naudé, the still-banned Afrikaans leader of the banned Christian Institute; and Andrew Boraine, the once-detained former president of the English-speaking National Union of South African Students, whose father is a leading member of the Progressive Federal Party. Among Black Consciousness personalities are Reverend Smangaliso Mkhatshwa, the formerly detained secretary-general of the Catholic Bishops' Conference, Aubrey Mokoena, Popo Molefe, and Mosiuoa Lekota.

As reflected in the UDF, the ANC's appeal is not difficult to see. As a national movement rather than a party, it symbolizes the historic struggle for equality. While other movements and organizations have risen and fallen, it has endured. In exile, the ANC has built organizational strength and won international legitimacy. In appealing for unity, it has been nondoctrinaire, with room for Christians, liberal pragmatists, communists, and members from all classes. As above-ground forces within South Africa have been harassed and their leaders repressed, as the [Pan-Africanist Congress] PAC outside has waned, the ANC has inherited support almost by default. Leaders who have left South Africa and joined the ANC have represented diverse backgrounds and orientations. . . .

V

The ANC is of course far from being the only organization in opposition to the South African government. In the parliamentary arena, the white Progressive Federal Party carries on its minority role of constant critic, led by Frederik Van Zyl Slabbert and Helen Suzman, and supported by many important business and mining leaders such as Harry Oppenheimer. Many PFP members, however, did not follow the party line of opposing the constitution proposals in the November 2 referendum.

Outside the parliamentary arena, the South African Council of Churches and the increasing number of black labor unions are active. And Bishop Desmond Tutu—described by Joseph Lelyveld of *The New York Times* in 1982 as "probably the most widely accepted black leader in South Africa today"—has great impact and influence both as an individual and as a church leader. Other organizations appealing to blacks include AZAPO (the Azanian People's Organization), the Black Consciousness successor to the groups banned in 1977, and Inkatha, the Zulu-based national movement led by Chief Gatsha Buthelezi, chief minister of the KwaZulu homeland. Other homeland leaders have built local political parties, but neither they nor AZAPO and the underground PAC are serious rivals of the ANC.

Inkatha is thus seen by many outside observers as the only real competitor for widespread black support. Unlike the ANC, it is a legal organization and Buthelezi is able to travel widely outside South Africa. Inkatha poses a difficult problem for the ANC both at home and abroad. Although Black Consciousness spokesmen have treated Buthelezi with contempt because of his homeland role, the ANC during the 1970s maintained informal and fraternal relations. They considered it important that the strategically situated KwaZulu have a sympathetic leader who would refuse independence, as Buthelezi has. Furthermore, Inkatha, whose uniforms and colors resemble those of the ANC, was regarded as a potentially important mass organization that might eventually mesh with the ANC.

Black hostility to Buthelezi within South Africa has intensified, however. And after he was seen as antagonistic to school boycotts and other popular campaigns in 1980, Tambo and other ANC officials attacked him publicly. Buthelezi has, in turn, responded to such criticism with increasingly bitter rhetoric. A resolution of the KwaZulu Legislative Assembly in April 1983 declared that the ANC had become "opponents of the black people." Senior ANC leaders continued to hope for reconciliation, but their number has now dwindled. Those who have appreciated Buthelezi's potential role are concerned that he has a hidden agenda of displacing Mandela and the ANC.

Buthelezi's hypersensitivity has limited his ability to act as a unifying force. He has talked of workers' and consumers' power but made little progress in organizing it. Inkatha has also failed to sponsor protest campaigns that would attract youthful or militant support. Claims regarding its membership, most of it Zulu, are open to question; and, because of pressure to join, loyalty may be limited. As late as October 1982, Buthelezi was saying that Inkatha had about 360,000 members; by January 1983 his claim was 750,000.

In that month, Buthelezi's leadership suffered a humiliating blow. In a political breakthrough for the government, the middle class leaders of the Coloured Labour Party decided to participate in the proposed constitutional scheme. The party had been Buthelezi's most important ally in the South African Black Alliance, a loose coalition centered on Inkatha. Still more damaging has been the decision of the broad-based United Democratic Front [UDF] to exclude Inkatha from affiliation.

Nevertheless, as a politically astute Zulu leader who makes African nationalist appeals, Buthelezi will continue to be a consequential personality. He has calculated that as pressures mount for radical change, whites will be compelled to turn to him as the most acceptable black leader. He opposes armed struggle (while threatening to undertake it), is prepared to compromise on one man one vote, endorses free enterprise, and promises reform and stability within South Africa's capitalist system. For a time, he was developing links to the National Party, but during the referendum campaign on the constitutional proposal he allied himself to the official white opposition, the Progressive Federal Party. As protest is mobilized, Buthelezi's warning that the alignment of black political groups with the ANC will trigger a "black civil war" may become a self-fulfilling prophecy.

The relative appeal of the ANC and other black groups cannot be evaluated with any precision. . . .

. . . A detailed poll [in 1981] for the Johannesburg *Star* . . . asked Africans in Johannesburg, Durban, and Cape Town how they would vote in a parliamentary election among candidates from the ANC, Inkatha, AZAPO and the PAC. The ANC emerged first in each city including Durban, in all the main African language groups including Zulu, in all age groups (although Inkatha was close among those over 40), and in all occupational groups except among the unskilled, where it was roughly equal with Inkatha. The more skilled or professional and the younger tended to be pro-ANC. The three leaders most liked were Mandela, 76 percent; Dr. Ntatho Motlana (the Soweto leader who opposes government-sponsored black councils), 58 percent; and Buthelezi, 39 percent, with Mandela and Motlana outranking Buthelezi even in Durban. Buthelezi's low standing among educated Africans was evident three years earlier in a survey designed by Schlemmer of men in Soweto over 16 whose education was mid-high school or above. Asked who people like themselves saw as "their real leaders," only five percent gave Buthelezi's name.

VI

Whatever their longstanding tactical differences, all African leaders without exception appear to be united on the issue of the government's constitutional proposals. Indeed, the ANC's 30-year-old call for a national convention has been revived by a group of government-recognized black leaders, including both Buthelezi and Matanzima, who are calling for a "nonracial democratic society." Their South African Federal Union includes leaders of semi-autonomous and independent homelands, urban councils, and business organizations.

Leaders such as these are constrained by vested interests and temperament from joining a radical struggle. Both internal and external pressures are also strong on homeland leaders to cooperate with the South African military, as several are now doing, to resist insurgency. Some homeland leaders do have popular support. Unlike the dictatorial and corrupt leadership of Transkei, Ciskei, and Venda, Dr. Cedric Phatudi of Lebowa, for example, commands a good deal of local respect. An elderly gentleman genuinely committed to the creation of a federal system that would be nonracial, he has little to say about programs for the redistribution of wealth and is averse to mass protest.

Black politics appears to be in disarray, although the extent of that disarray can be exaggerated. More fundamental than questions about armed struggle and boycott are deeply rooted differences about the role of whites. Thus AZAPO is strongly opposed to the ANC's Freedom Charter. One of its spokesmen, Saths Cooper, who recently completed a six-year term in prison, has even criticized Mandela as an "accommodationist" for dealing with prison officials.

Disagreements also reveal, however, a vitality in debate that augurs well for the future of democracy in South Africa. At the same time, antagonists display encouraging efforts to accommodate divergent views. Acting in a conciliatory spirit, AZAPO was instrumental in organizing a National Forum on June 11–12, 1983, which brought together representatives of nearly 200 black organizations, excluding those involved in government-sponsored institutions. The organizers discouraged any criticism of the Freedom Charter, but, on the assumption that the Charter was "dated," a "Manifesto of the Azanian People" was produced. Unlike earlier expressions of Black Consciousness, the Manifesto was reconcilable with the Charter—both are loosely socialist—but the ANC's National Executive Committee reacted by warning against those who diverted the people from the goals "enshrined" in the Freedom Charter.

Responding to recent efforts to fuse Black Consciousness and class consciousness, the Manifesto identified the enemy as "racial capitalism."

. . . Ideological differences will not easily be submerged. Nevertheless, influential leaders are impatient with such differences and recognize that there is room in the liberation struggle for many different approaches.

Meanwhile, an important influence for unity is exerted by prominent personalities with credibility in both the "Charterist" and Black Consciousness camps. Three were on the National Forum organizing committee: Dr. Boesak, Bishop Tutu, and Dr. Manas Buthelezi, the Lutheran bishop who was recently elected president of the South African Council of Churches and who has been compared with Martin Luther King. . . .

That alignments are blurred and overlapping can be seen in the relation of the two leading federations of black trade unions to each other, to the National Forum and the UDF, and indirectly to the ANC. The four-year-old Federation of South African Trade Unions (FOSATU), with over 106,000 signed up members, has earned a reputation for professionalism and avoidance of politically provocative actions. It accepts that workers should be "part of the wider popular struggle" but criticizes the ANC for tending "to encourage undirected opportunistic political activity." . . . Because it sees the struggle as one more of class than of race, its gravitation is toward the UDF. Constituent unions have expressed sympathy for the UDF, but FOSATU has not affiliated with it.

The rival Council of Unions of South Africa (CUSA), a three-year-old federation with an estimated membership of over 100,000, opposed the inclusion of whites in FOSATU's leadership although it has no problem itself in using white assistance. Its constitution calls for "a nonracial democratic society based on black leadership." In ongoing unity talks with FOSATU and strong unaffiliated unions, CUSA has argued for a framework that is worker-controlled, that is, black-controlled. Its leaders point to the ANC model: a nonracial membership whose national executive committee is all-African. Because of the priority it has given to opposing the government's constitutional proposals, CUSA participated in the National Forum and, despite criticism, has become affiliated with the UDF.

VII

. . . [I]deological inclinations vary among ANC members generally. An uneasy balance exists between those whose primary goals are political and those who believe liberation can come only with socialist reconstruction. At this stage, doctrinal differences within the ANC can easily be overstated and their importance exaggerated. The ingredients are present, however, for a vigorous debate if or when a democratic system comes into being. Both the ANC and the

Communist Party recognize that the organizations are separate and independent from each other, that the ANC is the leader of the alliance, and that Communists who are members of the ANC are obliged to be loyal to it. The burden is on critics to demonstrate that practice contradicts understandings on which everyone agrees. Influence within the relationship is difficult to estimate, but it is undoubtedly reciprocal. To assume that in any collaboration between African nationalists such as Tambo and Communists the latter will inevitably dominate is to underestimate the experience and sophistication of nationalist leaders.

VIII

. . . Responding to a persistent question about Soviet influence, Oliver Tambo said in 1982:

> The Soviet Union has no influence on the ANC any more than Canada has. What has really happened is that we found ourselves, decades ago, fighting against racism —and relatively weak. We went in search of friends, to Canada, the United States, Europe, India, and elsewhere. Some received us well, some were lukewarm, some turned us down. The Soviet Union gave support. So did other countries—Sweden, for example. Sweden gave us assistance without strings except that no funds may be used to buy guns. The Soviet Union does not have to say that because it gives us the guns. The Soviet Union does not have to say that because it gives us the guns. The supposed stigma of getting assistance from the Soviet Union has no meaning whatever in southern Africa. There would be no independence for anyone without those weapons. That's what ordinary people think. Where would we be without that assistance? Could we go to Washington?

Today the ANC receives some 90 percent of its military support from communist sources (that is, from the Soviet bloc). However, these sources probably supply less than the Reagan Administration's estimate of 60 percent of overall support. Although early aid from China dried up after the Sino-Soviet split, the ANC maintained contact, and following Tambo's most recent visit to Beijing in May 1983, China has given some financial aid and has promised to supply arms.

Both the Organization of African Unity (in 1963) and the United Nations General Assembly (in 1973) recognize the ANC and the PAC as national liberation movements. ANC spokesmen make a point of saying that arms from the Soviet Union come to the ANC through members of the OAU in accordance with its resolutions and those of the United Nations that call on member states to provide material aid. Military training takes place mainly in Africa.

U.N. recognition of the ANC and the PAC gives them the kind of official standing from which much follows. Both have observer status and can take part in debates in the General Assembly, the Security Council, and specialized agencies on matters of direct concern to them. The General Assembly contributes annually to the cost of the ANC's New York office ($107,696 in 1982–1983). The total amount of non-military aid from U.N. specialized agencies is unusually difficult to ascertain because most of it goes to individuals rather than to the ANC as an organization. . . .

In its quest for international legitimacy, the ANC has established a presence in some 33 countries around the world. ANC officials have often met with prime ministers and other high officials. In 1978 Tambo and three other leaders of southern African movements were received by Pope John Paul II. . . .

Governments on the African continent extending some form of aid include Nigeria and Algeria (each has recently granted $1,000,000), Egypt, Gabon, Ivory Coast, and Senegal. Tambo recently visited Saudi Arabia, which is also providing aid. Western governmental donors include Sweden, where ANC representatives meet annually with officials ($4,210,000 in 1982); Norway ($1,650,000); Denmark, the Netherlands, Austria, Italy, Finland ($236,000), and (in the past) Canada.

The ANC's network of fraternal relations extends to democratic socialist as well as communist parties. The Socialist International recognizes the ANC and has given it observer status. The West German Social Democratic Party supports a foundation that provides aid. In Italy, for example, virtually all political parties have donated non-military goods for a "Ship of Solidarity," due to arrive in Dar es Salaam in December 1983, destined for the ANC and the South West Africa People's Organization (SWAPO). . . .

IX

Not until 1959, the year before Sharpeville, did an American ambassador meet with an ANC leader. Philip Crowe, although concerned with the maintenance of "correct relations with an ally in the cold war," met Chief Albert Lutuli and found him "a moderate man." Not until the Kennedy Administration did U.S. anti-apartheid rhetoric include praise for black leaders, and not until the fourth of July, 1963, did the American Embassy invite a black guest to its annual reception. During the Johnson Administration, Embassy officials attended political trials and spoke privately to South African authorities in mid-1964 about the repercussions of a possible death sentence for Mandela and others on trial. The potential political importance of South Africa in the United States was evident in 1966 when Senator Robert Kennedy made an emotion-filled visit to the Republic, including a call on the rusticated Lutuli.

President Nixon tilted U.S. policy toward white South Africa. His Administration's signals of reassurance to the white regime included relaxation of existing restrictions on U.S. military sales, and private meetings in Washington between U.S. and South African military officials. Incredible as it may seem, his ambassador, John Hurd, went pheasant hunting with government leaders on Robben Island, where ANC and other political prisoners were serving life sentences.

During the Carter Administration, ANC contact with Ambassador Andrew Young and other officials in New York became "easygoing," as ANC leaders put it, but there was no "critical dialogue" between the ANC and the State Department. Within South Africa, the wide-ranging contact of the American ambassador with black opposition leaders was unprecedented.

Because of this "rhetoric of disapproval," South African blacks "by and large, held the U.S. in high regard" during the Carter period, Bishop Tutu wrote in 1982. But they were "aghast" when the Reagan Administration "sided with the status quo." Arguments against sanctions to help blacks in South Africa lost all credibility, said Tutu, when sanctions were used to help whites in Poland. . . .

President Reagan's State Department, even at the junior level, has had no communication with the ANC. The ANC's representative has not set foot inside the U.S. mission to the United Nations since January 1981, and his formal request for a meeting with Ambassador Jeane Kirkpatrick has gone unacknowledged. On the other hand, the President met with Chief Buthelezi in a small group before a mass prayer breakfast in January 1983 and spoke of his admiration for him. Buthelezi had also met Presidents Nixon and Carter. The Reagan Administration has wisely avoided, however, responding to Buthelezi's standing invitation for an "overt alliance" between the United States and Inkatha, initially made in 1980. . . .

XI

The Reagan Administration's "constructive engagement" with South Africa carries grave risks for the national interest of the United States. . . .

If the perceived U.S. alignment with the white minority continues, the disastrous consequence would follow of being on the losing side of a conflict in which the Soviet Union is seen by most blacks as on the side of liberation. The United States would be repeating the mistake it has made elsewhere in the world in supporting reactionary and dictatorial regimes. Compounding the mistake would be the unique racial dimensions of the conflict and the passions it would evoke in the United States and elsewhere.

Revolution is in the making in South Africa, and violence will be a part of it. In the case of South Africa, black leaders will continue to calculate that mass pressures, including strikes and boycotts, will be more efficacious than violence. Minimizing violence should also be an important goal for the United States. To this end, it should contribute to pressures on South Africa for genuine negotiation, although one can hardly envisage this except under domestic and external pressures that are overwhelming.

In pressing South Africa to change direction, the United States cannot be ambiguous on a step that symbolizes such a change: the universal franchise. As recognition of an equal stake in society, it has been endorsed by nearly every black leader in South Africa since the end of World War II. It is crucial to any settlement.

So is the role of the ANC. The United States can hardly stigmatize the ANC for its failure to eschew violence so long as the American alternative is unilateral change by a minority government based upon institutionalized violence. Fruitful negotiation cannot be limited, as the Reagan Administration would have it, to those who are "committed to peaceful change."

It follows that the United States should maintain contact not only with black groups tolerated by the government but also with the ANC. It should recognize the ANC as a legitimate political force whose guerrillas are freedom fighters entitled to treatment as prisoners of war under the Geneva Convention. . . .

The imponderables in the South African situation are too many for long-range prediction. Yet one can say with confidence that the United States is now proceeding down a blind alley. Nor is light likely to be seen in any "internal settlement" detour comparable to that led by Bishop Muzorewa in Zimbabwe. Future stability and growth depend upon the emergence of a government that has popular legitimacy. If the leadership of that government has the qualities of individuals like Frederik van Zyl Slabbert, the late Steve Biko, Desmond Tutu, Oliver Tambo, and Nelson Mandela, the United States will see in power leaders with the independence it hopes for.

29. *THE COLOURED AND THE INDIANS**

by GWENDOLEN M. CARTER

Gwendolen M. Carter, Professor of Political Science and African Studies at Indiana University, was formerly Director of the Program of African Studies at Northwestern University and Melville J. Herskovits Professor of African Affairs. Her classic study of white politics in South Africa, The Politics of Inequality, *has been followed by work on that country's racial policy of separate development in* South Africa's Transkei: The Politics of Domestic Colonialism *(Northwestern University Press, 1967), of which she is coauthor, and of black politics in the series* From Protest to Challenge: A Documentary History of African Politics in South Africa, 1882–1964, *four volumes (Hoover Institution Press, 1972–77), of which she is coeditor with Thomas Karis.*

*From *Which Way Is South Africa Going?* (Bloomington, 1980).

The Coloured

The Coloured sometimes speak of themselves ironically as the link between South Africa's people, meaning, of course, the miscegenation process that created them. Historically, as well as genetically, they have a special relation to the Afrikaners. They speak Afrikaans or sometimes a kind of "black" Afrikaans that has evolved over the years. They have always lived close to Afrikaners, whether in the farming areas of the Cape or in town. They trekked with them in the nineteenth century, and their densest living quarters have traditionally been near those of the Afrikaners. This closeness has evoked two diametrically opposed reactions from Afrikaners: one is to see the Coloured as the natural allies against the African masses; the other is to brutally underscore, in law and practice, their difference from whites.

Some of the Nationalists' earliest apartheid legislation—in particular, the Prohibition of Mixed Marriages Act and the clause in the Immorality Amendment Act prohibiting intercourse between whites and Coloured—was aimed directly at the Coloured because both had long been banned for Africans. But the purpose was, in the words of one Nationalist in Parliament, "to make our colour sense clear before the world." The Group Areas Act affronted the Coloured still more than it did the Africans because the latter had always had living centers separated from the white towns. The bitterness caused by implementation of the Group Areas Act was intensified by the ruthless bulldozing carried out in Cape Town's centrally situated District Six, a historic, picturesque Coloured area slated for occupancy by whites but unwanted by them and now scarred by bare patches of ground. Farther from town, recent Portuguese immigrants from Mozambique have taken over numerous houses formerly occupied by Coloured; this situation is all the more galling because the newcomers are welcomed as whites, and will ultimately be enfranchised.

The Coloured retained their vote on the common voting roll in Cape Province long after the Africans were removed, in 1936. A similar removal of the Coloured became a prime objective of the Nationalists once in office. . . . Like the Africans in the thirties, the Coloured were placed on a separate roll to elect their own white representatives. This took place shortly before the Africans lost even that possibility. In 1968, the Coloured lost theirs.

Nothing has embittered the Coloured more than their loss of the franchise. . . .

In a field in which South Africans are particularly sensitive because of their passion for sport, Coloured leadership has played, and continues to play, a significant role in fighting apartheid by mobilizing external pressure to exclude South African teams from international competition because of the country's policies of racial discrimination. . . . Dennis Brutus [an internationally known coloured poet now living in the United States] helped to organize the nonracial South African Olympic Committee (SANROC), whose international efforts led to the exclusion of South Africa from the 1964 Olympic Games in Tokyo. Despite constant attempts to be readmitted, South Africa has been excluded from Olympic competition ever since.

Dr. Koornhof, when Minister of Sport and Recreation, made substantial and, to a considerable degree, successful efforts to open up multiracial sports in South Africa in the hope that his country would be reaccepted into international competitions. His new, revised sports policy, announced September 1976, met some hostile Nationalist reactions, particularly over efforts to organize racially mixed sports at the club level, and considerable black skepticism. But already that year, sixty-three competitions between different racial groups were held on both national and international levels, according to Dr. Koornhof's report to the Cape Congress, in August 1977, and they have continued. . . .

Government spokesmen point out that substantial economic improvements are being made to enhance the position and opportunities of the Coloured. The Western Cape, where most of them live, is an area of Coloured "preference" over Africans in employment (one of the problems besetting settlements of African "squatters" from the impoverished "homelands"). The government has made the elimination of differential standards in wages and salaries between Coloured and whites a matter of priority. The Coloured university at Bellville, with its able Coloured rector, Dr. Richard van der Ross, is impressive. Middle-class Coloured housing has been built in an attractive area near Cape Town, and there can be little doubt that a major political objective is to build up a substantial and, by government expectations, satisfied Coloured community there.

Whether it succeeds is problematic. A striking feature of the 1976 demonstrations was that for the first time Coloured youth joined with African youth in expressing their resentment at discriminatory conditions and attitudes. The scars of District Six have not faded from people's minds any more than from the physical area. Requests to rezone that area for Coloured housing have been denied. Until the obvious roots of Coloured discontent have been dealt with —the franchise, discriminatory legislation, and bureaucratic arbitrariness—it seems unlikely that more than an uneasy relation between Coloured and whites will develop.

The Indians

Status in South Africa is based on race, not only in the major distinction between white and black, but also between Coloured, Indians, and Africans, who rank in that order in terms of what are called "privileges." Coloured are exempt from the influx control restrictions applied to Indians and Africans and are admitted to certain trades not open to the others. Indians, who are settled mainly in Natal and on the border of Johannesburg, are excluded from the Orange Free State and certain areas of Northern Natal. Up to June 1975, Indians required special permits to travel from one province of South Africa to another.

The nearly 800,000 Asians (nearly all Indians) form the smallest minority in South Africa, about 3 percent of its total population of 27.201 million in 1978. The Coloured, who numbered 2.553 million, came next, making up 9.4 percent; the whites, with 4.393 million, had 16 percent; and the Africans, with 19.463 million, composed 71.6 percent of the population. Among the blacks, the Indians are by far the most urbanized: 86.6 percent in 1970, exactly the same proportion as for whites.

Indians have suffered in the past from being defined as an "alien group," although their position as a settled part of the population is now assured. Brought to Natal between 1860 and 1911 as indentured labor for the sugar plantations, where local Zulus refused to work, many of them preferred to remain in South Africa rather than use their free passage home. Most of the workers were Hindu, but they were joined in considerable numbers by Moslem traders. Fear of their competition led to a series of discriminatory provisions, against which Indian communities periodically staged passive resistance campaigns. The most famous of these campaigns was led by Mahatma Gandhi, who founded the Natal Indian Congress in 1894. . . .

The so-called Pegging Act of 1943, which made interracial property transactions in Durban illegal, was followed by a more rigorous measure, in 1946, that offered a limited franchise in return for severe restrictions on land ownership and occupancy. This arrangement was refused indignantly, and the South African Indian Congress, which had been formed in 1920, appealed successfully to the Indian government to impose economic sanctions on South Africa and refer the treatment of South African Indians to the United Nations. The Natal Indian Congress embarked on a campaign of passive disobedience by squatting on land they were forbidden to occupy, and the Passive Resistance Council in the Transvaal similarly dramatized Indian grievances.

In January 1949, long-existing friction between Indians and Africans flared into violence by largely tribalized Zulus against Indian families. Shocked by the riots, African and Indian leaders developed a new relationship, which shortly took form in the Joint Action Committee of the African National Congress and the South African Indian Congress. This group helped to support the 1952–53 nationwide African passive resistance campaign. It also presented a joint memorandum to the Indian government on the disabilities of the nonwhite peoples of South Africa for use by the United Nations, thereby initiating the long series of still continuing protests and proposed actions by that body against South African practices of racial discrimination. Although the Joint Action Committee was forced underground after 1953, the association of Africans, Indians, and Coloured powered the Congress movement, is still a feature of the exiled African National Congress, and took a new and more cohesive form in the Black Consciousness Movement. . . .

Although all blacks suffer painful disabilities, those of the Indians have a special poignancy. A recent study of prejudice and intergroup relations carried out at the Durban-Westville Indian University suggests that Indians feel trapped between the whites, who hold political power, and the overwhelming numbers of Africans. Aware that both groups possess strong prejudices against them, the Indians tend to take out their frustrations in self-hate and intragroup aggression, the study disclosed, because they fear retaliation should they show their feelings too obviously against the source of their resentment.

There are group distinctions among Indians that lend themselves to such reactions. Those distinctions stem from different religions, languages, economic status, and international connections. The Moslem group is numerically smaller but wealthier than the Hindu; about 5 percent of Indians are Christian. Although not all the Moslems came originally from what is now Pakistan, they tend to support its side in disputes with India and to favor Moslem interests in Middle East issues. At least five different Indian languages are spoken within the local Indian community; this is a considerable barrier to social intercourse and intermarriage. In the past, caste divisions among the Hindu also tended to hamper intermarriage, but this seems much less the case with the younger generation, largely because of mixing in school. Indian education is administered by the Department of Indian Education and is separate from that of other groups. In 1979, a six-year phasing-in program was completed, and, as with the Coloured, education for Indian children will henceforth be compulsory up to age fifteen.

Although the Coloured retain bitter memories of the removals from District Six, the Indians have equally strong reactions to the rezoning of Cato Manor, a deep valley behind Durban. . . . Whatever the outcome, it is Indians who have suffered the most from implementation of the Group Areas Act, either through removals or the inadequate provision of living space. . . .

The Coloured and Indians are not only important in their own right but also for their role in the national economy, trade unions, and the Black Consciousness Movement. Their solidarity with Africans within that movement underpins a black front that not only pits numbers against power within South Africa but also can appeal to the international community. Moreover, Coloured leaders, by stimulating the international sports boycott against South Africa, have not only brought noticeable, though far from adequate, changes in the conditions under which sports are played within the country but also have initiated one of the few effective means of mobilizing international action.

Like the whites and the Africans, the Coloured and the Indians are subject to divisive interests and pressures that are often exploited by the government. They compete with Africans for jobs and never forget the Africans' dominant numbers. They are also well aware that from their side Africans often resent the more favorable economic position that Coloured and Indians have acquired, particularly within the professions and commercial life. Although they are long in the past, the 1949 Durban riots by Zulus against Indians have never been forgotten.

All blacks suffer from common disabilities vis-à-vis whites, but it is only Africans who must carry passes. In Cape Province, there is a legislatively endorsed Coloured preference in jobs, and when squatter settlements are destroyed, shacks occupied by equally poverty-stricken Coloured are allowed to stand. Such obvious differentiations make the development and maintenance of black unity difficult, but it appears increasingly that the common black disabilities and common objectives for political rights have a greater effect.

30. FREEDOM CHARTER*

PREAMBLE
We, the people of South Africa, declare for all our country and the world to know:

> That South Africa belongs to all who live in it, black and white, and that no government can justly claim authority unless it is based on the will of the people;
> That our people have been robbed of their birthright to land, liberty and peace by a form of government founded on injustice and inequality;
> That our country will never be prosperous or free until all our people live in brotherhood, enjoying equal rights and opportunities;
> That only a democratic state, based on the will of the people can secure to all their birthright without distinction of color, race, sex or belief;
> And therefore, we, the people of South Africa, black and white together—equals, countrymen and brothers—adopt this FREEDOM CHARTER. And we pledge ourselves to strive together, sparing nothing of our strength, and courage, until the democratic changes here set out have been won.

The People Shall Govern!

> Every man and woman shall have the right to vote for and stand as a candidate for all bodies which make laws.

*Adopted by the Congress of the People, 26 June 1955.

All the people shall be entitled to take part in administration of the country.

The rights of the people shall be the same regardless of race, color or sex.

All bodies of minority rule, advisory boards, councils and authorities shall be replaced by democratic organs of self-government.

All National Groups Shall Have Equal Rights!

There shall be equal status in the bodies of state, in the courts and in the schools for all national groups and races;

All national groups shall be protected by law against insults to their race and national pride;

All people shall have equal rights to use their own language and to develop their own folk culture and customs;

The preaching and practice of national, race or color discrimination and contempt shall be a punishable crime;

All apartheid laws and practices shall be set aside.

The People Shall Share in the Country's Wealth!

The national wealth of our country, the heritage of all South Africans, shall be restored to the people;

The mineral wealth beneath the soil, the banks and monopoly industry shall be transferred to the ownership of the people as a whole;

All other industries and trade shall be controlled to assist the well-being of the people;

All people shall have equal rights to trade where they choose, to manufacture and to enter all trades, crafts, and professions.

The Land Shall Be Shared Among Those Who Work It!

Restriction of land ownership on a racial basis shall be ended and all the land re-divided amongst those who work it, to banish famine and land hunger;

The state shall help the peasants with implements, seed, tractors and dams to save the soil and assist the tillers;

Freedom of movement shall be guaranteed to all who work on the land;

All shall have the right to occupy land wherever they chose;

People shall not be robbed of their cattle, and forced labor and farm prisons shall be abolished.

All Shall Be Equal Before the Law!

No one shall be imprisoned, deported or restricted without a fair trial;

No one shall be condemned by the order of any Government official;

The courts shall be representative of all the people;

Imprisonment shall be only for serious crimes against the people, and shall aim at re-education, not vengeance;

The police force and army shall be open to all on an equal basis and shall be the helpers and protectors of the people;

All laws which discriminate on grounds of race, color or belief shall be repealed.

All Shall Enjoy Equal Human Rights!

The law shall guarantee to all their right to speak, to organize, to meet together, to publish, to preach, to worship, and to educate their children;

The privacy of the house from police raids shall be protected by law;

All shall be free to travel without restriction from countryside to town, from province to province and from South Africa abroad;

Pass laws, permits and all other laws restricting these freedoms shall be abolished.

There Shall Be Work and Security!

All who work shall be free to form trade unions, to elect their officers and to make wage agreements with their employers;

The state shall recognize the right and duty of all to work, and to draw full unemployment benefits;

Men and women of all races shall receive equal pay for equal work;

There shall be a forty-hour working week, a national minimum wage, paid annual leave and sick leave for all workers and maternity leave on full pay for all working mothers;

Miners, domestic workers, farm workers and civil servants shall have the same rights as all others who work;

Child labor, compound labor, the tot system and contract labor shall be abolished.

The Doors of Learning and of Culture Shall Be Opened!

The government shall discover, develop and encourage national talent for the enhancement of our cultural life;

All the cultural treasures of mankind shall be open to all, by free exchange of books, ideas and contact with other lands;

The aim of education shall be to teach the youth to love their people and their culture, to honor human brotherhood, liberty and peace;

Education shall be free, compulsory, universal and equal for all children;

Higher education and technical training shall be opened to all by means of state allowances and scholarships awarded on the basis of merit;

Adult illiteracy shall be ended by a mass state education plan;

Teachers shall have all the rights of other citizens;

The color bar in cultural life, in sport and in education shall be abolished.

There Shall Be Houses, Security and Comfort!

All people shall have the right to live where they choose, to be decently housed, and to bring up their families in comfort and security;

Unused housing space to be made available to the people;

Rent and prices shall be lowered, food plentiful and no one shall go hungry,

A preventive health scheme shall be run by the state;

Free medical care and hospitalization shall be provided for all, with special care for mothers and young children;

Slums shall be demolished and new suburbs built where all have transport, roads, lighting, playing fields, creches and social centers;

The aged, the orphans, the disabled and the sick shall be cared for by the state;

Rest, leisure and recreation shall be the right of all;

Fenced locations and ghettos shall be abolished, and laws which break up families shall be repealed.

There Shall Be Peace and Friendship!

South Africa shall be a fully independent state, which respects the rights and sovereignty of all nations;

South Africa shall strive to maintain world peace and the settlement of all international disputes by negotiation—not war;

Peace and friendship amongst all our people shall be secured by upholding the equal rights, opportunities and status of all;

The people of the protectorates—Basutoland, Bechuanaland and Swaziland—shall be free to decide for themselves their own future;

The right of all the peoples of Africa to independence and self government shall be recognized, and shall be the basis of close cooperation.

Let all who love their people and their country now say, as we say here:

"These Freedoms We Will Fight For, Side by Side, Throughout Our Lives, Until We Have Won Our Liberty."

31. MASSACRE AT SHARPEVILLE, 1960*

by GAIL M. GERHART

The following commentary on the 1960 massacre at Sharpeville is from Volume 3, Challenge and Violence, 1953–1964 *of a monumental and invaluable 4-volume series entitled* From Protest to Challenge: Documents of African Politics in South Africa, 1882–1964. *The general editors of the series are Thomas Karis and Gwendolen M. Carter. Volume 3 is edited by Thomas Karis and Gail M. Gerhart. The latter was responsible for the material on Sharpeville. She is also the author of* Black Power in South Africa: The Evolution of an Ideology *(1978).*

In February 1960, Sobukwe, Leballo, and Howard Ngcobo, a [Pan-Africanist Congress] PAC executive committee member from Durban, drove to Cape Province to assess the state of the PAC's organization there and to lay plans for the anti-pass campaign. Ngendane joined the group in Cape Town, and Elliot Mfaxa, the party's national organizer, accompanied them as they touched centers of PAC activity in the eastern Cape. In Port Elizabeth and

*From *From Protest to Challenge: A Documentary History of African Politics in South Africa,* Vol. 3., *Challenge and Violence, 1953–1964* (Stanford, 1977).

other urban areas where support for the ANC was traditionally strong, popular interest in the touring Africanist delegation was meager. In Cape Town, however, where the ANC was relatively weak and had made little effort in the 1950s to address itself to the grievances of the city's many migrant and semi-urbanized workers, the PAC leaders were enthusiastically received. A crowd of about 2,000 assembled to hear Sobukwe speak at Langa township on February 14. The PAC was guiding Africans toward the creation of a New Africa, Sobukwe told his audience. The first targets in its unfolding program were abolition of the pass laws and the achievement of a guaranteed minimum wage of £35 ($98) a month for all Africans. African men were to prepare themselves, he said, to receive the call from the national headquarters. When the call came, all were to leave their passes at home and surrender for arrest at their local police stations; no one was to resort to violence or to let himself be provoked by police or *agents provocateurs.*

The final aims of the campaign were left somewhat ambiguous. On the one hand, passes and low wages were singled out as the chief grievances of Africans. On the other hand, there was a strong suggestion in all PAC pronouncements that the campaign would not ultimately confine itself to these issues alone; rather, it would be the first step in a rapid march to total freedom. The PAC opposed every piece of the government's apartheid legislation, Sobukwe often told his audiences, but when a man's house was flooding, the solution was not to try to throw the water outside; instead, the PAC aimed at "closing the tap from which all this vile legislation flows," and it would not rest until all white rule was overthrown.

The problems the PAC might face once it had been decapitated by arrests were the cause of some concern to the organization's leaders, but they did not allow this concern to dissuade them from the course they had set for themselves. With some degree of foresight, they formulated a plan according to which subordinate "layers" of leadership within each region would be chosen and trained so that another set of leaders could come forward when top men were jailed. In practice, however, implementation of this plan had not progressed very far at the time of the March 1960 launching.

Over the doubts of some of the PAC's most influential supporters, including Jordan Ngubane and A. P. Mda, Sobukwe and Leballo pressed forward with plans to launch the campaign in early 1960. The ANC at its December 1959 conference had resolved to launch an anti-pass campaign of its own with March 31 as the date for its initial action. Its campaign was to begin with the sending of deputations to local authorities and Bantu Affairs commissioners throughout the country to demand abolition of the pass laws. The PAC, its national working committee felt, would have to launch its campaign before the 31st if it hoped to seize the initiative and set the tone of resolute action. The choice of an exact starting date was left to Sobukwe.

On March 4, Sobukwe sent his final instructions for the campaign to all branches and regional executives of the PAC. The people were to be instructed to observe the rules of strict nonviolence; no one was to resort to violence and emotionalism in the belief that the PAC was trying to engage in "revolutionary warfare." In a somewhat different vein, a party flyer issued at about the same time declared that the pass laws had to be "blown to oblivion this year, now and forever."

On Wednesday, March 16, Sobukwe wrote to Major-General Rademeyer, Commissioner of Police, to inform him that the PAC would begin "a sustained, disciplined, nonviolent campaign" and its members would surrender themselves for arrest on Monday, March 21. Warning of "trigger-happy, African-hating" police officers, he assured Rademeyer that the people would disperse if the police gave them clear orders and adequate time to do so.

On Friday, March 18, Sobukwe announced at a press conference in Johannesburg that the campaign would begin on the following Monday. PAC circulars announcing the launching date were already in the streets. "I have appealed to the African people," Sobukwe told the press, "to make sure that this campaign is conducted in a spirit of absolute nonviolence, and I am quite certain they will heed my call. . . . If the other side so desires," he went on, sounding a prophetic note, "we will provide them with an opportunity to demonstrate to the world how brutal they can be. We are ready to die for our cause. . . ."

On Saturday, March 19, a conference of FOFATUSA delegates met in Johannesburg and resolved unanimously to strike in support of the PAC campaign. On the following day the *Sunday Times* reported the response of the ANC to an invitation from the PAC to join the campaign on March 21. A letter from Duma Nokwe stated that the ANC was unwilling to support action which had "not been properly prepared for, and which has no reasonable prospects of success"; it would carry on instead with its own program of action against passes. Unmoved by this rebuff, PAC leaders geared themselves for Monday morning. On Sunday, March 20, on instructions from Sobukwe, two members of the movement's national executive committee, Nana Mahomo and Peter 'Molotsi, slipped across the Bechuanaland [now Botswana] border to carry abroad the case for the PAC's action.

Sharpeville

If police had not shot into the crowd of demonstrators that gathered at Sharpeville location outside Vereeniging on March 21, 1960, the day might have marked just one more abortive campaign in the history of African protest. Contrary to the expectations of the PAC's leaders, response to the PAC's call was almost negligible in Johannesburg. Publicity for the campaign had been inadequate, opposition from the ANC had been appreciable, Madzunya had decided to oppose the campaign in Alexandra township, and the relatively materialistic and sophisticated Africans of the southwestern townships showed themselves to be little disposed toward risky political protest. When Sobukwe, Leballo, and other members of the PAC executive presented themselves for arrest at the Orlando police station, they were followed only by some 150 volunteers. In Durban, Port Elizabeth, and East London, no demonstrations took place.

Thirty-five miles south of Johannesburg, however, in the industrial complex around Vereeniging, PAC militants had organized well with little or no competition from the ANC, which had never been strong in that area. The long bus boycott at Evaton (between Vereeniging and Johannesburg) in 1955–1956 had impressed political organizers with the strategic importance of the transport systems carrying Africans to their jobs in the white cities of Vereeniging, Vanderbijlpark, Meyerton, and Johannesburg. Local activists were adept at coercing and cajoling African bus drivers into cooperation, and in the hours before dawn on March 21, they brought transport out of Sharpeville to a near standstill. At Evaton, a predominantly African town, thousands of people gathered and were addressed by PAC organizers. Several hundred men presented themselves for arrest without passes, but police refused to imprison them on the grounds that jail facilities were inadequate. Military aircraft were sent to swoop low over the assembled crowds in the morning; by nightfall no violent incidents had occurred. At Vanderbijlpark, a large industrial town about 12 miles from Evaton, several thousand protesters who were gathered at the police station refused to disperse either when the aircraft dived at them or when police threw tear gas. Police fired at protesters who were throwing stones, and two men were killed. A police baton charge eventually scattered the crowd, and by mid-day police reinforcements began shifting from Vanderbijlpark to Sharpeville a few miles away, where the demonstration appeared to be getting out of control.

Eyewitness accounts of the "Sharpeville massacre" vary considerably in their assessment of the mood of the large crowd that surrounded the location police station there on March 21. Witnesses sympathetic toward the demonstrators testified, both at the official commission of inquiry and at the trial of the Sharpeville PAC leaders, that the crowd was unarmed, amiable, well-mannered, and unaggressive. They estimated that at the time the shooting occurred in the early afternoon, the size of the crowd was between 3,000 and 10,000. Police witnesses testified that the number of people was much larger (official reports placed it at 20,000), that many were armed with sticks and other weapons, and that the crowd's mood was hostile, aggressive, and volatile. Tear gas had failed to halt demonstrators marching through the town earlier in the day, and some witnesses estimated that diving aircraft had only attracted more people to the site of the demonstration. Moreover, apparently unknown to the police, a rumor had spread in the township that a high-ranking official was coming to address the crowd at the police station.

The size of the crowd, the insults and threats (including cries of "Cato Manor")[1] shouted by individuals in the throng, combined with the natural anxiety of white men surrounded and outnumbered by people whom they regarded as the "enemy," brought police nerves after several hours to the snapping point. No order was given to shoot, and no warning shots were fired to frighten the crowd back from the fence surrounding the station. In a moment of panic, a line of white police opened fire on the crowd and continued to fire (for from 10 to 30 seconds, according to the findings of the commission of inquiry) as the demonstrators fled. Sixty-seven Africans were shot dead, the great majority hit in the back as they ran; 186 others were wounded, including 40 women and 8 children. White press reporters on the scene recorded the carnage in a series of grisly photographs that were to appear in newspapers all over the world in the days that followed. . . .

State of Emergency and Banning of the ANC and the PAC

The widely publicized shooting at Sharpeville confronted the South African government with a political crisis of unprecedented magnitude. All efforts by Verwoerd and other Nationalist Party leaders to make light of the incident proved futile as the waves of reaction mounted in South Africa and abroad. In Cape Town and the Transvaal gun shops sold out their stocks within days to panicky whites, and inquiries about emigration inundated the offices of Canadian and Australian diplomatic representatives. International condemnation and isolation, merely a worrisome threat to whites before March 1960, now seemed an imminent reality as protests against South Africa's policies poured in from every corner of the world. In a surprising move on March 22, the American State Department released a statement directly rebuking South Africa for the deaths on March 21 and expressing the hope that Africans in the future would "be able to obtain redress for legitimate grievances by peaceful means." On April 1 the United Nations Security Council intervened in the South African situation for the first time. The United States voted for a resolution (9–0, with the United Kingdom and France abstaining) that blamed the South African government for the shootings and called upon it "to initiate measures aimed at bringing about racial harmony based on equality." To many whites it looked as though South Africa had reached a point where change might be unavoidable.

[1] Site of a January 1960 riot, in Durban, in which nine policemen were murdered by an angry mob.—ed.

Political uncertainty brought immediate economic repercussions. Massive selling plagued the Johannesburg Stock Exchange, and speculation grew that the crisis would retard or halt the flow of foreign investment so vital to white South Africa's prosperity. In Cape Town, where Parliament was in session, the African stay-at-home, which had begun on the 21st, spread in the days that followed until, by the end of the week, it was virtually total, crippling the city's docks and industries. In the Vereeniging area absenteeism among African workers was also high throughout the week. When Lutuli called for Monday the 28th to be observed with a nationwide stay-at-home as a day of mourning for the Sharpeville and Langa victims, the prospect of a general strike by Africans momentarily loomed large.

Pleas from the United Party, liberals, and businessmen calling for the government to restore stability by making concessions to Africans, met with refusal from Verwoerd, who took the characteristic Nationalist Party view that concessions would only cause Africans to make further and bolder demands. Nevertheless, in an effort to bring the situation under control, government orders went out on March 26 that pass arrests should temporarily be suspended. That evening in Pretoria, where he was appearing as a witness in the Treason Trial, Lutuli ceremoniously burned his passbook and urged all Africans to follow suit.

The government's moratorium on pass arrests was a purely tactical move to deflate the African spirit of rebellion. Accompanying the move were strong measures to counter the African challenge and to suppress all threats to white control. Armored vehicles moved in to patrol location trouble spots around the clock; all police leaves were cancelled; and white citizen reserve units were called up to supplement police and military forces. Meetings were outlawed in main centers throughout the Union, while raids and arrests systematically battered anti-government organizations.

Although the specter of violence and disorder hung over the African residential areas of Johannesburg and the Reef as the crisis entered its second week, it was in Cape Town that the security of whites appeared to be most directly threatened by African rebelliousness. After police had agreed to jail about 100 anti-pass volunteers surrendering at Caledon Square police headquarters in downtown Cape Town on March 24, a crowd of 2,000 men from Langa location gathered at the same place the next day to court arrest. Police refused to jail them, and they marched without incident back to the township, but not before many whites had become thoroughly alarmed at the sight of the large crowd massed in the city center. By this time the African stay-at-home that had begun on the 21st was virtually complete, and businesses and industries that relied on African labor found themselves at a near-total standstill.

On Monday, March 28, the day designated by the PAC for the funerals of the Langa riot dead, a crowd estimated at 50,000 (a figure nearly equal to the entire adult African population of Cape Town) jammed the township and heard PAC funeral orators call for the strike to go on until African demands were met. These demands, repeatedly stated since March 21, were for the abolition of passes, a £ 35-a-month minimum wage, and no victimization of strikers. Never had an African urban population been so solidly united in its determination to defy white authority.

On the same day, serious rioting erupted in Johannesburg, and several hundred thousand Africans across the country observed Lutuli's stay-at-home call. In Parliament, the government introduced a bill calling for emergency powers to ban the ANC and the PAC and to increase the legal punishments for political acts of defiance.

On Wednesday, March 30, the government declared a state of emergency and assumed broad powers to act against all forms of alleged subversion, including the power to arrest and detain indefinitely any person suspected of anti-government activity. Early that morning police had begun conducting nationwide swoops to arrest leaders and supporters of the campaign. In Cape Town they entered Langa and Nyanga, beat up striking workers, and began a systematic roundup of known PAC leaders. As word of the arrests and beatings spread, people began to congregate. By mid-morning a broad column of Africans began to move out of Langa along the ten-mile route toward the city. A white journalist who witnessed the march expressed the tension of Cape Town's whites:

> There were about 5,000 when the march began. By the time I saw them, coming along the curved dual carriage-way that leads around the side of the mountain to the heart of Cape Town, there must have been at least 15,000. They were marching about twelve abreast, dressed in their workingmen's shirts, trousers and coats, and looking exactly like some sentimental Leftist painting, "The Peasants' Revolt." But this was real.

Philip Kgosana was at the head of the marching column as it entered the city. He intended to lead the crowd to the Houses of Parliament and to demand an interview with the minister of justice, but was persuaded by police to divert the march into Caledon Square. As Saracen armored cars and troops barricaded the approaches to Parliament and an Air Force helicopter circled overhead, Africans poured into Caledon Square and the surrounding streets. Press reporters estimated the crowd then to be about 30,000 strong.

The spontaneous massing of such a large crowd of Africans in the center of a "white" city was unprecedented, and neither the marchers nor the police were prepared with any plan of action. The marchers were unarmed, but had they become violent, perhaps in response to a police show of force, the toll in lives and property could have been immense. The outcome rested in the hands of Kgosana, a 23-year-old Cape Town University student with a flair for leadership, who had dropped his studies a few months earlier to devote himself full time to politics. Negotiating on behalf of the demonstrators, Kgosana asked for the release of the arrested leaders, an interview with the minister of justice, and an assurance that police would stop using force to break the African stay-at-home. After consultations among high-ranking police, Kgosana was informed that his last two demands would be met if he would request the crowd to disperse. The gullible Kgosana, not realizing that his only bargaining power lay in his ability to keep the crowd behind him, took a police microphone and directed the people to return to Langa, telling them that the police had agreed to make concessions. The marchers returned home. That evening when Kgosana and several colleagues returned to the city for their promised "interview," they were arrested and jailed under the terms of the new emergency regulations. A decisive historical moment had come and passed by, leaving whites shaken but still firmly in control. . . .

32. *UMKONTO WE SIZWE (SPEAR OF THE NATION).* *

Units of Umkonto We Sizwe today carried out planned attacks against Government installations, particularly those connected with the policy of apartheid and race discrimination.

Umkonto We Sizwe is a new, independent body, formed by Africans. It includes in its ranks South Africans of all races. It is not connected in any way with a so-called "Committee for National Liberation" whose existence has been announced in the press. Umkonto We Sizwe will carry on the struggle for freedom and democracy by new methods, which are necessary to complement the actions of the established national liberation organizations. Umkonto We Sizwe fully supports the national liberation movement, and our members, jointly and individually, place themselves under the overall political guidance of that movement.

It is, however, well known that the main national liberation organizations in this country have consistently followed a policy of non-violence. They have conducted themselves peaceably at all times, regardless of Government attacks and persecutions upon them, and despite all Government-inspired attempts to provoke them to violence. They have done so because the people prefer peaceful methods of change to achieve their aspirations without the suffering and bitterness of civil war. But the people's patience is not endless.

*Issued December 16, 1961.

The time comes in the life of any nation when there remain only two choices: submit or fight. That time has now come to South Africa. We shall not submit and we have no choice but to hit back by all means within our power in defense of our people, our future and our freedom.

The Government has interpreted the peacefulness of the movement as weakness; the people's non-violent policies have been taken as a green light for Government violence. Refusal to resort to force has been interpreted by the Government as an invitation to use armed force against the people without any fear of reprisals. The methods of Umkonto We Sizwe mark a break with that past.

We are striking out along a new road for the liberation of the people of this country. The Government policy of force, repression and violence will no longer be met with non-violent resistance only! The choice is not ours; it has been made by the Nationalist Government which has rejected every peaceable demand by the people for rights and freedom and answered every such demand with force and yet more force! Twice in the past 18 months, virtual martial law has been imposed in order to beat down peaceful, non-violent strike action of the people in support of their rights. It is now preparing its forces—enlarging and rearming its armed forces and drawing white civilian population into commandos and pistol clubs—for full-scale military actions against the people. The Nationalist Government has chosen the course of force and massacre, now, deliberately, as it did at Sharpeville.

Umkonto We Sizwe will be at the front line of the people's defense. It will be the fighting arm of the people against the Government and its policies of race oppression. It will be the striking force of the people for liberty, for rights and for their final liberation! Let the Government, its supporters who put it into power, and those whose passive toleration of reaction keeps it in power, take note of where the Nationalist Government is leading the country!

We of Umkonto We Sizwe have always sought—as the liberation movement has sought—to achieve liberation, without bloodshed and civil clash. We do so still. We hope—even at this late hour—that our first actions will awaken everyone to a realization of the disastrous situation to which the Nationalist policy is leading. We hope that we will bring the Government and its supporters to their senses before it is too late, so that both Government and its policies can be changed before matters reach the desperate stage of civil war. We believe our actions to be a blow against the Nationalist preparations for civil war and military rule.

In these actions, we are working in the best interests of all the people of this country—black, brown, and white—whose future happiness and well-being cannot be attained without the overthrow of the Nationalist Government, the abolition of white supremacy and the winning of liberty, democracy and full national rights and equality for all the people of this country.

We appeal for the support and encouragement of all those South Africans who seek the happiness and freedom of the people of this country.

Afrika Mayibuye!

Issued by command of Umkonto We Sizwe.

33. *"I AM PREPARED TO DIE"**

by NELSON MANDELA

Sentenced to prison for incitement to strike and leaving the country without a valid permit, Nelson Mandela was again brought to trial—the celebrated Rivonia Trial —on a charge of sabotage. Despite the following statement from the dock in his defense, Mandela was convicted and sentenced to life imprisonment. After being held for nearly 20 years at the notorious maximum-security facility on Robben Island, he was moved, in 1981, to Pollsmoor prison, a modern penitentiary near Cape Town, where he remains today.

. . . We who formed Umkonto were all members of the African National Congress, and had behind us the ANC tradition of non-violence and negotiation as a means of solving political disputes. We believe that South Africa belonged to all the people who lived in it, and not to one group, be it Black or White. . . .

The African National Congress was formed in 1912 to defend the rights of the African people which had been seriously curtailed by the South Africa Act, and which were then being threatened by the Native Land Act. For thirty-seven years—that is until 1949—it adhered strictly to a constitutional struggle. It put forward demands and resolutions; it sent delegations to the Government in the belief that African grievances could be settled through peaceful discussion and that Africans could advance gradually to full political rights. But White Governments remained unmoved, and the rights of Africans became less instead of becoming greater. . . .

Even after 1949, the ANC remained determined to avoid violence. At this time, however, there was a change from the strictly constitutional means of protest which had been employed in the past. The change was embodied in a decision which was taken to protest against apartheid legislation by peaceful, but unlawful, demonstrations against certain laws. Pursuant to this policy the ANC launched the Defiance Campaign, in which I was placed in charge of volunteers. This campaign was based on the principles of passive resistance. More than 8,500 people defied apartheid laws and went to gaol. Yet there was

*April 20, 1964 [shortened from the original].

not a single instance of violence in the course of this campaign on the part of any defier. I, and nineteen colleagues were convicted for the role which we played in organizing the campaign, but our sentences were suspended mainly because the Judge found that discipline and non-violence had been stressed throughout. . . .

During the Defiance Campaign, the Public Safety Act and the Criminal Law Amendment Act were passed. These Statutes provided harsher penalties for offenses committed by way of protests against laws. Despite this, the protests continued and the ANC adhered to its policy of non-violence. In 1956, one hundred and fifty-six leading members of the Congress Alliance, including myself, were arrested on a charge of High Treason and charged under the Suppression of Communism Act. The non-violent policy of the ANC was put in issue by the State, but when the Court gave judgment some five years later, it found that the ANC did not have a policy of violence. We were acquitted on all counts, which included a count that the ANC sought to set up a Communist State in place of the existing regime. The Government has always sought to label all its opponents as communists. This allegation has been repeated in the present case, but as I will show, the ANC is not, and never has been, a communist organization.

In 1960, there was the shooting at Sharpeville, which resulted in the proclamation of a State of Emergency and the declaration of the ANC as an unlawful organization. My colleagues and I, after careful consideration, decided that we would not obey this decree. The African people were not part of the Government and did not make the laws by which they were governed. We believed in the words of the Universal Declaration of Human Rights, that "the will of the people shall be the basis of the authority of the Government," and for us to accept the banning was equivalent to accepting the silencing of the Africans for all time. The ANC refused to dissolve, but instead went underground. We believed it was our duty to preserve this organization which had been built up with almost fifty years of unremitting toil. I have no doubt that no self-respecting White political organization would disband itself if declared illegal by a Government in which it had no say. . . .

In 1960 the Government held a Referendum which led to the establishment of the Republic. Africans, who constituted approximately 70 percent of the population of South Africa, were not entitled to vote, and were not even consulted about the proposed constitutional change. All of us were apprehensive of our future under the proposed White Republic, and a resolution was taken to hold an All-In African Conference to call for a National Convention, and to organize mass demonstrations on the eve of the unwanted Republic, if the Government failed to call the Convention. The Conference was attended by Africans of various political persuasions. I was the Secretary of the Conference and undertook to be responsible for organizing the national stay-at-home which was subsequently called to coincide with the declaration of the Republic. As all strikes by Africans are illegal, the person organizing such a strike must avoid arrest. I was chosen to be this person, and consequently I had to leave my home and family and my practice and go into hiding to avoid arrest.

The stay-at-home, in accordance with ANC policy, was to be a peaceful demonstration. Careful instructions were given to organizers and members to avoid any recourse to violence. The Government's answer was to introduce new and harsher laws, to mobilize its armed forces, and to send saracens, armed vehicles and soldiers into the townships in a massive show of force designed to intimidate the people. This was an indication that the Government had decided to rule by force alone, and this decision was a milestone on the road to Umkonto. . . .

. . . What were we, the leaders of our people to do? Were we to give in to the show of force and the implied threat against future action, or were we to fight it, and if so, how?

We had no doubt that we had to continue the fight. Anything else would have been abject surrender. Our problem was not whether to fight, but was how to continue the fight. We of the ANC had always stood for a non-racial democracy, and we shrank from any action which might drive the races further apart than they already were. But the hard facts were that fifty years of non-violence had brought the African people nothing but more and more repressive legislation, and fewer and fewer rights. . . .

At the beginning of June, 1961, after a long and anxious assessment of the South African situation, I, and some colleagues, came to the conclusion that as violence in this country was inevitable, it would be unrealistic and wrong for African leaders to continue preaching peace and non-violence at a time when the Government met our peaceful demands with force.

This conclusion was not easily arrived at. It was only when all else had failed, when all channels of peaceful protest had been barred to us, that the decision was made to embark on violent forms of political struggle, and to form Umkonto We Sizwe. We did so not because we desired such a course, but solely because the Government had left us with no other choice. . . .

Four forms of violence are possible. There is sabotage, there is guerrilla warfare, there is terrorism and there is open revolution. We chose to adopt the first method and to exhaust it before taking any other decision.

In the light of our political background the choice was a logical one. Sabotage did not involve loss of life, and it offered the best hope for future race relations. Bitterness would be kept to a minimum, and if the policy bore fruit, democratic government could become a reality. . . .

This then was the plan. Umkonto was to perform sabotage, and strict instructions were given to its members right from the start, that on no account were they to injure or kill people in planning or carrying out operations. . . .

Umkonto had its first operation on the 16th December, 1961, when Government buildings in Johannesburg, Port Elizabeth and Durban were attacked. The selection of targets is proof of the policy to which I have referred. Had we intended to attack life we would have selected targets where people congregated and not empty buildings and power stations. . . .

The Manifesto of Umkonto was issued on the day that operations commenced. The response to our actions and Manifesto among the White population was characteristically violent. The Government threatened to take strong action, and called upon its supporters to stand firm and to ignore the demands of the Africans. The Whites failed to respond by suggesting change; they responded to our call by suggesting the laager.

In contrast, the response of the Africans was one of encouragement. Suddenly there was hope again. Things were happening. People in the townships became eager for political news. A great deal of enthusiasm was generated by the initial successes, and people began to speculate on how soon freedom would be obtained. . . .

Another of the allegations made by the State is that the aims and objects of the ANC and the Communist Party are the same. . . .

The ideological creed of the ANC is, and always has been, the creed of African Nationalism. It is not the concept of African Nationalism expressed in the cry, "Drive the White man into the sea." The African Nationalism for which the ANC stands, is the concept of freedom and fulfillment for the African people in their own land. The most important political document ever adopted by the ANC is the "Freedom Charter." It is by no means a blueprint for a socialist State. It calls for redistribution, but not nationalization, of land; it provides for nationalization of mines, banks and monopoly industry, because big monopolies are owned by one race only, and without such nationalization racial domination would be perpetuated despite the spread of political power. It would be a hollow gesture to repeal the Gold Law prohibitions against Africans when all gold mines are owned by European companies. In this respect the ANC's policy corresponds with the old policy of the present Nationalist Party which, for many years, had as part of its program the nationalization of the Gold Mines which, at that time, were controlled by foreign capital. Under the Freedom Charter nationalization would take place in an economy based on private enterprise. The realization of the Freedom Charter would open up fresh fields for a prosperous African population of all classes, including the middle class. The ANC has never at any period of its history advocated a revolutionary change in the economic structure of the country, nor has it, to the best of my recollection, ever condemned capitalist society.

As far as the Communist Party is concerned, and if I understand its policy correctly, it stands for the establishment of a State based on the principles of Marxism. Although it is prepared to work for the Freedom Charter, as a short-term solution to the problems created by White supremacy, it regards the Freedom Charter as the beginning, and not the end, of its program.

The ANC, unlike the Communist Party, admitted Africans only as members. Its chief goal was, and is, for the African people to win unity and full political rights. The Communist Party's main aim, on the other hand, was to remove the capitalists and to replace them with a working-class Government. The Communist Party sought to emphasize class distinctions whilst the ANC seeks to harmonize them. This is a vital distinction.

It is true that there has often been close co-operation between the ANC and the Communist Party. But co-operation is merely proof of a common goal— in this case the removal of White supremacy—and is not proof of a complete community of interests. . . .

Another instance of such co-operation is to be found precisely in Umkonto. Shortly after MK was constituted, I was informed by some of its members that the Communist Party would support Umkonto, and this then occurred. At a later stage the support was made openly.

I believe that Communists have always played an active role in the fight by colonial countries for their freedom, because the short-term objects of Communism would always correspond with the long-term objects of freedom movements. Thus Communists have played an important role in the freedom struggles fought in countries such as Malaya, Algeria and Indonesia, yet none of these States today are Communist countries. . . .

This pattern of co-operation between Communists and non-Communists has been repeated in the National Liberation Movement of South Africa. Prior to the banning of the Communist Party, joint campaigns involving the Communist Party and the Congress Movements were accepted practice. African Communists could, and did, become members of the ANC, and some served on the National, Provincial and local committies. . . .

I joined the ANC in 1944, and in my younger days I held the view that the policy of admitting Communists to the ANC, and the close co-operation which existed at times on specific issues between the ANC and the Communist Party, would lead to a watering down of the concept of African nationalism. At that stage I was a member of the African National Congress Youth League, and was one of a group which moved for the expulsion of Communists from the ANC. This proposal was heavily defeated. Amongst those who voted against the proposal were some of the most conservative sections of African political opinion. They defended the policy on the ground that from its inception the ANC was formed and built up, not as a political party with one school of political thought, but as a Parliament of the African people, accommodating people of various political convictions, all united by the common goal of national liberation. I was eventually won over to this point of view and have upheld it ever since.

It is perhaps difficult for White South Africans, with an ingrained prejudice against Communism, to understand why experienced African politicians so readily accept Communists as their friends. But to us the reason is obvious. Theoretical differences amongst those fighting against oppression is a luxury we cannot afford at this stage. What is more, for many decades Communists were the only political group in South Africa who were prepared to treat Africans as human beings and their equals; who were prepared to eat with us; talk with us, live with us and work with us. They were the only political group which was prepared to work with the Africans for the attainment of political rights and a stake in society. Because of this, there are many Africans who, today, tend to equate freedom with Communism. They are supported in this belief by a legislature which brands all exponents of democratic government and African freedom as Communists and bans many of them (who are not Communists) under the Suppression of Communism Act. Although I have never been a member of the Communist Party, I myself have been named under that pernicious Act because of the role I played in the Defiance Campaign. I have also been banned and imprisoned under that Act.

It is not only in internal politics that we count Communists as amongst those who support our cause. In the international field, Communist countries have always come to our aid. In the United Nations and other Councils of the world the Communist block has supported the Afro-Asian struggle against colonialism and often seems to be more sympathetic to our plight than some of the Western powers. Although there is a universal condemnation of apartheid, the Communist block speaks out against it with a louder voice than most of the White world. In these circumstances, it would take a brash young politician, such as I was in 1949, to proclaim that the Communists are our enemies.

I turn now to my own position. I have denied that I am a Communist, and I think that in the circumstances I am obliged to state exactly what my political beliefs are.

I have always regarded myself, in the first place, as an African patriot. After all, I was born in Umtata, forty-six years ago. My guardian was my cousin, who was the acting paramount chief of Tembuland, and I am related both to the present paramount chief of Tembuland, Sabata Dalinyebo, and to Kaizer Matanzima, the Chief Minister of the Transkei.

Today I am attracted by the idea of a classless society, an attraction which springs in part from Marxist reading and, in part, from my admiration of the structure and organization of early African societies in this country. The land, then the main means of production, belonged to the tribe. There were no rich or poor and there was no exploitation.

It is true, as I have already stated, that I have been influenced by Marxist thought. But this is also true of many of the leaders of the new independent States. Such widely different persons as Gandhi, Nehru, Nkrumah and Nasser all acknowledge this fact. We all accept the need for some form of Socialism to enable our people to catch up with the advanced countries of this world and to overcome their legacy of extreme poverty. But this does not mean we are Marxists.

Indeed, for my own part, I believe that it is open to debate whether the Communist Party has any specific role to play at this particular stage of our political struggle. The basic task at the present moment is the removal of race discrimination and the attainment of democratic rights on the basis of the Freedom Charter. Insofar as that Party furthers this task, I welcome its assistance. I realize that it is one of the means by which people of all races can be drawn into our struggle.

From my reading of Marxist literature and from conversations with Marxists, I have gained the impression that Communists regard the parliamentary system of the West as undemocratic and reactionary. But, on the contrary, I am an admirer of such a system.

The Magna Charta, the Petition of Rights and the Bill of Rights, are documents which are held in veneration by democrats throughout the world.

I have great respect for British political institutions, and for the country's system of justice. I regard the British Parliament as the most democratic institution in the world, and the independence and impartiality of its judiciary never fail to arouse my admiration.

The American Congress, that country's doctrine of separation of powers, as well as the independence of its judiciary, arouse in me similar sentiments.

I have been influenced in my thinking by both West and East. . . .

The Government often answers its critics by saying that Africans in South Africa are economically better off than the inhabitants of the other countries in Africa. I do not know whether this statement is true and doubt whether any comparison can be made without having regard to the cost of living index in such countries. But even if it is true, as far as the African people are concerned it is irrelevant. Our complaint is not that we are poor by comparison with people in other counries, but that we are poor by comparison with the White people in our own country, and that we are prevented by legislation from altering this imbalance.

The lack of human dignity experienced by Africans is the direct result of the policy of White supremacy. White supremacy implies Black inferiority. Legislation designed to preserve White supremacy entrenches this notion. Menial tasks in South Africa are invariably performed by Africans. When anything has to be carried or cleaned the White man will look around for an African to do it for him, whether the African is employed by him or not. Because of this sort of attitude, Whites tend to regard Africans as a separate breed. They do not look upon them as people with families of their own; they do not realize that they have emotions—that they fall in love like White people do; that they want to be with their wives and children like White people want to be with theirs; that they want to earn enough money to support their families properly, to feed and clothe them and send them to school. And what "house-boy" or "garden-boy" or laborer can ever hope to do this?

Pass Laws, which to the Africans are among the most hated bits of legislation in South Africa, render any African liable to police surveillance at any time. I doubt whether there is a single African male in South Africa who has not at some stage had a brush with the police over his pass. Hundreds and thousands of Africans are thrown into jail each year under pass laws. Even worse than this is the fact that pass laws keep husband and wife apart and lead to the breakdown of family life. . . .

Africans want to be paid a living wage. Africans want to perform work which they are capable of doing, and not work which the Government declares them to be capable of. Africans want to be allowed to live where they obtain work, and not be endorsed out of an area because they were not born there. Africans want to be allowed to own land in places where they work, and not to be obliged to live in rented houses which they can never call their own. Africans want to be part of the general population, and not confined to living in their own ghettos. African men want to have their wives and children to live with them where they work, and not be forced into an unnatural existence in men's hostels. African women want to be with their men folk and not be left permanently widowed in the reserves. Africans want to be allowed out after 11 o'clock at night and not to be confined to their rooms like little children. Africans want to be allowed to travel in their own country and to seek work where they want to and not where the Labor Bureau tells them to. Africans want a just share in the whole of South Africa; they want security and a stake in society.

Above all, we want equal political rights, because without them our disabilities will be permanent. I know this sounds revolutionary to the Whites in this country, because the majority of voters will be Africans. This makes the White man fear democracy.

But this fear cannot be allowed to stand in the way of the only solution which will guarantee racial harmony and freedom for all. It is not true that the enfranchisement of all will result in racial domination. Political division, based on color, is entirely artificial and, when it disappears, so will the domination of one color group by another. The ANC has spent half a century fighting against racialism. When it triumphs it will not change that policy.

This then is what the ANC is fighting. Their struggle is a truly national one. It is a struggle of the African people, inspired by their own suffering and their own experience. It is a struggle for the right to live.

During my lifetime I have dedicated myself to this struggle of the African people. I have fought against White domination, and I have fought against Black domination. I have cherished the ideal of a democratic and free society in which all persons live together in harmony and with equal opportunities. It is an ideal which I hope to live for and to achieve. But if needs be, it is an ideal for which I am prepared to die.

34. THE SOWETO UPRISING, 1976*

by ALAN BROOKS and JEREMY BRUCKHILL

Alan Brooks and Jeremy Bruckhill grew up in Zimbabwe, studied in South Africa, and later moved to England, where they worked in the Research Department of the International Defence and Aid Fund for Southern Africa, Alan Brooks as its director and Jeremy Brickhill as his assistant. Mr. Brooks currently lives in England. Mr. Brickhill has returned to Zimbabwe.

"The storm has not struck yet. We are only experiencing the whirlwinds that go before it."—Prime Minister Vorster, December 31, 1976.

The First Day—Wednesday 16 June

In Soweto on 16 June 1976 life began as usual for the million and a half inhabitants. Inside the crowded matchbox houses Sowetans began to stir well before dawn. Fires were lit to prepare the morning meal of maize porridge and to heat water for washing. Chamber pots were carried carefully to be emptied in the outside toilets. Workers and children hurriedly dressed as the winter sun slowly rose over the smoggy township. Those over 16 carefully checked that their passbooks were in their pockets. Those illegally in Soweto without correct passbooks faced another anxious day avoiding detection by the authorities.

Starting at 4 A.M. the steady stream of black commuters snaked through the dusty streets towards the buses and trains which would carry them to another day's labor in the white factories, offices and homes.

But today was not an ordinary day for all Sowetans. In many houses dotted around Soweto young school students were wide awake and had been throughout the night, planning a demonstration. Others woke early, dressed quickly and stepped out into the cold morning air well before their parents had begun their usual trek into the white cities.

For three days they had been involved in hectic preparations for a protest

---

*From *Whirlwind Before the Storm: The Origins and Development of the Uprising in Soweto and the Rest of South Africa from June to December 1976* (London, 1980) [as edited].

march and rally to demand an end to their discriminatory education and specifically to be allowed to be taught in the language of their choice. Opposition to the government's Bantu Education policy had been growing in the Soweto schools over the past few months. A meeting of representatives from the schools had called for action to be taken and three days previously this meeting had elected an Action Committee and charged it with the task of organizing a demonstration.

Details had been carefully worked out to ensure the maximum participation of Soweto's students at the same time as minimizing the risk of intervention by the authorities. Preparations had been conducted as far as possible in secret and so far the police were unaware of the students' plans. Placards had been prepared and stored and Action Committee members had been touring the schools to hold clandestine mobilizing meetings.

The demonstration was to be peaceful but the student leaders were well aware that the police would attempt to stop them. Hence the secrecy. The Action Committee had even prepared their tactics in such a way as to confuse the police to ensure that they could assemble for the demonstration before the police had a chance to intervene.

Over a dozen assembly points had been chosen at various schools in Soweto. Each school had a set time of departure to march to Orlando West. In this way the student leaders hoped that each time the police received a report that one group of students was marching, before they could react another group would begin, and then another. The police would be too stretched to respond and would probably be confused by all this dispersed activity. This would give the students time to gather en masse at Orlando West to march to Orlando stadium for a mass rally.

Shortly before 7 A.M. thousands of pupils began gathering at the various assembly points. Placards were distributed and student leaders announced the last minute instructions, emphasizing the need for a peaceful, disciplined demonstration. Then at 7 A.M. the first contingent moved off; ten minutes later somewhere else in Soweto the next, and so on. Soon over a dozen columns were marching through Soweto, singing freedom songs, chanting slogans and carrying placards made from torn cardboard boxes and exercise book covers on which were written:

DOWN WITH AFRIKAANS
BLACKS ARE NOT DUSTBINS—AFRIKAANS STINKS
AFRIKAANS IS TRIBAL LANGUAGE
BANTU EDUCATION—TO HELL WITH IT!

· ·

By the time several thousand pupils had converged near Orlando West Junior Secondary School there had already been several brushes with units of police. The atmosphere was tense and expectant, but the pupils continued to sing. Shortly before 9 A.M. a senior pupil and one of the leaders called for quiet and addressed the crowd:

> Brothers and sisters, I appeal to you—keep calm and cool. We have just received a report that the police are coming. Don't taunt them, don't do anything to them. Be cool and calm. We are not fighting.

While hundreds of demonstrators were still marching into Orlando, several police vans and cars drove up to face the main crowd. About 50 police emerged from the vehicles and spread out in an arc facing the pupils. Despite the tense atmosphere the huge crowd remained calm and well ordered. The pupils were singing the national anthem in Sotho: "Morena Boloka Sechaba sa heso" (God Save our Nation). Suddenly a white policeman lobbed a tear-gas canister into the front of the crowd. Pupils ran out of the smoke dazed and coughing. The crowd retreated slightly, out of range of the tear-gas smoke, but remained facing the police, waving placards and singing.

A white policeman drew his revolver. Black journalists standing by the police heard a shout: "Look at him. He's going to shoot at the kids." A single shot rang out. There was a split second's silence and pandemonium broke out. Children screamed. More shots were fired. At least four pupils fell, and others ran screaming in all directions. A black journalist described the events:

> I remember looking at the children in their school uniforms and wondering how long they would stand up to the police. Suddenly a small boy dropped to the ground next to me. . . . They were shooting into the crowd. More children fell. There seemed to be no plan. The police were merely blasting away. . . . Out of the blur of dust and fleeing children stones began to fly at the police.

Whilst some carried the wounded away others darted out and threw bricks, stones and bottles. More shots rang out. More children fell. The shooting continued and more stones were thrown.

One young student who was standing near the front of the crowd described how, as the police arrived, the students had given "peace signs" and shouted "peace!" As soon as the first shots were fired, the front ranks, mostly young girls, picked up bricks, stones and bottles and pelted the police. Within minutes a well-ordered demonstration had been turned into a riot.

The firing continued but the crowd advanced pelting the police with anything that came to hand. More children fell. A journalist commented:

> What frightened me more than anything was the attitude of the children. Many seemed oblivious to the danger. They continued running towards the police dodging and ducking.

Sophie Tema, a black journalist on *The World,* described how out of the dust and chaos she saw a group of children emerge after the first burst of shooting, carrying a young boy called Hector Petersen, aged 13, who was covered in blood. They rushed him to a clinic in her car but he was dead on arrival. Photographs of this scene appeared throughout the world, and the victim became a symbol of the massacre at Soweto.

On the verge of being overwhelmed, despite their weapons, the police retreated towards Orlando East pursued by a stone-throwing and furious crowd. As the police retreated the pupils began to collect the casualties: at least two dead and over a dozen wounded. Teachers from nearby schools, taxi drivers and black journalists on the scene were called to transport the casualties to hospital. Armed with makeshift implements, others began to block the roads to prevent police vehicles from returning. Large numbers of pupils were still arriving at Orlando West. News of the shooting spread quickly. Barricades were thrown across roads and pupils armed with sticks and assorted bits of metal and wood stood behind them, awaiting the police onslaught.

The unit of police involved in the first shootings had come from the nearby Orlando police station which normally has a complement of about 100 uniformed and CID police. They retreated across the Klipspruit River, blocked off the road with their vehicles and called for reinforcements, but those who were hurriedly rushed to the area were unprepared to face thousands of angry demonstrators. They joined the others at the Klipspruit River roadblock and awaited further assistance. An operational headquarters was set up at Orlando police station. Ammunition and rifles were flown in by helicopter. Throughout the rest of the morning the police maintained their positions. Reinforcements were moved in quickly and by midday a force of several hundred had assembled at the Orlando police station.

Meanwhile billows of smoke began to rise over nearby parts of Soweto as groups of demonstrators set the hated township administration offices ablaze. Vehicles belonging to the West Rand Administration Board (WRAB) were overturned in the roads and set alight. . . .

At 1:30 P.M. two army helicopters began swooping over the pupils' stronghold in Orlando West dropping tear gas. Among the police reinforcements the first contingent of riot squad arrived. An hour later a second contingent arrived. Although they numbered no more than 150–200 men the two riot squad units (one from Pretoria and the other from Johannesburg) appeared well briefed and equipped. Dressed in camouflage uniform, they were armed with automatic rifles, hand machine carbines and machine guns. . . .

By mid-afternoon the police had succeeded in moving back into Orlando West. In Jabavu the riot squad had swept through the area near Morris Isaacson School. The demonstrators had spread into other areas, however. To the west of Phefeni station, a number of buildings were blazing including the Urban Bantu Council offices in Dube. Numerous burnt out vehicles were strewn across the roads reducing police mobility. A police spokesman said that 36 gutted vehicles had been found.

A photographer described the police offensive:

> It was at this point of burning any building that was a symbol of Government oppression and the breaking of bottle stores that the police started to shoot indiscriminately—mowing down quite a number of teenagers and bystanders. Hundreds of youths were killed. I was personally nearly shot down when I started taking photographs of police and the smouldering buildings. At the Dube office and Bank, my camera was taken by the police and the film destroyed.

. . . .

Toward evening workers arriving home found a chaotic situation. They heard of the horrors of the day's events and many of them joined the pupils. The attacks on buildings escalated. Between 5–8 P.M. the police received reports of 20 buildings set ablaze. As darkness fell the army helicopters which had guided police operations throughout the day were grounded. The police were now unable to get an overall picture of events and were particularly ineffective where there was no street lighting. Large convoys of police moved through Soweto firing into crowds in the dark, and were pelted with stones and bottles in return. . . .

Fires burned late into the night and fierce fighting went on. Police reinforcements continued to pour into Soweto. At 9:30 P.M. 14 "hippo" personnel carriers arrived. These vehicles, initially designed to withstand land-mine blasts and used in the war zones both in Namibia and Rhodesia, were to become important features of urban "riot control." The army was placed on the alert and an army detachment moved into Soweto to guard Orlando power station. Heavily armed police were guarding the railway stations. Reinforcements were sent to police stations elsewhere in Soweto, some of which had been besieged for several hours.

The Second Day—Thursday 17 June

By dawn on 17 June 1,500 police armed with sten guns, automatic rifles and hand machine carbines were massed to move into Soweto. Army units were on standby. . . .

At 8:15 A.M. the first incidents of the day were reported. A school in Diepkloof was being attacked by several hundred youths. In the west similar reports quickly followed from Orlando and Jabulani. Police patrols were sent out to deal with the incidents. Then reports came in of further attacks on WRAB offices in various parts of Soweto—first came Zola, then Klipspruit, then Orlando East and Mapetla—all within half an hour of each other. Units of heavily armed police in hippos, landrovers and riot trucks were dispatched to each new trouble spot. The pattern for the day's events in Soweto was set. According to an eyewitness:

> The second day, 17 June 1976, was marked by uncontrollable fury and burning hostility of the people. . . . Police also assumed another attitude. They shot at random, and at anyone who would raise a fist and shout "Power," into their face.

By midday the fighting was again raging all over Soweto. Roving police squads repeatedly attacked youths manning barricades. Large groups of students moved swiftly through the townships setting fire to official buildings, and crowds gathered on the streets. Some stood their ground, retaliated with stones and bottles and fought pitched battles with police. "We tried to fight the hippos," explained one students, "but we had to retreat." . . .

Casualties were even higher on this second day and the police were again reported to be firing indiscriminately, often not even leaving their vehicles. A newspaper reporter described seeing a boy aged about 14 attempting to escape when police attacked a group in Rockville. The boy tried to hide in a yard not far from the bottle store where police were firing on a crowd, but was caught in the police fire. . . .

Police also fired out of the helicopters which were constantly flying overhead dropping tear-gas. Madoda Mdluli, aged 16, was standing with two other boys when a helicopter flew over their heads and opened fire:

> We were scared but did not move. . . . we heard gunshots and I saw Nunu drop and we ran for cover. From where I stood looking back, I saw Nunu crawl on all fours and then drop to the ground.

. . . .

On 16 June when news of the shootings was first heard about 200 students from the University of Witwaterstand took part in a spontaneous protest picket. On Thursday 17 June three hundred white students marched from the campus through central Johannesburg carrying placards protesting at the massacre of schoolchildren in Soweto. As they marched they were joined by several hundred black workers. They were suddenly attacked by about 100 white vigilantes armed with clubs, metal pipes and chains. Other white civilians joined in while traffic police cordoned off the street. Several of the injured had already been taken away in ambulances when a contingent of police arrived, and baton-charged the remaining demonstrators. The vigilantes moved out of the way as police continued the attack by clubbing the fleeing the crowd. There were numerous injuries and several arrests were made. One of the vigilantes told a reporter:

> We grabbed anything at hand—I had a piece of steel piping—and laid into them. The students were no problem but some of the Blacks gave us a bit of trouble.

The action by the Witwaterstrand students was severely criticized by the Minister of Justice, Mr. J. Kruger, that evening in Parliament. He said he would not tolerate such behavior, which amounted to incitement at a critical moment, and he spoke angrily of placards carried by demonstrators, one of which exclaimed: "Don't start the revolution without us!" . . .

In the Krugersdorp township of Kagiso, crowds of pupils and adults began to gather in the early afternoon of 17 June. Uniformed riot squad police armed with rifles and machine guns arrived soon after 3:30 P.M. They threw tear gas among the demonstrators who immediately retaliated with stones, bricks and bottles. Overwhelmed by the fierce attack, the police retreated and kept out of the way while the crowds began to attack official buildings. The numbers swelled as workers arriving back from work joined the demonstrators, and beer halls, bottle stores and WRAB offices were set alight. At about 8 P.M. police reinforcements advanced into the crowds. They opened fire immediately and screaming people scattered in all directions. At least three people were killed and many others wounded in the initial shooting. The Leratong hospital in Kagiso reported that 5 dead and 50 wounded people were admitted during the night. . . .

From June to December: An Overview of the Uprising

The explosion that started in Soweto was heard in every part of South Africa and throughout the world. Thereafter the days passed in a fevered rush of demonstrations and shootings, arson and sabotage, strikes and boycotts. From the welter of incidents and episodes a confused impression arose of "riots and disturbances" in the eyes of those attached to the existing order, of heroic battles and campaigns in the eyes of those against it. . . .

Towards the end of September, while arson incidents, funerals of riot squad victims, and schools boycotts continued in the black townships of Soweto and Pretoria, heavy raids and numerous arrests signaled the start of a counteroffensive by the police which ran on into early October. In the Western Cape Coloured students resumed their boycott of classes while African students launched a campaign against liquor and the shebeens, beginning on 11 October. A few days later the SSRC [Soweto Students Representative Council] returned to the charge with an appeal for a period of mourning until the end of the year. It was to be marked by the closure of shebeens and cancellation of parties, sporting events and Christmas festivities in solidarity with those killed, detained or victimized for taking part in the strikes. It was accompanied and reinforced by some of the largest funerals yet held, these being political rallies organized so as to circumvent a ban on public gatherings.

By late October thousands of young blacks had left the country and taken refuge in neighboring states. Most were motivated by the desire to acquire arms and training so as to be able to return and continue the fight more effectively. The return of some of these, and of others who had left with similar motives before June 1976, began to make itself felt in the form of a wave of sabotage incidents and intensified preparations within the country for guerilla warfare.

Events in the first week of November showed that a boycott of examinations was within the capacity of the school student movement but a five-day stay-at-home was not. By the middle of the month the level of mass activity had fallen lower than at any time since mid-July, but student action against black collaborators flared up again in Guguletu at the end of the month, triggering off intermittent clashes in which the police sought to turn migrant workers against the young people and residents in the Cape Town townships. This reached a fierce and bloody climax over the Christmas weekend. Meanwhile in Soweto a boycott of white-owned shops was widely supported and the SSRC's call for mourning instead of celebrations proved generally effective.

Ushering in the New Year with his customary address to the white nation Prime Minister Vorster struck an appropriately somber note. The storm, he said, had not struck yet. "We are only experiencing the whirlwinds that go before it."

Chapter VIII:

WOMEN UNDER APARTHEID: Blacks and Whites in the Struggle

35. *WOMEN IN APARTHEID SOCIETY**

by FATIMA MEER

Fatima Meer, Professor of Sociology at the University of Natal in Durban, South Africa, has, among other anti-apartheid activities, helped organize the Federation of South African women, and, as a result, been banned more than once.

Social and Legal Status

South Africa's women of all races take their positions within the framework of male domination in the family, in the polity, economy, and society in general. It is difficult to assess which of the component cultures: African, Indian or European was the most repressive before the advent of industrialization.

Coloured and white women share a common cultural system, which appears to be less repressive of women than the Indian and African ones. Coloured women, however, are not as liberated as white women are in their relations with men. The difference is largely due to the economic factor. White women attain a very much higher standard of education and are able to reach out to a far more varied and relaxed life. The "patriarch" plays his role in moderation and, even if overbearing at times, compensates by his effective role as "provider" and "protector."

*From United Nations Centre Against Apartheid: *Notes and Documents,* "Women in the Apartheid Society" (New York, 1985).

236

Coloured and African women appear generally to experience male domination without its compensating and complementary services; increasing numbers of Indian women are facing the same problem. Failing to find adequately paid jobs and therefore unable to fulfill the positive aspects of their patriarchal roles, they lean on the negative, aggressive part. Women often make equal cash contributions to the household and at times even greater than men, yet are all too often ignored when it comes to major issues.

Traditional African society accepted women as equal producers in the self-subsistent economy. Married women possessed land and livestock and controlled the products of their labor. Though subordinate to men, they were no more dependent on them than men were on women. The rights of both were in the final analysis entrenched in their undeniable claims to family and tribe.

Modern capitalist society, underpinned by materialism, defines rights in terms of accumulated property. The fact that women have poorer access to property than men places them at an immediate disadvantage. African women, the bottom of the pile, have the poorest reach in this respect, that reach being further attenuated by the law which places their property right in the custody of men.

South African law and/or tradition defines a woman as subordinate to a man. This definition reaches its penultimate excess in the 1981 Bantu Code which until a few years ago was operative throughout the Natal province. It has now been replaced by the KwaZulu code.

The black working class family, not having the intellectual reach to trace its problems to their roots outside of itself in society, often locates them within itself, and aggravates the physical ravage with the emotional. Women blame the men for depriving them of their "rightful" roles as mothers, and the men burdened with their role as breadwinners, and unable to win the whole loaf, blame their failure on "natural" bad luck and retreat into the bottle. The rate of alcoholism is very high among Coloured and African men.

· ·

African Women

The perpetrators of *apartheid* have grasped in some insidious way that the foundation of their system finally rests on the subjugation of the African woman. Her isolation in the reserve where she becomes conditioned to bearing and raising children and caring for the aged and ill, abandoned by industry and forced back into the homeland by law, is imperative to the monopolistic accumulation of wealth and power in the white sector. The only differential in the South African economy that yields the high profits essential to attract capital, foreign and local, which in turn sustains *apartheid*, is the uninterrupted flow of cheap labor—South Africa's black gold—as one homeland leader puts it. That kind of labor is in the final analysis dependent on the continued subjugation of women, not only through law, but through the manipulation of traditional attitudes of sexual dominance and subservience.

Large numbers of African women in Natal continue to be subjected to the 1891 Bantu Code, which makes them perpetual minors and lifelong wards of men—their fathers, husbands and in the absence of these the closest surviving male relations, including sons. They may not marry, continue in employment, defend nor bring any action in court without their authority. Their male guardians can claim their earnings and control their property. Upon marriage, the wife's assets automatically revert to her husband, but she does not acquire any right over his property. On his death, the family estate, including her contributions to it, automatically goes to the closest surviving male relative, and she becomes his ward.

African women throughout the country are more severely restricted from entering urban areas than African men are. Laws dating back to the 1930s made such entering dependent on the qualifications of their "guardians"— husbands. Wives of men who qualify for urban rights through ten years of continuous service with one employer or 15 years in one area, as well as their children under 16, may live in locations outside the homelands provided they have acceptable accommodation. Women never acquire these rights on their own and are forced to send their children to the homelands.

. . . .

Political Groups and the Mass Protests

It is the political arena that has drawn the most volatile response from the South Africa's women. White women, English and Afrikaner, have joined their menfolk in their conflicts with each other and against indigenous blacks, and some have been enshrined as heroines in white annals. Generally speaking, white women defend the *apartheid* system and resist change. The Women's Enfranchisement Association of the Union, established soon after the Union of South Africa came into existence in 1910, finally won the franchise for white women in 1930, but it did so mainly to stir up the white franchise against the blacks and gain in this way the necessary two-thirds majority to abolish the Cape native vote.

The most impressive white political group is the Black Sash, founded soon after the Nationalist Party took power in 1949, specifically to protest against the excesses of the system against human rights. The organization has grown in stature and work and it now runs valuable advice bureaus to assist black women.

The most spectacular records are those of the mass resistance of black women; African, Indian, and Coloured. In 1912, all campaigned against passes: Africans and Coloureds as a single body in the Orange Free State against residential passes; Indians in Natal and in the Transvaal against provincial barriers and poll taxes.

The resistance in the Orange Free State was provoked by an 1893 law which required all African and Coloured women to produce work permits on the request by the police in order to establish their "right" to be in the area. The women, supported by the menfolk, pleased for years with the authorities to abolish the law which humiliated them, and obliged young girls to leave school and seek employment or be removed to other areas. Their pleas ignored, they finally formed the Native and Coloured Women's Association and openly defied the law, marching on the local administration offices, dumping their passes and facing arrest. Over a thousand were arrested. In 1918, the movement spread to the Transvaal: in 1923, the passes were finally withdrawn.

At the beginning of the century, Indian women in Natal and the Transvaal virtually made Gandhi, and proved the efficacy of the new liberation dialectic of *satyagraha* that he introduced. The South African Indian resistance movement remained by and large an elitist protest, until the women *satyagrahis* from the two ashrams in Natal and the Transvaal, Phoenix and Tolstoy respectively, communicated it into a mass movement. In 1912, they defied the anti-Asiatic law, crossed the provincial border from both ends and provoked the miners of Newcastle to lay down their picks and strike. A thousand workers thereafter began the epic march, led by Gandhi, across the Natal border into the Transvaal and the entire Indian labor force of Natal went on strike, bringing the industry to a standstill. Arrests and imprisonment followed, and the Government was forced to modify some of the hardships against the Indians. The great figure of that struggle was not Gandhi, but the emaciated young Valiamma, who refused to surrender despite her fatal illness that developed as a result of repeated imprisonment. She died in the struggle.

In 1946, the Indian women again took the lead in launching the second passive resistance campaign against the anti-Indian Land Act: at the end of that campaign, almost 2,000 Indians had been imprisoned for defying segregatory laws.

. . . .

Co-ordination of Congress Women and Support for National Liberation

Women from the Natal Indian Congress and the African National Congress joined their forces and established the Duran and District Women's League in 1952. In doing so, they went ahead of their parent bodies, the African National Congress and the Natal Indian Congress which operated in consultation but not as a single body. The League had taken stock of the manipulation of Africans against Indians in 1949, and saw its prime object as that of restoring mutual confidence. It therefore concentrated its activities in Cato Manor, the area worst hit during the disturbance. A crèche and milk distribution center was established in a church hall and League members were bussed out daily to administer and to teach. The League was actively engaged in the 1952 Campaign of Defiance of Unjust Laws. When passes were introduced for African women, it organized a vigorous protest movement culminating in a mass march on the Department of Native Affairs in Pietermaritzburg and the arrest of 600 women, mainly African, but including a significant number of Indian women and a few white members of the Liberal Party.

League representatives were among the founding members of the Federation of South African Women in 1954, and Natal sent a deputation of 156 members to the historic march of 20,000 women on Pretoria in 1956, organized by the Federation of South African Women.

In 1960, the League organized a protest march of the women and children of those detained in Durban during the emergency. Some 60 women with their children were arrested and charged, the charges being withdrawn after a short spell in prison and an appearance in court. The League organized a weekly vigil outside the prison to keep the public mind focused on the inequity of detention without trial. This was the last of League's activities. The banning of its secretary in 1954 and the detention of its chairperson in 1960 had weakened the organizing committee, but it was the banning of the African National Congress and of key members of the Natal Indian Congress that spelt its demise. . . .

36. *APARTHEID AND THE ROLE OF WOMEN**

by HILDA BERNSTEIN

Hilda Bernstein is a founder of the Federation of South African Women. The Title of her book, For Their Triumphs and for Their Tears, *from which the following is excerpted, is from the "Women's Day Song":*

Remember all our women in the jails
Remember all our women in campaigns
Remember all our women over many fighting years
Remember all our women for their triumphs, and for their tears.

In South Africa, the oppression of women has a further dimension, the dimension of apartheid. This, based partly on fantasies of racial superiority and

*From *For Their Triumphs and For Their Tears: Women in Apartheid South Africa* (London, 1975).

partly on the labor requirements of an industrial capitalist society, has created an environment for women that is unique in our time.

Thus for example, although women in modern society have been repeatedly told that their place is in the home, this is a concept which has developed only with the industrial revolution when divisions between the home and the workplace first came into being. However, in South Africa, the reduction of women to "superfluous appendages" robs them of even the limited importance given to women under ordinary capitalist-productive relationships. The creation of a home centered around the family is not necessary for women under apartheid. The whole sentimental conception: the eternal female and mother serving her husband, caring for his needs and those of her children, painted in such false and romantic colors, falls to the ground. The only function left to the black woman is through the system of reproduction (a biological fact that apartheid has not been able to change, and even this must be limited to ease the fears of whites who find themselves so numerically inferior).

The extremely high infant mortality rates are not only a source of great suffering and deprivation for black women, but also a source of their further oppression. For the result is far more pregnancies—far more periods of physical hardship during which work, education or development outside the home become impossible. For the typical white mother, pregnancy occupies no more than two or three years of her life. For the black mother, it must occupy many times that amount. And thus biology becomes yet another disability, reinforcing her inferior position.

Black women also suffer from the fact that some white men wish to exert their sexual power over both white and black women, as the prosecutions under the Immorality Act show. At the same time, they like to create the fantasy of "pure" white womanhood, which the black man longs to defile.

And moreover, the black woman finds her role of motherhood reduced to that of a domestic nanny caring for white children while her own know only separation, suffering and neglect; the most intimate care and feeding of the white babies is handed over to black women. The extraordinary thing is that all the separation from her own children and hardships suffered by the black domestic has not deprived her of her ability to show tenderness and love in the care she gives to the children who are not hers.

The contrast with the white woman is overwhelming. White women in apartheid society are less than nothing. After parturition, the white mother is scarcely needed at all. Limited as the role of middle-class motherhood may be in other countries; in South Africa it becomes nothing; the mother is not essential to the smooth running of the home, the domestic role is played by the black domestics.

The primary role of white women becomes that of consumer and as a living display, through leisure and adornment, of her husband's wealth. The sad thing is that, freed from the destructively time-consuming and repetitive domestic chores that chain women of other lands, the white woman in South Africa is unable to utilize her freedom constructively and dissipates it in a trivial round of social activities—though there are of course notable exceptions, including those who have been persecuted for their opposition to apartheid and, to a lesser extent, the women of the Black Sash.

In South Africa black women, these most vulnerable of all people within the apartheid state, have been forced to embark on a struggle that takes them beyond their own specific oppression. The struggle of South African women for recognition as equal citizens with equal opportunities is primarily the struggle against apartheid, for national liberation. Nor is it a question of putting one first, then taking up the other. The victory of this struggle against apartheid is the absolute condition for any change in the social status of women as a whole; their participation is an expression not only of their desire to rid all South Africa of the curse of apartheid, but also of their deep concern for their own status as women.

And they have shown repeatedly the capacity to understand and the willingness to fight for changes that lift them further than their own very harsh immediate predicament.

Thus under the conditions of apartheid South Africa's oppressed women cannot limit their objectives to those of simply trying to establish their legal rights in a modern industrialized society, nor can they hope to emerge with a few privileges in what is still largely a male-dominated world; but to destroy the whole basis of racial exploitation, and in so doing open up the prospect of a free development for both women and men.

37. DEMONSTRATION AGAINST THE PASS LAWS*

by MARY BENSON

Mary Benson, a South Africa-born writer, edited The Sun Will Rise: Statements from the Dock by South African Political Prisoners *(1981). She is one of many South African women who have been "banned" for anti-apartheid activities.*

As always for the African people, the difficulties and obstacles in organizing [a protest rally] were immense. There was police harassment with bannings

*From United Nations Centre Against Apartheid, *Notes and Documents,* "The Struggle in South Africa Has United All Races" (New York, 1984).

and frequent arrests. There were also the problems deriving from poverty, exacerbated by the great distances between towns and villages: how to afford fares and how to communicate with outlying branches when telephones, stenographers and typewriters were virtually non-existent. Nevertheless, there were countrywide protests which were to culminate in a mass demonstration in Pretoria. . . .

Port Elizabeth women raised $800 for the railway fares and filled two coaches in the train, while from Durban, twenty-three women set off in cars driven by Indian friends. As thousands of women approached the capital from all corners of the country, the authorities announced that it would be illegal to go in procession through the streets. Early on 9 August 1956,[1] there was therefore no procession. But everywhere there were women, not more than three in a group, dressed in the colors of the African National Congress, some with babies on their back, some in saris, striding toward the Union Buildings. They were determined to tell the Prime Minister that they totally rejected the Pass Laws. Twenty thousand women converged on the Government offices, and at their head were Lilian Ngoyi, Helen Joseph and Rahim Moosa.

Watched by the Security police, Lilian Ngoyi knocked on Prime Minister Strijdom's door. The Prime Minister was not there, declared his Secretary. The three women delivered their stack of protests[2] and then rejoined the huge crowd in the amphitheatre.

With one accord, the women rose to their feet and stood with hands raised in the Congress salute. For thirty minutes, they stood in complete silence. Not a child cried. Then they burst into the warrior's song of the women of Natal with its topical words:

"Strijdom, you have struck a rock once you have touched a woman!"

They sang the anthem: *"Nkosi Sikelel'i-Afrika"*, and afterwards they dispersed.[3]

Lilian Ngoyi and Helen Joseph were among those charged with treason a few months later.

---

[1] Since designated "Women's Day" in South Africa.—Ed.
[2] See Reading 38, a copy of the women's petition.
[3] But the protest ultimately failed. As Hilda Bernstein writes:

> The protests continued, but so did the issue of passes. The authorities made it inevitable; old women who went to collect their tiny pensions were told "no pass book—no pension." Mothers could not obtain the registration of the birth of a child unless they had their pass book. Teachers and nurses were dismissed if they refused to take passes. Gradually more and more women were forced to accept them. (*For Their Triumphs*, p. 47)

38. *PETITION FOR THE REPEAL OF THE PASS LAWS**

Pass Petition of August 9, 1956

We, the women of South Africa, have come here today. We represent and we speak on behalf of hundreds of thousands of women who could not be with us. But all over the country, at this moment, women are watching and thinking of us. Their hearts are with us.

We are women from every part of South Africa. We are women of every race, we come from the cities and the towns, from the reserves and the villages. We come as women united in our purpose to save the African women from the degradation of passes.

For hundreds of years the African people have suffered under the most bitter law of all—the pass law which has brought untold suffering to every African family.

Raids, arrests, loss of pay, long hours at the pass office, weeks in the cells awaiting trial, forced farm labor—this is what the pass laws have brought to African men. Punishment and misery—not for a crime, but for the lack of a pass.

We African women know too well the effect of this law upon our homes, our children. We, who are not African women, know how our sisters suffer.

Your Government proclaims aloud at home and abroad that the pass laws have been abolished, but *we women know this is not true,* for our husbands, our brothers, our sons are still being arrested, thousands every day, under these very pass laws. It is only the name that has changed. The "reference book" and the pass are one.

In March 1952, your Minister of Native Affairs denied in Parliament that a law would be introduced which would force African women to carry passes. But in 1956 your Government *is* attempting to force passes upon the African women, and we are here today to protest against this insult to all women. For to us an insult to African women is an insult to all women.

We want to tell you what the pass would mean to an African woman, and we want you to know that whether you call it a reference book, an identity book, or by any other disguising name, to us it is a PASS. And it means just this:—

*Presented August 9, 1956.

- That homes will be broken up when women are arrested under pass laws
- That children will be left uncared for, helpless, and mothers will be torn from their babies for failure to produce a pass
- That women and young girls will be exposed to humiliation and degradation at the hands of pass-searching policemen
- That women will lose their right to move freely from one place to another.

In the name of women of South Africa, we say to you, each one of us, African, European, Indian, Coloured, that we are opposed to the pass system.

We voters and voteless, call upon your Government not to issue passes to African women.

We shall not rest until ALL pass laws and all forms of permits restricting our freedom have been abolished.

We shall not rest until we have won for our children their fundamental rights of freedom, justice, and security.

Chapter IX

THE "REFORMS"

39. *NEO-APARTHEID: REFORM IN SOUTH AFRICA* *

by KEVIN DANAHER

Kevin Danaher was, until recently, an associate fellow of the Institute for Policy Studies in Washington, D.C. He currently works for the Institute for Food and Development Policy in San Francisco.

Introduction

For many years, South African government officials have been telling the world that they are reforming their system of apartheid, and given more time, free from outside pressure, everything will work out for the better. . . .

The reforms of the Botha regime are neither a dismantling of apartheid, as Pretoria's defenders claim, nor are they "cosmetic" changes, as some critics charge. The recent government reforms were designed to 1) gain better control over the African workforce, by cultivating more skilled workers while keeping the majority locked up in the rural labor reserves ("bantustans"), 2) create class cleavages in the African community, by giving black businessmen and industrial workers some economic and social privileges while keeping the black masses in a state of abject poverty, and 3) upgrade the state security apparatus, giving it a greater role in general policymaking.

From In Whose Interest? (Washington, 1984) [condensed].

Background to Recent Reforms

In the 1970s, a conjuncture of economic and political developments set the stage for changes in labor policy by the South African government. A succession of victories by black radicals in neighboring states, massive civil unrest by black South Africans, and growing guerrilla insurgency in Namibia and South Africa convinced officials of the South African Defence Force (SADF) that white privilege could not be preserved solely by military means. Top South African commanders argued that an effective defense against the "total onslaught" confronting white supremacy would consist primarily of political, not military, techniques.

Moreover, by the late 1970s, many of the political groups representing big business in South Africa were pressing for changes in the system of black labor control. They complained that the strict regulations governing the mobility of African workers resulted in labor supply bottlenecks which impeded the profitable utilization of African labor. Big business sought to reorganize production more along lines of productivity than race. They also saw a need for greater discipline among African workers and therefore favored some form of trade union rights that would permit collective bargaining while maintaining government control. White business leaders pushed for reforms aimed at expanding the "black middle class," giving the black elite a greater stake in the capitalist system and creating a buffer against revolution. White corporate leaders were necessarily more sensitive to international criticism than were the white workers and small businessmen who supported the more conservative politicians. . . .

The Wiehahn Reforms

In 1979, a government-appointed study group, the Wiehahn Commission, issued a series of six reports on legislation affecting African workers. Since that time, the government has implemented some of the Wiehahn recommendations. It expanded training and employment opportunities for some Africans; relaxed its enforcement of laws requiring segregation in workplace cafeterias and restrooms (but this type of segregation is still widespread); and created two new institutions, the National Manpower Commission, which researches labor issues and advises the Minister of Manpower Utilisation, and the Industrial Court, designed to speed up the resolution of labor disputes by taking them away from the civil courts.

The most important change based on the Wiehahn proposals was the legalization of African trade unions. Prior to 1979, Africans were permitted to form unions but these were not officially recognized by the government. . . . While granting unionized Africans greater bargaining power with their employers, legal recognition would bring them under the controlling mechanism of the government's industrial conciliation system. . . .

If the African unions continue to grow in size and militancy as they have over the past decade, they may reach a point at which the government's traditional repression becomes ineffective. A strong African trade union movement capable of shutting down the economy could not be trifled with as were the small, isolated African unions of the past. African trade union rights are the only area of reform that hold potential for challenging apartheid. The government's powers of repression, however, should not be underestimated. In short, it is still an open question whether Pretoria's limited trade union reforms will succeed in coopting and controlling African industrial workers, or whether the reforms will be burst wide open by an organized sector of the black population that is vital to the white economy.

The Riekert Reforms

Another set of changes was based on the Riekert Commission report issued in May 1979. Under the general rubric of improving "manpower utilization," the Riekert report examined influx control (the system of state controls on the movement of African workers from rural to urban areas) and made suggestions for upgrading the effectiveness of this system. Although the reforms eventually implemented by the government were not as broad as those suggested by the Riekert report, the contents of the report itself were well within the bounds of apartheid as envisioned by its founders. . . .

The basic goal of the Riekert reforms is to strengthen government control over African migration to the urban areas by means of more systematic manipulation of two factors: housing and jobs. As the report stated, the goal was "more effective control over migration than in the past, and the avoidance of much of the friction that accompanied such control in the past, in that emphasis will be placed mainly on the *control of employment and control of accommodation.*

The existing system of labor bureaus, which had been established to allocate jobs and regulate the flow of African workers from the bantustans to the white economy, was proving unworkable. Many white employers simply neglected to register with the labor bureaus and hired their African workers illegally. Employers were not only put off by the cumbersome bureaucracy of the labor bureaus, they also found that African workers who were in the urban areas illegally were more docile than those employed legally. The penalties for circumventing the labor bureaus were mild for the employer (a small fine, seldom exacted), whereas the illegal African worker would lose his job and be "endorsed out" to the impoverished bantustans.

At no time were the proposed reforms intended to improve the lot of the African majority. Rather, the changes were designed to 1) meet the needs of the white business community for a more well-regulated African workforce, and 2) divide the African workers into several distinct strata with a hierarchy of rights and wealth, thus dividing Africans along class as well as ethnic lines.

The labor bureau system was strengthened to gain better control over migrant workers. Employers hiring outside the registration system can now receive stiffer fines than in the past. More effort has been put into coordinating job registration with the legal status of the worker. The goal is to make it impossible for an African worker to come into an urban area and find work unless he has been recruited and signed a contract in his rural area.

Pass laws are more strictly enforced to separate the one-fourth of African workers who qualify for urban residential rights from those who do not. In June 1983 *The Economist* reported that, "arrests for pass law offences have almost doubled in the past three years, and the government plans to tighten influx controls, imposing much heavier fines on employers of 'illegal' blacks."

The privileged African workers with Section 10 rights are no longer required to register with a labor bureau when taking a new job, and they are allowed to move from one area to another if they have a job and housing in the new location. Section 10 Africans are also given preference in employment.

By linking the right to accommodation with legal job status, the government gained greater control over African migration to the cities. Only by being registered with and channeled through the labor bureau system can a rural African gain legal housing in urban areas. At the same time, the government cracked down on "squatters," those coming to the urban areas illegally and setting up makeshift dwellings. The government's policy has been to demolish the squatter camps and forcibly to remove the residents to their assigned bantustans. . . .

The government lifted some restrictions on the African business class. Africans can now run more than one business, employ people of other races, and are not limited to business sites under 350 square meters. White and black entrepreneurs can now do joint ventures in the African townships on a 51 percent black/49 percent white basis. Although African business has grown in recent years, creating an elite group who may have a greater stake in the system, the government keeps a tight rein on black "free" enterprise. Blacks cannot do business in the white cities, suburbs, and industrial parks. . . .

Another Rickert proposal, one that has gotten much publicity, involves a limited form of self-government for urban blacks. The Black Local Authorities Act (1982) provides for local self-government through the election of community councils in the African townships. These councils, however, are restricted to dealing with mundane infrastructural problems such as roads, sewage, and electricity. They cannot affect broad policy questions; they can be dissolved at any time by the white government; and they do nothing to change the fact that even this urban black elite can only participate in "national" politics via the bantustan governments. But perhaps the most telling criticism is that the overwhelming majority of Africans reject these government-sponsored institutions. In council elections held in late 1983, less than one of every five Africans registered to vote bothered to do so. In Soweto, the largest and most politically significant African township, voter turnout in the thirty administrative wards ranged from 1.6 percent to a high of 13 percent.

The main goal of the Riekert reforms was to weaken further the Africans by stratifying them according to wealth and social privilege, in addition to separating them ethnically. A detailed post-Riekert study of the labor control system found that it "helps foster a hierarchy of living standards, market opportunities and rights within the African population."

Educational Reform

Like the other areas of reform, changes in the education system were sparked by the political protests and economic stagnation of the 1970s. The appallingly low standards of African education limited the supply of skilled African workers and presented a security problem due to the frequent protests against the education system.

To deal with these problems within the bounds of the "separate development" strategy, Pretoria has increased funding for African education but has targeted it to intensify the class divisions within the African population. While devolving African educational responsibility onto the bantustans—currently over two-thirds of African students are in the bantustan schools—the government has focused its upgrading measures on the minority of African students whose parents possess urban residential privileges. This reinforces the effort to create a black elite whose skilled labor is vital to the white economy, and whose political quiescence contributes to the survival of white supremacy. . . .

In June 1980, the government commissioned the Human Sciences Research Council, a state-funded body, to conduct a comprehensive study of the South African educational system. Led by the Rector of the Rand Afrikaans University, Professor J. P. de Lange, the committee put together a report that challenged some of the basic premises of apartheid schooling. The committee argued for opening up the education system and reducing inequalities. It called for a single department of education capable of unifying, at least administratively, the many strata of apartheid schooling, and moving the various ethnic school systems toward eventual parity. The committee recommended voluntary racial integration at the local and regional level. It also suggested that universities be given the freedom to admit students based on academic rather than racial standards.

The Botha regime rejected the key recommendations of the de Lange report, emphasizing the government's intent to retain the racial and ethnic divisions of the current school system. The regime reaffirmed its support for "the principles of Christian education" and the "national character of education," that "each population group should have its own schools," and that "each population group should also have its own education authority/department." The combination of the government's vague pledges to work toward "equal opportunities" in education, and its insistence on retaining a segregated system, conjures up visions of the long-discredited notion of "separate but equal." When asked about the government's response to the de Lange Committee report, one of the committee members remarked: "this, in fact, reestablishes apartheid education and places us back where we started." . . .

The Constitutional Reforms

In the early 1980s, the Botha regime developed a detailed plan for restructuring the legislative and executive branches of government. This constitutional reform plan was approved by white voters on 2 November 1983. Because the new structure involves some nonwhite participation in the central government, the reforms have gained considerable attention in the western press and have caused some people to conclude that South Africa is moving toward democratic rule. However, a detailed examination of the plan reveals that an opposite conclusion would be closer to the truth.

The most important part of the plan—other than its exclusion of the African majority—is the concentration of power in the new chief executive. Under the new system, the President is head of the Republic and chairman of the cabinet, combining the powers of the offices of Prime Minister and President. . . .

The pre-existing white chamber of parliament (178 members) is supplemented by a Coloured chamber (85 members), and an Indian chamber (45 members). Each of the three chambers legislates separately on "group affairs" but the three can collaborate on "matters of common interest." The President holds the crucial power of deciding whether any particular issue should be defined as a matter of common or ethnic interest. On matters of common interest, in the event of a deadlock—unlikely due to the preponderance of white members—a final determination is made by another body, the President's Council. Like the cabinet, electoral college, and parliament, the President's Council has a majority of white members. . . .

Top officials in Pretoria, however, have made it clear that the constitutional proposals are not a step toward one-person-one-vote democracy. Prime Minister Botha explained that, aside from the community councils, the exercise of African political rights "will have to be done by means of independent and national states," i.e., the bantustans which have not been recognized as "independent and national states" by any government in the world except Pretoria. . . .

Aside from its inherent weaknesses, the constitutional reform plan is opposed by a broad spectrum of interests within South Africa and internationally. The far-rightists within Botha's National Party and the parties to the right of the NP denounce the reforms as the thin end of a wedge that will lead to the destruction of white power. The strong electoral showing of far-right parties in recent years indicates that a significant number of whites agree with this position.

Representatives of international business are critical of the constitutional reforms for not going far enough. *The Economist* criticized Botha because

> . . . his proposals are not really reformist at all. They purport to breach the political colour bar by extending parliamentary representation to the coloured (mixed race) and Indian minorities. In fact the proposals are aimed at strengthening the position of whites by coopting the coloureds and Indians as allies but in such a way that Afrikaners still dominate the system. Other regulations would further distance the blacks from power. . . .

The Financial Times complained that under the new constitution the President "would be a dictator in all but name." . . .

Opposition from South Africa's non-white majority has been extremely broad-based and vehement in its denunciation of the constitutional reforms. . . .

When some leaders of the (Coloured) Labor Party agreed to participate in the new tricameral parliament, the party was split down the middle and the collaborating faction was immediately denounced by some sixty civic associations, trade unions, and student groups in the Coloured community. Opposition to the collaborationist Coloured leaders was so intense that they were no longer able to hold open meetings in Cape Town.

Those members of the Indian community willing to collaborate with the new plan were previously associated with the South African Indian Council (SAIC), a body established by the white government to solicit advice from the Indian elite. Like the Coloured collaborators, the popular base of these Indian leaders is dubious. In the 1981 SAIC elections only 10.5 percent of registered Indian voters bothered to cast a ballot.

Among Africans, not only the more militant groups denounced the plan and campaigned against it, but even more conservative voices such as Bishop Desmond Tutu and six bantustan leaders spoke out forcefully against the constitutional reforms. Chief Gatsha Buthelezi, head of the KwaZulu bantustan, has always been careful to cultivate support in U.S. ruling circles. But when the Reagan administration praised the Coloured leaders who decided to collaborate with the new constitutional plan, the Zulu leader complained of being "slapped in the face" by the U.S. government.

The most important effect of the constitutional reforms will be to contribute to the growing polarization of South African society. State power will be concentrated in the hands of the chief executive, and a small percentage of the Indian and Coloured elites will be incorporated into the white establishment, but the most important group—the African majority—will intensify its opposition due to its total exclusion from the political process. . . .

The Basic Strategy: Denationalization and Retribalization

The core feature of "grand apartheid," the systematic denationalization of the African population via the bantustan program, continues unabated. The government claims that each African ethnic group must have its own area, to "develop separately." Although the government uses *ethnic* criteria to divide the African population, all whites—including Portuguese, Polish emigrés, white Rhodesians, Afrikaners, and British descendants—are judged by *racial* criteria and officially lumped together as one group.

Through the creation of so-called independent states—Transkei (1976), Bophuthatswana (1977), Venda (1979), and Ciskei (1981)—the white government has officially deprived some *eight million* Africans of their South African nationality. This denationalization applies not only to Africans forced to live in the rural areas but to the Section 10, urban Africans as well. Under the provisions of the National States Citizenship Act, any African with genetic, cultural, linguistic, familial, or residential ties to a particular bantustan is automatically deprived of South African citizenship on the day that bantustan is declared independent.[1] Although the statutes are carefully worded to avoid withdrawing citizenship on racial grounds, no whites, Coloureds, or Asians have been denationalized under the bantustan program. In a 1978 speech to parliament, the Minister of Bantu Administration and Development explained the central goal of the denationalization program: "if our policy is taken to its full logical conclusion as far as the black people are concerned, there will be not one black man with South African citizenship.

Even under the leadership of the so-called reformer Botha, the government has pressed forward with its denationalization/retribalization strategy. This is in spite of unanimous international refusal to recognize the independence of these mini-states. It is also in spite of generalized opposition to the plan from black South Africans. For example, in the 1982 elections for the Bophuthatswana National Assembly, of the estimated 300,000 Tswana nationals living in the Johannesburg area, only 135 voted. A telling rejection is the fact that millions of Africans "vote with their feet" to escape the abysmal conditions

[1] The clearest historical precedent for the bantustan/denationalization program was the 1941 Nazi law denationalizing German Jews. It is more than mere coincidence that the National Party supported the Nazi cause in World War II and now implements a similar policy.

of these labor reservoirs. The most complete study on the subject found that, not counting pass law removals, the government since 1960 has forcibly resettled some *3.5 million* Africans from "white South Africa" to the bantustans.

The program also proceeds in spite of the well-known fact that these bantustans do not possess the economic resources to achieve true independence from South Africa. The government's own figures show that as of 1982, "only 13 percent of the total income of blacks in the national states is self-generated. *The Christian Science Monitor* described the homelands as "economic disaster areas." Only one of the bantustans—Bophuthatswana—has advanced economically, but this has been achieved by erecting casinos and flesh houses catering to South African tourists.

Despite the lack of economic viability or international recognition, Pretoria will persevere with its bantustan strategy. Not only does the program lower the number of Africans officially considered citizens of South Africa, and divide the majority by forcibly retribalizing them, it also creates an administrative elite who cooperate in the suppression of trade unions, guerrilla groups, and other opponents of the regime. As part of Botha's "constellation of states" idea, the SADF is creating surrogate security forces in the bantustans. . . .

Some bantustan authorities have done important work for Pretoria by suppressing African trade unions and student groups. For example, security forces and vigilantes in Ciskei and KwaZulu have carried out mass detentions, torture, and even mass murder against antiapartheid students and trade unionists.

The bantustan program, like many other programs of the white minority regime, increases the polarization of South African society. The bantustans serve as labor reservoirs where "surplus" African workers can be dumped at will, but they are also breeding grounds of discontent, ripe for the appeals of revolutionaries. Bantustanization has been used to cultivate an African elite willing to collaborate with the white minority regime, but these so-called black leaders are denounced around the world and detested by the people they are supposed to govern. When Pretoria declares a bantustan independent, it conveniently denationalizes millions of African citizens, no longer counting them in its statistics on unemployment, malnutrition, and the like. But the bantustan farce is universally condemned and fools only those with some interest in being deceived. The bantustan program sows seeds of suffering and bitterness. The longer it continues, the more prolonged and difficult will be the struggle for justice and peace.

Conclusion

What has changed under "neo-apartheid" is the strategy of control: the government is more actively seeking Coloured, Indian, and African middle class allies to strengthen its resistance to the democratic demands of the African majority. The labor control system has been updated and streamlined. The security forces have been greatly expanded and given a central role in formulating general policy.

Although some blacks have benefited from recent reforms, the overwhelming majority has not. This is precisely the government's intent. By increasing economic and political opportunities for a select minority of blacks, the government hopes to coopt the better-educated strata, driving a wedge between them and the black masses. Although some government reforms tend to create a popular momentum for more change, the regime is prepared to repress that momentum.

The South African government has made it clear, for anyone who cares to see the truth, that it will continue forcibly to divide the black majority, and to deny full citizenship to all in a unified South Africa. The reforms of the recent past and foreseeable future are designed to provide a better-controlled African workforce for white industry, create class cleavages in the black community, and placate foreign criticism.

The central premise of the Reagan administration's "constructive engagement" policy is that by catering to Pretoria the United States can strengthen reform-minded elements of the white elite and thereby facilitate gradual movement away from apartheid. But the recent reforms have neither democratized nor liberalized South African society. Instead, they have served to reinforce minority rule and to ensure control of the black majority. . . .

40. REFORMS, CLASS CONFLICT, AND THE NATIONAL PARTY SPLIT*

by CRAIG CHARNEY

After studying South African politics at Oxford, Craig Charney worked as a reporter in South Africa for four years for the London Times Higher Education Supplement *and the* Johannesburg Star. *He is currently on the faculty of the political science department at Yale University.*

The split in South Africa's ruling National Party (NP) delivered the *coup de grace* to the traditional image of white South African politics as a contest between English- and Afrikaans-speakers, but the new conventional wisdoms are hardly more satisfactory. After the myth of the Afrikaner monolith was shown up by the events of February and March 1982, most observers switched from ethnic to ideological analysis, attributing them to the differences in

*From *Journal of Southern African Studies,* April 1984.

outlook between *verligte* ("enlightened") and *verkrampte* ("narrow-minded") Afrikaners. Some on the left wrote off the split as inconsequential, due to the NP's unwavering support for white political control and capitalism. However, both these types of ideological exegesis ultimately offer only another way to describe the split, not an explanation of its origins or significance. While the split was precipitated by disagreements between verligtes and verkramptes over responses to the political and economic crises facing the South African state, its roots lay in a process of class realignment. They can be traced to the evolution of the National Party into a party dominated by the Afrikaner bourgeoisie, who need new strategies and new allies. The split freed the NP to restructure the training, use, and living conditions of black workers, as capital demands, while attempting to broaden the base of the regime.

Nevertheless, liberals who viewed the split as a "step in the right direction" are likely to be disappointed. While the class character of the NP now encourages a degree of economic liberalization, it still seems to rule out political liberalization. Although the Afrikaner bourgeoisie shares the interest of English-speaking capitalists in the efficient employment of black labor, it is still too dependent upon state power and patronage to accept genuine power-sharing or majority rule. . . .

The Party Split

The motive force in the realignment of the white parties was . . . "the emergence of a class of aggressive, self-confident Afrikaner capitalists, whose interests went beyond those of the narrow class alliance out of which they emerged." The NP took power in 1948 as a coalition dominated by the Afrikaner petit bourgeoisie, a handful of Afrikaner finance capitalists, and the Cape agricultural bourgeoisie, drawing votes from farmers and the Afrikaans-speaking majority of the white working class. In office, it fostered an Afrikaner state capitalism, filling the expanding parastatals and civil service with its supporters, while using state patronage to promote Afrikaans business. As a consequence, Afrikaner control of private industry rose from 10 percent to 21 percent between 1948 and 1975, while, including the parastatals, Afrikaners' control of industrial output rose to 45 percent. The proportion of Afrikaners in the professions doubled, and the percentage of Afrikaners in white-collar jobs increased from 28 percent to 65 percent, while the numbers of farmers and blue-collar workers fell sharply. Increasingly, the view of the new Afrikaner middle class converged with those of affluent English-speakers on economic and social questions.

. . . The election of P. W. Botha as Prime Minister in 1978 confirmed the ascendancy of the Afrikaner bourgeoisie at the summit of the party. . . . Despite hesitations and deliberate ambiguity, Mr. Botha's government defined a new strategy to meet the crises confronting the state after the Soweto uprisings, developing verligte ideas and policies first broached or initiated under his predecessor, John Vorster. These policies—restructuring the position of the black working class and courting allies among the coloured and Indian minorities—addressed the needs of a mature Afrikaner bourgeoisie and the dangers posed by black working-class, nationalist, and guerilla struggles. As a party of the bourgeoisie, the NP developed an ideology presenting its class interests as "general interests," while still trying to retain the image of an Afrikaner ethnic party. However, the party's new line was increasingly incompatible with the NP's traditional alliance of Afrikaners of all classes, bound by rigid racism and exclusive access to the state.

The over-arching theme in NP ideology in the Botha era became the pursuit of economic growth. Overtly racist themes, already de-emphasized under Mr. Vorster, were abandoned. Instead of the Verwoerdian dictum "better poor and white than rich and mixed," accumulation was presented as in everyone's interest. Whites could continue to enjoy their privileges, while growth would offer higher living standards to blacks. As Hermann Giliomee puts it: "in the Botha Administration . . . a strong tendency has developed . . . to present the whites as a modernising elite and to portray economic growth, training, job creation, food production, and above all political stability, which is seen as making all these things possible, as sufficient justification for National Party rule." . . .

The NP's major substantive policy changes occurred in respect of labor, to meet the needs of a capitalist class worried by an under-skilled and angry black work force. . . . Deeds lagged behind words, but the intent was clear: to close the skills gap and increase demand by incorporating an organized urban African working class into the labor aristocracy. However, the renegotiation of the labor process with the black work force could hardly fail to anger white workers whose wages were already falling behind inflation. It represented the reversal of the NP's old view that "economic integration" would inevitably lead to "political integration."

Almost as striking were the overt changes in the NP's attitude toward capital. . . . "We have our differences," he [Botha] argued, "but we are creating reciprocal channels to plan national strategy in South Africa as a team." Contrast this to the attitude of Mr. Vorster: "in my time, I also talked to all the leading English businessmen; but I never involved them in planning and decision-making." The ghost of Hoggenheimer, the capitalist caricature against which the NP used to rail, has been laid, along with Nationalist solicitude for the "little man" in the fields and factories.

There were also reductions in petty apartheid, in line with the NP's commitment to the elimination of "unnecessary and hurtful" discrimination, such as the opening of many theatres, hotels, and restaurants to blacks. Although these changes will only benefit a few blacks, they still represented a departure from policy up to the 1970s, when the NP tried to make it impossible for South Africans of different races to meet other than as masters and servants in the workplace. The new line is both a gesture to the black petit bourgeoisie and a crack in apartheid's front of racial privilege. Finally, Mr. Botha abandoned the Verwoerdian shibboleth of "division of power" between the races and accepted a circumscribed notion of "power sharing" between white, coloured, and Indian. . . . However, to many Nationalists, accepting coloureds and Indians in Parliament threatened white control of the state, on which their vital interests depended. More specific anxieties were felt by civil servants over black competition and by working-class whites over the leveling down of state services.

Mr. Botha's policies consequently intensified the class conflicts in the NP's base. Three months after he took office, white miners struck to defend racial job reservation, while their former allies in the Nationalist government sided with management. During the year which followed, the Prime Minister's endorsement of labor law liberalization and reformist speeches (along with the Information Scandal) provoked by-election swings to the far right of up to 40 percent in traditional NP farming and mining seats. In the white General Election of 1981, support for the Herstigte Nasionale Party (HNP) and other far right groups increased almost six times, to over 200,000 votes. The last straw fell when the new constitutional scheme came before the NP caucus on 23 February 1982. A group of 23 MPs stormed out, including Transvaal leader Andries Treurnicht; 15 left the NP to establish a new Conservative Party (CP) in March. Soon almost one-fourth of the Transvaal NP district and branch committee members—often the most committed—defected, shattering many constituency organizations. What many thought impossible had happened: the National Party had split from top to bottom.

41. *OFF BY A THOUSAND MILES**

by *THE NEW YORKER*

And a young man writes:

Last winter, I was talking with this guy I know. It was snowing, so we talked about, you know, snow. "It's not so bad here—I used to live in Minneapolis," he said.

*From *The New Yorker*, September 9, 1985.

"Minnesota's pretty far north," I said. (I could have added that *I* used to live in Canada, but that would have been boasting.)

"Yeah, Minneapolis is on the same parallel as Juneau, Alaska," he said. We were about to go on to some other topic—Patrick Ewing, probably—when a rough map of the continent appeared in my head. (It may have been the radar weather map from Channel 7.) Anyway, Alaska looked to be significantly north of Minneapolis. We tracked down an atlas, and found that the Twin Cities lie at a latitude of about forty-five degrees, while Juneau, a snowball's heave from the sixtieth parallel, is about a thousand miles to the north. "Someone told me that about Juneau, and I've been passing it on for years," this guy said. "I guess I'll have to stop." And he did, I bet. He just happened to be wrong about this one thing. No big deal.

I started thinking about that conversation when I read the papers last Tuesday and found that President Reagan had praised the "reformist" government of South Africa. "They have eliminated the segregation that we once had in our own country—the type of thing where hotels and restaurants and places of entertainment and so forth were segregated—that has all been eliminated," the President told radio station WSB, in Atlanta. "They recognize now interracial marriages and all. . . . Blacks can buy property in the heretofore white areas, they can own businesses in some forty white-dominated districts," he continued. Mr. Reagan's point, in each instance, was that his policy of "constructive engagement" had helped bring about these improvements. Taking his statements in reverse order, blacks in fact cannot own businesses in white-dominated districts. Under the country's Group Areas Act, each inch of South Africa has been zoned white, colored, Indian, or black. Only whites can own property in white areas, only Indians in Indian areas, and so on. A new law, proposed by the government but so far not put into effect, would allow blacks to *operate* businesses in some white, central-city areas. But they cannot own the buildings, or the land beneath them, and, under the strictures of the Influx Control Act, they cannot even enter the white neighborhood where the businesses are situated without written government permission. In shanty-towns like Soweto, blacks were recently granted the right to acquire a ninety-nine-year lease on the land beneath their homes, but, according to the Washington *Post,* "that policy has been mired in red tape," and very few leases have been granted. As for the idea that the government now recognizes interracial marriages "and all," it is true: the ban on mixed marriages was repealed. A black married to a white cannot live with his or her spouse in a white area, though.

Mr. Reagan's assertion that all hotels and restaurants and places of entertainment have been opened to black people was his most powerful rhetorical point, because in this country true political freedom for blacks followed closely on the demise of Jim Crow laws. On the first day of February, 1960, four students from North Carolina Agricultural and Technical State University staged a sit-in at a Greensboro lunch counter. In August of 1965, the Voting Rights Act was signed into law. Petty apartheid and political domination were closely linked. In South Africa, Jim Crow was breached very slightly a decade ago (during the Nixon and Ford Administrations). Certain hotels and restaurants catering to international travelers were permitted to rent rooms and serve meals to black people. But this did not lead to widespread integration. Almost all places of public accommodation, including buses and trains, are still strictly segregated. In all of South Africa, there is not a single movie theatre that a black person and a white person (including a couple married under the newly relaxed miscegenation laws) can both be admitted to. More telling, though, is the fact that political reforms did not flow from the minor breaches of apartheid. Schools are still entirely segregated, and the money spent on white children far surpasses the amount granted to blacks. (No one can say, however, that the authorities aren't concerned with educating black children. Just last week, they jailed several hundred students, some as young as eight, for cutting classes.) Last month, of course, President P. W. Botha pledged that South Africa would never countenance giving each man and each woman a vote.

And South Africa is much worse than all that. All of us, not just Ronald Reagan, forget how bad. Every night, it seems, the evening news opens with pictures of black teen-agers scattering at the approach of tanks. "FOUR MORE DEAD IN SOUTH AFRICA," "THREE DIE IN DURBAN FIGHTING," "SIX KILLED AT FUNERAL"—day after day the drone continues, until the casualties and the riots all seem alike to us distant observers. We have so little experience with domestic violence in this country that it is hard to imagine how it must shred hope and faith. Consider that the Boston Massacre, which claimed the lives of five people in 1770, still sticks in our national memory. The killing of four young people at Kent State in 1970 convinced—briefly—large numbers of young Americans that they lived in a police state. In South Africa, they have a Boston Massacre most mornings and a Kent State nearly every afternoon. It is a sick, sad, ugly country.

That the real South Africa bears so little resemblance to the South Africa in Ronald Reagan's mind is mildly alarming. He has the resources of the State Department and the Central Intelligence Agency to call upon when he wants information; he has a National Security Adviser and a National Security Council; every morning, an aide hands him a digest of all the world's news; he can summon any expert on any topic to the Oval Office and the expert will catch the next flight; the White House library subscribes to two hundred and fifty magazines; he has a bank of television sets with enough damn screens to look at all three networks and CNN simultaneously. And yet he is wrong about South Africa—not "wrong" philosophically or morally but *wrong,* factually. He is off by a thousand miles. And that is somehow reassuring. Surely it explains why he has shown so little concern, why he has kept whispering softly to the South Africans, why he has spoken so often of progress. He didn't understand; he just got it wrong. Other people have known about South Africa for years, but then other people have known where Alaska is for quite a while, too. When I was a kid, I thought for some reason that Los Angeles and L.A. were two different cities. We get things mixed up in our heads, and they stick until someone explains the mistake. By now, someone has certainly told the President the truth—told him blacks can't go to the white movie houses in South Africa—and from this time on he will obviously act differently.

Chapter X:

THE DEEPENING CRISIS

42. *THE CURRENT CRISIS**

by GAY W. SEIDMAN

Gay Seidman is a leader of the University of California Berkeley Divestment Coalition. She has periodically lived and worked in southern Africa during the last eight years.

A year ago, if you said South Africa was reaching a turning point, people responded incredulously: Americans had grown used to the idea that the South African government would brutally repress any opposition to minority rule, and would continue indefinitely to preserve apartheid. Today the statement sounds almost cliched. But to say the situation is more fluid today than it has been for years begs further questions. How is the present crisis likely to develop? What can we expect to see in the next few months? And for those who believe only a democratic system will end the institutionalized violence that is apartheid, there is a third question: what can we do to block the government's efforts to preserve white supremacy?

Three main forces have shaped the current situation: internal resistance, government efforts to enact limited changes in the apartheid system, and international pressure on the economy. Perhaps the least understood element in this country has been the roots of the current uprising. Foreign journalists

*From *Democratic Left* (A publication of the Democratic Socialists of America, New York), November–December 1985.

tend to make regular comparisons with the 1976 "unrest," when high school students inspired by the Black Consciousness movement took to the streets. A common analysis of the present uprising rests on a generational argument, which suggests that the students we see in street demonstrations now are simply the latest age cohort to come up against the state. But this view is superficial at best.

The Black Consciousness movement was oriented towards intellectuals and activists; the students in 1976 were never very successful in mobilizing support from other parts of their communities, from workers or community groups. The roots of the present uprising lie in a much broader-based, grass-roots mobilization; although activists across South Africa have been jailed, killed or forced to go underground, the uprising has not died down.

In 1977, the government was able to crush the Black Consciousness movement by detaining leaders and banning its organizations. Since then, activists have learned to use another strategy. On one side, there has been the development of a strongly grass-roots-based union movement; today, some 12 percent of the black work force belongs to unions, and many more workers feel allegiance to the union movement. On the other, there are a range of other types of groups, which have allowed activists to mobilize new groups in the black communities. There are tenant groups, formed to fight rent increases on government-owned housing; squatter communities, organized to resist forced removal to the bantustans; community organizations fighting increases in government-regulated fares on the buses that carry workers from black residential areas to industrial sites. There are women's organizations, which fight apartheid's impact on black South African families; and student groups, which object to the segregated system of inferior education.

To varying degrees, these groups have set up democratic structures and decision-making processes, and have learned to use what power they have to confront the regime directly. Unions, of course, use recent modifications in labor legislation to organize workers and back up their demands with both legal and illegal strikes. Tenants organize massive rent strikes, denying the local township authorities the funds they need for local administration. Commuters refuse to ride buses or trains, walking miles to work for months until the fare comes down. Students refuse to attend classes, or even more threateningly, organize their own learning groups inside the school buildings. Since late 1979, groups have also learned to coordinate their struggles and strategies in specific campaigns. Obviously, linkage between different groups makes all of them stronger, and makes it harder for the government to crush resistance.

It would be misleading, I think, to talk about the rise in open mass-based resistance to apartheid in the last few years without talking about the rising awareness inside South Africa of an intensifying guerrilla struggle. Although strict censorship laws prohibit most descriptions of guerrilla activity inside the country, there can be no doubt that since the late 1970s, most anti-government activists have been aware of attacks by the armed wing of the African National Congress on police stations, oil refineries, electrical power stations and even military offices. During the 15 years after the ANC and other black political groups were banned in 1960, the ANC's armed wing slowly built up an underground network, infiltrating, according to Western intelligence reports, some 2,000 trained guerrillas into the country by 1980. Certainly, this effort was aided by changes in the whole Southern Africa region: the independence of Angola and Mozambique in 1975 and '76, and the independence of Zimbabwe in 1980, removed the buffer belt of colonial states that had once protected South Africa's and Namibia's borders from guerrilla infiltration.

By 1979, an independent report published in South Africa argued that the country was already engaged in a low-intensity war, and the government was already talking about the need to build up its defense capacity against ANC guerrillas. In 1981 and 1982, there appears to have been an average of a guerrilla attack every two weeks somewhere in the country. The ANC's armed wing, *Umkhonto We Sizwe,* is well known for its efforts to avoid unnecessary civilian casualties, but its attacks on empty government buildings and on military personnel, including police, undoubtedly offered activists a new sense of the possibilities of armed struggle against the regime. From about 1981, this awareness was heightened by an apparent conscious strategy on the part of guerrillas, who chose targets that could either damage the regime's economic or military capacity or that were directly linked to popular, open struggles.

For example, in 1983, there were attacks on police stations, Bantu administration buildings, electric power stations and railways. But the two attacks that stood out were the bombing of the air force and military intelligence headquarters in Pretoria, and the destruction of the "consulate" of the nominally-independent Ciskei in Johannesburg at a time when the Ciskei authorities were involved in brutally repressing a bus boycott, which underlined the links between the Ciskei and white-ruled South Africa, and which showed the links between popular resistance and guerrilla activity.

There is little doubt that the growth of visible support for the ANC during this period is partly linked to the impression made by such attacks on young activists: from the early '80s, ANC slogans and songs appeared more and more regularly at meetings and rallies, and the ANC colors, green, gold and black,[1] began to appear at activists' funerals.

But the ANC's influence goes beyond the armed struggle; the ANC is both a political and a military movement, and in fact places as much emphasis on the role of popular struggle as it does on military opposition to the regime.

---

[1] Green for the land, gold for the riches underground and black for the African people.—Ed.

From about 1980, the ANC's influence on political activity became increasingly evident: many of the community and union groups which emerged expressed a clear commitment to the non-racial, democratic tradition of the ANC. Turning away from the Black Consciousness approach, which argued that blacks had to create separate organizations within the black community, activists in the early '80s argued that anyone willing to fight for majority rule, including progressive whites, should be able to find a place in the movement.

In 1980, a campaign to recognize the 25th anniversary of the Freedom Charter, adopted as the ANC's fundamental principles in the late 1950s, allowed activists—including older ANC activists, who had been involved in the movement when it was still legal and who were emerging after long jail sentences or bannings—a forum in which to discuss the ANC's approach to the liberation of South Africa. The Freedom Charter begins, "South Africa belongs to those who live in it, both black and white," and calls for one-person, one-vote in a unitary state, as well as for the nationalization of monopolies and land reform.

The clearest indication both of the resurgence of popular organization and of the growing importance of the ANC came in 1983, with the formation of the United Democratic Front—today, the organization most clearly suffering from government attempts at repression. A coalition of more than 600 groups, the UDF allowed any group that wished to affiliate to join a broad front opposing the new constitution—including groups with white members. By creating a non-racial democratically organized front against the regime, the UDF hoped to plant the seeds of the new order within the old. Although the UDF's leaders and members are overwhelmingly black (a term that encompasses people classified "Asian" and "coloured" as well as "African"), a few sympathetic whites have also participated actively. More symbolically, perhaps, but also important, the UDF chose as patrons for the fledgling organization all the long-term ANC prisoners, including Nelson Mandela, and Helen Joseph, a white woman who spent some 20 years under house arrest for her resistance activities.

The UDF's formation and strategy can only be understood in the context of government initiatives during the late '70s and early '80s. In the late '70s, the South African state embarked on what was called a "total strategy," designed to meet the total onslaught it believed was coming from the north. Recognizing the inherent tensions in the old apartheid system, which allowed the growth of an urban black working class that had no stake at all in the status quo, government commissions began to recommend granting limited rights to urban blacks, while speeding up the process of cutting the 13 percent of the land area set aside as bantustans off from white-ruled South Africa. You can find the same approach in statements by P. W. Botha even today: on one side, he will grant limited autonomy to black residential areas, but on the other, he insists on retaining the Group Areas Act, under which different areas are set aside for each racial classification.

Alongside this limited autonomy, however, went an increase in the power of the central government: even white parliamentary opposition leaders, who reject one-person one-vote, say the new constitution grants dictatorial powers to the executive. Elections might be held for representatives to black urban councils or Asian or Coloured houses of parliament, but the white minority government would continue to decide the issues on which those bodies could vote, limiting the power of those elected representatives to participation in meaningless shop talk. This August, when the international community responded with horror at State President Botha's refusal to consider a democratic system for South Africa, the leader of the white parliamentary opposition, Van Zyl Slabbert, commented, "P. W. Botha has never lied about what he intends doing. . . . Anyone who believes P. W. is trying to bring about a major political reform is a victim of his own wishful thinking."

Leaders in the United Democratic Front would undoubtedly agree with Van Zyl Slabbert's analysis; in fact, they began to argue along these lines when the government first began discussing a new constitution in late 1982. They believed that the effort to create separate autonomous bodies could divide black opposition: people classified Asian and Coloured might be split off from the broad movement, while urban blacks might be split off from people living in rural areas or working as migrant laborers. Further, they argued that any participation in elections for new black urban councils or Asian and Coloured houses of parliament might create a stratum in black communities that derived its power from the apartheid system, and would therefore defend that system.

From 1983, the UDF began to mobilize its nearly two million members to oppose the new constitutional proposals, calling for a complete boycott of any forms of administration that were imposed on the black population. Only a constitution drawn up by what the UDF calls the "authentic leaders" of the country's population would be acceptable; and that means, UDF leaders say, that it must include leaders who have been jailed or forced into exile because of their demands for majority rule.

The UDF strategy of boycotting elections was overwhelmingly successful, with voter turnouts of one percent in many parts of the country. But in September 1984, the new constitution went into effect anyway. The opposition movement broadened its strategy: instead of simply refusing to participate in new administrative bodies, it tried to make the new system unworkable. Black councilors and Asian and Coloured parliamentary delegates were asked to resign; those who did not were threatened with property or personal damage. Today, only two townships still have functioning town councils. Townships near Johannesburg refused to pay rent increases, which were to fund the new administrative bodies; those rent strikes quickly turned into massive demonstrations, leading to a two-day stay-away in November that crippled the nation's industrial center.

In early 1985, ANC president O. R. Tambo called on the country to make itself ungovernable; by the end of the year, it was clear that that strategy was succeeding. The "unrest" had spread into small towns in rural areas; in larger townships, resistance continued despite military occupation of the streets. Local administration and control was virtually impossible: by the middle of 1985, not only whites but blacks who worked for the regime could no longer move safely through townships.

Most of the UDF's national leadership now faces treason charges, for promoting a pre-revolutionary climate; nearly 200 UDF activists have disappeared or been found dead over the last year. But across the country, local groups continue to come up with tactics suitable to their organizations and local contexts, sometimes imitating other areas' efforts, sometimes inventing new techniques for making the country ungovernable.

From the late '70s, while the government carried out limited modifications in apartheid, it also began to build up its military capacity in earnest, recognizing and sometimes overstating the threat from guerrilla activity. Its defense of Namibia, the colony South Africa controls illegally, today involves about $2 million daily, and some 100,000 white troops in an area with a population of only a million. It has steadily built up defenses along the other borders, and become about 75 percent self-sufficient in arms production. It also began a concerted policy of destabilizing neighboring states, with direct bombing raids, assassinations, and support of contra groups against neighboring governments who support the liberation movement. Support for a contra group in Mozambique led to the 1984 Nkomati Accords, where Mozambique finally agreed to restrict ANC activities inside its borders; but recent evidence proves conclusively that South Africa continued to fund the contra group anyway, apparently figuring that a trouble-free Mozambique on its borders could still provide a dangerous example of socialist development policies. South African invasions of Angola over the past ten years have cost Angola over $10 billion in damages, to say nothing of lives lost and homes destroyed.

Inside South Africa, military input into decision-making bodies has increased dramatically, so that military advisers sit on every city council and a state security council advises the cabinet. By 1984, the South African military budget was up to R3.75 billion, about half a billion more than the combined budgets for health, social welfare, tertiary education and all black education.

This military build-up has been costly: South Africa now owes some $20 billion to foreign banks, and has become increasingly dependent on foreign technology in its effort to be self-sufficient in arms and energy production. It is because of this dependency that the state of emergency has proved disastrous for the regime: international concern over the murders of some 700 people by police turned to outrage at the imposition of the state of emergency.

Today, it is difficult for even the Reagan administration to claim that Botha's reforms mean very much; even *Fortune* magazine no longer considers South Africa's strategic minerals crucial to American interests. International sanctions may not have much practical impact on South Africa, but they will make possible investors wary. Already in the grips of a deep recession, and already in debt, South Africa cannot pull out of the recession without new sources of capital—and that capital is unlikely to appear while the "unrest" continues. When South Africa announced a moratorium on debt repayments, causing massive panic among foreign investors in South Africa's gold mines, it became clear that the country's economy was teetering on the brink.

Into this conflict between growing internal resistance and an apparently intransigent government stepped a third force: South African and multinational capital, which in recent months has begun to look for new alternatives. Unlike Botha, who must answer to a white electorate, and unlike the ANC, which believes that majority rule must involve some redistribution of South Africa's assets, South Africa's business community is likely to seek a centrist solution. In Zimbabwe, the terms of the Lancaster House agreement have limited the government's ability to nationalize large resources or carry out widespread land reform; South African businesspeople are already beginning to think about a similar deal, where blacks could elect the government but where private property would be protected. A recent meeting in Lusaka between businessmen and the ANC failed to produce much common ground, since the ANC leaders told their visitors that their businesses, all large conglomerates, would have to be nationalized when the Freedom Charter is implemented. On their return to South Africa, the businessmen appear to have returned to an earlier effort to push the government to abandon racial discrimination before it is too late.

At the same time, there seems to be significant business support for a new grouping, the Convention Alliance, which is trying to bring black leaders inside the country together with moderate white politicians to discuss possible forms of future governance. By mid-October, this alliance seemed to have little hope of succeeding: only Gatsha Buthelezi, head of the KwaZulu bantustan who is widely hated for the way his followers attack and sometimes kill activists who reject the bantustan system, had agreed to join the new group. UDF leaders were unwilling to join the alliance, arguing that while their "authentic" leaders remain in jail or in exile no negotiations can be meaningful. Without the UDF's participation, it seems unlikely that the Convention Alliance will amount to a serious option.

Where does this description leave us? Neither resistance nor apartheid is likely to disappear overnight; at the moment, it seems probable that the struggle will continue for years, until there are free and open elections, and representative black leaders have some say in designing the system of government. In this scenario, what can the international community do? So far, international pressure has proved to be of immeasurable importance, more in staying the government's repressive actions than in forcing meaningful concessions. If we stop now—if we let international attention turn away from South Africa, where two or three people are dying daily already—the process of attaining a non-racial, democratic future could take much, much longer. In 1960 and 1976, international capital pulled out because of internal resistance; in both cases it returned, helping the state build up its ability to repress and control the black population.

As long as we continue to fight for sanctions, as long as we push institutional investors to put more pressure on American companies, we deny the South African regime the capital it needs for its economy; we deny the regime the technology it would need to make its repressive apparatus even more efficient. And we deny the minority regime an important psychological prop, its confidence that in the end, the United States will back the minority government against some mythical communist threat. If we allow Congress to aid Angolan contras, we help South Africa protect its borders against guerrilla attacks; if we allow Reagan to make distinctions between black South African leaders who have used violent and non-violent tactics, we help South Africa divide the resistance movement. South Africa will be free; there will be a non-racial democratic future, no matter what happens in the United States. But what we do can certainly help make that day come sooner.

43. *QUICKENING CHANGE IN SOUTH AFRICA**

by PETER GROTHE

Peter Grothe is professor of international policy studies at the Monterey Institute of International Studies.

MONTEREY, Calif.—A visitor returning to South Africa after an absence of five years is reminded of the story of the old fellow who heard the clock strike 13 and said, "It's never been this late before."

When I was in South Africa in 1980, giving guest lectures at universities, a highly respected Western diplomat told me that the most likely model for change in South Africa was not Mount St. Helens but rather a boiling caldron.

*From *The New York Times,* September 29, 1985.

In his view, then, a large and sudden eruption was unlikely. What he expected instead was limited black violence that would be met by repression from the Government, followed by limited accommodation and then a period of relative quiet. A series of such cycles of violence, repression and limited accommodation would, he thought, take place over a period of years until fundamental change had been accomplished.

At the time, I found this prediction plausible. It may still be, but my recent trip suggested that the Mount St. Helens metaphor is perhaps more appropriate today than it was five years ago.

The returning visitor finds nine significant differences between South Africa in 1980 and 1985.

First, unlike five years ago, blacks now feel a genuine sense of power and a decreasing reluctance to use it. Many blacks recognize that the South African Army and police are the strongest in Africa and that, in a violent confrontation, blacks would come out the losers. Nevertheless, many militant young blacks are ready for violence—including violence in white areas. Perhaps more important, the power to withhold one's labor and to boycott white stores gives blacks enormous economic clout, and they are now aware of it.

Second, the perceptual gap between ruling Afrikaners and blacks has widened. Whites point with pride to abolition of some of the worst aspects of apartheid—many of the better hotels and restaurants have been integrated, for instance, the mixed-marriage law has been abolished and many blacks are being promoted to middle-level jobs. Many Afrikaners speak about the enormous significance of these changes and the sacrifices they have made. The black view was summed up by one resident of Soweto: "Man, that's nothing but cosmetics. I'll only be satisfied when I get the vote."

Blacks and Afrikaners also have different timetables for change. Members of the Government talk about gradual, long-range solutions. The patience of the blacks is wearing thin. They want one man, one vote—and they want it now. The Rev. Beyers Naudé, the general secretary of the South African Council of Churches, told me: "My fellow whites have no idea of the deep sense of outrage in the black townships."

Third, five years ago the economy was strong. Now it is in turmoil. Many white business leaders, terrified by economic alarm signals and by the specter of foreign banks refusing to roll over their short-term loans, have urged the Government to release Nelson Mandela, negotiate with the banned African National Congress and immediately dismantle the apartheid system. This would have been unheard-of even six months ago.

Fourth, Afrikaners—once called "the white tribe of Africa"—are no longer unified. A significant and vocal minority has bolted the ruling National Party and formed their own ultraright group, the Conservative Party. Many observers see this faction, which argues against all concessions to blacks, as a constraint on President P. W. Botha's announced intentions of reform.

Fifth, there have been perceptible shifts in the attitudes of many whites in the last five years. The Afrikaner students I met seemed to be troubled and searching. Most seemed to hold views more liberal than those of their parents' generation. English-speaking students, who have traditionally held more liberal views than Afrikaners, have gone even further. Many of them now seem willing "to put their bodies on the line," as they did last month when hundreds of demonstrating Cape Town University students were whipped and teargassed by police. Further, many more English-speaking whites are now considering emigration. One English-speaking businessman told me: "More than half of my friends are planning to leave the country."

Sixth, there are growing fissures among blacks. Militant young blacks are becoming increasingly impatient with the moderate views of their parents' generation and with moderate leaders like the Zulu chief, Gatsha Buthelezi, and Bishop Desmond Tutu. Meanwhile, the Government continues to jail or ban moderate black leaders who want peaceful change, causing young militants to ask: "Look, the Government arrests the peaceful moderates. What option is there other than violence?"

Seventh, although President Botha denies it, it is quite clear that white South Africans are much more sensitive to outside political and economic pressures than used to be the case. Talks with many whites and a perusal of the press leave no doubt about this, and it would suggest that President Reagan's tranquilizing notion that the Botha Government has substantially solved its problems makes for the wrong strategy at the wrong time.

Eighth, blacks are experiencing what the American historian Crane Brinton once called "the revolution of rising expectations." When Rhodesia became Zimbabwe, South Africa became the last white domino on the continent. President Botha said to whites, "Adapt or die." Those and other events have given blacks the expectation that the complete dismantling of apartheid is within reach—not for their grandchildren's generation, but for them.

Finally, in the fall of 1980, President Jimmy Carter was extremely unpopular with South African whites and extremely popular with blacks. In sharp contrast, Ronald Reagan is extremely popular with whites and arguably the most unpopular President in American history with blacks.

What conclusions can one draw? No one can accurately predict the future, and the caldron may continue to simmer, more or less quietly, for some time to come. Yet most of the trends I noticed suggested to me that a volcanic eruption becomes more and more likely with every passing month.

In Alan Paton's classic novel, "Cry, The Beloved Country," a black South African clergyman says about whites, "I have one great fear in my heart—that one day when they are turned to loving, they will find that we are turned to hating." It strikes me now as a sadly accurate prophecy.

44. THE ROOTS OF SOUTH AFRICA'S CREDIT CRISIS*

by ROBERT A. BENNETT

Robert A. Bennet is a reporter for The New York Times.

The usually unflappable senior vice president of a major New York bank sat in his Westchester home a few weeks ago watching television excerpts from a long-awaited speech by South Africa's President, P. W. Botha. Like many other people, the banker had expected Mr. Botha to be conciliatory and indicate that his Government would change its racial policies.

But the banker was stunned—more by what he saw as Mr. Botha's pugnacious tone than by the words themselves. The banker turned to his wife and said, "There's financial trouble ahead."

No Chance to Withdraw

Indeed there was. As weeks went on, more and more banks, fearful that racial tension would undermine the South African economy, refused to lend new money or renew maturing loans to any South African borrower. It caused a plunge in the value of the rand, South Africa's currency, and eventually forced the Pretoria Government earlier this month to take the drastic step of forbidding South African companies to repay billions of dollars of principal on their foreign debt for the rest of the year.

Bankers, still shaken by the experience, are asking how the South African situation could have deteriorated so quickly before they had a chance to get their money out.

A picture of what went wrong has been coming into focus. Interviews with bankers around the world show that the problems had been developing for some time but that there were some critical turning points, including these:

- A surge in borrowing from abroad by South Africa's private sector that began about three years ago.
- Worldwide coverage of growing civil unrest over the country's racial policies.
- A shifting by major international banks of their South African loans to smaller banks, beginning last fall.

*From *The New York Times,* September 16, 1985.

- The widely publicized decision by the Chase Manhattan Bank in late July to stop all lending to South Africa.
- President Botha's speech, made in late August, which shattered hopes of a voluntary easing of the nation's racial policies.

What makes the crisis so unusual is that South Africa's economy was robust, the Government's coffers were full and the country's trade position was strong. Never in recent history, in fact, has a country so economically sound defaulted and risked a cut-off of credit for years to come from the very banks that are its financial link to the rest of the world.

Bankers say the story began about three years ago when a tight monetary policy at home encouraged South African companies to borrow overseas where interest rates were much lower. But it was only a year or so ago, as racial disturbances were increasing and coming to world attention, that most international banks began to realize just how great South Africa's debt burden had become.

Last fall, for example, the executive in charge of a major New York bank's African business took one of the bank's top officers to meet clients in Johannesburg.

The senior banker did not like what he saw. He found that over the previous three years South African commercial banks had borrowed heavily abroad. The borrowings consisted mainly of short-term loans that had to be repaid in a few months. But the banks used the proceeds for making longer-term loans to South African companies. In banking, such a practice is considered a classical error.

If South Africa's creditors suddenly decided not to renew those short-term loans, the borrowing banks could not quickly get repayment from their customers, who had borrowed on a long-term basis. And with racial disturbances spreading, the New York banker realized that political problems could touch off a financial crisis.

At a meeting with Finance Minister Barend du Plessis, the New York banker warned that South Africa had a "tremendous vulnerability" as a result of its debt situation.

The New York bank began reducing its lending to South Africa. Caution also spread among other banks. Bernard Shuttleworth, chief financial economist for the Standard Bank in South Africa, said he believes that "foreign banks had become increasingly nervous after September 1984." He said, "It was then that they began looking at us far more carefully."

Most of South Africa's traditional creditors, such as the North Carolina National Bank, began cutting back then on loans to South Africa. A spokesman for the North Carolina bank said it reduced its loans there from $217 million at the end of 1983 to $101 million this June.

Loan Participations Sold

Among banks in the United States, Citibank remains the one with more loans outstanding in South Africa than any other.

Many banks began reducing their exposure on loans in South Africa by selling participations to other banks. This sharing of the loans was not always apparent to the borrowers.

In some cases, instead of telling the South Africans of the credit cutbacks, large American banks began selling pieces of their South African loans to other, less informed banks around the world—especially in Japan.

The big New York banks liked this procedure not only because it helped reduce their exposure to South African debt but also because they could make a profit on the transactions. If the bank were earning three-fourths of a percentage point over its own cost of funds, it would try to sell a participation in the loan at a yield of only one-half point above the cost of funds—keeping one-fourth percentage point for itself.

"If you have four or six banks brokering South African loans, you might have as much as $1 billion in participations out there," said a New York banker. "Those participations were held by banks with the weakest knees." He added that they were the first to "cut and run" last August after Chase's decision.

In March the Bank of Boston, a large regional bank, announced that it would cease all lending to South Africa. Ira Stapanian, the bank's president, said last week that the bank feared it might lose business at home because of its dealings with South Africa but that the main reason for the cutback was fear that racial problems would destabilize its economy.

The bankers had to deal with economic problems, which they believed could be managed. At the same time, however, they faced political problems that made it impossible to focus only on economic reality.

While they worried that increasing violence in South Africa might destroy the country's economy, making repayment of the loans impossible, they also had to worry about the domestic repercussions of doing business with South Africa amid increasing public antagonism in the United States and Europe toward the Pretoria Government. Bankers said the news media, especially television with its almost daily vivid accounts of rioting, played a key role.

A South African banker said, "If there were no television, there would be no crisis."[1]

Chase's Decision to Stop

As racial tension mounted, the Chase Manhattan Bank decided in late July to cease all lending to South Africa. Financial sources in Johannesburg say the decision was made by Willard C. Butcher, Chase's chairman. Chase refuses to comment on the issue or even to acknowledge that it changed its policy.

Word of the decision spread in South Africa as Chase's officers told their clients of the new policy. South African companies began unloading the rand. One reason was that if foreign banks refused to renew maturing loans there would be a run on rands as borrowers converted them to repay in the original currency.

To find out if the reports about Chase were true, Gerhard de Kock, head of South Africa's central bank, telephoned Mr. Butcher in New York, according to banking sources. Sitting in his 17th-floor office at One Chase Manhattan Plaza, Mr. Butcher confirmed Dr. de Kock's fears.

Following Chase's precedent, the banks overseas and in the United States that had bought participations in South African loans began to refuse to renew the loans as they came due.

Reluctance to Expand Debt

These banks' refusal to re-lend had an important effect because every dollar not re-lent to South Africa by one bank had to be replaced by another. And no bank wanted to increase its debt exposure there.

"Chase, being such a large bank, probably tipped the balance for a lot of other banks," said Mr. Shuttleworth of the Standard Bank. In late August, for example, the First Bank System of Minneapolis announced that it would no longer lend to South Africa. Although its exposure was relatively small—about $39 million—its action added momentum to the belief that all banks were refusing to lend to South Africa.

It was the fear that such pullouts would drain South Africa of its foreign exchange that caused a panic among banks and others. While South African companies had about $10 billion of debt falling due over the next year, the country's readily available foreign-exchange reserves stood at about $2.5 billion, and South Africa expected to clear another $2.5 billion from its foreign

---

[1] On November 2, 1985, The South African government imposed sweeping restrictions on the media, including the barring of television coverage of unrest in areas affected by the emergency decree.—Ed.

trade surplus. So if no loans could be rolled over, the country would come up short.

As a result, during August dozens of banks acted to protect their own positions by stopping all lending to South Africa. They were trying to heed an old banking adage: Don't panic—but if you do, be the first.

45. THE EMERGENCE OF POWERFUL BLACK UNIONS*

by ROGER KERSON

In the early hours of August 28, South African security forces arrested John Gomomo at his home here. He was being taken in for questioning, the police told him, in accordance with South Africa's security laws that permit warrant-less arrests and detention without trial for indefinite periods.

Pre-dawn arrests are a fact of life for activists in South Africa. More than 2,000 people have been detained since the government declared a state of emergency on July 21. About half of them have been released, but the rest will remain behind bars until the government is good and ready to let them go. With little or no legal recourse, friends and supporters use petitions, prayer vigils and consumer boycotts to pressure the authorities.

Fortunately for Gomomo, his friends had a more powerful weapon to use on his behalf: they were able to stop production at a major industrial facility.

Gomomo is a shop steward at Volkswagen auto factory in Uitenhage and a vice president of the 20,000-member National Automobile and Allied Work-ers Union (NAAWU). He was arrested along with several other senior shop stewards from the Volkswagen plant. Police wanted to question them, Gomomo recalls, about their trade union activism.

"We had to tell them that we couldn't answer any questions about our union without a mandate from our members," he says with a smile. "So they said they would have to keep us locked up for a few weeks."

Meanwhile, one of Gomomo's neighbors, also a Volkswagen worker, spread the word at the plant about the arrest of the union officials. In response, the 3,000-strong black work force put down their tools and went outside for a mass meeting. They would not return to work, they told management, until the imprisoned union leaders were released.

*From *In These Times* (the Independent Socialist Newspaper published by the Institute for Public Affairs, Chicago), October 16–22, 1985.

At police headquarters the detained unionists overheard a conversation between officers and Volkswagen executives. The iron fist of the South African legal system relaxed shortly afterward and Gomomo and his colleagues joined a cheering crowd at the factory at 9:30 A.M.—less than six hours after they had been arrested.

The aborted attempt to detain a group of labor officials demonstrates the growing power and militancy of South Africa's independent black trade unions. With most opposition groups under constant attack by the government —virtually the entire leadership of the United Democratic Front, for example, is in detention, awaiting trial or in hiding, and several people have been mysteriously murdered—trade unions are one of the few remaining aboveground outlets for black resistance.

Powerful black unions are a relatively new phenomenon in South Africa. They received official sanction six years ago and have enjoyed tremendous growth since then, now claiming more than half a million paid up members. That represents some 20 percent of the black work force, and the unions have gained a solid foothold in such industries as mining, metalworking, retail trade, automobile manufacture and food processing.

After black unions were recognized in 1979, unions belonging to the two major labor federations—the Federation of South African Trade Unions (FOSATU) and the Council of Unions of South Africa (CUSA)—at first kept a low-profile on nonfactory political issues, focusing instead on workplace organizing. But with their trade union base solidly established, both federations are participating actively in the current explosion of political activity.

In the summer of 1984, FOSATU sent organizers door-to-door in the Eastern Cape, urging coloured and Indian voters to boycott elections for the discredited tricameral parliament. In November, several unions participated in a student-initiated, two-day stay away in the Transvaal region near Johannesburg. This year FOSATU and several independent unions have joined other opposition organizations in calling for consumer boycotts to protest the detention of political prisoners and the continuing state of emergency.

"There's no way we can divorce ourselves from the popular struggle," says Chris Dlamini, president of FOSATU. "It emanates from the fact that people don't have the right to vote—that our people do not have equal access to the wealth of this country, even though we pay taxes. . . . Trade unions are the only platform we've got."

Although Dlamini is one of South Africa's most important leaders, he still spends each day as a full-time shop steward in a Kellogg's cereal plant in Springs, a small city about an hour outside of Johannesburg.

The emerging black unions are run on the principle of "worker control." Only active workers can serve as union officers, and officers cannot speak on behalf of members without receiving a specific mandate from the rank and file.

Accountability is enforced with an effective shop steward system, creating democratic unions with broad-based popular support.

New Federation

The black union movement will take another step forward in November with the formation of a new, enlarged federation expected to have more than 400,000 members. The new federation is the result of four years of negotiations, which began in 1981 when black unions gathered to decide on a coordinated response to the government's labor reforms. The unity talks have been stormy at times, and some of the differences within the black labor movement parallel similar disagreements between competing opposition political organizations.

Now that the dust has settled, it appears that the new federation will include FOSATU and several major independent unions. CUSA has dropped out, following a dispute over the question of black leadership. CUSA subscribes to the Black Consciousness philosophy, which sees the black working class as the vanguard of the liberation struggle and insists on black leadership for black organizations.

FOSATU and the independent unions joining the new federation, by contrast, follow a policy of non-racialism. In South Africa's twisted political lexicon, non-racial organizations are those that are open to members of all races and that specifically welcome liberal whites in the struggle against apartheid. Whites hold key staff positions in several non-racial unions.

According to its draft constitution, the as-yet-unnamed federation will be based on the principle of industrial unionism and a strong effort will be made to create a single affiliate for every major industry.

The federation's leaders are convinced that strong, single-industry unions are the only effective means to combat the growing power of South Africa's major employers. The South African economy, like that of many other industrialized nations, is becoming ever more concentrated. A single corporation, Anglo American, controls more than 50 percent of the companies traded on the Johannesburg stock exchange.

Oddly enough, at a time when the independent black trade unions are escalating their struggle against the government, the same large corporations that do their best to defeat black workers on the industrial front are suddenly painting themselves as supporters of black political aspirations.

"Apartheid is dead," says Anton Rupert, head of the Rembrandt Corporation and one of the nation's leading Afrikaner businessmen, "and the corpse must be buried, not embalmed."

The Anglo American Corporation has gone so far as to call for the release of imprisoned African National Congress (ANC) leader Nelson Mandela, and it was Anglo American's chairman, Gavin Relly, who organized the recent talks between businessmen and exiled ANC leaders in Zambia.

Strange Bedfellows

It is undeniably strange to see prominent capitalists behave like seasoned anti-apartheid campaigners, taking out full-page ads calling for reform and jetting off to Lusaka over government objections. But their behavior becomes more understandable in light of the severe economic pressures being caused by South Africa's current political crisis.

Despite worldwide condemnation of apartheid, South Africa has remained, up until this year, a good place to do business. A spokesman for the American Chamber of Commerce in South Africa, for example, proudly told *In These Times* that investments in South Africa earned an average return of 15 percent, as compared to 10 percent in the U.S. and 8.5 in Great Britain. But that picture is changing by the minute for the following reasons:

- The administration of apartheid requires high government expenditure, and therefore high taxes, which can no longer be easily supported by business interests, now that black unions have pushed up the cost of black labor.
- The substandard living conditions of most black workers, and the restrictions on their movement imposed by the pass laws and the influx control system, are becoming a major impediment to creating a stable, productive workforce. Leading industrial concerns realized long ago that many aspects of apartheid are incompatible with modern capitalism's needs. Black workers must be "free," so to speak, so they can be more properly exploited.
- Political instability in South Africa is beginning to destroy the South African economy. The government suspended repayment of foreign loans this summer to head off an impending financial collapse, but business leaders are acutely aware that the economy will not function normally again until the country's political problems are resolved.
- The recent surge of activism by business leaders relates not only to economic difficulties, but also to an undeniable political fact: sooner or later, apartheid will fall. South African businessmen would like to make sure that capitalism doesn't crumble along with it.

". . . The free enterprise system," warns a worried A. M. Rosholt, executive chairman of Barlow Rand Ltd., "is threatened by the fact that the majority of blacks are not supporters of capitalism. They identify capitalism with the overall political system, which they reject." Rosholt's solution is for businessmen to speak out more forcefully for the need for reform and to take steps to guarantee that blacks "enjoy their fair share of the fruits of the system."

Rosholt's warning may be a classic case of too little, too late, since black workers are not willing to trust their future to the white business community.

"The business people want us to see them as being on our side," says a skeptical Chris Dlamini. "They're very involved in trying to reform certain aspects of the system. They wouldn't mind staging a *coup d' etat* and putting the [white liberal] Progressive Federal Party in power, which would protect their capitalist interests. We have to prevent that. That's why we say workers should lead the struggle."

While business and labor are both presently calling for an end to apartheid, they are obviously at odds over how the post-apartheid society will be structured. Nor can they agree on short-term tactics for bringing about change, one example being the sensitive issue of economic sanctions.

Businessmen, to no one's surprise, argue vociferously against sanctions, claiming that outside pressure on the South African economy will simply add to unemployment among blacks and "hurt those who are supposed to be helped." That argument, of course, has been picked up on this side of the Atlantic by Ronald Reagan.

Fortunately, black workers in South Africa don't seem to have much trouble figuring out who their real friends are. "If the employers are so worried about us," a shop steward said in discussing economic sanctions, "why don't they pay us a living wage."

Two recent opinion polls—by the *London Times* and Community Agency for Social Inquiry—show that more than 70 percent of blacks favor some form of economic sanctions or disinvestment to put pressure on the Pretoria regime. This contradicts the findings of an earlier poll—funded by the U.S. State Department—claiming that a majority of blacks opposed disinvestment. Critics have cited various methodological flaws in the earlier poll, and the climate of opinion may have changed since it was taken more than a year ago.

Labor leaders estimate that far more than 70 percent of blacks are in favor of sanctions. As a matter of policy, most trade unions strongly support divestment campaigns abroad, and international anti-apartheid activities are given significant attention in the labor press. But the black unions stop short of urging foreign companies to withdraw from the country.

". . . The pressure for disinvestment has had a positive effect and should not be lessened," says a statement of FOSATU's Executive Council from April 1984. "FOSATU is definitely opposed to foreign investment that accepts the conditions of oppression maintained by this regime. . . ." However, the union notes, the ultimate goal is to "ensure that the factories, machines and buildings presently in South Africa will be retained in South Africa to the ultimate benefit of all."

The bottom line is that South African workers don't want to see foreign companies leave the country with assets that they have helped to create.

"The legal ownership of these assets may rest with foreign companies," says Alec Erwin, FOSATU's education director. "But they have been developed . . . by the hard work and labor of South African workers. We can see absolutely no sense in handing over part of the social wealth of this country in order to place pressure on this regime."

The desire of South African workers to protect their long-term "social wealth" should not be confused with a reluctance to take short-term economic risks. Black workers have shown repeatedly that they are willing to put their jobs on the line to fight for political change. The Volkswagen workers in Uitenhage—where unemployment is running higher than 30 percent—could all have been fired when they walked off their jobs to demand the release of John Gomomo.

Those same workers took a similar risk in July, when they went on strike to protest Volkswagen's decision to donate a dozen vans to the All-Blacks, a New Zealand rugby team scheduled for a controversial tour of South Africa. The Volkswagen workers were determined not to let their labor be used to support an event that would have violated the international sports boycott of South Africa, lending credibility to the minority government.

The Uitenhage plant was shut down for several days, and the illegal strike ended only when a New Zealand court case cancelled the All-Blacks' tour.

Workers belonging to the Commercial, Catering and Allied Workers Union of South Africa (CCAWUSA) have also risked their jobs for political reasons in recent months. CCAWUSA was one of the unions endorsing a boycott of white stores in the Durban area in August. It was called to protest the state of emergency and demand the release of political prisoners. CCAWUSA represents workers at several major retail chains, and if the boycott is successful, as many consumer boycotts have been, one result may be that CCAWUSA members will be laid off.

Changing the System

Clearly, black workers are not afraid to use their growing economic power, even if they will suffer in the short run. "I'm not talking about a job, or no job," says Chris Dlamini. "I'm talking about changing the system."

Black South Africans have been fighting to change the apartheid system ever since it was introduced almost four decades ago, and the development of independent black unions have given them an important new weapon in their continuing struggle. More than a few policymakers in South Africa must long for the good old days before blacks had strong workplace organizations.

But black unions are here to stay. And they will continue to have an impact on their employers and the state. Just ask the harried executives at Volkswagen or the police in Uitenhage who tried to arrest John Gomomo.

46. THE CHURCH*

by GAIL HOVEY
Gail Hovey is executive editor of Christianity and Crisis.

No discussion of the current situation in South Africa would be complete without a discussion of the churches. On the one hand, the theology of the Dutch Reformed Churches has supplied the Afrikaners with a justification for white supremacy, with the belief that they are God's chosen people. The introduction to the new constitution, adopted in August 1984, well illustrates this conviction: "In humble submission to Almighty God, who controls the destinies of nations and the history of peoples; who gathered our forebears together from many lands and gave them this their own; who has guided them from generation to generation; who has wondrously delivered them from the dangers that beset them. . . ." According to this view, apartheid is the will of God.

On the other hand, well-known church people, black and white—such as Bishop Desmond Tutu, Dr. Allan Boesak, and the Rev. Beyers Naudé—are outspoken opponents of the apartheid regime and their opposition is fundamentally grounded in their understanding of, and faithfulness to, the Christian gospel. Less well-known church figures, including the Rev. Moss Chikhane and the Rev. Geoffrey Moselane, went on trial in late January along with twenty other members of the United Democratic Front, accused of murder and of seeking to overthrow the government, charges to which they have pleaded not guilty. Squatters in the town of Crossroads sang hymns while they waited for the police to come and destroy their homes, and victims of bannings and torture testify to the strength they have gained from their faith.

The people of South Africa, black and white, are overwhelmingly Christian, and the church is deeply divided. A group of Christians who call themselves the Kairos theologians put it this way: "Both oppressor and oppressed claim loyalty to the same Church. . . . There we sit in the same Church while outside Christian policemen and soldiers are beating up and killing Christian children or torturing Christian prisoners to death while yet other Christians stand by and weakly plead for peace."

*From *Monthly Review,* April 1986.

The policemen and soldiers are following orders which ultimately come from the Nationalist Party, from leaders who, with few exceptions, are members of the Dutch Reformed Churches. The theology of these churches has been called State Theology; it has allowed the Nationalists to rule South Africa with a clear conscience, convinced that their power to rule comes from God.

Those who stand by and weakly plead for peace are also much in evidence in South Africa, primarily in the so-called English-speaking churches. The theology of these churches has been called Church Theology; it is critical of apartheid but in an abstract and spiritual way. It avoids serious social analysis and its calls for justice are reformist.

Finally, adherents to Prophetic Theology believe that the church must be on the side of the poor and oppressed. This theology begins with social analysis and affirms the right of the people to resist injustice and oppression. The task is not to compromise with the apartheid regime but to replace it with one that will govern in the interests of all the people of South Africa. The vast majority of Christians in South Africa are, of course, black and oppressed. While not all of them would commit themselves to an understanding of Christian faith that requires radical action, for a growing number this is the only faith that can possibly be a source of life and hope.

In September 1985, a group of 151 individuals from all of South Africa's churches—English-speaking Protestant, Roman Catholic, evangelicals, pentecostals, and even Dutch Reformed—issued a challenge to the churches called the Kairos Document. After analyzing the three types of theology at work in the country, the Kairos theologians announced that the church in South Africa was in a period of crisis and that faithfulness to God demands allegiance to Prophetic Theology.

The political agenda of Christians responsive to Prophetic Theology includes an end to the state of emergency, the release of all political prisoners, support for the South African movements working for liberation (such as the African National Congress and the United Democratic Front), and immediate and comprehensive economic sanctions.

Throughout the decades of struggle in South Africa, individual Christians have fought for liberation. At a time when the churches themselves were captive to the state or afraid to take decisive action against apartheid, organizations such as the Christian Institute, which existed until it was banned for working for reconciliation between the races, have functioned alongside the churches. Black Theology, which took seriously for the first time black experience, played a critical role in the development of the black consciousness movement. Such organizations and individuals have been detained or banned —or worse—for their efforts.

What the Kairos theologians are calling for is a new formation of South African Christians to respond to the demands of this crisis time. It is too early to tell what their impact will be. But older leaders in the church are aware that the pressure for change is building rapidly, that if they are to have any credibility with the young, militant masses they will have to demonstrate a faith that is a resource in the liberation struggle. What they have to offer is hope—hope, they say, for oppressed and oppressor alike. In their words: "There is a hope. . . . But the road to that hope is going to be very hard and very painful. The conflict and the struggle will have to intensify in the months and years ahead because there is no other way to remove the injustice and oppression. But God is with us. We can only learn to become the instruments of his peace even unto death. We must participate in the cross of Christ if we are to have the hope of participating in his resurrection."

47. DETENTIONS UNDER THE STATE OF EMERGENCY*

by AMNESTY INTERNATIONAL

Amnesty International is an independent worldwide movement working for the international protection of human rights. It seeks the release of men and women detained anywhere because of their beliefs, color, sex, ethnic origin, language or religious creed, provided they have not used or advocated violence. These are termed prisoners of conscience. *It works for fair and prompt trials for all political prisoners and works on behalf of such people detained without charge or trial. It opposes the death penalty and torture or other cruel, inhuman or degrading treatment or punishment of all prisoners.*

More than 1100 critics and opponents of the South African Government's apartheid policies, including former prisoners of conscience, were detained by security police in the first week following the imposition of a state of emergency throughout large areas of South Africa from midnight on 20 July 1985. Those detained are held incommunicado and are believed to be in solitary confinement. Their places of detention have not been disclosed and they may be held for unlimited periods. The security police are not required to bring charges against the detainees nor to provide reasons for their imprisonment without trial. Amnesty International fears that some detainees may be tortured or ill-treated: they are liable to interrogation by security police who have been granted immunity in advance against prosecution for any acts committed in connection with their use of emergency powers. . . .

Once a state of emergency is declared, the government is empowered under

*From Amnesty International, External Document, August 6, 1985 [as condensed].

the Public Security Act to issue special regulations which remain in force throughout the duration of the state of emergency. This was done by the State President on 21 July 1985 by Proclamation R. 121 of 1985. The regulations so issued extended police powers of stop and search and conferred on the police and other law enforcement personnel, including the military, wide powers of arbitrary arrest and detention without trial. Section 3 of the regulations empowers the police or other law-enforcement personnel, of whatever rank, to arrest any person within the emergency area without warrant and detain them without charges for 14 days. Further detention on an unlimited basis may then be authorized at the end of this initial two week period by the Minister of Law and Order, at his discretion. Detainees are held incommunicado. . . . The authorities need not give any reasons for individual detentions, nor are detainees' places of imprisonment disclosed. Under the emergency regulations, it was also made an offense punishable by up to 10 years' imprisonment for any person to disclose the name of any detainee without prior written authorization from the Minister of Law and Order or his representative. . . .

The emergency regulations also confer on the police the power arbitrarily to impose curfews, control the dissemination of news, close any public or private place, control entry to and departure from particular areas, and remove from any area any person or section of the public in the interests of "public order." In addition, the Commissioner of Police and officers acting on his authority were empowered to take any action which they might consider "necessary or expedient" in connection with the safety of the public or the maintenance of public order. . . .

Security police raids on the homes of critics and political opponents of the government commenced shortly after the emergency took effect on Sunday, 21 July. More than 100 people were detained during the first day that the emergency was in force: by the end of July the total number of detainees had risen to more than 1300. Those arrested included many members of black student organizations, in particular the Congress of South African Students (COSAS), and community organizations in black townships throughout the Johannesburg and Eastern Cape areas. Many of these organizations are affiliated to the anti-apartheid United Democratic Front (UDF). . . .

Others detained during the first week of the emergency included at least 11 black church ministers, several of whom had previously been active in attempting to calm the situation in the black townships and to reduce the level of confrontation between the black population and the police. Officials and members of predominantly black trade unions were also among those detained. . . .

Political detainees held under the emergency powers have virtually no rights and may be subjected to a variety of punishments for what are termed "disciplinary contraventions." The contraventions, and the general conditions under which emergency detainees are to be held, were defined in a series of "Rules" issued by the Minister of Justice on 21 July. They provided that detainees may be held either in prisons or police cells and required that they should be searched on committal. The Rules stipulate that the detainees should be held incommunicado and are to have no contact with other categories of prisoners. However, provision was made for individual visits to detainees if approved by the Minister of Law and Order or the Commissioner of Police. . . . [T]he Rules imply that there may be some inspection of detainees' conditions and they do require that all detainees should be medically examined by a district surgeon, a government-employed doctor, on admission to their place of detention who should thereafter visit them "regularly." Provision is also made for ministers of religion to have access to detainees but the police may deny access to specific ministers.

Detainees held under the emergency are not permitted to communicate with the outside world through correspondence. They may not receive or send out letters, except with the express permission of the officer in charge of their place of imprisonment and the Commissioner of Police. Nor are they permitted reading matter other than the Bible or other holy books such as the Koran. . . .

The disciplinary contraventions include deliberately replying falsely to a member of the detaining staff, disobeying "a lawful command or order" and being "insolent or disrespectful" towards a police officer or other official. . . . The penalties for disciplinary contraventions include the requirement that the detainee should undertake "certain specific work" in the prison for up to 14 days; solitary confinement with full diet for up to 30 days; corporal punishment up to a maximum of six strokes with a cane, but only when the victim is a man "apparently under the age of 40 years" and when no other punishment has been imposed in respect of the same contravention. Detainees may also be sentenced to imprisonment in solitary confinement for periods up to 30 days during which they receive what is termed "spare diet" on not less than 18 days, "reduced diet" on six days and the full prison diet on the remaining six days. . . .

The imposition of the state of emergency follows widespread civil unrest affecting black townships in many parts of South Africa. . . . After simmering unrest . . . during the early part of 1984, serious unrest broke out in early September 1984 in the area south of Johannesburg generally known as the "Vaal Triangle," in particular in the townships known as Sharpeville, Sebokeng and Evaton. They appear to have been sparked off by local rent increases and the arrest of black community leaders who had opposed the constitutional changes, which were in the process of implementation in August and September. There were attacks by township residents on local black town councillors and black police officers, who were identified popularly as representatives of the authorities. Substantial police contingents, and subsequently army units, were deployed in the area and there was a further escalation of violence which extended in late 1984 and early 1985 into the Eastern Cape and East Rand, in particular, and parts of Orange Free State province. Large numbers of black township residents were shot by police and many were killed.

The most serious single incident of this nature occurred in the Eastern Cape on 21 March 1985, the 25th anniversary of the Sharpeville killings, when police opened fire on a funeral procession near Uitenhage. This incident was subsequently the subject of a judicial commission of inquiry which found that 20 black people, including several children, had been killed and others wounded. The police, who had been equipped with firearms and lethal ammunition but no other means of crowd dispersal on orders from above, were exonerated by the inquiry although at least 15 of those killed were found to have been shot in the back. There have been many further police shootings of civilians since the Uitenhage killings on 21 March 1985, particularly in the Eastern Cape area, and many people have been killed as a result. Since early September 1984, the total number of deaths associated with the unrest is reported to number around 500. Most are as a result of shootings by the police. . . .

48. *POLICE CONDUCT DURING TOWNSHIP PROTESTS**

by SOUTHERN AFRICAN CATHOLIC BISHOPS' CONFERENCE
The Southern African Bishops' Conference is a London-based organization.

Reckless, Indiscriminate, or Wanton Violence

A 20-year-old male resident of Sharpeville reports that at about 7 P.M. on the evening of September 3, he was sitting in his front garden chatting with members of his family and three neighbors. At about this time two police vehicles with policemen in camouflage uniforms drove slowly past the house. As the one vehicle passed the house a shot rang out. Immediately the youth's head jerked back and hit the wall. He fell grabbing his head. He was brought inside where he realized he had been shot. A local priest took him to the Sebokeng Hospital where he was told that the hospital was full and that they would transport him to Baragwanath Hospital in Soweto. At Baragwanath Hospital his left eye was removed—he now has an artificial eye. When he

*From Report on Police Conduct during Township Protests (London, November, 1984) [as excerpted].

returned to work on his release from hospital he found that he had been dismissed by his employers.

. . . .

Samson Mgudlwa, the father of Nicholas Mgudlwa, recounts the senseless death of his 10-year-old son as follows:

On the night of September 24 at about 8 P.M., Nicholas' family (four siblings and his father and mother) were watching television. Nicholas' father saw a white police kombi driving slowly along the street on which they live. Nicholas had gone into the backyard to chop wood. The family heard a shot being fired from the street. Mr. Mgudlwa closed the front door and called his son, Nicholas to come inside. From the kitchen door he could see Nicholas lying on the ground. He rushed up to him and heard the kombi speed off. "I carried Nicholas into the house. He was limp and bleeding badly on the left side of the head. I could see his skull. I took the child to a hospital. I found a rubber bullet on the ground where (he) had been shot." The following day he reported the incident to the Sebokeng Police Station. The police denied any knowledge of the incident. He explained that he was able to recognize the kombi as a police vehicle and he produced the rubber bullet he had found next to where Nicholas had fallen. He and his wife later went to Baragwanath Hospital, but Nicholas had been taken back to Sebokeng Hospital. He was unconscious. When they saw him on Thursday they were told that Nicholas had died that morning.

. . . .

The most savage example of this conduct is the incident involving Miss M. N., a standard three pupil from Soweto. While she was walking home, a hippo truck passed her and a policeman told her to board the truck and he would buy her sweets. When she refused to enter, another policeman pointed a small gun (revolver) at her and ordered her on to the hippo. When inside the hippo, she was told that the children in uniform were the ones who caused trouble. They sjambokked her and she screamed. One policeman then put his hand over her mouth and two other policemen continued to sjambok her for some time. Thereafter they told her to get out and go home. A medical practitioner at the Orlando Clinic examined her the following day and found the following injuries: 8 weals on her left thigh, 3 weals on her left buttock, 14 weals on her left forearm, 5 weals on her left chest, 12 weals on her right forearm and 7 weals on her right thigh. The beating was also found to have caused internal bleeding.

. . . .

Damage to Property

At about 6:30 P.M. on the same day the same deponent alleges that he saw five or six hippos drive up to a bottle store in Zone 14, Sebokeng. At the time that the police arrived a number of people were looting the bottle store. After shooting tear gas into the bottle store the police then entered. The police found five people inside the bottle store, four men and one woman, whom they ordered to lie on the tar road. After threatening to shoot them the police beat them and then chased them away. Thereafter four policemen entered the bottle store and called to some people nearby to help them remove the liquor. At this stage there were only two hippos at the bottle store. The police called out saying, "Kom, kom, julle ons sal nie skiet nie," (Come, come we're not going to shoot). Certain bystanders then assisted the police in loading the hippo with about ten sealed boxes of liquor. Shortly afterwards the policemen were seen drinking while shooting at crowds of people in the township. Real bullet shells were seen at that spot by the deponent the following morning.

· ·

Provocative, Humiliating or Insensitive Conduct

. . . Much of the conduct described in the sections dealing with actions by the police can be labeled provocative. Furthermore, many of the deponents who make allegations concerning the shooting or beating of the inhabitants of the Rand townships make reference in passing to such conduct as gratuitous abuse of blacks, or laughter while the involved policemen were beating people or humiliating bystanders. On at least two occasions police were seen drinking alcohol while patrolling the townships and in one case while physically assaulting a man inside a hippo. A particularly common allegation is that police laughed while perpetrating assaults.

Among the variety of abusive terms used by police at various stages included the following: "kaffir," "hond" (dog), "koelie," "you bloody fucking black men," "jou ma se gat," "jou ma se poes" (referring to his mother's private parts). It is incidents such as the following however, that create a suggestion that some of the police regarded their duties as a kind of sport.

· ·

Rape

. . . On November 21, 2 girls of 15 and 16 were allegedly raped by two white policemen in a police hippo. While returning from the shops, they were ordered into a hippo in Sharpeville at about 4 P.M. and kept inside until approximately 6:30 A.M. the next morning. During this time they were allegedly raped three times by two of the occupants of the hippo. They have been examined by a district surgeon and have identified their assailants to the police who are investigating.

. . . .

Concluding Remarks

. . . It was frequently asserted in the affidavits taken from township residents that the police appeared to believe they were at war. This attitude is reflected in the substance of the allegations contained in this report. The alleged refusal to discriminate between the innocent and the guilty, the callous disregard for the property and the lives of the "enemy," the ease with which the trigger is pulled or the baton wielded reveal an inability to recognize the humanity of other persons. The only remedy to assuage the legacy of bitterness these incidents have left behind and the responses that they have produced is an immediate enquiry into police conduct in the townships and the appropriate disciplinary action.

49. A SOUTH AFRICAN FIGHTS FROM EXILE*

by OLIVER TAMBO

Oliver Tambo is the exiled leader of the African National Congress. In the early 1940s, he and Nelson Mandela attended Fort Hare University together and founded the ANC Youth League. Together, they began the first African legal firm in Johannesburg in 1952. When the ANC was declared an illegal organization, it was decided someone—Tambo—had to lead it from exile. During most of the last 25 years, Tambo's name was almost unknown in the capitals of the West. However, it is not just the Communist bloc that has offered aid and recognition—the Soviet Union supplies it with arms while East Germany prints its monthly journal, Sechaba. Non-aligned countries, such as India, have long accorded Tambo the formalities due a head of state. Recently, with South Africa in turmoil, many Western publications have sought interviews with the exiled leader. In November, 1985, Anthony Heard, editor of The Cape Times, a South African newspaper, met with Tambo, who, as a "banned" person, may not be quoted in South Africa. Mr. Heard was arrested several days after the interview was printed. He faces the possibility of three years in prison. What follows is adapted from a longer text published Nov. 4 in The Cape Times.

Question: The A.N.C. is officially portrayed in South Africa as a Communist, terrorist-type organization. How would you answer this?

*From The *New York Times,* December 6, 1985.

Answer: It is true that the A.N.C. has members of the Communist Party. There has been an overlapping of membership from the beginning. But A.N.C. members who are also members of the Communist Party make a very clear distinction between these two independent bodies. We cooperate a lot, but the A.N.C. is accepted by the Communist Party as leading the struggle. There is absolute loyalty to that position. It is often suggested that the A.N.C. is controlled by the Communists. That has never been true.

As for the charge that we are controlled by the Soviet Union, this too is propaganda. We go to the Soviet Union as we go to Sweden and to Holland and to Italy to ask for assistance. The Western countries that support us do not give us weapons. But in the socialist countries, we get the weapons. So we go there to get what we can't get elsewhere. And that's all there is in it.

There is also a lot of exaggeration about terrorism. For the better part of 20 years, we were very, very careful in our sabotage actions to avoid hurting anybody. We could have been terrorists if we had wanted to, but we chose not to be. It is true that more recently, we have stepped things up. But this was after 20 years. We have been notoriously restrained in our armed actions—notoriously.

Q: What future do you see for whites in South Africa?

A: All of us in the A.N.C. have always considered that whites, like ourselves, belong to our country. We took the earliest opportunity to dispel the notion that we were fighting to drive the whites out. We have asked whites to join us in the struggle to get rid of the tensions that come with the apartheid system. We have hoped that together we could build a nonracial South Africa—and by nonracial we really do mean nonracial.

Our charter says that South Africa belongs to all who live in it, and we say that people who have chosen South Africa as their home are welcome there. There is plenty of room for them. We don't really see our white compatriots as whites in the first instance. We see them as fellow South Africans. We are all born in that country. We live on that continent. It is our country. Let's move away from these distinctions between Europeans and non-Europeans, whites and nonwhites.

It would be in the interests of all of us that everybody feels secure. Everybody's property is secure; everyone's home is secure. Let us not look at one another's color. Let us not address that. Let us see one another merely as fellow citizens.

Q: What about your economic policy? What about nationalization and the redistribution of wealth?

A: You have got to do something to end the poverty in South Africa—and the solution we see is one of nationalization. But there would be a debate about the level of nationalization.

Q: What sort of environment could that debate take place in? Would you see free media, free expression, freedom of newspapers?

A: Absolutely.

Q: What about violence? In what circumstances would you as leader of the A.N.C. be prepared to renounce violence and start talks?

A: This question of violence worries many people. The unfortunate thing is that people tend to be worried about the violence that comes from the oppressed. But there would be no violence at all if we did not have the violence of the apartheid system. We can stop our struggle. We can stop our violent actions. But on that basis? And in return for what?

Q: Is there a possibility of truce?

A: There is always a possibility of a truce. It would be very, very easy, if for example we started negotiations.

Q: With the Government?

A: Yes, with the Government—when they are ready. At the moment, we think they are not ready. A serious indication of readiness would be the release of Nelson Mandela and other political leaders in prison. They have got to be part of the process. Lift the state of emergency. Pull out the troops from the townships, and the police. Release the political prisoners. Even unban the A.N.C. Do all these things to create a climate. Then we would begin to see that the other side is ready to talk.

Q: On foreign policy, do you see South Africa as a pro-Western, nonaligned or as a Soviet-socialist-leaning country? For instance, in the sale of minerals and raw materials—would these be denied to anyone?

A: Nonaligned, developing trade with all the countries of the world.

Q: So the Americans can be sure of getting their needs?

A: The Americans will be sure to get it, if they are willing to pay for it. We would want to trade with all the countries of the world, in the interests of our own economy.

Q: I presume you favor sanctions. To the point where people lose jobs and the economy suffers seriously?

A: We think the economy must be put into difficulties because the economy strengthens the regime. As for losing jobs, for the victims of apartheid, it is nothing.

To be a victim of apartheid means many, many things worse than losing a job. And the way we look at it is: The more effective the sanctions are, the smaller the scope and scale of conflict.

Q: You strike me as a somewhat reluctant revolutionary.

A: I am angry and frustrated, like we all are, but I was once a full supporter of nonviolence because I thought it would fulfill our objective. When that failed, we had to look for an alternative. We found the alternative in combining political and armed actions—and it is one of those things that you have to do, as there is no other alternative. I don't think I am peculiar in this respect. I think that many people in the A.N.C. would be glad if there was no need for violence. But the need is there, and we have got to go ahead with it, bitter as it is.

PART FOUR

APARTHEID IN THE WORLD ARENA

Chapter XI

SOUTH AFRICA'S FOREIGN POLICY: Southern Africa, Namibia and Israel

50. *PAX PRETORIANA: SOUTH AFRICA'S REGIONAL POLICY**

by KENNETH W. GRUNDY

Kenneth W. Grundy is Professor of Political Science, Case Western Reserve University and the author of Confrontation and Accommodation in Southern Africa: The Limits of Independence *(1973).*

South Africa's Pact of Nonaggression with Mozambique was signed at the border town of Nkomati on March 16, 1984. Reportedly it was as psychologically and politically shattering for southern Africa as Egypt's pact with Israel was for the Middle East. Two implacable foes agreed not to attack one another and to halt their aid to the dissident groups that each harbored against the other.

For South Africa, the Nkomati Accord is only the most visible feature of a diplomatic offensive that involves all the governments in the region. What are the reasons for South Africa's apparent about-face? Has the face of southern Africa been significantly changed or will Nkomati be like Camp David, a symbolic accommodation amid insoluble conflicts of prejudice and interest?

From 1975 until 1983, but especially in the last three years of that period, South African policy in southern Africa was pugnacious and militaristic. In a word, South Africa tried to destabilize neighboring governments to force

*From *Current History,* April 1985.

them to forsake forces antagonistic to the white minority government in Pretoria. The diplomatic picture leading up to Nkomati and the other agreements was confusing, even contradictory. In the midst of violent incursions there were tentative overtures toward talks, behind-the-scenes negotiations and gestures of conciliation. By and large, however, Pretoria's thrust was uncompromising, and black governments were made to bend.

There is substantial evidence, occasionally circumstantial but generally more direct, that South Africa pursued policies designed to subvert the governments and to engage them militarily in order to keep them from supporting revolutionary and nationalistic liberation movements harbored on their territories. South Africa was determined to pursue a forward defense of the status quo, either by assisting dissident elements hostile to neighboring regimes, or by mounting direct incursions by regular or irregular units of the SADF (South African Defence Forces) and ancillary security forces. The South African government wanted to facilitate the search for a new government in Namibia that would pose no threat to the Republic of South Africa or to any government it implanted in Namibia. It also undertook raids into Zimbabwe, Lesotho and Mozambique aimed at alleged ANC (African National Congress) bases and at refugee concentrations that might be regarded as havens for the ANC. Presumably, it aimed to restrain any sort of revolutionary activity that might threaten a peaceful transition to the new constitutional order in South Africa.

A series of crossborder strikes into Angola (beginning in 1975 but increasing in intensity after 1977) engaged as many as 2,000 SADF members. In the years 1980–1984, South Africa virtually occupied extensive territory along the border. In addition, the SADF and the South African government are providing diverse support for UNITA (the National Union for the Total Independence of Angola), the largely Ovimbundu nationalist movement that effectively governs the southeast third of Angola. Ostensibly, SADF acted against Angola to prevent the SWAPO (South West African People's Organization) incursions southward. South Africa's defense of Namibia against SWAPO insurgents was to be a forward defense in depth. If the Angolan regime could be punished and forced to "pay" for its assistance to SWAPO, so much the better. If South African power could contribute to a change in government in Luanda, or at least a change in its policies vis-à-vis Namibia, then the aggressive policies favored by South Africa's Defense Department would be doubly rewarded.

The Mozambique file is also full, marked most clearly by "surgical" commando raids at alleged ANC offices outside Maputo in January, 1981, and October, 1983, and frequent air strikes into Mozambique. Far more damaging has been South Africa's sponsorship of the MNR (Resistência Nacional Moçambican, sometimes called Renamo). South Africa has provided sanctuary, arms, supplies, training and logistical support. The Mozambican economy, especially food distribution, has been disrupted, and sabotage and war have been widespread. Mozambique's Frelimo (Frente de Liberta ção de Moçambique) government came dangerously close to collapse.

Lesotho, of course, is even more exposed than Mozambique. Economic and political pressures (e.g., the impoundment of arms purchases at South African ports, sporadic border closings, harassment of Basuto laborers in South Africa and a December, 1982, SADF raid on "ANC terrorists" at Maseru, where 42 were killed) have forced Lesotho to expel some refugees. South Africa also assists dissident groups opposed to the government of Chief Leabua Jonathan.

Zimbabwe also charges South Africa with sponsoring anti-government forces. Propaganda, radio broadcasts, assassinations, espionage, "dirty tricks" of other sorts, economic influence (especially on transport facilities), the induced defection of top Zimbabwean white officials from the police and armed forces, and the incursion of SADF personnel into Zimbabwean territory contribute to a general sense of vulnerability in Zimbabwe, especially in the south and west. Elsewhere in the region, in Botswana, Swaziland and as far afield as the Seychelles, there is documented evidence of South African interference.

One cannot point with assurance to a specific decision taken by the South African government or agencies thereof to destabilize states in the region. But one can assess a number of policy lines and their cumulative impact on regional affairs. Although government rhetoric fastens on peaceful coexistence, constellation, and nonintervention as hallmarks of South African regional policy, actual policy includes an extensive dossier of reports of large- and small-scale open and clandestine raids into nearby states, the effects of which have been to heighten insecurities in areas near South Africa's borders. From close up, they may appear to be unrelated, ad hoc responses to diverse stimuli. But from afar what emerges is a recognizable pattern of coercive hostility toward governments already inclined to be hostile to Pretoria, insecure, and fearful about incursions from the only remaining white regime in Africa.

Once embarked on a course of aggressive "defense," South Africa found it easier to make a case for South African military operations elsewhere in the region. Apparent "success" provides its own rationale. Certainly, the SADF is convinced of its importance in the stabilization process. In its words, "forceful military action" has provided the time to allow Africans to experience "the dangers of Russian involvement in their countries, as well as the suffering and retrogression that follow upon the revolutionary formula." In short, Pretoria believes that South Africa's black neighbors have now had "their eyes opened to the dangers of Russian imperialism." By taking "firm action" and developing "a strong military potential," the SADF "has created a successful strategy of deterrence." In other words, without the SADF the negotiations that led to the cease-fires and to nonaggression pacts could not have been initiated.

Strength and Coercion

If peace has come to southern Africa, it is an imposed peace, a regional Pax Pretoriana based on strength and coercion. South Africa has adopted a disruptive doctrine of preemptive intervention and has engaged in direct military strikes into neighboring territory. Increasingly, the government of Prime Minister P. W. Botha has also found it useful to employ or to encourage dissident factions from neighboring countries to intervene against their home governments. Intervention may be justified as the exercise of the traditional right of self-defense. Alternatively, it may be rationalized as a form of counterintervention, i.e., intervention to redress a balance of force that has been disrupted by another country's outside intervention. The Cuban troops in Angola thus provide a standing alibi, enabling Pretoria to vindicate South Africa's refusal to come to terms with the MPLA or with SWAPO or to abandon UNITA.

The doctrine of hot pursuit, well established in international law, may also be used on occasion. But South Africa is hard-pressed to adopt that line in most cases, since crossborder, code-named operations are hardly spontaneous hot pursuit. Instead, Pretoria is engaging (like other countries in the world) in a form of anticipatory defense. According to this emerging political doctrine of preemptive intervention, the inherent right of self-help or self-defense justifies the use of preemptive intervention if: (1) a neighboring government is hostile; or (2) if, although it may not be hostile it is unwilling or unable to curb the activities of forces hostile to the intervening government in its own territory; or (3) even more minimally, if at some future time the target government might aid or be unable to control professed enemies of the intervening regime. According to this reasoning, the security of the intervening state is jeopardized if it fails to act. The consequent calculated policy of destabilization has been the Pax Pretoriana that has been punctuated by a series of agreements or near-agreements with neighboring governments.

The Triumph of Force and Fortuity

Eventually, South African military and economic power has prevailed, not in the sense that neighboring governments have been defeated or overthrown, but that important elements in those governments have come to realize that the costs of maintaining order in the face of internal unrest and external threat are beyond their immediate means. In Mozambique, poor economic planning and management, compounded by a widespread and long-lasting drought, have taken a heavy toll on the popularity of the Frelimo government. MNR forces, themselves not especially popular, have been able to thwart relief efforts outside Maputo. According to a report by Mozambique's National Planning

Commission, military intervention combined with South African economic "sanctions" have severely damaged the country's economy. The commission estimated that unrest has cost Mozambique R9.6 billion since 1975.

Mozambique's economy was dependent on services provided to South Africa and Rhodesia/Zimbabwe, and when those countries no longer used Mozambique's ports, railways and labor, Mozambique could not fill the minimal needs of its citizens. For these reasons, the vulnerable Maputo government approached the South Africans at least three times before the final phase of negotiations leading to Nkomati. South Africa did not reduce its pressure until it was absolutely certain that Maputo was prepared to end ANC activities in its territory. Even after signing the agreement, there is some question whether Pretoria immediately severed its aid to the MNR.

An agreement was reached in February, 1984, by which Mozambique would prevent the ANC from using its territory for attacks against South Africa in return for which Pretoria agreed to withdraw its covert (and always denied) support for the MNR. In 11 subclauses virtually every variety of subversive activity was detailed and forbidden, eliminated or controlled. A joint security commission was appointed to monitor the agreement.

Much to the ANC's chagrin, Mozambique moved swiftly to clamp down on ANC activities in Maputo. ANC facilities were searched, and many ANC operatives hastily left the country. For its part, South Africa closed the clandestine MNR radio station thought to be operating from the northern Transvaal. It also took active measures to help Mozambique with railways and harbors operations, and to supply drought and, ironically, flood relief. Pretoria also launched an economic blitz to relink South African private enterprise with opportunities in Mozambique. Although Maputo stated its belief that the South African government was determined to make the accord successful, it was "not satisfied" with Nkomati's security benefits. Economic activity was vigorous, but the extent of Pretoria's severance of its aid to the MNR is subject to debate.

A series of economic agreements were proposed. In late March, South Africa consented to pay higher charges for electricity from Mozambique's Cabora Bassa dam and to pay Mozambique for access to the power. (Portugal was a party to the agreement.) Talks were opened between South Africa, Botswana, Zimbabwe and Mozambique about building a storage dam on the Limpopo River. South Africa made a R10-million loan to Mozambique as part of a 10-point plan to rebuild Mozambique's faltering railway and harbor infrastructure. Other economic and technical assistance flowed from South Africa to Mozambique. But the MNR would not go away.

Finally, in October, as a result of vigorous South African mediation and Maputo's threat that the entire Nkomati exercise might be abandoned if the MNR's challenge were not contained, the MNR and the Maputo government agreed to a cease-fire. Significantly, the agreement was announced in Pretoria by South African Foreign Minister R. F. Botha. According to the agreement, President Samora Machel is acknowledged as the leader of Mozambique; "armed activity and conflict within Mozambique" is to be halted; and the South African government "is requested to play a role in the implementation of the declaration." Machel secured his ascendancy by granting the MNR equal status or a cease-fire commission. Foreign Minister Botha told reporters that SADF men would be responsible for implementing the cease-fire. Yet the prospects for success are suspect, because both the MNR and Frelimo officials expressed reservations.

Relations with Angola

Across the continent, Pretoria pursued accommodation with Angola. In February, South Africa and Angola agreed to a disengagement pact in Lusaka ostensibly brokered by the United States. A cease-fire to end the fighting in both Angola and Namibia is to be monitored by a joint commission that is to include a few United States representatives. South Africa agreed to a five-phase disengagement of its forces provided that neither Angola nor the SWAPO guerrillas took advantage of the withdrawal. South Africa promptly carried out four of the five planned phases of disengagement before the March 30, 1984, deadline.

But they halted at Ngiva, just 25 miles north of the Angola-Namibia border. According to Pretoria, SWAPO fighters were still crossing into Namibia, and the Angolans had not yet agreed to a joint policing of the border. Angola, for its part, said that it could agree only if South Africa set a date for Namibian independence. In response, South Africa refused to make such a commitment (it had been refusing for months) until the Cubans left Angola. Thus the main obstruction to a settlement remains the United States-South African precondition that Cuban forces must be withdrawn from Angola before Namibia can gain independence. Angola feels especially vulnerable to UNITA attacks and insists that South Africa must first end its assistance to UNITA. On these grounds the negotiations have been stalled for over two years.

Using Lusaka and the Cape Verde Islands as venues for negotiation, South Africa tried to arrange a Namibian settlement that would assure a role for its government alternative, the so-called Multi-Party Conference (MPC). But in time, the MPC lost standing as key member organizations drifted out of the MPC and toward SWAPO. The South Africans were left with no viable black conservative group to head an independent Namibia. Although press reports imply that the Namibia puzzle is close to solution, grave divisions still exist. Militarily, South Africa seems in control, but Pretoria's final victory is not possible so long as its regime in Namibia is totally rejected by the people. A military solution is not likely, and a political solution is tantalizing but elusive. SWAPO, the South African and Angolan governments, UNITA, and local Namibian parties insist on roles beyond their political-military means.

For South Africa, a settlement with Mozambique to reduce the ANC threat and a settlement with Angola to snuff out the SWAPO challenge in Namibia are high-priority regional issues. Protection of South Africa's distinctive and universally rejected sociopolitical order is its minimal foreign policy objective. That such settlements may lead to other, equally desired benefits must be factored into Pretoria's calculus. In the long run, South Africa seeks to create and institutionalize a grouping of regional states. In its latest guise, this grouping is termed a constellation of southern African states. If established, Pretoria hopes that it can secure for South Africa a measure of acceptance (in Africa and in the West), reduce economic pressures from abroad, permit South African industries to enlarge their fields of activity, and enmesh neighboring countries in an economic web too profitable and too complex to risk endangering it by political adventures against apartheid.

In addition to the high-profile peace offensive aimed at Angola and Mozambique, Pretoria has pressured other regional governments. Most maleable has been Swaziland. In March, 1984, after momentum had been established by the Nkomati Accord and the Lusaka Declaration, it was announced that, in fact, South Africa and Swaziland had entered into a security agreement fully two years earlier, just before the KaNgwane-Ingwavuma land deal was announced. The now-abandoned arrangement involved Pretoria's announced cession of the KaNgwane homeland (for South African Swázis) and a large tract of KwaZulu to Swaziland in May, 1982. The scheme was fought by homeland leaders, and eventually a South African appeals court declared the proclamation unlawful.

Speculation about the political and security arrangements (especially regarding Swaziland policy on the ANC and on the prospective South African-led constellation of states) attending the deal were reiterated when the February, 1982, nonaggression pact was made public in March, 1984. In the intervening years, Swaziland authorities had tried to crack down on ANC operatives in their country and Swaziland had increased the government's share of the largely South African-controlled Southern African Customs Union. The two-year delay in announcing the nonaggression pact (until after a regional image of accommodation had been established) appeared calculated to pressure other neighboring governments to enter similar agreements.

Zimbabwe, Lesotho and Botswana have charged intimidation by Pretoria. Some observers believe South Africa is stalling negotiations to revamp the Customs Union Agreement that Botswana, Lesotho and Swaziland are urging. South Africa has also angered Lesotho by delaying the negotiations over the R2-billion Highlands water project to develop and sell Lesotho water and power to South Africa, and by deliberately delaying at Durban arms shipments Lesotho has purchased from Italy and the United Kingdom. The links between Pretoria and dissident groups of Basuto add to the tension in Maseru. Early in 1984, leaders of all three governments spoke bitterly about Pretoria's tactics, but by the end of the year the rhetoric subsided. In Lesotho's case, a breakthrough may be imminent; the Highlands water project is back on track and so are the arms shipments.

As South Africa tried to build on its diplomatic initiatives, it also tried to sell its "reign of peace" abroad. In May and June, 1984, Prime Minister P. W. Botha embarked on a much-publicized tour of Europe, visiting Portugal, Great Britain, Germany, Italy, the Vatican, Belgium, Switzerland and France, the first official overseas tour taken by a South African Prime Minister in over two decades. Using the regional "peace" theme, South Africa tried to deflect threatened sanctions and international isolation, to depict South Africa as a broker of regional peace and not an ostracized pariah. But no apparent breakthroughs were achieved on outstanding international issues like Namibia or sanctions.

Probably knowing that nothing would come of it, Botha did offer to cede control of Namibia to France, West Germany, Britain, Canada and the United States. South Africa is obviously still searching for a way to circumvent the United Nations and its resolution 435. But South Africa also wants some kind of settlement. Namibia, the war and the administration of that war are expensive for Pretoria, economically and politically. Yet South Africa is not about to bail out precipitously. Disagreements in Windhoek and Pretoria pit hardliners in the SADF and the National party against the Department of Foreign Affairs on this and other issues.

With its regional successes and a renewed Western willingness to talk with Pretoria, the South African government appears to be making progress. Yet deep problems still remain. The MNR, originally created by Rhodesian intelligence and later handed over to South Africa, refuses to abide by Pretoria's dictates. It still receives funding from Portuguese business interests in South Africa and Portugal. The UNITA factor prevents peace in Angola and hence Namibian independence, and the Cuban troops provide Pretoria with a ready excuse for delaying final settlement.

Relations with Great Britain took a serious turn in the fall of 1984. In April, 1984, four South Africans were arrested in Britain, accused of helping to smuggle British military airplane parts and missile equipment to South Africa in violation of the arms embargo. From the start, the South African government worked to free the men from Britain. The accused were detained, and bail was at first denied. As a result of assurances from the South African embassy's first secretary to a British magistrate, the men were released on bail. The first secretary later agreed that, if the men were permitted to return to

South Africa until their trial, the State President himself would sign orders effectively extraditing them should they default. The South African embassy put up £200,000 cash and another £200,000 in guarantees. The men returned to South Africa.

But in September six political dissidents on whom detention orders had been served had taken refuge in the British consulate in Durban. The British refused to turn the men over to the South African authorities. In retaliation, the South Africans resisted the return of the "Coventry Four" to Britain. Moreover, they belligerently applied in a British court for a refund of the bail and relief from the additional £200,000 promise. In October, three of the "Durban Six" left the consulate voluntarily and were immediately arrested. In December, the other three left, and two were arrested and charged with treason. Still Pretoria refused to return the "Coventry Four."

Relations between Britain and South Africa are awkward. In the flap, anti-apartheid forces in Britain have been given a boost; South Africa's self-proclaimed reputation for respect for international law has suffered; international attention has been focused on detention without trial; and the government of Prime Minister Margaret Thatcher has suffered embarrassment.

Central to South Africa's vigorous diplomatic activity is a desire to project an image abroad of a flexible government, on the move, reformist, and able to live at peace with its neighbors. Free of international pressure the National party believes that it can manage its domestic challenges. But in fact, it is the domestic situation that has attracted attention to the inadequacies of Pretoria's reform process. The widespread boycott of the recent Coloured and Indian parliamentary elections signaled dissatisfaction with the new constitutional arrangements. Since then, nationwide unrest—transport boycotts, rent strikes, labor dissatisfaction, school strikes and boycotts, protests, and extensive violence—poses a direct challenge. The government's harsh responses, including the use of the SADF as well as the police, have led to extensive protest abroad.

The civil unrest across South Africa calls into question the elaborate but frail edifice of regional order. As Botswana's President Quett Masire said so perceptively of the Nkomati Accord, the treaty could bring stability and progress to the whole region "if it lasts." But if Pretoria were to use the accord to "keep down" black South Africans, "then I do not think it has a chance of enduring." President Kenneth Kaunda of Zambia, himself directly involved in the negotiating process on Namibia, said of the peace initiatives:

Yes, humble Swaziland agrees, humble Mozambique accepts, humble Zambia hosts meetings of unequal neighbors like South Africa and Angola. What else can we do? But we are not doing it with happy hearts. We do it out of fear, but that fear will end one day. It is bound to.

There is an imposed peace—a Pax Pretoriana. South Africa dominates the region, having bent its neighbors to its will. But they do not conform willingly. "This is our region," boasted Pik Botha. In his view, "it is raining peace in southern Africa." Still, the peace that Botha celebrates is fragile. The ANC, critically wounded in its operations against the South African regime, will not surrender just because it has been forced to relocate farther from the target. Governments compelled to humble themselves are not about to forget their humiliation.

As long as apartheid lives, anti-apartheid lives. The present semblance of agreement is not yet the substance of rapprochement. Peace is likely to be futile and short-lived because the underlying causes of the conflict, unequal wealth and power, have not yet been addressed.

51. UPSIDE DOWN IN ANGOLA*

by MICHAEL MASSING

The following article by Michael Massing, a New York writer and former editor of Columbia Journalism Review, *shows that in Angola, at least, it is hard to know who the enemy players are, even with a scorecard. While mostly concerned with American policy in Angola, Massing nonetheless provides valuable background for understanding South Africa's regional policies, especially its role in Namibia (which is covered in Readings 52–54).*

The current debate over U.S. investment in Angola is enough to make one's head spin. American liberals sound like flag-in-the-lapel conservatives as they glowingly describe the wondrous investment opportunities to be had in Angola. And conservatives sound like idealistic liberals as they vehemently attack corporate America for putting profits before principle. On top of it all, officials in this most Republican administration warn Big Business not to stand in the way of African liberation.

It's Third World war time again in Washington, which means that everyone is excitedly shouting slogans and uttering pronouncements about a part of the world they know little about. It's hard to tell who's behaving more hypocritically—liberals, conservatives, or the corporations themselves. Here's a scorecard:

When the Popular Movement for the Liberation of Angola (MPLA) came to power in 1975, the country's economy was a shambles. As the Portuguese retreated, they took just about everything that wasn't nailed down. And since

*From *The New Republic,* March 3, 1986.

native Angolans had been denied all positions of responsibility, severe short-ages of skilled labor developed. Recognizing that the Soviet Union had little to offer in the way of capital or technology, the MPLA swallowed its ideology and opened the door to Western investment. Luanda offered a host of incen-tives, among them generous tax allowances and easy repatriation of profits.

For American businessmen, such blandishments are hard to resist, even when coming from socialists, and over the last decade they have flocked to Angola. Chase Manhattan, Bankers Trust, Citibank, and Morgan Guaranty have all lent money to Angola. General Tire operates a manufacturing plant there, and General Motors is seeking to sell vehicles on a barter basis. Boeing provides spare parts for Angola's national airline, and a Louisiana sugar manufacturer is helping to manage a major mill. Caterpillar, IBM, NCR, Pfizer, and Xerox all do business in Angola.

Most important are the oil companies. With an output of 225,000 barrels a day, Angola is sub-Saharan Africa's second largest producer after Nigeria. An impressive collection of Western companies from France, Italy, Portugal, Brazil, and of course, the United States help pump the oil. Texaco, Mobil, Conoco, Marathon, and Cities Service all have operations in Angola. By far the largest, however, is the Cabinda Gulf Oil Company, a subsidiary of Chev-ron (which took over Gulf in 1984).

Although Gulf has been active in Angola for 30 years, it has most rapidly expanded its operations in the last ten, as the country's vast oil reserves became apparent. Gulf's current investment in Angola totals $600 million, most of it sunk into Cabinda province, site of the country's richest wells. Of the almost 700 people who work for Gulf in Angola, about 150 are Americans. In 1985 the company paid Angola $580 million in taxes and royalties. Along with the national oil company, with which it has a 49/51 partnership, Gulf accounts for three-quarters of Angola's oil production.

Earnings from oil help finance the government's war with Jonas Savimbi and his UNITA forces. That conflict, which is now more than ten years old, has been fueled by outside support on both sides. Savimbi has relied almost totally on South Africa; the MPLA has relied on the Soviet Union, which provides arms, and Cuba, which supplies 35,000 or so troops. Whereas the South African aid seems largely to come gratis, the MPLA pays for its help. No one knows precisely how much Cuba receives for its men; estimates range from $300 million to $800 million. All agree, however, that payment comes largely in the form of U.S. dollars—many of them supplied by Gulf.

And that has the right hopping mad. As conservatives frantically push U.S. aid for UNITA, they are simultaneously seeking to cut the flow of dollars to the MPLA. A coalition of right-wing organizations has mounted a national lobbying campaign seeking to pressure Chevron/Gulf out of Angola. Leading the charge is the Conservative Caucus, a Washington area activist group headed by Howard Phillips. In recent months the caucus has asked Chevron credit-card holders to protest the company's presence in Angola. It has mailed postcards to Chevron chairman George Keller, admonishing him that "patriotism must come before profit." The caucus has also bought Chevron stock in preparation for a proxy battle and encouraged members to pay "educational" visits to Chevron/Gulf service stations.

Howard Phillips explained the rationale for the campaign at a press conference in December: "Not only does Chevron generate more than two billion dollars a year in hard currency to keep a Soviet puppet regime in power [and] subsidize its 35,000 Cuban mercenaries . . . but Gulf's corporate executives have also been lobbying on behalf of the Soviet Union in Washington, urging Congress to reject U.S. aid to the UNITA freedom fighters led by Dr. Jonas Savimbi."

Gulf officials have been enthusiastic backers of the MPLA. In 1981 Melvin Hill, a Gulf executive, testified in Congress that the Angolan government was "businesslike and nonideological." Gulf officials have met with George Bush to urge a more accommodating U.S. stance toward Luanda. And last October the company co-hosted a dinner for Angolan President José Eduardo dos Santos. "We have a very good relationship with the Angolans," says Sid Anderson, vice president of Chevron's overseas operations. "They're businesslike and pay their bills."

All of which leads us to the Liberal Irony. As the campaign to support UNITA gained momentum in Congress last fall, liberal Democrats approached U.S. corporations for help in opposing aid. "We've needed that kind of support for our education efforts [on Angola]," says one aide to a Democratic representative. Last fall Chevron officials agreed to visit the offices of such key conservatives as Senator Steven Symms and Representative Robert Dornan. They left behind a three-page statement on the company's operations, which asserted that U.S. aid to UNITA would "jeopardize American property and commerce in Angola."

For the most part, though, Chevron has failed to fulfill the Democrats' expectations. "They've been extremely reluctant to get involved," the aide says. "They got scared very early on by the vehemence of some of the conservatives." Chevron rejected suggestions that it write a letter opposing aid for UNITA. Similar overtures were made to Boeing, Lockheed, and some other oil companies active in Angola, but all declined the invitation.

Not David Rockefeller. Last November the former Chase Manhattan chairman was asked if he might go public with his admiration for the Angolan government. In a letter to Howard Wolpe, chairman of the House Subcommittee on Africa, Rockefeller complied. Noting that trade between Angola and the United States had grown to more than one billion dollars a year, Rockefeller wrote that "Angola has become one of the largest and best economic partners [of] the U.S. in all of Africa. . . . I believe that the growing commercial partnership—as well as other extensive ties and relationships—between the U.S. and Angola merit important consideration in any policy determination." Aid for UNITA, Rockefeller added, would be most ill-timed.

On the face of it, this seems a real coup for the Democrats. It's not every day that a Rockefeller can be enlisted in the cause of African socialism. Such favor-seeking, though, carries some real risks. David Rockefeller is not exactly an innocent when it comes to dealing with the Third World. Under his direction, Chase Manhattan helped prop up some pretty unsavory dictators—all of them thoroughly businesslike and nonideological. Just a few weeks ago, Rockefeller was greeted in Argentina by violent street demonstrations, and several government officials refused to meet with him; one presidential adviser called him a "bloodsucker." Apparently the Argentines have not appreciated Rockefeller's businesslike ties to the military regime that ordered the disappearances of more than 9,000 people. (José Alfredo Martinez de Hoz, an economic minister during the junta's dark days, sat on Chase's international advisory board.)

Many of the companies active in Angola also do business in South Africa. There they have long resisted sanctions, arguing that the best way to further American interests in South Africa is to remain in the country. Such assertions are dismissed out of hand by liberals, who know that the corporations' real aim is to make a buck. It's hard to see much difference in Angola.

Back in my college days in the spring of 1972, black students occupied a Harvard administration building to demand that the university divest its stock in Gulf Oil. "Harvard out of Gulf, Gulf out of Angola," they shouted. At that time, of course, Angola was still a Portuguese colony, and the students accused Gulf of subsidizing Portugal's war against Angolan independence. In fact, Gulf was a frequent protest target in the early 1970s, when church groups mounted a campaign similar to the one being staged by conservatives today. Then, too, Gulf was unmoved, maintaining that the Portuguese were businesslike and nonideological.

The earlier campaign, however, did at least have a clear logic behind it, which leads us to the Conservative Irony. Angola is a war-torn, underdeveloped country located an ocean away from the United States. Why, then, have conservatives suddenly deemed it critical to our national interest? A major reason, they say, is Angola's rich natural resources. The country's already high level of oil production is expected to soar as vast new fields come on stream; last year Chevron declared that Angola might have the greatest oil potential of any country in West or Central Africa. The country also boasts lucrative diamond mines. Agriculturally, Angola is a potential breadbasket, and the surrounding waters contain some of the world's most bountiful fishing beds.

To conservatives, defeating the MPLA is essential if such riches are to be reserved for the West. "I believe the vital natural resources which are located [in southern Africa] must not fall into the hands of the Soviet Union and its proxies," Howard Phillips has said in reference to Angola, "and that our policy should proceed from that premise." Jeane Kirkpatrick recently wrote in the *Washington Post* that Angola's "mineral riches" help establish its "substantial long-range strategic importance," especially given the "Soviet determination" to incorporate such assets into the "socialist world system."

There is just one small problem with this line of reasoning: virtually all of Angola's resources already go to the West. The right may see Angola as a Soviet puppet, but somehow Western multinationals are managing to plunder it. The diamond mines under MPLA control are managed by a British company associated with South Africa's notorious De Beers consortium. And at least 95 percent of Angola's oil ends up in the West; half of Gulf's production finds its way into U.S. refineries. Last November, as pressure grew for sanctions against U.S. companies in Angola, the Congressional Research Service concluded that a withdrawal of Western technology might lead to a larger Soviet role in Angolan energy production, and "one of the likely consequences could be the loss of the bulk of Angolan oil for direct availability to the Western bloc."

The Reagan administration has played no small role in expanding the American presence in Angola. John Sassi, who worked for Gulf's international division for 19 years before leaving last summer to set up his own consulting firm, observes that "until the advent of the Reagan administration, there was little development of Angola's oil fields and not much major foreign investment." Since taking office, the administration has actively encouraged investment in Angola. In the last five years, the U.S. Export-Import Bank has approved three loans for Angolan oil and gas projects totaling $227 million. Since the United States does not have diplomatic relations with Angola, the loans required approval by the National Security Council. In each case, the loans were judged to be consistent with U.S. national interests. Angola may be Marxist, but today the United States is its largest trading partner—thanks in no small part to the Reagan administration.

As for the Soviets, what have they reaped in return for their massive military and financial investment? Very little. "The Soviets are not getting any economic benefits aside from ravaging the ocean floor with their fishing fleet," says a banker who has visited Angola frequently. "All they're getting is a satellite, another country that they can say is in their orbit." The Soviets receive virtually none of Angola's oil. They don't even get the satisfaction of offering their satellite economic counsel. Advisers in the key economic and oil ministries come not from the Eastern bloc but from Arthur D. Little, a consulting firm based in Cambridge, Massachusetts.

One final irony. In providing money to UNITA, the United States would be financing a group that has indicated its willingness to attack American facilities. Last February UNITA forces shot down a charter airplane that was transporting diamonds for De Beers; the plane's American pilot was killed. UNITA has attacked Gulf oil pipelines, and the South African commandos who targeted Gulf's Cabinda facilities last year carried UNITA literature claiming credit for the raid. Overall, according to American estimates, UNITA has caused more than seven billion dollars' worth of damage to Angola's infrastructure. Gulf's facilities have largely been spared—thanks to the presence of 2,000 troops in Cabinda supplied by Cuba.

It's unclear how effective the campaign against Chevron will prove. As of early February, the company had received 5,200 postcards and exactly two service station visits. Nonetheless, Chevron is clearly concerned: witness its reluctance to enter the political fray. Most worrisome is the position of the Reagan administration. In late January, Assistant Secretary of State Chester Crocker, who had previously encouraged corporations operating in Angola, suddenly declared that American businessmen "should be thinking about U.S. national interests as well as their own corporate interests as they make their decisions." President Reagan's recent sanctions against U.S. companies in Libya did not go unnoticed by those based in Angola.

Clearly, though, the Chevron question is only incidental to the real issue. Liberals should be able to advance better arguments against aid for Savimbi than the ability of American corporations to make good money in Angola. The liberal alliance with the David Rockefellers of the world seems a Faustian bargain that one day could easily backfire. By the same token, conservatives should be congratulated for recognizing, however belatedly, that U.S. foreign policy has more important ends than making the world safe for American investment.

But the conservatives are guilty of a deeper hypocrisy. "Strategic minerals" has become another Washington buzzword, one as drained of meaning as "freedom fighter." Those who use it don't really care about oil or diamonds: if they did, they would encourage American companies to remain in Angola and would do everything to make their stay a pleasant one. For conservatives, Angola and UNITA offer one overriding opportunity—the chance to inflict defeat on the Soviet Union.

Unfortunately, the war in Angola has already dragged on for more than ten years now, killing tens of thousands of people and devastating one of the richest countries in Africa. Foreign meddling has served primarily to increase the death and destruction. And there is no end in sight. Soon, perhaps, Washington will address the really important question about Angola: Will U.S. involvement help resolve this nasty conflict, or simply prolong it?

52. SOUTH AFRICA'S OCCUPATION OF NAMIBIA: NO END IN SIGHT*

by TRANSAFRICA

The following analysis of the situation in Namibia was produced by 24 different organizations. Salih Abdul-Rahim, legislative assistant for TransAfrica, was responsible for coordinating the research and drafting and integrating the varying institutional views that resulted in this report.

History

The original Namibians were the San and the Khoi Khoi; they were later joined by the Herero and the Nama peoples, who were traditionally cattle herders. It is believed that the Damara arrived with the Nama, and worked among them as herdsmen. The pastoral Ovambos, who grew maize and raised cattle, lived in the north. They were the largest group, and the only predominantly agricultural tribe. The Ovambos produced surpluses that supported development of skilled craftsmen such as blacksmiths, potters and woodcarvers.

By the time Europeans arrived, they found various highly organized social and political systems among the indigenous people. Collective ownership of natural resources prevailed. Grazing rights were a frequent cause for dispute, but the concept of individual ownership and large-scale dispossessions of land was introduced by whites.

The first Europeans to land on the Namibian coast were the Portuguese, who arrived in 1484. They were followed by other Portuguese, Dutch, and British expeditions. By the late 1700s trade relations were fairly well developed. Larger groups of European missionaries, traders and businessmen arrived throughout the latter part of the 19th Century. The Germans colonized parts of Namibia in the 1880s in an effort to build an empire in Africa. This marked the beginning of the conflict between Britain and Germany for possession of the coastal areas of present-day Namibia. The Germans expanded their control inland through purchases and so-called "treaties of protection" with

*From *Namibia: The Crisis in United States Policy Toward South Africa* (Washington, 1983 [as condensed].

rival chiefs. In 1890, they signed an agreement with the British to allocate acquired territories in the region. Thus, German South West Africa, a territory three times the size of Britain, was created, while the British retained Walvis Bay.

German Rule

German colonial exploitation was extremely brutal; it encountered sustained resistance from African communities and resulted in rebellions throughout the late 1890s with constant warfare between 1904 and 1908. The colonizers responded to these strong uprisings of the Herero and Nama peoples by conducting the 20th century's first genocide. Extermination campaigns in concentration camps resulted in the massacre of 54,000 of the 70,000 Herero people and 30,000 of the 50,000 Nama. Survivors were dispossessed of all their land, and their political and social structures were destroyed, leaving them to become a large, cheap wage labor pool for white employers. White settlement rapidly increased and laws were enacted that institutionalized racial oppression in a manner suggesting the system of apartheid that South Africa would impose years later.

League of Nations: South Africa's Mandate

During World War I, South African troops, acting on British orders, occupied the German colony of South West Africa. In 1920, South Africa was given a mandate by the newly formed League of Nations to administer the territory. Under the terms of the mandate, South Africa was to "promote to the utmost the material and moral well-being and the social progress of the inhabitants." These terms were ignored and additional laws were enacted to deny Africans political rights and to ensure a cheap labor supply. . . .

The United Nations

When the League of Nations was superseded by the United Nations in 1945, countries administering League of Nations Mandates entered into UN Trusteeship Agreements drawn to eventuate in full independence for the territories. However, South Africa refused the Trusteeship System—the only mandatory power to do so—and demanded the full incorporation of Namibia into the Union of South Africa. When the UN refused to accept this demand, South Africa proceeded to ignore the UN's authority over the matter.

In 1948, The Afrikaner National Party came to power in South Africa. The new regime made Namibia a fifth, *de facto,* province of South Africa, providing six seats for members of Parliament from Namibia in the South African parliament. In 1950, the International Court of Justice ruled that South Africa could not unilaterally change the status of Namibia and that the Mandate was still in force. South Africa ignored this ruling, enacting legislation that imposed the National Party's *apartheid* policy on the people of the territory.

With the passage of Resolution 2145 in 1966, the UN General Assembly terminated South Africa's mandate and placed Namibia under UN control. In 1969, the Security Council concurred in this action by adopting Resolution 264, which declared South African occupation illegal and called on South Africa to withdraw from Namibia. It also called for international diplomatic and economic isolation of South Africa whenever it acted on behalf of Namibia.

In 1971, the International Court of Justice at the Hague confirmed the UN action declaring South Africa's occupation illegal, and concluded that the only legal action South Africa could take would be to withdraw. Yet, South Africa continued to defy the world community and remained in Namibia. Despite South Africa's claims that administering Namibia was a financial drain and that it was charitable for Pretoria to govern Namibia, its determination to maintain control over Namibia reflected the extent to which Namibia was and is a source of wealth for South Africa.

. . . .

Inside Namibia

In 1964, South Africa directly imposed its apartheid policy on Namibia by dividing the country into separate "bantustans" or "homelands" for the African population along ethnic lines. . . .

The economy of Namibia is dominated by western transnational corporations and South African companies. Though Namibia is a country rich in mineral resources, the economy is profoundly distorted, with foreigners expropriating the wealth while the black population remains one of the poorest in the world.

While the forms of Pretoria's political control in Namibia have changed over the years, these changes have represented only tactical shifts rather than any dimunition of South Africa's absolute authority over the territory. . . . World opinion continued to oppose South Africa's occupation and when the political and military situation began to change in Namibia during the mid-1970s, resulting from the demise of the Portuguese colonial empire in southern Africa, South Africa began to look for alternatives to annexation that would nevertheless maintain the political, military and economic status quo in Namibia. The result was a conference called by the all-white National Party of Namibia for all "peoples" in the territory to discuss its future. Only organizations representing single ethnic groups were allowed to attend.

This conference, called the Turnhalle Constitutional Conference for the building in which it was held in Windhoek, continued sporadically for several years. Its final proposals for self-rule along ethnic lines under a two-tiered government were eventually adopted as Pretoria's scheme for an internal settlement. In the meantime South Africa had appointed an Administrator General to Namibia who was given the authority to rule by proclamation.

South Africa held elections in Namibia in December 1978 to form a 50-member "constituent assembly." Boycotted by SWAPO [South West Africa People's Organization] and almost all of the country's 40-odd political parties, the election was essentially a struggle between the two white-led political alliances that grew out of the Turnhalle Conference. . . .

On January 18, 1983, South Africa dissolved the National Assembly and announced that it was resuming "direct rule" in the territory. Few observers ever believed that South Africa had ever really abandoned *de facto* rule even during the tenure of the National Assembly and Council of Ministers.

· ·

SWAPO

On April 19, 1960, the OPO [Ovamboland People's Organization] was reorganized as the South West Africa People's Organization. SWAPO's stated objective is the complete liberation of the Namibian people and their land from colonial oppression and exploitation. . . .

SWAPO has established itself as a national movement representing the Namibian people, not just the Ovambo tribe, as is often claimed by its opponents. It has been noted by the International Defense and Aid Fund for Southern Africa that "Though Ovambos are among SWAPO's most numerous supporters, they are also the largest group of the Namibian population (40 to 50 percent) and will, in any independent government, form a majority of voters and representatives." SWAPO's Executive Committee also reflects the diversity of its national constituency. The SWAPO permanent representative to the UN and leader of their negotiating team is not an Ovambo.

The Organization of African Unity (OAU) recognized SWAPO as the liberation movement of the Namibian people in 1965, and in 1973 the UN General Assembly accepted it as the authentic representative of the Namibian people. SWAPO was granted full observer status in 1976.

Material aid to SWAPO comes from several organizations and countries. The OAU donates large amounts annually through its African Liberation Committee. Religious organizations, such as the World Council of Churches (through its Program to Combat Racism) and the Lutheran World Federation, provide money for educational and refugee relief work. Many African countries also provide bilateral aid, and some give sanctuary and provide facilities to Namibian refugees. The Eastern bloc countries and the Soviet Union also provide bilateral material support to SWAPO, as do several Western European countries, Sweden foremost among them. In addition, in Western countries that do not provide aid, community organizations and coalitions have raised monies and materials for SWAPO's refugee centers. . . .

Toward a Settlement

. . . .

Over the years, the UN has tried, in various ways, to pressure South Africa into acceptance of a Namibian settlement. The most forceful proposals for pressure have been consistently blocked in the Security Council by the "triple veto" of Britain, France and the United States. . . .

A confluence of military and political events in the mid-1970s caused Pretoria to reassess its position in Namibia. In response to continued international pressure and to new political and military realities of the region (largely due to the independence of Angola and Mozambique and the war in Rhodesia, now known as Zimbabwe), South Africa began to pursue a new strategy.

Characterized as a "two-track strategy" by former US Ambassador to the UN Donald McHenry, this strategy allowed South Africa to appear responsive to international opinion by negotiating for an international settlement while, at the same time, pursuing an internal settlement. . . .

The Western Initiative

Nowhere were South Africa's political intentions made more manifest than in the September 1975 Turnhalle Constitutional Conference. The conference was convened at the Turnhalle building in Windhoek and was attended by representatives from 11 separate "population groups" and a white delegation. South Africa claimed that the Conference was to be an open debate on all options for Namibia's independence, but only delegations accepting the racial and ethnic divisions imposed by Pretoria and representing only one "population group" were allowed to attend. This precluded the involvement of SWAPO and others who rejected racialism or tribalism as the basis for an acceptable national solution. . . .

The Contact Group [The U.S., Britain, France, West Germany and Canada] held four rounds of talks during the remainder of 1977, meeting separately with the South African government, SWAPO and the Turnhalle representatives. . . .

Though 1977 discussions conducted by the Contact Group were generally kept secret, they were reported to have gained the initial endorsements of the two principal contesting parties (South Africa and SWAPO) on certain compromises. The major issues agreed upon in the negotiations that year were as follows:

- The Turnhalle Conference would be disbanded. (It finally was dissolved in November 1977).
- South Africa would hold elections on the basis of universal adult suffrage with the participation of all political parties.
- An Administrator General would be installed in Namibia until independence. (This was an accommodation to what South Africa had already imposed.)
- UN supervision and control would be established through a Special Representative appointed by the UN Secretary General.
- The Special Representative's chief role would be to ensure that conditions were established allowing free and fair elections and an impartial electoral process.
- The Administrator General would repeal all discriminatory and repressive legislation.
- Law and order would remain the responsibility of South Africa.

. . . In addition to the principal agreements reached earlier in the negotiations, the proposal contained provisions for the following:

- The release and return to Namibia of all political prisoners.
- The return of all Namibian refugees.
- A cease-fire and the restriction of South African and SWAPO armed forces to bases.
- Phased withdrawal from Namibia of all but 1,500 South African troops within 12 weeks and prior to the start of the election campaign, with the remaining troops restricted to base.
- Demobilization of citizen forces, commandos and ethnic forces and the dismantling of their command structures.
- The peaceful return of SWAPO personnel outside of Namibia through designated entry points to participate in the elections.
- A United Nations Transitional Assistance Group (UNTAG) with military and civilian components to ensure the observance of the aforementioned provisions by all parties.

South Africa accepted the plan two weeks later, but expressed reservations over the issue of Walvis Bay. On May 4, 1978, the South African army and air force attacked a SWAPO refugee camp at Kassinga in Angola, killing nearly 700 people, mostly women and children, and injuring another 1,500. Many believed that this action was intended to prevent SWAPO from accepting the settlement plan but on July 12, 1978, SWAPO accepted the plan. Later that month the UN Security Council adopted Resolution 432, insisting on the reintegration of Walvis Bay with Namibia.

. . . On September 29, 1978, the Security Council adopted Resolution 435 endorsing the Waldheim Report [implementing the Western Plan]. The UN hoped to force South Africa to abandon its plan for ethnically based elections and to prove its commitment to hold free elections under UN supervision. In November 1978, the Security Council adopted Resolution 439, declaring that any South African-controlled elections would be void and that any person or body elected or created as a result of such an election would not be recognized.

Between 1978 and the present, South Africa has proved only its commitment to avoid the implementation of Resolution 435 at all costs while proceeding with its effort to impose an internal solution. . . .

During this period of South African stalling tactics, the Carter administration and the other Contact Group members defended their opposition to sanctions against Pretoria by arguing that these objections of South Africa could be overcome through negotiations. However, it was usually SWAPO, and not South Africa, that made concessions on several of these issues, in hopes of actually moving forward on implementation. South Africa consistently found new issues to raise as obstacles to the settlement plan. To its credit, the Carter administration did maintain that Resolution 435 was the only acceptable formula for a settlement and refused to allow any further weakening of the implementation plan.

. . . The Geneva Conference [which opened on January 5, 1981] marked the culmination of the Carter administration and Contact Group's four-year effort to achieve Namibia's independence. In Geneva, the Western Five had hoped to gain agreement on a cease-fire date and to begin implementation of Resolution 435.

. . . After assailing what it alleged to be the partiality of the UN in favor of SWAPO, South Africa walked out, causing the collapse of the conference, and refused to sign even a declaration of intent. South Africa's performance at Geneva was not surprising to many. Most observers had anticipated another dilatory tactic by Pretoria to slow the negotiations until the administration of U.S. President Ronald Reagan could take office in Washington. South Africa believed that the new U.S. administration would be more favorably disposed toward South African concerns in Namibia and that, in conjunction with a conservative government in Britain, a new U.S.-Britain alliance would mean new possibilities for policies of even greater accommodation within the Contact Group.

The Reagan Approach

. . . .

In a major television interview in early March 1981, President Reagan described South Africa as a "friendly country" and stressed that South Africa was "a country that strategically is essential to the free world in its production of minerals that we all must have." Two weeks later, the U.S. ambassador to the UN, Jeane Kirkpatrick, along with National Security Council and Pentagon officials, met with five South African military officers, including Pretoria's highest-ranking official in military intelligence. . . .

In April 1981 the assistant secretary of state-designate for African Affairs, Chester Crocker, made a two-week trip to 12 African countries to discuss the Namibian negotiations. He refused to meet with SWAPO leaders during the trip. During conversations with South African Foreign Minister Roelof "Pik" Botha and Defense Minister Magnus Malan in Pretoria, Crocker was informed that South Africa would not rule out an internationally acceptable settlement, but that it could not live with a SWAPO victory that left SWAPO with unchecked power. At this point, the U.S. began promoting the idea of drafting a constitution before elections. Such a constitution would be intended to guarantee white minority "rights" (encompassing land and property privileges) and to limit the authority and independence of a future Namibian government. On April 30, the U.S., France and Britain again cast a triple veto in the Security Council to defeat a resolution for sanctions against South Africa. The resolution had been introduced in response to the regime's intransigence on Namibia. . . .

In mid-May, South African Foreign Minister Roelef Botha led a delegation to Washington for talks with Secretary of State Alexander Haig and President Reagan. Thus, Botha became the first official from Africa to be received at the White House by the new administration. During this series of talks, the U.S. indicated to the South Africans that, "The political relationship between the U.S. and South Africa has now arrived at a crossroads of perhaps historic significance . . . the possibility may exist for a more positive and reciprocal relationship between the two countries based upon shared strategic concerns in southern Africa." The United States cautioned, however, that the problem of Namibia, which complicates U.S. relations with Europe and Africa, was a primary obstacle to the development of a new relationship with South Africa. Further, it was stated that the United States was willing to work with South Africa toward an internationally acceptable settlement that would not harm Pretoria's interests.

This policy of accommodation became known as "Constructive Engagement." Under this policy, the Reagan administration maintained that it would be far easier to influence South Africa to settle on Namibia and to begin a process of change internally if the United States built a closer friendship with the white minority regime than if the U.S. adopted a confrontational approach. Critics in Africa and elsewhere argued that this new U.S. policy was clearly racially and economically motivated and that it identified U.S. interests with those of white South Africa rather than with the legitimate aspirations of the 1.5 million people of Namibia whose land South Africa illegally occupied, or with the 22 million ruthlessly dominated black people inside South Africa. . . .

In August 1981, South Africa launched a massive invasion of Angola with widespread air and ground assaults. The international community condemned the invasion and called for the South Africans to withdraw. At the same time, the United States cast the sole veto against a UN Security Council Resolution condemning the invasion. . . .

In December 1981, the Contact Group presented its revised proposal, which incorporated Frontline States/SWAPO amendments. The group simultaneously offered an electoral system, however, that raised further objections. The group proposed a mixed electoral system, with half the members of the constituent assembly to be elected on a national basis by proportional representation and half on the basis of single-member constituencies. The Frontline States and SWAPO found this unacceptable because it was unnecessarily complicated and likely to cause confusion among a largely illiterate populace that had never before been given an opportunity to participate in free and fair elections. They maintained that the elections should either be based on proportional representation or single-member constituencies. Choosing one, they believed, would be practical and easy to administer, ensuring a genuine representation of all the people of Namibia. South Africa, on the other hand, accepted the mixed system and later insisted on it. . . .

The Collapse of the Negotiations

Suddenly, in early June 1982, the State Department announced that significant progress had been made in the negotiations and that there was now a basis for optimism that elections could be held in March or April of 1983. . . .

For all practical purposes, the formal negotiations were said to be finished, aside from certain details being worked out by the UN Secretariat. All that remained was for the South Africans to choose between the two electoral systems, The Contact Group already had prepared a draft letter calling on the Security Council "to set in motion the implementation of Resolution 435."

Yet, the letter, which had stated that "agreement has been reached among all the parties concerned" to begin implementation, was not delivered. Its conveyance became bogged down in the wash of a U.S. concern about the 15,000 to 20,000 Cuban troops in Angola. . . .

The matter of Cuban troops in Angola had been raised earlier by the Reagan administration in an attempt to link the issue to a Namibian settlement. Cuban withdrawal from Angola has been one of the primary U.S. objectives in the region—an objective the South Africans have embraced as the most recent in a long list of objections to implementation. This issue, however, is neither part of Resolution 435 nor is it within the mandate of the Contact Group in negotiating the UN settlement plan. The United States remains the only Contact Group member that has been attempting to make it a part of the settlement.

The Angolans have stated consistently that the Cubans would be withdrawn once Namibia was independent and the South African threat was removed. On February 4, 1982, Angola and Cuba issued a joint communique that stated that they were both ready to resume repatriation of Cuban troops as soon as South Africa withdrew its troops from Namibia. . . .

Underscoring Angola's security assistance needs was the third massive invasion, in August 1982, deep into Angolan territory by the South African forces and the continued occupation of parts of southern Angola by South Africa. This invasion fueled charges of U.S. duplicity, for while the United States was involved in on-going bilateral talks with Angola, principally regarding the Cuban troops, the United States had advance knowledge of South African plans for a major assault on Angola. South Africa's military aggression against Angola discredited its own claims that it was seeking a cease-fire. The escalation of its military presence inside Namibia also undermined U.S. diplomacy, which rested on the assumption that South Africa saw a Namibian settlement as desirable and in its own self-interest. . . .

Most observers now believe that American officials were being deliberately misleading with their sudden expressions of optimism. The statements have been criticized as an attempt to portray Angola as the uncompromising party and obstacle to independence. Observers argue that the joint U.S.-South African demand for a Cuban withdrawal is being used by South Africa to thwart implementation of the independence plan. Washington and Pretoria now place the responsibility for the failure on Luanda, while seeking to legitimize the South African occupation of southern Angola. . . .

. . . It is often overlooked that for Pretoria, a Namibia settlement has always posed two questions that have yet to be answered: Can the National Party government risk the domestic costs of a SWAPO victory in elections in Namibia? Do South Africa's military strategists believe they can better defend the white minority's rule in South Africa by conceding the war in Namibia and Angola? The available evidence suggests that neither the government nor the military believes that now is the time to settle on Namibia.

Using the American insistence on a Cuban withdrawal from Angola, South Africa now is able to block the settlement attempts by continuing to attack Angola, thereby assuring a continued Cuban presence. The Reagan administration, which initially prescribed a Namibia settlement as the necessary vehicle for closer U.S.-South Africa relations, now describes the South Africans as compromising and the Angolans as uncompromising. . . .

Conclusion

. . . .

There exist general theories about why the State Department had taken an optimistic view regarding the possibility of an early settlement and elections in Namibia. The prevailing theory, however, suggests that for the United States the issue was not Namibia's independence at all, but rather East-West rivalry and the maintenance of South African stability and dominance in the region.

"Constructive Engagement" must then be viewed as the diplomatic curtain behind which the United States can help Pretoria provide for its long-term security and maintain the status quo. It is a way of deflecting international criticism of U.S. support for South Africa. In the case of the Namibia talks, the belief is that if the Angolan government can be blamed for the failure of the negotiations, both international criticism and the issue itself can be diffused.

In the final analysis, the Reagan administration's perception of South Africa —as a bulwark against communism, reliable producer of strategic minerals required by the U.S., protector of the Cape sea lanes, and the center of a free enterprise system encompassing the southern region of the continent in a constellation of dependent states—will lead toward counter-productive results. Such perceptions as underpinning for policy will only make U.S. interests in the region hostage to an increasingly unstable and repressive regime, and will alienate the United States government from the majority of the nations of the world.

53. REPRESSION IN NAMIBIA: A LUTHERAN VIEW*

by MARTIN A. SÖVIK

Martin A. Sövik is an assistant director of the Office for Governmental Affairs of the Luthern Council in the United States. He testified on behalf of The American Lutheran Church, headquartered in Minneapolis, with 2.4 million members in 4,900 congregations, the Association of Evangelical Lutheran Churches, head-quartered in St. Louis, with 109,000 members in 273 congregations, and the Lutheran Church in America, headquartered in New York, with 3 million members in 6,100 congregations.

. . .[O]f the approximately 1.1 million Namibians, more than 540,000, about one half, are Lutheran. . . . It is fair to say that the church in Namibia plays as important a role in the political and social life of Namibians as, for instance, the Roman Catholic Church plays in Poland. . . .

As we consider the questions of the South African occupation of Namibia and how to end it, it seems useful to keep a few things in mind.

First, though it may seem that Namibia has been on the U.S. policy agenda for quite some time, we should never forget that for Namibians, the struggle for independence dates back to the turn of the century. Brutal colonial domination is part and parcel of Namibian life, going back to the first German colonists. We are Johnny-come-latelys to the matter.

Second, though apartheid is practiced by the authorities in Namibia, the real issue is the issue of independence from South African rule. Namibia remains virtually the last colony on the African continent. . . .

Lastly, we should remember that the sheer brutality of South African power is more in evidence in northern Namibia than anywhere else. . . . In Namibia, the South African government is waging war against people who do not seek a portion of political power in Pretoria (and never have), and are waging that war with far less restraint. One of the reasons that is possible is that for every atrocity in South Africa which gets publicized, there are others in Namibia, which rarely see the light of day. . . .

Part of the continuous danger which threatens all Namibians with random violence or detention by the occupying South African forces is the dusk to dawn curfew. The authorities have the right to shoot violators on sight, and I can assure you that people in the North take it seriously. At sunset, our group

*From *Namibia: Internal Repression and United States Diplomacy,* Hearings Before the Subcommittee on Africa of the Committee on Foreign Affairs, House of Representatives, Ninety-Ninth Congress, First Session, February 21, 1985.

was very unceremoniously hustled inside the compound of the church's guest-house by our hosts. Soon two or three armored personnel carriers rumbled down the road, searchlights panning, weapons at the ready. . . .

The most feared agent of South African terrorism is Koevoet, the secret police force. Reportedly established in the late 1970s information regarding it's activities is extremely closely held. So closely held, in fact, that when the President of the Southern African Catholic Bishops' Conference, Archibishop Denis Hurley of Durban, publicly accused Koevoet of atrocities, he was indicted for violation of laws which prohibit criticism of the police. . . . In the view of the people, it is there simply to exterminate those who oppose South Africa. The most common charge made against Koevoet involves the entrapment of Namibians. In the middle of the night, Koevoet, dressed in SWAPO fatigues and carrying Eastern-bloc weapons, will knock on a door, and demand food or temporary shelter. The next day the person will be arrested for harboring "terrorists," the South African label for SWAPO. It is difficult, to say the least to decline the demands of armed men. . . .

There is one more important fact that needs to be mentioned about Koevoet. Koevoet is a branch of the police, rather than the South African Defence Force. Under the rules of UNSCR 435, the South African Defence Force will be confined to discrete bases, and then return to South Africa. However, the police forces of Namibia, including Koevoet, will be used to keep order in the country, under the administration of the South Africans, with only supervision by the U.N. In addition, the peacekeeping force of the Transition Assistance Group will be responsible for disarming and repatriating SWAPO forces and monitoring the activities of the SADF. It will be important to monitor Koevoet especially carefully if and when 435 is implemented. . . .

There is no doubt that the churches of Namibia are targeted by the South African authorities, both as random victims and in a more directed manner. . . .

There is hardly a pastor in the North who has not been interrogated, or detained, or beaten. Everyday life is full of one indignity after another. Church vehicles are stopped and searched time after time. . . .

Though detention and torture of church personnel and church people is the most frightening means of pressuring the church, it is not the only one. In 1980, St. Mary's Anglican Seminary in Odibo was firebombed, for a total loss. In 1973, and again in 1980, the printing press of the ELOC church was bombed and completely destroyed. The press is used for the publication of hymn and prayer books, Christian education materials, and the church's newspaper, Omukwetu. Though no court has determined who was responsible for the bombing, I should tell you first, that it happened after curfew, and people living near the compound reported seeing army vehicles near it. . . .

The church leaders we talked to in Namibia leave no doubt as to their perception of South African intent. In the long run, it is to avoid giving up control of Namibia; in the short run it is to set up an internal government similar to the "internal settlement" attempted in pre-independent Zimbabwe. And especially, in the words of Bishop Hendrik Frederik of the Evangelical Luthern Church of Namibia, "South Africa is preparing us for a civil war." . . .

To create such a situation, the South Africans require three things, it seems to me. First, they need to have some sort of internal Namibian governing structure which has the appearance of legitimacy. Their boldest attempt was the establishment of the Democratic Turnhalle Alliance and the sham elections held in 1978. That attempt failed. The election was documentedly unfree and unfair, and the constitution of the ensuing internal government allowed the South African appointed Administrator General of Namibia to veto any laws passed by the so-called legislature and enact any laws he chose without its approval. . . .

The Multi-Party Conference is the latest South African attempt to create a political structure with the appearance of internal legitimacy. The MPC is even less broadly based than the DTA was, and is riven with internal strife among the parties within it's umbrella. Nonetheless, church leaders and others are convinced that in the near future another "internal settlement" will be formally announced.

I am often asked why any black politician in Namibia would cooperate with either DTA or the Multi-Party Conference. My short answer is simply to ask in return why Vidkun Quisling cooperated with Hitler during the Nazi occupation of Norway. They throw in their lot with South Africa because they don't think South Africa will lose the war, because South Africa is willing to give them some power over their own enemies, and because South Africa is willing to finance a quite nice life for them. These are all things they don't think they could achieve in a truly independent Namibia. . . .

The second thing South Africa needs to do, to give the Namibian reality the appearance it seeks, is to "Namibianize" the war, in order to make it seem like a conflict between a legitimate government and an illegitimate, Soviet-sponsored insurgency. To do that, South Africa has established the South West African Territorial Force, which fights along side of the SADF. The Territorial Force gets its personnel from two sources, enlistment and conscription. The conscription is particularly odius; it literally forces brother to fight brother or sister, father to fight son or daughter. In 1979, when conscription was extended downward to 16-year-olds the churches reported to us that in one month over 5,000 young men fled the country, either to SWAPO or to self-exile. In late 1984, South Africa extended eligibility for conscription upwards to the age of 55. The churches have time and time again publicly called for an end to conscription, and cited cases of both forced conscription and coerced registration.

Again, the question arises, why would a black Namibian enlist? Church officials cite two reasons. The first is economic. Not only is it a job, but it is a high paying job by Namibian standards. Given the extent of unemployment and poverty in Namibia, that is a highly seductive incentive. Secondly, church leaders complain that training and discipline in the armed forces is severely deficient. By enlisting, a young Namibian is transformed into a "big man"; he is given a weapon, but in many cases he is nothing more than a thug, able to bully, coerce and intimidate whomever he pleases, for almost anything he pleases. As a footnote to this discussion, it is interesting to note that in the Ovambo language, which is spoken by the majority of the people in the north, where the struggle is most intense, the popular term for Namibians fighting on the side of South Africa is "Omakakunya"—those contemptable little creatures who gnaw the people down to the bone. The popular term for the SWAPO forces is simply "amati"—friends.

Lastly, for the South African scenario to succeed, it must paint SWAPO as Marxist-terrorists, controlled by Moscow and seeking nothing more than the military power to turn Namibia into a totalitarian state serving it's own, and Russia's, ends. In the view of the churches of Namibia, this is as false as the legitimacy of the DTA or the MPC, as false as the idea that the war in Namibia is a civil war. Let me quote a variety of church leaders.

Bishop Kleopas Dumeni, of the 340,000 member Evangelical Lutheran Church of South West Africa/Namibia (ELOC):

> The South African government makes the propaganda that they are fighting against communism. . . . Who is SWAPO? Let me tell you. SWAPO is members, they are members, men and women, daughters and boys, of our families. Members of our churches. I said churches. . . regardless of denominations. Baptized, confirmed, married, have rights in their parishes, in their churches. Christians. . . . They are not communists.

Bishop James Kauluma, Bishop of the Anglican Diocese of Namibia, and President of the Council of Churches in Namibia:

> We hear all these allegations (about SWAPO), but we know some of these people who are fighting in the bush. We believe they are responding to an intolerable situation. They came out of Namibian society, which is a Christian society. Either they are Roman Catholics, or Lutherans, or Methodist, or Anglicans or another denomination in Namibia. We believe these people have respect for the church, and therefore we are not in agreement with these people who carry on, labeling these people as communist or Marxist. The South West Africa People's Organization, which is fighting against the South African army, has a chaplaincy service in the

movement itself. This is something those who claim that the movement is communistic or Marxist are not prepared to reveal.

. . . .

The church leaders do understand that some individual members of SWAPO may be Marxist in their analysis of Namibian history, and they certainly don't deny that many of SWAPO's policy prescriptions for an independent Namibia have their roots in the writings of Karl Marx—as do policy prescriptions of the British Labor Party, the Social Democrats of West Germany, or the French Socialist Party. Nor are they so naive that they don't understand the current political requirements of SWAPO, given the reality that only the Soviet-bloc has been willing to give them military support.

In a 1982 report, the Southern African Catholic Bishops Conference . . . concluded that "whatever the marxist tendencies of SWAPO, it seems to be a movement with powerful popular support, inspiring little apprehension in the majority of Christians in Namibia." And finally, I would like to quote Rev. Dr. Karl Mau, General Secretary of the Lutheran World Federation, and a pastor of the American Lutheran Church, on the roots of SWAPO.

> We have known the major movement in Namibia, the South West Africa People's Organization, from its inception . . . I have known many of its leaders personally, and have the highest respect for them. These were young men, mostly from our churches of the Anglican communion, who were committed to the freedom and independence and improvement of conditions for their people. They came over to New York as young men, completely inexperienced, wondering how they could get a hearing at the United Nations. And the church, from the beginning, tried to help them in this strictly non-violent course . . . Any number of times when we met with them they were absolutely committed to non-violence; they would not get involved with radical forces that were trying to push them in the direction of violent solutions.
>
> The major trials in 1967, '68 . . . [were] the first major attack on SWAPO, which was dubbed from that moment on as a movement supposedly being influenced by communists.
>
> You see, the strategy always is if there's any resistance to a system, it's being fomented by communists. . . . Finally, the decision had to be made by the movement that it could no longer remain committed to the non-violent approach. . . . The church was very much aware of this whole development because it was mostly church people providing the leadership.

It is impossible to believe that these church leaders . . . , are ignorant of the persecution of the church in Eastern Europe, especially since many of them work side-by-side with their counterparts from Eastern European churches in international ecumenical organizations like the Lutheran World Federation.

Yet they express no fear for the future of the church in Namibia if SWAPO were to win an election. In fact, it is interesting to note that last summer, when the South Africans released Herman Toivo ja Toivo, one of SWAPO's founders after twenty years in prison, the Council of Churches in Namibia served as his mailing address and temporary residence. . . .

Mr. Chairman, in your letter inviting me to testify today, you asked me to comment on the Namibian churches' view of U.S. diplomacy, and the effect of "constructive engagement" on the prospects for implementation of 435. I wish I did not have to, for it is distinctly uncomfortable for an American to travel to Namibia and hear their views. . . .

The individual churches of Namibia and the Council of Churches in Namibia have on many occasions criticized U.S. policy, especially the linkage of Namibian independence with the withdrawal of Cuban troops from Angola. I want to be explicit about this: in the view of the churches of Namibia, the domestic politics of Angola have no bearing on the right of South Africa to occupy and oppress their country; the Cuban troops pose no threat to them or the people of Namibia; and the linkage of Cuban troop withdrawal with the implementation of 435 is not only unacceptable, but an example of the United States and South African collaboration. The effect of this policy has been, in their view, to prolong the war, the killing, and the suffering of the Namibian people. . . .

The effect of this, Mr. Chairman, is that the church leadership of Namibia now distrusts the U.S. role in the diplomacy as much as it distrusts South Africa's intent. . . .

54. THE EMBODIMENT OF NATIONAL UNITY

by SWAPO [the South West Africa People's Organization of Namibia]

SWAPO is a national liberation movement rallying together, on the basis of free and voluntary association, all freedom-inspired sons and daughters of the Namibian people. It is the organized political vanguard of the oppressed and exploited people of Namibia. In fulfilling its vanguard role, SWAPO organizes, unites, inspires, orientates and leads the broad masses of the working Namibian people in the struggle for national and social liberation. It is thus the expression and embodiment of national unity, of a whole people united and organized in the struggle for total independence and social liberation.

SWAPO Constitution, 1976

The tasks before SWAPO at present and in the immediate future are:

1. The liberation and winning of independence for the people of Namibia by all possible means, and the establishment of a democratic people's government;
2. The realization of genuine and total independence of Namibia in the spheres of politics, economy, defense, social and cultural affairs.

To these ends, SWAPO has resolved:

1. To persistently mobilize and organize the broad masses of the Namibian people so that they can actively participate in the national liberation struggle;
2. To mould and heighten, in the thick of the national liberation struggle, the bond of national and political consciousness amongst the Namibian people;
3. To combat all manifestations and tendencies of tribalism, regionalism, ethnic orientation and racial discrimination;
4. To unite all Namibian people, particularly the working class, the peasantry and progressive intellectuals, into a vanguard party capable of safeguarding national independence and of building a classless, non-exploitative society based on the ideals and principles of scientific socialism.

SWAPO Political Program, 1976

55. ISRAEL AND SOUTH AFRICA: BUSINESS AS USUAL—AND MORE*

by BENJAMIN BEIT-HALLAHMI

Benjamin Beit-Hallahmi is a lecturer in Psychology at Haifa University.

When the subject of relations between Israel and South Africa was raised prior to 1977, there were those who disagreed with its designation as a major alliance. Today most observers, and the governments involved, would agree with that designation. The relationship is important, central and far-reaching for both countries. . . .

*From *New Outlook,* March/April 1983 [as condensed].

Diplomatic Contacts

There was a "secret" visit to Israel by Foreign Minister Reolof Botha, reported by the *Christian Science Monitor*. . . . All visits by South African leaders to Israel since then have been public. Visits by Israeli officials and dignitaries to South Africa in recent years have been commonplace and too numerous to mention.

Mr. Simha Ehrlich, then Finance Minister, visited South Africa in February 1978 as head of an Israeli economic delegation. He announced during that visit . . . that Israel would serve as a convenient way station for South African products, which would be exported first to Israel and then reexported (as Israeli-made) to the USA and EEC countries, avoiding higher taxes and political boycotts to the benefit of both countries.[1] . . . Israel's current Defense Minister, Ariel Sharon, has had extensive ties with South African military and political leaders for at least fifteen years. Sharon has visited South Africa scores of times, in his capacity as General, Member of Knesset, Agriculture Minister and Defense Minister. Leaders of the Labor Party, which has been in opposition since 1977, have paid frequent visits to South Africa since losing power. Yitzhak Rabin is a regular visitor. . . . Mr. Yossef Lapid, Director-General of the Israel Broadcasting Authority . . . , is a long-time admirer of South Africa and a frequent visitor there. In an emotional article entitled "For the Sake of South Africa I Shall Not Hold My Peace" . . . , Mr. Lapid expressed his support for the whites, stating: "If we have to choose between friendship with black Africa, as it is today, and friendship with a white, well-organized and successful country with a booming Jewish community,[2] then I prefer South Africa." This view, which is coupled in the article with citations of research proving the genetic inferiority of blacks, seems to reflect the feelings of many in the Israeli elite. . . .

At the United Nations, Israel has adopted a unique policy whenever matters of policy regarding South Africa are discussed and voted on. In such cases Israel informs the UN Secretary-General that it chooses not to participate. Thus, for example, when the General Assembly votes, as it has done several times, for an arms embargo against South Africa, Israel is listed in the official record as not participating which, in diplomatic parlance, means that it does not recognize the UN's authority in the matter. This is what happens annually, when the extensive program of the UN Special Committee against Apartheid is voted on. In response to the Security Council resolution imposing an arms

---

[1] According to James Adams, *The Unnatural Alliance*, 1984, it is probable that when *all* trade is accounted for, including military sales and diamonds (both kept confidential), Israel may be South Africa's biggest trading partner.—Ed.

[2] South Africa's 130,000 Jews are the highest per-capita contributors to Israel in the world.—Ed.

embargo on South Africa in November 1977, the then Foreign Minister Moshe Dayan stated that Israel would simply ignore the resolution. . . .

Military Cooperation

The full extent of military cooperation between South Africa and Israel has been kept secret by both sides, but significant aspects have been revealed. An undisclosed number of South African military men are training in Israel in connection with the sale of weapons. . . . According to the Stockholm Peace Research Institute (SPIRI), military cooperation between South Africa and Israel started as early as 1962, when Israel sold South Africa 32 Centurion tanks. The *Daily Telegraph* reported that Israeli officers were closely involved in planning the South African invasion of Angola. The *Guardian* reported on the involvement of Israeli counter-insurgency experts in Namibia, and on the cooperation of the two countries in weapon development and training. According to *Newsweek,* Israel has sold South African rifles, mortars, electronic equipment and missile boats. And according to report in the *Daily Telegraph,* Israeli technicians have built an electrified "wall" along South Africa's borders and Israel is remodeling all of South Africa's armored vehicles. *Davar* reported on a lecture by Mr. Colin Legum, an editor of the London *Observer,* in which details of military support by Israel to South African forces in Namibia were discussed. Mr. Legum referred to Israeli soldiers in uniform being seen in the villages of Namibia, and to their involvement with an electrical fence constructed along the Namibian-Angolan border.

. . . *Haolam Hazeh* reported on the joint military effort of the two countries against SWAPO in Namibia to keep the uranium mines under Pretoria's control. It also reported that Israel had sold South Africa radar stations, in addition to other electronic equipment. The *Rand Daily Mail* reported that Israel was involved in the training of UNITA forces, which fight against the Angolan government and are maintained by South Africa, in Walvis Bay (Namibia). The *Economist,* reporting on foreign troops on the African continent, stated that 200 Israeli officers teach "anti-terrorist" tactics to South Africa. . . .

Nuclear Cooperation

It is the most closely guarded secret of the alliance, but there is little reason to doubt that nuclear development plays a major part in the joint survival strategy of both countries. *Newsweek,* in an article on the Israel-South Africa alliance, reported on a joint nuclear weapons development program, and a nuclear test planned for the summer of 1977, which was cancelled under Great

Power pressure. The affair drew much attention in the world press to South Africa's nuclear capability and to its joint activities with Israel.

Both South Africa and Israel have refused to sign the Nuclear Non-Proliferation Treaty, and reports about the presumed nuclear programs of both countries have regularly appeared in the press all over the world. . . . *Ma'ariv* quoted an extensive report published by the London *Economist* on the Israeli-South African nuclear program. That report included details about the cruise missiles designed to carry the nuclear warheads, also under development, and visits to South Africa by Israel nuclear experts and Defense Minister Ezer Weizmann. According to the report, nuclear cooperation between the two countries started in 1966.

CBS Television News, in its nightly broadcast of February 21, 1980, carried a report by Dan Raviv, its Tel Aviv correspondent, who spoke from Rome, bypassing Israeli censorship. Raviv reported on the contents of a book by Eli Teichner and Ami Dor-On dealing with Israel's nuclear program. According to the report, nuclear cooperation between Israel and South Africa started in the mid-1950s, when South Africa started shipping uranium to Israel in return for Israeli technology. The report also dealt with the Israeli-South African nuclear test of 1979.

On September 22, 1979, an American spy satellite recorded a sudden flash of light appearing in the ocean near the southern tip of South Africa. This was interpreted by experts as a possible nuclear test, and speculation arose as to who was involved in conducting it. The US government has not made public any definite conclusions to this day. There has been conjecture about the possible relationship of this presumed nuclear test to the Israel-South Africa nuclear program. This conjecture received some confirmation in December 1980 when Israeli State Television carried, without any comment, a British-made program which offered a solution to the mystery. The program dealt in detail with Israeli-South African nuclear cooperation, and reported that the flash on September 22, 1979, was the result of a test of the newly developed naval nuclear shell, part of the joint program. There were no reactions in other Israeli media following the airing of this program, but *Yediot Aharonot* mentioned speculation in the USA that the September 1979 test was designed to try out a new neutron bomb.[3] The *Middle East* reported another nuclear test in December 1980, which was also monitored by an American satellite. According to this report, the latest test was part of the continuing joint Israeli-South African nuclear development program. The *Washington Post* carried a report by Jack Anderson detailing a joint project by Israel, Taiwan and South Africa to develop a strategic cruise missile. To quote Anderson, "US intelli-

---

[3] For more on this, see Samuel H. Day Jr., "The Afrikaner Bomb: Pretoria Marches Toward Doomsday," *The Progressive*, September 1982, and Robert S. Jaster, "Politics and the 'Afrikaner' Bomb," *Orbis*, Winter 1984.—Ed.

gence agencies have known for years that the three nations were working together on nuclear weapons development. But the addition of cruise missiles to their arsenals drastically alters the world 'balance of terror.' " . . .

The Alliance in Global Perspective

. . . Israel's role in southern Africa, according to . . . [one] analysis, is to support the apartheid regime as part of the struggle against "Soviet expansionism" and for the "Free World." Israel, indeed, has a special role to play because it can do some things which the USA is reluctant to be involved in.

Mr. Jacob Meridor, Cabinet Minister for economic planning, was quoted in *Ha'aretz* as follows: "We will say to the Americans: Don't compete with us in Taiwan; don't compete with us in South Africa; don't compete with us in the Caribbean or in other places where you cannot sell arms directly. . . . Let us do it. You will sell the ammunition and equipment through an intermediary. Israel will be your intermediary." Israel's mission as an intermediary with the South African government extends much farther than southern Africa, as it assumes a global perspective.

An almost unnoticed item in the Israeli press will illustrate the global dimension of the Israel-South Africa alliance today. On November 11, 1980, *Ma'ariv* reported, on page two of its weekend edition, that Israel and South Africa were supporting the Garcia Mesa regime in Bolivia and offering to extend "economic cooperation." For most readers this was probably an obscure, esoteric item. Its significance, however, was profound. It meant that the alliance had assumed a global role and was involved in supporting right-wing dictatorships in South America. The only achievement for which the Garcia Mesa government has been noted is supplying cocaine to rich North Americans looking for a new kind of thrill. Otherwise, it has been regarded as a tragedy in the history of Bolivia, a country that seemed on its way to achieving democracy. International support for the regime has been scarce, and all of a sudden two remote countries are offering it cooperation and support. . . .

It is quite clear that in these cases Israel and South Africa are exercising their responsibilities as bastions of the "Free World." . . . It should be remembered that . . . it was Dr. Henry Kissinger, US Secretary of State at the time, who encouraged Israel in its military involvement on the South African side in the Angolan war of 1975. The USA can well appreciate the utility of having Israelis, efficient and enthusiastic, with no public opinion and "human rights" voices to worry about at home, perform the necessary "strategic duty" for it. . . . Given the present administration in the USA, we can safely predict that the alliance will become stronger and closer still, and that it will assume a more global role in the future.

Chapter XII:

SOUTH AFRICA AND THE UNITED STATES: Constructive Engagement

56. *U.S. POLICY TOWARD APARTHEID: FROM TRUMAN TO FORD**

by THOMAS G. KARIS

Thomas G. Karis is identified in the headnote to Reading 28.

South Africa did not become a foreign-policy issue for the United States, and then only an incidental one, until after World War II, when American membership in the United Nations compelled it to take positions on resolutions dealing with South Africa. . . .

American economic interests in South Africa were negligible in 1945, but South Africa was thought of politically as an ally because it had taken a fighting role in both world wars. The South African government often cites this role today although South Africa became a belligerent in World War II over the opposition of many of those, including the former prime minister, who are now in power. The United States entered into a lend-lease agreement and established a small number of air bases in South Africa. . . .

Truman, 1945–52

. . . .

Cooperative relations with South Africa continued without interruption after Truman's election to a full term in 1948. . . .

*From *Southern Africa: The Continuing Crises* (Bloomington, 1979).

... [T]he Truman administration was preoccupied with the emerging cold war and welcomed all help. In early 1949 South Africa sent an air crew for the Berlin airlift and in 1950, under pressure from the opposition United Party, contributed an additional flag to the United Nations command when it sent a token fighter squadron to Korea. Beginning in the early 1950s, the United States and South Africa cooperated in both military and scientific matters. . . .

Eisenhower, 1953–60

· ·

U.S. policy toward South Africa has been reactive, but increasingly during the Eisenhower years a cautious administration came under pressure to respond affirmatively to the emergence of race as a preeminent domestic and United Nations issue. . . .

. . . [I]n 1957 the administration recognized, but in cold war terms, the coming importance of Africa when Vice-President Nixon, attending Ghana's independence celebration, reported that African developments "could well prove to be the decisive factor in the conflict between the forces of freedom and international Communism." In mid-1958, a Bureau of African Affairs, whose scope included South Africa, was finally established. And on October 30, 1958, after six years of abstention on General Assembly resolutions critical of apartheid, the United States finally came to the first watershed in its South African policy: it abandoned the "domestic jurisdiction" argument and voted for a watered-down resolution that omitted "condemnation." Voting alongside the Soviet Union and against Britain and France, the United States expressed "regret and concern" that South Africa had not reconsidered its racial policies. . . .

What became evident during Eisenhower's presidency was the gap between rhetoric and action—what a Congressional report later called "schizophrenia" —an ambivalence that continues to plague American policy today. But the low priority of South Africa for policymakers was not surprising. Neither the continent nor South Africa presented any critical problem or short-term threat to American interests; only violence in the Congo in 1960 won active presidential attention to Africa. Not only was the level of awareness of South African issues very low, but they had virtually no impact on politically influential groups. . . .

The contrast between rhetoric and action was dramatically evident after Sharpeville. Expecting that worldwide repercussions would be stunning, the State Department, without even consulting with the Embassy in Pretoria or the White House, issued a statement on the next day deploring police violence. For the first time a South African issue was taken up by the Security Council.

On April 1, 1960, the United States voted in the face of abstention by Britain and France for a resolution that blamed the South African government for the shootings and called on it "to initiate measures aimed at bringing about racial harmony based upon equality." Behind these words, however, there was no American intention or plan to confront South Africa with a choice between a change in the direction of its policy or acceptance of the psychological and economic costs of withdrawal of American support.

Within months, in September 1960, the United States and South Africa signed an agreement covering three NASA tracking stations. The South African government publicized this and other forms of cooperation as evidence of real and common interests; American criticism, on the other hand, could be dismissed as rhetoric intended to cater to pressure groups at home. . . .

Kennedy, 1961–63

. . . .

Rhetoric became critical of South Africa and reached eloquent heights during the Kennedy administration, and for the first time action in the form of an arms embargo was taken, at some cost to the United States, to make that rhetoric credible. But otherwise the gap between official statements and both public and private actions was wider than ever. Cooperative scientific and even some military relations continued. . . .

When a majority of U.N. members called for at least voluntary sanctions, the United States hardened its stance and decided to supplement moral exhortation with an acceptance of the principle of action to help induce change. On April 13, 1961, with Britain voting for the first time in criticism of apartheid, following South Africa's decision to leave the Commonwealth, the United States also supported a General Assembly resolution requesting all states to consider taking "separate and collective action" to bring about the abandonment of apartheid. On the other hand, it opposed a list of suggested voluntary sanctions, including diplomatic and commercial boycotts, as it continues to do today. The United States feared, Ambassador Plimpton said on April 5, 1961, that coercive measures would produce "an internal explosion in South Africa" and "embittered chaos threatening African and world peace and security."

"Abhorrence" became the standard word to describe the American attitude toward apartheid. . . .

[Ambassador] Plimpton . . . praised Chief Albert Lutuli, president-general of the banned ANC, who had been awarded the Nobel Peace Prize. . . . [O]n July 4, 1963, the American Embassy in Pretoria invited Africans to its annual reception for the first time. . . .

Meanwhile, an agreement was made with South Africa in 1962 for the establishment of a Defense Department space-tracking facility, separate from the NASA facility already set up; in exchange, South Africa would buy arms from the United States. But on October 11, 1962, replying to a Soviet accusation, Plimpton said that U.S. policy was not to sell any arms that the South African government could use to enforce apartheid. On August 7, 1963, the United States voted in the Security Council for a voluntary arms embargo. . . .

Plimpton had claimed that the United States had "reinforced the depth and strength of its public views on apartheid" by vigorous private approaches. In dealing with a wide variety of both official and private Americans, however, South Africans could hear what they wanted to hear. Thus, after Plimpton's attack in 1961, Eric Louw, the South African foreign minister, maintained in Parliament that the speech could not have been cleared with Secretary of State Rusk since shortly before its delivery Rusk and he had "a most friendly and cordial discussion." Stevenson, on the other hand, he said, was "dedicated to a hatred of South Africa."

Johnson, 1963–68

Lyndon Johnson, after the assassination of Kennedy, accepted a national responsibility "to strike the chains of bias and prejudice from minds and practices as Lincoln, a century ago, struck down slavery." Speaking in the United Nations, Adlai Stevenson said Johnson's "call for action to wipe out the remnants of racial discrimination in this country" applied equally to racial discrimination everywhere.

Some of the new administration's rhetoric exceeded earlier rhetoric in vividness, describing prisoners being brutalized into "a pitiful mass of flesh." And some action was taken, but the isolated steps were not part of a planned program of pressure. Naval cooperation apparently came virtually to an end, although South Africa continued to supply information on Russian trawlers, and, as noted later, the navy avoided South African ports after 1967. The United States tightened enforcement of the arms embargo, in part by forbidding the sale of materials for the making of arms, and at the end of 1965 made detailed claims of lost sales worth millions of dollars; but it continued to exclude multipurpose items and spare parts from the embargo. Embassy officials attended political trials and in mid-1964 spoke privately to South African officials about the repercussions of a possible death sentence for Nelson Mandela, leader of the ANC, and others then on trial. But because the trial was in progress, the United States abstained on a Security Council resolution dealing with it. The embassy's July 4 reception continued to be multi-racial, although many other official functions were for whites only.

South Africa as a concern of American foreign policy was at a near nadir because there appeared to be stability in that country and dangerous instability elsewhere, particularly in the Middle East and Southeast Asia. . . .

Nixon-Ford, 1969–76

It was not surprising that the election of a conservative president, strongly supported by business and with a "Southern strategy," should tilt U.S. policy toward greater sympathy—in effect, support—for white minority rule in Southern Africa. . . .

As in the Johnson years, concern about South Africa was at a near nadir; Vietnam and its repercussions at home and, later, Watergate preoccupied the president. In South Africa the status quo seemed safely entrenched. Superficial reforms bemused many Americans and fed their wishful thinking about fundamental change, but in fact controls over the African majority and the radical opposition were steadily tightened. . . .

The premises of policy in the Nixon-Ford-Kissinger era were set forth in the now well-known National Security Council Study Memorandum Number 39, prepared by August 15, 1969, and adopted in January 1970. Option two, which was essentially adopted, was to prove a gross miscalculation: "the whites are here to stay and the only way that constructive change can come about is through them. There is no hope for the blacks to gain the political rights they seek through violence. . . ." It also proposed that the United States continue its "public opposition to racial repression but relax political isolation and economic restrictions on the white states . . . broadening the scope of our relations and contacts gradually. . . ." Closer relations would be "to some degree in response to tangible—albeit small and gradual—moderation of white policies." To encourage change in white attitudes, "we would indicate our willingness to accept political arrangements short of guaranteed progress toward majority rule, provided that they assure broadened political participation in some form by the whole population."

There was no intention to make this shift known at the time or to open it up to public discussion. The National Security Council discussed the secret study on December 9, 1969, at a meeting in which Vice-President Agnew confused South Africa and Rhodesia in lengthy pro-Rhodesian remarks. Although the State Department has maintained that option two was not adopted as such, Kissinger recommended on January 2, 1970, and Nixon adopted "a general posture of partial relaxation along the lines of Option Two." . . .

The spirit of option two of NSSM 39 was evident in many signals of reassurance to the South African government during the early years of the Nixon administration. The arms embargo was relaxed through a redefinition of "gray areas" and an expansive interpretation of dual-purpose equipment such as small "civilian-type" jet planes, helicopters, and transport aircraft. On the economic front, the Commerce Department tacitly encouraged investment and trade, and both rose rapidly. Beginning in 1969, the Commodity Credit Corporation extended credit to South African buyers of agricultural products; and in 1971 restrictions on Export-Import Bank guarantees were secretly relaxed. In 1972 the Bank guaranteed a $48.6 million sale of locomotives.

In the United Nations, the United States voted against the annual anti-apartheid resolution in the General Assembly rather than abstaining on it; it opposed a Security Council resolution to set a date for South Africa's withdrawal from South West Africa; and in October 1974, arguing that the principle of universal membership should not be breached, it joined Britain and France in a triple veto of a Security Council resolution to expel South Africa. Some observers have alleged that beginning in the early 1970s secret agreements made South Africa "a backdoor member of NATO." with NATO furnishing equipment for the underground surveillance and communications base known as Silvermine, near Cape Town.

The new spirit was also evident in personal relations. Because of either insensitivity or ignorance, John Hurd, a conservative political appointee who became ambassador in 1970, went pheasant-hunting with government officials on Robben Island, where Nelson Mandela and other political prisoners were serving life terms. C. P. Mulder, minister of interior and information, who was expanding propaganda and lobbying activities in the United States, met Vice-President Gerald Ford early in 1974, a meeting widely publicized in South Africa. And contrary to stated U.S. policy, he and South African military officials met privately with high Pentagon officials. Other signals were to be seen in the administration's nonactions. The 1960s program of support for Southern African refugees "withered away." . . .

The Portuguese coup of April 1974 and the train of events in Southern Africa that followed finally commanded the attention of the highest policy-makers. Dormant fears came to a head: fears of radicalization, major revolutionary violence, and deepening Soviet involvement. The black Marxist governments coming to power in Mozambique and Angola in 1975 transformed the region, speeded up the timetable of the guerrilla struggles in Rhodesia and Namibia, and heightened black confidence and expectations in South Africa. Black-consciousness leaders publicly welcomed the new ruling parties, applauding the MPLA and Cuban forces while they were fighting South African soldiers during the Angolan civil war.

South Africa's military intervention in the latter part of 1975 proved to be a fiasco for South Africa and also for the United States, which had intervened covertly. Although the State Department has denied that the United States encouraged South African intervention, South Africa cooperated closely with the Central Intelligence Agency and believed that the United States welcomed its actions.

Secretary of State Kissinger took initiatives in 1976 that can be seen either as a new level of ambivalence regarding South Africa or as a coherent policy of cynicism. In order to preempt Soviet-Cuban intervention Kissinger committed the United States to majority rule (and presumably to a moderate black government) in Rhodesia by means of "a rapid negotiated settlement." Presenting detailed proposals for Rhodesia in a speech in Lusaka, Zambia, on April 27, 1976, he also affirmed a general commitment to "majority rule . . . for all the peoples of southern Africa." But his brief discussion of South Africa made no reference to majority rule and rapid change. What the United States looked for in South Africa "within a reasonable time," he said, was the ending of institutionalized separation of the races and "a clear evolution toward . . . basic human rights for all South Africans." The immediate need, however, was for South Africa to use its influence in Rhodesia, an action that would be "viewed positively."

Kissinger's Lusaka speech was intended, in his words, "to usher in a new era in American policy." A new era of active U.S. involvement in Southern Africa was, indeed, begun: but although the South African government was initially unhappy with the speech, it quickly realized that the new emphasis on majority rule was not focused on South Africa itself. The American actions that followed enabled white South Africans to convince themselves that the United States looked on them as a useful ally. . . .

While cooperating with the United States, the South African government may have hoped that it would recognize the independence of Transkei. The administration never seriously considered taking such a step, which would fly in the face of official opinion in Africa and would give some legitimacy to the unilaterial action of the South African government in depriving a large number of blacks of their citizenship. But Kissinger did not want to upset the South African government, and not until four days before Transkeian independence on October 26, 1976, did the administration announce a policy of nonrecognition. Even on that day only the United States abstained on the unanimous resolution in the General Assembly requesting states to prohibit any dealings with Transkei or other Bantustans. The U.S. position was based on "minor legal quibbles," a Republican citizen-member of the U.S. delegation said later; "once we were thought of as the world's conscience; now we seemed to be the world's lawyer."

More important as an issue for the incoming Carter administration was that posed by a resolution introduced by Scandinavian members and overwhelmingly adopted by the General Assembly a week after the election: it urged the Security Council to consider steps for ending new investment in South Africa. The United States and its major Western allies abstained.

57. THE CARTER YEARS: OPTION TWO WITH LIBERAL CLOTHING*

by ROBERT FATTON, JR.

Robert Fatton, Jr., is an Assistant Professor in the Department of Government and Foreign Affairs at the University of Virginia, Charlottesville. He is the author of the forthcoming book: Black Consciousness in South Africa: The Dialectics of Ideological Resistance to White Supremacy, *State University of New York Press.*

. . . [I]t is not surprising that the American foreign policy toward South Africa in the past thirty years and under seven different administrations has been characterized by continuity rather than discontinuity. What has changed throughout the years is the style and form of the conduct of this policy, but not its substance. Whether it be the liberal, moderate or conservative wing of the ruling class, the conviction has been that change in South Africa ought to be peaceful and gradual, and that it ought to take place under the aegis of the supposedly deracializing forces of capitalism. Moreover, the belief was and still is that change will come from the reforms of enlightened white politicians rather than from the revolutionary struggle of black nationalists.

Where differences have existed and still do relates to the tempo and substance of change occurring in South Africa, to the role of U.S. corporations in undermining white supremacy, to the economic benefits accruing from doing business in South Africa, to the nature of the black opposition, and to whether or not the apartheid regime represents an invitation to, instead of a bulwark against communism. It is within these clear and precise boundaries that the ruling class conducts the debate over its South African foreign policy.

This ruling class is generally divided into liberal, moderate and conservative factions. The liberal faction tends to believe that despotic and repressive right wing regimes provide a window of opportunity for communist forces and thereby that the U.S. should promote vigorously the democratization of these regimes. To a large extent the moderate faction accepts the principles of its liberal brethren, but it fears the consequences of U.S. support for democratization. Indeed, for the moderates democratization creates conditions of instability and uncertainty which may lead to "Marxist take-overs" rather than to "representative democracy." Accordingly, the moderates are hesitant to call for those type of policies conducive to U.S. backing for social change. Theirs is the equivocal position par excellence. In contradistinction, the conservatives express the determined conviction that U.S.-sponsored programs of change in

*From *African Studies Review,* March 1984.

the Third World are detrimental to the American "national interest." In their view, these programs are the vehicle through which "totalitarian communist" forces acquire power. Theirs is a reactionary policy opposing social change.

The competition between these three factions of the ruling class has generally resulted in a moderate-conservative consensus because liberals do not have "any major stronghold" of power and cannot therefore impose their objectives without the support of the moderates. In the process liberal policies lose their substance and essence; they become equivocal statements of purpose. . . .

It is now clear that Option Two[1] was seriously flawed. It underestimated the forces of the African revolution and misjudged the strength of white power. Yet, despite these flaws the major principles of Option Two continued to nurture the formulation of U.S. foreign policy toward South Africa. In the aftermath of the Portuguese coup and the coming to power of Afro-Marxism in Mozambique and Angola, the American ruling class still defined its objectives in terms of an accommodation with white South Africa. This accommodation, it was believed, was to facilitate the peaceful and gradual ascension of black moderate regimes in both Zimbabwe and Namibia and ultimately in South Africa itself.

In this context, and notwithstanding its rhetorical insistence on human rights which went as far as advocating through Vice-President Mondale "one man/one vote," the South African policy of the Carter administration embodied the basic principles of this Option Two. In fact, President Carter himself along with the major figures of his cabinet assumed that the capitalist penetration of South Africa by American corporations would bring a positive transformation of apartheid. "Economic development, investment commitment and the use of economic leverage [declared Carter to the *Johannesburg Financial Mail* was] the only way to achieve racial justice [in South Africa]." Andrew Young, then U.S. Ambassador to the U.N., introduced to a New York audience Harry Oppenheimer—the major figure of South African capitalism—as "a kindred spirit." Thus, both Carter and Young held the view that an enlightened capitalism would bring interracial harmony and contribute to the eventual demise of apartheid in the same way that it had supposedly undermined the entrenched racism of the American South.

Accordingly, the Carter administration strongly encouraged the "application of progressive employment practices" by American firms in South Africa, and it committed its full support for the implementation of the Sullivan principles. Not surprisingly, the Carter policymakers never contemplated or advocated a full-scale mandatory economic embargo against South Africa; neither did the more liberal wing of the ruling class.

[1] See previous reading.—Ed.

Indeed, in his report on U.S. Corporate Interests in South Africa (1978), Dick Clark, the then Chairman of the Subcommittee on African Affairs, rejected the "more extreme measures" of disengagement and investment sanctions despite his acknowledgement that the performance of American firms in South Africa had been "abysmal." He advocated a threefold strategy to discourage American investment in South Africa. Firstly, the U.S. government was to withdraw its facilities which promoted the flow of capital or credit to South Africa. Secondly, the government was to deny tax credits to those American firms contravening "fair labor practices;" and thirdly, it was to "withhold official endorsement of private groups which organize in defense of U.S. corporate investment in South Africa unless they satisfactorily support the corporate guidelines and fair employment principles laid down by the U.S. Government." . . .

The most determined challenge to constructive engagement ever produced by the ruling class was contained in the Democratic Party platform of 1980. Under the influence of the Black Caucus and the Kennedy wing the platform pledged to increase "political and economic pressure on [the] oppressive [apartheid] regime . . . [and to] divest, under legal procedures, South African holdings of all public institutions and deploy full legal economic sanctions until that government abandons its undemocratic apartheid system." Obviously, this platform vanished from the American political agenda with the Reagan victory. In any case, it is highly doubtful that it would have ever been given a chance even if Carter had won the election, for platforms in American politics are symbolic documents of high irrelevance to reality.

What is clear, however, is that the common thread of these different policies of the ruling class consisted of a strong determination to lessen Soviet/Cuban influence and protect American military and strategic interests in Southern Africa. The pursuit of these objectives always resulted in an accommodationist posture toward white supremacy.

Not surprisingly, in April 1977, the Carter administration depicted South Africa as "a stabilizing influence in the Southern part of the continent" in the face of what it described as the threat of Soviet expansionism. However, on November 4, 1977, in the aftermath of the revolts of Soweto and as a reaction to the repression unleashed by the white minority government against the black movements of opposition, the Carter administration joined in a unanimous Security Council vote to impose a mandatory arms embargo on South Africa. Although the embargo was largely symbolic because South Africa had achieved virtual self-sufficiency in military production, it marked an important departure from the consistent pattern of American opposition to mandatory U.N. sanctions.

Moreover, in its first two years in office the Carter administration developed a liberal tone and image. During this period it claimed that revolutionary social transformations in the Third World should no longer be perceived as necessarily originating in the machinations of international communism. In his Commencement address at Notre Dame University, President Carter declared: "We are now free of that inordinate fear of communism which once led us to embrace any dictator who joined us in that fear."

Nonetheless, by 1978 this very fear reaffirmed itself, and the Carter administration moved toward an increasingly cold war position. It defined the Shaba rebellion against the corrupt dictatorial rule of President Mobutu of Zaire as an instance of Soviet expansionism, and it adopted a conciliatory approach to South Africa by inviting Prime Minister Botha to visit Washington and promising him a "more normal relationship."

Under these circumstances Anthony Lake was correct in identifying the Nixon-Ford-Kissinger Option Two as the "tar baby" policy[2] since it remained effective under liberal clothing during the Carter administration. . . .

58. *THE CONSERVATIVE WORLD VIEW**

by ROBERT FATTON, JR.
Robert Fatton, Jr., is identified in the headnote to Reading 57.

The first element [of the Reaganite world view] is that of a new cold war attitude which is based on the belief that any radical disruption of the international status quo is masterminded by the Soviet Union and therefore that any revolutionary movement of national liberation constitutes a Soviet surrogate. In short, the Reaganites perceive in exogenous communist forces the cause of revolutions in the Third World. Accordingly, they are profoundly anti-revolutionary, indeed reactionary in both their vision and action. They see in the East/West confrontation an unfolding struggle for hegemony over those strategically located but potentially unstable regions of the globe. In this context, they assert that the United States must regain clear military superiority in order to both resist supposed Soviet aggression and overcome the so-called "Vietnam Syndrome," which allegedly has paralyzed the use and projection of American power.

The second element of the Reaganite world view places major emphasis on

[2] After the sticky doll in the Uncle Remus story, used by Brer Fox to capture Brer Rabbit.—Ed.

*From *African Studies Review,* March 1984.

peaceful and orderly change since it perceives revolutionary social transformations as portent of Soviet gains. For this world view the promotion of such orderly change embodies the most realistic and humane option available to the U.S. because it blocks the ascendancy of "communist tyrannies" and creates the necessary conditions for the development of liberal democracies. The development of liberal democracies, however, often requires American support for authoritarian regimes.

The third element of the Reaganite world view is based on the theoretical and political distinction between "authoritarian" and "totalitarian" systems. This distinction has profound implications for the making of U.S. foreign policy. On the one hand, it leads to either a benign opposition to, or an open embrace of authoritarian regimes, since these regimes are allegedly capable of democratic transformations. On the other hand, it leads to an unbending antagonism toward totalitarian regimes because these regimes are supposedly unchangeable tyrannies destroyable only through war.

The fourth element of the Reaganite world view is deeply embedded in economic and military considerations. According to the Reaganites the U.S. should promote vigorously the development of capitalism on a world scale because it brings economic benefits to both America and those regions touched by its rational spirit and free market. This promotion, however, entails social order, political stability and economic predictability, which in turn require a military and coercive apparatus capable of quelling any "Soviet-led" revolutionary encroachment. In the Reaganite perspective then, the U.S. should encourage the capitalist penetration of the Third World and protect it from revolutionary pressures. Thus, the worldwide expansion of capitalism demands a massive military establishment.

Finally, ethnic and cultural factors impart to the Reaganite world view a definite Anglo-Saxon ethnocentrism. These factors infringe decisively on the formulation of U.S. foreign policy since they contribute to the conviction that they are responsible for the development of liberal democracy in the West and for its absence in the Third World. In other words, ethnic and cultural factors engender the Reaganite belief that authoritarianism in Third World societies is legitimate since the populations of these societies have after centuries of suffering allegedly acquiesced in the "moral authority of injustice." Accordingly, American foreign policy toward authoritarian regimes is absolved of any wrongdoings since it cannot pretend to change the long and ingrained tradition of submissiveness engulfing the politics of these regimes.

59. IN DEFENSE OF AMERICAN POLICY*

by CHESTER A. CROCKER

Statement before the Subcommittee on Africa of the House Foreign Affairs Committee on April 17, 1985. Mr. Crocker is Assistant Secretary for African Affairs and the architect of "constructive engagement."

U.S. Policy and Public Opinion

Let me begin by stating what should be obvious to all of us at this time of heightened American interest in events in South Africa: there is no support for apartheid in our country. No respectable voice is being raised in defense of that odious system or in defense of the *status quo.* No one is suggesting that our policy should be a cozy partnership—business as usual—with a government that denies elementary political and other rights to a majority of the people on the basis of race. While there is much debate in our country concerning South Africa, that debate is not about apartheid. Rather, it concerns what we can do to support change toward a just society whose system is based on the consent of the governed.

This leads to my second point. At this time of protests and other expressions of moral indignation—about apartheid and the killings of blacks in South Africa—we should be able to agree on two things. We are fully justified in expressing our moral indignation. At the same time, moral indignation by itself is not foreign policy. If we are to play a positive, constructive role, it will not do to proclaim simply that we must "do something" about apartheid and then select among proposals according to how good they make us feel. Of course, there is a role for protest politics in any free society, and we respect it. But I do not believe the American people vote for their elected leaders in Congress and the executive branch to shape our foreign policies without regard to the practical results of those policies. Hence, the onus is on all of us to consider carefully the consequences of current and alternative policies. We cannot throw our hands in the air and say, in effect, "We are not interested in the results in South Africa."

We have heard arguments to the effect that, if nothing else, punitive sanctions would send a moral signal of our concern—a signal to black South Africans that we hear their voices and a signal to South Africa's white leaders that the time for basic change is now. In our view, there are better ways of

*From *Department of State Bulletin,* June 1985.

sending signals than those proposed by the critics of President Reagan's policy. What signal is sent by adjusting U.S. export licensing procedures so that South Africa's electric utility corporation imports German or Japanese computers instead of American ones? What signal is sent when we tell black South Africans that we are going to support their cause by stopping new or existing U.S. investment so that their chances of employment with the world's most enlightened and advanced corporations will be diminished? We submit that there are far more effective ways of sending signals, many of which are part and parcel of our current policy toward South Africa.

Setting the Record Straight

. . . [W]e frequently face a litany of warped statistics, misrepresentations, or outright falsifications of the facts with the clear purpose of discrediting U.S. policy toward that country and creating a false contrast between current policies and those of previous administrations going back to the early 1960s. The record needs to be set straight.

First of all, it should be clear to any objective observer that our relationship with South Africa is far from a "normal" one. The significant embargoes and restrictions already in place on our trade and cooperation in the military and nuclear areas, as well as in our commercial relationships, demonstrate, in a tangible way, that we find apartheid repugnant and are dissociating ourselves from it. Many of these policies and practices have existed for years. We have maintained them. U.S. arms sales to South Africa have been embargoed since 1963, and in 1977 the United States joined the United Nations in imposing a further mandatory arms embargo on South Africa. Our regulations are, in fact, more severe than the UN embargo and restrict U.S. exports to the South African military and police of items not covered in the UN embargo. In December of last year, the United States joined with other UN Security Council members in voting for an embargo on imports of arms and ammunition produced in South Africa.

In the commercial area, Eximbank is essentially prohibited from financing U.S. sales to South Africa except under very restrictive circumstances. OPIC [Overseas Private Investment Corporation] does not provide guarantees for South Africa. Our representative at the IMF [International Monetary Fund] must "actively oppose any facility involving use of Fund credit by any country which practices apartheid" unless the Secretary of the Treasury makes certain certifications to Congress. U.S. trade fairs do not travel to South Africa. We carefully review license applications for the export of, among other things, U.S. crime control equipment to prevent the use of such items in the enforcement of apartheid.

This information, vital to an understanding of current American policy, is too often ignored or misrepresented in our discussions. We hear claims that the United States supports the enforcement of apartheid by permitting the South African authorities to import mainframe computers to implement the pass laws which control the lives of approximately 22 million nonvoting South Africans. This, too, is absolutely false; it has no basis in fact. Administration policy is to prohibit the sale of computers to the South African military, police, or entities enforcing apartheid. We conduct regular prelicense checks on the end-use of these computers by such agencies as the Post Office, the Reserve Bank, or the Electricity Supply Commission and have insisted on our right to do postlicense checks as well. To my knowledge, there have been no violations to date. As far as we are concerned, this is a realistic approach, balancing our moral and political responsibilities with the realities of free trade.

We hear claims from critics that, since this Administration took office, the United States has sold $100 million worth of munitions to South Africa, including such items as shock batons. These allegations are a complete distortion of the facts. The Department of State has simply not licensed any export to South Africa of any item that is subject to the UN embargo. It is important to understand that our export controls go beyond the requirements of the UN embargo. There are items on the U.S. munitions list which are not subject to the UN embargo. For example, "encryption" devices, such as those used in bank teller machines, are on the munitions list. We will authorize their export to South Africa only for use by private entities like banks, financial institutions, and U.S. corporate subsidiaries, after careful checks on the recipients and their intended uses. These items comprise 90 percent of the value of licenses given for munitions list exports to South Africa. The remaining items, while on the munitions list, had similarly valid end-use by other entities, such as image-intensifier tubes for an astronomical observatory. There are no items approved for export for military purposes.

Yes, the system of controls is not perfect. A license was mistakenly authorized by the Department of Commerce some time ago for a shipment of shock batons to South Africa. This item was not controlled by the munitions list. It was not the critics who first brought this to our attention, but the Department of Commerce, which discovered the error and brought it to light. Such an export would not have been approved if it had been handled in the normal manner. It is blatantly untrue to accuse the Administration of approving or increasing arms sales to South Africa.

Our critics accuse us of supporting South Africa's acquisition of sensitive nuclear technology, claiming that South Africa could not have developed its nuclear potential without active assistance from the United States. It must be pointed out that South Africa has pursued an independent nuclear program for three decades. It stretches the imagination to envision how any U.S. Government could have prevented a technologically advanced nation like South Africa from developing an indigenous nuclear program. U.S. law and policy bar all significant nuclear transfers to countries like South Africa that have not accepted full-scope safeguards, and we have strict controls over transfers of nuclear technology. All applications for exports of nuclear-related equipment or assistance are thoroughly and carefully reviewed so that only limited, nonsensitive transactions are permitted. The United States has approved for export to South Africa only unclassified, nonsensitive items for use in fully safeguarded civil nuclear facilities. No U.S. help was given to weapons-related research.

On the other hand, by our efforts, the South Africans have agreed to follow the London Nuclear Supplier Group's guidelines on nuclear exports and are negotiating with the IAEA [International Atomic Energy Agency] for the application of safeguards at South Africa's semicommercial enrichment plant. We strenuously reject implications that we have an irresponsible attitude toward proliferation of nuclear technology in South Africa.

. . . The helicopters flying South African soldiers and police are not American. The nuclear power plants outside Cape Town are not American. Computers used by security forces and apartheid-enforcing agencies are not American. We have in place strong and effective policies that distance our country from such fields, sending both a tangible and symbolic signal that is clearly understood in South Africa. Our policies in this regard are the most rigorous of any of its major industrial trading partners.

The fact that we are one of South Africa's largest trading partners should surprise no one, given the vast size and strength of our economy. But it makes no sense to argue that overall U.S.-South African economic relations "support apartheid"—unless one is also prepared to argue that our policy should aim at the weakening and ultimate destruction of that country's economy as a device to end apartheid. Let me be very clear on that point: we have no intention of waging economic warfare on South Africa and its people. On the contrary, we firmly believe that economic growth has been—and will continue to be—a principal engine of constructive change in all fields in that country.

The Debate over Constructive Change

. . . There *is* a debate about the basic trend of events in South Africa, whether constructive change is occurring there or not. We believe the record, though no source of complacency or satisfaction on our part, is clear: South Africa is changing for the better. It also has a long way to go, and many basic issues have not yet been adequately addressed.

This is not the place for a comprehensive statement of the case. But allow me to make two brief observations about change.

First, we must recognize that the essential precondition for progress is change in the hearts and minds of white South Africans and in the white political alignments they give rise to. Winnie Mandela, the banned wife of the imprisoned ANC [African National Congress] leader, said it best when she told ABC's Ted Koppel that the Government of South Africa holds in its hands the key to the question of whether it is too late to avoid a catastrophe, too late for constructive change. In our judgment, she is correct. Despite the obvious limitations of change seen so far, we have witnessed, over the past three years, the crossing of a historical watershed by the National Party government, which has seen major defections in its own ranks as it undertakes reforms. We cannot afford in this country to underestimate the significance of this realignment in white politics, a process which is producing an electorate and a leadership committed to reform. Many factors have played a role in that process—including our policies—but the principal pressures for change are, and will remain, internal.

Second, it should surprise no one that wildly conflicting claims are made about what is really going on in that country. We are dealing with a highly politicized and polarized situation. It does not serve the political interest of white leaders to speak openly about the implications of specific reform steps or to define clearly in advance their current vision of their bottom lines in the bargaining that surely lies ahead. Similarly, it does not serve the political interest of black leaders to give credibility to a reform process from which they have been largely excluded so far or to speak positively about reform measures and models that do not yet offer them access to the corridors of political power. We are witnessing, in short, an effort by leaders of all races in South Africa to keep the faith with their own audiences and to hang onto their constituencies. Surely, that point will be understood in this House.

We in this country have a different role and responsibility. We are only indirectly participants in a vital political process taking place 8,000 miles away. It is unseemly for us to add to the polarization and distortions that occur there. It is also unseemly for us to dismiss as trivial changes—such as the repeal of laws on marriage and sex between races—that were made in this country less than 20 years ago.

In conclusion, we believe our policies are responsible and effective. Our position on proposed economic sanctions against South Africa is but one small part of a broader policy framework to which this Administration remains committed. We also remain open to constructive ideas on how we can do better. The case against such sanctions—which have been opposed by every administration for the past 20 years—is stronger than ever precisely because of what is taking place in South Africa.

60. WHY CONSTRUCTIVE ENGAGEMENT FAILED*

by SANFORD J. UNGAR and PETER VALE

Sanford J. Ungar, former Managing Editor of Foreign Policy, *was until recently a Senior Associate of the Carnegie Endowment for International Peace. He is the author of* Africa: The People and Politics of an Emerging Continent. *Peter Vale is Research Professor and Director of the Institute of Social and Economic Research at Rhodes University in Grahamstown, South Africa.*

I

Ronald Reagan's imposition of limited economic sanctions against the South African regime in September [1985] was a tacit admission that his policy of "constructive engagement"—encouraging change in the apartheid system through a quiet dialogue with that country's white minority leaders—had failed. Having been offered many carrots by the United States over a period of four-and-a-half years as incentives to institute meaningful reforms, the South African authorities had simply made a carrot stew and eaten it. Under the combined pressures of the seemingly cataclysmic events in South Africa since September 1984 and the dramatic surge of anti-apartheid protest and political activism in the United States, the Reagan Administration was finally embarrassed into brandishing some small sticks as an element of American policy.

The Reagan sanctions, however limited, are an important symbol: a demonstration to the ruling white South African nationalists that even an American president whom they had come to regard as their virtual savior could turn against them. . . . Mr. Reagan, beating Congress to the punch, signed an executive order banning the export of computers to all official South African agencies that enforce apartheid; prohibiting most transfers of nuclear technology; preventing loans to the South African government unless they would improve social conditions for all races; ending the importation of South African Krugerrand gold coins into the United States; and limiting export assistance to American companies operating in South Africa that do not adhere to fair employment guidelines. By any measure, this was a significant development, and Pretoria's reaction of shock, anger and defiance underlined its impact.

But the sanctions, applied at once with fanfare and apologies, do not represent a fundamental change in American policy toward South Africa. Nor do

*From *Foreign Affairs,* Winter 1985/86.

they portend or promote a meaningful evolution in the South African political and social system. On the contrary, they continue the recent American practice of attempting to reform the South African system by working entirely within it and honoring its rules. "Active constructive engagement" (the new, impromptu name the President seems to have given his policy during a press conference) is still a policy that engages the attention and the interests of only a small, privileged stratum of South Africans. It relies almost entirely on white-led change, as designed and defined by a regime that is becoming more embattled by the day. And it ignores the needs, the politics and the passions of the black majority in South Africa. The policy will continue to fail.

II

Constructive engagement has not merely caused the United States to lose five valuable years when it might have influenced South Africa to begin negotiating a settlement of its unique and extraordinary racial problems. Many would argue that constructive engagement was a necessary step in the evolution of American attitudes toward South Africa, but the cost has been great. American policy has actually exacerbated the situation inside South Africa by encouraging and indulging the white regime's divide-and-rule tactics—leading that regime, its internal and external victims and much of the international community to believe that, whatever the rhetoric emanating from Washington, American prestige is on the side of the Pretoria government.

Indeed, from the time constructive engagement took effect, American trade with and investment in South Africa increased, and the Reagan Administration expanded the scope of U.S. cooperation with the South African government. It lifted previous restrictions on the export of military equipment and equipment with potential military uses; permitted (until President Reagan's recent change of heart) the sale of American computers to the police, military and other agencies of the South African government that administer apartheid; and approved the sale of shock batons to the police. The Administration also allowed the return of South African military attachés to the United States and otherwise expanded diplomatic, military and intelligence relationships between the two countries—including the establishment of several new South African honorary consulates around the United States, the provision of American training for the South African coast guard, and the resumption of official nuclear advisory contacts.

In addition, the Reagan Administration frequently stood alone on South Africa's side in the U.N. Security Council—vetoing resolutions critical of South Africa on occasions when Britain and France abstained, and, in some cases, registering the only abstention when Western allies voted to condemn South African actions.

No specific conditions were imposed on South Africa in exchange for these American favors. On the contrary, they were granted at a time when many of the restrictions on black South Africans were being tightened and tensions inside South Africa were growing. One important consequence was that, while America's official gaze was averted, a whole stratum of black South African leaders who had appeared willing to negotiate over the country's future seem to have been pushed aside by groups that advocate violent solutions. The arguments in favor of American-style, if not American-sponsored, conciliation and negotiation in South Africa may now have lost their force, as the South African drama has taken new and significant turns toward a tragic resolution.

Viewed in the context of the events of the past 15 months, South Africa's problem today is a manifestly new one. Unless steps are taken to prevent further deterioration, that country is liable to drift into uncontrollable violence fueled from the extreme right and extreme left. What is needed from the United States is not a withering debate over disinvestment or a domestic public relations campaign on behalf of constructive engagement, but an entirely new and more imaginative approach to South Africa. A policy must be crafted that not only recognizes and works with the current grim realities there, but also tries to ease the transition to an altogether different, albeit unknown, future in which blacks will take part in the government of their country. There is no longer any question that this change will occur in South Africa; the question is how, according to whose timetable and with what sort of outside involvement.

Only by establishing much more direct communication with the South African majority and by granting it far greater and more practical assistance can the United States hope to influence the course of events there. In effect, a new, parallel set of diplomatic relationships is necessary. And only by taking further steps that risk hurting the pride of South Africa's current rulers can American leaders hope to win enough credibility among South African blacks to be listened to in the debate over the country's future—a debate that will have profound consequences in all of Africa, the United States and much of the rest of the world.

III

From the start, constructive engagement meant quite different things to the four constituencies that would be most affected by it: the Reagan Administration itself, and by extension the American public; the South African government and the white population it represents; the South African black majority; and other countries in southern Africa.

The policy of constructive engagement was spelled out in 1980 by Chester A. Crocker, shortly before he became assistant secretary of state for African affairs. One of its first principles was that the previous U.S. policy of putting overt, public pressure for change on the South African regime had seemed to promise much more to black South Africans than it could deliver. . . .

Ironically, the Crocker approach made its own very ambitious promises, this time to the American public and the international community. Among other things, it offered the prospect of increased American prestige in southern Africa (with the implication that Soviet influence there would correspondingly be neutralized); a solution to the diplomatic and military conflict over Namibia (or South-West Africa), the former German colony that South Africa has continued to rule in defiance of the United Nations; and a withdrawal of Cuban troops and advisers from Angola. The latter—the prospect of an apparent setback for the Cubans—carried particular domestic political appeal in the United States, and it alone seemed to justify the sudden focus of high-level attention on Africa.

Finally, and most fundamentally, constructive engagement promised that if the United States could, as Crocker put it, "steer between the twin dangers of abetting violence in the Republic and aligning ourselves with the cause of white rule," then it could contribute to the achievement of change in South Africa. The Reagan Administration seemed to believe that P. W. Botha, who had become prime minister in 1978 and elevated himself to state president in 1984 under a new constitutional scheme, was significantly different from other, more orthodox postwar South African leaders. Botha's program of limited reforms, Crocker felt, should be encouraged and applauded by the United States, if only to safeguard American interests in South Africa and the region.

In the early days of constructive engagement, Botha appeared to be impervious to, or at least capable of outsmarting, the increasingly assertive South African right wing, composed mostly of disaffected members of the ruling National Party. What is more, the domestic situation in South Africa seemed to be secure. The nationwide upheavals associated with the Soweto riots of 1976 had subsided. Despite localized incidents of black unrest and sporadic attacks inside the country by members of the exiled African National Congress, there was no obvious political force that might be able to dislodge, or even unnerve, the Botha government. When ANC attacks got out of hand, the South African government seemed capable of neutralizing the organization with commando raids into neighboring black-ruled countries.

Reinforcing all this was the widespread impression that the South African business community—led primarily by relatively liberal English-speaking men with extensive ties to the outside world—was not only poised to play a more active role in setting the pace of reform and determining the country's future, but was also being encouraged to do so by the Afrikaner-dominated political establishment. After the uprisings of 1976, business leaders had established new foundations that would attempt to improve the lives of black people in ways that the government itself was not yet prepared to attempt. At a widely publicized meeting in Johannesburg in 1979, Botha had explicitly asked the captains of South African business and industry to help him lead the country along a new political path, and they had, for the most part, responded enthusiastically.

The Reagan Administration seemed to believe that with its domestic situation under control and improving all the time, South Africa, with American backing, could also play the role of a regional power promoting peace. Once Namibia had achieved independence under U.N. supervision (in direct exchange for the withdrawal of the Cubans from Angola, a linkage that Washington introduced into the negotiations), other regional tensions would be reduced and, the State Department hoped, recalcitrant South African whites would see the advantages of peaceful coexistence with neighboring black-ruled states.

IV

The Botha government had different expectations of constructive engagement. Indeed, for Pretoria, Ronald Reagan's victory in 1980 stirred ambitious hopes. It seemed to signal a return to the days when the South African white regime could get away with portraying itself as a protector of the Western way of life, a bastion of freedom, decency and economic development at the tip of a continent afflicted by tyranny, chaos and abject poverty—above all, a bulwark against communism.

For the four previous years, that pose had been weakened, if not entirely rejected, by Washington. Jimmy Carter, with his emphasis on human rights and his public criticisms of apartheid (made, for example, during a visit to Nigeria) had come to be regarded as public enemy number one by many South African whites, who believed that he was trying to humiliate, or perhaps even destroy them. During a press conference at the end of a dramatic confrontation with then Prime Minister John Vorster in Vienna in 1977, Vice President Walter Mondale had appeared to advocate a one-man/one-vote system for South Africa. . . .

Anti-Americanism became a powerful force in South African white politics during the Carter Administration. In an election held some months after his showdown with Mondale, Vorster was able to add 15 seats to his majority in the white parliament simply by focusing the electorate's attention on alleged U.S. meddling in the country's affairs. Indeed, Carter's promotion of a climate of distrust between Washington and Pretoria, his refusal to acknowledge and endorse South Africa's dominant role in the region, may have contributed to the growing determination of the South African military to demonstrate the country's hegemony by destabilizing the governments and economies of neighboring states.

For the National Party government, Reagan's election raised hopes for more than just a return to a "normal" relationship between the United States and South Africa. There was the prospect of a valuable endorsement of the legitimacy of the white regime and the promotion of South African leadership in the region, perhaps through the "constellation of states" concept that Vorster had introduced and Botha had promoted. When President Reagan himself, in a television interview early in his term, extolled South Africa as "a country that has stood beside us in every war we've ever fought,[1] a country that strategically is essential to the free world in its production of minerals," some South African politicians began to fantasize that their wildest dreams might come true.

Pretoria was encouraged that the Reagan Administration viewed the problems of southern Africa in the context of East-West relations, a perspective that South Africa felt had been naïvely missing from Carter's policy. South Africa's suspicion of the Soviet Union bordered on paranoia, and the new American government's tough line toward Moscow was greeted in South Africa as "political realism." Indeed, white South Africans hoped they would finally be regarded as an integral part of Western defense requirements.

In a "scope paper" to brief then Secretary of State Alexander Haig for a meeting with South African Foreign Minister Roelof F. "Pik" Botha in 1981 (and later made public by TransAfrica, the black American foreign policy lobbying organization), Crocker gave every indication that the Reagan Administration might be prepared to trust South Africa with just such responsibilities. He wrote:

> The political relationship between the United States and South Africa has now arrived at a crossroads of perhaps historic significance; the possibility may exist for a more positive and reciprocal relationship between the two countries based upon shared strategic concerns in southern Africa, our recognition that the government of P. W. Botha represents a unique opportunity for domestic change, and willingness of the Reagan administration to deal realistically with South Africa.

If the South Africans cooperated on the Namibian issue, the Crocker memo went on to argue, the United States could "work to end South Africa's polecat status in the world and seek to restore its place as a legitimate and important regional actor with whom we can cooperate pragmatically." The United States was prepared to begin this process of new, "realistic" dealings with South Africa by taking "concrete steps such as the normalization of our military attaché relationship." In other words, the State Department leadership was so

---

[1] In World War II, the Union of South Africa did indeed cast its lot with the allies, but no thanks to those now in power in Pretoria. The National Party was sympathetic to the Nazis and one of its prime ministers, B. J. Vorster, was in fact arrested and interned as a threat to wartime security. See John C. Laurence, *Race, Propaganda and South Africa* (London 1979), Chapter 6, "Allies or Enemies of the Free World?"—Ed.

enthusiastic and hopeful about this course that it was willing to make symbolic gestures to Pretoria without any advance indication that reciprocal measures would be forthcoming.

Aware of this attitude, the Botha government expected still more concessions out of constructive engagement—perhaps even some form of American recognition of the South African-designed "independent homelands" of Transkei, Bophuthatswana, Venda and Ciskei, which had been scorned and shunned by the international community but remained an important part of the grand fabric of apartheid. . . .

As far as Namibia was concerned, given the rich enticements that were being offered, South Africa seemed willing to play along with Crocker's patient, if overly optimistic, efforts to secure a settlement. Pretoria was, of course, deeply suspicious of the United Nations and skeptical of any transition to independence in Namibia that would operate in favor of the South-West Africa People's Organization, which had been designated by the United Nations as the sole legitimate representative of the territory's inhabitants. SWAPO, although it included among its membership many old-line nationalists whose views were consistent with those of European social democrats, had long been aided by the Soviet Union and other communist countries and, as an organization, officially followed a Marxist political line. Once the connection of a Namibian settlement with the departure of the Cubans from Angola had been introduced by Washington, however, it was much easier for South Africa to cooperate—or at least to give the impression of cooperating—with the Reagan Administration's efforts, which most South African political analysts thought were doomed to fail anyway.

Whether the Botha government ever could have delivered on a Namibia deal without provoking a severe crisis in the ranks of white South Africans is another question; the South African Defense Force, whose influence over the country's regional policies is profound, was, and apparently remains, hostile to any negotiations to "give away" the territory.

When it came to the issue of internal reform, P. W. Botha found it relatively easy to satisfy the Reagan Administration with his own limited agenda. Botha, as a lifelong party organizer and long-standing member of the white parliament from southern Cape province, where the population is evenly divided between whites and so-called Coloureds, had very little direct experience with other blacks. Thus, when he promoted a new constitutional scheme in 1983 establishing separate chambers of parliament for the so-called Coloureds and Asians, he was still groping to construct an alliance of minority groups that would exclude, and defend itself against, the black South African majority. When the United States appeared willing to accept the new constitution as a step in the right direction, Botha and his reformist allies were encouraged to think that they had American support on this important front. It was the impression that the United States was identifying itself with the South African government's latest scheme for preserving and prolonging apartheid that was critical to the view of constructive engagement held by most black South Africans.

V

. . . .

For years, contacts between Americans and black South Africans had grown stronger, in part through greater journalistic attention to South Africa in the United States, and in part through the growing inclination of American civil-rights and other organizations to become concerned about the South African problem. An assumption gained currency in South Africa during the presidency of John F. Kennedy that the United States sympathized with the plight of black South Africans and tended to take their side during incidents of repression and violence. Among other gestures, Kennedy's State Department for the first time required the American embassy in South Africa to invite blacks to official functions; the President's brother, Robert, was particularly involved with South Africa, and his visit there in 1964 is still remembered as an important gesture of solidarity with those who were fighting apartheid.

The Carter Administration sought to rekindle this spirit in American relations with South Africa, especially during its first two years in office. After the death of "Black Consciousness" leader Steve Biko at the hands of the South African police in 1977, the Carter Administration led the international chorus of outrage, and for a time it seemed as if American protests had helped to end deaths in detention in South Africa. Although Carter's rhetoric on the South African issue subsided as the practitioners of realpolitik gained the upper hand in his Administration, and although he repeatedly disappointed those who were waiting for the United States to vote in the United Nations for international economic sanctions against South Africa, the Carter years are nonetheless regarded by some South African blacks as a time when America was ready to help.

In the heady early days of constructive engagement, however, the Reagan Administration seemed obsessed with a need to demonstrate classic American qualities of evenhandedness. In one speech in August 1981 to the annual convention of the American Legion in Honolulu, Mr. Crocker stressed that "it is not our task to choose between black and white" in South Africa, where the United States sought "to build a more constructive relationship . . . based on shared interests, persuasion, and improved communication." . . .

To some black South African leaders, not to choose sides between the oppressors and the oppressed was tantamount to buttressing the oppressors. Already, in March 1981, Bishop Desmond Tutu, then secretary-general of the

South African Council of Churches, had warned that "a United States decision to align itself with the South African government would be an unmitigated disaster for both South Africa and the United States." Tutu cautioned that the appearance of a reconciliation between Pretoria and the most influential government in the West would negate years of attempts by black South Africans to achieve a peaceful realization of their political ambitions.

Four months later, a well-known black South African academic, N. Chabani Manganyi, . . . called upon the Reagan Administration to fulfill its moral obligation to the people of South Africa and the international community by applying pressure for change; he said that whereas the Carter Administration had given blacks hope, "it could well be that President Reagan is preparing us for despair."

So preoccupied was the Reagan Administration with sending signals to South Africa's white minority, however, that it is not clear its representatives paid heed to such warnings. Crocker exacerbated the situation by failing to include formal, public meetings with black South Africans on the itineraries of his many trips to South Africa, which received prominent coverage in the South African press. . . .

Especially offensive to some black South Africans was the fact that the United States expressed no opposition to the Pretoria government's latest divide-and-rule tactic, the new constitution creating separate chambers of parliament for so-called Coloureds and Asians—nor to the conduct of a whites-only referendum in November 1983 for approval of the constitution. In a speech to the National Conference of Editorial Writers in San Francisco in June 1983, U.S. Under Secretary of State Lawrence Eagleburger stated:

> I do not see it as our business to enter into this debate or to endorse the constitutional proposals now under consideration. Nor do we offer tactical advice to any of the interested parties. Yet the indisputable fact which we must recognize is that the South African government has taken the first step toward extending political rights beyond the white minority.

In the view of black South Africans, who were almost universally opposed to the new constitution (even the leaders of six of the homelands urged a negative vote in the referendum), the United States could hardly have devised a clearer endorsement of the proposals. . . . Most blacks saw the new institutions as a farce. . . .

VI

American officials who spoke on behalf of constructive engagement liked to stress as often as possible that it was intended not merely as a policy toward South Africa, but as an effort to deal with the entire southern African region and its problems—thus Washington's promotion of direct talks between South Africa and Angola and its pleasure over the signing of the Nkomati accord between South Africa and Mozambique.

Most governments in the region, however, saw few benefits from constructive engagement. On the contrary, they saw evidence of a dangerous new South African military ascendancy, as the South African Defense Force seemed newly emboldened to strike across frontiers—into Mozambique, Lesotho, Botswana and, above all, Angola—in pursuit of ANC or SWAPO guerrillas and activists. The South Africans certainly supplied and trained the Mozambique National Resistance (MNR or Renamo), whose destructive war against the hard-pressed government of Samora Machel drove him to sign the Nkomati accord. (The accord called for Mozambique to expel ANC guerrillas in exchange for a suspension of South African aid to the MNR; documents recently discovered in Pretoria revealed that while Mozambique kept its part of the bargain, South Africa did not.) South Africa also kept up the pressure on the Marxist government in Angola by continuing to supply the rebel forces of the National Union for the Total Independence of Angola (UNITA) led by Jonas Savimbi. What is more, there have been few moments during the past ten years when there were not substantial numbers of South African troops inside Angola itself; last spring, South African commandos were captured in the Cabinda enclave (a part of Angola that is separated from the rest by a thin piece of Zaïre) as they were preparing to sabotage an American-owned oil-drilling installation.

At the same time, South Africa also found economic means of destabilizing its neighbors and demonstrating its political hegemony over weaker states. The United States tried to put distance between itself and the South Africans on the issue of destabilization, frequently condemning its cross-border incursions and finally, after the raids in Cabinda and Botswana, withdrawing the American ambassador to Pretoria, Herman Nickel, for several months. Yet it seems clear that South Africa felt comfortable taking these steps against its neighbors without fear of serious recriminations from Washington.

Indeed, the U.S. Congress has been pushing the Administration to resume American aid to UNITA; while intended as a means of demonstrating toughness toward Cuba and the Soviet Union, this action would have the primary effect of advancing South Africa's interests in the region. Savimbi is clearly Pretoria's client, and is regarded as such throughout Africa; in fact, there is no way to aid him without going through South Africa.

For a time it appeared that the Reagan Administration would be willing to complement its new closeness with Pretoria with substantial aid programs for nearby black-ruled states. But those programs rarely materialized, and when they did, as in the case of Mozambique, opposition from conservatives on Capitol Hill made them almost impossible to carry out. In the case of Zimbabwe, where the United States had made an international commitment of aid at the time of independence in 1980, the Reagan Administration decided to punish Prime Minister Robert Mugabe for his foreign policy positions—including his sponsorship of a U.N. resolution condemning the U.S. invasion of Grenada in 1983—by cutting back substantially.

VII

After nearly five years, then, constructive engagement has failed on every front and with all of its constituencies.

The American public has seen little to indicate new U.S. diplomatic or strategic strength in southern Africa; on the contrary, the region is in as much turmoil as ever, and the Soviets have suffered few notable setbacks. The Cubans are still in Angola, and Namibia is no closer to independence; indeed, the South Africans recently instituted a new internal regime there, in direct defiance of American wishes.

Within South Africa itself, the United States has given a great deal and seen little progress as a result. The only concrete achievements of constructive engagement, apart from the shattered Angolan-South African truce and the now-discredited Nkomati accord, were a brief period of leniency by the Pretoria government toward black trade unions and the granting of passports to black spokesmen invited to the United States, such as Tutu and [Dr. Nthatho] Motlana [chairman of Soweto's "Committee of Ten"].

But the Reagan Administration can hardly claim that constructive engagement has brought about genuine improvements in the lives of South Africans. On the contrary, the piecemeal reforms that have been enacted in the past five years have been the object of resentment. The introduction of the new tricameral parliamentary system has coincided with the most devastating internal violence the country has experienced since the formation of the unified South African state in 1910. Unrest has flared during the past year in every part of the country, and the imposition of the state of emergency has done little to quell it. In addition to the hundreds of known deaths and thousands of detentions that have occurred in recent months, more than one hundred South Africans have mysteriously vanished, many of them suspected victims of clandestine elements within the state security apparatus. The South African economy is in a shambles, and the country has been forced to postpone payment of many of its international debts. In some rural areas, such as the strife-torn eastern Cape, black unemployment is estimated to be as high as 60 percent.

The South African government, having expected so much, is itself disappointed with constructive engagement. It has reverted to old-style denunciations of American pressure as counterproductive, and it is furious over even the limited sanctions—worried that other nations may do the same or more and weaken the South African economy further. Far from strengthening its network of homelands, South Africa now finds itself having to think about dismantling them altogether or using them to create a new "federation." Its economic and military dominance of southern Africa is apparently intact, but it is not clear how long that will last if domestic turmoil continues. South Africa's formidable military machine is now required almost full time to help suppress internal unrest, despite a recently announced increase of 25 percent in recruitments into the police force. . . .

. . . With President Reagan appearing at times to justify the excesses committed by the South African government under the terms of the state of emergency and at other times seeming to exaggerate the degree of reform that has already taken place, the United States is viewed increasingly by black South Africans as part of the problem rather than part of the solution.

Similarly, other southern African states are blaming constructive engagement for much of their own distress. In some cases, overestimating the degree of actual American influence on the South African government, they have developed unrealistic expectations of what the United States can do to improve their situations, and they are bound to be disappointed.

VIII

It is time for a new American policy toward South Africa that will help restore the reputation of the United States as a defender of human rights and racial justice in that country and will serve the broader interests of all South Africans and Americans.

There are, of course, important limitations on the American ability to affect the situation in South Africa. The U.S. military is not about to intervene on any side in any current or future crisis; it is foolish for whites or blacks in South Africa to believe otherwise (as some of them do). Nor can American leaders wave political or economic wands that will transform South Africa overnight. Indeed, American sanctions or moves toward disinvestment from the South African economy are sometimes more important on both sides as symbols than as practical measures; when sanctions are invoked, they should be carefully calibrated and thoughtfully applied. Given the level of suffering that already exists in the country, it is in no one's interest to destroy the South African economy or to induce further chaos in the country. And despite the frequent declarations from many quarters about the willingness of black South Africans to endure sacrifices in exchange for eventual freedom, it is not for the United States to condemn them to more abject poverty and deprivation. Disinvestment efforts within the United States should be directed only against particular firms that are known to have conducted themselves in an antisocial, regressive manner within South Africa. As for the continued presence of American business in South Africa, individual companies, evaluating their risks on the basis of hard-nosed, pragmatic criteria, are making their own rational decisions on whether to stay or not.

But there are some official steps that the United States can take in an effort to move South Africa toward meaningful change and full participation by all of its people in the affairs of the country. If Americans still want to try to assure that the South African transition occurs relatively peacefully and with a minimum of vindictiveness on the part of blacks, then there is little time left to act.

The first step, uncomfortable as it may seem to many Americans, is to restore a forthright atmosphere of public and private confrontation to relations between Washington and Pretoria—precisely the sort of independent attitude that Mr. Crocker has eschewed. Internal and external pressure is the only thing that has ever produced meaningful change in South Africa. American officials need to become far more direct and persistent in their condemnations of apartheid. Speeches at the National Press Club in Washington alone cannot do the job. U.S. representatives in South Africa must be willing to denounce and even defy the system whenever possible, making clear their official and personal support for organizations like the UDF [United Democratic Front] and Black Sash, the women's group that represents the victims of arbitrary "pass arrests" and other government actions. Some things may have to be said or done many times before they are believed or credited by disillusioned blacks.

All of this would have the immediate effect of helping develop a healthier, more vigorous multiracial opposition within South Africa, which would be far more difficult for the regime to crush if it clearly enjoyed outside support. If an American decision to confront apartheid more boldly also stiffened the resolve of other Western nations and ultimately led to a growing international vote of no-confidence in the leadership of P. W. Botha, that too would be a desirable turn of events. It is now obvious that as long as he remains in power, the National Party will not be able to form or endorse the alliances with other political factions that are necessary to head off full-scale civil war.

The current South African government, under the short-sighted impression that it has profited from a five-year interlude of conciliation with the United States, would be bitterly resentful of such a reversion to prior strategy by Washington. It would undoubtedly attempt once again to profit politically from American hostility and would proclaim, as it must, that this is the surest way for the United States to lose, rather than gain, influence in South Africa. But the truth is that South Africa has few other places to turn. It is dependent on the United States, in spirit as well as in fact; fellow "pariah states," such as Israel and Taiwan—its other current friends—simply cannot do for South Africa what America can do. And if constructive confrontation hastened the start of negotiations over real power in South Africa, which constructive engagement has failed to do, that would be a step forward.

IX

Once having restored a proper sense of balance and confrontation to U.S.-South African relations, it would be important for the American government and private business interests to devise additional measures that might hurt the pride and prestige of the white South African government without inflicting undue economic damage on black South Africans. Some of the measures should be selectively instituted for predetermined periods, in response to particular events in South Africa, with the American government making it clear that they may be lifted if circumstances improve. Alternatively, if the situation continues to deteriorate, the pressures could be intensified.

The landing rights enjoyed by the state-owned South African Airways in the United States can be reduced or terminated. The availability of almost daily direct service between Johannesburg and New York, with only a stop in the Cape Verde Islands, is a great advantage to South African businessmen and officials, and since Pan American abandoned its service for economic reasons earlier this year, the South African state airline has a monopoly on the route's substantial profits. Far from considering this step, which has frequently been proposed in the past, the Reagan Administration actually expanded South African Airways' landing rights in the United States in 1982, permitting direct service between Johannesburg and Houston (later suspended). The cancellation of direct air service is a sanction the United States has frequently taken to demonstrate disapproval of actions by other governments—including the Soviet Union, Cuba, Poland and Nicaragua. Because of the importance to South Africans of their links to the outside world, this would probably be more likely to have an effect in South Africa than it did in those other countries.

The United States can take steps to reduce South Africa's privileged diplomatic status here. South African military attachés can be expelled, for example, especially in the wake of external raids and other objectionable actions by the South African Defence Force. The visa-application process for South Africans who wish to travel to the United States can be made as complicated and cumbersome as it is already for Americans who seek to visit South Africa. And if Pretoria proceeds with its policy of making it more difficult for American journalists to travel to South Africa, and to have the necessary access when they do get there, then the number of official South African information officers permitted in the United States can be reduced.

The United States has recently sought South African permission to open a new consulate in Port Elizabeth to establish an official American presence in the troubled eastern Cape. The Reagan Administration must take care not to grant unnecessary concessions in exchange; South Africa already has four full-fledged and four honorary consulates in the United States.

The flow of new American technology to South Africa can be further restricted, especially as it relates to the repressive domestic tactics of the South African government and its raids against neighboring countries. President Reagan's restriction on the shipment of computers to South Africa had little immediate effect because most of the material to which it applied was already in South African hands or could easily be obtained from other countries. Rigorous steps can be taken, however, including the use of U.S. Customs Service agents and other law enforcement personnel, to be sure that other American technological advances do not reach the South African police or military, directly or through third countries. It would also be possible to improve American compliance with the international arms embargo against South Africa and to take further steps to prevent nuclear material from reaching the country. It is widely known that some American companies operating in South Africa are involved in strategic industries, and therefore in the regime's domestic and international war effort; this could be prevented with new federal rules governing American corporate behavior in South Africa.

The U.S. government can severely restrict, or even suspend entirely, its intelligence cooperation with the South African government. There is reason to believe that these ties have helped the South Africans far more than the United States, and they carry the implication that the United States is complicit in some of the worst abuses committed by South Africa against neighboring countries. One of the most troubling aspects of this problem is that some operatives of U.S. intelligence agencies and some State Department employees who have served in South Africa are outspokenly sympathetic to the apartheid policies of the white regime and have occasionally used their positions to thwart official American actions and directives.

The United States can seek to internationalize discussion of the South African issue by putting it on the agenda of the annual Western economic summits. This would be a way of coordinating economic pressures on South Africa, and also of trying to persuade recalcitrant nations, such as Japan, which has richly profited from its pragmatic relationship with South Africa (the Japanese have status as "honorary whites"), to go along with the measures.

X

Even more important, perhaps, are positive, lasting steps that the United States can take to demonstrate its sympathy for the black majority in South Africa and to show that it does not believe all change there must be white-led.

The United States must open a dialogue with the African National Congress and other black organizations that have widespread support among black South Africans, just as Secretary of State George Shultz has suggested the white South Africans themselves should do. Not to know what the ANC, the oldest black nationalist organization in South Africa, is thinking and doing is not only bad diplomacy but also foolish politics. If South African businessmen and white opposition politicians have recently held such discussions, certainly American officials will be taking no great risk by doing so. As it is, there is a feeling among some black South Africans that the attitude of the ANC may now be too moderate, in view of the pace of events within South Africa, and thus the United States may have to open relations with much more radical organizations. This contact with black South African leaders should take place at the ambassadorial level, both inside and outside South Africa, as a means of stressing the American rejection of the notion that the white government is the only meaningful political institution in the country.

The United States should send a black ambassador—a man or woman of international stature—to South Africa as soon as possible, to demonstrate important points of principle to South Africans of all racial groups. Above all, this would be an opportunity to emphasize the valuable role that black people play in a multi-racial society and a system which South Africans often compare to their own. Some might complain that such an appointment smacks of tokenism, but if the ambassador behaved in an appropriate manner, his presence would be of more than symbolic value. For example, this new ambassador should attend the funerals of blacks killed by the police, political trials, and church services in black communities, as American diplomats in South Africa used to do. He should provide facilities for the meetings of groups that are trying to organize peaceful protests against the apartheid system and, in other respects, make it clear that he is the ambassador of all Americans to all South Africans, not just of white America to white South Africa. He should not take it upon himself to play American politics in South Africa—as the current U.S. ambassador did when he denounced Senator Kennedy while introducing him at a meeting of the American Chamber of Commerce of Johannesburg—but rather should take it as one of his jobs to convey to South Africans the depth of American feeling against apartheid and the so far inadequate steps to dismantle it.

Massive aid programs, funded by the American government, foundations and business, should be instituted to help black South Africans attain better educations in a broad range of fields, from engineering to international relations. The money for such programs should be distributed to all South African educational institutions, regardless of their nature, but special attention should be paid to encouraging the further integration of the mostly white elite universities. The committees that decide how this money is to be spent should have a majority of black South Africans. American-sponsored educational programs already available have barely scratched the surface; what is needed now is an effort to help black South Africans learn how to help run their country, an eventuality that seems not to have occurred to the ruling whites.

The United States should offer publicly to send forensic pathologists and other experts from the Federal Bureau of Investigation into South Africa to help find South Africans who have mysteriously disappeared and to help determine the cause of death of those who have been found. This has proved to be an effective technique in Central American countries such as El Salvador, where the police do not always care to solve crimes. The South African police are accused of acting to frustrate, rather than advance, the solution of some crimes against black people, and such outside help might well be appropriate. If the South Africans at first refuse such aid, the United States should offer it again and again, until its refusal becomes an embarrassment and a liability to the white government.

The United States government, in conjunction with professional groups such as the American Bar Association, should also send legal aid to black South Africans. Although the legal systems differ in certain important respects, the American experience with public defenders and government-funded legal services is an excellent example for the South Africans. American law schools and private foundations, for example, could help train black South Africans as paralegal workers, who in turn could establish elementary legal clinics in remote areas of the country, where the civil and human rights of blacks are the most egregiously and routinely violated; these paralegal workers could in turn report to lawyers, who make sure that the abuses are brought to the attention of the courts and the press. The American legal community could also assist the South Africans in the creation of a lawyers' organization in which blacks play a prominent role. (Such an association of doctors and dentists was recently established in South Africa, but unfortunately it is still not officially recognized by the American Medical Association.)

The United States should not only support the efforts of the black-led labor unions in South Africa, but where possible, should also send expert American union organizers to help them strengthen their institutions. Until and unless other structures are established, South Africa's black unions represent one of the few ways that the disenfranchised majority can become involved in political action, and American labor organizations have relevant experience to offer in this domain.

The American government should carefully monitor the performance of U.S. companies operating in South Africa, with a view toward creating and publicizing a list of those who treat their black workers badly. Indeed, American companies should be pressed by their government into playing a far more progressive role in South Africa—for example, by ignoring the Group Areas Act and establishing mixed housing areas where black and white South Africans can create de facto integrated neighborhoods. U.S. businesses operating in South Africa should also make every effort to visit any of their employees who are detained on political grounds and should establish a fund to be used for their legal defense.

The United States should help black South Africans increase and improve their means of communication with each other and the rest of the South African people. The exchange of South African and American journalists should be promoted, along with technical assistance in establishing black publications at the grass roots and black-oriented radio stations. Americans can help South Africans understand that a free press can often be one of the most important safety values available to a society where there is political discontent. Severe consequences should be invoked, such as restrictions on South African diplomatic personnel in the United States, if black publications are closed and banned in South Africa, as they often have been in the past.

XI

In sum, courageous efforts must be made to convince black South Africans that Americans identify with their plight and are willing to help. There have been times in U.S.-South African relations—before constructive engagement—when officials from the American embassy were the first to be called by black activists in moments of crisis, and there were even U.S. officials in South Africa who occasionally sheltered political fugitives or helped them escape from the country. This was a role more consistent with American principles than the current one of keeping a distance from anyone charged by the government.

Recent developments indicate that P. W. Botha, far from responding creatively to the American confidence in him, is resorting once again to repression rather than reform. Concerned about minor electoral losses on the right, he is ignoring the rumbling volcano of discontent on the other side, from blacks and whites alike. His recent curbs on domestic and foreign press coverage of unrest in South Africa are a sign that the last vestiges of decency—South Africa's last claims to be part of the Western democratic tradition—may soon be destroyed in the defense of apartheid.

The United States must clearly and unequivocally disassociate itself from such measures. And it must resist the ever-present temptation to use southern Africa as a place to score points in the East-West struggle. Only after America rediscovers its voice—and its principles—in South Africa can it hope to play a truly constructive role in the region once again.

61. DON'T PUSH SOUTH AFRICA TO THE WALL*

by KAREN ELLIOTT HOUSE

Karen Elliott House is The Wall Street Journal's *foreign editor.*

It's a whole lot easier to exert public political pressure than it is to fashion political solutions.

Nowhere is this so evident as in South Africa today, where the U.S. is trying to put the political and economic screws to the white Afrikaner government to speed the dismantling of apartheid and force the sharing of political power with the country's black majority.

But two weeks of travel throughout South Africa indicates the pressure isn't working. Indeed, it's having precisely the opposite effect. America's political strictures and economic sanctions have simply served to harden the attitudes of those who hold power, to raise unrealistic expectations among those who seek power, and to damage the economic fortunes and futures of the great majority of South Africans caught in between.

There is little doubt that this society and its abhorrent system of apartheid are going to change. Even the most hard-line Afrikaners see the handwriting on the wall and are talking about reaching accommodations that will leave them segregated in some white "homeland" enclave much like those apartheid has created for the blacks. Less militant whites—and there are many more of these—hope for a multiracial society inevitably ruled by the black majority, but with some protection for white and other minorities. The only real issue here is *when* such change will take place, not *whether,* and the when is a matter of years, not generations. Yet in its rush to hasten change, America risks pushing the South African economy further along a downward spiral so that there will be little left for the victors to inherit.

Clinging to Survival

Already the signs of suffering are everywhere as South Africa's economy, plagued by continued drought and depressed gold prices, grinds to a virtual standstill. . . .

Businessmen and government officials all agree that the maximum economic growth possible without foreign investment is 3 percent. In other words, just

*From *The Wall Street Journal,* October 30, 1985.

enough to preserve the status quo; not enough to improve the lot of blacks.

To the extent that a bigger slice of the pie for blacks comes at the expense of whites—and it must if the pie isn't expanding—racial tensions are bound to rise. Sanctions and disinvestment cripple the economy, and the greatest pain is borne by its weakest and most marginal members—who are black. This obviously breeds frustration, anger and violence. The violence erodes international confidence in the economy, leading to further reductions in investment that lead to more layoffs, more anger and more violence.

In short, it's easier to sit in America and argue the moral justification for applying economic pressure to South Africa than it is to walk through the streets of New Brighton or Soweto and see the mounting practical effects.

Beyond all this, the U.S. insistence on economic sanctions and disinvestment also is hardening the right wing, which, like it or not, holds the reins of power in South Africa. Enlightened self-interest should lead the government to continue and accelerate reforms. And, in fact, it has. The decisions over the past two years to give the vote to coloureds and Indians, to legalize mixed-race marriages and to allow black labor unions all are due more to internal economic realities than to external pressure. "They [the Afrikaner establishment] discovered they couldn't run the country alone," says Zach de Beer, a director of Anglo American Corp. and a consistent critic of apartheid.

Undeniably, South African President P. W. Botha is a man of limited vision. . . . The betting is he'll step aside in a year or so. Given pressures inside the ruling National Party, as well as those from its liberal opponents and the business community, more significant reform seems inevitable though probably still slower than Americans and black victims of apartheid would like.

Regardless, Americans should resist the impulse to try to force a faster pace of change. Already, righteous rhetoric in Congress and presidential pronouncements about the impending doom of apartheid are creating unrealistic expectations among blacks.

And that worries even apartheid's more ardent opponents. "Blacks are getting the idea that external pressure and the nongovernability of the townships will give them victory just around the corner," says Helen Suzman, a tiny but tough woman in her 60s who is the longest-sitting member of Parliament and the grande dame of anti-apartheid. "The risk is that Western powers are inadvertently encouraging blacks to launch violence against whites, and then the government is really going to unleash its terrible power on these kids." . . .

Another reason for the U.S. to forswear more sanctions—and sanctimonious rhetoric—is that, historically, pressure hasn't worked very well. Rhodesia survived nearly 15 years of sanctions. Israel has survived more than 30 years of economic and political pressures from much of the world. Whether it's the Soviet Union or Taiwan, Iran or Nicaragua, no national power structures have proved very vulnerable to economic and political pressures from outsiders. Perhaps if every nation in the world refused any commerce or contact with white South Africa the regime would collapse quickly, but that seems far-fetched in a real world in which even black African nations are openly or surreptitiously trading with South Africa.

The U.S. also should drop its insistence that the white government negotiate with terrorists. It's hypocritical to ask South Africa to negotiate with the African National Congress, which vows the violent overthrow of the white government, when the U.S. doesn't press Israel to negotiate with the Palestine Liberation Organization, because it vows the destruction of Israel. Clearly America isn't standing on principle. It's simply letting domestic politics dictate foreign policy. American Jews and their supporters oppose talks with the pro-violence PLO. American blacks and their supporters favor talks with the pro-violence ANC. The point isn't that consistency is necessarily an absolute virtue, but rather than negotiating with terrorists is generally a mistake. Like Yasser Arafat, exiled ANC leader Oliver Tambo, safe in Zambia, repeatedly calls for youths to give their lives for the struggle.

Inherit the Ruins

The more the U.S. insists on negotiations with the ANC, the more it strengthens the violent extreme and undermines the moderate middle. Indeed, already Mr. Tambo is greeted as a hero at various international gatherings. South African businessmen traipse to Lusaka, Zambia, for a word with the exiled leader, who pointedly repeats his determination to dismantle not just apartheid but capitalism as well. Meanwhile, Chief Mangosuthu Buthelezi, leader of Africa's largest black tribe, the Zulus, is shunned by many South African businessmen and most international groups. Why? Basically, because he's a moderate who, while opposing apartheid, doesn't believe it makes sense to destroy the country in order to inherit the ruins a little faster.

Once the U.S. insists the ANC is the legitimate voice of black Africans, then the ANC becomes the only group with whom the Pretoria government can negotiate if it wants to retain some measure of international approval and investment. Yet the ANC has made it clear it isn't interested in sharing power, just seizing power.

Finally, America must be true to its belief that it is the rights of the individual that are sacred, rather than the interests of any particular group. South Africa long ago made the mistake of structuring its society on the rights, or lack of them, of racial groups. The U.S. shouldn't participate in schemes that simply transfer power from one racial group to another, while still guaranteeing no protection for the individual—regardless of color.

62. THE STRATEGIC IMPORTANCE OF SOUTH AFRICA*

by LARRY BOWMAN

Larry Bowman was a consultant to the Rockefeller Foundation-financed Study Commission on U.S. Policy Toward Southern Africa whose report, South Africa: Time Running Out, *was published in 1981. Professor Bowman is a member of the Department of Political Science at the University of Connecticut, Storrs.*

The Cape Route

. . . .

It is hard to think of the Cape route as a "choke-point," once the logistical requirements are considered of somehow blockading the sea between the Cape and Antarctica. Now, obviously, most ships circumventing the Cape pass close to the South African shore and would be most vulnerable there. But the logistical requirements that the Soviet Union would face in positioning its ships for such a blockade, let alone the likely political and military consequences that would quickly ensue, make the whole proposition dubious at best. R. W. Johnson has argued that "the whole idea of Russian submarines starving the West into submission by a strategy of protracted interdiction or blockade was . . . absurdly nineteenth century in its conception. The very first ship sinking, after all, would constitute a major act of war and the nuclear bombers and missiles would be in the air only a few minutes later.". . .

Robert Price . . . asks two key questions: If the Soviet Union wished to interdict Western oil shipments, why would it do so at the Cape? And if the Soviet Union was prepared for a war with the West, why would it want its navy in South African waters? . . . Obviously, if the Soviet Union wished to halt the flow of oil to the West, it could do so far more efficiently by bombing the oilfields or blockading the Straits of Hormuz. Because of their proximity to the Soviet Union, each of these operations could be carried out much more effectively than any operation off the Cape. As for the war that would certainly ensue from any such provocative Soviet behaviour, Price notes that the Soviet Union would need its navy in the North Atlantic and Mediterranean, where it could assist in responding to the nuclear threat posed by US SLBMs (submarine launched ballistic missiles). Any ships based as far away as South African waters could be easily destroyed by US air power. It seems to me, therefore, in a view shared by many others, that there is no credible reason for

*From *Southern Africa in the 1980s* (London, 1985) [condensed].

the Cape route argument alone to be deemed a sufficient basis to build strategic ties with South Africa.

The Soviet Threat

Even if we agree that a superpower naval confrontation in Southern African waters is unlikely, this does not detract from the legitimate concern that the United States and its allies have about communist influence in the continent. . . .

But how great really is the threat? There are numerous states in Africa—Egypt, the Sudan, Somalia, Guinea, Ghana and Uganda, among others—where the Soviet Union at one time or another has had what was believed to be considerable influence, only to lose it. . . . Today the two countries in Africa which have the preponderance of communist military and civilian personnel —Angola and Ethiopia—are far from being supine puppets of the Soviet Union. Indeed, there is evidence from both countries, and particularly from Angola, that they would like to broaden their ties with Western countries. The continuing refusal of the USA to recognize Angola only serves to induce Angola to remain close to the Soviet Union and Cuba, a result we presumably would wish to avoid. . . . In an extensive analysis of Soviet African policy for *Problems of Communism* David Albright argues that the Soviet Union has "no grand design" for Africa and they do not really anticipate any " 'genuine' Marxist-Leninist breakthroughs in Africa." None the less, he expects "continuing Soviet efforts to take advantage of whatever openings develop."

. . . But there is little evidence to suggest that deepening our strategic ties with South Africa is a sensible way to confront this possibility. . . . What is needed . . . is a policy focused on African realities rather than one which simply sees Africa through the prism of superpower competition. . . .

The West really has little to fear from directly competing with the Soviet Union on all issues of importance to Africa [Daird] Newsom [Assistant Secretary of State for Africa, 1969–73] summarizes:

> The Soviets do not provide a market for most African goods; they are not part of the world economic system; not members of the IMF; they have no multilateral companies to spread technology; their ruble is not convertible. . . .

Unless things in Africa change dramatically in directions not now foreseen, there is little reason to believe that Western strategic ties with South Africa would be helpful for stemming opportunities for Soviet penetration of the continent. . . .

Access to Strategic Minerals

This final argument for maintaining strategic ties with South Africa is probably the most commonly heard. . . . No one really disputes the importance of South African mineral deposits. Once the raw figures are adduced, many jump to the conclusion that South Africa is strategically important and must be supported. . . .

At almost exactly the same time that the [1980] Santini Report [confirming U.S. dependency on South African mineral supplies] was being presented, the Subcommittee on African Affairs of the US Senate was receiving a report on exactly the same topic that it had commissioned from the Congressional Research Service. The key conclusion of this report was that "South African minerals are of significant, but not critical, importance to the West."

Three questions seem to dominate the debate about South Africa's mineral importance to the USA. One has to do with the likelihood of a cut-off of mineral supplies from South Africa; the second has to do with the possibility of South Africa and the Soviet Union conspiring as to supply and price of key minerals; finally, there is the question of US and Western vulnerability to the loss of South African minerals in either the short or long term, given the range of alternatives available. Taken in turn, each seems to me to clearly counter the facile reasoning that often underlies the mineral-dependency argument.

In 1980 the South African mining industry generated 67 percent of South African export earnings, up from 57 per cent in 1979. To say the least mineral exports are vital to the health of the South African economy. Can anyone really foresee the circumstances when *any* South African government would be in a position to forego these massive earnings ($25.6 billion in 1980)? . . . If a radical or leftist government were to come to power in South Africa, it would be even more dependent on mineral earnings in as much as it would presumably be seeking to improve the lot of all South Africans. And the hard truth of the mineral world is that only the USA and its Western allies (plus Japan) are likely purchasers of these minerals. . . .

A second concern has to do with the fear that a liberated South Africa might join with the Soviet Union in a minerals cabal against the West. . . .

. . . [It] does not seem plausible to argue that African states would want to cut off mineral sales; their economies could not stand it and there is no evidence to suggest that the USSR and its allies would step in as alternative buyers. The speed with which Angola and Zimbabwe have sought to stabilize their resource sales to the West underscores this point; would South Africa really be any different? Secondly, it needs to be noted that South Africa and the Soviet Union *already* collaborate on the world minerals market. Several recent reports have revealed that these two countries talk regularly together about the marketing of diamonds, gold and platinum; there are even suggestions that they may move into further collaboration on mining expertise and metals technology. While future projections about these contacts can only be speculative, it can at least be said that a pattern of co-operation with the USSR has been undertaken by apartheid South Africa and it need not await a South African revolution.

Finally, there is the matter of vulnerability to a minerals cut-off, and the industrial and defense problems that could cause. The Rockefeller Foundation-funded Study Commission on US Policy Toward Southern Africa looked at this problem in detail; it also had the benefit of other recent studies. The commission concluded that there were only four minerals—chromium, platinum-group metals, vanadium and manganese—that posed any real problem. The commission carefully reviewed the supply situation with respect to each mineral, but in no case did it foresee a problem that could not be overcome with foresight and planning. . . .

Taken together it simply does not seem to me that the Cape route, the Soviet threat, . . . and the minerals issue, sufficiently make a case for the necessity of building strong strategic relations with the present South African government.

63. *SOUTH AFRICA: A STORY IN BLACK AND WHITE**

by E. IMAFEDIA OKHAMAFE

E. Imafedia Okhamafe is Assistant Professor of Humanities at the University of Nebraska, Omaha. He is at work on a transvaluational critique of African literature.

The South African situation has racial strategic, economic, religious, social and political dimensions. But the current attempt by one vocal and influential wing of American conservatism or fundamentalism to paint the basic conflict in South Africa as apartheid versus Marxism rather than apartheid versus freedom masks the fundamental cause of this historic conflict: the institutionalization of a religiously and governmentally sanctioned white supremacy. Racist apologists usually preface their defense of Pretoria with an anti-apartheid rhetoric: we strongly condemn apartheid, but we don't want to push Botha too much, too quickly or too far lest we push South Africa into Marxist hands.

*From *The Black Scholar,* November/December 1985.

Consequently, this monomania, this sole concern with Marxism, aims not at the death of apartheid but at the reformation of apartheid.

But is there an acceptable form of apartheid? Is a reformed slavery, a reformed Stalinism, a reformed Nazism, a reformed fascism or a reformed Idi-Aminism acceptable? Is apartheid not Nazism? What, in a hierarchy of evils, surpasses apartheid? How can any system which is legally entrenched in and militarily or violently committed to the notion of separate and unequal development for the different races be reformed? Are there some palatable forms of apartheid? History teaches us that every form of apartheid is inedible.

Until the Bothas face the fact that no form of apartheid is palatable, South Africa will know no civic peace. Therefore, changing the image of apartheid is not a workable solution. Apartheid, for black South Africans or nonwhites, is a terminal cancer which must be terminated.

Reagan's policy of "constructive engagement" is a euphemism for the reformation of apartheid. This policy is not quite new. It has never worked as an apartheid-ending mechanism. It did not bring down the Verwoerds or the Vorsters. It has not and will not bring down the Bothas. When apartheid eventually falls or dies, it will not be because of "constructive engagement." Apartheid's death will come from deconstructive engagement.

Rightist Marxiphobia, which overshadows the debasement of a black majority by a white minority, is understandable in light of the history of the American ultra-right wing but somewhat unjustifiable, epecially in the South African context. The Red-based case for apartheid is a red herring. The Richard Vigueries and Jerry Falwells profess to reject apartheid on moral or religious grounds but defend it on political grounds. For them, apartheid may be evil, but its evilness fades when compared with Marxism. As Richard Viguerie put it in a recent appearance on television (CNN's *Crossfire*): "If I were black, I would prefer apartheid to communism."

Viguerie (who here reversely echoes Mandela's much maligned statement that even though he is not a communist, communism is preferable to apartheid), does not understand the reality of influx controls which leads suffering but resolute Mandela to say that Marxism is a lesser evil. Furthermore, the Vigueries believe that there is no acceptable alternative to apartheid since, for them, the only alternative to apartheid is Marxism. As Viguerie again put it, South Africa will continue to "have white rule for the foreseeable future. The question is whether that white ruler will be South African or Soviet."

Black Capacity to Rule

Inherent in this position is the assumption that blacks are incapable of ruling themselves, or as apartheid managers will bluntly put it: blacks are incapable of ruling themselves because they are, by nature, intellectually inferior; this, after all, is the major premise of apartheid; hence, each time apartheid managers and apologists are confronted with the democratic principle of one person, one vote, they usually point to political instability in black African countries; they also usually assert that black South Africans are economically better off than those in black-ruled African countries.

Hence Botha tells the world in his Durban speech, "I am not prepared to lead South Africans and other minority groups on a road to abdication and suicide. Destroy white South Africa . . . and this country will drift into factions, strife, chaos, and poverty." Therefore, the South African question is framed as a choice between white "civilization" with an apartheid face and black barbarism with a Marxist face. One confusion in rightist discourse is equating Marxism with communism. However, it is fair to acknowledge that any definition of communism or Marxism ultimately depends on one's interests or one's values or one's history.

In other words, one's positions often rest on where one is coming from, but where one is coming from is not usually linear or singular or straightforward. To equate communism with Marxism is to see the USSR as synonymous with communism or as the embodiment of communism. Even the first Western Christians (whom many of these critics claim to follow), practiced a modicum of some communism, as Luke tells us in Acts of the Apostles (4:32–37; 5:1–12).

For me, contemporary Marxism has its problems but my point here is that communism need not be an automatic pejorative: there are several kinds of communism just as there are several kinds of capitalism. It is possible to develop a system that is mindful of both the individual and society.

Nevertheless, the issue is not what ideology is acceptable to me or the Falwells; such decision best rests with the people of South Africa. It is for this reason that I ask: what would be wrong with South Africa going communist if such a decision is democratically determined? Does Viguerie's U.S. no longer stand for self-determination, for people choosing or deciding for themselves how they should govern themselves?

South Africa has so far effectively sustained and invigorated apartheid by sowing the myth that South Africa is a nation of minorities. This myth has the goal of negating or diluting the clamor for one person, one vote—the only democratic weapon that can dismantle apartheid. Apartheid has instituted this "new" society by stripping black South Africans of their citizenship and "enfranchising" them in about ten ad hoc apartheid camps called "tribal homelands."

Thus pre-homeland apartheid South Africa, which consisted of four racial groups (about 23 million blacks, 4 million whites, 3 million "coloreds," and one million Asians), artificially becomes, in post-homelands apartheid South Africa, a "new" nation of minority groups: about 4 million whites, 3 million "coloreds," one million Asians, and about ten black groups: Bophuthatswana, Ciskei, Transkei, Gazankulu, Kwazulu, Lebowa, Qwaqua, etc.

First, even if South Africa were a nation of such minorities, what makes South African whites the only group qualified to rule? Second, who wants to destroy white South Africa or white South Africans? Why equate or confuse the intent to destroy apartheid with a desire to destroy white South Africa or white South Africans? Third, the Bothas often point to political instability in some black African countries and use it as an excuse for rejecting one person, one vote—an exercise they rightly fear will usher in a nonapartheid government.

It is humorous that the Pretoria regime sees itself as a stable government and perhaps a model for black African countries that want political stability. Of course, as long as apartheid lives and as long as only blacks lose their lives, their liberty and their properties, the South African government can claim to be politically stable. Here is not the place to discuss political upheavals in much of black Africa, but the fact that much of one generation of African political leadership has failed to fulfill the aspirations for a better life that independence heralded, does not warrant or justify the racist conclusion that black Africans are inherently incapable of political leadership.

If the ANC or United Democratic Front do not typify the thinking of the majority of black South Africans as alleged by the Bothas, the Vigueries and the Falwells, why are these same Falwells afraid of the democratic principle of one person, one vote? And if, indeed, South Africa is a nation of minorities and if, indeed, South African blacks are groups of minorities speaking with divergent and divisive voices that are mostly pro-Botha and if, indeed, Botha's stooges such as Kaizer Matanzima of Transkei or Lucas Mangope of Bhophuthatswana are the true leaders or representatives of the majority of black South Africans, why are the Vigueries afraid of one person, one vote?

The "tribal homelands" is in truth a diversionary strategy forming part of South Africa's policy of destabilization. It aims at fomenting the fragmentation of anti-apartheid organizations in South Africa and anti-apartheid governments in black Africa. No amount of posturing, however, will cover up the fascist, war-mongering character of the apartheid state. At will and with impunity, South Africa openly violates the territorial integrity of several neighboring countries: Angola, Mozambique, Botswana, Lesotho and Zimbabwe. Of course, the territorial invasions are usually carried out in the name of protecting democracy against Marxism or terrorism. As CIA chief, William Casey, noted recently, to offend Botha is to loose U.S. intelligence on black Africa.

The Falwell rightists call Nelson Mandela and the African National Congress (ANC) Marxist terrorists. They forget that the ANC, which was founded in 1912, did not turn to a military strategy until the 1960s, in the wake of the governmental 1960 Sharpeville massacre of 69 blacks. The Falwells further forget that Mandela worked peacefully against apartheid from the 1940s until the 1960s when Sharpeville and its aftermath convinced him and many others that a system which violently imposes itself on others cannot be changed peacefully.

South African apartheid is a classic illustration of the Kennedy saying that those who make peaceful changes impossible make violent changes inevitable. It is now apparent (as 25 years after Sharpeville have confirmed with the Sowetos and the Bikos), that apartheid will not commit suicide. That apartheid causes and continues to cause violence is usually never underscored.

Who are the real terrorists? And what is terrorism? Again, one's answer will depend on where one is coming from. Is a terrorist anyone who uses violence? Is terrorism limited to nongovernmental individuals or groups? Why is the binary structure of social violence often overlooked or unstressed when the violence involves nonrightist freedom fighters as in the case of today's South Africa? Falwellian support or nonsupport is usually based on whether or not the group is perceived as struggling for freedom from leftism or for freedom from extreme negative rightism.

In other words, any leftism is automatically bad, but only extreme negative rightism such as Nazism or fascism is bad, and even a bad form of rightism (as Viguerie has told us), is better than any form of leftism. Therefore, such rightists never work to overthrow (even by their own admission), fascist or authoritarian regimes. At most, they only work to reform them. Hence, it is proper to support or arm the Shah's Iran but improper to support or arm the South African ANC or any other organization that insists on the immediate dismantling of apartheid.

But this distinction between leftism and the evil forms of rightism, which presumably enables these conservatives to support or arm Polish Solidarity or Savimbi's UNITA or the Nicaraguan "contras," is untenable. How is Marxism demonically worse than apartheid to the extent that apartheid enjoys preferential treatment in rightist thinking? What makes rightist evils only fit for reformation while extermination is reserved only for leftism?

On Social Violence

This rightist distinction should be considered in evaluating the rightist attitude toward the use of military means to achieve social change. Botha arrogates to himself the right to use violence (through the police, army, etc.) against those who vocally oppose or actively defy apartheid, but denies these opponents the right to fight back forcefully. Pretoria's violence is often characterized as enforcing law and order; it is seen as nonterrorist action motivated by black barbarism, whereas the retaliatory or defensive or apartheid-motivated violence of blacks is dismissed outright as Marxist terrorism.

Consequently, a picture of civilization versus savagery is drawn and disseminated. Such misleading portraits are often used to justify the continuation of some form of apartheid and "validate" or "confirm" apartheid's major credo that blacks are, as a group, incapable of ruling themselves because they are inherently inferior intellectually.

Botha declares, "I am not prepared to lead South Africans and other minority groups on a road to abdication and suicide." And Reagan describes Botha's State of Emergency as "a governmental reaction to some violence that was hurtful to all of the people." Note that Reagan ignores the violence (apartheid) which prompted black violence. Apartheid as the basic cause of the historic and current violence in South Africa continues to go unacknowledged.

Reagan adds, "We have seen the violence between blacks there, as well as from the law enforcement against riotous behavior. I think we have to recognize sometimes when actions are taken in an effort to curb violence." What "laws" are being enforced? Is apartheid not also the direct or indirect cause of much of the black-on-black violence mentioned by Reagan? The violence by blacks against blacks is, in general, specifically directed not at blacks as blacks but as managers or enforcers of apartheid.

Black freedom fighters treat apartheid managers and their accomplices the same way; they do not discriminate because what matters is not the form or color of apartheid. Apartheid, no matter how it manifests itself, deserves death. The paramount immediate objective is to attack all those black and white managers and promoters of apartheid. The black South African revolutionaries are doing what American revolutionaries during the U.S. war for independence did to Benedict Arnold, and what other revolutionaries (in France, Britain, Germany, etc.) did to traitors. Historically, revolutionaries have summarily dealt with traitors. The ongoing revolution in South Africa is no exception.

One can understand Bishop Desmond Tutu's advice to the blacks who killed a black woman traitor in Duduza. He said, "You cannot use methods to attain the goal of liberation that our enemy will use against us." The Nobel laureate continued, "When they saw that woman burning on television, they must have said maybe we are not ready for freedom."

But one can also understand the motivation and rationale of such action and the fruitlessness of Tutu's advice as Tutu himself pointed out later when he admitted to the impossibility of not resorting to such violence when the managers of apartheid have clearly and repeatedly and even boastfully stated that they will not "now or tomorrow" abandon apartheid. As Botha put it, "don't push me. . . ." Tutu also noted that the government has put itself in a "Catch-22 position" when it maintains that it "won't talk until the unrest has been quelled." Tutu declared, "The unrest is not going to be quelled because apartheid is there."

Recently in Soweto, about 900 children (including seven-year-olds) were arrested for boycotting school; most of them were released only after Bishop Tutu pleaded and pleaded. The remainder were detained without charges. South Africa's police commissioner said of the situation, "We are cracking down. We will not allow 5,000 stupid students to disregard law and order." To apartheid managers, those who engage in anti-apartheid activities are stupid.

One apparent self-delusion these apartheid managers continue to maintain is that anti-apartheid agitation is the work of only a few vocal individuals or a small minority group of black activists. In other words, apartheid is popular with many blacks. Therefore, cracking down on dissenters or locking up freedom fighters such as Mandela or Rev. Alan Boesak will eventually eliminate any significant or potent opposition or threat to apartheid. Apartheid managers and apologists continue to underestimate or ignore the mental and physical capability of blacks. South African blacks will not and cannot be manipulated or intimidated by apartheid's sophisticated and life-negating strategies. Black South Africans know how to read between the lines of apartheid.

U.S. Policy Shifts

Recent moves by Reagan and Botha have been hailed in certain quarters as steps in the right direction. Reagan's executive order, which imposes some mild economic sanctions on South Africa, is not a policy reversal as some have indicated. The text and especially the context suggest only a tactical shift. The order is a toothless bulldog: it lacks a timetable and has no legal force; and it was born only to deflect the Congressional sanctions bill.

Reagan's order is in line with his position on Botha's South Africa: reform apartheid but do not destroy it. He has already characterized Botha's administration as a "reformist" one. The recent announcement that there is a plan to make about ten million blacks citizens of South Africa is insulting; what gives the Bothas the right or power to decide for blacks what they should or should not do or be?

The UDF states the situation better, "the right of our people to land, property and full South African citizenship is non-negotiable and can never be seen as a favor from the master's table." Black South Africans are saying, we do not want any form of apartheid; we do not want apartheid reformed; we want apartheid removed. "Constructive engagement" or "active engagement" will not remove apartheid.

The present token tricameral legislature initiated to give apartheid a new face or a face-lift in order to make apartheid less objectionable and thus more manageable is another attempt to break up the solidarity that was growing among nonwhites ("coloureds," Asians, and blacks). It is the very same colonial method of divide and rule that is at work here again. The only reformation that can placate most blacks now is one that ends the emergency, withdraws the army and police from black areas, unconditionally releases all political prisoners, and institutes a national convention where all South Africans (black, white, "coloured," Asian), can, through their freely chosen leaders, discuss and decide their national future.

One would have thought that principle and self-interest would have induced the U.S. government and its Falwellian supporters to play a creative role in ending apartheid. They have not only refused to support or arm the fighters of apartheid, they have also condemned them outright as Marxist terrorists for getting arms from the Soviet block, the only source that has been willing to help them. Just as other freedom fighters in the world have never hesitated to accept any help from anywhere, the South African situation is no exception. To insist that because of this arms connection with the Soviets a predominantly black South African government will automatically become Marxist or automatically be pro-Soviet or anti-United States is to underestimate or ignore the intelligence of black people.

Lastly, no responsible, thoughtful, and honest apartheid fighter has maintained that the assumption of power by blacks is going to cure all the economic, social, political and educational problems of South Africa. Of course, no government cures all, but the deinstitutionalization of racism can only be a step in the attempt to establish a society where no particular racial group will be permanently, inherently or constitutionally privileged.

The struggle in South Africa is primarily a struggle against the racist appropriation of liberty, justice and property in South Africa. Racism will not necessarily end with the end of apartheid, just as the official end of Jim Crow has not ended racism in the U.S., but the end of apartheid will at least remove the government from the business of racism.

Chapter XIII:

U.S. CORPORATIONS, DIVESTMENT, AND SANCTIONS

64. *THE SULLIVAN PRINCIPLES*

by REV. LEON SULLIVAN

In the mid-1970s Reverend Leon Sullivan, a black Baptist leader from Philadelphia, and member of the Board of Directors of General Motors, wrote an employment code for American businesses in South Africa that have come to be known as the Sullivan Principles. Although he believes "these little principles have done more than the U.N. and all the other nations [in] making a difference," he nonetheless acknowledges that the cycle of repression and violence may require new pressures be put on the apartheid government. He is on record as favoring a complete economic embargo against South Africa if it does not dismantle its system of apartheid by June 1987.

Statement of Principles of U.S. Firms with Affiliates in the Republic of South Africa: Fourth Amplification, November 8, 1984.

Principle I: Nonsegregation of the races in all eating, comfort and work facilities.

Each signator of the Statement of Principles will proceed immediately to:

- Eliminate all vestiges of racial discrimination.
- Remove all race designation signs.
- Desegregate all eating, comfort and work facilities.

Principle II: Equal and fair employment practices for all employees.

Each signator of the Statement of Principles will proceed immediately to:

* Implement equal and fair terms and conditions of employment.
* Provide nondiscriminatory eligibility for benefit plans.
* Establish an appropriate and comprehensive procedure for handling and resolving individual employee complaints.
* Support the elimination of all industrial racial discriminatory laws which impede the implementation of equal and fair terms and conditions of employment, such as abolition of job reservations, job fragmentation, and apprenticeship restrictions for Blacks and other nonwhites.
* Support the elimination of discrimination against the rights of Blacks to form or belong to government registered and unregistered unions and acknowledge generally the rights of Blacks to form their own unions or be represented by trade unions which already exist.
* Secure rights of Black workers to the freedom of association and assure protection against victimization while pursuing and after attaining these rights.
* Involve Black workers or their representatives in the development of programs that address their educational and other needs and those of their dependents and the local community.

Principle III: Equal pay for all employees doing equal or comparable work for the same period of time.

Each signator of the Statement of Principles will proceed immediately to:

* Design and implement a wage and salary administration plan which is applied equally to all employees, regardless of race, who are performing equal or comparable work.
* Ensure an equitable system of job classifications, including a review of the distinction between hourly and salaried classifications.
* Determine the extent upgrading of personnel and/or jobs in the upper echelons is needed, and accordingly implement programs to accomplish this objective in representative numbers, insuring the employment of Blacks and other nonwhites at all levels of company operations.
* Assign equitable wage and salary ranges, the minimum of these to be well above the appropriate local minimum economic living level.

Principle IV: Initiation of and development of training programs that will prepare, in substantial numbers, Blacks and other nonwhites for supervisory, administrative, clerical and technical jobs.

Each signator of the Statement of Principles will proceed immediately to:

- Determine employee training needs and capabilities, and identify employees with potential for further advancement.
- Take advantage of existing outside training resources and activities, such as exchange programs, technical colleges, and similar institutions or programs.
- Support the development of outside training facilities, individually or collectively—including technical centers, professional training exposure, correspondence and extension courses, as appropriate, for extensive training outreach.
- Initiate and expand inside training programs and facilities.

Principle V: Increasing the number of Blacks and other nonwhites in management and supervisory positions.

Each signator of the Statement of Principles will proceed immediately to:

- Identify, actively recruit, train and develop a sufficient and significant number of Blacks and other nonwhites to assure that as quickly as possible there will be appropriate representation of Blacks and other nonwhites in the management group of each company at all levels of operations.
- Establish management development programs for Blacks and other nonwhites, as needed, and improve existing programs and facilities for developing management skills of Blacks and other nonwhites.
- Identify and channel high management potential Blacks and other nonwhite employees into management development programs.

Principle VI: Improving the quality of employees' lives outside the work environment in such areas as housing, schooling, recreation and health facilities.

Each signator of the Statement of Principles will proceed immediately to:

- Evaluate existing and/or develop programs, as appropriate, to address the specific needs of Black and other nonwhite employees in the areas of housing, health care, transportation and recreation.
- Evaluate methods for utilizing existing, expanded or newly established in-house medical facilities or other medical programs to improve medical care for all nonwhites and their dependents.
- Participate in the development of programs that address the educational needs of employees, their dependents, and the local community. Both individual and collective programs should be considered, in addition to

technical education, including such activities as literacy education, business training, direct assistance to local schools, contributions and scholarships.

- Support changes in influx control laws to provide for the right of Black migrant workers to normal family life.
- Increase utilization of and assist in the development of Black and other nonwhite owned and operated business enterprises including distributors, suppliers of goods and services and manufacturers.

Increased Dimensions of Activities Outside the Workplace:

- *Use influence and support the unrestricted rights of Black businesses to locate in the Urban areas of the nation.*
- *Influence other companies in South Africa to follow the standards of equal rights principles.*
- *Support the freedom of mobility of Black workers to seek employment opportunities wherever they exist, and make possible provisions for adequate housing for families of employees within the proximity of workers employment.*
- *Support the recension of all apartheid laws.* [1]

With all the foregoing in mind, it is the objective of the companies to involve and assist in the education and training of large and telling numbers of Blacks and other nonwhites as quickly as possible. The ultimate impact of this effort is intended to be of massive proportion, reaching and helping millions.

Periodic Reporting:

The Signatory Companies of the Statement of Principles will proceed immediately to:

- Report progress on an annual basis to Reverend Sullivan through the independent administrative unit he has established.
- Have all areas specified by Reverend Sullivan audited by a certified public accounting firm.
- Inform all employees of the company's annual periodic report rating and invite their input on ways to improve the rating.

---

[1] The italicized clauses were added to the code in 1984.

65. *THE SULLIVAN PRINCIPLES: A CRITIQUE**

by ELIZABETH SCHMIDT

Elizabeth Schmidt is a doctoral candidate in African history at the University of Wisconsin, Madison. She is the author of the authoritative critique of the Sullivan Principles: Decoding Corporate Camouflage: U.S. Business Support for Apartheid. *In the spring of 1981, she spent two-and-a-half months in South Africa as a correspondent for* Maryknoll Magazine.

Since early 1977, a number of U.S. companies with operations in South Africa have been endorsing—and to some extent implementing—an employment code called the "Sullivan Principles." Consisting of six principles, the code calls for desegregation of the workplace, fair employment practices, equal pay for equal work, job training and advancement, and improvement in the quality of workers' lives. As of October 25, 1984, 126 of approximately 350 U.S. companies doing business in South Africa had signed the employment code. These companies employ 64,724 African, "colored" (mixed ancestry), Asian, and white workers out of a total national work force of 10.6 million. . . .

Although worthy in principle, the employment code must be considered within the South African context. U.S. companies in South Africa participate in a political-economic system called "apartheid," which has legally deprived the African people—72 percent of the South African population—of their citizenship and political rights and dispossessed them of their land. . . . As a result of South Africa's apartheid policies, the 72 percent of the population that is African takes home only 29 percent of the nation's wages, while the white 16 percent of the population walks off with 59 percent of the national wage packet. . . .

A cheap and docile labor force has been a major drawing card for foreign businesses in South Africa. In April 1981, South African Prime Minister P. W. Botha (now the State President) told the press, "Through the years we have brought about a situation in which the Republic is one of the best countries to reside and invest in." Indeed, South Africa's white population maintains one of the highest standards of living in the world, and the economy attracts major investors from North America and Western Europe.

---

*From *One Step in the Wrong Direction* (New York, January 1985) [condensed].

U. S. Corporations—Agents or Obstacles to Change?

U.S. companies have taken advantage of South Africa's "good investment climate," rapidly expanding their investments in the apartheid economy. Between 1943 and 1978, U.S. direct investment in South Africa grew from $50 million to $2 billion—an increase of 4,000 percent. Stimulated by the Reagan Administration's policy of "constructive engagement," U.S. investments in South Africa rose to $2.6 billion in 1981. This sum accounts for 20 percent of South Africa's total foreign investments and is surpassed only by the investments of Great Britain.

The $2.6 billion figure indicating U.S. direct investment in South Africa seriously underestimates the value of American financial involvement in that country. A classified cable to the State Department from the U.S. Consulate in Johannesburg, leaked to the press in July 1983, reveals that U.S. financial involvement in South Africa is probably in excess of $14.6 billion. This figure includes direct investment, bank loans, and portfolio investment in South Africa-based companies, particularly in gold mining and other strategic mineral concerns. It does *not* include indirect investment in South Africa through U.S. subsidiaries based in Europe or Canada.

Perhaps even more important than the dollar value of these investments is their strategic significance. U.S. companies control the most vital sectors of the South African economy—33 percent of the motor vehicles market, 44 percent of the petroleum products market, and 70 percent of the computer market. Even more critical is the transfer of American technology and expertise—the training of technicians and the transfer of licenses. All of these factors are helping South Africa to become strategically self-sufficient. Once this goal has been achieved, the white minority regime will be able to defy international economic sanctions, resisting external pressures for internal change. In the final analysis, the assessment of a 1978 Senate Foreign Relations Committee Report is still germane: "The net effect of American investment has been to strengthen the economic and military self-sufficiency of South Africa's apartheid regime."

In spite of their vital contribution to the apartheid economy, U.S. businesses have insisted that they constitute a "progressive force" for change in South Africa. By adopting the Sullivan Principles, they hope to bolster their claim, promote a better image for U.S. companies on the home front, and diffuse the rapidly growing divestment movement.

Critique of the Sullivan Principles

Criticism of the "progressive force" strategy in general, and of the Sullivan Principles in particular, has centered on two points. The first, and most important, focuses on the fact that American businesses have never used their leverage to force fundamental change in South Africa. . . . Their employment practices are little—if any—better than those in South African companies and affect only a fraction of the black work force nationwide. What minimal benefits these corporations provide are of little significance compared to their strategic importance to the South African economy. With the help of American investments, technology, and expertise, the white minority regime is able to maintain a strong economy and a sophisticated security apparatus that quashes all political dissent. According to this logic, U.S. companies have no business operating under such conditions, where their presence simply serves to preserve and perpetuate the *status quo.*

The second point focuses on the implementation of the Sullivan Principles themselves. Although of less significance than the first point, the second must be considered because there is a general misconception that the principles *are* actually being implemented.

Before analyzing the effectiveness of the code, it is important to note that American companies are highly capital-intensive, employing a disproportionate number of skilled (i.e., white) workers. Thus, although white workers constitute only 18 percent of the work force nationwide, they compose 37 percent of the workers in the Sullivan signatory companies. While Africans constitute 71 percent of the national work force, they make up only 43 percent of the Sullivan signatory workforce. These companies employ only 0.4 percent of the African work force in South Africa, and only 0.5 percent of the African, "colored," and Asian work force combined.

The impact of the Sullivan reforms must be considered within this limited context. Such progress that occurs affects only a minute fraction of South Africa's black population. The following analysis assesses the achievements of the signatory companies more than seven and one-half years after the initiation of the fair employment code.

The Myth of Fair Employment

Since the Sullivan Principles were introduced almost a decade ago, they have made a minimal impact on the lives of black workers. As the corporate record deteriorates, fewer companies are willing to expose themselves to public scrutiny. As a result, a dwindling number of signatories are reporting on their South African employment activities. The number of corporate signatories reached a peak in 1982, with a total of 145 U.S. endorsers. However, that year half the signatories either did not bother to report or received a failing grade. Between 1982 and 1983, 29 signatories dropped out of the Sullivan program, including 17 companies that had never reported or had received failing grades, and others that objected to the annual per company fee of $1,000-$7,000 to support the Sullivan/Arthur D. Little monitoring apparatus. (The fees are prorated according to the companies' worldwide sales.) By 1984, given the addition of new signatories, the reinstatement of dropouts that had belatedly paid their fees, and a series of new withdrawals, there were 126 U.S. signatories. More than a quarter of these received the lowest possible rating.

In terms of Principle 1 (nonsegregation of facilities), the *Eighth Report* asserts, "All of the reporting units stated that they have achieved complete, *de facto* non-segregation of their facilities." Since no supporting evidence is provided, it is impossible to assess the validity of this claim. A similar claim in an earlier report exposes the complexity of the issue. In 1981, the *Fifth Report* asserted that in 95 percent of the reporting companies, "all races in a particular work area (are) able to all use the same locker room *which is associated with the work area*" (Emphasis added). The *Fifth Report* did *not* note that African and white workers rarely share the same jobs, and thus, rarely occupy the same work areas. It did *not* state that until all job categories are integrated, *de facto* segregation will remain. Rather than shedding new light on the subject, the *Eighth Report* obscures the issue even further.

Under the heading for Principle 2 (fair and equal employment practices), the *Eighth Report* states that "all of the reporting units continue to support the right of Africans, 'coloreds,' and Asians to form and belong to trade unions or representative labor groups, whether registered or not." The report does not indicate the criteria used to determine the representativeness of labor groups, nor whether the standards are established by management, labor, or a combination of the two. Significantly, the number of signatories that have actually negotiated and signed contracts with black trade unions was not revealed. While paying lip service to the principle of "freedom of association," a number of Sullivan signatories have indicated their antagonism to trade unions. In the *Sixth Report,* for instance, one signatory indicated that, "We do not believe unions to be necessary or desirable." Similarly, in the *Seventh Report,* a Sullivan endorser claimed that its employees rejected unions because "the company was looking after them and . . . they did not require a union."

As late as 1983, Colgate-Palmolive, a top category Sullivan signatory, was sharply criticized by members of its black workforce for its anti-union activities. The Chemical Workers' Industrial Union, which represents 80 percent of the company's black workers, waged a 16-month battle for recognition during 1980 and 1981. In the face of a workers' strike and a nationwide boycott of its products, the Sullivan signatory finally agreed to negotiate with the black union. According to a CWIU branch secretary, the company's managers "fight every issue tooth and nail. Their attitude is still very anti-union."

Another top category Sullivan signatory implicated in serious anti-union practices is the Fluor Corporation. This California-based firm built South Africa's strategic coal-to-oil conversion plant (SASOL) and maintains the facility under contract. Following their participation in the two-day general strike in November 1984, 6,500 African workers were fired from their jobs at SASOL and forcibly expelled to the bantustans. The general secretary of the Chemical Workers' Industrial Union, which organized SASOL as well as Colgate workers, claimed that this action was but the latest of the workers' grievances. For African employees, the SASOL plant meant "danger, hazardous working conditions, barracks-like hostels, racial oppression, rumors of men killed in accidents during the night and whisked away and, generally a very repressive environment."

During the sixth reporting period, Sullivan signatories recognized three times as many government registered as opposed to unregistered unions. (Comparable figures were not included in the *Seventh* or *Eighth Reports.*) Independent or unregistered unions tend to be far more militant and broadly political than government registered unions, and hence, less easily coopted or controlled. Historically, employers have favored registered unions, even when workers select independent unions as their representatives. Given the lack of information in the Sullivan compliance reports, it is impossible to determine whether employers chose to negotiate with registered in-house unions even when workers threw their support behind unregistered alternatives. Clearly, it is one thing for all of the reporting units to "support" the right of blacks to belong to trade unions, "whether registered or not." To act upon that principle is quite another.

Also under the heading for Principle 2, the *Eighth Report* claims that, "All benefits available to whites are also available to other races, and the benefits for Africans, 'coloreds,' and Asians are at least equal to those for whites. An exception is health care, where the benefits are technically equal, although the institutions providing the services may be administered separately." Implicitly accepted is the apartheid policy of "separate development" and the tired myth of "separate but equal." In South Africa, health care services *must* be administered separately to each race—by force of law. The segregated services and facilities offered to blacks and whites in South Africa are about as "equal" as inner-city and suburban schools in the United States.

Finally, the *Eighth Report* notes that while many signatories have "traditionally required all whites to have medical coverage . . . they have not had the same requirement for the other races." The rationale behind this discrepancy was the availability to Africans of low cost state administered medical care. While the *Eighth Report* rejects this position on the grounds that it "ignores the issue of the *quality* and *accessibility* of care," it offers no real solution to the problem. Instead it urges signatory companies "to encourage Africans to take advantage of the health care system that is now available primarily for South Africa's whites"—an impossible feat in apartheid South Africa.

In terms of Principle 3 (equal pay for equal work), the *Eighth Report* notes, "For the fourth year in a row, all reporting units stated that they are paying all races at the same rate for equal work." The report does *not* point out that very few African, "colored," and Asian employees work in the same job grade as white workers. Those who do usually find themselves at the low end of the wage range for that particular grade, with whites at the high end. Furthermore, the *Eighth Report* shows that in 1984, 77 percent of the unskilled workers were African, while only 0.4 percent were white. Of the professional workers, only 7 percent were African, while 85 percent were white. Two percent of the managers were African; 95 percent were white. Nearly three-quarters of all African workers employed by the signatory companies were engaged in unskilled or semi-skilled work, while only 2 percent of the white workers were so employed.

Given the overall concentration of Africans in unskilled and semi-skilled labor and whites in skilled and white collar jobs, it is not surprising to find a huge discrepancy between African and white workers' wages. Corporate backsliding in black training and advancement (see Principles 4 and 5) has projected this pattern far into the future. In the final analysis, the significance of Principle 3 is this: where there is no equal work, there can be no equal pay.

During the past several years, signatory progress in implementing Principle 4 (the training of African, "colored," and Asian employees for supervisory, administrative, clerical, and technical jobs) has declined significantly. While 56 percent of the clerical and administrative trainees were African, "colored," and Asian in 1980, these groups constituted only 45 percent of such trainees in 1984. Similarly, 72 percent of the supervisory trainees were black in 1980, while only 43 percent were black in 1984. Finally, in 1980, 25 percent of the managerial trainees were African, "colored," and Asian, while these groups composed only 13 percent of the trainees four years later. Conversely, during the same period, white worker representation in signatory training programs improved dramatically—at the expense of black workers.

The *Eighth Report* does not indicate the number of African, as opposed to "colored" and Asian, trainees involved in these programs. Historically, the number of "colored" and Asian workers trained for skilled and professional jobs has been proportionately—and sometimes absolutely—far greater than the number of Africans trained for these positions. Hence, lumping these groups into one category paints a picture for black employees as a whole that is far brighter than that of Africans alone.

In the same vein, white workers continue the pattern of filling skilled and professional job vacancies in far greater numbers than do black workers. In 1984, white workers filled 51 percent of the new supervisory jobs, while Africans filled 26 percent, "coloreds" 13 percent, and Asians 10 percent. Africans filled only 5 percent of the new managerial jobs, ("coloreds" 4 percent, Asians

6 percent), while white workers assumed 85 percent of the managerial vacancies.

As for Principle 5 (increasing the number of African, "colored," and Asian workers in management and supervisory positions), data contained in the *Eighth Report* indicates that white workers hold 95 percent of the managerial positions and 61 percent of the supervisory positions. Africans fill 2 percent of the managerial and 21 percent of the supervisory job slots. Three years ago, when statistics for managerial and supervisory positions were first separated from one another, whites filled 97 percent of the managerial jobs (Africans, 2 percent) and 62 percent of the supervisory jobs (Africans, 21 percent). In other words, there has been no advance for African workers in terms of managerial and supervisory jobs for at least the past three years.

The *Seventh Report* indicates that only 300 Africans, "coloreds," and Asians —or 0.7 percent of the black work force of 41,443—hold jobs wherein their responsibilities include supervising whites. Comparable figures have been omitted from the *Eighth Report.* Again, it can be assumed that most of the blacks supervising white workers are "colored" or Asian rather than African. The *Eighth Report* does indicate that 29 percent of the reporting units "had at least one" white employee supervised by an African, "colored," or Asian. In other words, in 71 percent of the reporting units, there is *not even one* white employee who is supervised by an African, "colored," or Asian worker.

Under the heading for Principle 6 (improvement in the quality of workers' lives), the *Sixth Report* states:

> Principle 6 has as its objective the constructive use of the Signatories' symbolic and economic presence in South Africa to improve the quality of life for all citizens, with particular emphasis on ameliorating conditions for (African, "colored," or Asian) individuals.

It is apparent from the above statement that the authors of the report are well aware of the potent "symbolic and economic presence" of U.S. corporations in South Africa. They do not seem to be as well-informed about the political system in South Africa, which has dispossessed the very Africans the corporations claim to benefit of their South African citizenship. The *Seventh* and *Eighth Reports* have completely dispensed with the above statement.

According to the terms of Principle 6, Sullivan signatories are required to provide services, facilities, and financial assistance to their workers' communities. Corporate activities in this regard have stayed well within the framework of the apartheid system. A favorite project has been the government-endorsed Adopt-A-School program. By 1984, signatory companies had "adopted" 250 black schools, providing them with financial assistance and improved facilities and donating employee time to school activities. According to the *Sixth Re-*

port, "The most popular forms of assistance in Adopt-A-School projects seem to be physical additions/renovations, including building classrooms, electrification, heating and plumbing." Landscaping and clean-up operations, support for sports, teaching, fundraising and meal subsidization were among the other types of school support provided by signatory companies. The *Seventh Report* indicated that the signatories assisted their "adopted" schools with "cash and assistance with renovations and expansion." In one school, the corporation "helped start an annual award program to recognize the 'best student' and 'best teacher.' " The pattern of providing financial and technical assistance to renovate or expand school facilities continued during the eighth reporting period with the construction of new classrooms, sports fields, and playground areas.

None of these forms of assistance interfere with the apartheid structures inherent in the South African educational system. The *Eighth* and all preceding reports ignore the fact that signatory companies are simply helping to finance inferior "colored," Asian, and "Bantu" education. The latter system was designed, in the words of former Prime Minister Hendrik Verwoerd, to teach African children "to realize that equality with Europeans is not for them." The Sullivan signatories are contributing to a system of indoctrination that is based upon the notion of white supremacy. They are adhering to government-imposed curricula that teach African children to be "hewers of wood and drawers of water" for white South Africa. By building new classrooms for the "Bantu" schools, and supplying them with heat and light, U.S. corporations are simply helping to make apartheid more comfortable—and longer-lasting. . . .

Black workers have been equally critical of signatory projects which they describe as showy public relations gimmicks, or worse, internally divisive. According to press reports, black employees at Ford Motor Company were disturbed by management's decision to spend millions of dollars on new (desegregated) locker rooms and cafeterias, at the same time claiming that it did not have the funds to increase black workers' wages. They also resented company projects that enhanced class distinctions among the black employees. While a black auto workers' union urged Ford to use the funds associated with Principle 6 in low-income areas, installing water taps, improving the roads, etc., Ford chose instead to build luxury homes for 70 upper-income African families, not all of whom were Ford workers. The houses cost about $12,000 to $15,000 each—far beyond the means of the vast majority of African families. Ford explained that it was providing African managers and supervisors with the opportunity to live at a higher standard than most township inhabitants. However, Fred Sauls, general secretary of the National Automobile and Allied Workers Union, indicated that Ford was merely "safeguarding its own interests by creating a black middle class, a black elite" with a stake in the system—a strategy associated with the policies of the current regime. The press did not indicate the fate of the shantytown residents whose homes were razed to make way for the Fordville development project.

. . . The *Sixth Report* states,

> At times during the past year, there have been elements of controversy about the Sullivan Principles and the role they play in helping justify the continuing presence of American corporations in South Africa. Much of this controversy is a result of confusion about what the Principles cover and therefore, what the ratings actually imply about a company's conduct.
>
> The Principles do not cover what some have called the "strategic issues": loans made to South Africa, imports of certain types of equipment, etc. What the Signatories are doing in these areas is outside the scope of this report.

In effect, the *Sixth Report* admits that signatory companies are contributing strategically important goods and expertise to the apartheid system and that the employment code was never intended to address this issue. In a few brief lines, the fundamental weakness of the Sullivan Principles is laid bare: the Principles address corporate employment practices as if they occur in a vacuum, as if the bottom line is the desegregation of toilets and recreation areas, rather than U.S. corporate support of apartheid structures. The *Sixth Report* ultimately exposes the Sullivan Principles for what they are—absolutely irrelevant to the struggle for freedom and justice in South Africa.

Corporate Complicity in Apartheid

Even more serious than their discriminatory employment practices and the irrelevance of their workplace "reforms," is the complicity of U.S. corporations in the overall subjugation of South Africa's black population. U.S. companies literally grease the wheels of the apartheid machine. It is the model Sullivan signatories—usually those corporations with the largest assets and annual sales—that are bolstering the most strategic sectors of the South African economy. Such companies have the resources to spend on upgraded cafeterias and recreation areas. They also have the most to lose if they are forced to withdraw from South Africa, and hence, the most to gain from a well-orchestrated public relations campaign.

Among the highest ranking Sullivan signatories are Ford ("Making Progress") and General Motors ("Making Good Progress"). Both companies sell motor vehicles to the South African military and police forces. Firestone ("Making Progress") and Goodyear ("Making Good Progress") sell tires to South African government agencies, products that can be transferred to the security forces.

Caltex, Mobil, and Exxon ("Making Good Progress") are producing petroleum products in South Africa that keep the military and police forces running and fuel the war of occupation in Namibia. . . .

The California-based Fluor Corporation ("Making Good Progress") is helping to build and equip a massive coal-to-oil conversion plant (SASOL) that is scheduled to provide an estimated 30 to 50 percent of South Africa's oil requirements. Fluor's SASOL contracts, worth about $4.2 billion, charge the corporation with managing and coordinating the total project, including responsibility for a major portion of the engineering design, procurement, and construction. With the assistance of the Fluor Corporation, South Africa is managing to circumvent the 1973 OPEC oil embargo and advance its long-term program of strategic self-sufficiency.

U.S. computers are used in every sector of the South African economy. The motor vehicles, petroleum, tire and rubber, and mining industries, South African banks and financial institutions, and large corporations could not function without U.S. computers. IBM, Burroughs, Sperry, and Control Data (all "Making Good Progress") have produced equipment that helps to run the "Bantu" administration boards and the prison system, implements the pass laws, and controls the flow of African labor. IBM alone controls 38 to 50 percent of the South African computer market. One-third of its business is with the South African government. IBM computers run the Johannesburg Stock Exchange and military communications in Namibia. . . .

Abiding by South African Law

As long as American companies are operating in South Africa, they must adhere to South African law. The implications of this fact were made all too clear in 1980 when the South African government passed the National Key Points Act. This law requires all companies designated as "key" industries to cooperate with the South African Defence Forces in the event of "civil" (i.e., black) unrest. Under the terms of the act, "key" industries will be offered financial incentives to buy weapons and other security equipment and to train company security guards. A number of subsidiaries of foreign corporations have been asked to form military commando units among their *white* workers. These military units will be responsible for guarding industrial plants from sabotage and unrest—presumably perpetrated by black workers and members of the black community. Under penalty of heavy fines and/or imprisonment of their top executives, foreign subsidiaries would be forced to obey the commands of the South African Defence Forces. They may not inform their parent companies whether they have been designated "key points." Nor may they report on any of their security-related activities.

Although the details of the key points plan are secret, it is considered likely that American auto companies, such as Ford and General Motors, and petroleum companies, such as Caltex, Mobil, and Exxon, have been designated "national key points." If such is the case, the operation of these companies in South Africa is far more detrimental to South African blacks than beneficial, no matter what the companies' employment practices.

Another critical law to which corporations in South Africa are bound to adhere is the National Supplies Procurement Act. Under the stipulations of this act, oil companies may not impose conditions on the sale of their oil. According to Standard Oil of California, a joint-owner of Caltex:

> It would be a crime under South Africa's laws were Caltex South Africa to undertake a commitment to not supply petroleum products for use by the South African military or any other branch of the South African government.

. . . .

Given the above statements and past practice, it is interesting to note that the most recent amplification of the Sullivan Principles (November 8, 1984) has called upon the signatories to break with this tradition [of conforming to local legislation]. According to the new stipulations, all signatories are to:

- Use influence and support the unrestricted rights of (African) businesses to locate in the Urban areas of the nation.
- Influence other companies in South Africa to follow the standards of equal rights principles.
- Support the freedom of mobility of (African) workers to seek employment opportunities wherever they exist, and make possible provisions for adequate housing for families of employees within the proximity of workers' employment.
- Support the recension of all apartheid laws.

. . . [Despite contrary reports in *The New York Times* and the (Johannesburg) *Star*], the "Fourth Amplification" to the "Sullivan Statement of Principles', Rev. Sullivan's press release, and his statement to the press, all dated November 8, 1984, make no mention of "ending," "repealing," or "rescinding" apartheid laws. Rather, they call for the "recension" of all apartheid laws, that is, their "revision."

. . . Rev. Sullivan told the *New York Times* that signatories would be required to use both legal and illegal means in their compliance with the new guidelines. Legal means could include public statements, articles, and position papers, and meetings with South African government officials. Among the illegal means that could be employed were the development of integrated housing projects and the employment of African workers without regard to their status under South Africa's influx control laws. Sullivan finally concluded that the signatories "must go beyond mere statements." . . .

Given that the South African government and its agencies are among the major purchasers of U.S. corporate goods, it is unlikely that U.S. firms will go out of their way to antagonize their number one customer, which also defines the terms under which the companies operate in that country. It is conceivable that U.S. firms will encourage the government to relax some controls—those that are bad for business. Even the South African business establishment has called for an easing up of restrictions on the movement of skilled African labor —in an effort to redistribute this vital but scarce resource.

South African businesses and government officials are encouraging the formation of a small African middle class—in order to bolster the number of skilled workers, to expand the domestic market for consumer goods, and to forestall gains by black militants, who are perceived to be anti-capitalist. Sullivan signatories are likely to support those amplifications that fulfill their business needs and those that give blacks a stake in the system, providing an illusion of political security. However, to those amplifications that might threaten the foundations of the system, Rev. Sullivan will be lucky if they are paid, even lip service.

Blacks Say No to Employment Code

Few black South Africans have been fooled by the corporate claim that U.S. businesses constitute a "progressive force" in South Africa.

Desmond Tutu, the new Anglican Bishop of Johannesburg and recipient of the 1984 Nobel Peace Prize, has described the "progressive force" argument as "humbug" and declared that the corporations are "lying" if they say they are helping the black population. He added, "They must know that they are investing to buttress one of the most vicious systems since Nazism."

Elaborating upon this theme, Tutu asserted,

> Involvement in South Africa is as much a moral as it is an economic issue. Black suffering is part of the economy from which the corporations are benefiting. Migratory labor, the deliberate starvation of people through (forced) resettlement—the corporations are involved in all of this.

Tutu dismissed the claim that economic prosperity leads to the liberalization of society. "There have been many economic booms in South Africa," he said. "But the benefits have not percolated down to the black population." In fact, the reverse is true. Large corporations have profited at the expense of cheap black labor. As for the argument that corporate withdrawal would lead to black suffering, Tutu retorted, "Since when have these companies been such altruists? The companies benefit from black suffering and the repressive policies of the apartheid regime." . . .

. . . Bishop Tutu [also] claimed, "Our rejection of the code is on the basis that it does not aim at changing structures. The Sullivan Principles are designed to be ameliorative. We do not want apartheid to be made more comfortable. We want it to be dismantled."

The Motor Assemblers' and Component Workers' Union of South Africa (MACWUSA), an unregistered black union that has organized workers at the Ford and General Motors plants, criticized the code on similar grounds. In a document submitted to Ford in 1982, MACWUSA called the Sullivan Principles a "toothless package" that "circles around apartheid's basic structures. The code does not demand apartheid to be abolished but merely to modernize and ensure its perpetuation."

Other critics concur that the codes are in fact "counter-productive," disguising the true nature of corporate involvement in South Africa. According to Bruce Evans, the Anglican Bishop of Port Elizabeth (the home of Ford, General Motors, Firestone, and Goodyear), "The employment codes disregard the economic role of multinational corporations in the South African economy. The whole problem is an economic one. Apartheid is there to hold up the economic system." Whether or not the corporations implement the employment code, they continue to bolster the apartheid economy.

The Federation of South African Trade Unions (FOSATU), the largest federation of black unions with at least 120,000 members, charged that the Sullivan Principles "merely serve as camouflage for employers."

Fikki Ahshene, whose FOSATU-affiliated union is among those that represent black workers at Ford, General Motors, Goodyear, and Firestone, asserted "We don't accept the Sullivan Principles. They were drawn up by the employers. Sullivan is on the Board of Directors of General Motors. He is part of the management." Ahshene added,

> South African workers had no say in the Sullivan code. If Sullivan wanted a big change in South Africa, he would have asked the workers what they wanted. Corporate priorities are not the workers' priorities . . . The desegregation of eating facilities is not important to us. The Sullivan Principles are just a means of taking pressure off the American multinationals.

. . . .

— Band-Aid
on a broken arm
(Sullivan Principles)

66. PROGRAMMING OPPRESSION: U.S. COMPUTER COMPANIES IN SOUTH AFRICA*

by NARMIC/AMERICAN FRIENDS SERVICE COMMITTEE

The American Friends Service Committee is an independent Quaker organization that works for disarmament, human rights, justice and development in the United States and around the world. The goal of AFSC's work on Southern Africa is to build public awareness and action in this country for the total abolition of apartheid and for self-determination of the peoples of Namibia and South Africa. NARMIC is a research project of the AFSC's Peace Education Division.

Apartheid's Memory Bank

With headquarters in Pretoria, the Plural Affairs Department, formerly known as the Bantu Affairs Department, plays a key role in the government's regulation of the African population. The Plural Affairs computer network, which is based on British-made ICL hardware, stores fingerprints and personal details on the 16 million South Africans whom the regime classifies as blacks.

Not far from the Plural Affairs Department in Pretoria, at the start of every business day, nearly 100 faithful state employees report for duty to a restricted area of the headquarters of the Department of the Interior that houses the "Division of Data Processing." Access to the Division is off-limits for good reason; it is a sensitive installation which houses the other major part of the apartheid system's registry—a computer base with files on another seven million people who are considered to be nonblacks.

Together, the Plural Relations and Interior Department's data systems make up apartheid's automated memory bank, giving the minority regime a degree of control that is unrivaled throughout Africa.

Interior Department Computer System

Since at least 1970, the Department of the Interior has relied on IBM hardware for its portion of the computerized population registry. Over the last ten years, new computers and peripheral equipment have been added to expand and upgrade the system's capability. Today, Interior Department operators use two IBM Model 370/158 mainframe computers. Files stored on magnetic tape and disc drives are retrievable by operators working at several terminals. The

---

*From *Automating Apartheid: U.S. Computer Exports to South Africa and the Arms Embargo* (Philadelphia, 1984).

IBM system processes and stores a vast quantity of details about the seven million South Africans including data such as identity numbers, "racial classification"—white, coloured, Cape Coloured, Malay, Chinese, Indian or Griqua—names, sex, date of birth, residence, photo, marital status, driver's license, dates of departure from and return to the country, and place of work or study. The same IBM computer functions as the basis for the "Book of Life," an internal identity document issued to all South Africans covered by the Interior Department databank. When questioned about IBM's role in the expansion of this system, an IBM official replied, "We feel that the fact that it is being done with computers hasn't any appreciable overall effects on the apartheid situation. This pass system could be done in many other ways besides computers."

In January 1981, Interior Minister Chris Heunis proposed an expansion of the identification system. Under the new plan, all population groups would have to submit to government fingerprinting, a requirement which currently only applies to people the regime classifies as black. "Fingerprints are the only irrefutable proof of identity;" the compulsory nationwide fingerprint program would help limit "increasing attempts to infiltrate strategic installations and national key positions with a view to espionage and/or sabotage," according to Heunis.

The IBM computer system used by the Department of Interior facilitates the very system of racial classification that undergirds apartheid. It also provides an efficient method of tracking South Africans' movements for security purposes. In the face of all this evidence however, IBM insists that it is politically neutral, and claims that it won't do business where its equipment will be used for repressive purposes.

Since exports to Pretoria's Interior Department are generally allowed by the U.S. government, IBM will likely continue to provide hardware to the Department's Data Processing Division. As the Interior Minister reported in 1978, the Department has been considering establishing new regional data-gathering facilities to back up its central computer installation. New satellite data processing centers of this type would extend the reach of the apartheid memory bank and would likely result in new contracts for IBM.

Watching the "Bantu" Public

Although the prospect of a new string of Interior Department computer centers, and mass compulsory fingerprinting both signal Pretoria's intention to tighten its grip on Indians, Asians, coloureds, and whites, the black population still endures the greatest degree of government surveillance and repression. Much of it is inflicted by the Department of Plural Affairs, the agency whose purpose, the government claims, is "to aid with the administration of blacks and guide them in their advancement toward self-determination. One of the Department's main functions is to administer the country's influx control system, a key feature of the Total Strategy. Influx control is the government's method of channeling needed black workers into the labor force and confining other blacks to South Africa's marginal, desolate reserves, known euphemistically as homelands. Influx control would not be possible without the hated passbook, which, if properly endorsed, gives its bearer the right to work or live in "white areas." Improper endorsements or failure to produce a pass can lead to arrest and jail.

The passbook system is based on a sophisticated computerized system which stores identity records and fingerprints from millions of Africans designated as blacks. "The fingerprint record," says the Department, "is absolutely essential because it guarantees positive identification and precludes the possibility of foreign blacks infiltrating into the Republic. . . ." All blacks are automatically subjected to fingerprinting at the age of 16. With fingerprints and personal data being fed into the automated system every day, the volume of the Plural Affairs Department's grim operations is staggering. In 1978, the Department had 15 million sets of prints stored in its central computer, and during the same year, the agency issued nearly 900,000 new passbooks and identity documents to South African blacks.

The repressive nature of the Department's computer bank has not gone unnoticed even in South Africa's white business community. One business writer described the system as "Computers flashing out reference numbers, photocopies relayed by telephone, perhaps even instant transmission of fingerprints—all to keep track of members of the population. Sounds like George Orwell's *1984,* doesn't it? Well it's SA's way of modernising and streamlining its pass and influx control system."

The British manufacturer ICL supplied the Plural Affairs computers. Although ICL is based in the United Kingdom, the company has a manufacturing facility in Utica, New York, which produces video terminals that could have been supplied to the Plural Affairs Department as part of the system. According to one U.S. computer industry guide, the type of computers ICL sells to the South African government contain "many U.S.-built components and peripherals."

Plural Affairs Network

Pretoria's Plural Affairs Department operates through a network of fourteen regional Bantu Administration Boards, which, the government says, "will, to an ever increasing extent, become the bodies on which the black laborer will rely for his physical and spiritual welfare while he is employed in white areas." The Boards, which serve as the arm of the minority government in the black townships, are made up of whites only and represent sectors of the economy with an interest in using and controlling the black urban population, such as industry, commercial organizations, the white unions, and local white government agencies. The Bantu Boards run the hostel system that houses many of the black workers who are not allowed to have their families with them. They also collect rent for group housing, run the Bantu tax system, and administer a complicated system of permits and controls which govern the movements of blacks.

Little information about the Boards' computer system is disclosed in South Africa, but the local computer industry press has indicated that the Bantu Boards have at least eight computers—all of them supplied from outside the country. Four of the computers are from ICL; four are furnished by U.S. corporations. Of the U.S. installations, three were apparently put in place before the U.S. began to place some controls on sales to the Department of Plural Affairs in 1978. One was installed in 1980.

The East Cape Administration Board, one of the largest in South Africa, uses a computer configuration based on a Burroughs 711, an ICL unit, plus printers and terminals. Burroughs' South African subsidiary rents this computer to the Board for R1300 per month. The system uses magnet tape and discs, which can locate and retrieve data within seconds.

Like other Bantu Boards, the East Cape Board is responsible for administering a series of repressive laws and directives which regulate the lives of all blacks in the large area under Board control. Police actions against blacks in the area are common. South Africa's Institute of Race Relations keeps a running account of them: ". . . In January, raids were conducted against squatters in East London's Second Creek and Mpuku Streets. Twenty-one people were arrested, convicted and sentenced to R10 or twenty days imprisonment each. . . . In February, East Cape Administration Board officials commenced with the removals and 'repatriation' to the homelands of squatters from these camps. Many squatters were reported as fleeing into the bush to escape removal. . . . Raids by board officials were conducted against Parkside (East London) squatters in November. . . . The squatter camp at Frankfort (King Williamstown) was demolished in March and the 150 families were resettled in an adjacent area. . . ."

Two U.S. computer suppliers furnish hardware to the East Rand Bantu Administration Board, which has jurisdiction over thousands of blacks in a large area to the east of Johannesburg. The Board's computer installation, in place since 1976, is based on a large Burroughs 3700 unit, and a model 1200 minicomputer supplied by Mohawk Data Science. The East Rand Board pays

Burroughs and Mohawk R228,000 per year to rent the computers—over a fourth of what it spends on housing for blacks in an average year. These computers are used to register blacks for the labor allocation system, and to administer the Board's financial matters. Although the Bantu Boards are directly involved in the implementation of apartheid, the flow of hardware to them has not stopped. Despite the embargo, the East Rand Bantu Administration Board installed a model 399 unit supplied by NCR some time during 1980. Blacks in the East Rand area are at the mercy of Administration Board police and the national police. Over 70 people are arrested in the area on an average day for pass law violations.

Expanding the Apartheid Memory Bank

In November 1980, the regime announced that it was considering a plan to expand computer surveillance of blacks by establishing a national network linking the Administration Boards and the police to a central computer in Pretoria. The new system was trumpeted as a measure that would reduce unemployment "by providing instant information on where jobs are and where workers are who can do the jobs." The network, which is under consideration in senior government circles, would amount to a vast national tracking system for the country's blacks, even more comprehensive than the one already in place.

Personal details fed into the computer would include educational qualifications, test results, employment histories, criminal records and "ethnic origins" of urban blacks and their status under influx control laws. The press also reported that the computer network would be programmed for "message input" by the police to pinpoint people who are required for questioning.

Apartheid critics denounced the proposal as marking a new era of control which, according to opposition spokeswoman Helen Suzman, "will make the pass system seem like child's play." Activist Sheena Duncan, a leader of the white women's organization called Black Sash, saw the regime's Total Strategy at work behind the plan. "Obviously, now they plan to link up and keep a stricter watch on black people's movements," commented a black leader.

The new computer system would be managed by the Department of Manpower Utilization, an agency authorized by the U.S. Commerce Department to receive U.S. exports on a case-by-case basis. U.S. computer companies in South Africa would presumably be free to bid on this project and supply the new equipment as long as they can make a case that the system would not enforce apartheid. . . .

67. SOUTH AFRICA: RUNNING SCARED*

by BROOKE BALDWIN

Brooke Baldwin is a graduate student in American studies at Yale University. An advisory board member of the Southern African Program for the Peace Education Division of the American Friends Service Committee, she is a member of the Yale Coalition Against Apartheid, and has done extensive research on the implications of U.S. investment in South Africa.

. . . .

U.S. financial involvement in South Africa currently stands at about $14 billion, including bank loans, shareholding and $2.3 billion in direct investment by some 300 U.S. based multi-national corporations with on-ground subsidiaries. While the South African foreign ministry claims that this investment is "not of determinant political importance in a country which draws the lion's share of its investment capital from domestic and other foreign sources," the government's own actions and admissions are among the evidence which contradicts this claim.

As early as 1982, Dr. Van der Merwe, head of the Reserve Bank's balance of payments section, admitted that increasing political pressure on foreign companies to limit their investments in South Africa had contributed to a shift in investment patterns away from direct investments toward [more vulnerable] loans. . . .

The *Rand Daily Mail* has reported that gross domestic fixed investment has been in decline since the end of 1981. This has partly been due to the business cycle, but also because the fear of disinvestment has diminished business confidence. In addition, John Chettle of the South Africa Foundation, a "foreign agent" registered with the U.S. Justice Department, who only two years ago was predicting the impossibility of successful divestment legislation, told the South African press that this withdrawal of existent direct investment was only the tip of the iceberg. The real damage to the economy, he said, had come from the loss of incalculable new investment:

> In one respect at least, the divestment forces have already won. They have prevented —discouraged, dissuaded, whatever you call it—billions of dollars of new U.S investments in South Africa. They have discouraged new companies, new investors who were looking for foreign opportunities from coming to South Africa.

*From *Economic Action Against Apartheid: An Overview of the Divestment Campaign and Financial Implication for Institutional Investors* (New York, 1985) [condensed].

. . . .

It would seem that the Foreign Ministry's claim that U.S. investment is of no "determinant political importance" lacks credibility in light of these facts. Far more credible is the *Financial Mail*'s conclusion:

> The build-up of foreign political pressures, and the willingness of some foreign interests to liquidate long-standing South African investments, suggests that the disinvestment campaign could have a cutting edge that should not be lightly regarded [by a country where] imported capital will continue to be vital to economic growth in the foreseeable future.

The South African government's own actions also belie its pretense of nonconcern with the importance of continued U.S. investment. Examples are plentiful:

- As the divestment movement has gained momentum, government lobbying has escalated in response, with almost 25 percent of its total $7 million lobbying expenditures for the the ten-year period from 1974 to 1983 being spent in 1983 alone. . . . In 1982, the South African Consul in Chicago produced a detailed twelve-page analysis claiming that Michigan divestment would run counter not only to the fiduciary responsibilities of university trustees but also to U.S. national interest. Also in 1982, the Washington law firm of Smathers, Symington and Herlong, on a $300,000 annual retainer to the South African government as a registered agent, sent a lobbyist to Boston to fight Massachusetts' landmark total divestment bill. And in 1983, the Pretoria government provided four Nebraska state senators with a $25,000 three-week tour, intended to win their anti-divestment votes. These efforts and expenditures are representative of lobbying which continues throughout the country.
- In 1982, when the South African government rewrote portions of its repressive legislation and replaced the Terrorism Act by the Internal Security Act, Section 54 (1)(a) and (2)(b) of the latter defined the support of divestment as "subversion" punishable by five years to life imprisonment. . . .
- On March 1, 1985, amidst interruptions and racial insults from other Members of Parliament (MP), a National Party MP, usually noted for his cautious conservatism, defended the failure of the government to evict Indians and "Coloureds" from a white residential area, arguing that such evictions would offend the rest of the world and add further impetus to the growing divestment threat. The *Rand Daily Mail* . . . contended that MP Meyer was reflecting the views of the Cabinet, who seemed to have come to realize that world opinion cannot be ignored when that opinion is backed up by the threat of damaging economic sanctions.

- Meyer's speech came only two days before the government created the new post designed to counter divestment, a move which the *Sunday Times*, Johannesburg, assessed as an "indication of the seriousness with which the government is treating the campaign." The *Times* added that further evidence of concern was an all-party seminar held that week to inform public representatives about the "extent and implications of the anti-South Africa drive." It also concluded that Botha's recent defensive speeches disclaiming government responsibility for the UDF treason trials came "as a clearing of the decks before the onset of the major disinvestment campaigns in the U.S. Congress and Senate." . . .

- [A memo presented to visiting Senator Edward M. Kennedy by the South African business community] is but one piece of compelling evidence that the local business community in South Africa is just as concerned as its government with the threat of the divestment movement. The *Financial Mail* termed the signatories of the memo, spokesmen for six influential South African employer bodies, including one Afrikaans group known for its government support, "Mr. Botha's Mutineers." The memo called for sweeping fundamental changes in government policy, including meaningful political participation for Africans, full black participation in private enterprise and an end to forced removals. The *Mail* emphasized that this was not a manifesto from the Left, but a "challenge to the government" from moderate business leaders "to change its ways before it draws down on South Africa universal odium, sanctions and disinvestment."

- The Federated Chamber of Industries' signatory spoke against forced removals as "only aiding those who want steps like U.S. disinvestment." The Associated Chamber of Commerce spokesman admitted that to some extent the memo was a "preemptive strike against disinvestment." . . . A factor which looms even larger [than the loss of vital revenue] is the government's fear of loss of investment and the technology which accompanies that investment in specific sectors vital to national security and economic viability. United States firms control, for example, 70 percent of the computer market, 45 percent of the oil market, and 33 percent of the motor vehicle market. Steven Bisenius, in warning against the dangers of disinvestment, is only one voice in a chorus who has declared that at stake is "the cut-off of new technology which accompanies U.S. investment in South Africa. I don't think South Africa's economy can afford to lose this important input." The *Rand Daily Mail* declared that South African corporations "could not hope to substitute adequately" for U.S. technology and managerial skills and added that their loss "would be such a hammerblow to business confidence" that it might actually discourage new South African investments.

· ·

A South African business analyst concurred, stating that "no other sector of the economy is as utterly dependent as the computer industry is on the multinationals . . . it is a sector through which a stranglehold can be applied on the whole economy."

Recent events suggest that oil is equally vulnerable to a U.S. stranglehold. On August 17, 1984, the *Financial Mail,* in considering the impact divestment could have on South Africa, stated, "No doubt, ways can be found to circumvent whatever divestment laws come into existence in America, or elsewhere. South Africa, after all, was able to overcome the oil boycott and the arms embargo—but in both cases at heavy financial cost." Several months later, the *Star,* Johannesburg, indicated how heavy those costs are, as an announced 40 percent increase in oil costs was predicted to bring inflation to a record high of 20 percent. The *Star,* reported that while politicians and businessmen alike were despairing over the tidal wave of price increases which was sure to follow, the Energy Ministry was warning that the 40 percent increase might not be the only one of 1985.

In March 1985 the African National Congress of South Africa (ANC) and the South West Africa People's Organization of Namibia (SWAPO) issued a report reviewing the impact of the 1979 United Nations General Assembly resolution calling for an oil embargo on South Africa. This study indicated that just under $2 billion a year is being devoted to overcoming the embargo imposed by most of the world's oil exporting countries. This amount exceeds South Africa's military budget for 1984.

The ANC/SWAPO report indicates that South Africa remains dependent on imported crude for 60 percent of its energy needs, despite development of the cost-inefficient SASOL coal-to-oil conversion plants, thus underscoring the impact withdrawal of U.S. corporations in this sector could have.

The *Rand Daily Mail* labeled as bravado government claims that there is no reason to fear American divestment because other foreign investors will rush to fill the void. Citing the American penchant to believe that "what is good for America is good for the world," the report predicts that once U.S. corporations have begun to withdraw, they will pressure others to act similarly.

This prediction is backed up by the opinion of Dr. Albert Wessels, a leading member of the Afrikaans business community, who, through his Toyota links, has come to believe that Japan would find it "exceedingly difficult to stay in South Africa once the Americans have gone." And, on March 20, 1985, in an interview on *Nightline,* Harry Oppenheimer, former chairman of Anglo-American, echoed his Afrikaans colleague when he declared that those who predict European countries will step in if the U.S. withdraws are "just whistling to keep their courage up." . . .

68. SOUTH AFRICA LOOKS CAPABLE OF SURVIVING SANCTIONS FOR YEARS—BUT AT A STIFF PRICE*

by STEVE MUFSON and LAWRENCE INGRASSIA

Steve Mufson and Lawrence Ingrassia are Wall Street Journal *staff reporters based in Johannesburg and London, respectively.*

In 1965, shortly after the first economic sanctions were imposed against white-ruled Rhodesia, then British Prime Minister Harold Wilson declared that the Rhodesian government would last "not months but weeks."

Fifteen years and a long, brutal civil war later, whites finally accepted majority black rule. The fact that Rhodesia—now Zimbabwe—held out so long is one indicator of how difficult it would be for economic sanctions to force political change in South Africa, experts on the region say.

In some ways, South Africa—also ruled by a white-minority government—is better equipped to survive sanctions than was Rhodesia. "South Africa is richer, has a better industrial base, and pretty much feeds itself," says Prof. Jack Spence, an expert on southern Africa at the University of Leicester in England. "It can engage in import substitution and there are always maverick states that will find ways to evade sanctions."

But while South Africa might be able to survive sanctions, it won't thrive. The sophistication of the economy makes it stronger, but also links it to the rest of the world. "It wouldn't have mattered if the world banned computer sales to Rhodesia, but it makes a big difference here," says Johan Cloete, chief economist for Barclays Bank in South Africa.

The Desirable Way

"While South Africa can certainly survive after a fashion without any capital inflow from abroad, this is undesirable in terms of the maintenance of a satisfactory growth rate," says Zach de Beer, chairman of LTA, a construction firm in the Anglo-American group of companies. "We can best achieve our socio-economic aims if we can arrange our lives in such a way that foreigners continue . . . to find us an attractive investment field."

The biggest companies in Rhodesia were South African firms that never considered withdrawing from the country. South Africa, by contrast, has

*From *The Wall Street Journal,* September 11, 1985.

many American and British companies, while several large South African companies have interests overseas.

South Africa desperately needs foreign investment to expand the economy for a black population that is growing rapidly; while the number of jobs for South African blacks hasn't changed in nine years, almost a quarter of a million blacks are entering the job market each year. Black unemployment of around 30 percent is fueling the current unrest.

"We want to grow at 4 percent to 5 percent a year in order to raise living standards at reasonable rates for our rapidly expanding population," says Mr. Cloete. "We have been getting less than 3 percent a year and that really isn't sufficient. There are only two ways to get it to go higher: export more or get direct foreign capital investment." As to the argument that any sanctions would directly hurt blacks more than whites, Lord Wilson, the former British prime minister, says: "I'm afraid there may be some truth in that. On the other hand, I think blacks will accept that suffering."

Adapting to Survive

Indeed, Rhodesia's example suggests that an embattled nation can adapt to pressure rather than make swift concessions. In the first decade after the sanctions on Rhodesia were imposed, the nation's industrial output doubled and mining output increased by two thirds. No longer able to import many products, Rhodesian companies began making everything from toothpaste to nails to shoes to home appliances. When black majority rule arrived, Tanzanian president Julius Nyerere said Zimbabweans had inherited the "jewel of Africa."

Oil sanctions against Rhodesia failed, as they have so far with South Africa. It was disclosed in the late 1970s that both British Petroleum Co., then state-controlled, and Royal Dutch/Shell Group supplied oil to Rhodesia despite the sanctions. The oil apparently made its way into Rhodesia from Mozambique and South Africa.

"It was impossible to stop them from getting essential equipment, essential food, essential raw materials," says Lord Wilson.

South Africa already has demonstrated how certain sanctions can be circumvented. It has acquired all the oil it needs through traders and built up a synthetic fuel industry. "Oil isn't a problem for South Africa," says Prof. Spence. "They allegedly have enough oil to keep themselves without rationing for two years and four years with rationing. Also, 70 percent of their energy needs come from coal, and they have enormous coal resources."

Arming Itself

South Africa also has managed to get around an arms embargo that has been in effect since 1965. Though the military could use replacements for some aging planes and ships, it has built a big arms-manufacturing industry for all the guns it needs. It even has exported some military equipment.

"Given time, we can probably replace whatever we can't import," says Mr. Cloete. "Everything we make in South Africa has an import content of about 20 percent" he adds, much of it in the form of machinery, ranging from baking ovens to mining equipment. The chemical and pharmaceutical industries rely largely on imported feedstocks.

U.S. sanctions so far fall well short of requiring any such import substitution. President Reagan's measures include banning computer sales to the government agencies dealing with apartheid, barring bank loans to the government, ending cooperation on nuclear technology, and stopping American purchases of Krugerrands. But IBM says it already falls within the guidelines restricting computer sales, most nuclear cooperation had already ended, and Krugerrand sales to the U.S. have dropped by more than 70 percent in the past year anyway because of Americans' reluctance to invest in the country.

Applying the Boot

Lord Wilson estimates that it would take at least six months to a year for tough sanctions to have any impact, but declines to predict how long it might take to actually force change. The fact that the U.S. has approved even limited sanctions is important psychologically because it is the one country that South Africa thought it could count on, he says. "I welcome the approach that the president is taking. . . . It's important that the U.S., almost for the first time, has started to apply the boot home."

"Sanctions will be imposed more for the West to be seen to be doing something than to impact the South African economy," says Prof. James Barber, an expert on southern Africa at Durham University in England. "The economic impact it might have had in South Africa is to undermine business confidence, but that is going now anyway. Sanctions may add to it a bit."

The psychological effect on investors seems clear but the psychological effect on the government isn't. S. J. Terreblanche, professor of economics at the University of Stellenbosch, warns that sanctions could have the opposite effect on the largely Afrikaner National Party. Lord Wilson agrees: "In the first instance, I think (sanctions) would make them feel lonely, hated, and they would be tougher than ever."

If the military and police burden of keeping peace in black townships increases, however, the combination of that with sanctions and the drain on capital investment could make the government's survival more difficult.

"Sanctions in Rhodesia became effective in undermining the regime when they were combined with revolutionary warfare," Prof. Barber says. "Sanctions made it more difficult (for the government) to fight."

69. SOUTH AFRICA-FREE INVESTMENT*

by *DOLLARS & SENSE*

Dollars & Sense *is a monthly magazine published by the Economic Affairs Bureau in Somerville, Massachusetts. It is edited and produced by a collective of economists and journalists who offer interpretations of current economic events from a socialist perspective.*

Over the past 10 years, colleges, universities, and pension funds all over the United States have divested their portfolios of stock in companies doing business in South Africa. Anti-apartheid activists have persuaded institutions such as Columbia University and the New York City Employees' Retirement Fund that divestment is a moral imperative.

Opponents of divestment—often institutional trustees, investment bankers who manage pension funds and university endowments, and executives of corporations with business in South Africa—maintain that divestment will lower the return or increase the riskiness of institutional stock portfolios because divestment narrows the universe of possible stocks from which portfolio managers can choose. But experience with South Africa-free funds (portfolios which contain no stock in companies doing business in South Africa) now shows that divestment actually leads to better portfolio performance.

According to the Investor Responsibility Research Center, 57 of the 100 largest Fortune 500 companies were operating in South Africa as of December 1984. The market value of firms with South African operations measured between one-fourth and one-third of the total market value of all stocks traded in the United States. Still, the South Africa-free companies are generally smaller than their counterparts doing business under apartheid.

Divestment opponents claim that fiduciary responsibility laws (the so-called prudent man rules), which govern the management of institutional portfolios, prevent them from investing in any manner which lowers the performance of·

*From *Dollars & Sense,* December 1985.

a portfolio below that which could be attained by any "prudent man." But studies which take into consideration both the risk and return of South Africa-free investments have found otherwise.

Several studies have evaluated the performance of South Africa-free funds, and found that, over a 5- to 10-year span, South Africa-free funds have consistently outperformed the Standard & Poors (S&P) Index of 500 large companies. Moreover, a survey of the largest institutional money managers in the United States showed that the median money manager not only did worse than the South Africa-free portfolios, but underperformed the Standard & Poors 500 as well! Experience has also shown that portfolio managers have been able to manage with Africa-free funds with significant less risk than funds containing South Africa-related stocks.

There's no reason a South Africa-free portfolio shouldn't do as well as a traditional portfolio. Even though South Africa-free companies tend to be smaller than those with operations in South Africa, they are still large in absolute terms. For instance, the South Africa-free companies in the S&P 500 have a median worth of $1.3 billion, compared to $1.4 billion for those in the S&P 500 doing business in South Africa. The universe of large, medium, and small firms available to South Africa-free investors remains enormous. According to modern professional thinking, any money manager worth his or her fee ought to be able to produce an optimal diversified portfolio drawing on the stocks of these companies.

Transaction costs—the costs associated with selling off South Africa-related stocks—are frequently cited by critics as a key obstacle to divestment. But if that's seen as the real obstacle, transaction costs can be held to a minimum by divesting gradually rather than all at once. For instance, the New York City Employees' Retirement Fund, worth $8.5 billion, is being fully divested over a five-year period.

A final argument in favor of divestment is that the business climate of a turbulent South Africa worsens every day. In response to the recent crisis, at least one firm specializing in corporate risk analysis recommends that firms doing business in South Africa de-emphasize their South African operations and prepare to shift production elsewhere. A recent *Business Week* listed 18 U.S. companies who have decided to divest part or all of their operations in South Africa, among them Ford Motor Co., Apple Computer, Pan Am and Singer. All cite declines ranging from 5 percent to 20 percent in the average return on their investments in South Africa. The "prudent man" rule may suggest that institutional investors should divest now.

70. DEAR EARTHA KITT*

by AFRICAN NATIONAL CONGRESS

The following article, in which the African National Congress is critical of stars who perform in South Africa, appeared in Sechaba, *the ANC's monthly magazine.*

. . . .

What we have said about Mr. Thorpe, Polaroid and Pepsi Cola goes as well for people like Eartha Kitt, Margot Fonteyn, Evonne Goolagong and all the others who have chosen off their own bat to break the boycott of South Africa. They all go for the profits they make in South Africa, and they all find reasons to justify their betrayal of our freedom fight. A reporter of the Johannesburg *Star* reported on May 27: "Singing sex-kitten Eartha Kitt told me before flying to Rhodesia at the end of her South African tour this week that she believed her visit had knocked a significant dent in apartheid.' " She hopes to come again, and to pave the way has also worked out a plan to salve the consciences of artists who want the pickings they can get in South Africa so badly they are even prepared to perform before segregated audiences.

In conjunction with OK Bazaars, Eartha has started an organization called SPEED (Stage Performers' Endowment for Educational Development) to raise money for African education. SPEED will ask every entertainer who comes to South Africa to give 2 per cent of his or her earnings toward African education. (Only 2 per cent, Eartha? Do you think you can buy us with 2 per cent?)

She said her visit had pricked White consciences, and claimed to have done more for the benefit of the Coloured people than the Coloured Labour Party which criticized her for coming. Well, Miss Kitt, all we can say is Mr. Vorster doesn't think so. He bans leaders of the Coloured Labour Party, but he hasn't done a thing to stop you, because he welcomes your help in breaking the international boycott of South Africa. He is prepared to dine with Dr. Banda, to allow you to sing to segregated audiences, and to let in any other person who is willing to perform on his conditions, because he knows what you do hurts us. Yes, Miss Kitt, hurts us, both physically and morally. You not only break the boycott we want imposed, but you hurt us, as a Black woman who has suffered the indignities of apartheid, by taking the side of our enemies in this struggle. You do what Vorster wants you to do; you don't do what we,

*From Sechata, September 1972.

the oppressed, want you to do. Whose side are you on? Are you just a good girl?

Moreover, Eartha, you encourage other people to overcome their doubts and follow in your footsteps. Two days after you spoke, Margot Fonteyn said in the *New York Times:* "What pleased me most, and made me feel justified in going was that Eartha Kitt was in Cape Town at the time I was there, and she was totally sympathetic and understanding and thought I had done the right thing. That made me very happy." Margot Fonteyn is a principled person. She even told Coloured demonstrators in Cape Town who objected to her performing before segregated audiences, that she was glad they had come. "I understand why you're here. I am happy to see you here with your posters. For 15 years I have refused many invitations to perform here, and nobody knew about that. At least my coming here has given you this opportunity to demonstrate." Please Dame Margot. We've got Vorster and his gang here already to demonstrate against. We have no lack of opportunities to get hit over the head with police batons. We don't need this sort of assistance from you or anybody else.

The time has come to say firmly to those who claim to be our friends that they must make their choice. South Africa is our country. We have chosen to fight and suffer to free it. If you are not in our camp you are in the camp of the enemy. There is no room in between. Please don't try to take the weapons out of our hands. If you can't join us, then at least leave us alone. We don't tell you how to dance or sing. What makes you think you know better than we do what must be done to "dent" or smash apartheid?

Above all, please don't sell us out for 40 pieces of silver and then pretend it is all for our own good.

71. *BOYCOTTING APARTHEID: ENTERTAINMENT AND SPORTS**

by UNITED NATIONS CENTRE AGAINST APARTHEID

This second [consolidated] register of entertainers, actors and others who have performed in *apartheid* South Africa since the beginning of 1981 is published

*From United Nations Centre Against Apartheid: *Notes and Documents,* "Register of Entertainers, Actors and Others Who Have Performed in *Apartheid* South Africa" (New York, December 1984); "Register of Sports Contacts With South Africa" [1 January–30 June 1984] (New York, December 1984); "Register of Sports Contacts With South Africa" [1 July 1982–31 December 1982] (New York, August 1983).

at the request of the United Nations Special Committee against *Apartheid*—as part of the campaign for a cultural boycott against South Africa called for in a number of resolutions of the General Assembly. . . .

Entertainers, Actors and Others *(January 1981–December 1984)*

Jim Abrahams, film maker
America, country rock group, composed of: Gerry Beckley, Darvey Bernell
Bob Anderson, singer
Paul Anka, singer
Susan Anton, singer
Beach Boys, band[1]
Bellamy Brothers, country music singers
Shelley Berman, comedian
C. L. Blast, singer
Norman Boehm, pianist
Ernest Borgnine, actor
Gwen Brisco, singer
Shirley Brown, singer
Glen Campbell, country music singer
Clarence Carter, singer
Ray Charles, singer
Cher, singer
Chicago, pop group
Rita Coolidge, singer
Chick Correa, jazz pianist
"Devine," singer-comedian
Valerie Errante, singer
Rénee Fleming, singer
Carla Fontang, jazz trombonist
Milos Forman, film director
George Forest
Midel Fox, jazz musician
Don Francisco, gospel singer
Buddy de Franco, clarinetist
Terry Gibbs, jazz vibraphonist
"Glide," breakdancer, member of the Dynamic Rockers
Jack Gregg, jazz musician
Michael Gunt, pianist

Susan Haine, dancer
David Hasselhof, TV star
Richard Hatch
Goldie Hawn, actress
Joe Henderson, saxophonist
Richard Groove Holmes, jazz musician
Jimmy Bo Horne, singer
Susan Howard
Peanuts Hucko, jazz clarinetist
Suzie Hyde, dancer
Janis Ian, singer
David Jackson, jazz musician
Willie "Gator" Jackson, jazz musician
Marine Jahana, dancer
Oliver Johnson, jazz musician
Jack Jones, singer
Garry Karr, bass virtuoso
Fern Kinney
Louis Lane, symphony conductor
Audrey Landers, actress-singer
Judy Landers, actress-singer
Jaime Laredo, violinist
Liberace, pianist
Love Machine, dancers and singers
Barry Manilow, singer
Ann-Margret, actress-singer
Barry Martin, dancer
Johnny Matthis, singer
Kevin Elliot Maynor, opera singer
Mighty Clouds of Joy, gospel singers
Liza Minnelli, actress-singer
Ella Mitchell, gospel singer
Marion Vernett Moore, opera singer
The New York Barbers' Shop and Agrupación Coral de Elizando
Linda Oliphant, singer
Charles Pace

---

[1] Have pledged not to perform in South Africa and had their name deleted from the register.

Alan J. Pakula, film director
Dolly Parton, singer
Peter Mancer Dancers and Reborn
Russell Peters, pianist
Jack du Pree, singer
Tim Reid, "Venus Flytrap," TV star
Kenny Rogers, country music singer
Linda Ronstadt, rock singer
Telly "Kojak" Savalas, actor
Shirley Scott, singer
Neil Sedaka, singer
Sharon Shackleford
Sha Na Na, rock group
Frank Sinatra, singer
Diane Solomon, singer
Candi Staton, singer
Dakota Staton, jazz musician
Joseph Swenson, violinist

Buddy Tate, jazz saxophonist
John Thomas, jazz musician
Stanley Turrentine, jazz artist
Lee Variety (leader of Variations Band)
Village People, band
Lovelace Watkins, singer
"Wavey" Legs, breakdancer, member of the Dynamic Rockers
Ronny Whyte, pianist
Aaron Williams, ventriloquist
Willy, juggler
William C. Witter, actor
Robert Wright
Pia Zadora, actress
Saul Zaentz, film director
Mark Zeltser, pianist
Efram Zimbalist, actor
Mike Zwerin, jazz musician

* * * * *

The South African regime and its racist sports bodies, despite their intensified efforts to break their international isolation, have so far failed to achieve any meaningful success. . . .

The International Rugby Board (IRB) is one of the few international sports federations which continues to accommodate *apartheid* sports and sanction international competitions with teams from South Africa without any reservation. . . .

Recent reports indicate that the regime provided large-scale financial assistance, through a series of tax concessions, to sponsors of sports events in order to enable them to lure sports persons from abroad.

White South African sports personalities are now complaining that overseas stars are being excessively pampered in South Africa. . . .

One [South African] player revealed that in 1983, when a South African team played Billie Jean King and Susan Mascarin of the United States in a "Test," the Americans were paid a fortune compared to the local players. "Billie Jean King brought in the crowds, so we have no complaints there," said the player, "But Sue? (Susan Mascarin) She was ranked nowhere, and got twice as much as our best player. We virtually played for nothing."

White South Africa's efforts to be represented at the Olympic Games and other major competitions has been repeatedly thwarted by the collective opposition of sports administrators from African, Asian, Latin American and East European countries. However, in collusion with the supporters of *apartheid,* South Africa is trying to penetrate into Olympic Games and other competitions by allowing its athletes to acquire passports of convenience or by registering its members with overseas clubs.

. . . Zola Budd, a South African athlete, was granted British citizenship in a record period of ten days in order to enable her to participate in the 1984 Olympic Games as a member of the British team. This was achieved with the assistance of a London newspaper, *Daily Mail,* and of the authorities concerned in the United Kingdom. The Government of the United Kingdom, despite a public outcry in the country, defended its action by saying that the "(Government) gave her exceptional treatment—but she (was) an exceptional girl."

South Africans are also reported to be competing in prestige athletic events as members of teams from the Federal Republic of Germany, Israel, Lesotho and Portugal. So far, the International Amateur Athletics Federation has been silent on this matter.

Internal Developments in South Africa

Most black South Africans participate in nonracial leagues. A few black South Africans who still participate in sports events authorized and supported by the regime continue to be humiliated by *apartheid* legislation.

The black government-recognized National Professional Soccer League (NPSL), which frequently boasts that its activities are nonracial, continuously falls into the *apartheid* trap when it is prevented from using most of the major football stadiums in the white "group areas."

In 1984, Witbank Black Aces, a member of the National Professional Soccer League, engaged a Peruvian player-coach, Augusto Palacios. He was prevented for some time from staying in the same house with his white wife in a white suburb because he was black.

The Sowetan, Johannesburg, aptly summarized the situation in South Africa on 4 April 1984:

> It is because of such laws that campaigns such as the sporting boycott have been launched vigorously. Palacios might have been one of those sportsmen who believed that politics and sports do not mix. In South Africa, they do. Maybe only now can he understand why the like of him should never have ventured to come and play in this country. . . .
>
> Oh! we are aware that red carpet treatment is laid on for black cricketers visiting the country. But much as sporting exchanges will enhance South Africa's claim of non-racial sport, a black still remains a black. To put it more crudely, South Africa's draconian laws will not be compromised because of a few sporting ventures. Palacios is no different. He is still a black man.

Alvin Kallicharran, the West Indian cricketer now playing in South Africa, had to obtain special dispensation from the Department of Internal Affairs to play in the Orange Free State. Kallicharran, of Indian origin, was forbidden by a provincial ordinance to live and work in the province.

A 60-year-old Indian businessman from Krugersdorp applied for membership in a local golf club in May. This immediately inspired an intense debate at the Krugersdorp Town Council; the matter was referred back to the management committee whose chairman said it should be a policy of the town council not to allow other race groups membership to white sports facilities.

The son of an Indian Councillor who cooperates with the regime had his application to join the Greytown Country Club (golf) turned down for the fifth year running. He now practices his game on the local polo and rugby fields.

Blacks playing in the government-authorized league of the South African Cricket Union in the Transvaal have been told by the Town Clerk of Potgietersrus that only whites could use the municipal grounds.

The group of West Indian cricketers who were lured to South Africa now find themselves unwanted both in their home countries and in South Africa. The wife of one of the Jamaican rebel cricketers said they cannot return home as they "are definitely outcasts." If the cricketers had been white, South Africa would have invited them to settle there as they previously did with white cricketers. But as blacks they could be accommodated only as third-class citizens and could not receive the "honorary white" status which was temporarily given to them while they played cricket.

Athletes (January–June 1984)

Professional Boxing
Buster Drayton
Billy Thomas

Golf
D. Abell
D. Allen
M. Allen
W. Ashwander
M. Blakey
M. Bodney
B. Brask
M. Buros
B. Buttner
B. Byman
J. Carr
T. Deber

E. Evans
B. Ford
D. Games
J. Grund
Rich Hartman
T. Jackson
G. Johnson
J. Kent
D. Kestner
D. Kluver
R. Kramer
K. McDonald
T. McGrew
R. Molt
B. Norris
T. Nosewics
D. Robertson
David Sann

E. Smith
J. Spelman
R. Stallings
P. Teravainen
M. West
B. Williford
N. Zambole

Horse Racing
Cash Asmussen

Motor Sport
E. Cheever
Eddie Lawson
Wayne Rainey
Freddie Spencer
Rex Staten
Jim Tarantino

Tennis

Sherry Acker
Jan Blackstad
Sandy Collins
Mary Anne Colville
Caryn Copeland
Christi Dorsey
Chris Evert Lloyd
Anna Maria
  Fernandez
Ann Hendrickssen
Jean Hepner
Andrea Jaeger
Suzie Jaeger
Jackie Joseph
Andrea Leand

Peanut Louie
Heather Ludloff
Ashara Maranon
Tina Mochazuki
Betsy Nagelson
Mary Lou Piatek
Barbara Potter
Mickey Snelling
Pam Teeguarden
Robin White

Water Skiing

Elaine Lundmark
Danny Aldrich
Don Aldrich
Mike Avila

Chris Bam
Mike Barnes
Ted Hoffman
John Straus
Mason Thompson

Weight Lifting

Dave Wagner

**Professional
Wrestling**

John Strongbo
John Studd
"Killer" Kowalski
  (manager)

(July–December 1982)

Golf

Johnny Miller
Jack Nicklaus
Jerry Pate
Craig Stadler
Lee Trevino

Gymnastics

Jay Foster
Lynn Lederer
Shari Mann
Jon Omori
Gary Rafalosky
  (Coach)

Mary Lou Retton
Noah Riskin

Tennis

Billie Jean King
Susan Mascarin
R. Akel
V. Gerulaitis
Brian Gottfried
Mark Groetsch
Johan Kriek (formerly
  South African)
P. Lehnhoff
T. Lucci

G. Manning
Jacques Manset
Sandy Meyer
Andrew Pattison
  (formerly South
  African, believed to
  be holding USA
  passport)
B. Schultz
Roscoe Tanner
Mark Wagner
Karl Yorston

PART FIVE:

SOUTH AFRICA'S FUTURE

Chapter XIV:

PROSPECTS AND SCENARIOS

72. *GUERRILLA PROSPECTS**

by R. W. JOHNSON

*R. W. Johnson, who was born in England but grew up in South Africa, is a tutor
in politics and sociology, Magdalen College, Oxford.*

. . . .

In order to extend the perspective of black working-class action beyond the
point of local wage disputes it is necessary to start conjuring with notions of
a concerted general strike leading to a violent confrontation between workers
and the state. Such notions, it may be seen, have more to do with the wilder
flights of Sorelian revolutionary syndicalism than with the more mundane
expectations suggested either by traditional Marxism or historical experience.
Labor history elsewhere in the world suggests strongly, after all, that the myth
of the mass general strike *is* a myth. Even should such an initiative be launched
it is difficult to see how it could be victorious. The workers lack coordinating
organization. They do not have funds to support a long strike. There are
blacklegs a-plenty. The townships will be sealed off by the police—they have
been built to specification to allow tight surveillance and control by small
numbers of police from prepared, strategic positions. Attempts at violent
confrontation will be met with the full force of the state's repressive machinery.
As yet little of this has been deployed—there is much more in reserve. The

**From *How Long Will South Africa Survive?* (London and Basingstoke, 1977).

Soweto disturbances saw the widespread use of armored cars and helicopters against the rioters. Pretoria has tanks and jet fighters too. How long will even the most determined workers' protest march last if it is being strafed by Mirages? Black workers—who are not fools—have understood this equation better than many of the revolutionary enthusiasts who would urge them toward fresh confrontations. Their political and industrial activity is likely to take such facts well into account. They may risk such confrontation if pressed, if desperate, or just possibly as part of some broader black movement of protest (as seems to have been the case at Soweto, where their action seems to have been one of communal rather class solidarity). They are unlikely to take such action out of revolutionary élan or mere principled loathing of white supremacy.

It seems not unlikely that the frustrations of black workers and unemployed may find outlets in attempts at urban guerrilla warfare. Toward the end of the Soweto events there were, indeed, signs of such a development with petrol-bombing forays into the white suburbs and arson against white business establishments. There is no doubt that urban guerrillas could wreak very great havoc and that there is no shortage of either targets or opportunities for such a movement. It is worth pointing out, though, that an urban guerrilla movement is constitutionally incapable of generating a mass movement behind it. A small number of militants act stealthily; their actions are as likely as not to have uninvolved blacks directly among its victims, and will quite certainly make them victims of the likely mass reprisals. For such reasons urban guerrillas have never led a successful campaign anywhere in the world. This tactic has failed throughout Latin America and it also failed under the more "promising" conditions of colonial Algiers. All the evidence suggests it would be a bloody dead end in South Africa too. . . .

Some of the same considerations apply to the possibilities of political action by rural Africans. These fall into two groups—those in the "white" countryside, and those in the homelands. The first group—perhaps 4 million strong —is politically invisible but not unimportant. . . . As white farms become increasingly mechanized their labor is required less and less, a fact which, in the government's eyes, provides a compelling reason for shunting this "surplus" population where it properly belongs—the homelands. Between 1960 and 1970 around a million rural Africans were thus uprooted. At some point the fear of starvation in the homelands may become so great that rural Africans, historically a politically quiescent group, heavily dependent upon their white farmer employers, may be pushed into open and violent resistance. The prospects for such a movement of resistance are, it must be said, extremely poor. The farmers themselves have a legendarily heavy hand with "awkward" Africans—among the African population in the towns rumors of horrific atrocities on the farms circulate continuously. In case of "trouble," the farmers would receive the full backing of the police against Africans who are usually illiterate, unorganized and only parochially conscious. For all their *de facto* preponderance in the "white" countryside such rural Africans have no land there of "their own" to retreat to. The possibility of rural risings against individual white homesteads can hardly be ruled out, but such activity would have a short life indeed unless it were part of a much more general movement of insurrection.

Finally, what of the prospects of political activity amongst the "homeland" Africans? . . . The question mark which hangs over the political activity of homeland Africans is not so much the chance that they may democratize the political systems of the Bantustans themselves, but whether the homelands in time will become the *foci* of guerrilla action threatening the white towns and countryside. There is no doubt that the build-up of a large, starving population, gradually radicalized by the experience of migrancy, poses such a threat.

Again, it must be said, the prospects for such action are rather poor. The homelands are bled of their young and active men. Only 42 percent of the population there is male; 49 percent are under 15 and a further 5 percent over 65. Secondly, one must not reason simplistically from starvation to revolt any more than one should argue from unemployment straight to urban protest. An overcrowded population at or beyond the edge of starvation does not necessarily provide a comfortable base for guerrilla action. Those who starve only sometimes rebel in anger; more frequently they die quietly of starvation, or live pleading for succour. Third, any such movement will, of course, have the power of the White Establishment with which to reckon—and, inevitably, the hostility of the Bantustan authorities themselves.

This last point is fairly crucial, for it means that such a guerrilla movement would not be able to regard the Bantustans as sanctuaries. There is no recorded instance of a guerrilla war being successfully waged without the benefit of a sanctuary. (Even the Cubans had the Sierra Maestra.) The sanctuary must provide not merely a place to which to retire after combat, but food, access to arms, and military training. In a number of recent guerrilla wars—the Vietnamese case is the most striking—the sanctuary has also provided a strongly supportive host government which supplies help in the most tangible form of all: its own professional army. A glance at the map, moreover, will show that most of the Bantustans are broken up into a multitude of small, unconnected fragments of land and that many are overshadowed by neighboring centers of white power. They could provide some sanctuary—but not much.

There is, finally, the point, argued by many, of the inevitability of the collapse of the White Establishment due to the sheer and growing numerical preponderance of the nonwhites. . . . Nonetheless, one must again warn against any simple jump in logic from such figures to the assumed inevitability of black majority rule in South Africa. There have been other white regimes in Africa and many have survived for years in the face of adverse black-white population ratios much greater than the 6.8:1 predicted for 2020 (or 9:1 if the ratio of all nonwhites to whites is preferred). At the time of writing, the Smith regime in Salisbury survives despite a ratio of blacks to whites of at least 20:1. The mind may well boggle at the prospect of over 70 million nonwhites being held in varying degrees of subjection by 9 or 10 million whites in the year 2020. The human costs of such a holding operation would be higher (they are high now), if only because there would be more humans, but there is nothing in historical experience to suggest that such a picture is inherently impossible. The figures can, of course, be projected onward to 2100 or beyond; at some point they must, doubtless, become conclusive on their own of black majority rule. But the history until now of white regimes in Africa does not suggest that the population ratio for, say, the next 50-year period provides an insuperable obstacle to continuing white supremacy. Rather, the history of such regimes very strongly suggests that the continuation of white supremacy for such a period is more likely than not. History, in a word, is again on the side of the *verkramptes.* . . .

. . . [A] guerrilla initiative [based in Mozambique] is, nonetheless, likely to come in the end. Reportedly the South African army already has contingency plans which envisage that areas such as the northeastern Transvaal and northern Natal may need to be abandoned as zones for free-fire operations. Even more fantastical schemes—for the withdrawal of the white population to a laager in the Cape, for example—are sometimes spoken of but may, effectively, be dismissed. The moment of truth comes long before that—if and when the great concentration of power, wealth and population in the Pretoria—Johannesburg area comes under threat. White South Africa cannot abandon that and survive. The crucial battles of a South African guerrilla war, one may fairly safely predict, will take place amongst the lions and zebras of the Kruger National Park and along the northern chain of the Drakensberg Mountains. The game reserves of northern Natal would seem equally likely areas of combat but they are strategically less significant.

To sum up, the position which faces South Africa in her frontier region is still extremely uncertain and one cannot predict with any confidence which direction events there may take. All that one may say is that the future of white supremacy in the Republic is likely best to be served by retaining the strategy of military nonintervention for as long as possible. This does not "solve" the long-term problems posed by the frontier balance but it would mean not having to face them fully for some time to come. To put it bluntly: if the

Pretoria regime adopts a sufficiently ruthless and brutal policy at home it may be able to repress black rebellion well into the twenty-first century; if it is willing to be sufficiently tough and flexible over Rhodesia and Namibia (allowing truly representative regimes to emerge there) *and* it is wise enough to keep its troops at home, its future would seem secure enough well into the 1990s. The margin is narrower but it is still considerable—and, of course, a 10–20 year period of respite places the decisions to be faced then comfortably beyond the time-horizon of working politicians now.

. . . .

If we take these trends together—the growth of Soviet power, the increasing use of Afro-Arab economic pressure on the West (in a period of recession), and South Africa's growing military and economic reliance on the West—there is the possibility that the West (and in practice it comes down to the U.S.) will gradually come to assume, however informally, a "metropolitan" role *vis-à-vis* South Africa. In our examination of the fate of other white regimes in Africa we saw how crucial to the transition from white supremacy to black rule was the key role of the metropolitan power. First it protected the whites from the military threat of black rebellion—and then used the leverage so acquired to force the whites into acceptance of majority rule. South Africa, we have said, was unique in good part because she lacked any relationship to such a power. But, if all the trends above continue, she may acquire one with the U.S. As Soviet power grows, so South Africa will feel increasingly threatened; at the same time she will be driven into ever greater dependence on the West militarily and economically; and the West will be under ever greater pressure from the Soviet bloc and the nonaligned states to use her leverage to ensure black majority rule in South Africa. That is, the U.S. will find herself placed in relation to South Africa as South Africa is now placed in relation to Rhodesia. It is exceedingly unlikely that America will ever play a metropolitan role to the extent of actually providing troops to stand between South Africa's whites and their black opponents internally or on the frontier. . . . Meanwhile the prospect of becoming either a protectorate of one of the big powers or a bone of contention between them has occurred to South African politicians. They do not like it, and are already beginning to strike heroic, "go-it-alone" stances. This does not necessarily mean very much—Smith did it in 1965. In the end reality has to be faced.

It has to be faced in the West too, particularly in the U.S. In the long run there are only two alternatives. Either the West must dig in and support white supremacy in South Africa or it must exercise a general pressure for its "reform," and, ultimately, its complete dismantlement. . . .

73. *THE ANC ROLE IS CENTRAL* *

by THOMAS G. KARIS

Thomas G. Karis is identified in the headnote to Reading 28.

Scenarios of the future can only be speculated upon, but it is difficult to envisage any in which the ANC will not have a central role. It is also impossible to see how violence can be ended so long as the regime is dug in and refuses to negotiate. From the American Revolution to Zimbabwe, the struggle for self-determination has often been accompanied by violence.

That negotiation with representative black leaders cannot be avoided is a principle endorsed by many white South African opinion-makers. Only occasionally, however, do they confront the reality of the political movement symbolized by the ANC. Such recognition was expressed on January 9, 1981, in a quickly deflated trial balloon in *Boeld,* the most influential Afrikaans newspaper and the Transvaal mouthpiece of the prime minister. Ton Vosloo, the editor, compared the ANC's "black nationalism" and support for it with the Afrikaner nationalism of the National Party. After identifying some non-negotiable conditions, he concluded, "The day will yet arrive when a South African government will sit down at the negotiating table with the ANC."

Bishop Tutu, who has met with ANC leaders while abroad but is not authorized to speak for them, volunteered in mid-1983 to act as a go-between in arranging negotiations. He had "little doubt," he said, "that the ANC would stop the armed struggle if it heard the government wanted seriously to negotiate dismantling apartheid." One condition would be that "our leaders in prison and exile" be participants in negotiation. There are undoubtedly additional prerequisites the ANC would insist upon before agreeing to a cease-fire. Given the current imbalance of white and black coercive power, the scenario is fanciful. Nevertheless, it seems important to note the issues that appear negotiable and those that do not. There is an encouraging possibility of some common ground with such men as Vosloo.

The ANC's primary aims—that South Africa should be nonracial, unfragmented, and governed according to a system of majority rule based upon universal suffrage—are not negotiable. Nor can the ANC be expected to accept any entrenchment of white economic privilege or rights to land. But if one accepts the positions of senior leaders at face value, the ANC would accept a bill of rights that guaranteed rights essential to a free political process. Since it has not arrived at any position regarding political institutions and proce-

*From *Foreign Affairs,* Winter 1983/84.

dures for the protection of minority rights, it is not committed to a "winner take all" system. Open to negotiation would be a federal system ("unitary" is often used loosely to mean an undivided country, not a unitary form of government), a bicameral legislature, electoral procedures, and judicial review.

Economic policy remains to be worked out, although the aim of a redistribution of wealth is essential. The ANC's orientation is toward an economy that is socialist, but pragmatic about free enterprise. On the question of attendance at the negotiating table, the ANC expects that other black groups who share historic aims would be included. Furthermore, no prescribed timetable exists for movement toward the goals set forth above.

Although ANC leaders still envisage some form of national convention, their expectation is that this could happen only after the liberation movement had transformed the climate for foreign business and imposed unacceptable costs on the whites. A persistent hope is that violence could be minimal if the wheels of the political system and the economy are stopped from turning. The vision is an old one: that masses of workers on whom the economy depends can bring down the regime. Over 30 years ago, the plan of the Defiance Campaign envisaged sustained and spreading strikes. Hoping for peaceful change, Buthelezi talks of grass-roots organization leading to a "groundswell" of numbers that will confront and overwhelm the oppressor. Thus, there is a romantic dimension to his realism. It also can justify postponement of interim action such as boycotts or civil disobedience while bolstering popular faith in eventual victory.

Another long-range strategy is that of the Federation of South African Trade Unions. In a careful mid-1982 statement, it praised the ANC as "a great populist liberation movement" of the 1950s but argued that changes—concentration of capital and the rise of a large industrial proletariat—have created conditions for a self-conscious workers' struggle. The important long-range task, therefore, is to build "non-racial, national, industrial unions, based on shop-floor strength." Prudently, FOSATU does not elaborate on how its strategy will mesh with popular movements or the nature of the political transition to a "society controlled by workers." But it foresees "bitter struggles" ahead. In commenting on the argument that only black workers and not armed struggle can win. Tambo has conceded that "the workers are potentially decisive" but insists that this is so only if accompanied by "the armed component."

Just what combination of legal, extra-legal, and illegal pressures will create a crisis for white power is unclear. The ANC talks of preparing the ground politically for the eventual involvement of masses of people in military action. This longer-range strategy envisages armed insurrection for the seizure of political power. How the rhetoric of "a war fought by the entire people" can be translated into reality in South Africa is conjectural. Presumably many would participate by using simple forms of sabotage. Discipline and control would be obvious problems. Already there are defendants in security trials who are untrained revolutionaries with no ANC connections.

Popular pressures to hit "the Boer" appear to be mounting. The racial dimensions of the struggle are recognized by the ANC's 14-year-old basic document on strategy and tactics. It gives primacy to African "national consciousness" in the face of a growing "all White solidarity" and foresees a "confrontation on the lines of color—at least in the early stages of the conflict." Yet there are strong constraints against indiscriminate killing of whites. Counteracting the "terrorist" image and comparison to the Palestine Liberation Organization propagated by the government is important for the ANC's standing in many Western countries. In 1980 the ANC became the first liberation movement to sign the protocol extending the Geneva Convention to wars of national liberation.

The most important constraint is the ANC's policy on racial cooperation. It places a high priority on facilitating the growth of white groups within South Africa that support its aims and would be prepared to cooperate with it. The ANC is genuinely anxious, in short, not to exacerbate racial bitterness, thus jeopardizing the goal of a nonracial society.

74. WHAT CAN BECOME OF SOUTH AFRICA?*

by CONOR CRUISE O'BRIEN

Conor Cruise O'Brien, the prochancellor of Dublin University and a contributing editor of The Atlantic, *is a graduate of Trinity College, Dublin, from which he holds a Ph.D. in history. In 1956 he was named assistant secretary-general of the Irish Foreign Office and deputy chief of the Irish delegation to the United Nations. In 1961 he served in the Congo as the personal representative of UN Secretary-General Dag Hammarskjold. He was subsequently the vice-chancellor of the University of Ghana and the Albert Schweitzer Professor of Humanities at New York University. O'Brien is the author of many books, including* To Katanga and Back *(1962),* Writers and Politics *(1965),* Camus *(1969),* States of Ireland *(1972),* Herod *(1978), and* Neighbors *(1980). His most recent book,* The Siege: Zionism and Israel, *was published in March 1986.*

"When is a black president going to rule South Africa?" The question was put to State President P. W. Botha at a rally in Springs, Transvaal Province, in one of the critical by-election campaigns of late last year. The questioner appeared to be a supporter of one of the two parties to the right of Botha's

*From *The Atlantic Monthly,* March 1986.

National Party—parties then gaining ground at its expense—and the point was that the policies of Botha's government might open the way to the coming of black power.

President Botha's reply was: "If we respect minority rights, we won't have black majority rule."

"Minority rights," together with "mutual respect," "participation without dominion," "co-operative coexistence," and "joint responsibility," is Botha-speak for what used to be called apartheid. The official language, used in Botha's 1983 constitution, is "the self-determination of population groups and peoples" *(selfbeskikking van bevolkingsgroepe en volke).* But it appears from all this lexical fumbling that the regime has not yet been able to find a new designation for apartheid which satisfies even itself.

The term *apartheid* ("separateness," often anglicized as "separate development") is just fifty years old. It belongs by now in the embarrassing category of discredited euphemisms and is far more often heard from the lips of those who denounce it than of those who invented it. Some of the more "enlightened," or *verligte,* Nationalists—basically those who are most concerned with trying to make a relatively favorable impact on international public opinion —have been saying for nearly ten years now that apartheid is dead, or dying. This is an acceptable official position. Dr. Piet Koornhof, who told the National Press Club in Washington in 1979 that apartheid was dying, was minister of cooperation and development. "Cooperation and development" is in fact another euphemism for apartheid, and Dr. Koornhof was chief administrator of what he said was dying. President Botha, personally, doesn't go so far verbally as Koornhof has done; Botha has spoken of "outgrowing apartheid in the discriminatory and negative sense."

The term *apartheid* is out of favor, but the main structures—such as segregated residence—set up in the name of that concept are still in place. The concept is that of the separate development of the different peoples of South Africa, according to legal categories defined exclusively by whites, within political institutions established exclusively by whites, and within an overall system controlled exclusively by whites. There is no apparent disposition on the part of a majority of whites to change those realities of power. The argument that most interests most whites is over how best to protect those realities: whether by going down P. W. Botha's road of limited reform (that is, by removing irritations associated with apartheid but not those essential to its maintenance) or by digging in and telling the blacks and the outside world to go to hell.

The "mini-general election"—five simultaneous by-elections at the end of October—showed the second school of thought as gaining, but not gaining very fast. The Nationalists have been losing Afrikaner votes to the parties on the right: the Conservative Party and the Herstigte Nasionale Party (which won a seat from the National Party in October). But these losses have been partly made good by a drift of English-speaking whites to the Nationalists, which enabled the Nationalists to hold four seats out of the five contested in the by-elections. Botha has had some success in projecting himself as not just the leader of the Afrikaner *volk* but the leader of "South Africa," meaning all the whites, including those whom Afrikaners used to call *Neef Brit,* "Cousin Brit."

This need to attract Anglophones may have something to do with the disfavor into which the purely Afrikaans euphemism *apartheid* has fallen and the tendency to replace it with woozier formulas—like those quoted above—mostly drawn from the richer rhetorical resources of Anglo-Saxon hypocrisy.

Neef Brit has been welcomed and wooed at Nationalist election meetings for years past, although (or because) all these elections have resulted in a strengthening of the Afrikaner monopoly of power in Parliament, as well as in the civil service, the army, and the police. Nationalist platform orators—almost invariably Afrikaner—are careful to alternate paragraphs of Afrikaans with paragraphs of English. Even the warm-up music for the National Party rallies includes not only old Afrikaans favorites but British tunes as well, slightly refracted through dim memories of Afrikaner schoolrooms. Thus the first three items on the musical program for Botha's election rally at Springs ran:

(1) She'll be coming around the mountain when she comes
(2) My Bonnie lies over the ocean
(3) Daizy, Daizy, give me your anser do

Daizy (sic), Daizy (sic), give me your anser (sic) do. Nobody seemed to notice anomalies. There were obviously very few born English-speakers present, and any who were would be so fully committed to the politics of Afrikanerdom as to be past worrying about how to spell Daisy.

As you can sense, the atmosphere of a modern National Party rally is significantly different from what is presumably imagined by those who call the South African Nationalists Fascists and Nazis. At Nationalists rallies there is (so far) nothing reminiscent of the Fascist or Nazi *style:* no dramatic light-and-sound effects, no military precision or paramilitary presence, no apparatus for inducing hysteria, and no manifestations of hysteria. At Springs, I was reminded not of Nuremberg but of a meeting of the Parti Québecois at Rivière-du-Loup (except that the Québecois would never have sung "Daizy"). These were middle-class (or upper-working-class) people from the same province, related to one another, speaking the same language, practicing the same religion, familiar with the same history books, worried about the same things. They were stolid, undemonstrative people, a bit puzzled and a bit nostalgic. Most of them seemed to like P. W. Botha, without being wild about him. A few right-wingers in the audience didn't like him much but weren't wildly against him either. Any fanaticism that may have been present was not lying around on the surface.

Too much, of course, can be made of that impression of normality. This was an all-white meeting in an electoral district most of whose inhabitants are black and consequently disenfranchised for all elections on which power in South Africa depends. The only black person in sight was an American cameraman. If South African blacks had gained admission to that meeting, even without heckling the stolidity level would have dropped dramatically. So also in Northern Ireland: Orange rallies are generally stolid, casual, and good-humored, but the detected presence of a Catholic, presumed hostile, can evoke some latent hysteria and violence; I speak from experience. (The Orange/Afrikaner comparison is quite a fertile one, provided it is not being used just for the stigmatization, or demonization, of one community or the other, or both.)

Similarly, if movie footage of South African police bashing black youths had been shown in that hall, it would have elicited sounds of approval, not disapproval. There is an organic connection between such orderly and peaceable gatherings as those election meetings and the episodes of violent repression required for the maintenance of apartheid (alias "minority rights" and so forth).

The connection should be noted, but preferably without too simple an assumption of moral superiority over those respectable-seeming people who sustain all those brutal, *sjambok*-wielding, buckshot-firing policemen we have seen on television. For there is a scarcely less intimate connection between the international agitation against the apartheid state—the pressures for disinvestment and sanctions—and the internal violence applied against the servants and suspected servants of that state.

The greatest victory in the struggle against apartheid, so far, has been the replacement of white indirect rule in the black urban ghettos by the rule of those who are known as "the children." The children are those who attend school, when they choose to do so. Some of them are as old as twenty-four; most of them are teenagers; pre-teens, down to eight or so, play supportive enforcement roles. It is the children—in this context the militants among them —who have made life impossible, often literally, for the agents of white power in black townships. It is the children who enforce the boycotts, whether of schools or of white shops. It is the children who discipline those who are seen to step out of line.

The children see themselves as the pacemakers of the revolution, and, like other revolutionaries, they make use of terror. But the guillotine was merciful compared with the children's chosen method of execution: burning alive, with a gasoline-filled rubber tire, "the necklace," around one's neck. The children humorously refer to each such case as a "Kentucky," after Kentucky Fried Chicken. A Kentucky and its necklace do not represent spontaneous outbreaks of popular rage. They are a standard ritualized penalty applied to black men and women designated as informers or collaborators.

On a university campus one bright afternoon in the South African spring I discussed the children and their works with an elderly black theologian, a clergyman resident in one of the townships—as the segregated urban locations for blacks are known. For obvious reasons, connected with the laws of South Africa, I don't identify this source; let us call him Ezra. I found Ezra in his study, reading a work by a mid-Victorian Methodist missionary. Ezra was chuckling, and read out the passage that tickled him. It was one of those "mysterious Africa" bits, a purple patch about the almost infinite depths of the black man's inherent incapacity to comprehend anything whatever. "He's talking about *my grandfather!*" Ezra cried with delight.

Ezra has been a member of the African National Congress since the early days—long before the ANC was banned, in 1960—and is still a firm supporter, and therefore committed, at least in theory, to aiding the armed struggle, ordered by the ANC, against apartheid. He doesn't like the Marxist tendencies of some of the present ANC leadership but doesn't take them too seriously. "I don't fear an African who, while he is fighting, utters voluminous words of Marxism," he says.

I asked Ezra a question about the state of the Church in the townships today. Very satisfactory, Ezra thought. The churches were always full on Sundays. "The ministers are with the people definitely. In a tremendous way. Ministers were among the first detained—especially Methodist ministers. The black side of the Church is tremendously radicalized." Ezra went on to talk about the police, who cause most of the violence, he said, especially by their attacks on funeral crowds as they disperse. "You get disgusted by such clumsy forceful-ness." The pulpits of the townships, it is clear, condemn all that.

I asked whether the parish clergy also condemned what I called "examples of popular violence." The wording was mealy-mouthed, because the question was fraught. Somehow it seems difficult to ask a Christian clergyman who is also a supporter of the ANC exactly what he has to say about the children and their necklace. The ANC's position on this matter is equivocal. According to a source generally sympathetic to the ANC, Roger Omond's recent *Apartheid Handbook*, "[The ANC's] leaders say that it attacks military and security targets, and tries to avoid civilian deaths, but that it is impossible for civilians to be completely unaffected by an armed struggle." It is certainly impossible to be completely unaffected by being burned to death.

Ezra did not care for my question, put though it was with almost Proustian delicacy. At first he tried to brush it aside. "There are generally not incidents on Sunday," he informed me.

How about Saturday? I wanted to know. Suppose an "incident of popular violence" happened in a certain parish on a Saturday night. Would the parish clergyman take that as a theme for his Sunday sermon?

"No," Ezra said. "He would fear for himself." Similarly, if a clergyman were asked to allow his church to be used for a political meeting, he could not refuse, in such circumstances. "They are really in sympathy. . . . It is a ministry to a very angry people."

True, there was the case of Bishop Tutu. The Bishop had not only condemned violence—whether popular or police—but had actually successfully interposed his person, at a funeral, between some children and their intended victim. But this transaction, Ezra seemed to think, had done little to enhance the brave Bishop's popularity among the young in the townships. Ezra had watched the scene on television. There were some children in the audience and they "jumped up and down with rage" at the Bishop's intervention. Ezra himself clearly thought that the Bishop had made a mistake in antagonizing the children in this way. Yet Ezra seemed to have his own reservations, very mildly expressed, about the temper of the young. Older people were "a bit more irenic than the young ones," as he put it. "You sober down. The children don't know how change works. . . . They are very optimistic." The thought of what all that childish optimism might entail seemed to depress his spirit, for he added: "I can't visualize what is going to happen. . . . I don't see much that is good in the future."

In another region of South Africa, more deeply stricken than Ezra's home territory by what white South Africa calls the unrest, I got a slightly different perspective on a world run by children. My informants were a middle-aged businessman, Bob, and a young clergyman, Mark. Both lived in the local township. Both were resolute supporters of the ANC and prominent members of the United Democratic Front (UDF), the umbrella group of organizations following the ANC's political line. Mark had recently been detained. These men were more political than Ezra, and also more closely involved with what was going on politically. Mark was highly articulate, obviously used to dealing with liberal sympathizers, and good at this kind of party work. I found Bob more illuminating, probably because his English was not quite good enough to conceal the complexities and contradictions of his actual thoughts and feelings.

Both were concerned about what was happening in their township and about the tendency for criminals to take over from the politicals. This would get worse, they both thought, as long as the government continued to refuse freedom of political organization. Nelson Mandela and other prisoners and detainees would have to be released unconditionally, and the ANC exiles allowed to return, also unconditionally, before the growth of anarchy in the townships could be checked. The Progressive MP for the area, who had brought us together, thought that was reasonable, and so did I. Reasonable, and therefore probably remote.

Both Bob and Mark spoke like men who have a lot more to lose than their chains and who thought they might be on the way to losing it. They supported the call for the withdrawal of the troops and riot police from the townships. But for ordinary policing, as was known in the townships before the Emergency (declared in July 1985), they seemed to feel a certain ambivalent nostalgia. Mark said, "People did retain a fair amount of faith in the police. If my house is burgled, for example. But now there's a tendency to say, 'Get rid of them all.' But some say, 'Let them stay and operate as police' " (that is, not politically).

"Rev. is right," Bob said, but corrected him slightly: "Everybody respected the police before the riot police. But now there's no difference." Bob is a big, stout man with a lot on his mind. Suddenly, out of the blue, he said, "That type, now, of that little youngster . . ." Instead of finishing the sentence, he related an incident:

"On Friday night"—we were meeting on Tuesday—"six thugs armed with pangas attacked an Indian home, beat the husband, and repeatedly raped his wife, who later died."

Then, after some thought, Bob added a political gloss. In this urban area the Indian housing estate is "a buffer zone" between the black and the white areas. So one had to "get rid of the buffer zone, to get at the whites," he said. "These youngsters, just seeing the white face, they attack."

Bob's remarks lacked logical connection, and were therefore convincing, in the context. The six were seen in the first place as "thugs": criminals, not comrades. But they were also seen as agents of a political-racial purpose: breaking up a buffer zone and clearing the way for the revolutionary attack on the white area, the heartland of apartheid. The dividing line between criminality and politics may be clear in theory and rhetoric; in practice, and emotionally, it is liable to get blurred.

Rhetoric and reality also tend to drift apart where Indians are involved. According to ANC-UDF rhetoric—as engaged in certainly by Mark, and probably also by Bob in formal party contexts—Indians are fellow blacks. In practice, it would seem, this is not exactly so. The youngsters of whom it was said, "seeing the white face, they attack" were in fact, on this occasion, seeing Indian faces and attacking Indian people.

The children, it is plain, have a grip on the imagination of their elders. And it is not just through fear that this grip is maintained; admiration enters into it too. The elders are a bit ashamed of their own past submissiveness to things like the pass laws and are proportionately proud of their children's bravery in defying apartheid. The system is loathed—and not just by the highly politicized—and no less so for being rebaptized "minority rights" or "self-determination." The system's black agents have been correspondingly hated, and the children are admired for taking on those agents, even though the frightfulness of the children's favored penalty may be quietly deprecated by some of the elders.

Yet the children with the necklace are only some of the children. "These youngsters, seeing the white face, they attack" is not, or not yet, true of most of the youngsters. I was able to find that out for myself—not altogether voluntarily—one Sunday morning, on my way to hear Bishop Tutu conduct a religious service at St. Matthew's Church, Embeni, Soweto.

I went to Soweto because it was an opportunity to see Bishop Tutu—whom I know already in the white context—at work among his black parishioners. Entering Soweto in a taxi that morning, I felt a bit nervous, and not only because of Bob's dramatic generalization. There were other reasons, both political and personal. Politically, it looked like being a rough weekend. On the previous Friday the political activist Benjamin Moloise, convicted on a murder charge, had been hanged in Pretoria Central Prison after two years' imprisonment, despite a general expectation that his sentence would be commuted. A commemorative service was held in Johannesburg—not Soweto—later that morning. As the mourners left the service, having been addressed by Winnie Mandela and others, a resident in a neighboring white apartment block dropped a flowerpot from an upper window into the middle of the mourning crowd. This precipitated a riot—the first black riot in downtown Johannesburg, legally a white area. There were riot pictures in the Johannesburg *Business Day* the following morning. These aroused a lot more attention among the paper's white readers than the usual riot pictures. The usual riot pictures were taken in Soweto (when they could still legally be taken there) and showed either "white on black" (white policemen bashing black demonstrators, or at any rate blacks of some description) or "black on black" (black militants lynching black collaborators, or at any rate blacks of some description). For most white people, who never go near places like Soweto, all that seems almost as remote as it does to people looking at these same Soweto pictures in New York or London. But the pictures that appeared in *Business Day* on the morning of Saturday, October 19, were taken not in Soweto but in downtown Johannesburg, and they belonged to a hitherto quite rare category of picture—"black on white." They showed black demonstrators shoving white people around—not shoving them all that drastically, and nothing remotely comparable to some of the horrors of black on black, but they were still more startling and more ominous than anything shown before, since those shoved were whites, those shoving were blacks, and this was Johannesburg, 1985.

Business Day is a pretty dull newspaper, but it made compulsive reading that morning.

Black on white is still rare among politically motivated happenings, but it is not so rare in what you might call the private sector. On the afternoon of that same Saturday, I myself became a small statistic of black on white in the field of urban crime. It was a warm afternoon, and I was taking a walk in the neighborhood of the Carlton Hotel, where I was staying. There were not many people around—shops and offices close at one o'clock on Saturday—and most of those who were around were black. Suddenly, quietly, and quite gently, one of these grasped my arms from behind. Another appeared in front of me, very close. From a distance he might have seemed to be asking for a light. In fact he had a knife with a four-inch blade pointed at my throat. A third man frisked me expertly and removed all my valuables, but left me my passport and notebook. Then they made off, without physically molesting me in any way. They were not children but middle-aged men, and from their age and relative restraint you might infer that they were non-political: "ordinary decent criminals," as they say in Northern Ireland.

So what? the reader may reasonably ask. A person can be mugged in any modern city. I know this. In fact, the last time I had been mugged—almost exactly twenty years before—was in Manhattan, at Morningside Park. Although that event occurred during a break in a Socialist Scholars' Conference at Columbia, it had no political significance and did not portend the imminent eclipse of the United States Constitution or the collapse of the capitalist system. Nor would the corresponding happening in Johannesburg justify conclusions about the impending collapse of law and order in South Africa, although it does suggest that the forces of law and order may be stretched thin by the combined impact of escalating political unrest and escalating ordinary crime, both drawing on the same huge and expanding pool of black unemployed. (With an additional 350,000 seeking work each year, South Africa's director general of manpower, Dr. Piet van der Merwe, expects unemployment to have more than doubled in ten years: from 10.6 percent of the labor force in 1977 to 21.9 percent in 1987.) I mention the mugging not because of any such wider implications but mainly because of the slight subjective jolt that such a happening imparts to the perspective from which the writer so affected views the phenomena about which he is writing. If you have recently had a knife held at your personal and non-metaphorical throat even for fifteen seconds, you are unlikely to be able to write about violence with the same degree of composure and fluent capacity for abstract generalization on the subject as you could attain had you not been obliged to concentrate, intensely if briefly, on the blade of that knife. The middle-aged men whose acquaintance I made that afternoon in von Brandis Street, Johannesburg, were altogether silent for the whole period of our life together, but if you listen carefully during the discussion of violence which inevitably pervades this essay, you may occasionally be able to detect the faint sound of their breathing.

* * *

No, reader, I have not forgotten that I was about to proceed to St. Matthew's Church, Embeni, Soweto, there to witness Bishop Desmond Tutu conduct an Anglican service. The sequence of events, both macro and micro, runs as follows:

Friday morning. A black man is hanged in Pretoria, and mourned in Johannesburg, mainly by blacks. A white hand drops a flowerpot, from a height, onto the mourners. The mourners riot.

Saturday. Black-on-white pictures in the paper. I get mugged (coincidentally).

Sunday. To Embeni, Soweto, to witness Bishop Tutu, and so forth. But before I go on to Embeni, please allow me yet another digression. It is through such digressions, I think, that I can best share with you a personal experience of South Africa.

Brief digression on having been mugged as a topic of conversation in white liberal circles in today's South Africa.

First of all, it isn't a topic of conversation. "I have been mugged" is a conversation-stopper, and a veritable bazooka among conversation-stoppers. I found that out at a party in Johannesburg's northern suburbs on the evening of my little mishap.

The presence of a mugging victim, I found, is a great begetter of pregnant silences, the pregnancies being strictly of the unwanted variety, to judge from the expressions of those so affected. That much is a matter of observation. Why it should be so can only be guessed. My own guess is based on placing myself in the shoes of those concerned. This I do without much difficulty, because I am a white liberal myself (subspecies *Homo Candidus Liberalis Pessimisticus*) and I have lived in Africa (Central and West, not South). So I hear their underground train of thought as rumbling along the following lines:

> *By blacks, of course, though of course he doesn't say so. He would say so if they were white. But whites have other ways of robbing people, with less risk. And what can a black do, if he's out of work and has no one to help him, except rob, whatever the risk? There's no social welfare, and millions of blacks are unemployed.*
>
> *So how can you tell the muggee how frightfully sorry you feel about his trouble? The muggers are far more deserving of sympathy than he is. He can stop his credit cards and traveler's checks and be very little the worse for his experience. They continue their desperate, hand-to-mouth existence until they get caught and go to jail.*
>
> *Yet the muggee's hard-luck story is hard to take for some other and quite different reasons. We ourselves are potential muggees, and worse than muggees, and we shall remain here, at high risk, long after this character has gone back from whence he came. And we ourselves hardly deserve more sympathy, even from ourselves, than we could legitimately offer this hard-luck man—perhaps even less. We, too, are affluent, within a system we oppose and despise, so we are also—at least to some extent—legitimate*

targets, not only of the violence of the black unemployed but also of the revolutionary political enemies of apartheid. Ideologically, we have to be on the side of those who pose a threat to our lives and property; existentially, we are unable to be on that side. Also, we are unable to change the color of our skins, a matter that ought not to be of the slightest importance but that the white community over many generations has made into the touchstone of everything, the be-all and the end-all: a be-all that looks more and more like an end-all.

We have had to contemplate that desolate range of subject matter for quite a long time, and we never much like being gratuitously reminded of it. So I'm afraid our accident-prone friend would do well to pass on, without undue delay, to some other topic of conversation.

The words are imagined, but the predicament reflected in them is real. Like other predicaments—the Irish one, for example—it is fraught with ironies. In noting the ironies, in attributed language, it is very much not my intention to satirize those who are caught in the predicament, which is probably the grimmest that any liberals have ever been caught in. These South Africans are coping with it, in many cases with admirable courage, resourcefulness, and cheerfulness combined with intellectual rigor. I am thinking in particular of South African scholars and writers who over many years have combated apartheid by all the means appropriate to their functions.

It is a crowning irony that while the apartheid regime is punishing the journalists in their function, by elaborate and expanding censorship provisions, some of the dottier foreign enthusiasts of anti-apartheid are trying to inflict precisely symmetrical damage on South Africa's academic community. Thus a group of Irish lawyers, with Mr. Sean MacBride, the Nobel and Lenin International Prize for Peace-winning former director of Amnesty International, as its most eminent member, recently urged an academic boycott of South Africa. The institutions that would be worst hit if this disgusting proposal were acted on are those—like the University of Cape Town—that are totally desegregated and are major sources of accurate information about the workings of apartheid and agents of exposure of attempts to camouflage apartheid. The zealots of apartheid will be absolutely delighted if this scheme of the zealots of anti-apartheid ever catches on. The fact is that both lots of know-nothings hate liberalism and associated manifestations of disinterested intellectual activity.

After writing the paragraph above I learned that the South African scholars invited to the World Congress of Archaeology in Southampton next year have had their invitations withdrawn by the organizers.

End of digression and on to Embeni. When I ordered a taxi, giving that destination, on the Sunday morning, the hotel porter told me that I should get a police escort. But somehow I didn't feel I would be all that welcome in

Bishop Tutu's congregation if I turned up supported by a Casspir armored personnel carrier—full of South African police. In any case, such support would be likely to attract a lot more trouble along the way than it might avert. That was my hunch, and it turned out to be right. So no police.

My taxi driver rated as "coloured" (mixed-race) in terms of the basic document of apartheid, the Population Registration Act of 1950, so he wasn't a resident of Soweto (by virtue of the Group Areas Act of the same year). He told me he knew the way to St. Matthew's, Embeni, but actually he didn't; he just knew the way to Soweto, a sprawling city of small houses, encompassing more than a million and a half people. Once in Soweto, he had to ask the way, and this he did about twenty times. The first few times, I sweated a bit. I have driven with Protestants through Catholic South Armagh, and with Jews in the vicinity of Hebron, and felt a bit nervous each time, but I felt more nervous this time remembering Bob's dictum "seeing the white face, they attack" (and a white face is a lot more conspicuous in Soweto than, say, a Protestant face in South Armagh). They all saw the white face, but there was no attack. Among the first people consulted by my driver was a group of young males: children. They showed no signs of color prejudice but gave directions in a friendly way. The same was true of all the people we talked to in other areas of Soweto. It was rather different from what you might think Soweto is like, and different also from what Soweto actually *is* like under other conditions— for example, at a funeral and in the presence of the police. Considering the high proportion of politicized militants among the youth of Soweto, it is improbable that there were not some of these among the people consulted by my taxi driver. My guess is that any militant children who took note of my presence considered that the only kind of white person fool enough to ride around Soweto in a taxi looking for directions would be a foreign sympathizer with "the cause of the people"—that is, the ANC.

In any case, violent hatred of all whites as such is not a general condition among the people of Soweto. That much I can claim to have established experimentally, with the aid of my consultative taxi driver. Black leaders claim that their people hate apartheid without hating whites. That claim may seem improbable, but my experience is certainly a small piece of evidence in its favor.

St. Matthew's, Embeni, is an unfinished church, only half roofed over, but entirely usable on such a bright, warm, South African spring morning. The church was crowded, for the most part with smartly dressed men, women, and children, including choristers in brightly colored gowns and boys in blazers. All eyes, all the time, were on Bishop Tutu. My notes taken in the church read:

> Tutu baptizing: firm plunger of struggling lambs; [not babies but] big kids. Tutu preaching in Xhosa; simultaneously translated into Tswana. Great facial mobility

and range of gestures. Clutching lectern with both hands, then reaching out and seeming to snatch things out of the air. Dead-pan, with wide-open eyes, for jokes. Laughter, applause. Then he relaxes, smiles. Affection, approval, amusement, confidence of congregation/audience. A "good turn" and spiritual solace, all in one. Then a few words in English. Change of persona: no comic effects; grave, academic tone. Limited range of gesture now, using left hand. [He said] "God looks down on South Africa and weeps when he sees how some of his children are treating his other children. . . . Christ's religion [is] a religion of the poor, the marginalized, the ghetto people. . . . But the others, whom we disagree with, are not to be killed."

After that, my concluding note reads simply, "Dances high-life in full Episcopal regalia."

There is a danger of that sounding funny. It wasn't funny at all; it was profoundly moving, and precisely appropriate. Only once before had I seen a sight that moved me in the same way. (There is a danger of this comparison sounding funny too, but I intend it in the most reverent appreciation.) Twenty years ago I watched a ground hornbill, in a clearing in the bush in northern Ghana, dancing all by himself a solemn and triumphant dance, as if celebrating the Creation.

Even so, in the half-roofed Church of St. Matthew in Embeni, Soweto, did Desmond Tutu dance before his Lord.

In what I have written up to now, I have followed a train of personal experience, and one that was far from newsworthy. In so doing, I hoped to supplement the impressions of South Africa that you may get from the media, especially television. Daily life in South Africa at present is not so charged with hatred and violence as the selected images on the screen suggest. There is no deliberate distortion; it is in the nature of news coverage to reflect not daily life but what is startling, alarming, shocking. There are a lot of such things in South Africa, but not everything is like that. As that veteran enemy of apartheid Alan Paton said to me in Durban, "[The foreign media] seem to see nothing in South Africa but white wickedness and black suffering. Those things are there, but they're not everything."

No. Those Afrikaners in Springs were not like Nazis; those blacks at Embeni were not exclusively preoccupied with suffering or hating. Correction is needed, but there is a danger of overdoing the correction. To convey a reassuring message would be much more misleading than the television coverage is.

Television cannot reflect the routine of daily life, but the violence shown episodically on the screen pervades daily life, mostly in latent form, and governs the contexts in which daily life is lived. Those stolid Afrikaners are behind their police, in every sense, and all the talk of police brutality leaves them at best unmoved. That relaxed and joyous congregation at St. Matthew's may see the children as their champions, though the champions are also scary. Bishop Tutu's warnings against violence seem to be taken as appropriate, coming from him, more than as binding on those addressed. I was reminded of Pope John Paul II in Ireland condemning political violence. Everybody, including IRA supporters, thought the Pope was a lovely man, but support for the IRA and its armed struggle was not in any degree diminished.

Afrikaners, for their part, are cynical about the Bishop's condemnation of violence, as veiled collusion. Across the gulf that separates the ruling Afrikaners from the rebellious blacks, even such conciliatory sounds as are wafted to the other side bear sinister connotations. At a Supreme Court session in Pretoria, I heard a judge refer sardonically to a priest who was supposed to have told his congregation, "I don't know how long you can be held back from burning vehicles." Clearly, the judge heard that priest as actually inciting to violence, egging the congregation on, in coded language. Across such a chasm constructive dialogue appears unattainable.

If the televised images and printed reports convey to you that South Africa is already in a state of civil war, then that impression is exaggerated. But if they convey to you that South Africa is drifting, at an accelerating rate, toward civil war, then that impression is, in my belief, correct.

What can be the outcome of this incipient civil war? That remains a difficult question.

In my visits to various South African cities—Cape Town, Port Elizabeth, Grahamstown, East London, Durban, Johannesburg—I put to a number of well-informed people the following three propositions:

The maintenance of the status quo is impossible.

Reforms acceptable both to the white electorate and to politicized blacks are impossible.

Revolution is impossible.

The first of those three propositions needs no discussion here, since nobody disputes it. To the second proposition most of my informants replied, in substance: "Maybe not impossible. We must continue to hope that reform is not impossible. But it will be extremely difficult, certainly."

As regards the third proposition, most informants, black and white, thought that if reforms acceptable to most politicized blacks continued to be denied by the white electorate, revolution would become inevitable, but in the fairly long term. Hardly anyone considers revolution possible in the here and now— within the next five years or ten years; even the ANC is said to put the remaining life of the apartheid regime at no less than ten years.

I should now like to consider the forces making for acceptance of major change, those working for resistance to change, and how the resistance might be overcome.

*   *   *

The argument in favor of the feasibility of major reform, as I understand it, runs more or less as follows:

Already a sizable portion of the white electorate is in favor of major reform. That support is likely to grow, as white South Africa begins to understand the magnitude of the external pressures on it, of which the fall in the value of the rand—from fifty-four cents in July of 1985 to thirty-six cents in October of 1985—is the most telling symbol and most painful symptom for the white population generally. The business community is enthusiastically in favor of sweeping reforms.

It certainly is. If Marx were right and capitalists were the real controllers of the political systems of societies with capitalist economies, then Nelson Mandela would now be ensconced in Pretoria as state president, with Oliver Tambo, the ANC leader, as his minister for defense.

I talked in Port Elizabeth, in the Eastern Cape Province, with the secretary of the local Chamber of Commerce. Port Elizabeth's commerce was brought very nearly to a standstill by the almost-hundred-percent-effective black boycott of white business in the city. The secretary, representing a business community on the verge of desperation, sounded rather like a spokesman for the ANC, although he had earlier supported the Nationalist Party. I was reminded of Herman Melville's story "Benito Cereno," in which, as you will recall, the man who is apparently master of a slave ship is in reality the captive spokesman for the slaves, who have successfully rebelled.

The business leaders who went to talk with the ANC leadership in Lusaka in September are already in a sort of "Benito Cereno" condition in relation to the future—prisoners by anticipation of a slave rebellion of whose inevitable success they have begun to be convinced.

Also, the case for radical change is now vigorously and skillfully presented in Parliament by the small but compact and effective Progressive Federal Party, led by F. van Zyl Slabbert. (I should say that I am using *Parliament* here to mean what everyone still thinks of as the *real* Parliament—the white one. But strictly speaking, since the enactment of P. W. Botha's 1983 constitution, Parliament consists of three houses—the House of Assembly [white], the House of Representatives [coloured], and the House of Delegates [Indian]. The institutions of revamped apartheid are confusing, like its vocabulary, and for the same reasons. Although the House of Representatives and the House of Delegates are generally considered as facades masking the continued white monopoly of real power, and although fewer than 20 percent of the eligible coloured and Indian voters bothered [or dared] to vote in the elections for their respective houses, it was the provision of these concessions to the coloured and Indian communities, while failing to offer *even* a façade to the black majority, that enraged blacks generally and precipitated the present wave of unrest, beginning in late 1983.)

For years after the National Party came to power in 1948—a power that it has maintained unbroken since then—the demoralized opposition, the United Party, offered no serious challenge to apartheid. That challenge came, indeed, and incisively, but from just one member of Parliament, Helen Suzman. Now the old United Party, rebaptized the New Republic Party, is in terminal decline, as was manifest in the mini-election of last October. Its parliamentary place has been taken by the Progressive Federal Party, "the Progs." Helen Suzman is still going strong, and is as astringently alert as ever, but she is now a member of a PFP group with twenty-seven seats in the House of Assembly. That is still a small minority—twenty-seven out of 178—but it does represent a significant rise in the level of rejection of apartheid in a section of the white community.

The quality of this opposition is exceptionally high. Dr. Slabbert is an attractive and inspiring leader, forty-five years old, energetic, highly intelligent, humorous, and entirely unpompous. In style he is rather like Pierre Trudeau. He was an academic, and he is quite startlingly candid for a politician, but he seems well able to live down those handicaps.

I talked with Progs in different parts of the country. I was struck by the strength of the respect and affection that Dr. Slabbert inspires in his following. I didn't hear a single sour note, and this is rare, in my experience, when one talks in private with party members anywhere about their leader.

I heard Dr. Slabbert address a rally in Cape Town on the eve of the mini-election. It was a large and enthusiastic gathering, very different from the turnout for State President Botha at Springs (although the difference was not reflected in the election results). The leader outlined the present demands of the PFP:

1. Dismantle apartheid completely.
2. Release political prisoners and all who are detained without trial.
3. End the state of emergency, and allow freedom of organization.
4. Call a national convention to determine the new, nonracial, democratic constitution for South Africa.

These demands correspond fairly closely to the current demands of the ANC-UDF leadership, and Dr. Slabbert, like the business leaders, has visited the ANC leadership in Lusaka.

The business leaders and the Progs are mostly drawn from the English-speaking community (although Dr. Slabbert himself is an Afrikaner). The English-speaking community—about 40 percent of the white population—has, however, been excluded from power since 1948 by the representatives of the Afrikaner community, the majority community within the all-white electorate for the House of Assembly. There can be no progress in the direction of radical change—by constitutional means—unless there is first a significant change in Afrikaner attitudes. What signs are there of such a change?

Well, there are *some* signs. Afrikanerdom is no longer such a monolith as it appeared, say, in the first decade after 1948.

It is not only representatives of English-speakers who have taken—or at any rate tried to take—the road to Lusaka. Students at Stellenbosch, the oldest and most distinguished Afrikaner university, announced their intention of traveling to Lusaka to talk with the ANC. The Botha government withdrew the students' passports, a step that, interestingly enough, it did not take in the case of the business leaders; apparently such conduct may be grudgingly accepted on the part of *Neef Brit* but may not be tolerated where children of the *volk* are concerned. Nonetheless, opinion at Stellenbosch, both student and faculty, supported the students and their right to travel. I myself found that one can spend an agreeable day on that beautiful campus at Stellenbosch, and have many instructive conversations, without ever meeting anyone who appears to support the National Party. And it's not only Stellenbosch. What some people call the Afrikaner thaw has also reached the Dutch Reformed Church, the central spiritual institution of Afrikanerdom, whose blessings in the past legitimized and sustained apartheid. Dr. Beyers Naudé, the most eminent pioneer of anti-apartheid within the DRC, was deprived of his ministry in 1963 and remains an outcast from Afrikanerdom (greatly to the benefit of his reputation in the outside world). Last October, Dr. Nico Smith and other DRC clergymen followed the example of the business leaders, of Dr. Slabbert, and of the Stellenbosch students by announcing their intention of traveling to Lusaka to meet the ANC leaders.

When this announcement came, it caused shock waves throughout South Africa. It seemed to some that a breach had appeared in the ideological citadel of Afrikanerdom.

There have also been signs of change within the medical and legal professions, change that could not have occurred without the consent of the (mainly) Afrikaner members. In October of 1985 the South African Medical Council struck off its rolls one of the police doctors implicated in the death in September, 1977, of the Black Consciousness leader Steve Biko, from injuries received while in police custody. And in December, before the Supreme Court, the state was obliged to withdraw the charges of treason that it had brought against a number of prominent members of the UDF. There have been several other signs of professional unease at some of the practices and demands of the apartheid state.

Afrikaner writers and intellectuals have also turned against apartheid, rejecting it not in the Botha sense but really and fundamentally. Afrikaans writing—some of it now translated into English—is full of a sense of foreboding and evil. I talked in Cape Town with J. M. Coetzee, the author of a number of novels, including *Life and Times of Michael K,* which I had just read. *Michael K,* like several other impressive Afrikaner novels and stories, is set in a desolate, ruined South Africa, felt as the South Africa of the future if the country's rulers persevere on their present course. "I used to wonder," Coetzee told me, "why it couldn't become Brazil." He has stopped wondering about that, but by even wondering about it he had already broken, as others like him have done, with the traditions of his people and the governing ideology of the state. He is a thin, controlled, matter-of-fact man; you might take him for an accountant. But his view of the facts and figures tallies with his artistic vision: "When things begin to break down, people should start starving pretty soon. Whites live in pockets. They can be cut off. One single highway leading into Cape Town . . ."

(And, indeed, along that highway you already get a whiff of incipient siege. On my last day in Cape Town my friend and host, David Welsh, drove me out that way to the airport. David is a well-known political scientist and the co-author with Dr. Slabbert of *South Africa's Options: Strategies for Sharing Power.* As we got into the car, David handed me a cushion. This was in case people threw stones at the car. Stoning cars, along this and some other high-ways, has become perhaps the most prevalent form of black-on-white activity —or more likely, this being the Cape, coloured-on-white. Coloured militants seem to be more hostile to whites as such than black militants are. A white University of Cape Town student told me, "It's mainly the coloured people who call you whitey." As it happened, there were no stones that morning. But the Casspirs of the South African police could be seen occasionally, strung out along that "single highway.")

Academics, churchmen, writers, doctors, lawyers . . . It is clear that a significant number of Afrikaner intellectuals are at least beginning to desert apartheid. And this must cause some concern to the regime. An ideology needs intellectuals to impart it, by writing and teaching. And intellectuals who can do this properly need themselves to believe in the ideology they try to impart. True, intellectuals can always be hired to say and write the proper things. But intellectual mercenaries seldom carry conviction. So the ideology of apartheid is in trouble.

The modern tendency for intellectuals to desert apartheid is a little ironic, since apartheid is largely the creation of intellectuals. Intellectuals, mainly teachers and *predikants* (Calvinist clergymen), were the originators and dis-seminators of Afrikaner nationalism, the politico-cultural movement that eventually produced the doctrine and system of apartheid, and it was also intellectuals who shaped and refined that doctrine and system.

To understand the present predicament of Afrikanerdom, and the significance within that predicament of the (partial) defection of Afrikaner intellectuals, we must here consider briefly the history of Afrikaner nationalism within the general history of South Africa.

The Afrikaners are the oldest white community in South Africa. They are descended from Dutch people who settled in, and spread out from, the vicinity of the Cape of Good Hope, after a fort and a vegetable garden had been established there, for the Dutch East India Company, by Jan van Riebeeck, in 1652. For nearly a century and a half these Dutch-speaking people— absorbing a number of Huguenot émigrés from France—were the only white inhabitants of South Africa, which they came to regard as their country. Their language evolved away from the original Dutch—similar to the evolution of Canadian French away from metropolitan French—to what is now Afrikaans. Their attitudes toward the native peoples they encountered in South Africa were similar to those of English-speaking settlers in North America toward the natives of that continent, during the same period. Many Afrikaners also owned slaves.

As a result of the French revolutionary wars, the Netherlands lost control of South Africa. By the peace treaties that closed the Napoleonic wars, victorious Britain's rule over South Africa was internationally recognized. Emigration to South Africa from the British Isles was encouraged.

Friction soon developed between the new rulers and their Afrikaans-speaking subjects. British policy toward the natives was influenced in the early nineteenth century by English-speaking missionaries, as well as by Whig Enlightenment philanthropy. Afrikaners resented these novel ideas and also resented the new British settlers. In 1834 the Parliament of the United Kingdom declared slavery abolished throughout the British Empire. And by 1838 the new anti-slavery laws came into force in South Africa (then consisting of what is now the Cape Province).

Many Afrikaner farmers decided to get away from the British and their meddlesome innovations, and the Great Trek began. Thousands of Afrikaners —or Boers, as they were then known—set out in their ox wagons with their families, their arms, and their black ("Hottentot") servants for the north, well beyond the then existing zone of white settlement. After many vicissitudes (and historic clashes with the Zulus, to be considered below) the Afrikaner emigrants established two internally autonomous Afrikaans-speaking republics of their own—the Transvaal and the Orange Free State—under British "suzerainty."

Suzerainty seems originally to have meant little more than a warning from Britain to foreign powers to keep out of the Boer republics. However, everything changed in the mid-1880s, with the discovery of gold in large quantities on the Whitwatersrand, where Johannesburg now is ("The city with the heart of gold," as a 1985 poster has it). Foreign immigrants—"Uitlanders"—arrived, and British governments promptly took on an active role as protectors of the Uitlanders. By the 1890s, the heyday of jingo imperialism, concern for the Uitlanders had become merely a pretext for escalating British demands, whose eventual rejection would be the *casus* for a war of annexation of the Afrikaner republics and their wealth—a war that was expected to be brief. It wasn't. The resistance of the Afrikaners proved unexpectedly stiff, and the Anglo-Boer war went on for three years (1899–1902). The last phase of the war involved severe measures against Afrikaner civilians: Lord Kitchener established "concentration camps"—the first official use of that term—in which about 26,000 Afrikaner women and children died.

In the aftermath of the Anglo-Boer war a new British government decided on a policy of reconciliation in South Africa, and members of the Afrikaner elite, led by Generals Barry Hertzog and Jan Smuts, met them halfway. This process led, in 1909–1910, to the creation of a self-governing Dominion of the British Empire: the Union of South Africa. The Union (which became today's Republic of South Africa in 1961) was governed from its foundation until 1948 by a "white coalition" of English-speakers and Afrikaners. In this period the earlier tendency of English-speakers to protect the blacks—a tendency that had already faded during the nineteenth century—was replaced by a rhetoric of "racial reconciliation." Racial reconciliation meant reconciliation between Afrikaner and British and joint supremacy of both over all blacks.

But against that ruling concept there was a rising tide of Afrikaner nationalism. Afrikaner nationalism aimed at—and eventually got, in 1948—an Afrikaner monopoly of political power in South Africa. Afrikaner nationalism, as a conscious movement, began in the mid-1870s, but it gained greatly in emotional power as a result of the Anglo-Boer war and a felt need to cancel out that defeat.

"Afrikaner nationalism, as a conscious movement, began in the mid-1870s." That statement of mine is firmly based on modern Afrikaner historical scholarship. But it is also—and symptomatically—a proposition passionately resented by modern Afrikaner nationalists, because the modern Afrikaner nationalist credo lays it down that the Great Trek itself, in the 1830s, was the birth of Afrikaner nationalism. Afrikaner historiography can be a dangerous business. For having challenged some aspects of the received nationalist version of Afrikaner history, a distinguished historian, Professor Floors van Jaarsveld, was tarred and feathered in front of a theological conference at the University of South Africa, Pretoria, on March 28, 1979. The subject on which Professor van Jaarsveld had proposed to address the conference was the historiographical reassessment of the Day of the Covenant.

The Day of the Covenant is Afrikanerdom's National Day, celebrated on

December 16. It commemorates the crowning event of the Great Trek: the victory of Andries Pretorius's Boer *commando,* on December 16, 1838, in the Battle of Blood River, over the *impis* (regiments) of the Zulu king Dingaan —that same Dingaan whose *impis* had the previous February massacred a party of more than 300 Boer trekkers, mostly children, under Piet Retief. The Battle of Blood River is commemorated on the spot by sixty-four life-size bronze ox wagons. That battle is also the central event commemorated in the great Voortrekker Monument at Pretoria, probably the most impressive shrine of sacral nationalism to be found anywhere on earth.

It is unlikely that there was much sacral nationalism, or nationalism of any kind, among the followers of Piet Retief or Andries Pretorius in 1838. What there was was the sense of being a chosen people in a promised land, something closely corresponding to the sense of the Puritans of New England in the seventeenth century—a good seedbed of nationalism, but not yet nationalism itself. Sacral nationalism made its appearance about forty years later, bringing with it the legend of the Covenant with God supposed to have been sworn and repeated by Sarel Cilliers—the *predikant* who accompanied Pretorius—that if the Zulus were defeated, the day would be observed every year as a day of thanksgiving.

This sacral nationalism, still the creed of South Africa's governing National Party, was born in South Africa in a period when European nationalisms were increasing in intensity. Afrikaner nationalism was a latecomer, but tardiness seems to intensify nationalism: German nationalism, too, was a latecomer. The men who gave Afrikaner sacral nationalism its first expression, in the 1870s, were teachers and *predikants,* meeting in Die Genootskap van Regtes Afrikaners (the Society of True Afrikaners), which had been founded in Paarl on August 14, 1875. It was a prolific and enthusiastic society. It produced, in 1876, its own newspaper, *Die Afrikaanse Patriot,* the first publication in Afrikaans, a medium that had hitherto been regarded, even by those who spoke it, as a mere patois of Dutch. And the same movement brought the basic text of the new Afrikaner sacral nationalism: *Die Geskiedenis van ons Land in die Taal van ons Volk (The History of Our Land in the Language of Our People).*

That title contains the three key words—*land, taal, volk*—of modern Afrikaner nationalism and of the rhetoric of the governing party of today's South Africa. The words *land* and *volk* have emotional associations corresponding to those of the same two words in German. They may also have a *potential* charge corresponding to what happened to the same two words in defeated Germany after the First World War, when *völkisch* nationalism turned from obsessive into manic, and Nazism was born. I shall come back to the question of that potentiality and what might release it.

At the time of the British victory in the Anglo-Boer war, in 1902, Afrikaner nationalists became divided into *bittereinders* and *hensoppers* ("hands-uppers"). The same sort of division continued inside Afrikaner politics throughout the first half of the twentieth century. One set of Afrikaners—considered by the others as little better than *hensoppers*—favoured "unity," meaning the unity of white South Africans. From the coming of autonomy, with the foundation of the Union of South Africa in 1910, South Africa was ruled, essentially, by coalitions based on (and usually led by) Afrikaners of this type, together with the English-speaking community.

The other set of Afrikaners regarded themselves as the only *regte* Afrikaners, the only true nationalists. They saw the Afrikaner community—now 60 percent of all whites—as the rightful rulers of South Africa, with *Neef Brit* in second place, and all South Africa's other inhabitants outside the political process. To that end they worked to establish the solidarity of the *volk* against the Afrikaner leaders—notably Generals Hertzog and Smuts—who preached and practiced Caucasian ecumenism, the solidarity of whites in general.

After its founding, in 1918, that extraordinary institution the Afrikaner Broederbond set out to provide the leadership of the *regte* Afrikaners. The Broederbond was a secret society, but it was no ordinary secret society. By the late 1930s it had attained the leadership of resurgent Afrikaner nationalism, and within thirty years of its founding it had led the National Party to a monopoly of political power that has never since been interrupted.

Since the victory of the National Party, in 1948, the Broederbond has been the establishment of Afrikanerdom: every head of government has been a member, as P. W. Botha is now; almost all ministers have been members; and all *regte* Afrikaners of consequence are members. It is now—and this is a symbol of the malaise of the Afrikaner elite—a *divided* establishment, with members divided between the National Party and the smaller Afrikaner parties to the right of it. Though divided, the Broederbond remains an establishment.

But in its beginnings the membership was young and hungry. As with the earlier Genootskap, many of the members were teachers, *predikants,* intellectuals. And as with the Genootskap, much of its work consisted in nationalist indoctrination, through the churches, the schools and colleges, the press. The nationalism was sincere in its fervor; it was also connected with a deliberate effort of social promotion for Afrikaners generally, and in particular for members of the Broederbond, through mutual help. The Broederbond soon came to see the eventual winning of permanent political power in South Africa—political power as an Afrikaner monopoly—as the key to the fulfillment of both its nationalist and its social ambitions. By the 1930s—under political conditions very different from those of the previous century—the fanning of nationalist excitement had definite political objectives, the first of which was the casting out from the *volk* of men like Hertzog and Smuts, the allies of *Neef Brit*. And this objective was largely achieved by December 16, 1938, the centenary of the Day of the Covenant.

Carefully prepared and organized by the Broederbond, the celebration of the centenary was a culminating event in the liturgy of the sacral nationalism of the *volk.* During the preparatory months ox wagons traversed the land from Cape Town to Pretoria, stopping at all the holy places of nationalism. Nationalist excitement steadily mounted. Henning Klopper, the first chairman of the Broederbond and the chief organizer of these celebrations, wrote: "The whole feeling of the trek was the working not of man, not of any living being. It was the will and the work of the Almighty God. It was a pilgrimage, a sacred happening." It was. It was also a political happening. The temperature of Afrikaner nationalism had been raised so high as to make it impossible for either Smuts or Hertzog to be present at the ceremonies. The Broederbond had succeeded in the first of its major objectives. The second—the conquest of political power—was achieved just ten years later.

(It is worth noting at this point that the hundred-and-fiftieth anniversary of the Day of the Covenant falls in less than three years' time.)

It was in the same period, the late 1930s, as the Broederbond was methodically preparing itself for the advent of Afrikaner power over all the other peoples of South Africa, that the framework for the doctrine and system of apartheid was created. The practice of white supremacy, in a rough-and-ready sort of way, had been around ever since the Dutch came to South Africa, and while Boers and English-speakers had their different ways of legitimizing the practice, they were generally agreed on the necessity for it, whatever the reasons for the necessity might be. What was new about apartheid was its doctrinal and systematic character: the fact of being an ideology. And the ideology, once its exponents came to power, made for a far more pervasive and insistent form of white supremacy than anything known before: more drastic, more pedantic, more innovative, imaginative, bureaucratic, and meddlesome, and therefore far more tormenting to those subjected to its maddening attentions than the old, relatively easygoing routines of white rule had been.

The Broederbond was the creator of the apartheid ideology, through the writings of three of its academic members, high pundits of nationalism: Dr. N. Diederichs, Dr. P. J. Meyer, and Dr. G. Cronjé.

This was the late thirties, and the early ideologues of apartheid were influenced to some degree by the language and concepts of contemporary European right-wing authoritarianism—usually in its milder forms. (Though many leading Afrikaner nationalists were "pro-Nazi" during the war, the affinity seems to have been less ideological than a matter of "the enemy of one's enemy," as with other subject peoples' nationalists in the same period; compare the "pro-Nazism" of Flemish, Breton, and Palestinian nationalists. Many Afrikaners, as well as English-speaking South Africans, fought on the side of the British in both world wars. But Afrikaner nationalists—those who regarded themselves as the only *regte* Afrikaners—were opposed to South African involvement on Britain's side in either war. Some were pro-German; some favored neutrality.)

In the main, however, apartheid was an Afrikaner answer to an Afrikaner problem. The problem was this: Afrikaner nationalists saw themselves as essentially freedom-fighters. They had fought for their freedom, at the dawn of the century, against the greatest empire on earth, and had given a good account of themselves. And now, under the leadership of the Broederbond, they were headed for the recovery of their freedom, in their own home. But black people were a large majority in that home. Were the Afrikaners, once they had liberated themselves, going to liberate the blacks, by giving them real votes, and so power over whites, including Afrikaners? Obviously not, since such a conclusion would make nonsense of the whole epic struggle of the *volk* for freedom. Were they, then, going to deny to others the freedom they prized so much for themselves? The accurate answer was yes. But the accurate answer was unacceptable to people who were, like all fervent nationalists, self-righteous in the extreme. A sham answer was needed, and was believed, since it was needed. And so apartheid was born.

"The Boer nation," said the ideologue G. Cronjé, "can fully understand the sufferings of the Bantu. It is that same imperialism and capitalism, having them believe that the foreign is better than what is their own, which seeks to destroy their tribal life." So the liberation of the blacks by the Afrikaners would consist in the restoration of their tribal life.

The liberation of the Afrikaners, however, would entail a monopoly of state power. "In the future Afrikaner national state [*volkstaat*]," P. J. Meyer wrote, "the undivided power granted by God rests with the Afrikaner state authority."

So the circle was squared; the two liberations were fully compatible. The apotheosis of Afrikaner sacral nationalism under God's ordination *(Godsbestemming)* would also liberate the blacks.

The invention of apartheid was a major achievement of liberation theology.

That is not so outrageous a paradox as it may sound to some ears. In the early part of the twentieth century the Afrikaner nationalists were not merely accepted internationally as a national-liberation movement. They were admired by fervent nationalists in all the countries of the British Empire, and the other colonial empires, as the archetypal example of a national-liberation movement, the most heroic and determined of fighters against imperialism. It was the Anglo-Boer war that set the pace for the worldwide process of decolonization in the twentieth century. The Irish nationalists were the next to strike a blow against imperialism, and they were consciously imitative of the Boers. Mr. Sean MacBride is an advocate of extreme measures against the Afrikaners, but his father, Major John MacBride, fought with the Boers against the British. And I suspect that many Irish people today actually do not know that the brutal Afrikaners whom they occasionally see on their television screens are the same people as the valiant Boers of Irish nationalist tradition.

The fact that a genuine national-liberation movement should invent the ideology of apartheid, and erect its institutions, should not surprise us much. People fight for freedom, but what some of them win is power. And the use they make of their power may not look at all like the freedom their admirers saw them as fighting for. That generalization is relevant not only to the past Afrikaner struggle for freedom but to the *anti-*Afrikaner freedom struggle of today. Joseph Stalin and Pol Pot were once fighters for freedom, champions of the cause of the people. And it would hardly be an inconsistent development of present revolutionary activities if among the children with the necklace, who are currently burning people alive in the name of the cause of the people, were to be found a potential Joseph Stalin or a future Pol Pot.

To come back to the Afrikaners, and to the Afrikaner intellectuals in particular: those among them who talk to us in the 1980s about minority rights, self-determination, and so on may be conscious hypocrites, and I suspect they mostly are. But those who created apartheid, its theoreticians and early practitioners, were not hypocrites at all. It might have been better if they had been, because then they would have left apartheid where it began: in the domain of words.

Like Pygmalion, the creators of apartheid were in love with their creation and brought it to life. As soon as the Nationalists came to power, in 1948, the building of the institutions of apartheid began, and it proceeded apace after the appointment of a dedicated apartheid intellectual, H. F. Verwoerd, in October of 1950, as minister for native affairs (he later became prime minister). The principal institutions were the "Bantustans," later "Homelands" (under apartheid, euphemisms atrophy quickly). The Homelands are supposed to be nation-states, in which the Bantu is free to live his own tribal life, even if he doesn't want to. Under Verwoerd the Nationalists set up Bantustans with the same confident elan with which the Jacobins of revolutionary France had set up their sister republics *(Républiques soeurs):* the Cisalpine Republic, the Parthenopean Republic, and what have you. The sister republics of the Afrikaner state have names like Ciskei, Transkei, Bophuthatswana, and Venda. (These are the four that are supposed to be fully independent. There are also six others.) There is a crazy poetry about it all, but the attempt to turn crazy poetry into reality, an attempt sustained with fanatical energy, has produced vast amounts of unnecessary human suffering: peremptory uprooting, colossal movements of populations, constant police investigation of passes, the separation of families, unusually long journeys to work—the catalogue of evils is well known. But it is different to see it. Traveling through a densely populated resettlement zone in a remote and desolate valley in the Ciskei, I noted the general impression in my diary: "Mad child scattering packets of shacks over valley floor."

Nor was apartheid applied with any real respect for its supposed guiding principle: tribal affiliation. The theory of the thing was that the identity of each tribal group was to be cherished—that each was a kind of *volk,* which, given its own land, might aspire someday to become like the Afrikaners, in a black sort of way. The architects of apartheid might have believed all that intellectually, but in practice they couldn't bring themselves to respect any black *volk,* and they chopped up the land to suit themselves—the Afrikaners, the real *volk.* Thus a certain group of people, having once been South African, suddenly found themselves citizens of Transkei. Then they were out of Transkei and back into South Africa, because the boss of Transkei, Kaizer Matanzima, didn't like them. Then they were out of South Africa again and found themselves citizens of the newly created and now "independent" state of Ciskei. And so on. The term *Homelands* became a mockery.

Nationalist faith in apartheid continued strong for nearly thirty years. It survived the enormous demonstrations against the pass laws, in March of 1960, which led to large numbers of arrests and to the killing of sixty-nine blacks by the South African police, at Sharpeville. Sharpeville sent shock waves round the world, but Nationalists saw it as a flash in the pan. It was not until June 16, 1976, when school riots began in Soweto and spread across South Africa, that Nationalist complacency began to be shaken. The riots were precipitated by a desire to reject the enforced teaching of certain subjects in Afrikaans. But it soon became clear that far more was involved. Young people, who had never known any institutions other than those of apartheid, were in rebellion against those institutions. Apartheid had failed conspicuously in the one area indispensable to its success: the education of young blacks.

If Nationalist complacency was shaken by Soweto, it has to be shaken even more profoundly by the present unrest. Sixteen years had separated Sharpeville from Soweto; less than half that time span separated Soweto from the unrest that broke out in the autumn of 1983, almost simultaneously with the introduction of P. W. Botha's new constitution. And the unrest that began in 1983 has continued without a letup ever since, with an extent and intensity never previously known, and it has been accompanied by an unprecedented measure of international displeasure, all leading to the collapse of the rand, and the South African moratorium on repayments.

The defection of a significant part of the intellectual elite of Afrikanerdom set in after Soweto. But an even more disturbing kind of intellectual defection seems to have set in among the Nationalists who remained, especially the leaders: a partial defection of their own minds.

Watching members of the nationalist establishment in South Africa both in the flesh and on television, and reading or listening to their words, I formed the impression that these gentlemen had become incapable of thinking, at least on the subject about which they talked the most. It is understandable that this should have come about. The initial strain of attaining a belief in the fantasies of apartheid must have exacted a considerable mental toll. That was followed by the strain imposed by the divergence, combined with the denial of the divergence, between apartheid in theory and apartheid in practice. And that was followed in turn by the growing discredit of apartheid, leading to the combined necessities of assuring the international community that apartheid was to all intents and purposes dead while reassuring the Nationalist rank and file that apartheid in all essentials was very much alive. And on top of all that was the frantic quest for some euphemism adequate to describe the new reality that was to replace apartheid. This quest is doomed to failure, because the new reality—this is the minimum requirement of Nationalists—has to have at its core the prime substance of the *old* reality: white supremacy, and Afrikaner supremacy within white supremacy. And that is the reality that apartheid was created to disguise, not only from others but—and especially—from the creators of apartheid themselves.

All that is more than enough to boggle the mind, and the minds in question appear by now to be well and truly boggled.

While I was in Pretoria, I collected, from the State President's splendid offices in Union Building, a big bunch of P. W. Botha's speeches. I read all of these, and the experience went far toward boggling my own mind. Botha and his aides, it seems, have been so long in the business of churning out nonsense of the ideological sort that they can no longer discern and eliminate ordinary nonsense. Take the following gem, from a speech delivered by the State President on the occasion of the unveiling of a monument at the Burgher Memorial in Delareyville, on October 10, 1985. Botha was speaking in honor of Delareyville's eponymous Boer War hero General J. H. De la Rey, to whom he paid the following tribute:

> General De la Rey, after whom this town is called, laid down his life in the service of freedom and the principles of justice. Later, for the sake of these same principles, he revolted against the unfair attempts on South West Africa.

General De la Rey's posthumous exploit eclipses that of Hilaire Belloc's hero of the Napoleonic wars, who "Lost a leg at Waterloo,/And Quatre-Bras and Ligny too!"

I have seen Botha in action in person twice—addressing the faithful at Springs and addressing a critical audience, the Foreign Correspondents' Association, in Johannesburg—and I have often watched him on South African television, which his picture dominates. On television his face in close-up doesn't look like much—it is puffy, the mouth a bit slobbery. But on the platform he is more impressive—a big, well-built man, with a demeanor that contradicts the flow of bland, conciliatory euphemisms that often pours from

his mouth. When he is being abrasive—as he was with the foreign correspondents—he appears to mean what he says. But whether what he says is meant
to please or to rasp, he looks the same: grim, unsmiling, determined—his little,
rather porcine eyes darting from side to side as if searching for enemies, his
gestures suggestive less of oratorical emphasis than of chopping something or
somebody. His mind may be a bit gone, but his will appears intact.

I don't believe that Botha and his colleagues are anywhere near to agreeing
to hand over a significant share in power to any blacks. They may eventually
agree, in order to ease the international pressure, not only to gestures like the
release of Nelson Mandela but to quite far-reaching reforms: to end influx
control, to reform the pass laws, even to abolish the Group Areas Act (although most groups would have to remain in the areas in which they were put
during the imperious heyday of apartheid). These reforms would make life a
bit easier for ordinary blacks, but it is not likely that they would do anything
to reduce the unrest. The unrest at this stage is a struggle for power, conducted
on the black side by people who believe that the apartheid regime is beginning
to collapse under the combined pressure of the unrest itself and the international pressure it generates. Quite rightly, these people see such reforms as
have come and such as may be coming as fruits of the unrest, and so they will
keep up the unrest, and pile on the pressure, by every means they can. And
the elemental hatred of large numbers of blacks for the whole apartheid system
will support them in keeping the pressure up as long as the regime refuses to
begin handing over power to the revolutionary leaders.

So, because the National Party will refuse, the unrest will continue—no
doubt with ups and downs in intensity—at least as long as the National Party
remains in power. It will do so for a little under three years, until the next
general election. But for how long after that?

Not all that long, runs one line of argument. There are those defections, that
confusion at the top: premonitory signs. There is that queue to Lusaka, leaving
the sinking ship. More generally, the Afrikaners of today are not the stern,
embattled colonial farmers of Nationalist legend. They are urbanized, *embour-
geoisés,* softened—part of the consumer society, part of the permissive society.
They are no longer securely hooked to the culture represented by the Voortrekker Monument.

They spend less time, the argument goes on, in contemplating the exploits
of the immortal General De la Rey, or the vexed question of what Sarel Cilliers
may or may not have said to Andries Pretorius on the eve of the Battle of Blood
River, than they do in contemplating the latest American situation comedy,
courtesy of South African Television. They, whose ancestors so staunchly
resisted anglicization, have shown far less resistance to Americanization. Even
the hold of the Afrikaans language, the sacred *taal,* is weakening. It was
weakening prior to television; as early as the fifties the circulation of the

English-language press was rising faster than that of the Afrikaans press. But televised entertainment is a far more effective agent of Anglophone acculturation than the printed word is. And televised entertainment is overwhelmingly American (and depicts an integrated society). Where *Neef Brit* failed, *Neef Yank* has won.

And—continues the argument—these Americanized bourgeois are not going to die in the last ditch, on some kind of spiritual ox wagon. Ox wagons are for the birds. Once these people realize that the game is really up, they are going to desert the National Party in droves. In such a situation the only Afrikaner tradition that can make sense to the Americanized Afrikaner is that of the *hensoppers*.

I can accept a large part of this argument—even the bit about the permissive society. In Pretorius Street, Pretoria—of all places—I saw a conspicuously placed poster supplying the telephone number of the Rentagirl Escort Service. I don't know what Sarel Cilliers may be saying, in heaven, to Andries Pretorius about *that*.

I agree with most of the descriptive part of the argument. White South Africans, English-speakers and Afrikaners together, respectfully attended by cheap black servants, may form, as has been said, "the most spoiled society in the world." What I find much less convincing, though, are the political inferences from all this. In particular I think that the argument greatly overstates the *political* (and politico-cultural) impact of television in deeply divided societies.

In Northern Ireland, Catholics and Protestants have been watching virtually the same television programs, and very often the programs that Afrikaners have been watching, for about a quarter of a century. But this common experience has in no way mitigated the ancient antagonism of the two communities. While the set is switched on, both communities are in the world of admass. But when the set is switched off, each is back in its separate world, Green or Orange. Similarly, I suspect that many an Afrikaner, switching off his set, returns to the *laager* as if he had never left it.

Basically, I think people distinguish between reality and make-believe more precisely than some commentators give them credit for. The stuff on the screen is make-believe. The alien community, on the ground and near you, is unfortunately part of the world of reality. You have to wake from the sweet dreams on the screen and keep your guard up.

If the "softening up" argument proves to be correct, there should be a poor turnout for the commemorative ceremonies culminating on December 16, 1988—the 150th anniversary of the Battle of Blood River.

My own guess is that there will be an impressive turnout. True, the mood will be far from the ebullient one in which the centenary was celebrated, in

1938. At that time Afrikanerdom was on the way up, and on the road to power. The ox wagon was also a bandwagon. Nothing of that now. The mood required in 1988 will be one of grim determination, because the *volk* is confronted with the greatest perceived threat to its existence since the Zulu king Dingaan treacherously murdered Piet Retief and his followers, in the *kraal* at Umgungundhlovo, on February 6, 1838. But the very fact of enhanced danger is likely to make the year 1988—commemorating in February the disaster at Umgungundhlovo, as well as in December the deliverance at Blood River—a most appropriate time to display the determination of the threatened *volk*.

I think it probable that many of those who take part in the commemorative ceremonies of 1988 will be drawn from the ranks of the Afrikaners who are supposed to have become Americanized. And it may be that their determination will be registered a shade more grimly for a certain sense of guilt about having, in those long leisure hours before the TV screen, allowed their attention to wander far from the Vow that Sarel Cilliers swore, on behalf of all Afrikaners, in the terrible days between Umgungundhlovo and Blood River.

It is not, of course, all a matter of Afrikaner pride, legends, memories. There are also Afrikaner *interests*. Some of these are general interests, shared by all whites. But some are specific to Afrikaners, and the nature of these makes it particularly difficult for Afrikaners to contemplate a transit of power to blacks. The basic problem here is that the power that would be in transit is *political* power, which has been an Afrikaner monopoly since 1948. And the political power in question here is not a matter that affects just a few elected officials. The fruits of political power have become the mainstay of life for a very large number of Afrikaners.

This phenomenon, like much else in South Africa, dates from 1948 and the first electoral triumph of the National Party. Dr. D. F. Malan, the first Nationalist prime minister, found an elegant and unchallengeable formula for turning the South African Civil Service into an Afrikaner monopoly. He simply decreed that future entrants into the civil service would have to be competent in both Afrikaans and English. And what could be fairer than that in (white) South Africa's bilingual society? In practice most Afrikaners knew at least some English—perforce, since English was the language of business. True, the English of many Afrikaners was not very good. But any reasonable Afrikaner candidate could attain a degree of competence in English adequate to satisfy a selection board made up mostly of Afrikaners.

However, whereas almost all English-speakers had acquired the rudiments of Afrikaans at school, hardly any of them had bothered to acquire a real command of the language, because they had never needed to. True, young English-speaking aspirants to public employment could start brushing up their Afrikaans. But it was not likely that many of them could acquire such a mastery of the finer points of the language as would satisfy a selection board made up mostly of Afrikaners.

With one neat stroke Dr. Malan had Afrikanerized the civil service of South Africa. And there was more to it than that. Selection procedures controlled by the Broederbond ensured that all top posts went to Broederbond members and the remaining posts to *regte* Afrikaners of lesser social standing.

The relevance of these transactions to the present situation is that Afrikaners —and especially *regte* Afrikaners—have much more to lose than English-speakers by a transfer of political power. Under "one man, one vote" the private sector, where most of the English-speakers are, could hope to carry on with business more or less as usual, as in Robert Mugabe's Zimbabwe. Some businessmen—especially in Port Elizabeth—believe that business would be a lot *better* under "one man, one vote" than it is now. The blacks, if they were well led, would in their own interest be inclined to lay off the private sector. But they would take over the public sector. They would Africanize it just as surely as Dr. Malan Afrikanerized it in 1948, and for the same reason: jobs for their own people.

And so, without that power scores of thousands of Afrikaners would find themselves out in the cold and—unlike the English-speakers—with nowhere outside South Africa to go. Many of them—with few skills that are in demand in the private sector—would be likely to sink back to the condition of poor whites, which was the condition of many of their families in the days before the resurgence of Afrikanerdom.

More generally, the Afrikaners, who came up from their nadir, in 1902, to make themselves, forty-six years later, the masters of the great, rich, and beautiful land of South Africa, would now fall back to an even more unacceptable position than was theirs in the aftermath of the Anglo-Boer war. Then they accepted defeat at the hands of the mightiest empire in the world. Now they would be lorded over by those over whom they themselves have lorded for so long.

That, no more and no less, is what Afrikaners have to fear—*that,* and not immersion in some generalized doom, such as being "driven into the sea," in store for all whites (nowhere in Africa have whites been driven into the sea, though some other peoples have). What is at stake is the Afrikaner monopoly of political power. That is why the admonitions of the leaders of the business community fell on deaf ears, as far as the Afrikaner beneficiaries of political monopoly are concerned. Afrikaners see themselves as asked to sacrifice their own, deeply cherished, specific interests for the convenience of *Neef Brit.* Nothing in their history or in the nature of their present situation suggests that they are likely to do this.

Afrikaners are neither the uniquely virtuous *volk* of their own rhetoric— "the highest work of art of the Architect of the Centuries," as Dr. Malan once put it—nor yet the moral monsters depicted by outside rhetoric. They are ordinary human beings, with the normal human quotas of greed, arrogance, and so forth, operating within a unique predicament, which they have inherited and are now thrashing around in. I suspect that some of the righteous who denounce them from afar might behave quite like them if they were caught in a similar predicament—if, for example, there had been a black majority in America in the 1950s.

Pride and economic interest are here intertwined. There is probably no people that would willingly accept such a precipitous fall in power, status, and income as would be required of Afrikaners in the event of the great transition. So Afrikaners, despite their shaken morale, despite the defection of a certain intellectual elite, and despite their partial Americanization, seem likely to go on voting for the parties of the *laager*—the Nationalists and the Afrikaner parties to the right of them—so as to hold the Afrikaner monopoly of political and military power. The mini-election of last October reflected no weakening —rather the contrary—in the determination of Afrikaner voters to hold on to that monopoly.

While holding on to that monopoly to the very last possible moment, the Afrikaner leadership is likely to try various schemes involving the co-optation of blacks or the delegation of subordinate authority to blacks. That is already happening, in a crude but partly effective way, in the Homelands, where black elites and their dependent clansmen have common interests with the Afrikaners rather than with the black revolutionaries (generally the most deadly enemies of the Homelands elites).

But there is available a bolder and more radical form of co-optation than any yet attempted. This is called the Zulu option or the Buthelezi option. This option is already much discussed and is likely to be attempted, in some shape or form, well before the apartheid regime reaches the end of its tether.

So, before we come to consider the possible character of that end game, let us take a look at the Zulu option.

In its roughest outline the Zulu option runs as follows: There are about six million Zulus in South Africa and about five million whites. Under apartheid lines of division, in South Africa's population of 27 million (excluding the four supposedly independent Homelands), blacks (Africans, Asians, coloureds) outnumber whites by more than four to one: whites make up 19 percent. But if Zulus could somehow be made allies of the whites, then the number of whites and their allies would rise to 41 percent—more than twice as nice as the way it is now. (It is all more complicated than that, but that is the general idea.)

But how to get Zulus out of the apartheid classification and into an alliance with whites? At this point the Zulu option becomes the Buthelezi option.

Chief Mangosothu Gatsha Buthelezi (he prefers the "Mangosothu," but the press, for obvious reasons, prefers the "Gatsha") has been chief minister since

1976 of the Homeland of Kwa Zulu, but he is much more than that. In general the Homeland chief ministers are local bosses, each a ruthless master of his allotted patch of territory, with few ambitions or capacities beyond that. But Buthelezi is a national and international figure, who has followed a line independent of both the South African government and the ANC-UDF leadership. Because he operates within the Homelands system and because he has campaigned internationally against sanctions and disinvestment, ANC spokesmen depict him as a stooge. But his track record is not that of a stooge. He refused "independence" status for Kwa Zulu at a time when the South African government was pushing its fiction of independent statehoods for the Homelands. In 1983 he campaigned against P. W. Botha's disastrous tricameral constitution, at a time when that document was being widely touted (especially in the business community) as "a step forward." He is very much his own man.

Buthelezi is often described as "a Muzorewa"—a comparison to Bishop Abel Muzorewa, who emerged briefly to nominal leadership in the last stages of Ian Smith's Rhodesia (Zimbabwe) and who was repudiated in the British-organized elections that brought Robert Mugabe to power. There is some point in the comparison, since white South Africans look at Buthelezi as white Rhodesians looked at Muzorewa: as a black option for when things get very bad, a late way of staving off the worst.

But Buthelezi has far more going for him than Muzorewa ever had. Buthelezi has his own power base, in Kwa Zulu, and his own large and dynamic political party, Inkatha, with an embryo militia in Inkatha's Youth League.

The Inkatha youth are a tough lot; they are often referred to as the *Impis,* after the dreaded regiments of the Zulu kings Shaka, Dingaan, and Cetshwayo. There is a romantic aura about the whole movement—a fascist potential, according to its opponents (the ANC and the UDF).

Inkatha today claims a paid-up membership of one million, and even its adversaries do not dispute that the membership is large. The bulk of the membership is drawn from the northeastern province of Natal (including Kwa Zulu), but there are also many members in urban areas outside Natal. Buthelezi has addressed large meetings in Soweto.

Buthelezi's adversaries accuse him of splitting "the people"—which consist of all blacks, including Indians and coloureds—along ethnic lines. Buthelezi retorts that Inkatha membership is open to all. Still, almost all the members appear to be Zulus. In a conversation at Jan Smuts Airport with Buthelezi, who had with him John Mavusu, the top Inkatha man in Soweto, I put a question about that. Mavusu replied, "Inkatha is not a Zulu organization. But the Zulus have always provided the leadership for other Africans." Chief Buthelezi did not appear to dissent.

The ethnic factor in South African politics is very difficult for an outsider to assess. Perhaps even for an insider—inside *what,* after all? Apartheid, of course, insists on the transcendent importance of ethnicity, and assigns and reassigns ethnicities with ponderous and capricious rigor. The enemies of apartheid sweepingly dismiss ethnic categories as irrelevant. In fact ethnic affiliations—not necessarily as defined by Afrikaners—appear to remain important, though their manifestations can be extremely confusing. I was told by a distinguished and judicious resident of Soweto, Dr. Nthato Motlana, of a remarkable incident that occurred during my visit. A mob came down the street chanting, "Get the Zulus." What was remarkable was that the words shouted were *in Zulu.* And the shouters were themselves Zulu: Zulu Soweto residents attacking Zulu migrant workers holding Kwa Zulu passes. There are urbanized Zulus, politicized and de-ethnicized by the ANC, who hate Buthelezi and the very name of Zulu. But it seems that most Zulus are less complicated. Intertribal fighting has been a significant—though relatively little-noted—part of the unrest, and Zulus have often played a leading part in this. About sixty people were reported killed in fighting in Natal between Zulu and Pondo tribesmen on Christmas Day, 1985. Such clashes are triggered by local disputes—over matters like access to water—but they can also have some political overtones. The non-Zulu party to any such conflict is much more likely than the Zulu party to use ANC-UDF slogans, and is likely also to accuse the Zulus—and Buthelezi's Inkatha in particular—of tribalism and collaboration with Pretoria. And it is the very fact of this continuing contention among blacks that attracts the attention of some of Pretoria's planners to the Buthelezi option.

Buthelezi himself is a proud African, proud of his people's martial history and of his own dynastic connections: he is a descendant on his mother's side of the last independent Zulu king, Cetshwayo. Buthelezi's manner is aristocratic, in a European rather than an African manner. Some other African chiefs whom I have met are rather obviously indifferent to the opinion of their interlocutor; they have a somnolent, inward-looking hauteur. Buthelezi, though, is charming, affable, considerate. On his visits to Britain he goes down very well, I believe, with members of the House of Lords.

Buthelezi is austere in his personal life. He doesn't drink or smoke, and there is no touch of scandal or corruption about him anywhere. In these respects he is very different from most of the other Homelands chiefs.

The trouble with the "Buthelezi option" is that Pretoria seems unable to deal with a proud African, or even to register the existence of such a phenomenon. The Buthelezi option, on Buthelezi's terms, would mean power in Natal Province: Natal as a predominantly Zulu state. There can be little doubt that this revival of Zulu glory would rally great numbers of Zulus around Buthelezi and that Pretoria could reap at least some of the benefit of the Zulu option. But that would still mean blacks ruling whites in Natal—even though the whites there are mostly English-speaking, not Afrikaners—and Pretoria still cannot stomach that. The Botha government at the end of 1985 was still thinking essentially in terms of buying off this (to them) awkward black with some kind of showy job in Pretoria. This is a hopeless version of the Zulu option. But the National Party seems incapable of envisaging any way of dealing with blacks except bludgeoning or bribery.

Racism, like other forms of hubris, tends to blind people to some of their true interests and to the nature of their predicament. And racism wrapped in layers of euphemism—as in contemporary South Africa—remains as blind, and as racist, as before.

But even in Pretoria at a later stage brings itself to take the Buthelezi option seriously, it will probably still only be buying a little more time for itself. For the serious trouble, which will not go away, is not in Natal but mainly in the Transvaal and the Cape, and there the pressures are bound to increase. All the demographic odds are heavily against the whites. In 1983, according to official South African statistics, black births outnumbered white by *ten to one.* (And these statistics are geared to *understating* the demographic disparity, by omitting the figures from the four all-black "independent" Homelands.)

The more black children, the more turbulent the black children. Politicization spreads fast in an expanding population with expanding unemployment, especially as the more energetic and ambitious children realize that politicization brings with it power within the ghettos. The children who count for most are the children with the necklace.

The more children, the more unrest; the more unrest, the more repression; the more repression, the more international pressure and the more economic misery.

Let us suppose that this vicious spiral develops to the point where it overcomes the stiff resistance to change of a large part of the Afrikaner electorate. I doubt whether that will happen, even when things get much worse, but let us suppose it does happen. At some future general election—let us say the next one, in less than three years—large numbers of Afrikaner voters desert the *laager* parties and join forces with the Progressives. You have once again, as before 1948, a British-Afrikaner coalition. And you have a white state president who is pledged to enter into serious negotiations with the ANC about "one man, one vote."

Could such a state president count on the loyalty of the South African Defence Force?

I raised that question, in my Proustian way, in conversation with an Afrikaner political analyst who—because his specialty is Marxism—has been in close touch with South African military intelligence.

Could he, I asked, envisage some possible future circumstances in which the South African Defence Force might no longer be amenable to civilian control?

He looked at me, deadpan, and said, "You are supposing that there is civilian control at the moment."

Partly he was referring to a matter of structures. Security is the concern of a joint committee—the State Security Council—which includes the head of the Defence Force and the commissioner of police as well as members of the Cabinet. But many well-informed South Africans believe that the security forces are already, at least to some extent, a law unto themselves, prepared to ignore government policies of which they disapprove. Thus in Mozambique an apparently highly successful South African government line of policy seems to have been sabotaged and scorned by the South African military.

On March 16, 1984, the governments of South Africa and Mozambique concluded a pact—the Nkomati Accord—under which each government pledged itself to ensure that its territory would not be used for the planning or launching of a military attack on the other. Under that accord—which scandalized former admirers of Mozambique's ruling left-wing party, Frelimo —Mozambique reduced the ANC presence there to a small, purely diplomatic mission. It all seemed quite a coup for South Africa. But in practice the accord was ignored—or rather, systematically violated—on the South African side. The South African military continued to provide logistic backing for the Mozambique Resistance Movement, Renamo. And during October the Mozambique government published captured documents—the authenticity of which is officially disputed by Pretoria but generally accepted by well-informed South Africans—according to which the military authorities advised Renamo to treat the Nkomati Accord as null and void, and spoke disrespectfully of South Africa's foreign minister, Mr. "Pik" Botha. (As it happens, I have never met a single South African, of any persuasion, condition, or color, who did *not* speak disrespectfully of Pik Botha; but that, of course, is not the point here.)

So it does rather look as if P. W. Botha's government may not be in full control of its own armed forces. The "wars" the South African forces have been intermittently waging or supporting beyond South African borders—in Angola and Namibia, Botswana and Lesotho, as well as in Mozambique and possibly in Zimbabwe—may well not be P. W. Botha's idea at all; he may have no alternative but to go along, much as the last governments of France's Fourth Republic rubber-stamped the actions of an army over which they had lost control.

And it does seem that the South African Defence Force may already be to a great extent "Algerianized." An important recent book, *Pretoria's Praetorians: Civil-Military Relations in South Africa,* by Philip Frankel, suggests as much. It appears that the lectures given at the South African Joint Defence College are entirely based on the work of the French general André Beaufre, a specialist in counterinsurgency, and that they draw on the lessons of France's experiences in Algeria and Indochina (presumably in order to avoid repeating those experiences). The quotations from this martial guru suggest that the boggling of the Afrikaner mind must be proceeding at an especially accelerated rate in the Joint Defence College. Beaufre, whose doctrine is that of "the indirect mode," says that the strategist in the indirect mode "is like a surgeon called upon to operate on a sick person who is growing continuously and with extreme rapidity and of whose detailed anatomy he is not sure: his operating table is in a state of perpetual motion and he must have ordered the instruments he is to use five years beforehand."

It doesn't sound as if the chances of a successful operation are all that high. All the same, it is clear that the graduates of the Joint Defence College are being conditioned to get their hands on that unfortunate "sick person" and try out their surgical skills.

It doesn't sound, either, as if the Afrikaner-dominated South African Defence Force would—even in much worsened circumstances—be likely to obey what they would regard as a *hensopper* state president, bent on making a deal with the ANC. Apart from their pride, traditions, and anti-Marxist, anti-ANC ideology, they have (like the Afrikaners in the civil service) their professional interests and status to think about, which would be prime casualties of such a deal.

So it seems that even if a majority of the white electorate were prepared to throw in the sponge, the struggle to maintain white, and Afrikaner, supremacy would be carried on by the armed forces, presumably under martial law, with the suspension of the constitution (which is, in any case, not a document that inspires any great veneration, even among white South Africans).

True, there might be questions, under such conditions, about the discipline of some elements of the armed forces. English-speakers—a number of whom already try to evade national service—might desert or be allowed to resign. And there might be even more serious problems concerning the reliability of blacks (including Indians and coloureds) in the Defence Force.

Blacks make up at present about 40 percent of the South African Defence Force and the South West African Territorial Force (and about 50 percent of the police). Most of these are "other ranks," but some have recently been promoted to lieutenant. Most are noncombatants in support roles, but significant numbers have seen active service: it has been reported that at least 20 percent of the forces serving in Namibia have been blacks. There continue to be more black applicants for places in the Defence Force than there are places. Military analysts report that morale among the black troops is high, and, remarkably, there have apparently been no black desertions to the enemy.

This last phenomenon may be due in part to the extreme ferocity with which the champions of "the cause of the people" treat not only collaborators but at least some ex-collaborators. In October an army jeep carrying two black soldiers drove past a "political" funeral, always a dangerous gathering of mainly militant people. One of the black soldiers jumped out and gave the clenched-fist salute of the Revolution. He was immediately surrounded by a group of mourning children. Perhaps he thought they were coming to congratulate him. They tied a tire around his neck and burned him to death. It was not a news item likely to incite black soldiers to desert.

Of course, the discipline of the black soldiers may weaken under the rising pressures. But even the desertion of many blacks would hardly inflict crippling damage on the Defence Force. Armed blacks are confined to the infantry, with infantry weapons and training only. The armored units, the artillery, and the air force are all-white and mainly Afrikaner; the navy is still predominantly English-speaking but is becoming increasingly Afrikaner.

Even at an advanced phase of the unrest the South African Defence Force would probably still be able to hold, for a prolonged period, those parts of South Africa they would want to hold: primarily the Cape, plus the mineral-rich areas of the Transvaal. The 1977 Security Council embargo on the supply of weapons to South Africa has had the effect of making South Africa largely self-sufficient in conventional arms manufacture. (South Africa is also said to possess a nuclear capability.) The economic difficulties attendant to such unrest would be very serious but probably not crippling. Afrikaners would be prepared to tighten their belts quite a lot rather than abandon their power and status. Sanctions and disinvestment would hurt, but a country with South Africa's resources will always be attractive to the international black market. "Gold," as the poet Horace remarked, "has a way of getting through the guards."

It is true that a general strike, a complete withdrawal of black labor, could defeat this last stand of Afrikanerdom. But it should be noted that the present wave of unrest in the townships is almost exclusively confined to the *unemployed* young. The employed have been mainly quiescent; the black trade-union leaders, once the focus of protest against apartheid, have taken a back seat politically since the children took over. A recent strike, in the principal hospital in Soweto, failed in November despite ferocious intimidation designed to keep it going. One nurse accused of strike-breaking was burned alive. The strike ended a few days later. The children are now threatening to enforce a general strike during this year, but they may find that miners don't burn so easily as nurses. Yet trade-union leaders by the end of 1985 were sounding more militant than they had during most of the year. The combination of pressure from the children and resentment at police actions may produce more strikes this year, though probably not the general strike the children call for.

In conditions of high unemployment and no social security, a job (any kind of job) is a most precious possession: hence, among other things, the flow of black recruits into the South African Defence Force. And a black rebel in

South Africa is not in the relatively happy position of an IRA rebel in Northern Ireland, able to devote all his time to killing the soldiers of the enemy government, in the secure knowledge that the welfare services of the enemy government will keep the family of the "unemployed" rebel supplied with all the necessities of life. So a general and protracted withdrawal of black labor seems unlikely.

Up to almost the end of 1985 the unrest consisted mainly of what the children did, together with sporadic and relatively minor attacks, mostly with grenades but more recently with land mines, in border areas. The township unrest, led by the children, precipitated the brutal police repression, which caused most of the deaths in 1985 and attracted almost all the international attention. According to (admittedly approximate) figures published in *The Times* of London on December 20, 1985, there were 685 people killed in the period from January 1 to October 31, 1985, compared with 149 killed in all of 1984. More than half of those killed in 1985 were "blacks killed by police": 360 people. As against that, only eighteen policemen were killed; significantly, seventeen of these were "killed by township residents," as against only one "killed by guerrillas." The next largest category of killed after "blacks killed by police" was "residents killed by residents": 201 people. These included the victims of the children, and this category may be more subject to underestimation than the others; in any case, in 1985 this category by itself exceeded all of the deaths in 1984. The category "blacks killed by police" increased nearly five times from 1984 to 1985 (79 to 360), but the category "residents killed by residents" increased more than ten times (17 to 201) over the same period. The category "police killed by residents" increased even more sharply: from one in 1984 to seventeen in 1985.

Those *Times* figures showed only one white killed by blacks in 1984 and only one white killed by blacks for 1985 up to October 31 (the latest date covered by the *Times* survey). But in the last days of 1985 the figure for whites killed by blacks suddenly shot up. Six white civilians—including four children—were killed on December 15 by land-mine explosions in a game reserve near the Zimbabwe border. The ANC claimed that these explosions were "justified." On December 23 a bomb in a crowded shopping center at Amanzimtoti, a white beach resort south of Durban, killed another six white civilians. No organization claimed responsibility for the Amanzimtoti bomb, but Michael Hornsby, the experienced South African correspondent of *The Times,* commented on the incident: "It is arguably the most indiscriminate act of urban terror to date except insofar as it seems to have been aimed mainly at whites. It has long been predicted that pressure on the ANC leadership from impatient young members of the organization to attack white civilians directly would become irresistible."

So by the end of 1985 the children seemed to be setting the pace for the guerrillas as well as for the townships. And several correspondents noted a hardening of mood also among whites, especially in the Afrikaner community, following the two major black-on-white incidents of December. Pressure for a tougher military response to black terrorism was rising.

A military—or simply more deeply militarized—government in South Africa might be expected to get a lot tougher than the government of P. W. Botha has yet felt able to be. The model might be General Jacques Massu's successful repression of the Front de Libération Nationale (FLN) in Algiers in the late 1950s. (The Massu repression was itself a response to FLN indiscriminate terror-bombings of Europeans, very much on Amanzimtoti lines.) If an Afrikaner Massu is to persuade people in the townships that he is more frightening than the children with the necklace or the bomb, he is going to have to become very frightening indeed. The least that might be expected—under martial law and a total news blackout—would be house-to-house searches backed by uninhibited use of firepower; torture (on a larger scale than now practiced) and execution of suspects; and deportations and concentration camps.

General Charles de Gaulle, by about 1960, was able to bring Massu-style repression in Algeria to an end, and then to abandon French Algeria (in 1962). But there is no Afrikaner De Gaulle and no possibility of one, no general or statesman with anything corresponding to that commanding prestige. For the post of an Afrikaner Massu, though, there would be plenty of competition.

I rejected earlier the current facile tendency to equate present-day Afrikaner nationalism with Nazism. But like all exalted nationalisms, the Afrikaner kind probably has a potential for something like Nazism, which could be evoked by events as they develop. In general, Afrikaner nationalism up to now has been like *pre*-Nazi German nationalism, with a similar tendency to idolize the *volk*. But the idolatry of the *volk* can turn into something very dangerous when the *volk* feels humiliated and deeply threatened. That was how the metamorphosis set in in Germany after 1918, and events in South Africa, in the terminal stages of Afrikaner power, could precipitate a similar metamorphosis.

If South Africa were left to itself, I think Massu-style (or Nazi-style) repression could be a success, in its own ghastly way. I don't see how the ANC or the children could stand up against it.

If South Africa were left to itself . . . But even already it isn't. I'm not talking about sanctions and disinvestment, which—even combined with the internal unrest—are quite unlikely to end Afrikaner domination over the peoples of South Africa. I'm talking about external *military* intervention.

On South Africa's border external military intervention already exists. About 30,000 Cuban troops are in Angola, where some of them have been (briefly) in combat with South African forces. And the Soviet Union is believed to have warned South Africa in November of 1983—through its ambassador at the United Nations—that any attempt by South Africa to challenge the Cuban defense positions south of Luanda "would not be tolerated."

South African propaganda makes, of course, the most of the red shadow on its borders. And it even appears that some of the more feverish military minds in Pretoria have been hoping to provoke direct Soviet intervention in Angola, in the belief that the United States would then throw its weight behind South Africa.

But to appear as the champion of South Africa is not a coveted international role now. It will be even less coveted if the rulers of South Africa meet rising unrest with far more thoroughgoing repression (as envisaged above). No news blackout could prevent word of Massu-style repression in South Africa from reaching the outside world, probably even in an exaggerated form. The word *genocide* has already been used, wildly, to characterize the actions of P. W. Botha's government. But future forms of repression may be such as to lead many people not only to throw the word around but also to believe that genocide is actually happening. And then there will be an international call for someone to stop the genocide.

In a book about the United Nations (published in 1968) I put forward as a possible scenario, in some such situation, the following:

The General Assembly passes a resolution calling on its members to supply contingents for military intervention in South Africa. The Soviet Union and its allies announce that they will contribute to such a force and participate in such an intervention. The Soviet Union is then casting itself in the same role —champion of international legality and of aroused world opinion—that the United States did over Korea, with the mandate of the General Assembly's "Uniting for Peace" Resolution of 1950.

I don't think that unilateral Soviet intervention will actually happen. But I think that the possibility of something on that order happening is already influencing the course of events. Indeed, the recognition of the existence of the possibility is the principal reason why the possibility is unlikely to come to fruition.

If the Soviet Union seemed to be moving toward assuming the kind of role I have described, the United States would have three options, all of them unattractive.

The first option would be to do nothing. Since the effect of that would be (or be seen as being) to hand over South Africa, its mineral resources and its strategic position, to the Soviets, I take it that this option is in practice impossible.

The second option would be to tell the Soviet Union, "Hands off South Africa!" Because the Soviet Union seems quite unlikely to want to risk inter-superpower war over a remote region in which it has only contingent interests, it would presumably back away. But as it backed away, it would unleash a propaganda barrage, to which the United States would be extremely vulnerable. The United States would be credibly represented as the protector of a white regime practicing genocide against blacks. There are already signs— under the present *relatively* mild conditions—that the United States is increasingly reluctant to appear in the role of protector of South Africa. So the second option seems improbable (though not impossible, like the first one).

The third option is for the United States itself to back a military intervention, which would then become a United Nations operation backed by both superpowers—and probably sanctioned by the Security Council as well as the General Assembly. Under this option the United States could hope to protect its own interests in the region with international approval. So this option— though no doubt repugnant to many U.S. policy-makers—looks like being less repugnant than the other two.

Under certain freak circumstances the normal condition of superpower rivalry can turn into limited superpower consensus. That happened in November of 1956, over Suez, when both superpowers—in different tones of voice— ordered Britain, France, and Israel to get out of Egypt, which they did.

And it happened in 1963, when United Nations forces, with the support or at least the acquiescence of both superpowers, put an end to the Independent State of Katanga, which with West European support (and also South Africa support) had seceded from what is now Zaire.

The case of Katanga seems especially instructive in relation to U.S. options regarding South Africa. Katanga was of course a much smaller and less significant territory. But like South Africa, Katanga was exceptionally rich in strategic minerals, and like South Africa, Katanga made much of its anti-communism. Its motto, everywhere displayed, was, "Katanga: Central Africa's shield against Communism." Under the Eisenhower Administration the United States bought the "shield" idea, and protected Katanga. But under Kennedy the United States slowly and hesitantly reached the conclusion that Katanga, and its anti-communism and its unpopularity, had become a liability to the United States and an asset to the Soviet Union. The process of thought by which this conclusion was reached is set out in *To Move a Nation,* the memoirs of Roger Hilsman, the director of the Bureau of Intelligence and Research in the Kennedy State Department. Those memoirs make interesting reading today, in the context of South Africa. Because when the United States reached the conclusion that Katanga was a liability, the United Nations put an end to Katanga, by force—a policy that the Soviet Union had long urged and so could not oppose.

A kind of limited superpower consensus on South Africa emerged in 1977, when the Security Council decreed a mandatory embargo against the supply of arms to South Africa. Under such conditions as are contemplated above, that consensus could develop into something much more formidable, on mega-Katangan lines.

October 24, 1985, was the fortieth anniversary of the United Nations. On that day I took part in a debate on South African Television with Dr. Brand Fourie, whom I had known when he was South Africa's permanent representative at the United Nations; he was later ambassador in Washington. Before the cameras I talked about the possible line of development examined above: limited superpower consensus, expressed through the United Nations, leading to the extinction of white-controlled South Africa. South African Television is government controlled, and this kind of thing is not generally discussed on it. Dr. Fourie—who happens to be the present chairman of the South African Broadcasting Corporation—was naturally discreet in his reaction. All he said before the cameras about such a possibility was, "It can't be ruled out."

As Dr. Fourie and I walked out of the studios, after the televised discussion, we went on talking about limited superpower consensus. He told me, "I said just there it couldn't be ruled out. But there's more than that. That thing is my nightmare and has been for years."

Of course, it is one thing to snuff out little Katanga and quite another to deal with the South African Defence Force. Presumably there would be a United Nations naval blockade, with superpower participation, and a blockade along South Africa's land frontiers, combined with a build-up of forces on those frontiers, and followed by an ultimatum requiring South Africa to bring the repression to an end and to assent to the organization, under the United Nations, of free and non-racial elections.

And what would the South African reply be?

I put that question to two Afrikaner political scientists, with whom I discussed this possible scenario. Both of them thought that the South African government (or junta) might use its "nuclear capability" against the United Nations.

The Götterdämmerung of the *volk!*

Obviously, there would be *bittereinders* who would favor that course; that is what *bittereinders* are for. But on the whole it seems more likely that the *hensoppers,* in that extremity, would prevail, as they did at the end of the Anglo-Boer War. Militarily, and nationally, there would be no disgrace in capitulation to such overwhelming force. Pride would be saved: it would have taken nothing less than the whole world to overcome the *volk.* And interests could at least be better protected by capitulation than by Götterdämmerung.

In some such way as that, the immensely difficult transition of power might be achieved. In all the above I have of course been guessing. But I have tried, in my guessing, to respect existing patterns of force. Obviously, it would be foolish to attempt any similar analysis of what might happen after the transition. Still, certain shapes can already be dimly made out, looming in the fog.

Even after apartheid and all its elaborate mutations have been thrown to rust on the scrap heap of history, South Africa will still have enormous problems. There will be more and more children, and more and more of the children will be unemployed. It may be nearly as hard for a black government to control Soweto as it is for a white government.

But the new black South Africa, unlike the other African countries, will have a large black middle class. "We are the fittest for independence, and we shall be the last to get it." It was Oliver Tambo who said that to me, back in 1960, when I was a delegate to the General Assembly, and he was a "nongovernmental observer" on behalf of the ANC. What he meant was that South Africa, unlike the countries of West, East, and Central Africa, then beginning to flock into the United Nations, had a large class of educated blacks: a black bourgeoisie, though he didn't put it that way. (Tambo himself is essentially a liberal; he will get on very well with Dr. Slabbert.)

I think that after that transition South Africa's first elected black government is likely to be responsive to, and reliant on, those educated blacks. It will be essentially a middle-class government, though it may be "middle-class Marxist," like the government of Robert Mugabe.

Such a government would probably be supported by organized labor—the employed—but would be immediately challenged by all the "outs" of black society, including the politicized unemployed. There likely would be doubts about the loyalty of the lower ranks in the expanded black contingents of the reconstituted armed forces.

In these conditions the new black government would need such allies as it could find. And it would be likely to find allies among the whites. A multiracial coalition, probably a tacit one, could be expected to emerge: a coalition of all those with something to lose, whatever the color of their skin.

The multi-racial bourgeois coalition might not be wholly attractive, though it might, with luck, work quite well. But it would be better than apartheid, and better than the Bothaesque mutations of apartheid. It would be a lot better than a possible coming "Massu apartheid." And it would be a lot better also than the rule of the children with the necklace, or rather of whichever ominous child emerged as the victor out of the internecine competition for power within a political movement whose sanction, symbol, and signature is the burning alive of people in the street.

75. A BLACK SOUTH AFRICA?*

by XAN SMILEY

One of the weirder products of apartheid is the crippling of language in a maw of euphemism, hypocrisy and sociologese. You talk about the Afrikaner "right to self-determination"—meaning power over everybody else. There once was a minister of "plural affairs." His job was then divided into "constitutional affairs" and "co-operation and development" and now another title has been invented—all roundabout ways of saying "minister for the blacks." The very word apartheid—literally, "apartness," "separatehood"—was coined as a euphemism. Apartheid itself begs definition.

The word actually means two rather different, though overlapping, things, one social-economic, the other political. As the economy has become more sophisticated, social-economic apartheid—the idea that blacks are born to live at an inferior material level of life, and should be encouraged to do so—has been falling to bits. Yet, though people of every color work together, the law still forces nearly all of them to live in segregated residential areas, to send their children to separate schools, to be treated in different hospitals.

What has changed is that the argument sustaining these laws is disintegrating; and the laws themselves are rotting away quite fast at the edges. The fiction that skilled urban blacks who are vital to the economy are "foreigners" in Johannesburg has been abandoned even by President Botha's supporters. The white-black prosperity gap is enormous, but, at least in the towns, it is narrowing. Though still rife, the humiliations of "petty apartheid"—the separate lavatory, the separate canteen, the separate bus—are being reduced. The economic and social obstacles confronting blacks remain huge, but at least whites now nearly all accept that they and the blacks share the same material aspirations. Social-economic apartheid is dying, slowly; few whites, except the 20 percent or so who vote to the right of Mr. Botha's National Party, would care nowadays to justify it.

But that is only half the battle. The end of apartheid is not just the end of segregation and a fairer share of the economic cake. It must also mean, bluntly, the end of white political power. That must mean, even more bluntly, black power. Even liberal whites find this hard to stomach. They prefer to talk about "power-sharing." In the past year, blacks really believe that for the first time they have smelt power. They argue, rightly, that de facto social and economic

*From *The Economist* (London) February 1, 1986.

apartheid will not be swept away completely until there is a substantial switch of political power.

Most of them do not even want to share power, if that should mean a share-out of patronage on a racial basis. Mr. Botha's tentative talk of a "confederation," almost certainly meaning a devolution of power into an assortment of racially determined regional entities, with whites hanging on to the mainspring of government at the center, is therefore not acceptable to blacks. Even non-racial federalism, the liberal whites' alternative, is looked at askance because blacks think, with some reason, that it smacks of an attempt to stop them having untrammeled political power.

When foreigners—and most South African blacks—demand the end of apartheid, what they generally mean, in the end, is a predominantly black central government, probably run by the African National Congress, with Mr Nelson Mandela—if he is still alive—at the head of it. Is that achievable? Is it desirable? And what, given the extraordinary peculiarities of South Africa, is the best (or the least bad) that busybody foreigners should be aiming at?

Those questions are worth addressing only if it is clear that the current unrest is so serious that the government is bound, sooner rather than later, to start surrendering painfully large hunks of power. *Verligte* ("enlightened") Afrikaner Nationalists and liberal white businessmen still fondly argue that a dramatic improvement in the quality of black life may take the revolutionary sting out of the black townships—and persuade "responsible" blacks, led by the emergent black middle class, to accept some power-sharing formula. Militant blacks and liberal-to-radical whites, however, argue that life for South African blacks is so ghastly that the patchwork of revolts in the townships has already turned into an unstoppable revolution. Has it?

Revolt or Revolution

Blacks are not materially as badly off as before. Working conditions and real wages of urban black labor, especially skilled labor, have improved sharply in the past decade or so. For this the blacks can thank an impressive economic growth rate, which, as the Oppenheimers and their liberal big-business friends so assiduously point out, is also a good way of breaking down social-economic apartheid and its growth-stunting restrictions; they can also thank international companies, who have led the way in liberal employment practice; and they can thank the burgeoning black and multi-racial trade union movement, even though it has been legal only since 1979.

In real terms, average black income per head outside farming and the homelands rose in the 1970s by 63 percent (the rise for Indians, Coloureds—people of mixed race—and whites was 25 percent, 7 percent and 2 percent) and went up further this decade until the recession began to drag standards down a year or so ago. But the growth of a black labor aristocracy and professional class has been particularly rapid. The wage gap between white and black miners' average pay has narrowed from a ratio of 18:1 in 1972 to 4:1 today. Black workers in the car industry get a minimum of Rand 2.5 an hour (1 Rand = $0.39; a year ago it was worth more than $0.80); higher paid black car workers get nearly R6 an hour, compared with a low-grade white clerical worker's R3.75 per hour. Black consumption is now much greater than white. By next year there should be about 370,000 blacks in professional and managerial positions—more than a third of the total, and more than twice the figure of 1970.

Blacks have become far better educated. The number of black secondary school pupils has leaped from 123,000 in 1970 to 615,000 today. The old system of permits to allow blacks to attend "white" universities has been dropped: about 12–15 percent of students at most of the English-speaking universities are not white. Middle-class black South Africans are among the most sophisticated in Africa, and tend to regard their counterparts even in the more dynamic African countries such as Zimbabwe and Kenya as rather bumpkinish. There is also, especially in the eyes of black nationalists, a disturbing gap in attitude as well as prosperity between skilled-and-upward blacks in the "first world" of the great urban centers of South Africa and those in the ten rural cesspits known as "homelands"—often described by whites as well as blacks as the "third world" bits tacked on to "first world" South Africa.

That is where the real grinding poverty lies. Since 1970 about 3m "surplus" blacks from the townships and white farms have been dumped there. And it should not be forgotten that, for many of the luckier ones who do live in the white areas, wages for the un-unionised are paltry. At the grimmer end of the black scale, many farmworkers still get a paltry R1.2 a day, with a food ration and housing thrown in, and domestic workers often as little as R1. Rising unemployment also means more crime and more "illegals" in the townships. Last year in Soweto alone there were over 1,200 nonpolitical murders.

Yet, even for the luckier "insiders," as the better-placed blacks are sometimes known, the brutal realities of life under apartheid have hardly altered a jot. The one exception—already mentioned—is the law allowing trade unions to jostle for power and money. And government's greater sensitivity to outside opinion has meant that most of the forced removals of people from "black spots" (areas surrounded by white-designated land but where blacks hold land title) have stopped. The overwhelming majority of blacks, however, are unaffected by the reforms that have caused such Angst among whites.

Most blacks are unmoved by being allowed in white ("international") restaurants; by being allowed to have sex with or marry a white person; by being allowed to send a child to an expensive predominantly white private school;

by being allowed to buy leasehold and even free-hold property in the urban areas (a privilege that a mere few thousand rich blacks, a large number of them in Soweto, have been able to afford); by being allowed on to beaches specially designated as "mixed" as opposed to "exclusive" (another nice euphemism there); by being allowed in multi-racial railway carriages (which tends to mean whites can sit in shoddy black carriages, while the former whites-only carriages remain "exclusive"); by being allowed in the same lavatory as a white person in the place of work (and there may still be differentiation by professional grade, which often amounts roughly to the old distinction); by being entitled to play rugby or cricket for the national or provincial teams (when public sporting facilities in the townships remain grossly inferior—pebble-strewn dustbowls versus manicured lawns—to the parks run by white municipalities, which are still entitled to withhold permission for mixed-race sport); by being able to join a multi-racial political party, though, if black, you cannot stand for parliament.

The new black middle-class and skilled workers may have the money to soften the edges of apartheid. But even they still crack their heads against what Mr. Botha says are the "non-negotiable" corner-stones: the Group Areas Act, which tells people by their color where they can live; and the Reservation of Separate Amenities Act (the latter amended to make sport at the higher level look better for international consumption), which tells people by their color what facilities they may share.

Even the hated pass-laws, under which some 200,000-plus blacks were arrested in 1984 for their inability to prove their permission to be in a "white" area, are still in place, though the president's council, an advisory body nominated by Mr. Botha, has recommended their abolition; instead, there may be another euphemism, called "planned urbanization," meaning less harsh control of black movement around the country. A wider range of urban insiders, if they have fulfilled certain long-term job or residential qualifications, may be allowed to dispense with renewable permits. And another suffocating dehumaniser, which still lies at the heart of discrimination, is the Population Registration Act, whereby every South African is racially tagged from cradle to grave (unless you are one of the 100-odd yearly unfortunates whose race classification is altered) in order to decide what school, hospital, residential zone you are destined for.

Above all, there is that little matter of the vote. No change there. The whites' hope that middle-class blacks could be co-opted as a buffer against black nationalism has been proved horribly false. There are quite a few blacks with something material to lose, yet many of those are nonetheless at the forefront of the protest movement. Indeed, the much-sung parliamentary reform of a year ago, when Indians and Coloureds were each given a chamber, was viewed by the still-excluded-blacks of all classes not so much as "step in right direction" (the hope of many reform-minded white businessmen at the cautious end of the liberal spectrum) as a declaration of war. Since then, with many townships descending into anarchy, blacks have even less say than they did a few years ago because so many urban councils, always despised, have been rendered powerless.

Civil Strife without End?

Since the state of emergency was imposed by Mr. Botha on July 20th last year, the death rate has gone steadily up. From September 1984, when the present unrest began in earnest, just under one person a day until the end of that year was dying violently. Then, in the first half of 1985, the rate rose to more than 1.6 a day. Since the emergency it has gone up to 3.6. After press restrictions were brought in two months ago, the rate has risen a shade further. More than 1,100 people have been killed as a result of the past 17 months' unrest.

Nearly 8,000 people have been arrested under the emergency regulations, most of whom have been released. Last year another 3,600 were detained, of whom about a third are still behind bars, under security laws already in force before the emergency. The police's own figures show how ready policemen are to shoot unarmed rioters. Police mistreatment of prisoners has been as widespread as ever, with techniques such the "helicopter" (hooded prisoners twirled upside down from a pole), electric shock and thorough beatings all commonplace.

Before 1984, government managed to contain opposition by chopping off its head—by rounding up the leaders. This time, the national opposition is so scattered, through the 680-plus groups affiliated to the United Democratic Front, that there are few easily identified national leaders whose imprisonment would hamper the protest movement. Most of the UDF's national executive has been imprisoned or forced underground. Many of its regional or town leaders are on the run. But the little civic organizations that form the backbone of the UDF have made people so politically conscious that there always seems to be somebody available to fill the gaps caused by death or detention.

The UDF is very broad ideologically and draws its members from every class. Middle-class blacks, traders' associations, schoolteachers' groups, church organizations are all prominent. The rough end of the UDF is the unemployed township youths, who are often very violent—and brave—in the face of police sjamboks or bullets. They have nothing to lose. They themselves are often particularly brutal towards blacks suspected of backsliding from the struggle.

The threat of mass trade union action, together with township ungovernability and the deteriorating economy, is another of Mr. Botha's worries that is unlikely to go away. The mainly black unions have cautiously built up their strength, especially in key industries such as mining, engineering and car manufacturing, and now embrace about 16–18 percent of the active black and brown work force (excluding domestics and farmworkers). A new "super-federation" of 33 unions, the biggest in South Africa's history, was formed in December. It will further increase labor muscle by breaking up community-based and "general" unions and reassembling them in national industrywide unions.

The unions have until now been rather careful not to get too enmeshed in overt politics. As a result, their leadership has not been badly hit by the state of emergency. But the new Congress of South African Trade Unions (COSATU) promises to become increasingly political. Though most of its members probably sympathize with UDF/ANC, it has been careful not to affiliate itself formally to any political party. But there is no doubt that it will use its muscle to assail the government when it thinks it can hurt it most. There has been an especially meteoric growth of the unions on the mines, which produce a good half of South Africa's export earnings.

It is clear that the UDF is an overground version of the African National Congress—even though the government cannot prove it. The aims are identical, though the UDF cannot officially advocate violence, as the ANC does, and stay legal. It is equally clear that, with the possible exception of Natal and Zululand, where Chief Mangosuthu Gatsha Buthelezi and his vast Inkatha movement have managed to keep most blacks under their grip, the UDF/ANC is hugely popular. Opinion polls among blacks are pretty fallible in South Africa, but they all show that the ANC leader, Mr. Mandela, is unquestionably the blacks', and now also the Coloureds', national hero. The UDF leaders and patrons nearly all have long ANC pedigrees. If the ANC were unbanned, it would absorb the UDF in a trice. If elections were held, it would win an overwhelming victory. If, theoretically speaking, there were an agreement between the government and the just-legal black opposition, the ANC would certainly have the authority to seal it.

And yet there is little evidence that the ANC is actually responsible for the unrest. Its achievements lie elsewhere. Military action in South Africa is not one of them, though it does carry out about a hundred pinprick attacks, mostly on economic targets, every year. Its heralded switch to "soft" targets will have practically no military effect. The death of four white children and two adults from a landmine explosion near the Zimbabwe border on December 16th and the killing of five people by a bomb put in a Durban shop a few days later will merely tarnish the ANC's image abroad, make South African whites angrier, and the country's black neighbors even more vulnerable to reprisals. The white government's ability to batter any neighboring black countries suspected of harboring ANC people (and even, in the recent case of Lesotho, to help overthrow the leader) has already reduced, though not ended, the movement's ability to slip activists in from outside.

All the same, the ANC has managed, by setting up cells manned by about about 2,000 or so underground political activists and guerrillas within the country, to make its presence felt. More important, the ANC-in-exile has managed to stay, by the standards of exile groups, remarkably united. It retains the old Christian, liberal, economically and ideologically moderate element led formerly by the late Chief Albert Luthuli. It has managed to absorb many of the post-Soweto militants who left in the late 1970s. It has absorbed much of the "black consciousness" movement whose magnet was Steve Biko, killed by the police in 1977.

It has also, since 1955, maintained its alliance with the tightly Moscow-linked South African Communist Party, whose members have risen to positions of influence in the highest councils of the ANC. This, understandably, has made many western governments and South African business and liberal leaders a bit queasy. Recently, however, the ANC's leader-in-exile, Mr. Oliver Tambo, who is ideologically to the right of Zimbabwe's Mr. Robert Mugabe, has glided into the board rooms and cabinet offices of the West and persuaded many of their occupants that his movement, though it would nationalize quite a chunk of the mines and banks, is essentially moderate and would favor a mixed economy.

It is not the ANC but the UDF that has "made the townships ungovernable," to use the language of black protest. The UDF's most telling weapons of protest are the consumer boycott, the school boycott, which has just been called off for a few months, and hostility toward any blacks considered to be "sell-outs" or "system blacks." The consumer boycotts have hurt white traders, especially in small towns, so hard that for the first time far-from-liberal whites have had to think about black grievances and to try, within their local context, to redress them. The school boycotts have dinned into thousands of young blacks the slogan "liberation before education."

The thousands of youths idle on the streets provide a steady crop of riot fodder—and provide the intimidation to cow the waverers. They have forced people who have ignored the consumer boycott to drink the detergent or eat the packets of flour they have just bought from the shops. They have stoned and burned buses carrying school boycott-breakers. They have killed several hundred black stooges or informers, known as *impimpis.*

Perhaps the most important new weapon of the protest movement is the violence, or threat of it, against the blacks that the government has been banking on co-opting. Hundreds of black policemen and urban councillors have had their houses burned down. Many have been killed. Though more than two-thirds of the blacks killed have fallen to police bullets, the rest, dubbed quislings, have been victims of their fellow blacks' wrath. Wealthier blacks have had to pay protection money to informal township committees. In many townships, entire town councils have resigned. Many mayors have had to run away. The informer system is breaking down, and special branch intelligence is starting to dry up.

A strident multi-racialism is another important feature of the UDF. It lies at the core of the protest. It is fair shorthand to talk about the "black opposition," but in fact the UDF leadership is about two-thirds non-black. South Africans of Indian origin and "so-called Coloureds," as UDF sympathizers refer to people of mixed race, are prominent. Throughout the UDF, from top to bottom, there is a small but noticeable sprinkling of influential whites, as there is in the ANC. This is particularly noticeable in Cape Town, where even a residents' association in a white-designated area has joined the UDF. Much of the white church leadership, too, is UDF-inclined.

The multi-racialism of the UDF/ANC has made it harder still for President Botha to make piecemeal changes likely to placate the blacks. Government concessions based on race, offers to blacks as blacks, are rejected. For instance, he is trying to create about eight "regional services councils" which, from April, are due to combine the old white provincial councils with a collection of black urban councils, so that, together, whites and blacks can co-operate on the administration of such services as roads, sewerage, electricity. Ten years ago this would have been astonishing. Even the blacks might have been favorably impressed.

Today, however, they will spurn the new regional bodies, just as they have spurned the black town councils, because they will be viewed merely as an extension of the same old racially based set-up. Blacks want one education system, one health system, one parliament. Nothing the government has yet talked about suggests a readiness to move away from "group identification" as the starting point of reform. That is why the townships will probably continue to burn.

So What's New?

Yet, despite the relentless array of injustices still afflicting black and brown South Africa, it is untrue to say that nothing has changed or that Mr. Botha's reforms are meaningless. Though they mean almost nothing to most blacks, to whites they are pregnant with meaning. Since whites have power, that is not irrelevant.

What has changed, dramatically, is that white ideology has collapsed. That is what National Party people mean by the death of apartheid. There remains —in the words of the country's top Afrikaner businessman, Mr. Anton Rupert —apartheid's "stinking corpse," which Mr. Botha, in *verligte* eyes, has been far too slow to bury.

This ideological collapse has greatly demoralized the ruling white tribe, the Afrikaners, because it has divided it down the middle between Mr. Botha's agonized would-be-pragmatists, who probably make up two-thirds of the tribe, and the others who still cling on to the old beliefs and argue—probably rightly —that their president's tentative stumblings will lead him inexorably to a point where he will find himself willy-nilly sitting down beside blacks to discuss political power.

So far there is no real physical threat to white power; so far there is little threat to white lives, of which less than 30 have been lost in the past year. The white state is mighty, and well-equipped. It has the capacity to repress the township revolts far more bloodily. The blacks have virtually no urban or rural guerrilla capacity, practically no guns, few safe havens within South Africa or without. It is premature to talk about the overthrow of apartheid within a year or two. As Mr. John Kane-Berman, director of the Institute of Race Relations and leading liberal critic of government, bleakly puts it: "This government is entrenched well into the next century; that is a view, not a wish."

But is it wise to assume that, because white physical power is unchallenged, the white will to govern will remain constant? Not any more. It is the will, not the physical strength, that is under question. It is the will that is undermined by the collapse of ideology.

That is why President Botha's government looks so weak, even though his party has 126 out of 178 seats in the white chamber of parliament (with help from a little bit of pro-rural gerrymandering), the Indian and Coloured chambers have no power to affect anything outside their "own" affairs, Mr. Botha has extremely close relations with the army (sometimes thought to be interested in running the political show itself), and his presidency has another four years to go.

And yet against him there is a surge of tribal disaffection, both from *verligte* Afrikanerdom and from the right wing. There is no obvious alternative leader with qualities that Mr. Botha lacks. The academic Mr. Gerrit Viljoen is cleverer, perhaps more imaginative, but lacks political experience and worldliness. Mr. F. W. de Klerk, the other front-runner, has political acumen, but lacks imagination. One of them may replace Mr. Botha quite soon.

A change of leader might not make that much difference. The trouble with the entire National Party is that it has no idea where it is going. Collectively it has accepted that apartheid cannot work. It has disavowed the ideology and gradually begun to dismantle the machinery. But it cannot, understandably, come to terms with the idea of ending political apartheid—that is to say, losing power. That is why Mr. Botha lacks conviction. The new tri-cameral parliament may have been a "step in the right direction." But it has also emphasized the point at which even liberal Afrikanerdom reckons it can go no farther— unless it is coerced.

A Zulu Red Herring

A diversionary tactic would be to give the Zulus under Mr. Buthelezi and the despised "English" in Natal a chance to experiment with the so-called "KwaZulu/Natal option," which could become the model for a future federation of South Africa.

Mr. Buthelezi has become the *verligte* Afrikaners' favorite black man. Though he has consistently denounced apartheid, he is frequently on the radio and television, particularly because he opposes economic sanctions against South Africa. He is against consumer and school boycotts, and is not especially friendly to the trade unions. He has also declared a readiness to discuss federal forms of black rule that fall short of one-person-one-vote in a unitary state, which is the aim of the UDF/ANC. Though he denounces the system of homelands and refuses to accept "independence," as four of the ten homeland leaders have, his passionate and publicly articulated sense of tribal pride—"I am the leader of six million Zulus, the biggest tribe in the country"—is honey in the ears of Afrikaner leaders, for whom the playing up of black tribal divisions is a key to white survival. Mr. Buthelezi says that he is still loyal to the "old ANC" but that it has been taken over by Communists and Xhosas, the country's second tribe.

Mr. Buthelezi is high in Mr. Botha's esteem. There is talk of an Afrikaner-Zulu alliance. Already, Zulu police have been sent into action in Cape Town to help quell disturbances there. Not surprisingly, Mr. Buthelezi has become the most detested figure in the eyes of the UDF/ANC.

He cannot yet be written off. His Inkatha movement is more than 1m strong. Through deftly dispensed patronage, he controls the housing and a lot of jobs in his KwaZulu 44-bit patchwork, some of which includes the townships of Durban. Though authoritarian and excessively sensitive to criticism, he is a good organizer and polemicist. But he increasingly lacks the support of educated and middle-class Zulus. Most of the students at the university of Zululand outside Durban loathe Inkatha, especially since Inkatha heavies killed some anti-Buthelezi students there two years ago.

His urban following, even in Durban and certainly other cities, has been steadily shrinking. Mr. Buthelezi's main problem is that he has not been able to deliver the political goods. That is why his future may hinge on the KwaZulu/Natal option. The trouble is that the idea is very vague, couched in academic waffle, and far from implementation.

There is no sign that the English-speaking whites of Natal are readier to surrender real power to a moderate Zulu leadership than Afrikaners are to blacks as a whole. The party with which Mr. Buthelezi is negotiating the KwaZulu/Natal option is the moribund New Republic Party, the relic of

General Smuts's old United Party and still the main force in Natal's provincial council. Some of its members are still against even abolishing "exclusive" bathing on Durban beaches. It would probably be years before Mr. Buthelezi could get a real hunk of power for blacks in Natal.

So the much touted Natal option still looks pie-in-the-sky. That means that Mr. Buthelezi, for all his ability, will probably end up a loser, a sort of cross between Zimbabwe's Joshua Nkomo, driven back to a tribal constituency heavily outnumbered by a combination of other blacks, and Bishop Muzorewa, suffocated to death by white kisses.

The Argumentative Whites

The climate of political opinion has changed at all points of the white spectrum. Intellectual Afrikanerdom and the Afrikaner churches are in a state of intense ferment. Courageous Afrikaner editors, such as Mr. Harald Pakendorf of *Die Vaderland,* are voicing thoughts that would have astounded their readers ten years ago. To such Afrikaners, who are ahead of the tribal pack but still part of it, the idea of unfettered ANC rule is not yet conceivable. But the sort of power-sharing ideas that were the preserve of a small white liberal minority are now seriously contemplated by these molders of Afrikaner opinion. Afrikaner big business has, for the first time, come right up alongside the old liberal Anglo-Jewish business establishment that it once regarded with unremitting hostility.

In the middle of the spectrum, quite a few ordinary small-town white businessmen and traders have been forced by the consumer boycotts to sit down and argue with the real black township leaders, as in Port Elizabeth. Within the limits of the law, they have even submitted to local agreements which have sharply altered the old relationship between black and white. There is a new readiness to take black demands seriously.

White liberalism, too, is undergoing similar drastic introspection farther down the ideological road. The Progressive Federal Party accepts that the 18 percent of the vote it won at the last election will probably fail to get much bigger. Liberals are informally divided between those who reckon that the UDF/ANC is the force of the future, and should even be encouraged in its battle against apartheid, and those who fear the ANC and look to Mr. Buthelezi as their ally.

The PFP leader, Mr. Frederick van Zyl Slabbert, probably sides with the radicals, and wants his party to back away from a PFP-Inkatha alliance. Many of the business leaders feel more at home with the distant idea of the KwaZulu/Natal option, the qualified franchise (though it was dropped from the PFP manifesto eight years ago), and a power-sharing arrangement which really does prevent "domination by any one group."

The radical white liberals are no longer an insignificant minority, especially in the Western Cape, where the rainbow of skin-color makes visible nonsense of the requirement that everybody should be neatly classified by race. The Reverend Allan Boesak, a UDF patron and deputy head of the Coloured bit of the Dutch Reformed Church, preaches to several hundred whites mixed up in multi-racial congregations. At the university of Cape Town, where about 15 percent of the students are not white, an alliance of white left-liberals and radical blacks and browns has taken over the official students' council—and affiliated to the UDF. That means the students of one of the country's most important English-speaking universities have quasi-voted ANC.

But whatever the changes within liberal circles, the ferment within Afrikan-erdom matters much more. And there the main struggle for supremacy is between Afrikaners of the pragmatic middle-right and Afrikaners of the fanta-sy-right, though Mr. Botha's relative pragmatists are increasingly coming to rely upon the votes of the tougher English-speakers.

Even if, as is likely, Mr. Botha's relative pragmatists prevail over the die-hards, moral persuasion will not be enough to make Afrikaners just hand over power. That can come only by coercion. The most potent coercive combination would be continued internal violence, leading to white exhaustion rather than collapse; internal labor unrest, strikes and consumer boycotts, leading to eco-nomic weakness for the country and hardship for all, in turn leading to greater unemployment fueling further township violence; further ferment in white consciences, especially Afrikaner ones, which, despite the brutalities of the past, are still sensitive to mighty agonizing twinges of Calvinistic puritanism and desperate introversion; general white demoralization—and emigration—leading to a weakening of the will to govern; and external hostility, to pump up all these pressures.

Coercion and Sanctions

The economic sanctions issue is complex. Many good people and plausible arguments are ranged against the economic sanctions' lobby. It is unfair, in America especially, that the sanctions debate has descended into a crude test of "How strong is your commitment against racialism?": pro-sanctions equals anti-apartheid, and vice versa. That is wrong.

One of the worst—and most popular—arguments against economic sanc-tions, however, is that they hurt blacks hardest, the very people they are designed to help. That is true as far as it goes. But the leaders of the blacks, the black trade unions and a growing number of ordinary blacks say they are prepared to make the sacrifice. The don't-hurt-the-blacks argument looks shabbiest when it is deployed by outsiders who have never shown the slightest interest in black welfare before. A better argument is that sanctions would seriously damage half a dozen of South Africa's black neighbors just when their economies need help to increase foreign trade. But, there again, those black neighbors say they are prepared to make that sacrifice.

Sanctions are reasonable as moral gestures in foreign policy—so long as they do not actually have the reverse effect to that intended. The best anti-sanctions argument is that they could actually prolong apartheid by driving Afrikaners behind the stockaded wagons of the laager, thereby encouraging greater repression and a siege economy which the country will be able to sustain. This argument is ultimately based on two separate assumptions: first, that sanctions will not destroy or dramatically enfeeble the economy; second, that—if sanctions do hurt—the Afrikaners would rather commit suicide than be forced to accept black rule. It is now looking more and more as if the first assumption is false. The second, though not disprovable, depends on the accuracy of a picture of the average Afrikaner that may well be out of date.

Can economic sanctions hurt? Some types can. Others are likely to be less effective. Some are "private"—that is to say, people will dish South Africa because common sense tells them to, irrespective of government diktat or moral argument. But purely commercial anxieties and government-imposed measures—"public" sanctions—feed on each other.

Last year's tumble of the Rand was caused by a combination of hard-nosed foreign self-interest and anti-apartheid lobby-pressures which could pull the Rand down even farther. The prevention of new loans from abroad would hurt too—much harder than "disinvestment" if that simply meant foreign companies selling off their South African assets to local conglomerates. The ultimate sanction would be a trade embargo enforced by a blockade—a seemingly outlandish idea today, but one that could become more serious. If, for example, an alliance of third-world countries, with Russian help, began to threaten embargo-breaking ships, would America have the nerve to come to South Africa's rescue? Quite possibly not.

The picture fast building up, and reflected in gloomy (sometimes even panicky) faces of businessmen in Johannesburg, suggests that, yes, sanctions can hurt very hard indeed. They are unlikely to make the economy crumble, but over a period, perhaps as long as a decade, they will grind it down.

The second question, then, is whether they will have the right effect. Liberal businessmen in South Africa say they will not. Their argument has a hollow ring. Few businessmen could advocate a course that, in the short term at any rate, is bound to make them much poorer. At first they used to say sanctions were pointless—they would not hurt. Now they say, yes, they would hurt, but they would drive the government in the wrong direction—back into the laager. They argue that the reforms that have been made, though not radical enough, have at least split Afrikanerdom and altered the nature of the political debate. True. That is why, five years ago, there was a case for "constructive engagement," for encouraging Mr. Botha to challenge the doctrine of his own tribe. But the game has changed again. Mr. Botha has come just about as far along the reform path as he voluntarily can. Subtle persuasion looks very much as though it has run its course.

The Laager Mentality

Many intelligent businessmen and a majority of white liberals, however, still insist that, if coerced, Mr. Botha's government would then disappear, sjambok flailing, into the laager—or even lose an election to the primitives of the far right. But the "laager mentality" is a cliché. The idea that Afrikaners are so different from anybody else that, if kicked, they are bound to go backwards underestimates the intelligence and overestimates the do-or-die heroism of modern Afrikaners, 90 percent of whom are no longer bible-thumping *boers* (farmers). Like their English-speaking white compatriots, they have become part of a spoilt, affluent suburban society, whose economic pain threshold may prove to be rather low. That, at any rate, seems to be the message of the white response to the black consumer boycotts.

As for the possibility of collective suicide, that suggests that they are special people, almost mad. They are reluctant to accommodate themselves to black power. That is not madness. It is merely human. The record of black rule elsewhere in Africa is bound to discourage whites from handing over power. However selfishly the Afrikaners—and the English-speakers—may have behaved, their dilemma demands sympathy.

One of the risks of the pro-sanctions argument is that once the West has turned its back on the South African government, a large element of leverage disappears. There is a decent case for a stick-and-carrot approach, with a set of requirements, a timetable for their accomplishment, and a clear list of punishments and rewards.

Fine in theory. The snag is that you need far greater international cohesion than you are ever likely to achieve. Even the small group of "wise people" from the Commonwealth is most unlikely to agree to a timetable for the removal of apartheid or the penalties that should be inflicted if it is not adhered to. More to the point, a large section of the anti-apartheid lobby is already locked into a maximalist position: the pressures can be lifted only when a clear-cut black-majority government—such as Mr. Mugabe's in Zimbabwe—is in place. No more, no less.

Bishop Desmond Tutu, at the soft end of black nationalism, has toyed with the stick-and-carrot game. Two years ago, he said that sanctions should be applied unless the pass laws were abolished. Now that that may happen, it is certain he will feel obliged to up the ante. Sanctions, unless they are to be symbols designed merely to salve the consciences of people in the West, have to be thorough. If a decision is taken to apply them, they will have to be heaped on until Mr. Botha or his successors are prepared to sit down with blacks and discuss losing power.

The uncomfortable all-or-nothing nature of the process towards ending apartheid is precisely mirrored in the riddle of Mr. Mandela's release from prison. If he came out, he would insist on being allowed to do politics again. He would insist that his ANC be unbanned. He would insist that the state of emergency be lifted and that the thousands of prisoners be let out too. This would provoke the sort of explosion of popular excitement that would lead either to a massive wave of repression or to massive further concessions.

If Mr. Botha shrank from repression, he would probably be cornered into promising to hold a national convention. If that were to happen, the blacks would insist, as another pre-condition, that the remaining pillars of apartheid —the Group Areas Act and so on—be knocked down. Such a train of events is at present too drastic for Mr. Botha, beleaguered as he is, to contemplate. So Mr. Mandela may well remain behind bars.

All the same, the question is whether Afrikaner tribal survival depends on making that fateful accommodation with an overwhelming black majority or pretending that it can be fended off. If the Afrikaner tribe decides that the blacks cannot, in the long run, be fended off, it would be shrewd to make that accommodation as soon as possible. If the Afrikaners continue to say no, the case for coercion is strengthened. Sanctions would certainly not work overnight. Much would depend on the continuing determination of the blacks to keep their urban areas ungovernable. But the quicker the white tribe submits, the better its chance of a bearable future in a black-ruled South Africa.

To What End?

If white demoralization and economic deprivation take their toll, a national convention would have to lead inexorably to a new constitution in which blacks would be given the chance to have the main say in government at the centre. It is then that parties such as the Progressive Federal Party could come into their own—as creative thinkers.

The ANC, too, almost certainly the chief beneficiary of any new deal that is likely to stick, might then start being flexible. After all, the more flexible it is, the quicker it is likely to get a toe in the door to power. It might even accept an element of representation-by-race for a limited period, as Mr. Mugabe did. It might stop sneering at federalism, too.

Actually, if the white liberals of the PFP were clever, they could sensibly drop federalism and start arguing for proportional representation in a central parliament, with possible blocking or delaying powers for minority parties (not based on race). There could, at the same time, be a large extension of local government which, because most people would at first live among fellows of their own color despite the riddance of race laws, would amount to a way of reassuring frightened minorities. Mr. Tambo or Mr. Mandela would run the show at the center, but he would have to take careful account of minority wishes round the edges.

There could even be an electoral requirement, as in Nigeria before the soldiers took over, whereby a prime minister/president has to win a specific proportion of votes from all over the tribal/racial/regional board, so as to get somebody acceptable to as wide a spectrum of South Africans as possible.

It would be silly, however, to expect an ANC government, once in power, to be any keener on western-style democratic pluralism than any other African nationalist movement. It is not in its heart. The ANC instinct, whatever its newly projected image of tolerance and moderation, would be to dominate the press, the judiciary, the army and police, in fact all the institutions of state, just as virtually every government on the African continent does. At best, the ANC would be authoritarian.

But there has been nothing to suggest that either Mr. Tambo or Mr. Mandela is racialist. They need the skills of 5m whites and would be eager to persuade a good chunk of them that life under black rule could be bearable. The odds are that the ANC would rapidly come to terms with big business (the state would take a big stake), accept a mixed economy, and—at any rate to begin with—let whites get on with running a lot of it. The calmer men in the ANC might allow private schools (Mr. Tambo sent his son to a well-known one in Britain) and private medicine to continue, to soften the transition. There is little, for that matter, to suggest that most black South Africans are bent on a puritanical socialism, though there would be some immediate redistribution of wealth.

Then, however, a bitter struggle would probably break out within the ANC between the Nationalists and the Communists. The current 30-strong top body of the ANC contains a very strong contingent from the South African Communist Party. It probably has a good dozen of them, some in key places, several of them Indian, Coloured and white. Mr. Mandela is left-wing (how could he not be?) but probably not a Communist. He has written of his admiration for the British parliamentary system. And Mr. Tambo is certainly not a Communist. Within the trade unions many would welcome wholesale nationalizations, but many would not. Despite its deprivation, it is highly unlikely that the bulk of the black population would voluntarily rally to a Communist banner.

The likelihood of the Communist faction taking over gets bigger the longer today's struggle drags on. A handover to the ANC, with as many checks and balances as possible but on the assumption that at the end its supremacy is likely, is a big risk. But eventually there could be no alternative. Therefore the sooner the better. That is the best cool-calculating argument for sanctions.

The irony is that the Afrikaners, after a generation of pain, probably stand a better chance of coming to terms with the new state than do their English-speaking compatriots. The Boers have less liberal baggage to lose than the English. Most of them are more fiercely wedded to the country. The old paradox is that they have treated the black people worse, yet relations have on the whole been closer than those between black and English. Witness the 2.8m Coloureds, 90% of them Afrikaans-speaking. Witness recent studies showing that three-quarters of supposedly white Afrikaners have black blood. Strangely, despite the hatreds, the cultural gap between white and black in South Africa is narrower than it is anywhere else in Africa. All is not lost.

76. THE COSTS OF DISINVESTMENT*

by GAVIN RELLY

Gavin Relly is chairman of the Anglo American Corporation of South Africa, the country's largest corporation. In September 1985, he organized and led a visit of South African business executives to leaders of the outlawed African National Congress in Zambia.

. . . The fundamental principle that South African business leaders adhere to is the importance of individual freedoms and of a free enterprise economy. This view brings them into conflict with apartheid on both moral and pragmatic grounds. Apartheid, after all, seeks to restrict such fundamentals of the free enterprise system as labor mobility, the ability to choose where to live and educate one's family, and one's ability to participate freely in the country's political life.

Abundant evidence shows that apartheid and its associated economic policies have restricted the quantity as well as the quality of opportunity for all South Africans. This explains why business executives oppose restrictions, racial or otherwise, placed on these freedoms. . . .

But business leaders oppose apartheid for another important reason—it has become an ethnic, quasi-socialist system of government pursued by an Afrikaner oligarchy not hitherto imbued with free enterprise principles. In this respect, apartheid has incorporated some of the worst features of other centralized, bureaucratic, socialist systems. Fortunately, these central features of apartheid also have increasingly conflicted with an industrializing society's need for high economic growth. And the process of reform instituted in the late 1970s and pursued somewhat unevenly in the 1980s has resulted partly

*From *Foreign Policy,* Summer 1986.

from the changing economic interests of the Afrikaner community and partly from domestic and international pressures.

What, then, can South African business (and its overseas counterparts) do to accelerate the dismantling of apartheid and to promote the kinds of fundamental political negotiations needed? Political negotiations among South African business leaders start with the assumptions that there can be no quick fixes, whatever the situation's urgency, and that a sweeping, business-led, efficiently managed transformation of society is not in the offing.

First, contrary to many foreign misperceptions, neither domestic nor foreign business can force the South African government to act against its will. One cannot simply assume, as many do, that because American business often can influence Washington in its favor, South African firms have the same power. . . .

An Afrikaner Transformation

During the rise of Afrikaner nationalism in the early 20th century, and certainly since World War II, business—until recently, dominated by whites of English descent—has been cast in an adversarial role with respect to government. Afrikaners used their numerical preponderance among the white electorate to seize power and then, through essentially statist and socialist measures, redistributed wealth in favor of the Afrikaner community. Business had exceedingly limited influence over this process. In fact, after the Sharpeville tragedy of 1960, then Prime Minister Hendrik Verwoerd reacted angrily to urgings from English- and Afrikaans-speaking executives to end the system of reserving categories of jobs for whites. He refused to address a major gathering of business leaders, whom he charged with "paving the way for black domination." He also denounced as "traitors" the Associated Chambers of Commerce (ASSOCOM), the most liberal and vocal South African business organization. . . .

As economic growth and successful political mobilization combined to transform the Afrikaner nation from a rural and blue-collar background into a modern Western people, a class of Afrikaner business leaders emerged whose interests increasingly clashed with apartheid. This class's influence was not unimportant in contributing to the erosion of apartheid in fields such as job assignments and trade union rights for blacks.

But on the central question of political power, the state—the very instrument of Afrikaner modernization—emerged as the key obstacle to political reform. More than 40 percent of employable Afrikaners now work in the state sector, many having retreated there from the agricultural and mining sectors. Political reform threatens the livelihood of such people. The prospect of sharing power—with the inevitable loss of jobs in the state sector to black South

Africans—let alone surrendering power, must look doubly unattractive when a deteriorating economy makes job alternatives hard to find.

The state sector has been the chief beneficiary of apartheid, and bureaucrats and nationalist politicians have been able, in most instances, to pass on the costs of apartheid policies to other groups. Where this has not been possible, these leaders sometimes have concluded that apartheid's costs are cheaper than submitting to pressures that they believe threaten their very security.

Many of the costs of disinvestment, increasing sanctions, and isolation can be passed on to others: black migrant workers from neighboring southern African states, black South Africans, and South African industry and commerce in the form of higher taxes, for example. Yet if sanctions continue to multiply, Pretoria probably will have been fully committed to a repressive and destructive siege by the time the government fully feels their adverse effects. This course of action will have been promoted by the polarizing effect of sanctions that could encourage black and white extremists and discourage those willing to negotiate.

These realities support the South African business view that there are no quick fixes for South Africa and that economic growth is essential to dispel notions of a zero-sum game, as well as to stimulate socioeconomic development. But any realistic assessment of black politics leads to the same conclusions. . . .

Undoubtedly, the banned African National Congress (ANC), the political group supported by the largest number of South African blacks, is an important political actor. Consequently, for practical as well as philosophical reasons, South African business advocates the release of the ANC's leadership and the "unbanning" of the organization—and indeed supports the same for all other detainees of conscience and banned organizations. . . .

But the sad fact is that conflict and divisions among black and predominantly black political groupings based on ideology, interest, tribal identity, and sheer competition for influence are deepening. The black consciousness groups such as the Azanian People's Organization and the Pan-Africanist Congress have strong ideological differences with multiracial organizations and coalitions such as the ANC and the United Democratic Front, and have clashed violently with them in local conflicts. Zulu Chief Gatsha Buthelezi is regarded with intense suspicion by many black groups because of his participation in the homeland system and his opposition to sanctions. But much of this opposition reflects recognition that Buthelezi is a formidable contender for power. The Zulu Inkatha movement he heads is a disciplined mass political movement with a coherent set of principles.

Further complicating the situation are the homeland elites with their vested interests; uncontrolled, radical youth; and a wide range of trade unions that sometimes overtly support the above major groupings, but whose interests often differ importantly from theirs.

Whites should derive no comfort from these divisions because they simply make the whole inevitable process of reaching an accommodation in South Africa messier and more protracted, and the task of a postapartheid government more difficult. But they do exist, and only romantics and revolutionaries believe that they can be conjured out of existence or forcibly removed. Witness the history of Africa to the north of the republic.

Still, such difficulties and complexities in no way prevent South African business from constantly reiterating to government its view that only a process of negotiation with truly influential black leaders on issues of political power will make possible the final transition to a postapartheid society. And only such talks will remove the growing international political vote of no-confidence manifest in the disinvestment-sanctions movement. But rational persuasion obviously has its limits, and South African business leaders realize that constructive domestic and international pressures are essential.

A third reality that hampers rapid change in South Africa is the nature of the South African economy. Sooner or later, apartheid will go, and most of the problems associated with a modernizing, industrializing state with a peculiar mix of First and Third worlds will remain. . . .

All South Africans need to be acutely aware of the limited resources available to government and the importance of maintaining and, if possible, increasing resources in the interests of postapartheid society. This is a long-term commitment requiring steady adherence to free enterprise principles and a proper appreciation of the South African economy's real nature.

As a trading country, South Africa can preserve its mining and manufacturing base only if it retains its membership in the Western-dominated international economic system. South Africa must therefore both maintain and expand the capital and technology inflows essential to an industrializing society, and also maintain an ability to compete in international markets.

But South Africa has to run harder than its widespread image in the West as an industrialized country might suggest. Despite all its minerals and diamonds, South Africa is wealthy only in comparison with its less fortunate African neighbors: Its gross national product (GNP) per capita in 1982, when its population was estimated at 30 million, was two and one-half times larger than the average for its 20 subequatorial African neighbors, but only 25 percent of Canada's.

Further, South Africa has an annual population growth rate of 2.7 percent and a typical Third World population profile—more than one-half of the population is under the age of 20. Fulfilling even the basic needs of a growing population, such as health, education, employment, and general contentment, is very difficult. Currently, an annual average economic growth rate of 6 percent is required to create employment for more than 300,000 new job seekers every year. Yet not even this growth rate will help the existing pool of unemployed, estimated at up to 25 percent of those blacks able to work.

Without foreign capital inflows, the South African economy can grow at little more than 3.5 percent per annum. In fact, recent growth has been even lower, averaging only 2.5 percent during the last decade and a shocking 1.1 percent during the last 5 years. Contributing to these dismal statistics have been the cessation of capital inflows over the last decade and the increase of outflows recently. . . .

Without international development capital, dismantling apartheid will present both serious problems and major opportunities. . . .

Among potential dangers, even during the current transition period, satisfying the black population's pent-up socioeconomic demands is requiring ever greater wealth. Black expectations are constantly rising and will no doubt continue to do so when blacks have access to political power.

Meeting those expectations will require development capital as well as transformed business and government policies. Such development capital cannot come solely from South African sources, whatever the economically liberating effect of dismantling apartheid. Currently, government spending stands at a very high 27 percent of the GNP. But that spending has gone to civil service salaries rather than to essential infrastructure, thereby gravely inhibiting economic growth. Moreover, higher individual and corporate taxes have diminished available investment capital. Similarly, private savings have dropped, exacerbating a vicious circle. Not only will remedying all these shortcomings still leave South Africa short of investment capital, but transformations in South African politics surely will introduce new constraints on the economy.

New Initiatives

Concerning its own policies, South African business is coming to the conclusion that it cannot adapt itself to the new South Africa by carrying on much as it has in the past. . . .

Specifically, my company, Anglo American Corporation of South Africa, is following three important strategies. They all reflect our general belief that what we do now will determine whether we are seen as a credible, nonracial organization in a free enterprise society. First, Anglo American is making a determined effort to visualize what "credible" will mean in 10 or 15 years. It certainly will not mean a simple linear projection of current practices, however progressive our manning and industrial relations policies may be. Credibility will require an absolute, mind-wrenching effort to grasp the future and translate it back to the real action we should be taking now.

Second, we must support and nurture effective and responsible trade union activity. . . .

Third, the company must be a stalwart advocate of the free enterprise theme, with the important obligation that we position ourselves to be seen both practicing and encouraging free enterprise. As a very large corporation, Anglo American naturally has the capitalist label hung around its neck. It will be deeds, rather than words, however, that determine whether we are acceptable to a society that, with the best intentions in the world, will have simplistic views about wealth.

Business operates on a long-term basis. Anglo American needs to plan for a long-term future to encourage industrial and economic growth. If we can show that we are taking a long-term view of the future of South Africa, organizations like the ANC and the trade unions will be encouraged to do the same. . . .

Business leaders realize that the form of the state will have to change just as dramatically as the shape of their businesses. But for all their specificity and agreement on the steps needed to dismantle apartheid, executives seem less united and articulate on what constitutional structure should replace the current system. This matter will have to be negotiated, and business leaders' roles will in one sense be confined to mediating among various political forces. . . .

In regard to appropriate political systems, some business voices favor the federal option. It seems to provide the most scope for devolving and sharing power in a way that reflects South African social diversity, and to be most conducive to ensuring the survival of individual freedoms and free enterprise.

Many, to be sure, fondly imagine that federalism can serve as a device to ensure continued white domination; the ruling National party's constitutional vision of an ethnic confederation or federation certainly qualifies as an example. No thinking business leader, however, believes that this is a viable political goal for white South Africans any longer.

At the same time, devices to ensure the protection of individuals and, possibly, minorities—for example, bills of rights and systems of voting such as proportional representation—reflect genuine and valid concerns. Indeed, the adoption of a bill of rights, now widely advocated in liberal and business circles in South Africa (witness the important business charter published by the Federated Chamber of Industries), is one way of helping to restore the classic Western democratic concept of the rule of law so tragically eroded during the apartheid era. A bill of rights would not be worth the paper it was written on unless it was supported by the majority of the population of South Africa. Yet one of the most positive and exciting developments in South Africa currently is the effort being made by many, including prominent business leaders, to find common ground in the area of commitment to various freedoms and common-law principles as a preliminary to getting a real negotiating process off the ground.

Realistically, it would be foolish not to expect that at least a measure of social welfarism will be present in postapartheid society; that the state—just like its Afrikaner predecessor—will try to redistribute wealth; and that some centralization and bureaucratization will ensue. What business can and must do is constantly stress the importance of maintaining a wealth-generating private sector, hampered as little as possible and able to compete in both domestic and international markets.

Whatever one's political persuasion, one lesson from the first 25 years of independence in African countries has been absolutely clear: Massive state intervention in the economy through nationalization, through the creation of parastatal enterprises, and through the building of vast bureaucracies that ignored the interest of agriculture and the bulk of the rural population has been uniformly disastrous. The 1980s have seen a growing realization of the inappropriateness, not to say destructiveness, of such policies, and country after country, even if ostensibly maintaining a socialist line, has moved to stimulate or reestablish its private sector: Mozambique, Tanzania, and Zambia are three examples close to South Africa. The pragmatic economic policy thus far pursued by the impeccably socialist Prime Minister Robert Mugabe of Zimbabwe owes much to the advice of Mozambican President Samora Machel, who exhorted Mugabe not to repeat Mozambique's mistakes, to retain skilled whites, and to stimulate agricultural production.

. . . Of course, South African companies must live out their free enterprise faith in South Africa, pressure government to create circumstances in which all South Africans are free to participate in the capitalist system, and involve themselves in all of the affirmative action programs mentioned above. But they must also engage black political groups in a dialogue about the economic future of South Africa. That was one of the key motivations behind the visit by a group of seven South African business leaders that I led last year to the ANC in Zambia.

The ANC's freedom charter, however admirable it may be in many respects, is a distinctly vague and woolly document on economic matters. Conceived in the circumstances of the mid-1950s, when South Africa was a vastly different place politically and economically, the charter asserts that "the mineral wealth beneath the soil, the banks and monopoly industry shall be transferred to the ownership of the people as a whole: all other industry and trade shall be controlled to assist the well-being of the people."

Yet the goal of continued competition in the international economy is incompatible with nationalization: Large and sophisticated organizations where efficiency is at a premium are rendered less efficient by state intervention, and in the international marketplace, that is their death knell. Even attempts to break down the allegedly monopolistic large companies in South Africa are entirely misguided. Small, open economies like South Africa's benefit from the international operations of large companies. A corporation like Anglo American, employing some 300,000 South Africans, can finance very large projects that generate jobs at home and much needed foreign earnings from sales abroad. It also prides itself on its expertise and efficiency.

Some U.S. companies present in South Africa already have launched innovative efforts, placing considerable development capital in areas such as education, training, and housing. The best American companies are living out their nonracial faith, not just in words, but in deeds. Although they are not breaking the law in South Africa (problematical in a country that needs more respect for the concept of the rule of law), American companies are nevertheless finding ways of challenging existing apartheid legislation that sometimes catalyze the slow process of reform. Thus Americans have helped break down still existing separation of amenities, such as the reservation of certain beaches for certain racial groups, and some are planning to build racially integrated residential areas for their employees as an exception to the Group Areas Act. Such moves do not dramatically sweep apartheid aside. But they do serve a pioneering or path-breaking function that helps government and the rest of the community follow in their footsteps. . . .

South Africa is not a country for the faint-hearted. It presents immense challenges but also immense opportunities, as well as the excitement of involvement in one of the great historical processes of change seen in the 20th century. South African business is rapidly adapting, planning, and mobilizing to participate in that great experiment, but it knows that its resources, even when combined with the economic forces liberated by the abolition of apartheid, will be inadequate to the challenge. The American counterparts of South African executives therefore face an awesome responsibility. Many have made good profits in South Africa for decades. But faced with lean times and a host of pressures, they are attracted to the easy option of withdrawal, especially if the ignorance, mischief making, and mythology underlying those pressures are ignored. Greater participation in South Africa and the structural reform initiatives proposed by South African business are much harder roads to walk. But they may also be in one of business's best and most prominent traditions— business risk taking.

77. SOUTH AFRICA: THE CRISIS DEEPENS*

by JOHN S. SAUL

John S. Saul is a member of the editorial collective of Southern Africa Reports *and co-author, with Stephen Gelb of* The Crisis in South Africa *(Monthly Review Press), the second edition of which includes this article and was published in the summer of 1986.*

. . . Change? Reform or repression? From its first days, of course, Botha and company's "total strategy" to defend their system was defined as including both reform and repression, a point reiterated by Botha himself in a recent gloss on widespread police and military action in the townships: "Official security action [sic] protects the process of peaceful reform and ensures the necessary stability without which reform will be undermined by violence and revolution." Certainly preemptive "security action" became, with Botha's ascendancy in 1978, an ever more marked feature of South Africa's policy beyond its borders in southern Africa. Building on the precedent of the 1975 invasion of Angola and subsequent destabilization efforts there (via UNITA), Botha proceeded to generalize this approach throughout the region, unleashing, most dramatically and brutally, its MNR puppet against the Mozambican regime while employing a mix of similarly shadowy bands of counter-revolutionaries and occasional direct attacks elsewhere as well (Lesotho, Botswana, Zimbabwe). One goal of such actions was to weaken logistical support for the African National Congress (ANC), although South Africa has also been interested in undermining the credibility of the nationalist and/or socialist experiments being attempted in such countries and in forcing their damaged economies back in under South African regional hegemony.

The apartheid government has paid a surprisingly low cost for such ruthless aggression, both internationally and domestically—even being praised in some quarters as "peacemaker" when Mozambique's government finally capitulated to South African military pressure at Nkomati. Moreover, the destabilization tactic may have scored some success in disadvantaging the ANC, however temporarily. Perhaps if use of the stick had proved to be as effective inside South Africa itself, less criticism would have been heard, in business and other circles, of Botha's overall policy package. Fortunately, this has not been the case, though not for want of trying on the part of the state. Of course, repressive state action has always been close to the surface in apartheid South Africa, but its scope expanded markedly in 1984 and 1985 as resistance grew. At the

*From *Monthly Review,* April 1986 (as condensed).

beginning of 1984 it was directed primarily against student protestors, in August against those working to boycott the tricameral elections in the Indian and "Coloured" communities. Yet, as already noted, it was the dramatic scale of police and military response to developments in the Transvaal beginning in September—dozens killed, hundreds detained—that really set the tone for what was to follow. When the state of emergency was declared in many parts of the country in July 1985, it was primarily a formalization of the prevailing situation, even if it did give the forces of repression a somewhat freer hand.

. . . The targets have been carefully selected, the UDF being especially prominent among them. As Trevor Manuel of the UDF's national executive wrote in August 1985, "Two years and one month after its inception, the UDF finds itself bearing the full brunt of the government's onslaught. Two-thirds of our national and regional executive members are out of action through death, detention or trial. At least 2,000 rank and file members of the UDF are in detention. A major UDF affiliate, COSAS, has been banned. . . . This repression . . . is the consequence of the effective challenges we have mounted to the government's 'reforms.' " Moreover, this grisly national pattern could be extended with examples drawn from virtually every South African black community, though the small town of Cradock in the Eastern Cape provided a particularly graphic instance. There Mathew Goniwe—"the dead man who haunts all our futures," in the words of Anton Harber—helped lead the Cradock Residents' Association (CRADORA) to mount an impressive, broad-gauged program of political mobilization (among other things, convincing local councillors to resign their posts and then effectively facilitating their reintegration back into the community). The result? One night in June 1985, the car driving Goniwe and three of his close associates was "intercepted" on the road by unknown assailants; over the next four days, according to Harber, "the mutilated and charred bodies of the four men were discovered in isolated posts on the outskirts of the city."

Not surprisingly, the UDF, in an official statement regarding Goniwe's murder, felt "forced to conclude that the 'defenders of apartheid' were bent on a 'murderous path' to eliminate all popular leaders." At the same time, such developments did begin to make some spokesmen for vested interests in South Africa uneasy. Was it possible that the "leaders" who were thus being peeled away were in fact important potential intermediaries in the kind of dialogue with the mass of the population that might eventually become necessary? Was the day arriving when a more rather than less organized resistance movement would be welcome as providing some minimal guarantee of a reasonably orderly transition to a new dispensation? These were questions given all the more urgency by the fact that the government's fierce crackdown seemed merely to heighten the black population's spirit of resistance, rather than the reverse. . . .

In consequence, . . . it is the business community that has been most desperate to discover a more adequate reform agenda. Thus when P. W. Botha appeared to fumble the ball with his ill-starred "Rubicon" speech to the National Party Congress in Natal in August [1985]—a speech much ballyhooed as likely to announce significant change but, in the event, characterized by an all too familiar defensive truculence—the headline for the story in the influential *Financial Mail* was a blunt "Leave Now":

> . . . the man has gone as far as he can—he has nothing more to offer—and he should therefore pay the appropriate penalty. . . . [He] is hopelessly out of his depth and should, forthwith, go into a well-earned retirement.
> Nothing new. Nothing specific. No timetable. Influx control to be "reviewed," Mandela stays in Pollsmoor. The backtracking on the denationalization policy implicit in the homelands policy was done in guarded and obscure terms. Everything, in short, suggests that if Botha ever had a "hidden agenda" for change, it was that the blacks would be linked to the homelands; urban blacks given their say in community and regional service councils; and everyone else represented through the tricameral Parliament.
> There have been tinkerings—or, to be more correct, promises of tinkerings—to the system. But it is in shambles. That is where P. W. has led us.

. . . What, then, of the business community's own reform agenda? Certainly the most prominent and powerful of capitalist interests are relatively less boxed in by the ideological parameters of "white supremacy" than is true of denizens of the state structure and, as Gelb and I observed, can thus more readily conceptualize a shift away from racial capitalism. For all the benefits that have accrued historically to capital (the availability of cheap black labor, in particular) from South Africa's unique marriage of economic exploitation and racial oppression, this marriage can begin to have its costs, economic costs (as we have mentioned), but, perhaps more importantly, political costs. After all, South African-style racial oppression tends to etch class contradictions in color, race and class contradictions then reinforcing each other in a manner that can become quite revolutionary. . . .

In consequence, the business community has begun to hedge its bets, the current sense of urgency producing, as its most adventurous outcome to date, an expedition to Lusaka, Zambia, by a group that included several of South Africa's most important capitalists—Relly, and Tony Bloom of Premier Milling for example,—in order to hold exploratory meetings with the banned and exiled African National Congress. We must be circumspect, however. As Gelb and I noted in 1981, even for the most sophisticated actors in the capitalist camp "the passage from racial capitalism to liberal capitalism seems a particularly hazardous one. . . . [The] dominant classes, mounted on the tiger of racial capitalism, now find that they can neither ride it altogether comfortably, nor easily dismount." Thus, even if they could hope to deliver a quite advanced model of reform through the dense underbrush of the whites-only polity (a considerable challenge in itself), such actors sense that they might not easily keep the democratization process within its "proper" channels. Given the deeply engrained social and economic inequalities that would continue to exist in South Africa, they have the nagging fear that the granting of any real political power to blacks must lead to a revolutionary challenge to those inequalities as well. . . .

Reform if necessary, but not necessarily reform. But just how do the "liberal minded" propose to become half-pregnant in South Africa? The formulation by the aforementioned Gavin Relly, published almost simultaneously with his meeting with leaders of the ANC, is among the most sophisticated . . . [omitted but see Reading 76]. A slippery text indeed—typical of what happens to the reform impulse when it moves beyond the eternal (albeit newly rediscovered) verities of freeing up the marketplace (removing the "irrationalities" of influx control, for example) toward the question of "one person, one vote, in a unified South Africa." There is the arrogance of power, of course, the same arrogance that led "reform-minded" Anglo American offhandedly to sack 14,000 workers from its Vaal Reefs mine in early 1985 when they had the temerity to take strike action. Nor is the kind of constitution-mongering bruited about by Relly something new. It surfaced in Natal at the beginning of this decade with the report of the Buthelezi Commission, which sought to theorize a novel (and highly qualified) redivision of power between Chief Buthelezi's KwaZulu administration and Natal's white polity. And Frederik van Zyl Slabbert and his Progressive Federal Party, the voices of liberal capitalism in South Africa's white parliament, have long been hawking just such "confederal" and "consociational" constitutional models, models that reflect the PFP's stated preoccupation with what they choose to label South Africa's "plural society" and with the dangers of "majority domination."

Put more honestly, such proposed constitutional gimmickry seems chiefly preoccupied with so dividing and counterbalancing black political inputs—all in the name of democracy—as to blunt any eventual challenge to white social and economic power. But perhaps under such a dispensation the qualifier "white" would become somewhat less important, giving further point to Roger Southall's conclusion to his careful study of the Buthelezi Commission that the "common objective of consociational strategy at this point is to recruit subordinate racial elites to a front that is deliberately counter-revolutionary"—thus marking one further and quite sophisticated attempt, in the name of reform, "to forge a class alliance across racial lines." We shall no doubt hear more of such schemes, if, as, and when a third round of "formative action" gets underway. Indeed, recent evidence suggests that the government, too, is laying the groundwork, through programs of industrial decentralization and regional administrative reorganization, for various possible "federalist" solutions of its own. It need scarcely be added that none of these possible developments has much to offer the mass of the African population. What will be evident, however, is just how much harder the state and business community will have to be pushed before the matter of genuine democratization and transfer of power to the black majority is likely to be placed firmly on the negotiating table.

It is one thing, however, [for the ANC] to win a "battle of ideas," quite another to win the struggle for power. As Lodge adds, "A bomb a week does not add up to a full-scale guerrilla war, and the prospect of the ANC being able to present a really formidable set of obstacles to the functioning of the state and the economy is still remote." Not that the struggle for power in South Africa is likely to look like some clearly recognizable rerun of guerrilla warfare elsewhere in Africa. Nonetheless, the mobilization of actions across a broad front which constitutes the "mass strike" (and which cumulatively saps the confidence and capacities of the defenders of the status quo) needs to obtain greater firepower if it is to shake more profoundly the powers-that-be. . . .

Events since June 1985 suggest that the ANC is still a long way from being able to provide enough of this kind of clout [the capacity to lend firepower and paramilitary clout to popular actions in the townships and workplaces in any confrontation with the South African army and police] to the resistance movement. Government bullets still tend to be met by sticks and stones; defenseless Africans die while white policemen escape reprisal and the rest of the white population remains cocooned in its comfortable suburban lifestyle. However, there are signs that this is changing. Africans are beginning to shoot back in the townships. There seems less reluctance on ANC's part—a point that was apparently discussed at length at the Consultative Conference—to eschew the kinds of attack in which white civilians might perish. Of course, this grim necessity, unwelcome to the ANC since it is the apartheid state and not the liberation movement that harbors the terrorists and psychopaths in South Africa, is merely one way in which the resistance movement must "take the struggle to the white areas," in the words of a recent ANC leaflet distributed inside South Africa. But it reflects an awareness that the large majority of the white population that continues to support the apartheid state, either actively or tacitly, must be made to comprehend more clearly the precise scope and seriousness of the black challenge that confronts it. Much depends on the ability of the ANC to deliver on its promise in this regard.

But what of consolidating the politics of the mass strike and giving it an ever stronger thrust in sheer mobilizational terms? Here, too, there are challenges. Thus the questions of the precise weight to be assigned to race consciousness and racial solidarity in developing South Africa's resistance movement has always been a problematic one. The Pan Africanist Congress's split from the ANC in the late 1950s had a distinctly cultural nationalist edge to it, and while the PAC has more or less self-destructed in exile, the Black Consciousness Movement (BCM), which did so much to revive the spirit of resistance in South Africa in the late 1960s and early 1970s, evoked some of the same sentiments. Though many BCM people have since found their way into the Congress Alliance, the cultural nationalist legacy lives on, providing, in the organizational forms of the Azanian People's Organization (AZAPO) and the National Forum, a current dissident from the UDF-ANC-Freedom Charter mainstream. This has led on occasion to inter-organizational tensions, although useful efforts have also been made to resolve them when they have threatened to get out of hand. It is worth noting, as well, that cultural nationalism has also had some impact on the trade union movement, the Azanian Congress of Trade Unions (AZACTU) and the more important Council of South African Trade Unions (CUSA) both having refrained from joining the impressive new trade union central, the Congress of South African Trade Unions (COSATU), launched in November 1985. At the same time, it should be emphasized that CUSA's intransigence on this question cost it the affiliation of what was far and away its most important unit, the National Union of Mineworkers (NUM), which did join COSATU.

In fact, cultural nationalism has been far less divisive than one might anticipate, given how graphic is the counter-reality of white racism. Certainly the UDF has eschewed it completely in stitching together its formidable alliance of some six hundred to seven hundred base organizations. Moreover, the UDF's firm line on this issue may have influenced the ANC, at its June conference, to remove its last remaining restriction on the role of non-Africans within the movement, membership on the National Executive Committee. Rather more complicated has been the question of the relationship between the UDF and the trade union movement. Thus a number of unions, particularly those linked to the Federation of South African Trade Unions (FOSATU), have held back from joining the UDF. One misgiving they had was historically rooted, springing from a sense that in the 1950s trade unions—given the close ties of the South African Congress of Trade Unions (SACTU) with the Congress Alliance—had rushed too readily into national level political campaigns without adequately consolidating the kind of shop-floor presence—power at the point of production—so necessary over the long haul. They were anxious to avoid making the same mistake.

Moreover, one of the most striking features of the independent trade unions that have emerged since the 1970s is their strong emphasis upon internal democracy and accountability to the membership. It was just such unions that tended to be most suspicious of the actual functioning of the UDF, being wary not merely of its size and the catholicity of the organizations affiliated to it, but also of the possibility that its top-heavy structure and commitment to high-profile political activity would, in Spauding's words, "almost inevitably

make [it] less democratically linked to [its] base than the unions themselves."
Nor is this all. As Spaulding continues:

> Some unionists have apparently worried that the UDF—and possibly the ANC—
> were just a bit too petty bourgeois in their make-up and too exclusively preoccupied
> with the mere transfer of formal political power to push big business on the questions
> of socialism and working-class power in post-liberation South Africa. For such
> unionists, further consolidating a working-class base on the shop-floor is crucially
> important, not only in order to make possible a continuing confrontation with capital
> but also to help pull to the left any ANC-led alliance which might eventually rise
> to power.

... This "workerist" tendency of FOSATU does not stand alone in the camp
of the independent trade union movement. There are certainly unions and
unionists of a more "economistic" bent, for example, whose reluctance to enter
the political arena has been grounded in a much narrower definition of the
legitimate scope of union activities. Moreover, misgivings about particular
kinds of political involvement have, upon occasion, even led to tensions between workplace and residence, between trade unions on the one hand and
civic and youth organizations on the other. This was notoriously the case with
the Eastern Cape stay-aways in March 1985—directed against massive re-
trenchments, the AMCAR-Ford merger and, most centrally, increased petrol
prices—and especially in Port Elizabeth (but less so in Uitenhage). Nonetheless, it remains generally true that all South African trade unions have been
drawn ever more firmly into the political arena. . . .

Thus Chris Dlamini, COSATU's first vice-president, led off the union's
inaugural rally at King's Park Stadium in Natal in early December by announcing that "time has run out for employers and their collaborators."
Indeed, the "unity gained through the formation of COSATU has foiled the
rulers' divide-and-rule strategy." Then it was the turn of Elijah Barayi, now
president of COSATU, to speak and he immediately called for the resignation
of P. W. Botha and all homeland leaders. Barayi also delivered a quite specific
ultimatum to Botha: abolish influx control laws within six months or
COSATU would take (unspecified) action. There were other pronouncements:
support for disinvestment now and for the nationalization of the mines and
other large industries in the future; for equal pay for equal work, especially
for black women; and for the immediate lifting of the state of emergency and
the withdrawal of troops from the townships. It remained to be seen how these
and other demands would be followed up on, but it was hard to avoid the
impression that another important step had been taken toward consolidating
a distinctive "working-class politics" in South Africa. . . .

It may be that this and other kinds of strong opinion will give rise to tensions
within the resistance movement, broadly defined. But as with the tensions that

we have seen exist specifically within COSATU itself, it is not inevitable that these will turn sharply antagonistic or become debilitating. Indeed, one of the most exciting things about contemporary South Africa—for all the likely horrors of the transition period still to come—is precisely the vibrant quality of its liberatory politics, the number of "big questions," which, being alive and well, give promise for the South Africa that will ultimately emerge. Not that all "antagonisms" within the black population can be so positively defined. The regime has found its allies, even in the black townships, although it is no accident that these latter have been markedly the targets of popular outrage there. Nor are the actions taken against them quite the outbreaks of anarchic "black-on-black" mob violence that the media (with South African official blessing) would often have us believe. As noted, an organizational infrastructure that exemplifies a very high level of political creativity generally underpins and guides township political actions (this in spite of the government's most brutal efforts to decapitate successful organizations whenever it can safely do so, as witness the Goniwe case). As the well-informed Catholic Institute of International Relations correctly insists, the so-called disorder in South Africa is, in reality, a "mass movement." The CIIR, is even more outspoken about the targets, both institutional and individual, of this "movement":

> South African blacks are proving that they cannot be governed as a people colonized from the white enclave, either by black collaborators, or by the naked violence of security forces and riot police. They reject the garrison state. . . . Most significantly, they have identified the new black local authorities, the community councillors, as the key to the state's attempt to control the townships and co-opt blacks. Community councillors have been dealt with mercilessly, killed and their houses burnt. Almost 200 have resigned; only 3 out of 34 councils set up in 1983 still function. Black resistance has thus struck hard at the lynch-pin of state strategy towards urban blacks.

Other "internal" enemies of liberation are even more familiar, if a little less immediately vulnerable: the bantustan elites, in particular. Thus, in 1983, the crackdown on SAAWU activists and on East London bus boycotters was even more vicious inside Lennox Sebe's Ciskei than it was outside. And such is the authoritarian and unapologetically servile nature of Mangope's regime in Bophutatswana that when, as 1986 dawned, over 20,000 miners were sacked by Gencor for striking its Impala Platinum Mines inside that bantustan, they had even less hope for redress than their 14,000 counterparts fired by Anglo American, a number of months earlier, in the so-called white area. Examples could be multiplied endlessly. However, it can safely be said that the actor in the "homeland" drama who is most deleterious to the cause of liberation has been Gatsha Buthelezi, chief minister of Kwazulu. The only black South African leader of any real visibility to have come out in strong opposition to economic sanctions against South Africa, this immoderate stance has made him the darling of certain influential Western circles and a boon to the South African business community and the apartheid government.

Yet his real value to the latter is manifested inside the country. Although he is just ambitious and independent enough to be an occasional embarrassment to it, the government has nonetheless found that, given a long leash, Buthelezi serves their basic game plan of divide and rule very well indeed. He is an outspoken foe of both the ANC and the UDF, and recent months have found his *impis* (squads of bully boys) and youth corps—working with tacit police support—acting as the physical hammer of the UDF and of community activists in Natal (while also exacerbating tensions between Africans and Indians there). This need come as no surprise. In fact, Buthelezi has built his power base among the Zulu at least as much by force and intimidation as by charisma and tribalist rhetoric. This is especially true in the most rural areas of Kwazulu, where the combination of isolation and of chiefly power structures has hung heavy over local communities. But the menace of Inkatha's strategy of intimidation has always spread more widely than that: among the ugliest of numerous relevant incidents was the 1983 assault on the Ngoye campus of the University of Zululand, where Inkatha thugs killed, beat, and raped dozens of students for the "disrespect" they had shown toward Buthelezi. Like so many other frightening facts about Buthelezi, this event was little publicized abroad.

Never quite the "spokesman for the 6 million Zulu" that his publicists have sometimes claimed him to be, Buthelezi's recent excesses in attempting to savage the growing mass resistance movement have reduced his popularity even further. According to the Community Resource and Information Centre:

> An opinion survey conducted by the Institute of Black Research showed that most Africans blamed Inkatha for the recent unrest in Durban. It was found that Inkatha and the police were seen as starting the trouble and being the most active in it thereafter. The survey reflected a considerable loss of support for Chief Buthelezi— a finding that was supported in other recent surveys.

Still, Buthelezi remains credible enough—and pliable enough—for van Zyl Slabbert to have taken him on board the PFP's "Convention Alliance," a recently proposed moderate "middle way" forward to constitutional reform. True, the fact that Buthelezi was alone among black leaders in linking himself to such an initiative is equally significant, while Slabbert's decision to join the trek to Lusaka to meet with the ANC may serve to remind us that it is definitely not Buthelezi who is "winning the battle of ideas." At the same time, there can be little doubt that he remains on offer for any "consociationalism"—he had, of course, attempted to take out a patent on that scenario with his own Buthelezi Commission—or "confederalism" that may be forthcoming. Other blacks may be available, if, as, and when the "endgame" bargaining process becomes a more pressing reality. For reasons that we have discussed, however, it will not be easy for any such blacks to deliver a sufficiently large popular constituency to render workable any of the (limited) range of formative options South African ruling circles seem willing to risk, now or in the foreseeable future.

The Revolutionary Dialectic

. . . What, then, of the future? Even if developments since 1981 seem to have confirmed much of the analysis of South Africa's crisis that Gelb and I advanced at that time, and even if that crisis has deepened along lines we might have predicted, it is not much easier now than it was then to set out with any real precision (or, indeed, confidence) a scenario for racial capitalism's ultimate demise. There will be some ebb and flow that springs from the degree of intensity of state repression (that degree of intensity being itself affected by the unpredictable balance of forces—and arguments—within ruling circles, even if unlikely to diminish markedly in the near future). In this regard, the dismissal at year's end of treason charges against a significant number of imprisoned UDF leaders has been hailed as a major political victory. Not that bannings, detentions, and killings will cease to take their toll. Nonetheless, the UDF's brand of above-ground, mass-based opposition seems likely to take fresh strength from these acquittals, the newly released leaders almost immediately throwing themselves back into political work.

Their renewed efforts, in combination with continuing pressure on the state on all the internal fronts we have examined (from the post-Consultative Conference ANC, from the post-unity trade union movement, from the township mobilization which will not disappear), must continue to take a toll of the state's capacity to repress the struggle. As for the precise "content" of this resistance movement, even the advances it has made since 1981 do not make its future entirely predictable. Gelb and I wrote then of the simultaneity, within the South African struggle, of the proletarian and the "popular-democratic" moments (the latter evidenced in broad organizational—and class—alliances and constructed around the ideologies of nationalism, racial consciousness, and democratic self-assertion that seem so effective in focusing much of the experience of lived oppression in South Africa). We suggested that the pressure of events in South Africa made it likely that these two moments would be complementary rather than contradictory, each drawing out the progressive potential of the other. As we have seen, the past five years have brought a further strengthening of both the "popular-democratic" and the "working-class politics" terms of South Africa's revolutionary equation and this has been, unequivocally, all to the good. Moreover, these two components have, indeed, tended to reinforce one another, the strength of popular-democratic assertions helping further to politicize the trade unions (to take one example), the growing assertiveness of the working class helping further to deepen the saliency of class considerations and socialist preoccupations within the broader movement.

Precisely how these strands will interweave, organizationally and ideologically, and in terms both of the further development of the liberation struggle itself and of the efforts to shape a new, post-liberation South Africa remains openended, of course. It may be true that the ANC, at least as regards organizational linkages, stands in most immediate and overt harmony with the UDF, this latter being, in turn, the most important above-ground manifestation of the "popular-democratic" current in South Africa. Moreover, the ANC remains most comfortable with a relatively populist projection of its programmatic intentions; it is reluctant, certainly, to proclaim any very straight-forward socialist vision of the future, a "two-stage" theory of the struggle (national liberation first, then, possibly, socialism) still being the most that many of its spokespersons will offer publically on this subject. Yet this need not imply that the ANC is fundamentally out of step with the most important bearers of "working-class politics" (those within the trade union movement, for example); nor that Jay Naidoo spoke to deaf ears during his Harare meeting with the liberation movement.

It is even less likely that the ANC, already so deeply rooted inside the country, could be very far out of step with the crystallizing mood of the black townships. There "popular-democratic" assertions are not easily distinguished from even more radical sentiments. As Patrick Laurence has written in assessing "capitalism's uncertain future," "South Africa's major extra-parliamentary opposition movements bristle with anti-capitalist sentiments. There is no doubt that there is a growing hostility towards capitalism among black youth. The reason is simple: capitalism is seen as the driving force behind apartheid."

It is not surprising, then, that the 1985 Consultative Conference underscored more strongly than ever a familiar ANC theme: the centrality of the working class to its revolutionary endeavors. As for its recent spate of meetings with businessmen, politicians, editors and churchpersons, not only has the ANC refused to compromise on the question of the full democratization of South Africa, but it has also stuck, quite explicitly, to the basic intimations of a socialization of production that are to be found in the Freedom Charter: "The national wealth of our country, the heritage of all South Africans, shall be restored to the people; the mineral wealth beneath the soil, the banks and monopoly industry shall be transferred to the ownership of the people as a whole."

Both resistance and radicalization have grown apace, then, and the process cuts across the entire field of organized opposition. Certainly there are strong grounds for reasserting—even reinforcing—the conclusion Gelb and I reached in 1981: "Just as the ANC is at the center of things, so the center of things is increasingly within the ANC: the continuing dialectic between this movement and the considerable revolutionary energies at play within the society has become the single most important process at work in South Africa's political economy." True, there is little more room than there was in 1981 for "jejune optimism"; it remains true that the "crisis is still a long way from being resolved in favor of the popular classes or in socialist terms." Nonetheless, the evidence and arguments presented above do suggest that as the South African crisis has deepened in recent years, it has moved much closer to a positive resolution on both counts.

78. SEVEN SCENARIOS FOR SOUTH AFRICA*

by ROBERT I. ROTBERG

Robert I. Rotberg is identified in the headnote to Reading 9.

South Africa has seven possible destinies. From left to right the seven rubrics are: (1) Revolution, (2) Substantial Regime Change, (3) Power Sharing, (4) Limited Power Sharing, (5) Concessions, (6) Change But No Change, and (7) Reaction and Retrenchment. . . .

Reaction and Retrenchment (7)

. . . Reaction and Retrenchment (Scenario 7) has the least analytical power of all of the scenarios. It presupposes the coming of the Conservative and Herstigte Nasionale parties to power . . . following a major lurch to the right as a result of adverse white reaction to reform initiatives of the present government. Theoretically, the general election results of 1989 could produce such a reversal. Or events before 1989 could lead to a military coup or a massive defection of sitting members of the National Party away from their government. . . . Scenario 7 presupposes a turning back of the clock, a withdrawal of present overtures to the world and to Africans, as insufficient and as unsatisfactory as those overtures may be. This is a larger scenario, but South Africa has never known political laagers. Its leaders, even in the darkest of days, have always known how to retreat. . . .

Revolution (1)

At the opposite end of the spectrum is Scenario 1, Revolution. Revolutions, in the classical sense, occur when the state loses legitimacy—when it can no longer impose its authority. . . .

*From *CSIS Africa Notes,* October 29, 1985 [condensed].

It is immensely difficult to devise a theoretical framework for a South African revolution. . . . [T]he potential revolutionaries may possess sufficient grievances, but they lack funds, arms, materiel, and the standard building blocks of a late twentieth-century revolution. . . . [For] analytical and practical reasons . . . sanctuaries are likely to remain unavailable and revolution as a total concept unrealizable. . . . If the struggle for South Africa is between white and black, and not between different classes or different ideological persuasions, then no revolution fueled by a shift in the allegiance of the army will occur so long as the state continues to recruit its soldiers from among the ranks of those whose very way of life is at stake. . . .

Change but No Change (6)

Scenario 6 describes South Africa in 1985. . . . The state may have difficulty restoring peace and tranquility, but its ultimate authority is mortgaged in no overwhelming sense. That is, ordinary police tactics of crowd control are barely sufficient to impose law and order, but the firepower of the army is held largely in reserve. . . . [Although] many of the townships are today ungovernable, it does not necessarily follow that this year's violence begets greater violence, and then even more violence, and that the state crumbles. . . .

Within the framework of Scenario 6, the state combines repression with the granting of concessions. . . . Naturally the state—any state—finding itself in this scenario knows that to negotiate the nature of change means a derogation of the authority of the state, and a weakening of its sinews of war.

Likewise, it is fundamental to Scenario 6 that protesters and their leaders believe that they will lose the momentum of their protest if they accept concessions as improvements decided upon unilaterally. . . . Thus, although the state wants to reform meaningfully (but more slowly than Africans desire), the state is not yet willing to accept the basic elements of the prevailing black demand for political participation and for *negotiating* its translation into practical policies.

. . . Yet the levels of rhetoric are high in this phase, the state attempts to persuade its own supporters, Africans, and foreigners that its intentions are good but that it needs time. . . . But in this phase either leadership or resolution is lacking for the kinds of strategic respositioning, rather than tactical readjustments, that would move South Africa from this scenario to Scenario 5, and beyond.

. . . What Africans want, what the West calls for, and what a peaceful (or at least non-cataclysmic) solution to the South African problem demands is a major strategic shift of a kind that happens only very occasionally in the life of any modern state. . . .

Concessions (5)

Scenario 5, Concessions, is not yet the scenario within which South Africa is operating. Since Scenario 5 is different more in degree than in kind from Scenario 6, however, South Africa could slide easily from the one to the other, but not back. Part of the regime's current dilemma is that a return to a Scenario 6 posture cannot be achieved once Scenario 5 has been entered. . . . And 5 has an open-ended quality unsettling to any government . . . seeking to control the pace and direction of reform rather than to begin a process over which authority could be lost.

. . . What differentiates 5 from 6 and others is that the entrance into this scenario would be hastened by a combination of continued or renewed violence and intensified pressure from the West. The introduction of stronger U.S. sanctions, the animosity of Europe (and Australia and Canada), would be but a part of the overall atmosphere of Western alienation.

A second distinction between this and lower-numbered scenarios is that the conferring of concessions would be preceded, in each case, by some form of consultation between the state and presumably "authentic" representatives of the protesting majority. . . . Any such consultation, by individuals or groups, risked a loss of credibility and the label "collaborator" or "stooge."

Nevertheless, it is theoretically possible for a government intent on believing that concessions would mute an opposition, or quiet protesters, to find Africans with whom discussions can occur. A government might also believe that the very contours of its concessions might defuse or defer protest. Clearly the government of South Africa could gain credibility overseas with the enunciation of an end to pass laws and influx control, broad new plans for housing and education, the introduction of an African franchise at the local or regional level, the provision of common citizenship, and so on. Nelson Mandela could be released. But such attempts to buy peace and time are bound to be insufficient if—from the majority point of view—they are introduced unilaterally and are not part of an overall restructuring of South Africa, including the homelands. In a more profound sense than most Africans realize, the majority seeks official recognition that South Africa can no longer progress without considering black preferences and opinions. Africans seek to become an integral part of the bargaining process.

Limited Power Sharing (4)

The government of South Africa has long ago realized that Africans prefer Scenario 4 to 5. That is, Africans want power sharing, even if limited, rather than concessions. . . . Yet the failure of 6, Change But No Change, signaled by violence without end and the inability to repress without embarrassing losses of life, could lead to a decision to move directly from 6 to 4—on the grounds that concessions would be refused or rebuffed, but that limited power sharing would have at least some chance of halting rioting and removing the sting of protest. This it might, but only if the shift to limited power sharing is negotiated with Africans. To decide to negotiate is the major step. To persuade Africans recognized as politically legitimate to negotiate is a second major move, and both are intertwined.

A result of open bargaining between whites with physical and economic power and blacks with numerical (and possibly historical) power could be the sharing of political control in the operational sense between white and black at local and regional levels. The black cities would become black-governed entities with full revenue raising and revenue expending powers. Blacks would receive the franchise at the municipal level. Municipalities would obtain statutory rights and also have influence at the regional level. Blacks would begin to experience autonomy—a measure of control over their destiny in the political sense. They would start to have a stake in their own country, and have real if limited power as against the central government.

. . . Further, although whites might be persuaded to concede limited power sharing in the sense described, they would want power sharing to remain limited, and not be a transitional stage. Africans, on the other hand, may have reached the point where they can only be persudaded to accept limited power sharing if they believe it to be a prelude to Scenario 3. Alternatively, but only after a period of bitter repression, Africans might become more willing to accept such "half loaves" rather than the full loaf that their leaders urge them to demand.

Scenario 4 would clearly become an option for the white government only after levels of violence reached new heights, Western pressure became even more insistent, and the National Party underwent substantial alterations in the nature of its leadership. . . .

Power Sharing (3)

Scenario 4 is an alternative to 5, and not as likely a progression from 5 as it is from 6. Scenario 3, Power Sharing, obviously flows from 6, and could result directly (as could 2) from 6. If violence is high and sustained for long periods, if police and military repression proves insufficient to quell or shorten the cycles of violence, if Western pressure grows more compelling and isolating, if prosperity fades (for whites as well as blacks), and if—decisively—the costs to the white way of life as well as the country's economy become too great (or are so perceived by large numbers of whites), then Scenario 3 becomes an operational possibility.

A shift to 3 is less abrupt, by definition, than a shift directly to 2. But it would nevertheless occur with comparative rapidity once the decision makers appreciated that the white will to resist or to continue fighting had snapped. That appreciation would occur subjectively, not objectively, but it would occasion a crisis of legitimacy.

There are two preconditions: (1) that Africans would, over the bargaining table, be constrained to accept less than "one man, one vote" by the existence of a still strong military machine in white hands, and (2) that leaders would assume power in the National Party and in the top echelons of the Defense Force who were prepared to settle for less than total victory and to demand more than total defeat. . . . Nevertheless, if there were unremitting agitation by Africans at levels five times greater than in 1985, white persons of power would be compelled to devise a new solution and Scenario 3 could be the negotiated result.

Substantial Regime Change (2)

Scenario 2—Substantial Regime Change—is less than a revolution, for the prevailing order changes, but the structure of society remains. It may sound farfetched in 1985, but South Africa could be transformed radically and rapidly without the classical revolution which, as we have reasoned, is highly unlikely. Substantial regime change means a shift from white to majority rule under conditions of uncommonly high stress, with limited time for adjustment, little preparation, and few safeguards for minorities.

Scenario 2 could prevail if, after a period of sustained violence at about, say, 10 times the 1985 intensity, with widespread loss of white as well as black life, the white government finds that the quenching of violence is possible only by open negotiations with Africans from a posture of weakness rather than strength. Prior to this point a National Party regime would have given way to a transitional white group, the military would have acknowledged an inability to continue fighting in a sustained way against Africans, and partition would be the solution on the lips of many.

The Odds

These are the logical alternatives for the future of South Africa. A simple conclusion is that there is every cause for anxiety, since none of the scenarios is promising, and each of the possible states would be reached only by the compulsion of events, not imaginative leadership. On the other hand, the 1984–85 cycle of violence does not necessarily and ineluctably presage repetitious cycles immediately. Historical determinism is not at work, but numerical superiority, international hostility, and the passage of time may nevertheless produce the same results.

TWO VIEWS FROM WASHINGTON

On June 12, 1986, President P. W. Botha proclaimed a nationwide state of emergency that in effect turned South Africa's racist regime into a police state: midnight knocks on the door, police empowered to fire at will—in essence a license to kill—and restrictions on the press that amount to almost total censorship. As Botha put it, he is prepared to do whatever is needed to preserve "our heritage of more than 300 years." A civil rights monitoring group has estimated that more than 8,000 people, mostly political activists in the black townships—especially supporters of the United Democratic Front—as well as trade unionists, journalists and clerics, had been detained without trial in the six weeks which followed. Ford and Rockefeller Foundation authorities have received alarming information about brutal mistreatment of those jailed, including the beatings of school children. The official death toll as of July 20 was 162.

The iron fist displayed by the Botha regime has predictably increased international pressures for tougher sanctions. In Great Britain, Prime Minister Margaret Thatcher's rejection of this course has caused a rift in the Commonwealth. President Kaunda, of Zambia, for example, regarded by many as a conciliatory African statesman, informed Foreign Secretary Geoffrey Howe upon his arrival in Lusaka that he was "not welcome as a messenger of your government." Thirty-one of fifty-eight nations, including India, withdrew in protest from the Commonwealth Games which opened in Edinburgh on July 24.

Here in the United States, President Reagan, in a major address on July 22, urged South Africa to free Nelson Mandela and move toward political peace, but reaffirmed his opposition to stringent economic sanctions, declaring they are an act of folly. Noticeably lacking in new initiatives, or forceful pronouncements, the speech made it clear that the President was not interested in cracking down on the Pretoria government. As *The New York Times* editorialized, President Reagan's "reassessment" of South Africa ended "without an iota of change or regret. . . . He came up deaf not only to one of the great moral issues of his time but even to the importunings of the Congress down the street. He would have been wiser to say nothing at all."[1]

It is not surprising, then, that the U.S. response angered many blacks in South Africa, including Bishop Tutu, who retorted: "I found the speech nauseating. . . . He sits there like the great big white chief of old," telling "us black people that we don't know what is good for us. . . . I think the West, for my part, can go to hell."

Less expected was the storm of bipartisan criticism in the U.S. Congress. Senator Richard G. Lugar, the Republican chairman of the Foreign Relations Committee, drafted new legislation that banned all new investment in South Africa, prohibited the importation from South Africa of such products as coal and steel and canceled the U.S. landing rights of South African airlines. Lugar's bill eventually passed Congress but was then vetoed by the President. However, on October 2, following similar action by the House, the Senate voted overwhelmingly to override the veto, a rare case of a dramatic political defeat for Ronald Reagan.

The message was clear: Americans do not support the Reagan Administration's policy of pampering Pretoria. The sanctions stop short, however, of requiring divestment by U.S. corporations operating in South Africa. New initiatives are needed if apartheid is to be overcome. Unfortunately, as the South African crisis deepens, the United States, under Ronald Reagan, is without a credible policy.

---

1. On the same day (July 23, 1985) the *Times* printed a remarkable report by the investigative reporter Seymour Hersh which revealed that the United States, working closely with British intelligence, had provided the South African Government with intelligence about the banned and exiled African National Congress, including specific warnings of attacks being planned. South Africa in return reported on Soviet and Cuban activity in the region. This sharing of informatin reversed the policy established by the Carter administration which banned any sharing of intelligence. Hersh could not determine whether the United States was still engaged in providing South Africa with information about the ANC.

I. SANCTIONS ARE IMMORAL

by RONALD REAGAN

On July 22, 1986, President Reagan delivered a major speech on South Africa and apartheid in which he denounced the idea of punitive sanctions as immoral and repugnant.

The root cause of South Africa's disorder is apartheid, that rigid system of racial segregation wherein black people have been treated as third-class citizens in a nation they helped to build. America's view of apartheid has been, and remains, clear: apartheid is morally wrong and politically unacceptable. The United States cannot maintain cordial relations with a government whose power rests upon the denial of rights to a majority of its people, based on race. . . . Many in Congress, and some in Europe, are clamoring for sweeping sanctions against South Africa. The Prime Minister of Great Britain has denounced punitive sanctions as immoral and utterly repugnant. Well, let me tell you why we believe Mrs. Thatcher is right.

The primary victims of an economic boycott of South Africa would be the very people we seek to help. Most of the workers who would lose jobs because of sanctions would be black workers. We do not believe the way to help the people of South Africa is to cripple the economy upon which they and their families depend for survival. . . . The mines of South Africa employ 13,000 workers from Swaziland, 19,000 from Botswana, 50,000 from Mozambique and 110,000 from the tiny landlocked country of Lesotho. Shut down these productive mines with sanctions and you have forced black mine workers out of their jobs and forced their families back in their home countries into destitution.

Southern Africa Like a Zebra

I don't believe the American people want to do something like that. As one African leader remarked recently, southern Africa is like a zebra: if the white parts are injured, the black parts will die, too. Western nations have poured billions in foreign aid and investment loans into southern Africa. Does it make sense to aid these countries with one hand and with the other to smash the industrial engine upon which their future depends?

Wherever blacks seek equal opportunity, higher wages, better working conditions, their strongest allies are the American, British, French, German and Dutch businessmen who bring to South Africa ideas of social justice formed in their own countries. If disinvestment is mandated, these progressive Western forces will depart and South African proprietors will inherit at fire-sale prices their farms and factories and plants and mines. And how would this end apartheid?

Our own experience teaches us that racial progress comes swiftest and easiest not during economic depression but in times of prosperity and growth. Our own history teaches us that capitalism is the natural enemy of such feudal institutions as apartheid.

. . . .

In defending their society and people, the Southern African Government has a right and responsibility to maintain order in the face of terrorists but by its tactics the Government is only accelerating the descent into bloodletting. Moderates are being trapped between the intimidation of radical youths and counter gangs of vigilantes. And the Government's state of emergency next went beyond the law of necessity. It too went outside the law by sweeping up thousands of students, civic leaders, church leaders and labor leaders, thereby contributing to further radicalization.

Such repressive measures will bring South Africa neither peace nor security.

. . . The realization has come hard and late but the realization has finally come to Pretoria that apartheid belongs to the past.

In recent years there's been a dramatic change. Black workers have been permitted to unionize, to bargain collectively and build the strongest free trade union movement in all of Africa. The infamous pass laws have been ended, as have many of the laws denying blacks the right to live, work and own property in South Africa's cities. Citizenship wrongly stripped away has been restored to nearly 6 million blacks. Segregation in universities and public facilities is being set aside. Social apartheid laws prohibiting interracial sex and marriage have been struck down.

It is because state President Botha has presided over these reforms that extremists have denounced him as a traitor. We must remember, as the British historian Paul Johnson reminds us, that South Africa is an African country as well as a Western country. And reviewing the history of that continent in the quarter-century since independence, historian Johnson does not see South Africa as a failure. "Only in South Africa," he writes, "have the real incomes of blacks risen very substantially. In mining, black wages have tripled in real terms in the last decade. South Africa is the only African country to produce a large black middle class. Almost certainly," he adds, "there are now more black women professionals in South Africa than in the whole of the rest of Africa put together."

Despite apartheid, tens of thousands of black Africans migrate into South Africa from neighboring countries to escape poverty and take advantage of the opportunities in an economy that produces nearly a third of the income in all of sub-Saharan Africa.

It's tragic and in the current crisis social and economic progress has been arrested. And yet, in contemporary South Africa, before the state of emergency, there was a broad measure of freedom of speech, of the press and of religion there. Indeed, it's hard to think of a single country in the Soviet Bloc, or many in the United Nations, where political critics have the same freedom to be heard as did outspoken critics of the South African Government.

To Dismantle Apartheid

But by Western standards, South Africa still falls short—terribly short—on the scales of economic and social justice. . . . But the South African Government is under no obligation to negotiate the future of the country with any organization that proclaims a goal of creating a Communist state, and uses terrorist tactics and violence to achieve it. . . .

Strategically, this is one of the most vital regions of the world. Around the Cape of Good Hope passes the oil of the Persian Gulf, which is indispensable to the industrial economies of Western Europe. Southern Africa and South Africa are repository of many of the vital minerals—vanadium, manganese, chromium, platinum—for which the West has no other secure source of supply. . . .

Apartheid threatens our vital interests in southern Africa because it's drawing neighboring states into the vortex of violence. Repeatedly within the last 18 months South African forces have struck into neighboring states. I repeat our condemnation of such behavior.

Also, the Soviet armed guerrillas of the African National Congress, operating both within South Africa and from some neighboring countries, have embarked upon new acts of terrorism inside South Africa. I also condemn that behavior.

The Region at Risk

. . . If this rising hostility in southern Africa between Pretoria and the front-line states explodes, the Soviet Union will be the main beneficiary and the critical ocean corridor of South Africa and the strategic minerals of the region would be at risk.

Thus it would be a historic act of folly for the United States and the West, out of anguish and frustration and anger, to write off South Africa. Ultimately, however, the fate of South Africa will be decided there, not here. . . .

The key to the future lies with the South African Government. As I urge Western nations to maintain communication and involvement in South Africa, I urge Mr. Botha not to retreat into the locker, not to cut off contact with the

West. Americans and South Africans have never been enemies, and we understand the apprehension and fear and concern of all of your people. But an end
to apartheid does not necessarily mean an end to the social, economic and
physical security of the white people in this country they love and have
sacrificed so much to build.

To the black, colored and Asian peoples of South Africa, too long treated
as second- and third-class subjects, I can only say: In your hopes for freedom,
social justice and self-determination you have a friend and ally in the United
States. Maintain your hopes for peace and reconciliation and we will do our
part to keep that road open. We understand that behind the rage and resentment in the townships is the memory of real injustices inflicted upon generations of South Africans. Those to whom evil is done, the poet wrote, often do
evil in return. . . .

But let me outline what we believe are necessary components of progress
toward political peace.

First, a timetable for elimination of apartheid laws should be set.

Second, all political prisoners should be released.

Third, Nelson Mandela should be released to participate in the country's
political process.

Fourth, black political movements should be unbanned.

Fifth, both the Government and its opponents should begin a dialogue about
constructing a political system that rests on the consent of the governed, where
the rights of majorities and minorities and individuals are protected by law.
And the dialogue should be initiated by those with power and authority, the
South African Government itself.

Sixth, if post-apartheid South Africa is to remain the economic locomotive
of southern Africa, its strong and developed economy must not be crippled.
And therefore, I urge the Congress and the countries of Western Europe to
resist this emotional clamor for punitive sanctions. If Congress imposes sanctions it would destroy America's flexibility, discard our diplomatic leverage
and deepen the crisis. To make a difference, Americans who are a force for
decency and progress in the world must remain involved.

Policy on South Africa

. . . I have directed Secretary Shultz and A.I.D. Administration McPherson
to undertake a study of America's assistance role in southern Africa, to determine what needs to be done and what can be done to expand the trade, private
investment and transport prospects of southern Africa's land-blocked nations.
In the past five years, we have provided almost a billion in assistance to South
Africa's neighbors, and this year we hope to provide an additional $45 million

to black South Africans. We're determined to remain involved diplomatically and economically with all the states of southern Africa that wish constructive relations with the United States.

This Administration is not only against broad economic sanctions and against apartheid, we are for a new South Africa, a new nation where all that has been built up over generations is not destroyed; a new society where participation in the social, cultural and political life is open to all peoples; a new South Africa that comes home to the family of free nations where she belongs. . . .

Blacks and Business

If we wish to foster the process of transformation, one of the best vehicles for change is through the involvement of black South Africans in business, job-related activities and labor unions. But the vision of a better life cannot be realized so long as apartheid endures and instability reigns in South Africa. If the peoples of southern Africa are to prosper, leaders and peoples of the region of all races will have to elevate their common interests above their ethnic divisions.

We and our allies cannot dictate to the government of a sovereign nation —nor should we try. But we can offer to help find a solution that is fair to all the people of South Africa. We can volunteer to stand by and help bring about dialogue between leaders of the various factions and groups that make up the population of South Africa. We can counsel and advise, and make it plain to all that we are there as friends of all the people of South Africa.

In that tormented land, a window remains open for peaceful change. For how long, we know not. But we in the West, privileged and prosperous and free, must not be the ones to slam it shut. Now is the time for healing. The people of South Africa of all races deserve a chance to build a better future. And we must not deny or destroy that chance.

II. WHY THE DOUBLE STANDARD?

by REPRESENTATIVE WILLIAM H. GRAY 3D

The Democratic response to President Reagan's speech on South Africa was delivered by Representative William H. Gray 3d of Pennsylvania.

Good afternoon. Today President Reagan declared the United States and Great Britain co-guarantors of apartheid. By joining Mrs. Thatcher in opposing economic sanctions, the President protects Pretoria from the one weapon it fears most.

The President failed to recognize what the American public, the Congress and the world community have known for a long time—the Administration's policies in South Africa have failed.

In 1985 the Congress bipartisanly passed the Anti-Apartheid Act, changing our policy and opposing sanctions. The President, through executive order, adopted weaker measures and asked Congress to wait nine months. We have waited, but conditions have worsened. That is why just one month ago the House of Representatives passed the toughest possible economic sanctions: total disinvestment and a trade embargo, the measures we already have imposed on Cuba, North Korea, Cambodia and Libya. However, the President tells us that sanctions will only hurt the blacks, the people we are trying to help.

But blacks have suffered for years, not because of sanctions, but because of apartheid. They suffer because by law they cannot vote. They suffer because they are 72 percent of the population squeezed onto 13 percent of South Africa's most barren land. They suffer because they can be arrested without charge or trial.

More than 6,000 blacks have been detained in the past month alone. They are allowed no contact with lawyers or families. The Government refuses to even identify the detainees. Under a sweeping state of emergency, they simply have disappeared. Killings, detentions, people disappearing—a modern-day Holocaust is unfolding before our very eyes. Against such a backdrop, how can sanctions hurt black South Africans when apartheid is killing them?

Jobs versus Justice

Out of 28 million black South Africans, only 47,000—one tenth of 1 percent —hold jobs with American companies. These numbers alone tell us that the issue in South Africa is not jobs, but the loss of life and the denial of justice. Archbishop Tutu, Reverend Boesak, Doctor Naude, Winnie Mandela, countless other South African leaders have pleaded with us to impose sanctions and raise the cost of apartheid—even the labor union leaders.

The Eminent Persons Group, representing 49 Commonwealth nations, urges economic sanctions as the only remaining non-violent pressure for change. The governments of six other nations surrounding South Africa have issued a joint statement supporting sanctions as the means to help end apartheid, even if it means some hardship for their own nations and economies. They all recognize that without economic sanctions, without pressure, without increasing the cost of apartheid, there is no reason for South Africa to dismantle apartheid.

President Reagan tells us that sanctions don't work. Why then have we imposed sanctions against Libya, Nicaragua, Poland and Cuba, and some 20 nations throughout the world? Those sanctions express our profound distaste of the policies and the actions of those nations. We imposed them not because we thought they would bring down those Governments, but to disassociate us from all that those Governments stand for while raising the cost of behavior we abhor.

Why not South Africa? Why the double standard? That's the question the oppressed majority keeps asking the land of freedom and liberty.

The President says our strategic interests would be jeopardized if violent elements assume power in South Africa, but the President's own policies put our strategic interests at risk. He condemns apartheid but he refuses to back it with meaningful action. In doing so he gives black South Africans no choice but to accept support from other nations who offer it. That does not serve our long-term strategic interests. That does not put us on the side of the future in South Africa.

The Fight for Freedom

The President has always stressed a single message in his foreign policy. That message is strength. Why does he refuse to show strength toward South Africa? The President has preached that the Reagan doctrine is to fight for freedom wherever it is denied. Why is the doctrine being denied in Pretoria? Where is that doctrine in Cape Town, in Port Elizabeth, in the hellholes of Crossroads and Soweto?

What is needed is not simply a condemnation of apartheid, while we provide economic support for South Africa's oppression through our loans and investments. What is needed is a new policy that clearly dissociates us from apartheid and calls for the complete dismantlement of that system, not cosmetic reforms.

Our policy must demand the release of all political prisoners and the start of negotiations between the black majority and the white minority to develop a timetable for full democracy, which is one person, one vote. We agree with the President on that.

The policies of this Administration, known as constructive engagement, clearly have not achieved these bipartisanly endorsed goals. Therefore, we are asking the question: Where is the progress that our President tells us about? Where is the influence when South African police are killing more blacks now than ever before?

Where is our influence when the regime keeps behind bars, bans or banishes the leaders with the widest popular support, including Nelson Mandela? Where is our influence when President Botha rejects President Reagan's personal request not to impose a new emergency restriction?

Today the President sent a message to South Africa. To the racist majority regime of Pretoria he said, "We are your friends, don't cut our friendship off. We want your minerals. We want to work with you and continue our investments and loans." Then the President said to the 28 million majority, whose rights have been denied, whose lives are being lost and whom justice is being denied, "Maintain your hope, but do nothing to end that oppression." Is this the message of America? Have we not learned from Nuremburg what will happen in Johannesburg? And why the Western democracies must raise the cost and totally disassociate from apartheid if we are to accomplish our goals?

GLOSSARY AND
ABBREVIATIONS

African	In South Africa, refers to indigenous people (Zulu, Xhosa, Tswana, etc.)
Afrikaans	Language spoken by Afrikaners and majority of "Coloureds"
Afrikaner	South African white descended from early Dutch, German or Huguenot settlers
ANC	African National Congress, most important black opposition group
ARMSCOR	Armaments Development and Production Corporation, a parastatal producing and exporting weapons
Azania	Name for South Africa used by PAC and Black Consciousness organizations
AZAPO	Azanian People's Organization, a Black Consciousness group
baaskap	Bossdom, term describing white domination
Bantu	Pejorative term for Africans; for linguists, the family of African languages spoken in sub-Saharan Africa
bantustans	Areas designated by the South African government as homes for the various African ethnic groups (also, "homelands," "reserves")
BCM	Black Consciousness Movement, broadly, groups originating in the 1970s espousing need for black pride and autonomy
blacks	Term used by opponents of apartheid and others to include Africans, Coloureds, Indians
black spot	Land in white areas "illegally" occupied by blacks. Black occupants are forcibly removed to the bantustans
BLS states	Botswana, Lesotho and Swaziland
Boer	Afrikaner (sometimes any white with Afrikaner mentality); lower case: Afrikaans word for farmer
Coloured	Racial classification for South Africans of African-European descent

endorsed out	Being expelled from an urban area if not entitled to be there under the pass laws
FRELIMO	Front for the Liberation of Mozambique, has ruled Mozambique since 1975
Frontline States (FLS)	Angola, Botswana, Mozambique, Tanzania, Zambia and Zimbabwe
grand apartheid	South African government policy to create independent "homelands"
Group Areas Act	Legislation that set up segregated zones in towns and cities, applied to residence and occupations
ISCOR	Iron and Steel Corporation, a parastatal
laager	An encampment protected by a circle of covered wagons
MNR	Mozambique National Resistance, South African-backed guerrilla movement opposed to FRELIMO
MPLA	Popular Movement for the Liberation of Angola, has ruled Angola since 1975
OAU	Organization of African Unity, since 1963 the main association of independent African states
PAC	Pan-Africanist Congress, breakaway from ANC, outlawed in 1960
parastatals	Corporations controlled and largely owned by the South African government
passbooks	Identity document required for Africans over sixteen (official name, Reference Book)
PFP	Progressive Federal Party, liberal white parliamentary opposition
petty apartheid	Laws enforcing racial segregation in such areas as public facilities, transportation, hotels, restaurants, etc.
rand	Unit of South African currency; on Jan. 10, 1986, equal to $0.41
Robben Island	Maximum-security prison near Cape Town, holding many political prisoners
SADCC	South African Development Coordination Conference, founded in 1979 to foster development and independence from South Africa; includes Malawi, Swaziland and FLS
SADF	South African Defense Force
SASOL	South African Coal, Oil and Gas Corporation, a parastatal engaged in converting coal-to-oil
Section 10 rights	Key section of Black Urban Areas Consolidation Act, defining the qualifications allowing Africans to remain permanently in "white" areas
sjambok	Animal hide whip used by police

Soweto	Largest African city, population over one million (acronym from *So*uth *We*st *To*wnships), near Johannesburg
total strategy	Botha's call for a combination of economic growth, military preparedness, and political reform to counter adversaries
townships	Black residential areas located near white cities
trekboers	Afrikaner farmers who traveled by ox wagons inland during the eighteenth and nineteenth centuries; *voortrekkers* are those who took part in the Great Trek (1834–37)
UNITA	National Union for the Total Independence of Angola, South African-backed rebels seeking the overthrow of the MPLA
veld	Open grassland with scattered shrubs and trees
verkrampte	"Narrow-minded" or reactionary Afrikaners
verligte	"Enlightened" or reformist Afrikaners
ZANU-PF	Zimbabwe African National Union (Patriotic Front), in power since independence, in 1980

SELECTED BIBLIOGRAPHY[1]

Recent Books

Bender, Gerald J., Coleman, James S., and Sklar, Richard L., eds. *African Crisis Areas and U.S. Foreign Policy.* Berkeley: University of CA Press, 1985.

Breytenbach, Breyten. *The True Confessions of an Albino Terrorist.* New York: Farrar, Straus & Giroux, 1983.

Crapanzano, Vincent. *Waiting: The Whites of South Africa.* New York: Random House, 1985.

Danaher, Kevin. *In Whose Interest? A Guide to U.S.-South Africa Relations.* Washington, D.C.: Institute for Policy Studies, 1984.[2]

Davies, Robert, O'Meara, Dan, and Dlamini, Sipho. *The Struggle for South Africa: A Reference Guide to Movements, Organizations and Institutions,* 2 vols. London: Zed Books, 1984.

De St. Jorre, John. *A House Divided: South Africa's Uncertain Future.* Washington, D.C.: Carnegie Endowment for International Peace, 1977.

Kuzwayo, Ellen. *Call Me Woman.* San Francisco: Spinsters Ink, 1985.

Lelyveld, Joseph. *Move Your Shadow: South Africa, Black and White.* New York: Times Books, 1985.

Leonard, Richard. *South Africa at War: White Power and the Crisis in Southern Africa.* Westport, CT: Lawrence Hill, 1983.

---

[1] See also the books excerpted or cited in this volume.
[2] Contains an extensive annotated bibliography of recent journal and magazine articles.

528

North, James. *Freedom Rising.* New York: Macmillan, 1985.

Omond, Roger. *The Apartheid Handbook: A Guide to South Africa's Everyday Racial Policies.* New York: Penguin, 1985.

Thompson, Leonard. *The Political Mythology of Apartheid.* New Haven, CT: Yale University Press, 1985.

Other Books and Documentary Sources

Adam, Herbert and Giliomee, Hermann. *Ethnic Power Mobilized: Can South Africa Change?* New Haven, CT: Yale University Press, 1979.

Biko, Steve. *I Write What I Like.* New York: Harper & Row, 1978.

Bissell, Richard and Crocker, Chester, eds. *South Africa into the 1980's.* Boulder, CO: Westview Press, 1979.

Bunting, Brian. *The Rise of the South African Reich.* London: Penguin, 1964.

Carter, Gwendolen. *The Politics of Inequality: South Africa since 1948.* New York: Praeger, 1958.

Cornevin, Marianne. *Apartheid: Power and Historical Falsification.* Paris: UNESCO, 1980.

Davenport, T. R. H. *South Africa: A Modern History.* Toronto: University of Toronto Press, 1978.

Davidson, Basil; Slovo, Joe; and Wilkinson, Anthony R. *Southern Africa: The New Politics of Revolution.* London: Penguin, 1976.

De Braganca, Aquino and Wallerstein, Immanuel, eds. *The African Liberation: Documents of the National Liberation Movements,* 3 vols. London: Zed Press, 1982.

Elphick, Richard and Giliomee, Hermann, eds. *The Shaping of South African Society 1652–1980.* Harlow, Essex, U.K.: Longman, 1979.

First, Ruth. *117 Days.* London: Penguin, 1965.

Frederickson, George. *White Supremacy: A Comparative Study in America and South African History.* Oxford: Oxford University Press, 1980.

Gerhart, Gail. *Black Power in South Africa.* Berkeley, CA: University of CA Press, 1978.

Gandhi, Mohandas K. *Satyagraha in South Africa.* Weare, NH: Greenleaf Books, 1979.

Hirson, Baruch. *Year of Fire, Year of Ash: The Soweto Revolt: Roots of a Revolution.* London: Zed Press, 1979

Hope, Marjorie and Young, James. *The South African Churches in a Revolutionary Situation.* Maryknoll, NY: Orbis, 1981.

Johnstone, Frederick A. *Class, Race and Gold: A Study of Class Relations and Racial Discrimination in South Africa.* London: Routledge and Kegan Paul, 1976.

Joseph, Helen. *If This Be Treason.* London: André Deutsch, 1963.

Karis, Thomas and Carter, Gwendolen M., eds. *From Protest to Challenge: A Documentary History of African Politics in South Africa, 1882–1964,* 4 vols. Stanford, CA: Hoover Institute Press, 1972–1977.

Legum, Colin, ed. *Africa Contemporary Record: Annual Survey and Documents.* New York: Holmes & Meier.

Luthuli, Albert. *Let My People Go: An Autobiography.* New York: McGraw Hill, 1962.

Magubane, Bernard Makhosezwe. *The Political Economy of Race and Class in South Africa.* New York: Monthly Review Press, 1979.

Mandela, Nelson. *No Easy Walk to Freedom: Articles, Speeches and Trial Addresses of Nelson Mandela.* Portsmouth, NH: Heinemann, 1973.

Marquand, Leo. *The Peoples and Policies of South Africa.* Oxford: Oxford University Press, 1969.

Mokgathe, Naboth. *The Autobiography of Unknown South African.* Berkeley, CA: University of CA Press, 1971.

Moodie, Dunbar. *The Rise of Afrikanerdom: Power, Apartheid and the Afrikaner Civil Religion.* Berkeley, CA: University of CA Press, 1975.

Price, Robert and Rosberg, Carl, eds. *The Apartheid Regime: Political Power and Racial Domination.* Berkeley, CA: Institute of International Studies, University of CA Press, 1980.

Sachs, Albie. *Justice in South Africa.* Berkeley, CA: University of CA Press, 1973.

Saul, John S. and Gelb, Stephen. *The Crisis in South Africa: Class Defense, Class Revolution.* New York: Monthly Review Press, 1981.

South African Institute of Race Relations. *A Survey of Race Relations in South Africa.* Johannesburg: Annual.

Study Commission on U.S. Policy Toward Southern Africa. *South Africa: Time Running Out.* Berkeley, CA: University of CA Press, 1981.

SWAPO of Namibia. *To Be Born A Nation: The Liberation Struggle for Namibia.* London: Zed Press, 1981.

Thompson, Leonard and Prior, Andrew. *South African Politics.* New Haven, CT: Yale University Press, 1982.

Walker, Cheryl. *Women and Resistance in South Africa.* London: Onyx Press, 1982.

Recent Magazine and Journal Articles[3]

Adam, Herbert and Uys, Stanley. "Eight New Realities in Southern Africa." CSIS, *African Notes,* Feb. 28, 1985.

---

[3] See footnote number 1, and also the magazine and journal articles excerpted or cited in this volume.

Dash, Samuel. "A Rare Talk With Nelson Mandela." *The New York Times Magazine,* June 7, 1985.

Davies, Robert and O'Meara, Dan. "Total Strategy in Southern Africa: An Analysis of Southern African Regional Policy Since 1978." *Journal of Southern African Studies,* April 1985.

De St. Jorre, John. "South Africa's Non-U.S. Economic Links." CSIS, *African Notes,* May 24, 1985.

Goodman, David L. "South Africa, Whites Who Won't Fight." *The Progressive,* Sept. 1985.

Klug, Heinz and Seidman, Gay. "South Africa: Amandla Ngawethu!" *Socialist Review,* Nov.–Dec. 1985.

Malan, Rian. "My Traitor's Heart." *Esquire,* Nov. 1985.

Mandela, Winnie. "A Piece of My Soul." *Mother Jones,* Oct. 1985.

Mishra, Brajesh. "Ending the Impasse." *Africa Report,* Sept.–Oct. 1985.

Naudé, Rev. Beyers. "Where Is South Africa Going?" Africa Report, May–June 1985.

Owen, Ken. "Inside South Africa: A Status Report." CSIS, *Africa Notes,* June 30, 1985.

Pogrund, Benjamin. "Falling Apartheid." *The New Republic,* Sept. 9, 1985.

Price, Robert M. "Southern African Regional Security: Pax or Pox Pretoria." *World Policy Journal,* Summer 1985.

Schwartz, Joseph. "Black Politics in South Africa." *Dissent,* Winter 1986.

Shepherd, George W., Jr. "The United States' South Africa Policy: The Failure of 'Constructive Engagement' and the Emergence of New Options." *Africa Today,* 2nd Quarter 1984.

Villa-Vicencio, Charles. "Twenty-Five Years After Sharpeville." *Africa Report,* May–June 1985.

Weissman, Stephen. "Dateline South Africa: The Opposition Speaks." *Foreign Policy,* Spring 1985.

Special Issues on South Africa

America, Aug. 3–10, 1985.
The Black Scholar, Nov./Dec. 1985.
Christianity and Crisis, Feb. 4 and 18, 1985.
Current History, April 1985.
Economic Notes (Labor Research Association), July/Aug. 1985.
Newsweek, Sept. 16, 1985.

Pamphlets

Benson, Mary, ed. *The Sun Will Rise: Statements from the Dock by Southern African Political Prisoners* IDAF,[4] 1981.

The Catholic Institute for International Relations and The British Council of Churches. *Namibia in the 1980's,* 1981.

The Catholic Institute for International Relations and Pax Christi. *War and Conscience in South Africa: The Churches and Conscientious Objection,* 1982.

El-Khawas, Elaine and McKenna, Barbara. *Perspective: College Actions on South African Investments,* Amer. Council on Ed., May 1985.

Hovey, Gail. *Namibia's Stolen Wealth: North American Investment and South African Occupation,* African Fund, 1982.

IDAF. *Apartheid: The Facts* (1983).

IDAF. *The Apartheid War Machine* (1980).

IDAF. *Children Under Apartheid* (1980).

IDAF. *Women Under Apartheid* (1881).

Konig, Barbara. *Namibia—The Ravages of War* (IDAF), 1983.

Mandela, Nelson. *The Struggle Is My Life* (IDAF), 1978.

Seidman, Judy. *Facelift Apartheid* (IDAF), 1980.

Sikakane, Joyce. *A Window on Soweto* (IDAF), 1977.

The South African Council of Churches and The Southern African Catholic Bishops' Conference. *Relocations: The Churches Report on Forced Removals,* 1984.

Selective List of Organizations Opposed to Apartheid

Africa Resource Center, 464 19th St., Oakland, CA 94612. (415) 763-8011.

American Committee on Africa/Africa Fund, 198 Broadway, Suite 401, New York, N.Y. 10038. (212) 962-1210.

Artists and Athletes Against Apartheid, 545 8th St., SE, Suite 200, Washington D.C. 20003. (202) 547-2550.

Association of Concerned Africa Scholars, P.O. Box 791, East Lansing, MI 48823.

Episcopal Churchpeople for a Free Southern Africa, 339 Lafayette St., New York, N.Y. 10012. (212) 477-0066.

International Defence and Aid Fund for Southern Africa, P.O. Box 17, Cambridge, MA 02138. (617) 491-8343.

---

[4] The London-based International Defence and Aid Fund for Southern Africa (see Reading 10 for its statement of purpose) is the publisher and distributor of more than two dozen books and pamphlets; portable photo exhibitions; postcards; posters; videos and films on South Africa and Namibia.

Southern Africa Media Center, 630 Natoma St., San Francisco, CA 94103. (415) 621-6196.

The U.S. Out of Southern Africa Network/PAM, 19 W. 21st St., New York, N.Y. 10010. (212) 741-0633.

TransAfrica, 545 8th St., NE, Washington, D.C. 20003. (202) 547-2550.

United Nations Center Against Apartheid, UN Secretariat, New York, N.Y. 10017. (212) 754-6674.

Washington Office on Africa, 110 Maryland Ave., NE, Washington, D.C. 20002. (202) 546-7061.

Southern African Political Movements in the United States

African National Congress (ANC), Suite 405, 801 Second Ave., New York, N.Y. 10017. (212) 490-3487.

Pan-Africanist Congress of Azania (PAC), Suite 703, 211 East 43rd St., New York, N.Y. 10017. (212) 986-7378.

South West Africa Peoples Organization (SWAPO), Rm. 1401, 801 Second Ave., New York, N.Y. 10017. (212) 557-2450.

U.S. Companies with Investments or Loans in South Africa and Namibia

A unified list with periodic updates has been compiled by Pacific Northwest Research Center, P.O. Box 3708, Eugene, OR 97403, and is available from The Africa Fund, 198 Broadway, New York, N.Y. 10038. Project managers were Roger Walke, now reachable at PNWRC/East, 1830 Ingleside Terrace NW, Washington, D.C. 20010, and Richard Knight of The Africa Fund. The unified list is a compilation of existing lists including those from the U.S. Consulate General in Johannesburg, South Africa, Investor Responsibility Research Center (IRRC), 1319 F Street NW, Washington, D.C. 20004, U.N. Centre Against Apartheid and Corporate Data Exchange, as well as other sources and information encountered in the press.

INDEX